Hotel Design

Planning and Development

From Raffles to E Walk and beyond

◄ Title page. *An incredibly welcome restoration* **Raffles Hotel, Singapore** (see p. 202). Creative developments of the mid-1980s such as the restoration of this quintessential icon of welcoming hotel design helped touch off the most astonishing wave of progress observed in the industry for many decades. The revival of this famed east-meets-west hotel demonstrates the value of restoring a masterful neo-Renaissance façade renovating 103 deluxe suites, and creating an adjacent mixed-use development comprising 65 specialty shops and a museum. Of key interest are the public interiors, highlighting the 1920s era, when the hotel served as both the workplace and playground of literary luminaries such as Somerset Maugham and Nöel Coward. The hotel is named in honor of Singapore's founder, Sir Stamford Raffles.

◄ *A super-luxury hotel to remember* **Four Seasons Hotel, New York** (see pp. 170 and 350). The innovative and elegant rotunda lobby of I.M. Pei's exciting design creates a warm arrival space for New York's tallest hotel. Located on 57th Street, amidst the best shopping and business destinations, the hotel receives accolades for its 370 oversized rooms and gracious style and service. The multilevel lobby offers guests a variety of positions from which to view others—and be viewed—magically turning the massive space into an intimate experience, even while at one of the world's busiest crossroads.

► *A taller ultratel* **Kowloon MTR Tower, Hong Kong, China** (see p. 205). Considered one of the most imaginative ultra-high-rise multiuse hotel designs, this colossus of 102 stories by SOM Architects features a peaked roof and ornamental spire, traditionally counted in a building's official height. More technically complex for being built as part of a land reclamation project in Kowloon Bay, the project combines a restaurant and observatory at its top, office floors in the middle, and a five-star hotel with a 23-story atrium at its base, atop a commercial podium and parking garage. The location of the hotel rooms, highlighted in the accompanying key diagrams, varies based on market trend analysis.

◄ *A panoramic ultratel* **Park Hyatt at Shinjuku Tower, Tokyo, Japan** (see p. 211). Kenzo Tange's triple-tower design provides an unusually large floor plate for the hotel to spread out on the top 14 floors of this immense 52-story structure. The glass-roofed sky lounge on the forty-first floor links the hotel public spaces and guestroom levels to the commercial functions below while providing dramatic views of the city.

► *The modern east-meets-west hotel* **Four Seasons Hotel Chinzan-so, Tokyo, Japan** (see p. 303). Situated across from a treasured 17 acre (7 ha) historic park and gardens, the hotel's architecture and interior design join eastern and western traditions to create a serene and intimate ambiance in the heart of a frenetic city.

▼ *The mixed-use luxury downtown business and tourist hotel* **Far Eastern Plaza Hotel, Taipei, Taiwan** (see p. 23). Adjacent to Taiwan's largest shopping center near the Taipei World Convention and Exhibition Center, this 422-room urban luxury hotel serves premier business and entertainment travelers to this thriving metropolis.

▲ *The ultratel transit hub* **JR Central Towers & Station, Nagoya, Japan** (see pp. 211–212). The 'skystreet' on the fifteenth floor links the 59-story hotel tower to a 55-story office building and a 20-story retail podium in a high-density multiuse complex that spans over a massive transportation hub in Japan's third largest city.

➤ *The top-of-the-line all-suite hotel gem,* **RIHGA Royal, New York** (see pp. 158 and 386). The late twentieth century parallels the opening of the vast domain of all-suite and extended-stay hotels, including its leading example of luxury design by architect Frank Williams for William Zeckendorf, Jr, scion of the fabled family of pioneering developers. The hotels contains 500 one- and two-bedroom suites with sweeping views of midtown Manhattan and Central Park.

➤ *The downtown luxury business and tourist hotel* **Manila Diamond Hotel, Philippines** (see p. 304). Hirsch Bedner's skillful interior design for the double-level lobby of this 500-room luxury hotel, located in the center of the city's business and leisure district, combines black granite, marble, gold leaf, and rich wood paneling with dramatic cove lighting in bringing a colorfully elegant style to the nucleus of the hotel's public spaces.

➤ *The Ginza's deluxe downtown hotel* **Hotel Seiyo Ginza, Tokyo, Japan**. This elegant 72-room hotel, a glistening 12-story tower of polished alabaster, is situated at the financial and fashion crossroads of the Orient, in Toyko's Ginza district. The interiors and restaurants and lounges blend the best of Japanese and western design and cuisine, offering international guests a memorable experience.

⮟ *The mixed-use downtown waterfront hotel* **Mojiko Hotel, Moji Harbor, Kitakyushu, Japan**. One of Aldo Rossi's final projects, the hotel is sited at the mouth of a cove facing Kanmon Strait, surrounded by water on three sides, and on axis with the Mojiko train station. The mixed-use building, which includes harbor offices and a theater, is the centerpiece of a redevelopment project bringing tourism and entertainment back to the historic Moji district.

▲ *The blended airport hotel* **Kempinski Munich Airport Hotel, Germany** (see p. 47). The hotel's huge glazed atrium lobby blends with the many surrounding hangar and terminal structures. Sometimes used for special receptions for up to 1,200 people, the oversized space is the centrepiece of the hotel, bracketed between two efficient wings containing 383 guestrooms and suites. The growth in business travel and the vastly increased demand for accommodation at international airports has created several new world-class airport hotels.

◄ *The office park hotel* **Hotel Kyocera, Kokubu Hayato Technopolis Center, Kagoshima, Japan** (see pp. 51 and 285). The guestroom corridors offer dramatic views through the hotel's 14-story curved glass and stainless steel façade to the bustling technopolis center and the tranquil Kirishima Mountains beyond.

▲ *The small city mixed-use hotel* **Martinspark Hotel, Dornbirn, Austria**. A green copper bulge that contains a fashionable restaurant hovers over the hotel entrance to this representation of Austria's distinctive New Modernism movement in a community complex that also houses a department store, boutiques, and residential apartments.

➤ *The mixed-use downtown business and tourist hotel* **Hyatt Regency Fukuoka, Japan**. The cylindrical hotel tower of this Michael Graves-designed mixed-use complex contains a spectacular central court featuring a seven-story copper-clad pyramid—a dramatic sculptural element whether viewed from the guestroom corridors or by looking up from the lobby below. The entry court leading to the hotel lobby is flanked by two wings of retail shops, a high-tech business center, and state-of-the-art function rooms above.

▲ *The eco-country inn* **Yusuhara Visitors Center, Yusuhara, Japan** (see p. 54). Architects Kengo Kuma & Associates employed the openness of modern design and the warmth and diversity of traditional local materials to create a lodging facility integrated with the pristine natural environment near the Shimanto River. Local cedar, bamboo, and rice-paper frame the guest quarters, restaurant, terraces, and communal bath against the emerald backdrop of wooded hills.

➤ *The futuristic country inn* **Noto Monzen Family Inn, Ishikawa, Japan** (see p. 54). Though not a quaint farmhouse with a porch full of rocking chairs, this privately owned and managed ultra-modern incarnation of a country inn nevertheless offers the essential qualities that define the traditional genre including generous hospitality, personal attention, owner involvement, comfortable ambiance, and unhurried surroundings. On a remote site overlooking the Sea of Japan, the owner and her husband manage all food preparation and the daily household tasks, providing the guests with the experience of being welcomed into a private home.

➤ *The deco boutique hotel* **Delano, Miami Beach, Florida** (see p. 27). A row of duplex bungalows line one side of the Water Salon and Orchard in this airy South Beach creation credited as Ian Schrager and Philippe Starck's third collaboration. From the all-white guestroom décor to the open-air stage of the pool area, a mixture of theatricality and simple elegance define this tropical oasis.

▼ *The futuristic boutique hotel* **St. Martin's Lane, London, England**). An ordinary office building in Covent Garden was transformed into a dazzling spectacle, especially at night when the exterior becomes a pulsating light show. Depending on their mood, guests may alter their room color by operating an ingenious lighting control device mounted behind the bed where they choose the color of light to flood their room and illuminate the grid of square windows on the hotel's façade.

▼➤ *Contrasting styles in boutique hotels* **Blakes** and **The Hempel, London, UK** (see p. 29). Anouska Hempel demonstrates opposite stylistic ends of the spectrum embraced by the burgeoning boutique segment with her skillful crafting of two London hotels. The Blakes is rendered in sumptuous dark colors and gilded carvings with ornate Victorian rooms filled with heavy upholstered furniture dramatically lit to theatrical effect. The Hempel, in contrast, is stripped of ornament and color, offering instead Zen-like atmospherics of calm simplicity detailed only by the play of delicate light on the clean lines of elegant materials.

◄ *The large-scale boutique hotel* **Paramount, New York**. After careful study, developer Ian Schrager opted not to combine or enlarge rooms of this 610-room urban hotel, instead preferring to keep all the rooms at their original tiny size. Philippe Starck rose to the challenge by instilling an ambiance of cool, glamorous style in each room, where every detail brings life to the whole experience in making this the first over-200-room boutique hotel.

➤ *The most exclusive boutique hotel,* **The Mercer, New York** (see p. 28). André Balazs transformed John Jacob Astor II's late-nineteenth-century factory in SoHo into a boutique hotel with a refined elegance that sets it apart from all others in that segment. Sensuous simplicity describes the décor that designer Christian Liaigre brought to the 75 guestrooms whose tall ceilings and wide industrial windows uniquely define their character.

◄ *The acrobatic adaptive reuse* **Adelphi Hotel, Melbourne, Australia.** The conversion of a rooftop club with a stunning 25 m saltwater lap pool, whose glass-enclosed end dramatically cantilevers seven stories over the sidewalk, offers guests of this intimate 34-room urban hotel a unique and thrilling amenity.

➤ *An adaptive 'mixed-use-reuse'*, **Le Meridien Lingotto, Turin, Italy** (see pp. 189 and 300). Architect Renzo Piano masterfully transformed one of the most important buildings of early twentieth-century Turin, the Lingotto Fiat Factory, a building that inspired the great Swiss architect Le Corbusier who marveled at its rooftop test track. The car factory was converted into an exclusive multipurpose complex that includes a congress center with auditorium, exhibition showcase, service center, shopping mall, and 240-room hotel. In the guestrooms the architect maintained the original features of the full-height French windows, a characteristic feature of the original building, inviting sunlight reflections on the red wood panels, adding a touch of warmth.

➤ *The Rykiel-designed interior landmark* **Hotel de Crillon, Paris, France** (see p. 169). One of Paris' most illustrious fashion designers was commissioned to decorate one of its most cherished and luxurious hotels. Sonia Rykiel used the precious stones of garnet, ruby, sapphire, and pearl as her inspiration for the décor of the presidential suites, while maintaining the original French *parti* with Louis XV-style furnishings. Shown here is Suite Presidentielle Blanche.

◄ *The 'un-adaptive' reuse* **The Crowne Plaza Hotel, Washington, DC** (see p. 190). The original Hamilton Hotel, built in 1922 with 250 rooms, was converted in the late 1970s to an office building. All floors were completely gutted leaving little of the original hotel, except for the elevator shafts, window locations, and the vaulted lobby ceiling. Under the guidance of the District of Columbia Preservation League, which was responsible for protecting the building's historic façade, Brennan Beer Gorman Architects recreated much of the original hotel architecture and interiors, introducing a new scalloped glass entrance canopy and decorative ceiling and column treatments, thereby restoring the hotel to its original grandeur.

➤ *The ecotourist resort perched on water* **Pangkor Laut Resort, Lumut, Malaysia** (see p. 103). On a remote 300 acre (121 ha) island in the Straits of Malacca, visitors to this tranquil Malaysian resort are offered a choice among forest villas, beach villas, or the thatch-roofed sea villas shown here. Perched on stilts and strung together by wooden boardwalks, these vernacular over-water cabins sway ever-so-gently with the motion of the tides.

▲ *The ecotourist resort at the rainforest's edge* **Sheraton Inn Timika, Irian Jaya, Indonesia** (see p. 104). Western amenities and covered porches bring visitors comfortably in contact with the wilds of a primordial rain forest in this architectural study of environmental sensitivity.

◄ *The ecotourist resort overlooking rice fields* **Amandari, Bali, Indonesia** (see p. 104). Perched on an escarpment high above the winding Ayung river gorge in central Bali, this quintessential ecoresort was designed as a walled Balinese village, with river-stone walkways linking 30 thatched-roof cottages. The gentle curve of the negative-edge salt-water pool mimics the original rice terraces that tumble below toward the gorge.

▲ *The ecotourist beach resort and museum* **Tanjong Jara Beach Hotel and Rantau Abang Visitor Center, Kuala Trengganu, Malaysia.** This is one of the very earliest ecotourist resorts built on the Terengganu coast on the eastern seaboard of the Malaysian peninsula overlooking the South China Sea. Winner of the coveted Aga Khan Award for Architecture, Wimberly Allison Tong & Goo's design was inspired by indigenous *istanas*, the elegant, wooden palaces built for ancient Malay sultans and crafted of native hardwoods using traditional building techniques.

◄ *The ecotourist desert resort* **Hotel Explora en Atacama, San Pedro de Atacama, Chile** (see p. 105). Located in one of the world's driest places at the foot of the Andes, this environmentally sensitive resort provides explorations into the wonderland of complex ecosystems that has sustained ancient tribes in the desert for thousands of years.

➤ *The ecotourist wilderness resort* **Hotel Explora en Patagonia, Lake Pehoe, Chile** (see p. 105). Set on a remote windswept site amidst giant majestic horn-shaped peaks, glacier-fed lakes, and primordial forests of the Torres del Paine National Park, this ecoresort serves as a base camp for challenging explorations into the spectacular untamed surroundings.

▲ *The planned community on the Gulf* **Seaside, Florida** (see p. 215). Architects Andres Duany and Elizabeth Plater-Zyberk devised a master plan for this 80 acre (32 ha) planned community on Florida's panhandle incorporating Gulf Coast vernacular architecture fostering a strong sense of place. The dominant building type is wood-frame cottages with deep roof overhangs, ample windows, and cross-ventilation, well adapted to the climate and enhancing the sensual pleasure of life by the sea. Among the wide variety of overnight accommodations available in the community, ranging from full-service luxury to modest limited lodging, the Honeymoon Cottages shown here are full-service duplex units safely tucked behind the dune.

◄ *The full-service retirement community* **TidePointe, a Classic Residence by Hyatt, Hilton Head, South Carolina** (see p. 218). Built on 63 acres (25 ha) with cottages and village homes laid out among the lagoons and salt marshes of eastern Carolina, this senior living community offers a retirement lifestyle that resembles an exclusive country club. The 34,000 ft^2 (3,160 m^2) clubhouse includes a club-style dining room, game rooms, art studios, bank, hair salon, small market, and connecting pier for crabbing and fishing. As a continuing-care retirement community, TidePointe also includes assisted-living quarters, skilled nursing care, and a specialized memory support center giving residents the security of knowing that, as they age, most of their long-term health care needs will be met within the retirement community, without the need to relocate.

▲ *The luxury conference retreat* **Rough Creek Lodge, Glen Rose, Texas** (see p. 147). Built on a bluff overlooking Mallard Lake, the lodge caters to executives on business retreats as well as leisure travelers and bird hunters attracted to the natural beauty of the ranch's plains and creeks. The architecture and interiors incorporate materials and colors reflecting its Texan roots, including hickory millwork, rough-sawn cedar, pine, pewter, limestone, granite, saddle leather, and naturally shed long-horns and antlers.

➤ *The super-luxury country inn* **Twin Farms, Barnard, Vermont** (see p. 53). Tucked away in the bucolic rolling hills and meadows of the New England countryside, the former farm houses of writers Sinclair Lewis and Dorothy Thompson provide the setting for an inn of impeccable style and graceful hospitality. Masterfully decorated by the late Jed Johnson, the two houses and surrounding cottages are adorned with authentic antiques, original art, and opulent finishes befitting a magnificent country estate.

▲ *The seaside site contextual resort* **The Westin Regina Golf and Beach Resort, Los Cabos, Mexico** (see pp. 64 and 66). The welcome rebirth of modern design in the late twentieth century, as well as the hotel's outstanding organic environmental siting, are enthusiastically applauded by sophisticated vacationers at this superb resort gem.

◄ *The sun-valley's 'found' site contextual resort* **The Buttes—A Wyndham Resort, Tempe, Arizona** (see p. 69). Revered by mainstream and super-sophisticated vacation markets alike, this innovative organically-designed desert resort and conference center defies previous notions of location in achieving its popular success.

▲ *The growing global golf resort experience* **The Greenbrier at West Village Golf Resort, Fukushima, Japan** (see p. 81). Japanese and American architectural influences are combined in this outstanding resort and golf clubhouse designed by Robert A.M. Stern, Architect.

➤ *The urban destination spa resort* **The St. David's Hotel & Spa, Cardiff, Wales** (see p. 83). This outstandingly creative urban destination spa rises out of Cardiff Bay, revealing a number of classic design features, including a transparent lobby canopy, a sun-filled atrium space sheltered beneath a soaring roof truss, and generous guestroom balconies and spa and pool decks overlooking the harbor. Spas such as this are the true stars of the turn-of-the-millennium design era.

▲ *The Caribbean Island resort* **Hyatt Regency Aruba Resort & Casino, Netherlands Antilles**. On the leeward side of the windswept island of Aruba, colorful tropical vegetation welcomes guests to this 361-room hotel overlooking the shallow blue waters of the Caribbean Sea. The public spaces and recreational areas, including a multilevel water feature and pool, were designed around the concept of ancient ruins with hand-carved replicas of huge stacked boulders drawn from the island's original gold smelting yards.

◄ *A Grecian resort table-top* **Hyatt Regency Thessaloniki, Greece.** Table-top design is an integral part of the guest's dining experience. Often conceived in collaboration with the chef and food and beverage director, the design of the table-top reflects the aesthetics and operational mode of the hotel and is designed in concert with the overall theme of the hotel and its restaurants. This table setting from Ambrosia, the hotel's main restaurant, draws its inspiration from elements of Greek antiquity.

➤ *The Alpine village ski lodge* **The Ritz-Carlton Aspen Highlands, Colorado** (see p. 101). One of the most exciting resort designs of the era based on the ski lodge as an all-seasons resort, the new genre includes vacation ownership and condominium units as well as shopping and entertainment villages. The additional recreation amenities and conference facilities support year-round operation. Themed with rustic Ahwahnee Lodge-style architecture compatible with the mountain environment, the building blends into the terrain. Subject to environmental approval by authorities, accommodations are limited to reasonable density as well as continued preservation of existing open spaces.

⮟ *The modern ski lodge* **Amangani, Jackson Hole, Wyoming** (see p. 100). With its superbly inviting pool and spa supplementing idyllic slopes and panoramic views, the lodge design combines the traditional texture of rugged stone inside and out with uniquely clean architectural lines creating an original vocabulary most applicable to new and luxurious ski country regions.

◄ *The sensitively blended multiresort destination* **Cala di Volpe Hotel, Costa Smeralda, Sardinia, Italy** (see pp. 98 and 107). This large-scale premier resort development personifies the pioneering accomplishment of one of the era's most significant design objectives—preservation of local cultural traditions through sensitive architecture and ecology and by not exceeding reasonable resort densities. Master planned in the mid-1980s, the inventive strategy continues to prove extremely successful aesthetically, environmentally, and in its major contribution to the long-term local and regional economies. The Cala Di Volpe Hotel, of the four widely separated and architecturally varied resort hotels encompassing this highly principled development, is bound to its neighbors by its use of the island's indigenous materials and by continuing the large-scale preservation of local detailing.

▲ *The new vocabulary Red Sea resort* **Sheraton Miramar Resort el Gouna, Egypt** (see p. 76). Architect Michael Graves created a challenging new design vocabulary, highly compatible with the indigenous Pharaonic style as well as with innovative luxury amenities, in one of the era's most original resort concepts.

▼ *The themed mid-rise multiresort destination* **Jumeirah Beach Resort, Dubai, UAE** (see p. 109). One of this era's most significant resorts raises the art of themed architecture to a level far beyond the concept's breakthrough success. As part of a composition of three luxury resort structures, designed to symbolize the seafaring tradition of Dubai, this mid-rise hotel of the trio recalls the form of an ocean wave.

► *The themed ultratel multiresort destination* **Burj al Arab Hotel, Dubai, UAE** (see pp. 108–109). The world's tallest resort structure symbolizes a wind sail, related to the mid-rise wave structure shown in the accompanying view. The third structure, a resort conference center, is designed in the form of a ship, whose tapered hull accommodates the resort's conference seating requirements.

➤ *A high-renaissance themed casino hotel* **The Venetian, Las Vegas, Nevada** (see p. 231). The concept represents one of the era's most extensive, authentic, and impressive triumphs in the application of historic architectural theming, from paintings and filigreed ceilings to ornate stone bridges and gondolas.

➤ *The sublime in themed casino hotels* **The Conservatory at Bellagio, Las Vegas, Nevada** (see p. 230). This superb atrium garden concept takes on a life of its own, exuding natural sensations of water and aroma without a single fountain or drop of falling water. A standing pool with flowering plants (changed on a monthly basis) affirms that great spaces are not confined to palaces and museums but, increasingly, grace hotels. Removable stone floors give access to the myriad of electrical, lighting, life-safety, irrigation, chemical, humidification, and other silent technologies.

➤ *Gaming history themed at a casino hotel,* **Silver Legacy Resort Casino, Reno, Nevada**. In the heart of the 'biggest little city in the world,' an immense composite dome encloses an unprecedented 120 ft (36.6 m) high, 100-year-old automated silver mining rig that stands at the center of the casino floor. With 75,000 ft^2 (6,970 m^2) of painted surface area, the interior of the dome is one of the largest indoor murals ever created and is illuminated by special lighting effects that depict an entire day from sunrise to nightfall and periodically simulate lightning storms. From a distance, the gigantic 18-story silver sphere forms an impressive futuristic vision against the sculpted backdrop of the 1,800-room hotel tower.

◀ *The oceanfront resort renovation and addition* **Wyndham El Conquistador Resort & Country Club, Fajardo, Puerto Rico.** Plans to rehabilitate the 265 acre (107 ha) mega-resort, closed for over a decade, include complete renovation of the grand hotel and casino and the addition of convention facilities and three new resort villages. This would provide the resort with 918 guestrooms and suites in four unique resort environments. Perched high above the water's edge at the confluence of the Atlantic Ocean and Caribbean Sea, the resort site is carefully planned to maximize views and maintain the characteristics of picturesque Spanish and Caribbean harbor and hill towns.

6:45

▲ *The most multifaceted mega-hotel* **Atlantis, Paradise Island, Bahamas** (see p. 194). Easily the era's most multifunctional resort, the virtual 'resort city' advances new concepts of fantasy theming, yachting marinas, and marine habitats to exponential heights.

➤ *The theatrical boutique in-town resort* **W Hotel at Times Square, New York.** The latest segment of entertainment hotels focusing on show business features a 55-story boutique resort of 550 guestrooms. The hotel's fourth floor sky lobby overlooks the newly revitalized Great White Way and the space below offers an array of Broadway-style amenities including themed shopping and restaurants. The hotel's signature feature is a 300 ft (91 m) illuminated sign tower. For decades a virtual museum of unique giant billboards known in the trade as 'spectaculars,' the area is now celebrated as a forerunner of the architectural ornamentation of the information age and, with the city's encouragement, the concept is sparking the unprecedented rebirth of the entire midtown district.

➤ *The towering 'sail' on the waterfront* **Yokohama Grand Inter-Continental Hotel, Japan** (see p. 40). The dynamic V-shaped hotel tower is sometimes mistaken for a huge ship at full-sail by seagoing vessels approaching the harbor. Internally linked to the Pacifico Yokohama International Convention Center and Exhibition Hall, the 31-story hotel symbolizes the city's energetic maritime history while signaling its enterprising future.

◄ *The resort theme park mega-hotel* **Portofino Bay Hotel at Universal Escape, Orlando, a Loews Hotel, Florida** (see p. 196). Universal Studios used a truly ingenious technique to create their resort in Orlando. They carefully selected and meticulously reconstructed the façades of a most picturesque Italian fishing village as exterior architecture, complete with its visually relaxing harbor, creating a stunning and most endearing setting.

▲ *The profound at themed casino hotels* **The Palace of the Lost City, Sun City, South Africa** (see pp. 229, 249, 280, and 293). One of the pivotal design accomplishments of the era, developed through the analytic methodology of Gerald Allison, principal of WAT&G Architects, the palace ensures the everlasting definition and promise of fantasy in design, architecture, and art.

◄ *The most varied downtown waterfront entertainment resort* **Sea Hawk Hotel and Resort, Fukuoka, Japan** (see p. 41). Catering to new heights of citywide events ranging from enormous wedding parties at the hotel's mammoth atrium to baseball double-headers hosted in the adjacent retractable-roof sports stadium, architect Cesar Pelli captures the passion of Japan's urban ethic.

➤ Overleaf. *Dubbed 'E Walk' by its developers, as the icon of the theatrical entertainment in-town resort* **The Westin New York at Times Square** (see p. 34). Charging forward on the frontiers of the once seedy area west of Times Square, Arquitectonica has delivered a futuristic design that trumpets the pioneering spirit of the red-hot entertainment hotel segment with a thrilling composition of colored glass and dazzling light. The development by Tishman features 863 rooms attached to entertainment amenities on a level not seen in Times Square since the Astor Hotel electrified visitors to the Great White Way nearly a century ago.

Beyond E Walk. *Emerging megatrends promise stunning new prototypes as fashionable as boutique gems and as far out as 'ultratels,' 'floatels,' 'spa-tels,' and other significant design concepts of the future.*

VOX
TV
LIFE IS SHORT
Hip Jeans
NYC
WSCB
78
Water for life
EAT HERE!
DINER
sports ca
ENTERTAINMENT
CLUB CHILI
SUPER STORE
SEGA
IMIX
URBAN MIDWA
SOUVENIR

Hotel Design

Planning and Development

Walter A. Rutes, Richard H. Penner, and Lawrence Adams

W.W. NORTON & COMPANY

NEW YORK • LONDON

This edition first published 2001 in the United States by W. W. Norton & Company

Previous edition published 1985 as HOTEL PLANNING AND DESIGN

Printed in the United Kingdom

The text of this book is composed in Helvetica Light
with the display set in Helvetica Medium and Bold
Composition by Gray Publishing, Tunbridge Wells, England
Manufacturing by Cromwell Press, Trowbridge, England
Book design by Robert Gray

Library of Congress Cataloging-in-Publication Data
Rutes, Walter A., 1928–
Hotels design, planning, and development/Walter A. Rutes,
Richard H. Penner, and Lawrence Adams.
p. cm
Rev. ed. of: Hotel planning and design.
Includes bibliographical references and index.
ISBN 0-393-73055-7
1. Hotels–Planning. 2. Hotels–Design and construction. I. Penner, Richard,
and Lawrence. III. Rutes, Walter A., 1928– Hotel planning and design. IV. Title.
NA7800 E87 2001
728'.5–dc21 00-062521

ISBN 0-393-73055-7

W. W. Norton & Company, Inc., 500 Fifth Avenue, New York, NY 10110
www.wwnorton.com

W. W. Norton & Company, Ltd., 10 Coptic Street, London WC1A 1PU

0 9 8 7 6 5 4 3 2 1

Acknowledgments

This book is the result of many years of experience in the specialized field of hotel architecture and interior design—the experience of the scores of people who generously provided us with their insights about design and with examples of their work. We credit the architects, designers, photographers, and others who encouraged us and provided us with material about their projects in the List of Credits because there are more than we can suitably acknowledge here.

We owe a special debt to three giants in the industry, architect Gyo Obata, designer Michael Bedner, and financial consultant Bjorn Hanson, who agreed to introduce the book with personal observations about their distinguished careers and with projections about the future of hotel architecture, design, and development. In addition, sincere thanks to Robert Kastner, Val Lehr, I.M. Pei, John Portman, Jr., Ian Schrager, Robert A.M. Stern, and Howard Wolff for providing a series of sidebar commentaries for specific chapters.

Our own associates and many good friends provided helpful comments throughout the writing of the book, and others went far beyond the call of duty in providing resources. Thanks especially go to Peter Aaron, Mustafa Abadan, Brandon Adams, Raj Ahuja, Dr. Erik Alexander, Robert Ashton, Fausto Barba, Robert Barry, James Belluardo, Jodie Benzer, Horst Binzer, Peter Blyth, Ted Brumleve, Wendy Brenman, Pope Bullock, Roberto Capponi, Jack Clark, Mark Coffee, David Dann, Arthur Dawson, Kenneth Demay, Jan deRoos, Peter Dixon, Sandra Dove-Lowther, William Eaton, Dr. Blair Ford, Robert Glazier, Emmett Gossen, Michael Gawron, Amy Hall, Sid Hartman, Greg Hartmann, Yoshiro Hashimoto, Alan Helman, Bill Hendrickson, Tiffany Highfield, John Hill, Frank Homiah, Mark Hornberger, Tom Hurley, Steve Jewell, Linda Kastner, Victor Kell, Peter Kuttner, Nick Leko, David O. Levine, Anne Lloyd-Jones, J. Michael Loughran, William Louie, Robert J. Lynch, R. Nicholas Loope, Allison D. Mehta, Alejandro Morales (ASW), John Nicolls, Michael Nowlis, Don Olson, David Oswald, Bradford Perkins, John Portman III, James Rappaport, Michael Redlin, Roque Rey (ASW), Forrest Richardson, Illona Rider, Debra Robinson, Stephani Robson, Corey Sannes, Eliot Soffes, David Stipanuk, William Tabler Jr., Garritt Toohey, James Tortorella, Kim Walker, John Wall, Dr. Mark Warner, Elizabeth Wedge, Monette Williams, Gail Wilson, George Wong, Kellogg Wong, Stanley Wong, Jim Wood, Asegul Yalim, and Larry Ziebarth.

We cannot offer enough thanks for the patience and enormous good judgment of the editors at Architectural Press in Oxford, Gray Publishing in Kent, and W.W. Norton in New York: Marie Milmore, Sian Cryer, Neil Warnock-Smith, Lesley Gray, Nancy Green, Julie Tiller and Robert Gray without whose assistance this book would not be possible.

Also, over the past few years, students at Cornell, New York University, and other universities took on individual research projects or assisted with the many drawings that illustrate the book. These include Jerome Chen (Cornell), Jean Dubyna (NYU), Carlos Fernandez (NYU), Naomi Hori (NYU), Keisuke Nakae (University of New Haven), Eduardo Quintero (Cornell), Carla Silva (Cornell), and Cassy Tristam (RMIT, Melbourne). Their interest and enthusiasm for the details of hotel planning issues are infectious.

There are too many individual contributors to acknowledge each one. We want to thank, however, the many hotel executives who identified their company's most exciting new properties, the representatives of the scores of architectural and interior design firms who provided material, the photographers who culled their very best shots, all of whom willingly met our endless requests for additional information. Most of all, however, we must recognize the sacrifices made by our families who have provided us with incredible support and encouragement to complete this project. Thank you all.

Dedication

We dedicate this book to our partners, children, and grand-children,
with love and deep appreciation for their support and encouragement.

Contents

Foreword

Architect's Perspective

Gyo Obata, FAIA
Co-Founder and Co-Chairman
Helmuth, Obata + Kassabaum, Inc
St. Louis, Missouri

As business and leisure travel become more intertwined, today's hotels must accommodate the overlapping desires and needs of the traveler. Hotels need to provide more things to more people—a place to work, relax, gather, entertain the family, eat, drink, and shop. Modems, computers, wireless phones, and fax machines are becoming room standards while entertainment expectations are now greater than just a tennis court or indoor pool. The convergence of the themed hotel has brought increased competition to the hotel industry.

But whether it is an urban high-rise or a remote retreat, human experience ultimately determines a hotel's success. What are travelers looking for? After all, they are not a homogeneous group. It is crucial that hotel designs take into account this diversity. Our designs must reflect the image of the owner and operator along with the nature of the local surroundings—and produce space that embraces these factors. My job as an architect is to create wonderful destinations of preference that provide the right financial returns for the owner and operator.

In this book, Rutes, Penner, and Adams dissect the emerging trends and essential planning and design criteria of many different types of hotels throughout the world. Each type offers its own rendition of a wonderful travel experience.

When I travel, size—or lack thereof—is very important. I prefer to stay in small, quaint hotels. On the Left Bank of Paris, rooms may be slightly cramped, but it is all about atmosphere. In boutique hotels the architect is given a great opportunity to create an interesting environment around every corner. Larger hotels, though, need not overwhelm visitors. A larger program provides an opportunity for designers to break the hotel into smaller components, bringing it down to a human scale. This gives visitors a more comfortable and personal experience.

Basic amenities also are important. Even the smallest details can affect a guest's experience. Do I have room to spread out my papers? Is the bathroom big enough to set out my toiletries? Can I easily get to the lobby from my room? Are the walls thick enough so I don't hear my neighbor's television? These all are questions we must consider as we design hotels and resorts for today's discerning traveler.

Second Homes for Business Guests

We should try to make hotels, especially urban, suburban, and convention hotels, feel like second homes for business guests. These hotels must offer a full range of business and leisure amenities. We recently completed a leadership center for a major corporation in St. Louis. The design was driven by the company's desire to create a collaborative learning environment—a place where people from throughout the company could come together to exchange information and redesign processes—to learn to think differently. This private 'leadership retreat' consists of a workshop area for lectures, break-out rooms, a dining room, lodges, and living areas. Because employees stay at the center for several days at a time, we spent a great deal of time studying the room features. The rooms had to be warm, comfortable and inviting, while also being conducive for conducting business.

Mixed-use Projects

Mixed-use centers that incorporate hotels offer unlimited options for the business and holiday traveler. These 'cities within cities' benefit the retailer, hotel owner, and guests. We designed The Galleria in Houston as one of the first shopping malls to incorporate mixed uses. Galleria guests can ice skate indoors between business meetings while watching colleagues shop. Over the years, The Galleria has captured the public's imagination and maintained its attraction to local, national, and international visitors.

The designer of mixed-use developments and hotels also must consider and study the surrounding area. Arena Central, a mixed-use facility we're currently designing in Birmingham, England, includes a 450-bed hotel, office and residential components, and an array of entertainment and leisure facilities. Reintegrating the site with central Birmingham's urban fabric was the major challenge. A comprehensive understanding of the site's history, context, and current condition—and appreciation for the city's architecture—helped formulate the redevelopment strategy.

Resort Hotels

Travelers expect today's hospitality facilities to reflect and enhance the environment in which they are located. This is especially true with resorts. The architect must understand the land, site, and environmental considerations in addition to the culture. The challenge for the architect is, first, to identify what's special about the location and, second, to capitalize on its strengths without mimicking other places.

Gone are the days when a beach and a hotel made a resort. Today's guests are active and demand to be entertained. For instance, they prefer interacting with nature instead of just gazing at it. In Hawaii, Hilton awaits final permit approval to begin construction of an artificial lagoon reef, complete with fish, walkways, waterfalls, and undersea caves.

Environmental and Cultural Sensitivity

I want to emphasize the importance of environmental and cultural sensitivity. We are designing resort projects all over the world and recognize that working in different countries requires an appreciation for different criteria. Unspoiled beauty and natural environments draw today's tourists—it's both responsible and great business.

The most effective way we have found to take advantage of environmental assets, local customs, and cultures is to use the owner's and operator's wealth of knowledge. We also form collaborative relationships with local design professionals, manufacturers, and suppliers to make sure that we incorporate indigenous materials throughout our resorts.

The Sheraton Timika Hotel, a remote resort at the edge of a tropical rain forest in Irian Jaya, Indonesia, is one of my favorite projects, and illustrates the importance of the relationship between a resort and its environment. Minimizing the impact of the guesthouse on the environment was a critical concern in the design. Supporting stilts elevate guestroom bungalows above the rain forest floor to preserve the fragile nature of the flora, fauna, and water table. The main lodge rests on an expressed base of local river stone. Interior lobby finishes feature a select palette of Indonesian woods, marble, and stone. All furnishings and textiles were designed and manufactured in Indonesia.

A 250-bed resort and health spa hotel on the Dead Sea in Jordan, owned by BTC of Jordan and operated by Marriott International, also shows how important it is to rely on the knowledge of the owner, operator, and local community. HOK, as the architect, relied on collaboration with the local design, engineering, and construction community in Amman. The resort plan uses indigenous Jordanian architecture, both in terms of materials and shading techniques. The scheme creates a lush inner court featuring a two-tier pool with waterfalls, whirlpools, and local plant life. The interior draws on local materials to create a welcoming, cool, and relaxing environment. Responding to the therapeutic wonders of the Dead Sea, a full-service health and beauty spa lies near the shoreline. The successful design of the scheme springs from a combination of technology and operational know-how, along with the skill and energy of the local client team.

I cannot talk about travel destinations without mentioning ski resorts. I love to ski. I've never designed a ski resort but I have a great idea for one. Because skiers are loaded down with boots and ski equipment, I think it's important to minimize the change in elevation where people walk, shop, dine, and catch lifts. Making it easy for people to move seems simple, but it's so important.

The point is that planning a successful hotel or resort is all about improving the human experience. Whether people travel to an urban hotel tower on business or to a ski resort on vacation, guests walk away feeling good, bad, or indifferent. If the feeling is not good, you've lost your audience.

An Unquenchable Thirst For More

I congratulate the authors of this book for preparing such a comprehensive reference piece. *Hotel Design, Planning and Development* provides practical advice on how to maximize the human experience in this ever-changing industry. I also applaud the owners and operators that have responded to travelers' unquenchable thirst for more. The demand for more specific and comprehensive hotels and resorts has helped create a more sophisticated design industry. Just turn the pages and take a look.

Interior Designer's Perspective

Michael J. Bedner
Co-founder and CEO
Hirsch Bedner Associates
Santa Monica, California

Hirsch Bedner Associates has been fortunate to play a significant role in the hospitality design industry for more than 35 years. During that time, we've introduced new concepts and helped redefine older ones. We've seen trends come and go, and sometimes come back again. Through it all, we've learned to distinguish between the timeless and the transitory in terms of emotions, lifestyles, and designs.

Like most types of design, the interior design of hotels and resorts evolves with the changes and advances in materials and technology as well as the shifting experiences and expectations of the guests. Unlike most types of buildings, hotels and resorts are designed from the inside out, with a greater emphasis on the interior spaces and how the guests will interact within them.

Adding to the challenges of creating functional, pleasing, and timeless designs for hotels and resorts are other complex variables. Today's tourists and travelers are better educated, more selective, and far more socially responsible. They demand more attention to, and sensitivity for, local cultural and environmental circumstances and concerns. Successful hospitality design must have a sense of style and offer a special feeling of place. Flashy gimmicks and temporary experiments with design elements are major impediments to achieving the ideal balance of grace and beauty while respecting practical operating considerations.

Those of us at HBA are pleased and proud to have worked with the authors of this book in a variety of ways over the past three decades. We share with them an interest in a dynamic and exciting enterprise—the design of hotels and resorts in all corners of the world. They share with us our understanding of what makes a project successful, not only in bottom-line business aspects, but in more important design and human terms.

Developer's Perspective

Dr. Bjorn Hanson, Ph.D.
Global Industry Partner, PricewaterhouseCoopers LLP
New York, New York

The past 10 years have been a period of extraordinary change in the history of the lodging industry with so many implications for development and financing. Just a few of these changes and their implications are given below.

Lower break-even

Our firm's analysis of US lodging data highlights an astounding structural change in the occupancy required for a hotel to break even: break-even occupancy has decreased from 65.5 percent in the late 1980s to 51.5 percent. The largest factor in this dramatic change is the cumulative effect of increases in the average room rate above the rate of inflation. Essentially, more revenue from rate means less revenue is needed from occupancy. Other factors lowering break-even occupancy is the reduced number of employees per 100 occupied rooms from a high of 81 in 1986 to about 75 today. This is the result of management actions such as employee empowerment programs, making some services optional (such as turn-down service), use of technology (reducing accounting, switchboard and other positions), and de-emphasizing less profitable departments, as well as the change in mix to limited-service hotels. Other factors that have contributed to lower break-even occupancy include lower debt leverage and relatively low interest rates. The result of lower break-even occupancy is that developers and lenders face less risk of the types of losses they encountered in the early 1990s than at any time in history and that debt-service coverage ratios, the primary test used by lenders, are at all time highs.

Increasing segmentation

There is a greater range of choices of lodging products than ever before. Many of these exhibit highly favorable economics, require very small parcels of land, have lower project costs and, therefore, are easier to finance. Some extended-stay and limited-service concepts can be developed on less than one acre. Guests may choose across a range of specialized lodging types and many price points, increasing demand, which, in turn, allows for the development of new properties in additional markets. This incremental demand is not only driven by price. It is fueled by emerging tastes and preferences for such offerings as eco-lodging, adventure travel, health-oriented holidays, and learning vacations.

New Sources of Capital

Dramatic changes also have occurred with sources of capital. For example, in the early 1990s, only five percent of hotel rooms in the United States were under public ownership. In 2000 the number is over 18 percent. Also important is that the number of rooms controlled by public companies, whether through ownership, management, or franchise, is now over 62 percent. In exchange for access to relatively inexpensive capital these companies are subject to the analysis and scrutiny of the public markets and, as a result, are highly focused on quarter-over-quarter and year-over-year growth in earnings. Returns from dividends to shareholders typically are only about one-fourth of the cost of private debt. Access to capital fuels new construction and consolidation. This access to capital, in turn, has fueled rapid consolidation with the five largest lodging companies now controlling over 40 brands.

Industry Globalization

In the 1980s, major international lodging companies were almost exclusively focused on their home country, whether it was in the United States, Europe, or Asia. But as the lodging consumer has become more international, so have the hotel management companies. This increasing globalization is supported by the lower cost of international travel, increased international business activity, and the increasing availability of technology. At the turn of the century, unlike only a few years ago, two of the five largest lodging companies in the world are based outside the USA.

These and other major issues will continue to shape the industry in the next decades. There has never been a time with so many complexities and possibilities for developers, lenders, and investors—or a future full of such challenges and opportunities.

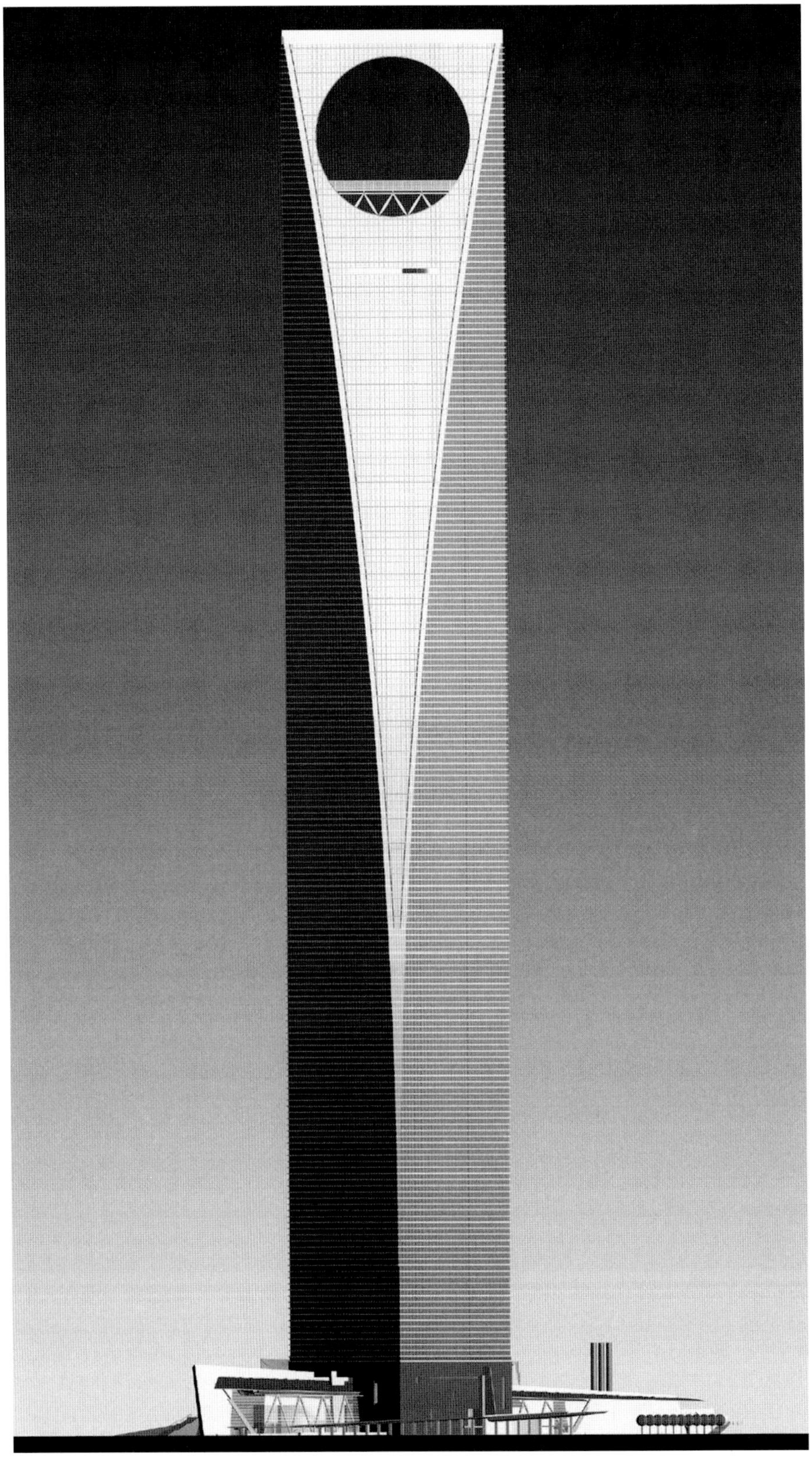

The ultratel **Shanghai World Financial Center, China** (see pp. 209–210). Ever-burgeoning Shanghai's proposed second multiuse vertically-tiered ultratel tower (94 stories), by KPF Architects, combines hotel, office, and related amenities in a unique and striking design, focused on a spectacular rooftop visitors' center near the top. The size and location of the hotel component within such structures, as highlighted in the accompanying key diagram, is based on predesign market-trend research.

Preface

For their kind Foreword illuminating the timeless goals of the world's largest industry, we immensely thank Gyo Obata, Michael Bedner, and Bjorn Hanson, who represent the major disciplines involved with hotel development and design.

As architects, we admit to a certain tingling sensation each time we hear of another 'ultratel' tower, one of the most impressive hotel prototypes developed in the 15 years since our previous book, *Hotel Planning and Design,* was published. Perhaps the next few decades will see as exciting concepts for new environments, such as 'spacetels,' and 'marinetels.' With an increasing proportion of development worldwide stimulated by hotels and new megatrends changing their essential character, it is again time to analyze the changing state of art in hotel design, planning, and development.

The inquiry begins with the word 'hotel,' meaning mansion, borrowed from the French soon after the American Revolution in an effort to express the sophistication of the new multifaceted inns that appeared. From their onset, these novel mixed-use establishments served the varied needs of a rapidly expanding society, freely incorporating new residential, commercial, and industrial features in hotels. These included the first grand ballroom in New York, an atrium and Merchants' Exchange in Boston, a domed European lobby in New Orleans, and a theater, shops, and laundry in London. Their competitive nature competitive nature advanced the newest technologies such as gas and electric lighting, central heat, telephones, and elevators.

Consumer needs and desires more than ever drive hotel design and development today, ranging from 100-story ultratels to a variety of new entertainment hotels literally illuminating locations such as New York's Times Square and Toronto's SkyDome stadium complex. Other novel concepts include the latest niche boutique hotels and the response to the health consciousness megatrend with urban resort spas.

Our imaginations happily pass through different prisms of experience as architects, educators, and hotel executives, but we are unanimous in never before having seen a more extraordinary succession of inspired designs created by the collaboration and wisdom of owners and developers, architects and designers, operators and consultants. They know full well that success lies in the most popular and forward-looking market design concepts. While supported by socioeconomic research, as in all growing industries, the hotel industry thrives on the market research of prevailing trends to shape future development.

Such trends include a vast emerging global marketplace and, most importantly, increasingly sophisticated consumers, freely pursuing highly personalized perceptions of choice and value. These often are combined with avid interests in ecotourism, environmental conservation, historic preservation, education and self-development, as well as the expanding health consciousness of a maturing population. Other expectations include increasing numbers of family vacations, in part enhanced by vacation ownership, and greater opportunities and business travel for women. Most guests clearly prefer informal but high-styled residential decor and functionality in the guestroom or suite combined with exciting cuisine and entertainment, dramatic themed shopping, exotic gaming venues, and unique sports experiences including spectacular golf, shared yacht ownership, and year-round skiing. New choices for getaways include vacation ownership and cruise ships, urban and suburban leisure parks, low-density multiuse communities, and pioneering ecotourist resort regions.

In the following chapters we expand upon the product trends of today's huge and budding demand generators, ranging from novel theming to the internet. We observe that many of today's product attributes did not even exist a decade or two ago. So sophisticated are today's markets that certain once-popular concepts have faded into oblivion while some previously negative traits are now considered positive attractions. Therefore, we are pleased to be able to interpret today's design, technology, and creative concepts which offer such bright prospects for the future.

Walter A. Rutes, Richard H. Penner,
and Lawrence Adams

Part 1

Mall Hotel

Hotel Types

With concepts ranging from resort theme parks to efficient extended-stays and from high-fashion boutique hotels to flexible virtual office suites, Part 1 reviews more than 50 different types of hotels now flourishing in today's increasingly customized marketplace. Separate chapters are devoted to each of 12 major categories. For example, suburban hotels offer many choices as varied as airport hotels are from country inns, while resorts encompass an ever-widening array as unique as the ecotourist retreat is from the convention resort. Countless downtown and suburban structures reinvent their ambiance through innovative renovations, restoration, additions, and adaptive reuse.

The successful conference center, which significantly differs from the convention resort or mega-hotel, for instance, is clearly addressed in terms of design options, planning, and development considerations as well as social and cultural implications. Future trends are outlined in each category and summarized in the final chapter of Part 3. A continuing theme is the emphasis on strongly targeting specific market sectors so that the hotel may better fulfill its function. For example, luxury resorts and super-luxury hotels need small, superb restaurants and health spas to maintain their clientele.

This part begins with an overview tracing the hotel's evolution and the latest forecasts of its future development, viewed in an historical perspective, and summarizes these in a chart on hotel milestones. The evolutionary tree diagram is another theme threading through these chapters.

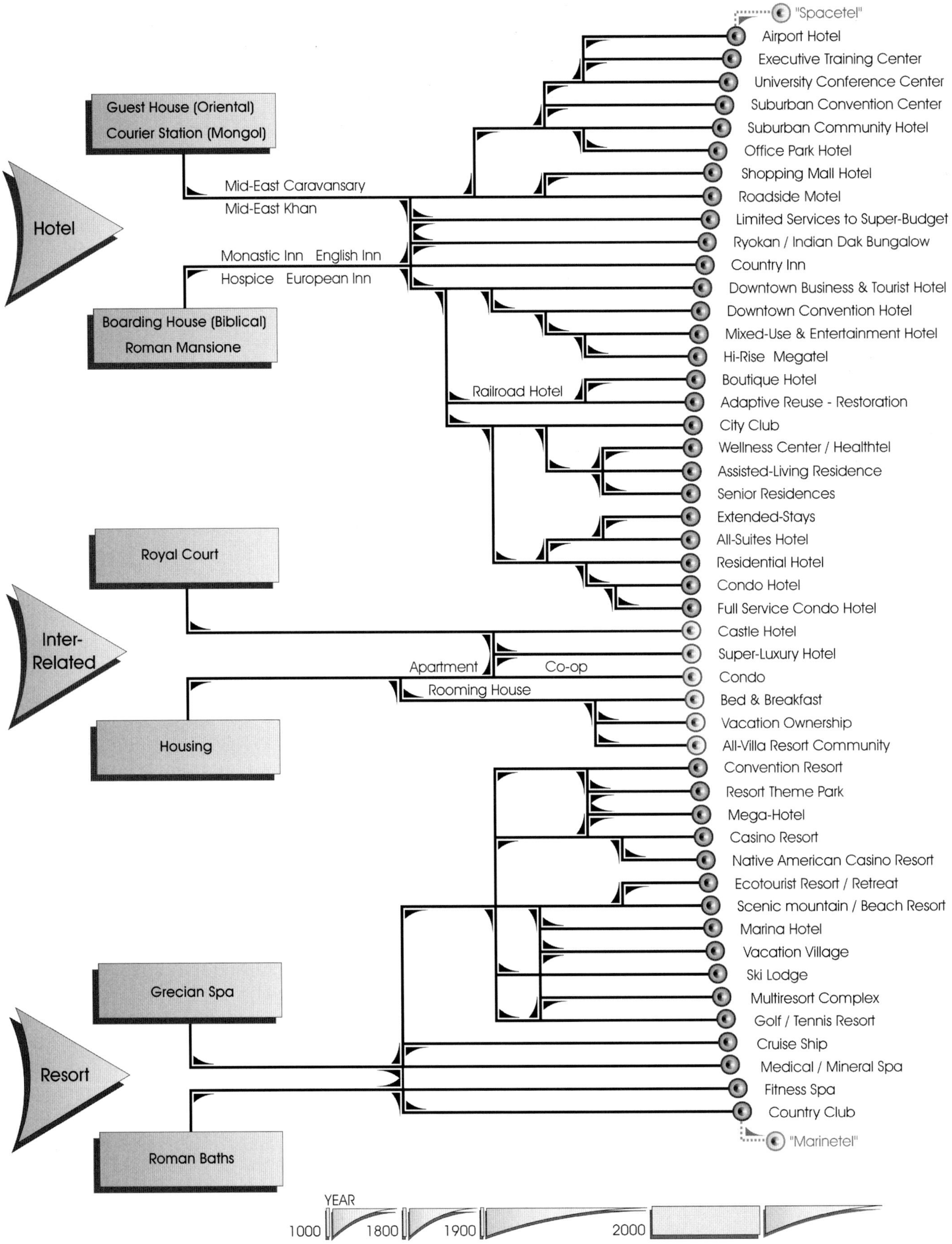

Hotel varieties multiply **Evolutionary tree diagram.** The diagram illustrates the increasingly diverse types of hotels, mostly emerging in the past few decades, and their related roots. Drawing by Adams Soffes Wood.

Overview 1

Arriving in Isfahan centuries ago, you could stay outside the city gates at a roadside caravansary now called the Sha Abbas. Or desiring better service, you might continue to The Khan, an intown hotel. As a 'frequent traveler' journeying to Rome, you could stay at a downtown mansione, a boarding house on the Appian Way, or at a spa resort.

While the quality of hotels has advanced immeasurably over several centuries, the basic elements remained almost as simple and familiar as in ancient times. But with growing guest sophistication and imaginative design and development, the world's largest industry anticipates a vast demand for the increasingly diverse and popular customized types of hotels, resorts and leisure-time amenities now appearing worldwide. Among the more than 50 different types of hotels illustrated and discussed in this part of the book, many variations are being refined and their markets assessed. They range from sensible extended-stay residential-feel units to sensitively designed urban boutique hotels. Hotel development encompasses many diverse fields from senior and assisted-living residences to authentic ecotourist retreats as well as exemplary adaptive reuse and restoration of existing urban infrastructure. And the latter provides a variety of fine hotels and entertainment amenities that dramatically upgrade inner-city environments. With ongoing 'imagineering,' family theme parks increasingly continue to serve as multiresorts for major corporate trade exhibitions and conventions as well as for advanced leisure park communities.

Based on resort examples ranging from Costa Smeralda, Sardinia, to Branson, Missouri, regional economies are benefiting from innovative tourism planning (see Chapter 4). For example, the latter features a unique galaxy of star performance palaces, showcasing favorite regional country and western entertainment, stimulating the development of new resorts. Also, at numerous Native American reservations, casinos are attracting additional hotel and resort developments upgrading the areas' economies, including one in Connecticut valued at $1 billion (see Chapter 13). And one of the most successful new prototypes of the era, a 2,145-room complex adjacent to the Orlando Convention Center, is the first major convention resort designed for cost-sensitive consumer groups (see Chapter 5), a sector for which the industry traditionally provides high standards at affordable rates, often at prices below those which are feasible. Targeting the design is a good way of giving each group more choice in their preferred benefits.

Other major prototype and 'protopart' developments include hotels with themed shopping and entertainment atriums, cruise ships, all-villa enclaves and various types of vacation ownership resorts, spas and 'healthtels' as well as ultra-high-rise towers, dubbed 'ultratels,' with various vertically integrated mixed-uses including offices and trade centers with flex-suites affording virtual officing. A wide range of the era's most significant hotel types, extending from future concepts for world-class multiresort destinations to the most innovative and cost-effective limited-service prototypes are illustrated in their full global arrays of settings.

Parts 2 and 3 provide information on how to program and develop the various hotel types, while the latest examples in each category are illustrated in the chapters of Part 1, where different features of each type of hotel are described with examples. For instance, for one of the newest types, see the section on the entertainment hotel in Chapter 2.

Varieties

Earlier studies charted significant growth of over 30 diversified hotel prototypes developed largely in US markets. Not surprisingly, the count of major types shown on the accompanying tree diagram is now up to 50 worldwide, and still rising.

For the first time the hotel classification system has

expanded its basic categories to recognize new hotel types such as all-suites and extended-stays and the parameters of new and redefined rate categories such as super-luxury, luxury-deluxe, luxury, upscale, mid-rate, limited-service, economy, and budget (see Appendix C).

Genealogy

Visualize an evolutionary tree reaching from its historic roots to its highest branches, a tree budding new hotel and resort concepts. Consider the roadside motel, descendant of the coach inn and posting station, in turn rooted in the monastic inn and caravansary of the Middle Ages, as well as the Roman *mansione*, all catering to the travelers of their times. Then consider a type still in relative infancy, the all-suite hotel, which was developed as a hybrid of the residential hotel and condominium, while a third type, the vacation ownership unit, as we know, combines the condominium with the destination resort, creating a superb family destination with tradability. For an illuminating historical view, trace the origins of different types of hotels in the list of hotel milestones later in the chapter as well as in the tree diagram.

A clear understanding of how a successful prototype evolves is essential in developing new concepts and projecting their growth (see Chapter 22). For example, China's major expansion of downtown and tourist hotels to better serve international tourists and business travelers and obtain foreign exchange credits moves steadily ahead, including two strikingly varied nearly 100-story mixed-use 'ultratels' in Shanghai (see Chapter 12). While China has greatly benefited from the latest worldwide experience in the design of hotels, initially catering to foreign travelers, as its economy advances it plans other types of ultimately needed hotels and resorts through adapting today's most innovative topology to its own required standards and traditions.

In industrialized nations, a familiarity with the new hotel types is essential in order for developers to plan their expansion strategies and devise more imaginative prototypical features that attract new groups. As some types of hotels are as different as a single-family home is from a high-rise apartment tower in the residential field, it is essential for the designer to understand the variations in facilities, areas, and circulation patterns required for each new form of hotel. Also, an overall familiarity of the diverse types encourages cross-fertilization of ideas: for example, introducing larger health spas to fill relaxation needs at conference centers, adding meeting rooms to turn country inns into instant conference retreats, and borrowing attributes of super-luxury hotels, such as original artwork, to upgrade other types of hotels. New ideas for better hotels come from each member of the consulting team, ranging from market researchers to food and beverage specialists, and including a variety of disciplines from high-tech systems experts to talented landscape architects and environmentalists. The fields in which consultants are recommended, and required, are considered in Chapter 19.

Classifications

Since hotels usually are classified by location, function, and other special characteristics, a given hotel may enter into more than one category. For example, the W Hotel in Union Square, New York, is both a boutique hotel and an example of adaptive reuse. However, the overlap should not impair the usefulness of the classification system referenced in this book, which permits easy access to information using subject headings that are used in the hotel field and are clear to the public.

While hotel classifications are necessary for the purposes of organizing and referencing information, they are by no means perfect and no substitute for specific knowledge of the individual character and detailed ingredients of the hotel. As the *New Haven Register* lamented:

> *Along with new hotel types and almost infinite combinations and varieties, it is increasingly difficult for guests to select a hotel when labels are inadequate or misleading. Downtown hotels have as many tennis courts, pools and saunas as resorts. Resorts have as many convention or conference guests as downtown convention hotels or airport meeting centers. Motor inns are not necessarily superior to motels. And 'inns' are not necessarily old. 'Lodge,' 'spa,' 'guest ranch,' are also unclear labels. Price is no indicator—expensive hotels may have small rooms, while budget hotels have larger, better appointed rooms. Buying on the basis of ingredients looks like the new wave.*

But continuing research says do not count on it, no matter what one may wish. It is likely that today's oxymoron marketing mantra of mass customization is increasing in the hotel field, after bringing gold to industries ranging from clothing to personalized vitamins. It responds to the consumer's desire for individual treatment in an increasingly impersonal world. If the typical guest buys designer clothes and made-to-order music CD's from a long questionnaire then why not a virtual Ritz at Times Square?

Therefore, in this book guest perception is emphasized as well as actual differences in types. In other words, what's *in* at the inn is even as important as *what's* in it.

Planning and Design Considerations

Since each hotel type has a different goal as to the kind of guest it seeks, its planning requirements will vary by the location selected, size, image, space standards, circulation, and other similar characteristics. For example, convention hotels and conference centers require proximity to airports, while vacation villages and ski lodges do not. Airport hotels and roadside motels need high visibility and signage, while conference centers, country inns, vacation villages, and ecotourist retreats seek seclusion. And while super-luxury hotels must be small to create an intimate atmosphere, luxury and upscale hotels must be large enough to justify the great number of restaurants, lounges, and banquet rooms required by first-class or five-star international standards.

Design considerations also vary by type. For example, resorts require larger rooms, closets, and drawer space than downtown hotels due to the longer stays of their guests and the greater number of occupants per room. Some roadside motels may need larger restaurants than other hotels for peak periods such as breakfast, but no room service. Casino hotels require a glittering design, while conference center décor needs to be more understated. Also similar design concepts are expressed differently in each hotel type. For example, the social pastime of people-watching in the downtown or suburban hotel is accommodated by its lobby or atrium space. The same purpose is served by the pool deck in a resort, the sun deck at the ski lodge, the commons area at the conference center, the outdoor bar at the piazza of the vacation village, the tea lounge of the super-luxury hotel, or the high-fashion lobby of the boutique hotel.

While the specific facilities, area programs, and technical requirements are discussed in Parts 2 and 3, this part summarizes the main variations and trends of current planning and design for each distinct hotel type.

Hotel Milestones

Reflecting social change as well as new technology, this list traces the most significant events in the development of lodging, from ancient times to today's worldwide advances

Ancient times	Boarding houses existed. First resorts at mineral and hot springs in Greece. *Mansiones* built along Roman roads to lodge government-sanctioned travelers; inns existed for others. Romans spread spa resorts to England, Switzerland, Middle East; introduced *campona* (inns) in England. Riviera popular with Phoenician and Greek traders. *Caravansaries*, cloistered courtyard caravan stops, provided by government along roads in the Middle East and *khans*, small inns, established in towns.
Middle Ages	Manorial lords, abbeys, and monasteries sheltered some travelers. Monastic inns run by religious orders. Hospices built as hospitals and shelters for travelers. Some inns developed in larger towns (no meals). Rooming houses used as relay stations for mail, government transport, rest stops, and changing horses. Hospitalers created shelters for Crusaders and pilgrims traveling to Holy Land.
1100s	Travel became safer in Europe. Inns prospered with freedom and right to travel, declined in times of lawlessness. The European inn gradually developed. The Three Kings Inn in Basle, Switzerland, opened; the earliest inn still operating.
1200s	Guest houses and courier mail stations developed in China and Mongolia. Rooming and relay stations opened for mail, government transportation, and rest stops. Cour St. Georges Inn opened in Ghent, Belgium. Angel Inn opened in Grantham, Lincolnshire, England.
1300s	The English country inn developed. Castle Inn founded in Taunton, Somerset, England. French law required innkeepers to replace stolen property plus three times its value as damages to victims.

1400s	French law introduced requirement for a hotel register. English law established regulations for inns. The Krone Inn in Solothrun, Switzerland, is earliest adaptive reuse—converted from a residence.
1500s	European spas revived in Carlsbad and Marienbad, present-day Czech Republic. Stagecoaches developed, using Roman road system; teams changed, carriages checked, and travelers accommodated at posting houses. English innkeeper set pattern for Europe and USA to follow; 6000 inns in England. Inn plan took form of enclosed cobble court with arched entrance, rooms along two sides, kitchen and public rooms at front, stabling and storage at rear. First travelers' guide published rating inns in France.
1600s	Hotel industry developed in Europe with well-placed and reliable cuisine 'at sign of insignia on a metal plaque, grating its rugged hinges in every wind.' Seaport inns developed in US cities, e.g. The Blue Anchor in Philadelphia. Village inns developed as required by Massachusetts law in all towns, e.g. Old Yarmouth Inn at Yarmouthport. First scheduled coach service established in England.
1700s	Clubhouses similar to British clubs and Masonic lodges developed in USA. Spa resorts developed in Yellow Springs, Pennsylvania, and White Sulphur Springs, West Virginia. Boodles and Coventry Clubhouses opened in London. Market Square Taverne founded in Williamsburg, Virginia. Place Vendôme, Paris, was the first mixed-use complex.
1780s	Dessien's, Calais, France, and Covent Garden Inn in London were early large inns.
1790s	Industrial revolution stimulated hotels in England, Europe, and USA; resorts developed. Corre's Hotel and City Hotel in New York were first downtown hotels. Hotel D'Angleterre opened in Copenhagen, Denmark, was earliest adaptive reuse. Saratoga Springs, New York, developed as a spa resort.
1800s	White Hart Hotel opened in Salisbury, and Royal Hotel founded in Plymouth, England. Luxury 'swagger hotels' established in major cities. Early resorts built along French and Italian Riviera. Imposing clubhouses built. Fulton's Cleremont steamship launched. Exchange Coffee House in Boston was first atrium hotel.
1810s	Ryokan guest houses developed in Japan. Dak bungalow, 24-hour guest stops, run by Indian government .
1820s	Catskill Mountain House in New York State was an early, major resort. City Hotel in Baltimore, Maryland, was first hotel with partial gaslighting. B&O Railroad began passenger service. Tremont House in Boston is first luxury downtown hotel with indoor toilets, door locks on rooms, and à la carte menu.
1830s	Saratoga Springs Hotel opened in New York State. American Hotel in New York City was first with gaslighting throughout. Astor House opened in New York City. St. Charles and St. Louis Hotels established in New Orleans, Louisiana. Holt's Hotel, New York City, was the first with a baggage elevator. Reform Club in London had courtyard roofed-in to become an early atrium. Euston Station Hotel, London, was an early example of a railroad hotel.
1840s	Railroads replaced coaches; coach-route inns declined. Shephard's Hotel in Cairo, Egypt, was an early major adaptive reuse. Hotel des Trois Couronnes founded in Vevey and Bar au Lac Hotel opened in Zurich, Switzerland. New York Hotel in New York City was first with private baths. Planters Hotel founded in St. Louis, Missouri. The Homestead established in Hot Springs, Virginia. Resorts developed in Coney Island, New York.

1850s

Spa resorts reached height of popularity.
Resorts developed in Niagara Falls, New York, and New Jersey shore.
Mills House opened in Charleston, South Carolina (rebuilt in 1970).
Parker House established in Boston (rebuilt in 1927).
Fifth Avenue Hotel in New York City is first with passenger elevators.

1860s

Railroad terminal hotels such as Charing Cross in London were main type developed through the 1920s.
Mohonk Mountain House established in the Catskills, New York State.
Central and Union Pacific Railroads were joined.

1870s

Coney Island, New York, is a themed seaside resort with Queen Anne and Oriental-style hotels and an amusement park with a roller coaster.
Fashionable Vendôme Hotel built in Boston. Sherman House founded in Chicago.
Palmer House opened in Chicago was largest at the time and the first built with a fireproof structure (rebuilt in 1925).
Palace Hotel in San Francisco was the earliest hotel with a large atrium.
Grand Hotel built in Point Clear, Alabama.
Continental opened in Paris (restored in 1970 by Inter-Continental).

1880s

Hotel Del Monte established in Monterey, California.
Hotel Everett, New York City, was the first with partial electric lights.
Sagamore Hotel at Lake George, New York, was first with electricity in all rooms.
Chelsea Hotel, New York City, was first large residential hotel.
Mountainview House established in Whitefield, New Hampshire.
Ponce De Leon Hotel, St. Augustine, Florida, was the first built of concrete.
Grand Hotel, Mackinac Island, Michigan, had the largest veranda.
Victoria Hotel, Kansas City, Missouri, was the first with baths in all rooms.
Hotel Del Coronado, San Diego, California, was the largest resort of its time.
Whiteface Inn and Golf Club founded in Lake Placid, New York.
Savoy in London was the first hotel with a theater, chapel, print shop, and laundry.

1890s

The Broadmoor opened in Colorado Springs, Colorado.
Brown Palace, Denver, Colorado, had the earliest hotel atrium still operating.
Copley Square Hotel opened in Boston.
Ecole Hotelière, Lausanne, Switzerland was first hotel school.
Hotel Netherland, New York City, was the first with telephones in all rooms.
The Breakers opened in Palm Beach, Florida (rebuilt in 1906 and 1926).
Lake Placid Club established in Lake Placid, New York.
Original Waldorf=Astoria built in New York City, tallest of its time, at 17 stories (later the site of the 102-story Empire State Building).
Wentworth-by-the-Sea opened in New Castle, New Hampshire.
Claridges, Berkeley, and Connaught all opened in London.

1900s

The Ritz founded in London.
The Willard opened in Washington, DC.
The Plaza, St. Regis, and The Astor built in New York City.
Taj Mahal Hotel opened in Bombay (restored in 1972 by Inter-Continental).
Ellsworth M. Statler of Buffalo, New York, set the main planning principles for modern multistory hotels.
First cross-country auto trip in the US.

1910s

Grand Central Terminal in New York City was an early mixed-use complex.
Boarding house resorts developed in the Catskills, New York State.
The Bellevue-Stratford opened in Philadelphia. Copley Plaza built in Boston.
Beverly Hills Hotel established in California.
The Greenbrier opened in White Sulphur Springs, West Virginia.
Asilomar near Carmel, California, was the first nonprofit conference center.
Kahler Hotel in Rochester, Minnesota, was the first medical hotel.
First trans-Atlantic flight and first scheduled airline.
Hotel Pennsylvania in New York City has 2,200 rooms—largest of the time.

1920s	***Hotel boom #1*** generated by economic prosperity. Grand Central Station, New York City was a transportation complex connected with five hotels. Miami Beach developed with Mediterranean-style architecture, e.g. Flamingo, Pancoast, and Roney Plaza Hotels. School of Hotel Administration established at Cornell University. First nonstop cross-country plane flight. Baker and Adolphus hotels opened in Dallas, Texas. Royal Hawaiian established in Honolulu. Prohibition caused decline of hotel/restaurant business. The Ritz-Calrton opened on the Boston Public Gardens. The Statler in Boston was first mixed-use hotel/office building. Ahwahnee Hotel built in Yosemite National Park in California. Biltmore founded in Santa Barbara, California. Arizona Biltmore built in Phoenix, Arizona. Stevens Hotel in Chicago had 2,700 rooms—largest of the time. The Cloister opened in Sea Island, Georgia.
1930s	Depression forced most US hotels into receivership. The new Waldorf=Astoria in New York City, largest of the time, built during the Depression.
1940s	Statler, Washington, DC, is one of few hotels built during World War II. Flamingo in Las Vegas is a first casino hotel. Statler hotels in Los Angeles, California, Hartford, Connecticut, and Dallas, Texas were among the first post-war hotels. San Souci in Miami was first new post-war resort.
1950s	***Hotel boom #2*** generated by expanded education and mass travel. Resorts developed in the Caribbean. Vacation village concept developed by Club Med. Holiday Inn was first motel with large rooms. Casino hotels developed in Las Vegas, Nevada. Fountainbleau opened in Miami Beach. First commercial trans-Atlantic jet service. Airlines began developing hotels.
1960s	In the USA 23,000 hotels, 40,000 motels, and 170 chains operated. Resorts developed in Spanish Mediterranean, Portugal, Balearic Islands, Scandinavia, Greece, and Yugoslavia. Hyatt Regency in Atlanta, Georgia, reintroduced atrium. Arden House of Columbia University, Tarrytown House in Tarrytown, New York, and General Electric Co. in Crotonville, New York, were first conference centers used extensively by businesses. Sheraton at Prudential Center in Boston was major hotel/mixed-use complex. Hilton Palacio del Rio Hotel in San Antonio, Texas, was first built with concrete prefabricated modules.
1970s	Boeing 747 introduced; airlines became active in hotel development through subsidiary chains. New hotel expansion took up slack caused by demolition and conversions of hotels to apartments and office buildings. Walt Disney World Resort near Orlando, Florida, opened as first major hotel/amusement destination center. Extensive hotel development in Middle East generated by oil prosperity. Luxury condominiums developed offering hotel services. Hotel restorations extensively developed. First suite hotels converted from condominiums. Timesharing and condominium resorts developed. MGM Grand casino hotel fire in Las Vegas caused changes in building and fire codes. Outbreak of Legionnaires' disease at The Bellevue-Stratford Hotel in Philadelphia causes bankruptcy and changes in engineering and maintenance operations. No-smoking rules take effect in US Federal buildings. Peachtree Plaza in Atlanta, Georgia, built with 70 stories—tallest hotel. Multiresort complexes developed in Maui, Hawaii, and Cancun, Mexico. China opened to foreign tourists; international hotel experts invited to participate in development of facilities. Mid-east investments in US real estate increase values of hotels and resorts.

1980s

Hotel boom #3 generated by innovative marketing and development of specialized types of hotels; many combined with large-scale commercial complexes such as Copley Place and Lafayette Place in Boston.
Airport hotels, conference centers, all-suite hotels, vacation villages, health spas, marina hotels, ski lodges, timesharing, and condominium resorts expanded rapidly.
Casino hotels developed in Atlantic City, New Jersey.
Condominium hotels developed, such as The Ritz-Carlton and Four Seasons in Boston and UN Plaza in New York City.
Limited-service budget motels continued rapid growth.
Popular revival of country inns.
Marriott Marquis in Atlanta was largest convention hotel.
Marriott Marquis in Times Square in New York City was highest cost hotel project.
Hyatt and Marriott opened mega-hotels in Orlando, Florida.
Hotel Boom in China; 50 major hotels under construction or design including 2,000-room Lidu in Beijing; increase from 200,000 visitors at beginning of decade to 5,000,000 per year expected by end of century.
Embassy Suites and Crowne Plaza by Holiday Inn, Courtyard by Marriott, and Residence Inn debut.
Japanese investments in US real estate increase values of hotels and resorts.
Americans with Disabilities Act (ADA) began to affect broad areas of hotel operation and design.
Electronic key card for hotel rooms introduced by Ving.

1990s

Gulf war slows tourism.
Recession of 1991 resulted in lowest financial record in hotel history, with majority of hotels not meeting debt service.
Growth through conversions became more prevalent.
Over 75 percent of top 25 US chains engaged in global hotels.
Casinos and hotels on Native American reservations gained acceptance.
Riverboat Gaming on Mississippi River and Gulf Coast.
Budget hotels became industry's leading money makers.
Saudi investor bails out Fairmont and Four Seasons Hotels as well as the EuroDisney (now Disneyland Paris Resort) development near Paris.
Palace of the Lost City in Africa was highest cost casino resort.
Vacation ownership booming with 5 million members.
Regent Four Seasons built in New York was highest cost hotel project per room.
Mega-casino themed resorts rapidly expanded in Las Vegas including New York, New York, Bellagio, Mandalay Bay, the Venetian, and Paris, attracting family market.
Cruise ships booming due to unmatched appeal to affluent elderly population.
Business centers with a self-service office available to hotel guests.
Universal Studios opened major resort theme park including mega-hotel in Orlando.
Walt Disney Company announced expansion of luxury resort, retail, dining, and entertainment center at Disneyland, Anaheim, California, and added theme park and mall at Disneyland Paris Resort in Marne-la-Valle, France.
Atlantis mega-hotel opened on Paradise Island, Bahamas.
Technology pervaded hotels with Internet connections, new communications, and entertainment systems.

Hotel boom #4 generated by advanced technology, imaginative design and the successful marketing of mass customization of hotels, resorts, and leisure-time amenities.
Spas booming to baby-boomers who perceive them as essential to health.
Boutique hotels booming to business travelers, with developers rapidly converting and building new properties as well as new chains by the originators, Ian Schrager Hotels, Kimco/Palomar, brand *W* by Starwood Hotels, and others.
Billion-dollar Native American mixed-use casino complex partially completed and still expanding in Connecticut, catapulting the region into a major gaming center.
Entertainment hotels being introduced in downtown areas including New York.
Hilton Hotels acquired Promus, owner of Embassy Suites/Doubletree, reordering leading worldwide chain rankings to Marriott, Starwood, Hilton, Bass, and Accor.
Over 250 luxury and upscale hotels announced for development worldwide.
Ultra-high-rise mixed-use hotels on rise in Shanghai, Bangkok, and other major cities.

The versatile boutique business and tourist hotel **W San Francisco, California** (see pp. 17 and 286). Clad in sculpted precast-concrete panels, the 30-story, 423-room hotel is built in Yerba Buena Gardens, a 25-year urban renewal project, South of Market in the heart of downtown. Located next door to Arata Isozaki's Museum of Modern Art and near Moscone Convention Center, the Sony Metreon Entertainment Center, and Union Square's luxury retail shops, the hotel serves a variety of downtown markets, including conventioneers, the fashion set, Internet entrepreneurs, and the never-ending stream of tourists to the 'city by the bay.'

Downtown Hotels 2

Downtown Business and Tourist Hotels

The City Hotel built in 1794 on lower Broadway in New York City trumpeted a new form of hospitality building distinct from European inns and US seaport and village inns of that period. Designed by Benjamin Latrobe and larger than any inn, the City Hotel was five stories tall, had 73 guest-rooms, but, most significantly, housed a ballroom and banquet hall—public spaces that forecast the new role that hotels would play as the center of downtown social and business life for centuries to come. Expanding on that new role in 1809, the Exchange Coffee House in Boston featured an assortment of public social and business functions including a ballroom, a restaurant, a coffee room, and a merchant's exchange floor beneath a 100 ft (30 m) diameter sky-lit dome making this the first atrium hotel and further defining this new downtown business and tourist hotel genre.

It was the Tremont House in Boston that established hotels as enduring monuments in the city-scape. Clad in Quincy granite, the Tremont was the most costly building in the USA in 1828. It earned the title 'The Adam and Eve of the Modern Hotel Industry' by setting the standard for deluxe innovations including private locked rooms, indoor bathrooms, à la carte menus, the first bellboys, and an annunciator system that allowed guests to call the front desk from their rooms. The architect, Isaiah Rogers, devised an ingenious floor plan of crossing corridors that splayed the public rooms across the front of the building with courtyards in the back and an intersecting guestroom wing that separated public from private realms. Envious of the Tremont's stature, John Jacob Astor hired Rogers seven years later to design the Astor House in New York City as the new best hotel in the country. Other US cities joined the competition as each major city sought to own the most prestigious hotel in the land. In New Orleans, French citizens boasted the St. Louis Hotel while the English had the St. Charles.

Innovative design continued to flourish as each new hotel vied to outdo the previous with such amenities as hot and cold running water in the rooms, bathrooms on each floor, gas lighting, steam heat, and room service. But no invention had a greater effect on future hotels and, indeed, the very skyline of the city than the passenger elevator first used in 1859 in the Fifth Avenue Hotel in New York City. The locals referred to the elevator as a 'vertical screw railway' while the English called it the 'ascending room.'

By the turn of the century, most major cities had at least one prestigious hotel. The Astor and Waldorf hotels were developed on New York's Fifth Avenue. The Palmer House and the Sherman House, the largest hotels of their time, became the pride of Chicago's State Street, while The Palace on San Francisco's Market Street and the Brown Palace in downtown Denver displayed their impressive atriums. Feeding off the frenetic growth in US cities, the Savoy in London advanced the mixed-use nature of hotels by including a theater and a chapel. The Savoy had its own in-house laundry and, with 67 bathrooms to its 400 guestrooms, the builder was prompted to ask the developer if he was catering to amphibian guests.

Perhaps no hotel exhibited the extraordinary role that they would play as epicenters of the urban social, political, and business activity as the original Waldorf=Astoria, designed by H.J. Hardenbergh as two separate hotels for the feuding Astor cousins. The eventual reconciliation led to one of the prize public concourses of the day as Peacock Alley married the two hotels and was permanently symbolized in the hotel's official spelling with the equal mark between Waldorf and Astor. As the 'unofficial Palace of New York,' the Waldorf=Astoria's huge ballroom and 40 public rooms were used for the most important social and political events of the day. Peacock Alley was a fashionable runway where elegant gowns

The new downtown 'city within a city' **The Ritz-Carlton, Millenia Singapore.** Pritzker prize-winning architect Kevin Roche designed this slender 32-story tower located in Marina Center, Singapore's new city within a city and its largest and fastest growing business and commercial center. Integration of exterior expression with interior experience is achieved on an urban scale as metal and glass canopies adorn each guestroom window creating a textural play of light and shadow on the building's skin while defining the character of the 608 guestroom interiors. All guest bathrooms are positioned on the outside wall with large octagonal windows directly over the tub providing panoramic views of the city's skyline and occasionally providing passers-by with sensational views into the hotel as well.

and the latest attire were on display for those who came to see and be seen. The Bull and Bear men's café was where J.P. Morgan and Henry Clay Frick met to cut deals after the close of the New York Stock Exchange.

The early twentieth century saw the advent of the modern commercial hotel. Ellsworth Statler established the main principles of modern high-rise hotels when he built the Buffalo Statler in 1908 in New York State, bringing the service departments up to the ground floor, surrounding them with restaurants, bars, and banquet facilities, and connecting them to the guestroom floors by means of service elevators. Although the Ritz in Paris was the first hotel to provide each guestroom with its own private bath, the Statler introduced the model for today's bedroom and bathroom set and exemplified efficient planning of double-loaded corridors and guest-level floor plans (see Chapter 15).

Statler's innovative prototype proved monumental as it defined a model of business–tourist hotels in cities for decades to come. Ever evolving and catalytic in the post-war downtown hotel boom of the 1920s and 1930s, its influence continues today finding new forms in the rapid expansion of new types such as boutique hotels, downtown entertainment hotels, and mixed-use complexes.

Development and Planning Considerations

Rail travel in the early twentieth century fostered development of hotels near city railroad terminals. New York Central Railroad made acres of prime sites available along Park Avenue in the Terminal City development around Grand Central Terminal and many hotels took advantage. Even after the decline of rail travel, many of these locations remain viable hotel development sites since they have evolved into centers of concentrated business and retail activity and the terminals themselves have become commuter stations. In fact, restaurants and bars of hotels built near commuter train stations are usually at their peak just after quitting time.

The location of a hotel in the city in many ways defines its market and its character. In addition to rail terminals urban hotels have gravitated to locations close to active business centers and fashionable shopping districts such as New York's Fifth Avenue, Chicago's Magnificent Mile, or Tokyo's Ginza Strip. The 12-story polished alabaster façade of the sumptuous Hotel Seiyo Ginza is surrounded by the world's highest priced real estate at the heart of Tokyo's

A credit to the icon of historic business and tourist hotels **The Fairmont, San Jose, California.** The developers directed the architects to design a modern hotel modeled on the traditional role that grand hotels of the early twentieth century provided as epicenters of downtown social activity. The 583-room hotel, sited at the crossroads of a multiblock urban redevelopment project, provides a strong civic presence and invites city dwellers as well as hotel guests to utilize and enjoy its facilities, amenities, and hospitality.

great fashion and finance center (see color section, p. C-7). High-end residential neighborhoods with fashionable shops, museums, and art galleries often provide a magnet for luxury hotels whose character borrows from the residential surroundings (see Chapter 9). Some hotels are identified with major city plazas and parks such as the Plaza Hotel on New York's Central Park, the St. Francis on San Francisco's Union Square, and The Ritz-Carlton on Boston's Public Gardens.

A new wave of urban entertainment venues, led by the resurgence of Times Square in New York City, the Hakata City development in Fukuoka, Japan, and the area around the Sony Metreon in San Francisco's South of Market area, have provided fertile ground for a new type of hotel exemplified by E Walk, The Westin New York on 42nd Street. As cites realize the value of their waterfronts after long periods of neglect; mixed-use developments that include hotels are prospering in the context of cruise-ship and ferry terminals, waterfront recreation facilities, and the air, light, and spectacular views afforded by the open expanse at the water's edge.

Boutique hotels originated in marginal neighborhoods where inexpensive and obsolete buildings were transformed into high-fashion lodgings. With their explosive popularity and heavy investment from major chains, boutiques have expanded to more central upscale locations in the city. Other markets that drive location in the city are for hotels located near major medical centers, government centers, convention centers, financial markets, courts, universities, and city halls.

Public incentives

Redevelopment and urban renewal efforts often seek hotel development as a catalyst to attract other development or to provide a necessary ingredient for the success of a project. The Miami Beach City Commission teamed up with several South Florida business and civic leaders in planning the renovation and expansion of the Miami Beach Convention Center but, in order to be successful in attracting large conventions and trade shows, the shortage of nearby first-class hotel facilities had to be solved. Following a highly competitive selection process, the developers for the Loews Miami Beach Hotel were awarded $29 million in city-backed financing, land valued at $20.6 million, and an 800-space parking facility from the city redevelopment agency as development incentives (see Chapter 5).

In downtown San José, California, the Fairmont Hotel provides a vital central element in the first phase of a multiblock redevelopment project. The hotel site is bordered by a new light-rail transit mall on the east, a retail mall on the south, City Hall Park to the west, and an urban plaza to the north that serves as a forecourt to a new office building and a museum addition. Responding to this pivotal location in the redevelopment master plan, the hotel's design displays a strong civic presence providing an arcade surrounding the hotel and a lobby plan that encourages pedestrian traffic to cross through the building. Here the hotel's public areas become part of the system of downtown pedestrian circulation, further unifying the hotel within the fabric of the city.

A deciding factor in hotel location is very often the influence of city zoning regulations that control use, density, and bulk on any given development site. City guidelines may also offer zoning bonuses or tax incentive programs that aim at fostering the beneficial qualities a hotel brings to a neighborhood. Zoning constraints can rule out a site for hotel development by not permitting the transient use, not allowing sufficient floor area to be built for the project to become feasible, or through some other regulation that stymies the developer's goals. For example, one prime downtown site could not be developed as a hotel because, although city zoning regulations required two loading berths based on the proposed size of the hotel, another regulation prohibited curb cuts along the avenue frontage. In order to solve the dilemma, the developer had to acquire an adjacent parcel of land that fronted another street so that the hotel could build the required loading berths.

Land values in urban areas normally are so high that development calls for building the maximum allowable floor area that a site can bear. City planners regulate density in different areas of the city based on the desire to keep the character of a residential neighborhood low-scale or to encourage large-scale development and high-rise construction in other areas. Density, therefore, is regulated by a formula relating the area of the zoning lot with a density factor sometimes called the 'floor area ratio' (FAR). FAR is a multiplier used to calculate the amount of floor area that can be built on the site. For instance, if we have a site that is 10,000 ft^2 (930 m^2) and the mandated FAR on the site is 15 then 150,000 ($10{,}000 \times 15$) ft^2 of zoning floor area can be built on the site. Cellars and subcellars usually are unlimited. If this area turns out to be insufficient then other options may be available such as FAR bonuses or purchasing air rights (also called unused development rights) from an adjacent property. The New York City zoning map describes a theater subdistrict that, in order to encourage the construction and renovation of theaters, provides floor area bonuses for developers who build or renovate legitimate theaters in that district in addition to their own development project.

Planning Controls

City zoning regulations also may control the shape of the building in order to define view corridors, street walls, and building height. But most often bulk regulations are aimed at preventing dark, stagnant streetscapes and are designed to permit light and air to penetrate down to street level and make it a healthier environment. These regulations sometimes are referred to as height and setback rules and are best illustrated by New York City's 1916 zoning ordinance that dictated specific prescriptions for stepping back upper floors from the street based on sun angle studies. The result of that law defined the character of skyscraper design for decades, as illustrated by the remarkable renderings of Hugh Ferriss. The Sheldon Hotel, the world's tallest hotel when built in 1923 with 34 floors and 1200 rooms, was a beautifully proportioned response to 1916 zoning and set the tone for many of New York's great buildings of the 1920s and 1930s.

Use regulations also can have important ramifications in the design and development of hotels. Retail continuity was a requirement for one hotel built on a fashionable shopping street in New York. According to the zoning regulation, only 20 percent of the street frontage could be anything other than

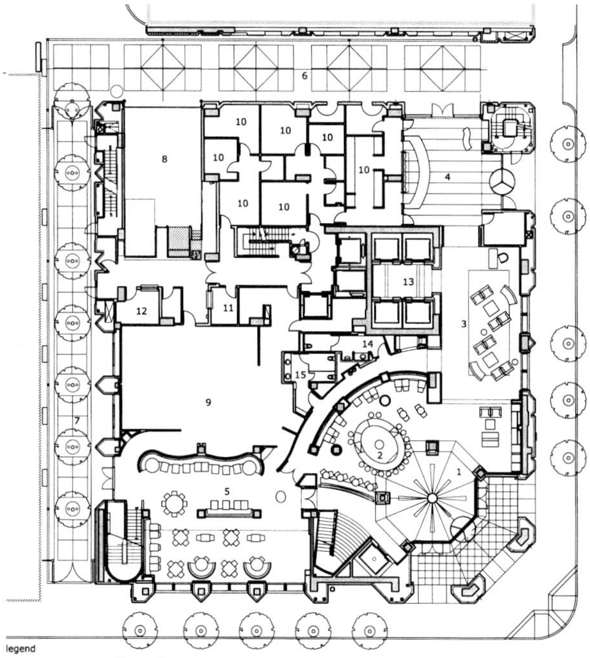

legend

1. main entry
2. cafe/lobby bar
3. living room
4. check-in lobby
5. restaurant
6. porte cochere
7. pedestrian walkway
8. loading dock
9. kitchen
10. office
11. security
12. purchase/receiving
13. elevators
14. men
15. women

Ground level

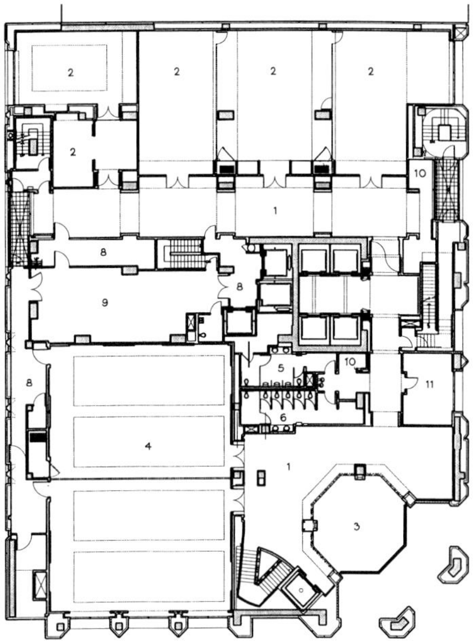

legend

1. pre-function
2. meeting room
3. open
4. ballroom
5. men
6. women
7. office
8. service
9. prep kitchen
10. telephones
11. business center

Third level

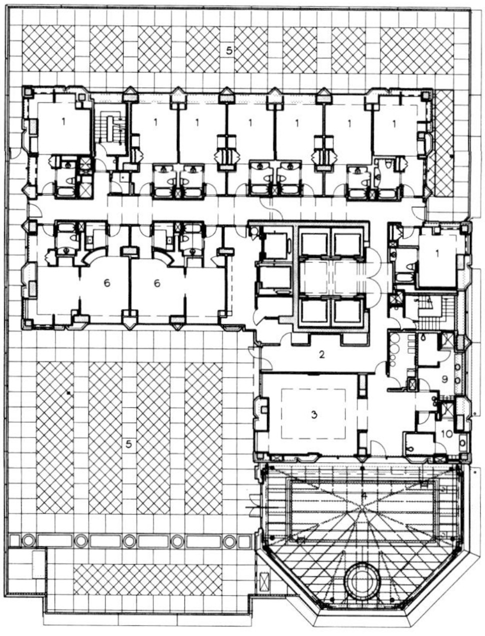

legend

1. guestroom
2. corridor
3. health club
4. pool
5. outdoor terrace
6. hospitality suite
7. hunt walkway
8. service
9. men
10. women

Fourth level

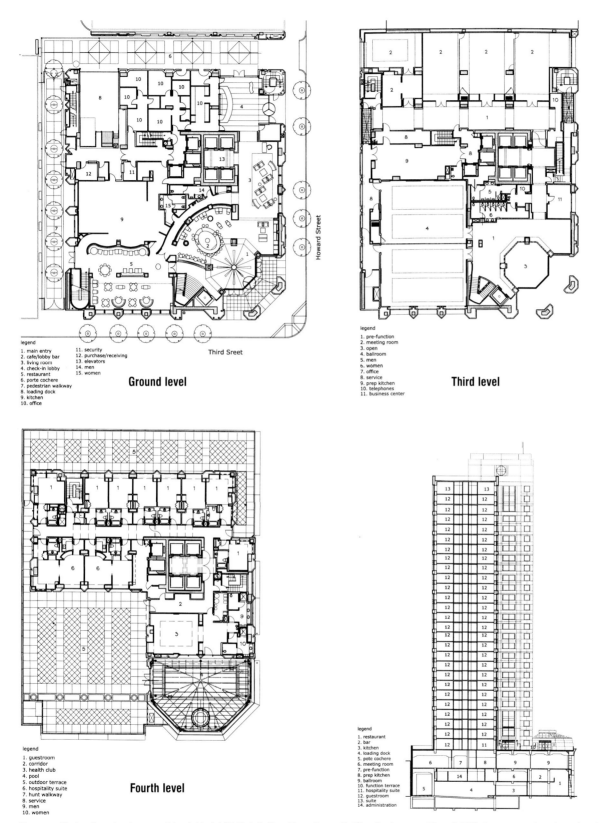

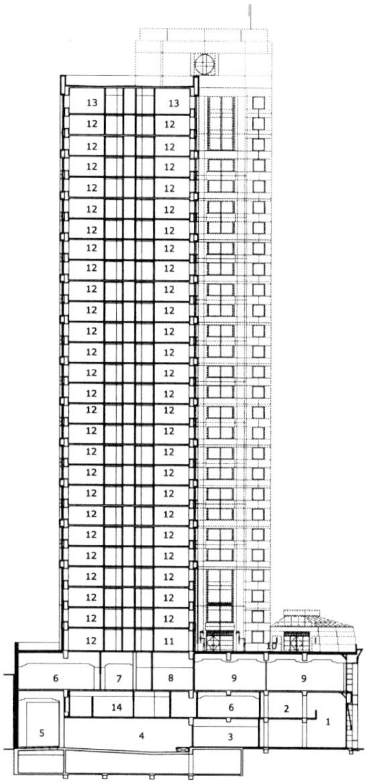

legend

1. restaurant
2. bar
3. kitchen
4. loading dock
5. pote cochere
6. meeting room
7. pre-function
8. prep kitchen
9. ballroom
10. function terrace
11. hospitality suite
12. guestroom
13. suite
14. administration

The versatile boutique business and tourist hotel **W Hotel, San Francisco, California** (see pp. 12 and 286). In response to urban planning goals the position of the guest tower elevator core and the through-block porte cochere dictated the location of the front desk at the opposite end of the plan from the main street-level entrance. Pedestrians enter a three-story octagonal rotunda that connects the restaurant, bar, and meeting facilities to the hotel lobby.

retail use. The hotel entrance therefore became very narrow, contradicting the developer's wishes for the hotel to have great presence on the street. The architects, therefore, were compelled to raise the lobby to the second level by terracing up over the stores that flanked the entrance. Similarly, the SoHo Grand was built in a district primarily slated for manufacturing use and zoning dictated that only a manufacturing company could occupy the ground floor. The hotel was permitted only an entrance and access to a stair and elevator to reach the lobby on the second floor.

The tower massing of the W San Francisco came about out of negotiations with the city planning agency and civic concern over visibility between important city buildings. Built adjacent to the San Francisco Museum of Modern Art and across from the Moscone Center convention hall, the architects set the tower of the hotel back from the corner to ensure sight lines between these two prominent buildings. A lower, three-story rotunda housing the grand stair of the hotel anchors the corner, successfully emphasizing its importance at street level in the delicate balance of urban planning goals.

Many cities now have commissions and agencies who oversee construction on or near its historic buildings and landmarks. In many cases, whole neighborhoods are designated landmark districts and any new building must be scrutinized for its contextual appropriateness. Architects and developers often must conduct exhaustive research and prepare convincing documentation to present to the landmark authority for approval before construction. The degree to which faithful reproduction of details and design is required usually depends on the value and status of the landmark itself. In Paris, Hotel de Crillon recently underwent an extravagant renovation under the auspices of the French National Landmark Commission and, in London, the extensive interior reconstruction of The Lanesborough was reviewed by four separate historical preservation organizations. Construction on The Mercer in New York City's SoHo cast iron district was closely monitored by the city's Landmarks Commission.

The boutique business and tourist hotel **SoHo Grand, New York.** The décor of the hotel's public spaces draws its inspiration from the architecture of the surrounding SoHo Cast Iron Landmark District. Zoning laws permit only manufacturing use on the first floor, so the hotel lobby, restaurant and bar occupy the second floor accessed from the entrance by a giant blackened steel and bottle-glass staircase.

Traffic, Parking, and Service

Parking is less of a necessity in downtown hotels than in most other hotel types, since business travelers are less likely to drive and there is an abundance of public transport. Many of the city's restaurants, museums, stores, and office buildings are usually within walking distance. Guests at a city hotel often leave their cars parked for the entire stay, since driving on city streets and trying to find parking is far less desirable than calling a cab, hopping on a bus, or using underground transit. Many cities now discourage the construction of parking garages in order to encourage use of public transport as a way of cutting down on congestion and pollution. This presents a problem for new hotels, since a moratorium may exist on creating new parking. In fact, many city hotels lease parking and use valets to park guests' cars. Where possible, hotels should provide 0.4–0.8 parking spaces per room in larger cities and 1.2–1.4 spaces in smaller cities where guests rely more on their automobiles.

Entrance courts and porte cocheres are rare in dense, urban settings. Exceptions include the New York Hilton Hotel which has a block-long covered entrance court, the W San Francisco, and The Ritz-Carlton on Nob Hill. More common is a hotel drop-off zone where taxis and limousines are permitted to wait for hotel customers. One important consideration when evaluating a site on a busy urban street is to make a note of bus stops, fire hydrants, and other features that could prevent the creation of a passenger drop-off area for the hotel.

While building signage is of utmost importance for many hotel types, including both roadside and suburban lodgings that depend on recognition from a speeding automobile, in downtown locations the building itself is relied on for identification.

Architectural critics historically have feasted on hotel designers who, due to their lack of imagination in giving the building personality and identity, have resorted to large signs on top. It is, however, important for a hotel restaurant to have some identifying feature in the way of a sign, canopy, or marquee that can be read by pedestrians. A separate entrance to a restaurant in a downtown hotel is a distinct advantage. Hotel restaurants do not share the luxury of a captive audience that resort restaurants or even suburban and airport restaurants have. The city is full of independent restaurants, often within walking distance, and so the hotel restaurant must compete at literally the same level—at street level. Without establishing a reputation with a noted chef or spectacular décor, a restaurant that is tucked away in the public areas of a hotel will be compromised.

As indicated above, off-street loading docks are needed and usually mandatory in city hotels. The problem that arises on tight urban sites is in locating the loading area with its odors and noise as distant from the hotel entrance as possible. In the case of sites that front on more than one street, provided that curb cuts are permitted, this should not be difficult. One hotel in Times Square had enormous site constraints and opted for a 40 × 14 ft (12 × 4.5 m) hydraulic truck elevator connected to a subcellar loading facility. The basement included a giant turntable to turn the truck around so that it could back up to the underground dock.

Garbage collection presents many special challenges in an urban setting, not least of which is noise. Traffic problems usually mean that collection is done in the middle of the night. Noise from the trucks echoes from surrounding buildings disturbing guests. Many luxury properties go to the expense of providing high-quality sound-resistant window systems such as triple-glazing on lower floors where this problem is worst.

Site Factors

As with any hotel development, a survey of elements surrounding the site is as important as surveying the site itself. The density of urban settings presents a multitude of special problems. Placing your entrance next to an adjacent property's loading dock may be worse than next to your own. Care should be taken when locating close to a movie theater where long ticket queues and exiting crowds may disrupt your entrance. Some cities have regulations that prohibit alcoholic beverages to be served within a certain distance from a place of religious worship so that a liquor license may be impossible to obtain. Due diligence to avoid these types of problems is essential.

Views add real value to a hotel property. Hotels routinely demand higher rates for rooms with great views of the skyline, the waterfront, or a park than those facing an adjacent office building. Therefore, it is important to know and, perhaps, to predict where views will exist. It may govern decisions on how high to build to ensure that upper floor specialty suites gain a spectacular view over surrounding buildings. A developer may be faced with an economic decision to build a 50-story hotel with 10 keys per floor as opposed to a more efficient and less costly 25-story hotel with 20 keys per floor. The added expense of building the taller structure must be weighed against the potential of higher room rates for the added value of spectacular views and the intangible value of a more significant presence on the city's skyline.

When designing the RIHGA Royal Hotel in New York City, the architects and developer were aware of plans for a large bulky office tower directly across the street that would limit any view facing south. In response they devised a system of bay windows so that every room had views facing east and west. Similarly, sunlight and shadows are another consideration when designing a hotel in the urban landscape: whenever possible, roof terraces and main entrances should be arranged to receive maximum light.

Size

Following the application of elevators to hotels, Americans developed large hotels in the mid-nineteenth century while Europeans cherished their small hotels, resisting the construction of hotels of over 500 rooms until well into the 1960s. Completing the circle in the 1990s, US cities embraced the boutique hotel in returning to a model that provides a European level of personalized service and atmosphere.

The optimum-size hotel often is determined by 'threshold' factors, or points beyond which:

- additional rooms are needed to offset the high land costs
- an extra elevator or second bank of elevators must be added
- an additional restaurant is needed
- the additional building height necessitates a more sophisticated structural system
- the added loads dictate more complex foundations
- another cooling tower, chiller, or boiler becomes necessary
- structured parking is needed.

But while such elements influence optimum sizing within a range of 50–100 rooms, they are relatively minor factors when compared with the inherent administrative efficiency of small versus medium and large-size hotels.

Two hundred rooms is a threshold beyond which management begins to shift from a direct hands-on style of operation to a more intricate system of multidepartment heads and assistant managers. In a hotel with fewer than 200 rooms, the management style can be more personal, with fewer supervisors required, more productive and happier employees, more satisfied guests, and reduced operating expenses. Any economies of scale to offset this usually are not achieved until a size of 500–600 rooms is reached. In other words, labor productivity peaks at 200 rooms, declines, and is not overtaken by size economy until there are at least 500 rooms.

Note that among independent nonchain hotels, most are under 200 rooms. This proves their size is basically efficient and profitable even without the marketing and reservation advantages of the large chains. Moreover, large hotel restaurants tend to be overstaffed and have oversized, over-equipped kitchens, in part because of additional banquet areas, while small hotels often lease out their restaurants to more effective individual operators.

Although less efficient to manage, hotels in the 200–500 range often are more convenient to market and finance. For example, lending institutions may prefer to invest in two 500-room hotels in different cities than in one more efficient 1000-room facility, no matter how great the market demand. But these midsize hotels need to economize more on their capital costs to offset their lower efficiencies. Conversely, the smaller and larger hotels can translate their superior profitability into more attractive designs, such as atriums or more elegant décor.

The tallest downtown hotel **Baiyoke Sky Hotel, Bangkok, Thailand.** While several hotels in large mixed-use projects share the glory of some of the world's tallest buildings, the 673-room Baiyoke Sky Hotel, with 94 hotel floors, lays claim to the title of tallest downtown hotel in the world.

Design Considerations

The prestige of Atlanta, Georgia soared after its first atrium hotel, the Hyatt Regency Atlanta, triggered a wave of new development and catapulted the city into the future, further defining its role as capital of 'the new South.' The symbolic image of Quebec has long been shaped by the commanding presence of Le Chateau Frontenac high above the bluffs on the St. Lawrence River. Hotels as highly visible monuments and prized trophies have elevated the self-esteem of cities since architect Isaiah Rogers produced the Tremont House in Boston and the Astor House in New York City in the early 1800s.

Making a dominant visual statement on the skyline has long been a goal of hotel owners and supported by architects and developers alike. The majestic domed roof of the St. Louis Hotel in early nineteenth-century New Orleans could be seen for miles away by boats on the Mississippi River and the superb twin copper spires of the Waldorf=Astoria have adorned New York City's skyline for 70 years. The RIHGA Royal laid claim to being the tallest hotel in New York City until the Four Seasons Hotel New York topped it a few years later. Usurped as world's tallest with the completion of the Burj Al Arab Hotel in

Dubai, the Baiyoke Sky Hotel in Bangkok still claims the title of tallest downtown hotel in the world. Unlike many of the huge mixed-use towers seen in other parts of Asia, at 94 floors, with the exception of a handful of floors in the base given over to a merchandise mart, the Baiyoke Sky is all hotel. Mixed-use projects such as the Shinjuku Tower in Tokyo or the Shanghai World Financial Center allow hotels to bask in the glory of these magnificent skyscrapers while occupying only a fraction of the floor area. The Grand Hyatt Shanghai sits on top of SOM's 1,380 ft (420 m) tall Jin Mao Tower and claims to be the world's highest hotel (as opposed to tallest). It also boasts having the tallest atrium ever built—and the longest laundry chute (see Chapter 12.)

Style and Theater

Interest in postmodern architecture in hotel design as an alternative to the international style has waned. Interest has been renewed in the fundamentals of modern architecture, and a new modernism has emerged. Explorations in this realm are affected strongly by the burgeoning boutique, waterfront, and entertainment hotels—discussed in separate sections of this chapter. Together they have turned the typical downtown business and tourist hotel into a more inviting location throughout the world's downtown areas, as illustrated in these pages. Examples include: in Japan, the harbor-front Yokohama Grand, Hotel Seiyo Ginza, Mojiko Hotel, Sea Hawk, D-Hotel, Hotel Kyocera, Park Hyatt Tokyo, and JR Central Towers; Riyadh's Al Faisaliah; Hotel Rey Juan Carlos I in Barcelona; Adelphi Hotel in Melbourne; the two ultra-towered Shanghai World Financial Center and the Jin Mao Tower in Shanghai; the Shangri-La Far Eastern Plaza in Taipei; Martinspark in Germany; and, in the United States, San Francisco's W boutique hotel, New York's pioneering E Walk entertainment hotel, Chambers, RIHGA Royal, and the Four Seasons Hotel, New York.

The attributes of high style and theater have come together as a welcome relief from the sameness of most downtown tourist and business hotels.

Place and Tradition

In the Imperial Hotel, Tokyo, Frank Lloyd Wright demonstrated early in the twentieth century that hotels must reflect place and tradition. Hotels that establish their primary aesthetic identity by creating a contextual fit to the architectural heritage of the city they inhabit reflect this same sensitivity and provide real value to preserving a sense of place in the city. The Four Seasons Hotel, Mexico City is an eight-story, 240-key luxury hotel located on Paseo de la Reforma near the famed Zona Rosa, Mexico's premier shopping area. The design of the hotel centers on a large inner courtyard that features a decorative central fountain and is surrounded by a graceful colonnade expressing the Spanish Colonial architectural heritage inherent in the city. The courtyard provides an oasis of quiet elegance that combines natural light, lush vegetation, and the soothing sound of the fountain against the tumult of this enormous bustling metropolis.

The contextual downtown hotel **Four Seasons Hotel, Mexico City, Mexico.** Located at the center of the world's largest city near the famed Zona Rosa, Mexico's premier shopping district, the design of the eight-story, 240-room hotel expresses the Spanish Colonial architectural heritage of the city. A large inner courtyard features a traditional decorative fountain and is surrounded by a graceful colonnade providing an oasis from the frenetic life on the street.

Sense of Place and Theater

Robert A.M. Stern, FAIA
Principal, Robert A.M. Stern Architects, and Dean, Yale University School of Architecture

A great hotel is more than rooms and services; it is an idea, a narrative, a story line that clearly draws the guest into a unique world that will help make business or pleasure travel special. The more we travel, the more things blur—so that those hotels that are sharply defined as architecture stand out and command our patronage.

A sharply-focused hotel architecture can make us see many different things: for the business traveler, who has little time to get out and about, the sense of the 'local' is perhaps the most important, not only anchoring the guest in a place but also introducing something of a cultural dimension. Because so much modern architecture is international in character, the place-based hotel is more important than ever before.

A hotel, even a business hotel, is an inhabited stage, combining architecture and showmanship—a mix that has been traditional to our profession since the Renaissance, when architects were put in charge of the grand entertainments of powerful patrons. Hotel architecture has a lot to do with theater and theatricality: the theater transports audiences to another time in order to suspend disbelief and free up minds for pleasure and for new ideas. So too must a hotel. There needs to be a sense of the 'other,' the exotic, the foreign, or the otherwise unattainable.

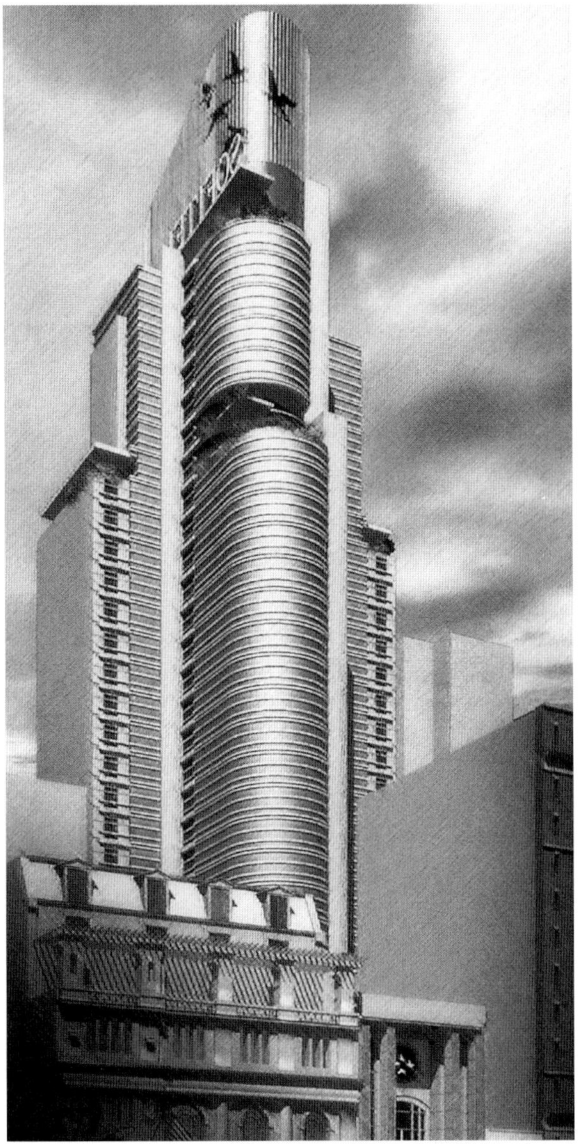

The efficient downtown 'sliver-site' hotel **Hotel Sofitel, New York.** Scarcity of buildable sites in many urban areas has resulted in hotels that require innovative planning and structural gymnastics to overcome the difficulties inherent in their small odd-shaped footprints. This 400-room hotel includes a 30-story 'T'-shaped tower with a bullnose-shaped wing that terraces back from mid-block.

Beyond hotels that contain facilities for performance and entertainment as discussed below in the section on downtown entertainment hotels, there is a fundamental quality of downtown hotels in providing a setting where the theater of human life is played. Morris Lapidus laid bare the theatrical aspect of hotels in the 1950s with his designs for the Fontainebleau and Eden Roc hotels in Miami, Miami Beach. Here, guests were cast as performers while dining on an elevated stage-like restaurant or descending a grand stair that might have been built for Loretta Young or Scarlett O'Hara. From the Astor Hotel to E Walk, hotels have long embodied an architecture of theatricality defining a place for the drama of human activity and experience.

Space Maximization

The density of urban sites requires a much tighter control over matters of efficiency and layout. The designer must make every square foot count to a degree not usually required in other hotel types where space is not such a premium such as at resorts and suburban hotels.

Where FAR limits the amount of area that can be built on a particular site, and since cellars and sub-cellars are usually excluded from FAR calculations, components of the hotel that do not require natural light and air should be located below grade. In addition to mechanical spaces, and if the governing building codes permit, this usually includes most back-of-house functions such as laundry, kitchen, storage, engineering, housekeeping, and employee areas. Executive offices, meeting rooms, and the health club even may be located below grade to allow valuable floor area to be utilized for additional guestrooms. The high cost of excavation is offset by the value added to the property by utilizing every allowable space for revenue-producing functions. There are locations where cellars are not possible, such as New Orleans where much of the city is below sea level and the water table is near the surface. Also, many of the hotels in the Terminal City development around Grand Central Terminal such as the Biltmore and the Waldorf=Astoria were not able to utilize cellars because they were built over the subterranean railroad tracks.

A convention hotel presents a particular design challenge for a tight urban site in that tower columns and core must be kept away from the clear-span ballroom. This generally means that the site must be large enough to contain both elements independently, otherwise enormous structural gymnastics are required to transfer the massive loads from the tower around the ballroom. In many cases, the use of huge transfer girders and mechanical offsets are needed in order to transfer tower columns and shear walls and to provide a feasible column placement in the public areas of the hotel. It's all part of the expense of building downtown.

The Hotel Sofitel, New York, a 400-room 30-story hotel, is built on a difficult 'T'-shaped mid-block site on 45th Street with a 35 ft (10.5 m) wide leg out to 44th Street. The architects found that the most efficient tower configuration resulted from placing the elevator core at the intersection of the two legs of the 'T'. The structural engineers devised a system of shear walls in lieu of columns that reduced the number of columns, thereby simplifying the construction process. A 5 ft (1.5 m) thick concrete transfer mat was required over the 2,500 ft^2 (325 m^2) ballroom to pick up 23 stories of tower columns.

Fierce competition in many cities over the short supply of usable hotel sites, coupled with extraordinary revenue growth due to increased downtown room rates, has developers vying for all types of odd-shaped sites. Holiday Inn abandoned its cookie-cutter, right-angles-or-die formula in order to build on a 4,000 ft^2 (370 m^2) trapezoid-shaped site near Wall Street. Hotels known as 'sliver' buildings, tall buildings wedged into small narrow mid-block sites, are on the increase as large sites are becoming scarcer.

The twin tower business and tourist hotel **Far Eastern Plaza Hotel, Taipei, Taiwan.** The elegant twin towers of the hotel are linked at the base by a dramatic circular rotunda that serves as the main entrance and as the fulcrum of the building's public spaces. The skillful geometric composition, reflected in its sculpted interior volumes, enhances Taiwan's burgeoning skyline.

Back-of-house Efficiency

Back-of-house operations in downtown hotels present many challenges not usually encountered in hotel types with less constrained space. Often relegated to cellars where valuable above-grade areas are limited to guest usage, many functions have to operate with clockwork precision to ensure that guest services are provided in a timely and efficient manner. Efficiency of operations was the battle-cry of Ellsworth M. Statler in developing the back-of-house functions for the Buffalo Statler in 1908. Following Statler's lead, Warren and Wetmore designed New York's Biltmore Hotel in 1913 with excellent functional organization and machine-like precision. Statler's theories on hotel organization have withstood the test of time as architects such as William B. Tabler have advanced his approach, improving on efficiency and economy in hundreds of hotels and widely influencing functional design.

Some hotel chains have centralized certain back-of-house functions, such as the laundry, offsite to support several properties in a region. This has proven beneficial to urban properties where space can be recaptured and reassigned, freeing up floor area for much-needed administrative functions, additional meeting space, or guestrooms.

Public Spaces

Since a hotel's architecture is often obscured and overwhelmed by its dense urban surroundings, the entrance lobbies in downtown hotels must make bold statements and lasting impressions. More than any other element, the lobby quickly sets the hotel's tone and ambience.

The grand hotels of the 1920s and 1930s saw dramatic swings in the size and extravagance of their public spaces. The original Waldorf=Astoria was rendered obsolete by the Plaza Hotel when it opened, offering New York society its immense ballroom and sumptuous Palm Court, parlors, and lobbies. The New Netherland, built in New York in 1926 during Prohibition, avoided lavish public halls and placed its emphasis on luxurious appointments in the private realms of guestrooms and suites. Then the new Waldorf=Astoria emerged in 1931 to reclaim the title as the 'unofficial palace of New York,' as vast lobbies and ballrooms once again became fashionable.

In the late 1960s, The Hyatt Regency Atlanta expanded on historic models, such as the San Francisco Palace Hotel and Denver's Brown Palace, and set the pace with its towering atrium for a bold, new dramatic form of downtown hotel lobby. With or without atriums, the trend in the 1970s and early 1980s was for large impressive lobbies. In reaction to the expense and perceived lack of warmth, many developers returned to more intimate interior spaces and focused interior budgets on high-quality materials, lighting, and artwork to achieve a sense of grandeur.

Far from dead, the atrium has found new life downtown in suite hotels such as The Embassy Suites at Battery Park City in New York, where in-line suites share in the atrium's daylight (see Chapter 8); mixed-use developments such as Jin Mao Tower and the World Financial Center in Shanghai, where the sky-lobby is found at the base of a sky-atrium (see Chapter 10); and in other hotels such as Hotel Juan Carlos I in Barcelona, where high-drama design still draws a crowd.

Erected in time for the Olympic Games of 1992, Hotel Juan Carlos I is a strikingly modern building embodying the highest aspirations of Catalonian design. A parabolic-shaped atrium is open to the north with a 14-story curtain wall that faces downtown Barcelona. Stylistically, the architects, Carlos Ferrater and Jose Maria Cartana, designed the atrium combining the shock-value drama of John Portman's famed hotel lobbies with the refined new modern elegance of a Philippe Starck interior. Undulating ribbons of polished metal rails form a glittering spectacle. The radial organization of functions at the lobby floor utilizes Portman's concept of shared space, as reception, two restaurants, bars, and other public amenities border the atrium at the ground floor.

Postage-stamp-sized sites, combined with security concerns about the overcrowded streets and occasional huge crowds in New York's Times Square, have prompted several hotels in that area to raise their lobby above the street level. The Embassy Suites Times Square, that shared a site with an historic theater, resorted to massive steel trusses and other structural gymnastics to build the hotel lobby and tower over the theater. These hotels must necessarily employ additional reception staff at ground level to ensure that guests are greeted appropriately and ushered up to the lobby safely with their luggage and to prevent unwanted sightseers from wandering into the hotel.

Guestrooms

The size of hotel rooms is difficult to quantify in the downtown context since there are so many subtypes to consider. Among these are adaptive-reuse of office buildings where very deep room layouts are generated, boutique hotels where micro-rooms charge top rates, and lofty suites of luxury style such as The Mercer. Standard rooms at super-luxury hotels such as the Four Seasons Hotel, New York start at 610 ft^2 (57 m^2). Size is constant only in the major chains and the result is similar to the suburban types.

Since the average length of stay and number of occupants per room are similar, guestroom sizes in downtown hotels are equivalent to those in suburban and airport hotels. The basic 12.5×18 ft

(3.8 × 5.5 m) clear room dimension varies only within 10 percent, based on special preferences of owners or operators who believe a slightly larger room will give them a competitive advantage. Experience has shown that a foot of width is less important in making the room seem larger than a lighter color or other decorative scheme. For example, in the restoration of New York's Inter-Continental Hotel, a mirrored wall was installed in one 11.5 ft (3.5 m) wide room. Most guests felt the room was larger and preferred it to a 12.5 ft wide standard room.

While increased width provides a small amount of additional space between the bed and the dresser, this space does not allow for additional furniture, whereas increased length can provide for an extra chair or sofa bed. Also, increased width adds more cost than length, since it increases structural spans, slab thicknesses, and the exterior façade. Therefore, lengthening the room is less costly and more beneficial to the guest than widening it.

No hotel prototype expresses the density and crowding issues faced by downtown hotels more than the capsule hotels in Japan. The Japanese, whose population density is 10 times greater than the US, have a long history of inventing ingenious ways of utilizing minimal space. The primary market for capsule hotels is young professionals who live in the outer suburbs of Tokyo where rent is cheaper than in the city. Often kept late at work and dreading the long train ride home only to turn around a few hours later to return, they frequently seek inexpensive overnight lodging. These hotels, conveniently located near railway stations, can contain up to 1,000 units, called capsules. A capsule is a sleeping compartment, not unlike those found on trains, except that they usually are entered from one end rather than from the side. Approximately 6.75 ft (2 m) long by 3.5 ft (1 m) wide by 3.5 ft (1 m) high, they are stacked two high and double-loaded on long corridors. For ¥4000 ($35) per night you get a clean, private capsule made of molded plastic, equipped with a firm mattress, a TV mounted to the ceiling, a radio, an alarm clock, a reading light with a dimmer switch, a mirror, a corner shelf and a controllable ventilation nozzle similar to those found on airplanes. Capsules for men and women are on separate floors. The public areas of the hotel usually include a cafeteria and a bathhouse with a communal pool, both of which are open all night. This epitome of no-frills accommodation serves an important market in a uniquely vibrant metropolis.

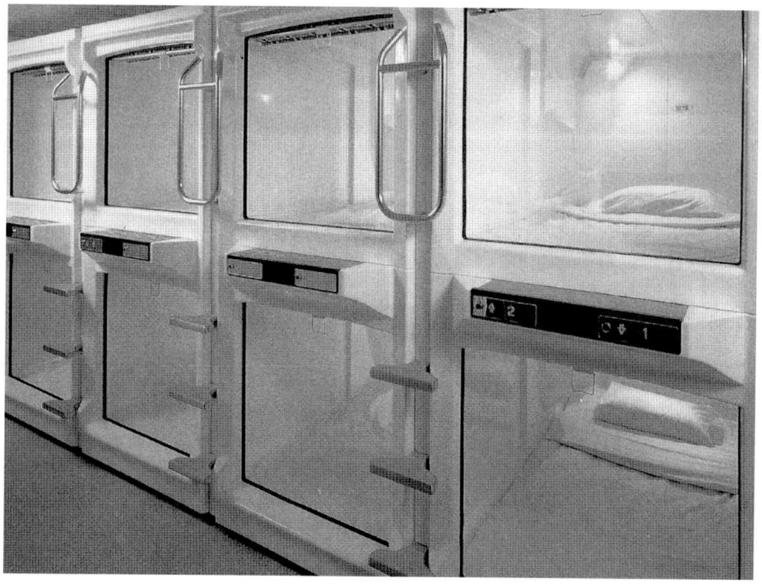

The downtown micro-hotel **Toyoko Capsule Hotel Ohmori, Tokyo, Japan.** Rented overnight or by the hour, the minimal accommodations provided by capsule hotels with guest modules often no larger than a sleeping compartment on a train serve an important market in Japan's business community. Young professionals working long hours in the city often find these inexpensive lodgings a welcome alternative to their long commute to and from their suburban apartments.

Adaptive Reuse

The past few years have seen a number of urban office buildings converted into hotels. Hotel chains are showing strong interest in establishing new properties in downtown areas, but suitable sites for new construction are scarce and expensive. At the same time, older office buildings are becoming functionally obsolete and devalued in the competitive office space market. Converting older office buildings to hotels has proved to be an attractive development opportunity. In most cases the cost of acquisition and renovation has been less than the cost of new construction. The feasibility often depends on several factors including zoning, building footprint, window modules, building façade, floor-to-ceiling height, and structural systems. (See Chapter 10 for more discussion on adaptive reuse.)

Trends

- Ecotourism will come to town. 'Green' hotels such as Sheraton Rittenhouse, Philadelphia, utilize environmentally friendly and nontoxic materials and systems aimed at providing guests with a healthier environment and encouraging environmentally responsible building technologies. Advances in these technologies will make it more economically feasible in urban applications.

- Brand segmentation and proliferation will make it possible for a single hotel to offer multiple-brand products under one roof and benefit from sharing hotel employees and most back-of-house facilities, while maintaining separate entrances, registration lobbies, restaurants and lounges, guestroom floors, and health clubs. For instance, we may see a Marriott Courtyard, a J.W. Marriott, a Residence Inn, and a Marriott Vacation Club functioning in harmony all within one building.
- Chains will consolidate service functions within a region. Hilton centralized their laundry facility for a large region that included New York City, western Connecticut and northern New Jersey. This allowed many properties to free up much needed space for back-of-house, administration, and, in some cases, additional guestrooms and meeting space. This trend should continue as centralization of other functions is made possible through increased computerization and Internet capabilities such as accounting, reservations, and some administration functions.
- Mixed-use developments that contain hotels will continue to flourish downtown. The services and amenities provided by hotels are recognized as a benefit to a multitude of building types including office buildings, residential condominiums, university campuses, transportation centers, entertainment complexes, conference centers, shopping malls, and medical complexes.
- Increasing technical sophistication of business travelers and the explosion of information technology has produced a dramatic new emphasis in downtown business hotels. Guestrooms made to function as office work spaces and high-tech business centers are becoming essential components of these hotels. Major chains are developing new concepts for the business traveler that include guestroom workstations with an ergonomic chair, a two-level desk, adjustable task lighting, and multiple power and data outlets. New guestrooms in these facilities also may include flexible furniture such as a table that converts to a small conference table and in-room terminals for Internet video conferencing.
- Virtual officing, particularly in mixed-use developments, will allow guests to lease office space on a transient basis in the same building, or in one adjacent to the guestroom tower, in order to conduct business on the road. With high-tech officing capabilities, advances in teleconferencing, and Internet communications systems, the possibility exists for office time-share products to emerge as add-on features to an urban residential time-share or extended-stay hotel.
- Many new forms and formulas of extended-stay, urban time-share, fractional ownership, vacation clubs, hotel condominiums, and other hybrid products will emerge to blur the line between residential ownership and traditional transient accommodations. This expansion is related to the increasing demand for personalized service where residential condominium owners seek the luxury of hotel services. This trend will not only have a dramatic effect on the way hotels are traditionally operated, but also the way urban residential apartments are rented and sold.
- The thirst for super-luxury accommodations will continue to grow as the economy remains prosperous and more guests can afford top-quality facilities and a higher level of personalized services.
- The term 'urban resort' will become more than an oxymoron. Urban resorts and spas will continue to propagate as 'baby boomers' make up a large percentage of health conscious consumers and fitness enthusiasts. They seek state-of-the-art exercise facilities, the latest spa treatment programs and techniques, fresh juice bars and organic restaurants. Look for these hotels to offer special diets and dining plans, health education training, medical supervision, and sophisticated massage and treatment programs in addition to exercise programs.

Boutique Hotels

The term 'boutique hotel' is largely attributed to developers Ian Schrager and his late partner Steve Rubell for the dramatic design makeover of Morgans, a small, dilapidated midtown building, to an independent high-styled hotel in 1984. The final decades of the twentieth century saw the emergence of hotels in small (usually fewer than 100 rooms), urban prop-

The beach boutique hotel **Delano, Miami Beach, Florida.** Adding to the surreal composition of the hotel's outdoor features, Philippe Starck's water salon gives new meaning to notion of the 'shallow end of the pool.' A large part of the pool's area is only 1 ft (0.3 m) deep and furnished with ornate cast-aluminum tables and chairs, with food and beverage service provided by barefoot waiters with their pant legs rolled up.

erties where the key descriptive elements are fashion, glamour, style, chic, hip, flair, elegant, and cool. Today, the term, 'boutique hotel,' transcends the earlier definitions and bridges multiple hotel classifications from small to large, luxury to affordable, urban to resort, modern to traditional, renovation to new construction, and, with the creation of the W brand, from independent to a rapidly expanding segment of a major chain. The boutique segment has, in fact, blossomed into multiple subsegments.

Many examples of small fashionable hotels existed in Paris, San Francisco, New York, and Los Angeles predating the term, including L'Hotel in Paris, the Lowell in Manhattan, and Hotel Vintage Court in San Francisco that, by our standard definition, would be considered boutique hotels. The term had just not yet been coined.

By definition a boutique is 'small, fashionable and independent.' A strong emphasis on high fashion is seen as the essential ingredient common to those of this genre.

In reaction to the mediocrity and dreary uniformity of conventional hotel design, entrepreneurs working in New York, as well as pioneering San Francisco developer Bill Kimpton, realized that unique and provocative architecture and design could be a very fertile marketing asset. A substantial market was discovered for fashion-minded travelers seeking an atmosphere where they could enjoy an artistic lifestyle; a setting that immersed them in the avant-garde where they could feel they belonged to a community of insiders whose taste was unequivocal.

The popularity of the boutique hotel may be attributable to the growing sophistication of the traveling

The luxury boutique hotel **The Mercer, New York.** The high ceilings and architectural fabric of the original factory building were recreated to provide guests with the loft living experience uniquely characteristic of New York's SoHo district. Innovative room layouts include spacious white marble and tile bathrooms that open directly into the room through a pair of folding doors, expanding the room spatially and inviting guests to bathe while enjoying daylight and views of SoHo (see p. C-13 for a further view).

public, especially the younger, style-conscious, business traveler, in reaction to the predictable blandness of the established hotel trade. According to Kimpton: 'The individuality of boutique hotels appeals especially to travelers in their 30s and 40s, a generation who has seen everything that the chain hotels have to offer.' Today's young travelers require something new and innovative. They demand sex appeal and excitement. They want surroundings that stimulate and astonish them, an antithetic to Kemmon Wilson's 'the best surprise is no surprise' Holiday Inn.

Schrager and Rubell were able to address this untapped market by instilling in their lodging properties the same theatrical magic and glamorous mystique that succeeded for them at their legendary nightclub, Studio 54. They realized that a whole generation had been overlooked by the lodging industry. With Morgans in Manhattan, arguably the progenitor of the species, with designer Andrée Putman they transformed a seedy hotel in an unstylish midtown location into a property that attracts movie stars, entertainment moguls, models, and designers. With designer Philippe Starck, the Royalton and Paramount soon followed in Manhattan, and some years later, Miami Beach's Delano and Los Angeles' Mondrian. Like Studio 54, these properties depended on hip cachet and chic renown for their popularity.

Attracting trendsetters and celebrities, boutique hotels have ushered in the return of the hotel lobby as a downtown social-gathering spot, an important urban function on the wane since the grand hotels of the golden age when hotels were at a city's epicenter of fashion, politics, and high society. Grand hotels have long been associated with their stylish interiors. Although at a different scale, but in greater quantity, this new attention to innovative style in many ways is a return to the grandeur of nineteenth-century hotels—cosmopolitan, elegant, and distinctive—a culture of design.

Size

The term 'boutique' connotes smallness and most often is used to refer to small, intimate hotels. While many automatically use the term to refer to a hotel with fewer than 100 rooms, this is not entirely accurate. Three forerunners of boutiques in New York City opened with more than 100 rooms: Morgans Hotel with 113, the Royalton with 170, and the Paramount with 600. Hence, from its inception, the boutique hotel has had much more to do with avant-garde design and stylish cutting-edge operation than size. The recent opening of the W brand, literally in the shadow of the Waldorf=Astoria, attempts to bring the boutique ambience to a 700-room hotel.

You can have a 2,000-room boutique hotel as long as it offers a fresh, original design approach and a distinctive original attitude, according to one pioneering developer. This may be true, but only at the expense of targeting a specialized audience, since a broader market is necessitated by increased size. The challenge for developers of large boutique hotels will be to maintain the high level of personalized service characteristic of this segment.

This hotel type includes many smaller hotels, not necessarily independent, not necessarily high-style, urban, retrofit, or upscale and sometimes not particularly small. With boutique hotels' financial success, many have come to use the term largely as a sales tool. However, when lacking innovative design or stylish operation, these smaller hotels are in violation of the fundamental boutique leitmotif and are merely small.

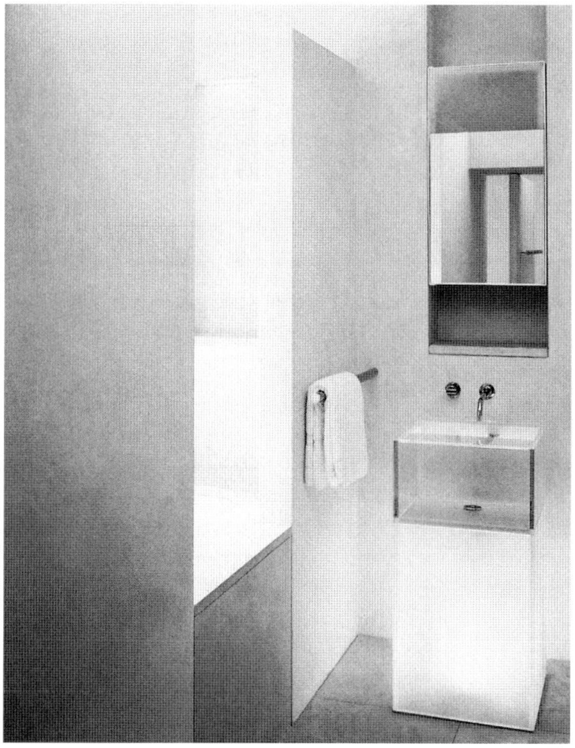

Stylistic diversity in boutique hotels **The Hempel** and **Blakes Hotel, London, England.** The contrasting styles of Anouska Hempel's two London creations is nowhere more evident than in the decorative treatment of the guest bathrooms (see p. C-12 for further views).

Luxury to Economy

The widespread appeal and financial success of boutique hotels has caused the label to be used very broadly to include segments and properties not originally thought of as boutiques. For example, a 370-key, ultra-luxury chain hotel, referred to in travel brochures as a boutique hotel, ostensibly because of its superb modern design by a world-famous architect, draws a chic and fashionable clientele. It is more useful to consider this hotel with other luxury properties.

On the other hand, The Mercer in Manhattan's SoHo district is an excellent example of a boutique at the luxury end of the scale. Conceived by Andre Balazs with designer Christian Liaigre, The Mercer offers large, sumptuously furnished rooms with high ceilings, lush materials, and impeccable, personalized service. The luxury accommodations at The Mercer are so opulent that fashion baron Calvin Klein reportedly postponed his expensive SoHo apartment renovation and opted to extend his stay there indefinitely.

In renovating the 600-room Paramount hotel the developer Ian Schrager made the decision not to gut the interior in order to combine rooms. Instead, he kept the original small room configurations intact and construction costs low in order to create an affordable alternative hotel. He declared that his goal with the Paramount was to create a Super YMCA. The approach was further compared to the accomplishments of the retail chain, The Gap, in offering affordable style. W has gone one step further by commissioning the creative staff of a highly regarded commercial design team to manage the styling of its expansion, cashing in on mass-market successes of trend-conscious retail chains such as Banana Republic, CK, and DKNY.

Boutique hotels on the luxury end of the segment cater to an upmarket clientele requiring a high degree of luxury and personalized service. The Leading Hotels of the World, Ltd, an organization that represents over 300 luxury hotels, includes in the five-star boutique category the Hotel Splendido in Portofino (65 keys) and the Hotel Bel-Air in Beverly Hills (90 keys). Lee Andrews of Leading Hotels noted that the smaller the hotel, the higher the guest's expectation for high-quality service.

The gallery boutique hotel **Chambers, New York**. This recently constructed boutique hotel draws inspiration from its art-conscious neighbors. Designed by the Rockwell Group and Adams Soffes Wood Architects, the hotel itself functions as a gallery exhibiting over 400 pieces of art by some 100 artists. Each of the 77 guestrooms is fashioned as an artist's loft containing a minimum of three original pieces per room. Clad in Macedonian limestone, the 15-story façade steps back from its narrow lot, punctuated with french doors opening to glass and blackened steel balconet railings.

Modern and Traditional

One only needs to look at the two London hotels conceived and designed by Anouska Hempel to appreciate the range of architectural style embracing the boutique model. A firmly traditional approach was taken with Blakes Hotel and twisted with just enough spin to cause a second look and to see deeper artistic intent. Black-painted walls trimmed with ornate gilded crowns and moldings and oversized tester beds cloaked with heavy rich-colored fabrics set the style of Blakes Hotel. Almost in exact contradiction the same designer created The Hempel with a stark, minimal achromatic Zen-inspired interior.

To fit the mold, traditionally styled boutiques need to express some distinguishing element of originality. Several of Kimpton Group's properties, including Hotel Monaco in San Francisco, are traditionally styled, but are achieved with a note of whimsy, flair, and humor that give them distinction from the more mundane trappings of conventional hotel design. New York's skillfully renovated Algonquin Hotel by Alexandra Champalimaud might be considered a boutique, but while highly creative in capturing the unique spirit of that famous hotel it is better characterized as historic restoration.

Far more prevalent contemporary design motifs are the palette of boutique hotels. The segment is replete with examples of those that embrace modernism in establishing a new and fresh imagery. The Metropolitan and One Aldwych in London, The Kirketon in Sydney, D Hotel in Osaka, the Time Hotel, and The Franklin in New York, and many others have adopted the iconography of a new modernism.

New Construction and Renovation

The attraction to develop boutique hotels may be at least partially attributable to the number of older hotels that can be refurbished for far less cost than building from scratch. Part of the reason that San Francisco has so many boutique hotels is due to a large inventory of older hotels that could be inexpensively acquired and upgraded. In the absence of suitable hotels to renovate, developers have also turned to adaptive reuse of outmoded downtown office buildings and other industrial buildings. The Mercer was converted from an old warehouse. In one of the most creative examples of adaptive reuse, Andrée Putman converted a watertower in Cologne into the spectacular 88-room Hotel im Wasserturm. Philip Pilevsky and Brian McNally have hired UK architect David Chipperfield to convert the American Standard Office building on New York's Bryant Park. Starwood converted the Beaux-Arts Guardian Life building on Union Square to its third W Hotel in New York.

The success of the genre has led many developers to construct from the ground up. Since boutique hotels have long been thought of as renovations, many regard new construction boutiques as a contradiction in terms. Examples include the 62-key

Il Palazzo in Fukuoka, Japan; the SoHo Grand, and the Tribeca Grand in New York, the Malmaison in Glasgow, and Art'otel Potsdam in Germany. D Hotel in Osaka was built on a tiny site with only two rooms on each of its seven floors above a miniature lobby. The guestrooms of Chambers, a new 77-key luxury hotel on West 56th Street in New York, will feature exposed sprinkler pipes, track lighting, and concrete bathroom floors alluding to the atmosphere of an artist's loft.

Independent to Chain

Reporting net operating income levels at 40 percent, boutique hotels have attracted the attention of major hotel chains which are attempting to draw the chic and glamorous crowd to their boutique hotels. The dynamic is instructive: to justify the high costs of chain operations and to recap the profits that big companies need they abandon the small, intimate nature original of the boutique ethos and go bigger. For example, the initial W in New York City was a 700-room boutique hotel; the concept then expanded to numerous major cities. While one independent developer was said to have warned: 'Boutique hotels are alternative products, and I don't see how a chain of them can be an alternative,' others are finding advantages in expanding corporately with financial partners.

Another pioneering developer, William Kimpton, working closely with his designers, formed The Palomar brand with a new philosophy of aesthetic expression creating 'more of a collection than a chain.' The first international boutique chain, Malmaison, based in the UK, emphasized the importance of creating sisters, not twins, when rolling out boutiques, each property fusing correlating design and operational style with regional attributes.

Andre Balazs' hotel in Los Angeles, The Standard, was conceived as a prototype for a chain of inexpensive hotels, combining classical modernism with futurist chic, for the young business traveler. Others expanding to chains include Art'otel, a small German chain, and Hotel del Sol by Chip Conley, who posits that when expanding boutiques into a chain it is important not to lose the owner/operator perception.

The boutique 'hotel of the Stars' **Mondrian, West Hollywood, California.** Schrager and Starck transformed this 1959 hotel of 245 rooms on Sunset Boulevard into one that recaptures the glamour of Hollywood. Just off the main lobby, the outdoor dining terrace of the hotel's specialty restaurant, Coco Pazzo, is covered with 8 ft (2.4 m) high terracotta flower pots that provide shade and privacy to diners while framing spectacular views of Los Angeles to the south.

Quirky Amenities and Gimmicks

The Hotel Monaco offers a pet goldfish during your stay. At the Mondrian, Raymond Chandler's *Farewell My Lovely* replaces the Gideons' *Bible*. At the Delano, poolside furniture is arranged in the water salon at the shallow end of the swimming pool where waiters will wade in to serve your *cuba libre*. Morgans is so hip its name doesn't appear on the building's façade. The New York City W refers to itself as an urban spa and resort. The International House Hotel in New Orleans holds voodoo ceremonies at an altar in the lobby. The Beach House at Hermosa Beach near Los Angeles features ocean lofts instead of rooms. The Franklin, New York City, places a teddy-bear on the pillow next to the mint. (It is rumored that toy czar Ty Warner may go one better at his recently purchased Four Seasons Hotel, New York and put an I.M. Pei 'beanie baby' on the pillow.) Boutique hotels are going to

More than a Place to Sleep

Ian Schrager, Chairman, Ian Schrager Hotels

I believe that the hotel business has descended to a commodity business. It has become generic; it has been institutionalized. The only opportunity for distinguishing your product from another company's product is on price, like all commodities. That's the myth of the brand. I don't think that anybody stays in a hotel, except for perhaps Four Seasons or Ritz-Carlton—which conjure up in your mind a whole bunch of anticipations—because of its name.

Therefore, we conceived our company on being an anti-brand, not being generic, not being institutional. There is something wrong when you stay at a hotel in Los Angeles and it is exactly the same hotel as when you go to London or Miami. A hotel should give a sense of time and place, and that basically was our opportunity. People like myself and my former partner Steve Rubell were able to meet with some success because there hadn't been a new idea in the hotel business, I think, since Statler invented the modern hotel room and Portman in the 1960s came up with the atrium hotel.

The hotels in the USA are predicated on the mass-market model. There was a virtue in everything being the same. There was a virtue in coming up with an idea and 'cookie-cutting' it across the country. Those who are old enough may remember the Holiday Inn advertisement from a few years ago that said, 'The best surprise is no surprise.' For me, there is nothing better than a good surprise when you go into a hotel and can have fun there.

The reason that there aren't any innovations in the hotel industry is because it is so capital intensive and the system doesn't encourage new ideas. The financial institutions, which are a necessary part of any hotel development, are not interested in seeing new ideas; they are not interested in getting people excited about something, about walking right up to the edge and doing something that hasn't been done before. They only want to see something that already has been done—but perhaps in a different color or a different finish. They want to see something that is proven to be successful and just redo it. Nobody is really willing to go out there and do something that hasn't been done before.

Well, that is what we're trying to do, come up with something that hasn't been done before. Treat a hotel as more than just a place to sleep—a place for somebody to have fun, a visual feast. Walk inside and see something that you haven't seen before. Walk in the lobby and excite people, be able to cut the electricity in the air. Something indefinable, the same kinds of things that make you want to purchase a car or buy a house or pick a mate. Those are the kinds of things that we deal in and it was very personal to us. These were the kind of hotels I wanted to stay in. I wasn't looking to do a hotel for a hundred million people. I was looking to do a hotel that I would like and, by chance, there would be other people out there who also would like it.

great lengths to differentiate themselves from the pack as even this segment is starting to get crowded.

Perhaps no one has shown the diversity and creativity in coming up with offbeat products targeting micro-niches of Chip Conley with Joie de Vivre Hospitality, a San Francisco boutique hotel group which boasts 13 boutique hotels, two boutique motels, and a boutique Japanese day spa. True to San Francisco's bohemian legacy and laid back charm, Conley has properties that offer everything from poetry readings, algae shakes, vitamin pills on the pillow, and in-house psychiatrists to free tarot card readings and back rubs. At the Bijou Hotel there's a miniature movie theater right off the lobby that shows films about the 'city by the bay.' Popcorn and junior mints are sold at the front desk. At one of its four-star properties, Joie de Vivre offers a special plastic surgery package for many who travel to San Francisco for these operations. Amenities include rides to and from the clinic, a nurse on call, and a foot massage to take your mind off the recovery. Joie de Vivre's Costanoa is a boutique camping resort south of San Francisco where guests can order a café latte to their tent after roughing it on a long hike through the woods. The idea here is to allow guests to connect with nature in an upmarket fashion.

The boutique hotel addition **Shoreham Hotel II, New York.** Phase two of the hotel's development included the transformation and addition of a small 1960s office building to the adjacent 87-key boutique hotel, a 1920s building that had been renovated just 4 years before. The two dissimilar buildings were joined at the ground floor, thereby doubling the hotel's key count. The textured glass back wall of the garden room, a private dining room off the hotel's main restaurant, is washed in natural light from a skylight above.

Planning and Design Considerations

The value of good hotel design is no longer equated with the use of expensive materials. Boutique hotels with linoleum floors and chrome-plated fittings are getting the same average daily rate (ADR) as conventional luxury hotels with marble floors and brass fittings. Quality design and architecture are essential values of the service that the boutique hotel must deliver. Notwithstanding the old adage, 'good design doesn't cost more to build,' it may, in fact, cost more in design fees as developers compete for celebrity designers to add market appeal to their properties and to stay ahead of the fashion curve. Andrée Putman, Philippe Starck, Christian Liaigre, Rafael Vinoly, David Chipperfield, David Rockwell, Richard Meier, Jean Nouvel, and others are in high demand to provide prestige value as well as originality and vision. Even fashion design giants Sonia Rykiel, Todd Oldham, and Giorgio Armani are courted for exclusive designs in this domain.

The nightclub boutique hotel **The Standard, Los Angeles, California.** A few doors inland from the Mondrian on Sunset Boulevard in West Hollywood, Andre Balazs' 142-room hotel delivers high style at budget prices. Catering to a decidedly younger set, the undulating balconies of the former retirement home overlook the LA basin and the electric blue Astroturf of the pool deck. With a DJ at the front desk, The Standard underscores the trend that hotels have become the nightclubs of the new century. (A) Guests checking-in are dazzled by performance artists in a large glass vitrine behind the front desk. (B) Styled by Shawn Hausman and The Standard design team in combination of classical modernism and futuristic chic, the large guestrooms feature Gio Ponti-inspired beds, silver vinyl beanbag chairs, Andy Warhol flower-print drapes, and 'day-glo' orange and white bathrooms.

As we have seen, design styles for this niche segment are as varied as the markets they serve. Whatever the market, the boutique designer's mandate is to bring to the project a high level of creativity and originality, to design an ambience that makes guests feel that they are staying in an exciting place where sleeping is the last thing on their minds. However, there is a danger of letting innovative design approaches overshadow other fundamentals of hotel design. Some fall into the trap of style over substance. In one example, guestrooms were designed with the bed floating in the middle of the small room with a long narrow ledge very close to one side. Unfortunately, this unique layout gave no room for the housekeeping staff to make the bed and resulted in the threat of a strike by the hotel union.

The icon of a theatrical entertainment hotel **The Westin New York at Times Square.** The main entrance to the 863-room hotel on 43rd Street and a second featured entrance on 42nd Street link the hotel public spaces to E Walk, the 200,000 ft^2 (18,580 m^2) retail, restaurant, and entertainment complex that extends 400 ft (122 m) eastward towards Times Square. The spectacular 45-story tower stands as a dramatic icon on the Manhattan skyline, marking the entrance to the heart of Times Square from the west (see p. C-32 for a further view).

Historically, boutique properties have had subfunctional back-of-house and administration areas with all emphasis going to visual pyrotechnics and hip persona. Since most early boutique hotels were renovations, they often inherited poor conditions from the start. Cramped basements, slow elevators, and lack of loading facilities are inherent conditions that cause undue hardship in the operation of these properties. The experimental nature of this type of hotel also presents unusual design challenges for operations and back of house. An all-white guestroom décor and bellmen in Armani suits place added burdens on the housekeeping department. Fresh exotic fruit in the room requires specialized food and beverage service. Pet goldfish for the guests may require an aquarium department for one chain. Demand for high-level personalized service in luxury boutique hotels normally requires a much higher staff-to-guest ratio that impacts all employee areas. Like any hotel, the back-of-house and administration areas need to be tailored to the operational style of the hotel. With boutiques this can be in many ways as unique and original as the physical design.

Trends

The boutique segment is getting crowded, leading some experts to caution against over-saturation. More than 30 boutique hotels exist, are under construction, or are being planned in Manhattan alone. Even so, with RevPAR (revenue per available room) running from 10 to 40 percent above industry average, the lodging giants are either already in development or are planning their participation in the boutique bonanza. We may very well see every large hotel chain with a line of boutiques in the near future. Meanwhile, the boutique pioneers are busy branding their products and creating mini-chains.

Perhaps the greatest appeal of the boutique hotel in a world of segmentation is its being the most segmentable segment. Boutique products continue to cross-fertilize with other hotel types to form unexpected hybrids. The Sheraton Paris Airport Hotel, whose interiors were designed by Andrée Putman, may well be the first boutique airport hotel. It is conceivable that we will some day see boutique casino hotels, boutique cruise ships, boutique office park hotels, and perhaps even a boutique assisted-living facility for aging 'baby boomers.' Just as we've seen boutique developers borrowing from the successful formulas of mass-market retail chains we may see design-conscious commercial companies enter the fray with hotels of their own such as Hotel Nike, Absolut Hotel, or Microsoft.hotel.com.

To date we have seen urban boutique development limited to the most elite cities with established cultural credentials. But as the traveling population continues to grow more sophisticated there is no reason to believe that the attraction will not spread to secondary and even tertiary markets. As the public becomes more sophisticated it values leading-edge design. The endurance of the boutique phenomenon may rest on the continuing demand for individual personalized service in a lodging environment that exhibits a high level of innovation and artistic expression.

Downtown Entertainment Hotels

Personifying the theatricality of the 'Great White Way', the Astor Hotel built in Times Square in 1904 was a vast amusement palace with early themed restaurants, elaborate banquet halls, and a famous rooftop wintergarden that brought a festive presence to Broadway. The Astor was a rousing forerunner of downtown entertainment hotels whose lobby included many theatrical and thematic elements, the most dazzling of which was the Orangerie, a room with amazing scenographics and lighting effects that provided guests with a virtual apparition of the Mediterranean. Hot summer nights in New York City rendered the nonair-conditioned Broadway theaters so uncomfortable that many closed their doors for the season. Outdoor performances, however, were staged in the cool night air of the outdoor rooftop theater of the Astor's wintergarden. The wintergarden roof was encircled in sparkling lanterns adorning the building's cornice line and presenting a spectacle to merrymakers of the night, perhaps foretelling the glittering light show that plays in Times Square today.

After years of decline, Times Square has been revitalized with massive new office buildings, television studios, themed retail outlets, renewed public and private investment in theaters, and entertainment-based hotel development. Two such entertainment hotels face each other across West 42nd Street like bookends embracing the evolving renaissance.

The Westin New York at Times Square

Heralded as a gateway to the new Times Square, Arquitectonica's design for the 45-story Westin New York is conceived as a sweeping multicolored tower split by a piercing arc of light into two dramatic high-rise elements, one blue-toned vertical tower set against a bronze-colored element with horizontal

An entertainment hotel at the 'world's crossroads' **Hilton Times Square, New York.** Rising 25 stories above the Crossroads of the World across the street from The Westin New York on 42nd Street, the 444-room hotel is attached to a 335,000 ft^2 (31,120 m^2) entertainment and retail complex that includes Madame Tussaud's Wax Museum, a 25-screen cineplex, a music store, and many other dining and retail outlets.

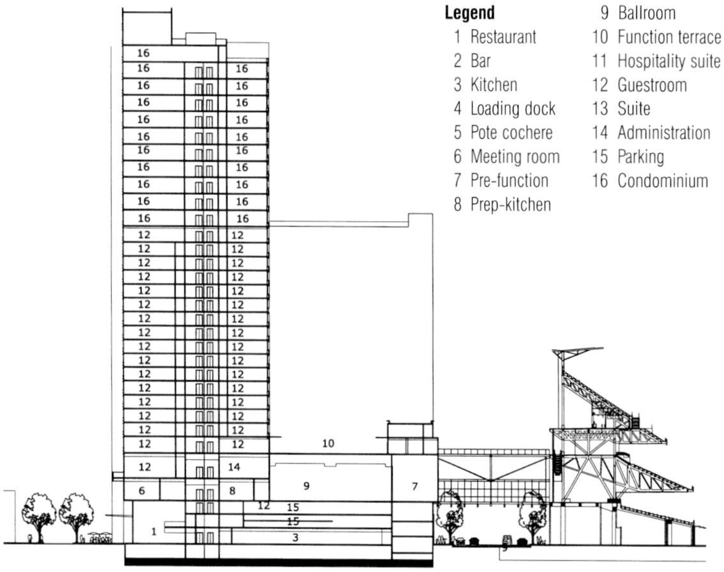

The sports entertainment resort **The Westin Park Towers, San Diego, California**. Connected to the San Diego Padres' new downtown baseball stadium, the 512-room hotel tower is oriented to give guests a view of the ball field while the ballroom prefunction lobby opens wide to the ocean breezes of the Pacific.

bands. The gently curving bolt of light symbolically connects the skyline to the street below. Developed by Tishman Realty & Construction, the 57,500 ft^2 (5,300 m^2) site is the centerpiece of joint efforts of the New York State Urban Development Commission and the New York City Economic Development Corporation to transform 42nd Street from a seedy strip with its ever-present hustlers and sex shops into a glitzy family-oriented entertainment center.

The first phase of the project is E Walk, a sculptured block that extends 400 ft (122 m) along 42nd Street as a series of stage-set-like buildings reminiscent of other façades on the street and layered with lights and signs. It contains a 200,000 ft^2 (18,500 m^2) retail, restaurant, and entertainment complex, including 13 multiplex movie theaters, numerous shops and restaurants, and a virtual-reality family entertainment venue called Broadway City. The complex, designed by D'Agostino Izzo Quirk Architects, also contains a 13,500 ft^2 (1,250 m^2) restaurant located on the ground and second floors and a nightclub featuring live entertainment evocative of the neighborhood's history. Rising behind E Walk, the glittering bisected tower of the 863-room hotel will be entered from 43rd Street, but internally linked to the entertainment complex.

Hilton Times Square, New York City

Directly across from E Walk on the south side of 42nd Street, the Hilton Times Square provides a similar concept with 335,000 ft^2 (30,000 m^2) of retail and entertainment functions including a 140,000 ft^2 (13,000 m^2), 25-screen movie multiplex, a 60,000 ft^2 (5,500 m^2) Madame Tussaud's Wax Museum, a 20,000 ft^2 (1,850 m^2) record and music store, and a 20,000 ft^2 (1,850 m^2) shoe store that will feature a basketball court for customers to try out the footwear. Developed by Forest City Ratner and designed by Beyer Blinder Belle Architects, the complex also includes 35,000 ft^2 (3,250 m^2) of franchised food and beverage operations with a food court, fast-food operations, and themed café restaurants. Like The Westin, the 25-story, 444-key Hilton hotel tower is set back behind a cluster of sculpted façades with themed signage and flashy lighting. Entrances are on 42nd and 41st Street. The hotel includes a sky-lobby restaurant and lounge to take advantage of views of the Times Square area and express elevators to transport guests from street level to the lobby.

Both of these hotels primarily are oriented toward middle-market leisure guests attracted to the

The educational entertainment hotel **Moody Gardens Hotel, Galveston, Texas.** Adjacent to the Pyramids of Moody Gardens, an elaborate complex of educational and entertainment venues overlooking Galveston's Offats Bayou, this 303-room hotel provides convention facilities, including a 15,000 ft^2 (1,390 m^2) ballroom, supplementing the neighboring Galveston Island Convention Center.

entertainment venues of Times Square. But they also will serve the needs of business travelers associated with the influx of media company businesses in the huge new office towers nearby such as Condé Nast, Viacom, and Reuters and from their proximity to the Javits Convention Center to the west.

The Westin Park Towers, San Diego, California

The San Diego Padres are building a new 46,000-seat baseball stadium as part of a $1 billion redevelopment enterprise that will include hotel, office, retail, and residential development within a 26-square-block section of the East Village, just outside the Gas Lamp Quarter of downtown San Diego. The owner of the Padres is also building The Westin Park Towers adjacent and attached to the stadium by a connecting bridge. Designed by San Francisco architects Hornberger + Worstell, the orientation of the hotel tower will allow most guests to view the ball games from their guestroom windows. On game day, these hotel rooms become super sky-boxes. Alternatively, guests may enter the stadium by crossing a bridge that connects from the hotel lobby level, raised above several parking levels. The 512-room Westin Park Towers also will include a ballroom level that opens to a large balcony overlooking the beach. The glass wall separating the ballroom prefunction from the balcony completely retracts, as does the ballroom wall itself, so that banquets may be held completely open to the Pacific sea breeze.

The sports entertainment in-town resort **SkyDome Renaissance Hotel, Toronto, Canada.** Built integral to Toronto's futuristic domed stadium, the hotel offers 70 of its 346 guest rooms with windows facing directly onto the playing field where guests may watch baseball, football, hockey, concerts and other sporting and entertainment events from the comfort and convenience of their hotel room.

Boston's gateway downtown water-front hotel **Boston Harbor Hotel, Boston, Massachusetts.** Water taxis from nearby Logan Airport are greeted by the hotel's grand arch that welcomes guests to the famed Rowe's Wharf redevelopment project, one that enhanced the city's waterfront while reclaiming its important seafaring heritage.

Moody Gardens Hotel

The sign invites you to 'experience the earth, the heavens, and the seas at the Pyramids of Moody Gardens.' Covering 242 acres (98 ha) in the city of Galveston, Texas, Moody Gardens is a premier 'edu-tainment' complex featuring a 10-story glass Rainforest Pyramid; North America's first IMAX 3D Theater, the Discovery Pyramid designed in conjunction with NASA, and the new 12-story high Aquarium Pyramid. Also featured at Moody Gardens are the Galveston Island Convention Center and the Moody Gardens Hotel. More than just an entertainment park, the goals of the complex are research-based educational programs dedicated to humanitarian and environmental issues.

Nestled in the valley of the Pyramids, the 303-room Moody Gardens Hotel and Spa, designed by Morris Architects, is an essential component of the complex. The immense educational/recreational campus is far more than anyone can experience in a single day, so the hotel serves the demands of the multiple-day guest who spends a weekend or longer. Also, the related activity of the Galveston Island Convention Center is served by the hotel which operates a 15,000 ft^2 (1,400 m^2) ballroom and other conference facilities to go with the 38,000 ft^2 (3,500 m^2) exhibition hall of the Convention Center.

Panoramic views of the gardens and pyramids are pervasive throughout the hotel's public spaces. The hotel blends with its surroundings, providing a large cascading water feature in the center of the lobby and special-effects lighting simulating a multicolored sky. A rooftop restaurant provides views of the Gulf of Mexico, Galveston's Offats Bayou, and a bird's-eye view of the entire campus of Moody Gardens.

Downtown Waterfront Hotels

The first hotels in North America were seaport inns located in the harbor districts of cities along the Atlantic coast. During colonial times, before the increase in travel by stagecoach, private carriage, and horseback that resulted in the construction of inns and taverns along the highway routes, ships from Europe were the most important means of travel and seaport inns catered to the needs of intercontinental travel and commerce.

In the world's seafaring towns, waterfronts have long been utilized for commerce relating to waterborne foreign trade. Technological developments in the shipping industry such as containerization coupled with expansion of trucking on the interstate highway system rendered obsolete many port city waterfronts and dock neighborhoods that depended on overseas maritime commerce for their prosperity. Urban renewal efforts now seek to reclaim the cities' waterfronts for recreation and leisure-time enjoyment. Waterfronts in many ways have become the cities last frontier. New York City alone has 578 miles (930 km) of waterfront, most of it inaccessible or underutilized.

Boston Harbor Hotel, Massachusetts

The Rowe's Wharf development in Boston is a prime example of a city reclaiming its waterfront. The relocation of an elevated traffic artery removed a significant barrier that separated downtown Boston from this former seaport area and restricted expansion to the east. Rowe's Wharf reconnected

The urban waterfront view hotel **Seaport Hotel, Boston, Massachusetts.** Located on the waterfront adjacent to the World Trade Center Boston, the 426-room hotel tower is oriented to maximize views of the harbor and of the downtown skyline.

The waterfront convention hotel **Pan Pacific Hotel Vancouver, Canada.** The 506-room hotel is situated on Canada Place, the heart of the downtown harbor-front that includes the World Trade Centre office complex, the Vancouver Conference and Exhibition Centre and Canada's largest cruise ship terminal.

The towering 'sail' at the water's edge **Yokohama Grand Inter-Continental Hotel, Japan.** Located adjacent to the city's Seaside Park, this 600-room hotel tower provides a dramatic central element to the Pacifico Yokohama Waterfront Development. The V-shaped plan configuration of the guest floors ensures that all rooms have views of the harbor (see p. C-28 for a further view).

downtown to the harbor and enhanced Boston's historic identity as a seafaring town. The city planning authority directed the development of the complex outlining goals that included a public interface to water transportation, preservation of specific city views, and encouragement of pedestrian circulation. The master plan called for the development of offices, condominiums, and a hotel, designed by Skidmore, Owings & Merrill. The acclaimed grand arch of the 230-key Boston Harbor Hotel prominently signifies the main entry to the complex from the water. Hotel guests as well as local citizens can launch from this point for a 7-minute ride by water taxi to Logan Airport.

Pan Pacific Hotel Vancouver, Canada

Canada Place, in the heart of Vancouver's downtown harbor front, began as the Canadian Pavilion for EXPO '86 and later was converted to the Vancouver Conference and Exhibition Centre. Today, in addition to the conference center, the complex contains Vancouver's cruise ship terminal, embarkation/disembarkation point for over 250 vessels carrying in excess of 550,000 passengers annually, the World Trade Centre with over 200,000 ft^2 (18,500 m^2) of office space, and the Pan Pacific Hotel with 506 keys and extensive meeting facilities. The cruise ship terminal, with its distinctive white sail design, is easily recognized in the distance by approaching vessels. The complex is situated at the hub of Vancouver's passenger transportation system with access to elevated rapid transit, commuter ferry service, heliport, seaplane, and bus services.

Perched on top of Canada Place above the World Trade Centre office complex, the hotel benefits from panoramic views of the city, harbor, and coastal mountains. The three-story lobby atrium, which includes a totem pole and a waterfall, houses the lounge, restaurant, and café, all with views of the harbor and mountains. The hotel tower is oriented so that 80 percent of the rooms have water views.

Yokohama Grand Inter-Continental Hotel, Japan

One of the leading ports of Japan, and second only to Tokyo in size, the city of Yokohama was almost totally destroyed in 1923 by an earthquake. Gradually reconstructed according to government designs, the city now is among the most sophisticated in Japan. The recently developed Minato Mirai waterfront area has become the new commercial center of Yokohama. Within this center, the Yokohama Grand Inter-Continental Hotel is built on the harbor connected to the vast facilities of the Pacifico Yokohama International Convention Center and Exhibition Hall. The dramatic 31-story tower design of the hotel draws from the city's nautical heritage and, from a distance, resembles a huge sailing vessel that has its massive sail filled with the wind. The V-shaped tower configuration provides all 600 guestrooms with excellent views of Yokohama harbor and Seaside Park. The oversized guestroom windows give guests the impression of being on a cruise ship in the harbor.

Sea Hawk Hotel & Resort, Fukuoka, Japan

Over 700 years ago on two separate voyages, the invading armies of Kublai Khan attempted to land near the ancient city of Hakata, Japan, the closest natural port to the mainland of Korea. Both attempts failed when typhoons came to the rescue of Japan's defending army and devastated the enemy fleet. These typhoons were nicknamed *kamikaze* meaning divine wind. Cesar Pelli's design of the Sea Hawk Hotel & Resort, built on this same site on the edge of the modern port city of Fukuoka overlooking Hakata Bay, embodies the spirit of the wind and the water with its elegantly slender tower resembling a giant ship's prow pointing out to sea. Composed against the taut curves of the 36-story tower, which locates all 1,052 guestrooms with a view to the water, is a voluptuous curving barrel-vaulted glass atrium whose horn-shaped volume wraps around the tower and faces the sea.

The hotel is conceived as an urban resort, a building that offers an escape from daily routine, yet provides valuable public amenities to the city. It is built adjacent to a 40,000-seat baseball stadium that has a high-tech three-part retractable dome and shares a downtown entertainment function (similar to San Diego's Westin Park Towers). Urban hotels in Japan depend on large public functions to support and bring life to the hotel. Unlike its western counterpart, the guestroom is a secondary source of revenue. The spectacular atrium of Sea Hawk supports lavish wedding facilities, elaborate restaurants, bars, health club, shopping concourse, meeting, and banquet rooms that all operate as destinations of their own, independent of the hotel. Planned as an urban plaza, the atrium is filled with fountains, trees, patterned paving, and copious sunlight. In stark contrast, the quiet elegance of the hotel lobby demonstrates the multiple roles of a large hotel in the life of a city in Japan.

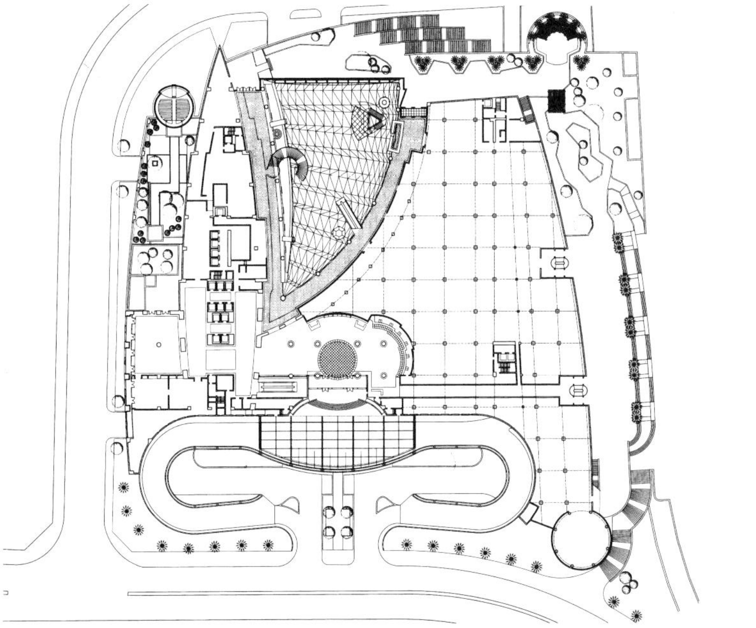

The downtown waterfront resort **Sea Hawk Hotel & Resort, Fukuoka, Japan.** Planned as an elaborately landscaped indoor urban plaza, the dramatic curving glass-vaulted atrium wraps around the 36-story hotel tower and provides a spectacular backdrop for weddings, meetings, dining, and shopping while serving as the central element of the hotel's public spaces (see p. C-30 for a further view).

The on-airport 'flagship' hotel **Hyatt Regency, Paris—Charles de Gaulle, Roissy, France.** When seeking its first foothold in the one of the world's greatest tourist and business centers, Hyatt did not choose the center of Paris, but the international business suburban region around Charles de Gaulle Airport in Roissy. Architect Helmut Jahn conceived the hotel design as a six-story high glass hall linking two silver wings of guest rooms epitomizing the high-tech world of aviation. Symbolizing the magic of flight, the atrium restaurant lies beneath a 12 ton (11 tonne) inclined metal disk suspended from above.

Suburban Hotels 3

In his 1898 treatise, *Garden Cities of Tomorrow*, Sir Ebenezer Howard described three options for living in the industrial age: town, country, or town–country. In promoting his utopian model he noted that cities had become alienating, unsanitary, and unlivable; while the country, offering natural beauty, fresh air, and healthfulness, lacked the social advantages of city life. Early suburban or 'pseudurban' development sought to offer a refuge from the noise, dirty air, crime, and congestion of late nineteenth-century urban life while mitigating the cultural deficiencies of the countryside.

The Riverside Hotel, one of the first suburban hotels, was built in 1870, 9 miles west of downtown Chicago in Riverside, Illinois—an early commuter suburb planned by Frederick Law Olmsted and Calvert Vaux. Riverside was founded in 1868 as a new suburban community combining 'the beauties and healthy properties of a park with the conveniences and improvements of the city.' Overlooking the Des Plaines River, the hotel was designed by noted Chicago architect William LeBaron Jenny, who also designed most of Riverside's houses. Even though this elite suburban development was tied directly to downtown Chicago by the Burlington Railroad line and a limited service parkway (also designed by Olmsted and Vaux), the developers went bankrupt as it was considered at that time too far out of town.

Following World War II, major investment in the interstate highway system and billions of dollars made available through the US Federal Housing Administration and the Veterans Administration for suburban home development fueled explosive suburban residential development. By 1950, 1.5 million new house starts per year in the US were spurred on by the post-war suburban baby boom. With expansive residential suburban development came the growth of the large-scale regional shopping center drawing patrons from a wide geographic area and further fueling suburban expansion.

In the 1950s, industry and commerce began relocating near major highways in the suburbs as trucking superseded railways. Suburban sites with good highway access, lower land costs, plenty of parking, attractive landscaping, and nearby services spurred development of industrial parks and research and development centers. Eventually, corporations began to realize advantages in decentralizing and relocating to the suburbs that were cleaner, less congested, less expensive, and safer than the city.

By the 1970s, mid-rise apartment buildings, business and science parks, mega-shopping malls, satellite universities, sports complexes, airport commercial developments, entertainment centers, theme parks, research institutes, industrial parks, medical complexes, and a wide variety of hotels made up the rich fabric of suburbia. As commuting patterns changed to accommodate the increasing population who live in one suburb and work, shop, and play in another, highway interchanges became the epicenters of commercial development. No longer just an interchange, the highway cloverleaf had become a destination in and of itself. Naturally, a strong demand arose for hotels near this burgeoning suburban business energy.

Prior to the 1940s, with the exception of resorts, most hotels were located in cities and towns. As highways superseded railroads, the market for accommodation along the roadways and near residential suburbs expanded rapidly. Early hotels in suburbia took the form of motels and motor inns catering mostly to the needs of the motorist. Motels located near airports served airline crews and stranded passengers and provided an inexpensive alternative to downtown lodging. As business activity in the suburbs increased, suburban hotels took on a different role and began to resemble downtown hotels with meeting rooms, restaurants, shops, health clubs, and other full-service amenities. Expansion of suburban growth, especially around airports, malls, and business parks generated a multitude of user segments and price categories. To a large extent, the broad market segmentation that has defined the hospitality industry in the 1990s grew out of the diversity reflected in the suburban hotel markets. In fact, it is perhaps in the suburban hotel types that we find brand proliferation and segmentation played out to the maximum. Some hotel chains have as many as seven separate brands tailored to subsegment markets, all found with suburban applications. Hotel chains, through extensive market research, have customized their products for broad-ranging cost categories and fine-tuned target markets beyond leisure and business to create applications appropriate to today's travel needs.

Roadside Hotels and Motels

Following World War I, when Americans first took to the road in great numbers, the need for roadside accommodation expanded dramatically. The majority of motorists were in search of convenience, economy, and informality not offered by the more upmarket downtown hotels. This gave rise to a variety of roadside inns, tourist cabins, and motor courts lining the major thoroughfares. These facilities often were a series of detached cabins operated by a family whose nearby home provided the registration office. Located on the outskirts of town, most offered a casual atmosphere, the convenience of parking next to your door, no tipping, payment-in-advance, and easy departure without the check-out ritual.

The budget roadside motel **Motel 6 prototype, North America**. Visibility from the road is essential for roadside inns—a large majority of their customers are walk-ins without reservations. Following the model of Howard Johnson's and McDonald's, architecture becomes signage for many that compete for the attention of passing motorists.

Individual cabins of tourist courts often were dressed up in a variety of fanciful ways to catch the eye of the passing motorist and to tantalize their imagination and fantasy. Wigwams, log cabins, igloos, adobe huts, and so on—these storybook cabins were hotel design's earliest examples of theme architecture. Less flamboyant cabins simply donned red roofs to be seen more easily. The dollhouse-like freestanding cabins eventually were replaced by linear one-story structures housing rooms under a single continuous roof.

Arthur Heinman opened the Milestone Motel in San Luis Obispo, California, in 1926 and immediately claimed credit for inventing the term 'motel.' The evolution of the building form from a series of unconnected cabins to a continuous line of rooms might be traced to early prototypes of the 1930s where a guest's automobile was sheltered beneath a roof that spanned between two cabins. Eventually, as lodging demand increased, these carports were closed in to make additional rooms, thereby forming a string of connected rooms facing an open parking lot. Later, as the significant economies of construction and maintenance of this new form were realized, a second floor was added.

By the early 1930s many of these roadside lodgings gained unsavory reputations as lodgings of ill repute. 'Hot sheet motels,' as they were called, were rented by the hour, no questions asked. In a 1940 article entitled 'Camps of crime,' FBI chief J. Edgar Hoover declared that many motels were dens of vice and corruption that harbored 'gangs of desperados who prey upon surrounding territories.'

Following World War II, the expansion of the interstate highway system in the US created an explosive demand for safe, clean, comfortable en route lodging. The potential of this lucrative market quickly drew the attention of hotel entrepreneurs like Kemmons Wilson who developed a respectable chain of family-style motels named after the Hollywood movie *Holiday Inn*. Holiday Inn's chief innovation was the inclusion of a restaurant that made the facility more hotel-like, thus completing the evolution from tourist court to motel to motor inn and motor hotel. By the late 1950s an explosion of motel, motor hotel and motor inn chains such as Howard Johnson's, TraveLodge, and Ramada Inn found key locations on the new interstate highway system. By 1954 there were more motel rooms than hotel rooms in the US. By 1972 motel room numbers doubled those of hotels.

(A)

(B)

(C)

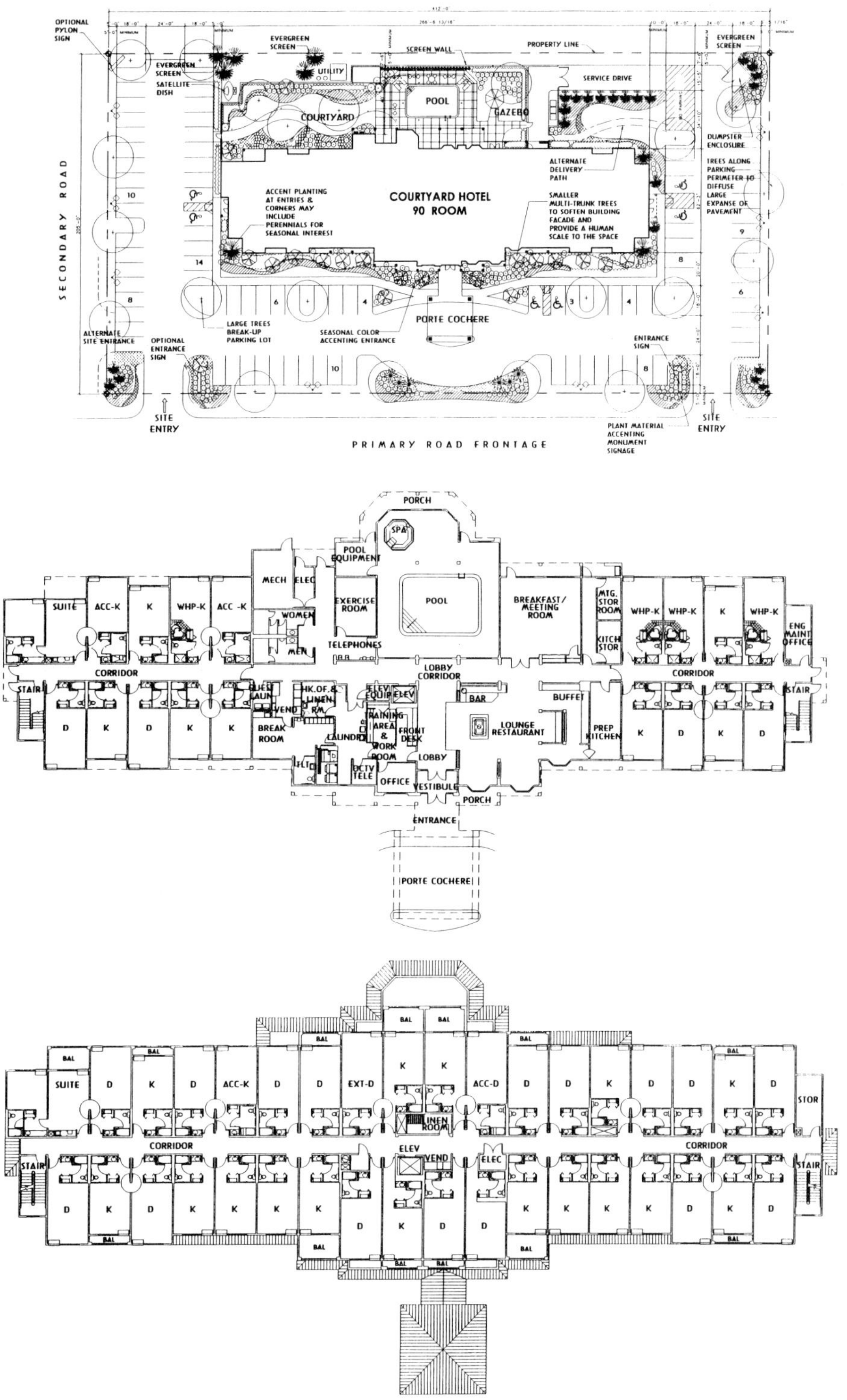

The versatile mid to upscale hotel/motel **Courtyard by Marriott prototype.** An example of research-based product development tightly focused on the transient business and leisure market segments, the Courtyard brand takes the form of a three- or four-story hotel ranging in size from 90 to 156 rooms. (A) Site design criteria focus on optimizing the number of units per acre while requiring good visibility from major roadways. Landscape design elements include the signature walled courtyard with a gazebo, outdoor pool, and patio area; self-contained parking with a 1:1 parking space-to-room ratio; service/trash enclosures out of sight from guestrooms and arriving guests; and perimeter landscape buffers to control undesirable offsite views. (B and C) The prototypical interior layout responds to guest preference for the added security of interior corridors; a modest but well appointed food and beverage outlet; and a residential atmosphere and amenities that facilitate business and social activity.

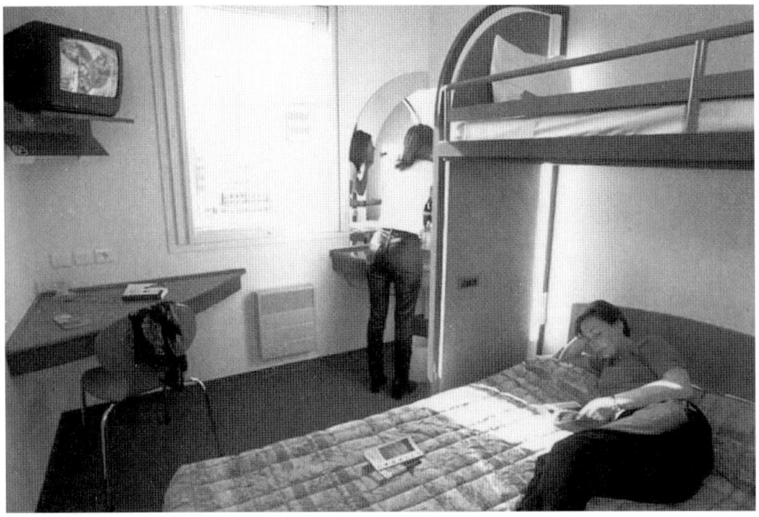

The super-budget roadside motel **Formule 1 prototype, France.** Low-cost tourism is well served by the highly efficient and innovative furniture arrangement that permits three guests to comfortably share a 96 ft^2 (9 m^2) guestroom.

In his autobiography, Frank Lloyd Wright described a new type of American architecture, related to and dependent on the roadway: 'The great highway is becoming, and rapidly, the new horizontal line of Freedom extending from ocean to ocean.' Wright, who was very interested in the marriage of automobile and building, designed two motels in 1956. The Wieland Motel was designed with ten bilevel circular guestroom pods splayed out on a shallow crescent in a garden-like field with cars tucked under a portion of the second levels. The Bramlett Motor Hotel, designed for a Memphis suburb, had three round, nine-story towers connected at the base with lobby, registration, and parking and linked at the top by a restaurant and outdoor dining with views of the Memphis skyline in the distance.

Enter segmentation. Products of the major chains began to become more elaborate, adding swimming pools, coffee shops, gift shops, meeting rooms, and amenities normally associated with fully fledged hotels. This competition drove most of the 'mom-and-pop' operators out but left a gap in the economy market. By the early 1960s a whole new generation of budget motels began to appear as stripped down versions of the big chain products. Motel 6 rented, appropriately, for $6 per night. Days Inn advertised luxury budget rooms for $8 per night. By the mid-1970s segmentation and branding had rendered the word 'motel' obsolete. No longer described in terms of its location on the highway, such products now were referred to by categories such as limited-service budget hotels or mid-priced full-service, with new brand names ending with Inn, Lodge, Hotel, or Suites, but not Motel.

Unfortunately, the corporatization of the motel resulted in a bland uniformity of design that prompted *New York Times* critic Ada Louise Huxtable to write 'Hospitality and the plastic esthetic' in 1973, where she condemns 'the totally uniform and cheap consistency of taste and manufacture' of the ubiquitous plastic room. A new appreciation of the earlier funky design styles of the 1950s and 1960s motels has emerged, however, in places like Wildwood, New Jersey where 'doo-wop' architecture is the retro-trend *du jour*.

To recapture markets turned off by both the higher prices of the more elaborate inns and the cheap, unimaginative designs of most budget motels, a new wave of well-managed motel chains has unveiled inventive designs combining low rates with a fresher, more sophisticated ambience. These include such rapidly expanding hotel companies as Accor and Choice, each of which has developed several innovative brands in the budget/economy sector.

Primarily located on the outskirts of European cities, Accor's Formule 1 hotels represent an ingenious development in low-cost tourism. This super-budget hotel's rooms, at 8 × 12 ft (2.5 × 3.5 m), are the smallest of any chain-operated hotel. Designed to sleep three people, the room features a unique arrangement of a loft-bed elevated over a double bed with a clothes rack suspended beneath, a retractable desk and stool, a ceiling-mounted TV/radio, and a small triangular sink in one corner. Every four rooms share a tub and shower along the hall which are accessible with the guest's credit card and are chemically self-cleaned after each use.

Microtel lays claim to being 'the only all-newly constructed interior corridor hotel chain in the budget/economy sector.' Microtel, an international chain, based its design prototype on careful market research to provide the basic needs yet keep amenities to a minimum so that the guest doesn't pay for what isn't used. The interior corridor is offered as an important security feature. The $35 per night MicroSaver rooms offer efficient built-in furniture, mattresses approved by the American Chiropractic Association, and free cable TV. Microtel proudly exhibits its Americans with Disabilities Act (ADA) compliant rooms, marketed as the best available in the budget sector. To introduce its new product, Microtel constructed exact replicas of its room prototypes on a 60-ft truck and toured 33 US cities.

Straddling economy and mid-price classifications, Rodeway Inn provides indoor corridors, a swimming pool, and a breakfast room in a three-story, elevatored building. Recognizing that senior citizens represent 30% of lodging demand and 50% of repeat business, Rodeway developed the Rodeway Choice Room featuring large-button telephones and remote controls, brighter lighting, lever handles on doors and faucets, and grab bars in the shower and bath.

To make food service available, and to avoid the expense of operating a restaurant, some budget chains lease or co-develop part of their site to a fast-food chain. Today, just off the exit ramps outside of major metro areas, you find highway villages, acres of asphalt where the weary traveler can choose from several brands of roadside inns and a variety of food outlets. Most are situated in a roadside mini-mall with laundry facilities, drug stores, book stores, groceries, and other retail outlets designed to serve the needs of interstate travelers.

Trends

One new variant of roadside accommodations is the new 'super truck stop.' At the new Travel Centers of America travel plaza in Commerce City, Colorado, although no actual sleeping quarters are offered, a weary driver may use the double-size marble showers, literally modeled on a Ritz-Carlton hotel bathroom, free with a purchase of 50 gallons of diesel fuel. The guest also can subscribe to the park-and-view system, which turns the truck cab into a virtual motel room, complete with 24-hour e-mail, cable television, and a wake-up call. Laundry service is also available. The Petro Company's Wheeler Ridge center near Bakersfield, California, has a 40-seat movie theater and an Internet lounge.

Airport Hotels

More than just places to arrive or depart for your flight, today's airports have, in many ways, become destinations in themselves. They are business and conference centers for fast-moving executives, shopping malls ideal for picking up family gifts; they sport restaurants and food courts, art galleries, museums and, more than ever, elaborate and sophisticated hotels.

Some of the most interesting hotels built in recent years have been at or near airports. A far cry from

The on-airport blended hotel **Kempinski Airport Hotel Munich, Germany**. Blending effortlessly with the runways, airline hangars, control tower, and terminal buildings, Helmut Jahn's hotel design forms part of a technologically advanced business and conference center linked to the airport terminal (see p. C-8 for a further view).

The on-airport interchange hotel **Sheraton Paris Airport Hotel Charles de Gaulle, Roissy, France.** Providing a glimpse into the future of transportation-based lodging, the 270-room hotel is located at the absolute intersection of air and rail travel, on top of a major regional train station and at the crossroads of people movers, monorails, and motorways.

yesteryear when airport hotels were dowdy, cheap, noisy one-night-stands of necessity, catering to disgruntled passengers on layover, pilots and airline personnel, and guests simply wanting to avoid the hassle and expense of staying downtown. While airport hotels still serve these markets, they have seen vast growth in the business and leisure segments that now represent 85 percent of their guests. Today, most hotel companies would not dream of building a full-service airport hotel without significant meeting facilities including a ballroom, a 24-hour high-tech business center, a health spa, some form of sport-ing facility, luxury suites on a concierge level, at least two restaurants, and other upmarket amenities previously limited to downtown hotels and resorts.

Much of the explosive growth in airport hotel development can be attributed to busy corporate executives asking the question: 'When you only go from the airport to the hotel and the hotel back to the airport why would you want to stay anywhere else?' The international corporate world has come to favor meeting at airports where the location is ideal for business guests to fly in from different cities, hold their sessions, and be off in minutes, avoiding long trips through downtown traffic. Airport hotels, with occupancy rates outperforming all other segments and with the highest average daily rate (ADR) in the industry, present serious competition to downtown hotels. As globalization continues to fuel the pace and reach of business travel, amenities for the individual business traveler to work and meet onsite are expanding rapidly.

Every major airport now has a major airport city next to it full of new hotels. Architect Helmut Jahn noted that airports, 'in addition to their role of moving people and freight, have become self-sufficient economic and cultural nodes, micro-cities that are no longer dependent satellites of the old downtown.' In setting forth a conceptual approach to airport hotels as a new building typology, Jahn contends that airport hotels must deliver the excitement of being at a crossroads and a sense of the romance and adventure of travel.

Jahn's design for the Kempinski Airport Hotel, the first building of the Munich Airport Center (MAC), a planned state-of-the-art business and conference center, is a prime example of this new typology. The building's form, with its huge glass atrium and transparent front and rear façades, is suggestive of a large aircraft hangar, a contextual nod to the community of airport structures next door. The hotel is tied to the main terminal building with an elaborate system of moving sidewalks that circulate through the entire airport.

Conceptually and typologically similar to the Munich model, Jahn designed the Hyatt Regency Paris—Charles de Gaulle Airport, touted by Hyatt as an architectural masterpiece. It has a spectacular six-story high atrium between two glistening metallic wings of hotel rooms. The hotel was built 5 minutes from the airport, and only a short distance from the Villepinte Trade Show and Exhibition Center and so serves this complementary market as well as the airport.

London's Heathrow Hilton is an example of an on-airport hotel, one that is actually on the property of the airport and attached to a terminal. Also styled as an aircraft hangar, its large atrium connects two parallel wings of the hotel and directs the view in one direction toward an active runway and in the other at the terminal building. Rooms on the north side of

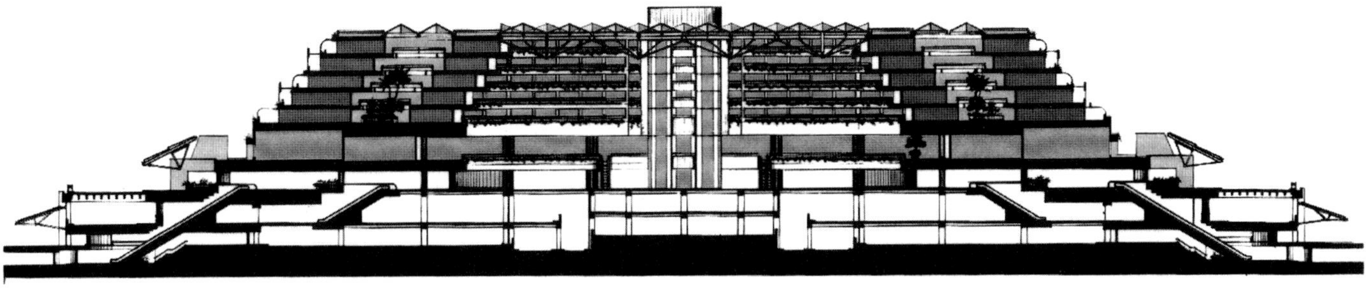

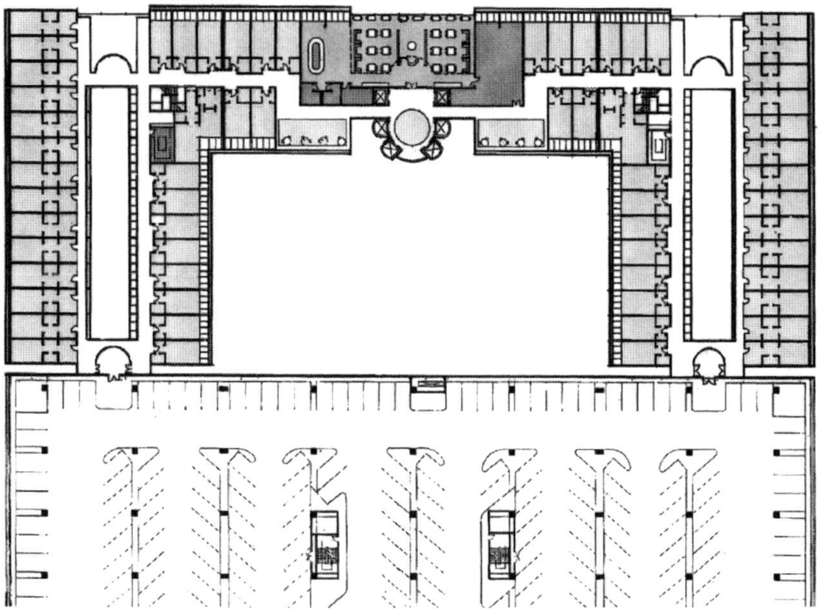

The integrated airport terminal hotel **Hyatt Regency Orlando International Airport, Florida.** The 446-room hotel's lobby and atrium is elevated one floor above the airport's main departure and arrival level, providing it with direct access to ticket counters and other amenities while separating it from the boisterous activity of the main terminal's operations.

the hotel have a view of the supersonic Concorde's docking station.

The 858-room Hilton Chicago O'Hare Airport, one of the first and perhaps the best-known of on-airport hotels, is centered between the airport's four terminals, which are easily accessible via underground moving sidewalks. The hotel has an airline ticket counter with baggage service in its lobby and arrival/departure information available on monitors in the lobby and on guestroom televisions. Frequent guests are given private mailboxes where they pick up their room keys and any messages on arrival.

Situated atop the Module d'Echanges, the central transportation hub in the heart of Charles de Gaulle Airport, the Sheraton Paris Airport Hotel represents not only a futuristic embodiment of an airport hotel, but a spectacular milestone in the evolution of transportation-related lodging. The 'module' forms the intersection of the travelator (people mover) that extends a short distance into Terminal 2, a monorail that connects to Terminal 1 and to remote car-parks, the primary airport roadway, and the TGV (high speed) and RER (regional) train stations which connect the airport to the rest of the Parisian metropolis. The hotel's reception and public spaces are located within the exchange module on the path that travelers take between train stations and the airline terminal and from the monorail that facilitates connecting flights. Above this level are four floors of guestrooms in an airfoil-shaped structure mounted entirely on vibration-isolation springs and clad with a double-framed noise-resistant exterior skin. Rooms surround a lozenge-shaped atrium, perhaps the first ever with a glass floor, open to daylight from above and below, expressing a sense of weightlessness and flight. The interiors, designed by Andrée Putman, are sleek and colorful, meant to evoke a sense of travel and transition, bucking the usual trappings and purposely avoiding the cozy atmosphere previously thought wanted by road-weary travelers.

The Hyatt Hotel at Orlando International Airport was built as an integral part of the terminal expansion in phase II of the airport development. This hotel, built one floor above the main terminal departure and arrival level, is directly accessible without conflicting with passenger circulation patterns. The hotel's large atrium connects to the terminal at the concourse level with the lobby situated on an open mezzanine overlooking the atrium on one side and the monorail stations that connect the terminal to the passenger gates on the other side. This hotel, in many ways, represents the perfect synergy between an airport hotel and an airport terminal. Aside from the guestroom accommodations, airline travelers may avail themselves of the 40,000 ft^2 (3,700 m^2) of meeting facilities, including a new 11,000 ft^2 (1000 m^2) state-of-the-art ballroom, ultra-high-tech business services, spa, health club, and two restaurants in the hotel. One of the restaurants is on the top floor with panoramic views of the airport. In turn, hotel guests, only minutes from the terminal concourse, may instantly avail themselves of ticket counters, travel services, high-end and moderate-priced retail shops, and multiple dining options.

Like the airport itself (and Bourbon Street for that matter), the Hilton New Orleans Airport and its facilities are open 24 hours a day. Built across the street from Moisant Field beneath the approach path to runway 10, the hotel has a 24-hour business center with vending machines for computer disks and other business supplies. The state-of-the-art fitness center, also open 24-hours, includes a built-in walking track, outdoor lighted tennis court, putting green, and swimming pool.

As we have seen with other hotel types, the airport hotel segment has sprouted subsegments. Airports in smaller markets or at smaller airports where full-service hotels might not make economic sense are seeing the development of limited-service facilities such as Comfort Inns and Hilton Garden Inns. In 1996 Marriott split its 782-room hotel at Miami International Airport to three separate hotels representing different market segments: a full-service J.W. Marriott, a less expensive Courtyard, and a Fairfield Inn, each with its own front desk.

A growing number of newlyweds stay at airport hotels with luxury accommodations including fine restaurants and fully equipped spas before leaving on honeymoon. Hotel companies, recognizing the diversity of this market, aim to provide amenities that encourage guests to stay more than the usual one or two nights. The Hilton Miami Airport & Towers resembles a resort hotel, built on a peninsula in the middle of a 100-acre artificial lake featuring tennis, water-skiing, and jet skiing. Down the road, the Hotel Sofitel, also near Miami International Airport, has a French restaurant and bakery that offers a free baguette to each guest at check-out.

If there is a downside to this remarkable transformation of airport hotels it is that airline crews and budget-minded travelers of the early 1990s have been pushed out and replaced by high-yielding corporate and group meeting accounts. Hilton reports that 68 percent of its guests are individual or group business travelers, 20 percent are leisure travelers, and only 11 percent are airline and airport personnel. Countering this trend, new hotels, such as Aurora International Hotel at London's Heathrow, are built specifically to cater to airline personnel. As for the budget-minded and delayed passengers, new forms of guest accommodations are surfacing for those waiting for flights and not in need a full-night's stay at an airport hotel. At Narita Airport in Japan, 'refresh rooms' are provided off the main terminal concourse that offer a clean and comfortable room with a shower where travelers can rest or sleep for a few hours. A similar facility, Cocoon, on the shopping level in Terminal 1 at Charles de Gaulle Airport, provides 59 micro-guestrooms of 70 ft^2 (6.5 m^2), which are rented by the hour with a maximum stay of 16 hours.

Planning and Design Considerations

The sky-lit lobby atrium, no longer popular for downtown locations where the expense and drama now is traded for more intimate luxury, find good use in airport hotels as a comfort to guests who have arrived from long flights in cramped aircraft cabins and who hunger for expansive space and air. These atriums provide a sense of light and transparency and of being closer to the sky, maintaining the milieu of flight. The atrium design also reduces airport noise for those rooms that face the interior.

The historically short guest length-of-stay characteristic of airport hotels and the need to respond to unforeseen arrivals due to flight problems, place special demands on the hotel's administrative and back-of-house areas. Rooms' division, accounting offices, front-desk areas, housekeeping, food service, and engineering divisions are all heavily impacted by the operational needs unique to airport hotels.

Eighty-five percent of airport hotels are affiliated with chains which require that these hotels be within 3 miles (5 km) or 10 minutes of a terminal, offer food service 24 hours a day, free airport vans, same-day laundry and pressing service, business centers, and multilingual receptionists. With a new focus on the individual business traveler and corporate meeting groups, design requirements suitable for conference centers and flex-office guestrooms discussed in other chapters should be reviewed. Airport hotel guestrooms should be equipped with large work desks with ergonomic seating, fax machines, two-line phones, Internet access, speaker-phones and voice mail, as well as other amenities appropriate to today's business traveler.

Height restrictions for all buildings in the vicinity of airports are strictly regulated by government agencies such as the US Federal Aviation Administration. Noise obviously plays an important role in site selection for a hotel; planning should account for the air traffic patterns including arrival and departure routes around the airport. Furthermore, sophisticated new noise reduction technologies are available and should be employed, including the use of triple-glazed windows, resilient wall-mounting clips, vibration-isolation springs, and amplified sound-cancellation systems.

The high-tech office park hotel **Hotel Kyocera, Kokubu Hayato Technopolis Center, Kagoshima, Japan.** In the heart of the Kokubu Hayato Technopolis Center, which adjoins Kagoshima Airport, the hotel serves the needs of international technology companies as well as local enterprises with its state-of-the-art business center and conference facilities while maintaining the atmosphere of a resort hotel (see p. C-8 for a further view).

Office Park Hotels

Office parks were established in the US as a natural outgrowth of suburban expansion. Many of the same qualities that attracted residential development to the outer boroughs—green space, lower costs, easier access, and safety—also attracted business developments in the form of suburban office complexes. The rapid decentralization of the central business districts to perimeter developments was a necessary phase in the evolution of the modern city, as major office-tower tenants moved to the suburban office market.

While industrial parks were the precursors of the genre, high-tech industries led the way to early office park development. Silicon Valley, California, was an early manifestation of a modern office/science park. In the early 1960s the area around Stanford University became a haven for computer science graduates wanting to establish their businesses in close proximity to the university's research facilities. Hewlett-Packard was the first major company to locate its California headquarters in Silicon Valley to take advantage of the research-rich environment. In the 1970s corporate giant IBM moved from its Manhattan office headquarters to suburban Armonk, New York, and split off entire new divisions to other suburban areas across the US. Other major corporations followed suit in their exodus from downtown.

In Europe, British developer Stuart Lipton created Stockley Park adjacent to London's Heathrow Airport as a US-style business park. Lipton's emphasis was on landscape design and quality architecture as essential amenities offered to his tenants. According to Lipton: 'It was all about PhDs rolling in the grass.' The theory was that fertile minds function better in the pleasant open environment of a business park than the crowded cacophony of a city office block.

Office parks usually fall under the control of a single entity that sets out a master plan and defines development guidelines and restrictions. Amenities are important to tenants and their employees and, if not available in the immediate area, they must be provided on the site. These include good parking, attractive landscaping, daycare facilities, food and beverage outlets, fitness centers, outdoor recreation, business support centers, meeting and conference facilities, and overnight accommodations. Since hotels can provide many of these amenities under one roof, they are a natural fit for office parks.

The Boeing Company built Longacres Park office campus in Renton, Washington with 2.9 million ft^2 (270,000 m^2) of facilities. Designed by the architectural firm SOM, the clusters of low-rise buildings were sited sensitively on a farmland meadow with ponds, trails, and green pastures. The designers took care to preserve the natural wetlands and to enhance the park-like setting so that office workers could interact with the environment by jogging through it or watching the seasons change as they walk to nearby meetings. A unique water filtration system purifies water run-off from the car park through a system of ponds, encouraging the growth of a variety of wetland plants, adding to the qualifications of Longacres Park as the first ecobusiness park.

The Seattle/Renton Hilton Garden Inn, a short and pleasant stroll from Longacres Park, is characteristic of a mid-priced hotel fitting the needs of office park business visitors and tenants. Each of the hotel's 150 executive-style guestrooms has an oversize desk, a halogen lamp, an ergonomic task chair, data cabling, and multiple two-line phone locations. The standard guestroom is 12 × 26 ft (3.6 × 8 m) and, in addition to the oversized work area, contains a hospitality center with microwave, refrigerator, and coffee brewer. Typical of Hilton Garden Inns, the public areas of the hotel are housed in a separate pavilion in front of the main guestroom wing and include the lobby, registration, two restaurants, a business center, and catered meeting facilities. The pavilion is designed as a centerpiece to the building and presents a comfortable residential scale while maintaining business functionality.

Airport hotels frequently provide accommodations and important amenities to nearby business/office parks being developed at major airports to serve the needs of international trade and business. Examples of these 'fly-in business parks' include Stockley Park at Heathrow, Munich Airport Center (MAC), and the Villepinte Trade Show and Exhibition Center near Charles de Gaulle. Developed for high-tech industries, Chipshol Park, next to Schipol Airport in Amsterdam, got its name from combining 'chip' from microchip and 'Shol' from Schipol. The Sheraton Schipol Airport Hotel and the Kempinski Munich Airport Hotel are representative of hotels designed to support the juxtaposition and dynamic synergy of contemporary business travel activity and the compatible functional requirements of corporate office park tenants.

The Kokubu Hayato Technopolis Center, which adjoins Kagoshima Airport, was planned as one of Japan's principal excursions into the information age by providing offices to high-tech enterprises for the future. In the heart of the Technopolis Center, the Hotel Kyocera was designed by architect Kisho Kurokawa to meet the needs of international business and local companies with two levels of conference facilities below grade and boardrooms, business center, restaurant, and bar overlooking a dazzling elliptical 13-story atrium. This business hotel has the feeling of a resort with views of the Kirishima Mountains and Kinko Bay through its transparent curved façade. A dramatic, glazed tent-shaped chapel at the base of the atrium caters to weddings and other festive activities. The Hotel Kyocera is exemplary of the hybrid nature of many suburban hotels as its serves international trade, local enterprise, leisure travel, and community functions (see plans on p. 285).

Country Inns and Bed and Breakfast Inns

Descended from eighteenth-century English and European inns, one of the oldest forms of hospitality has endured to become one of the industry's fastest growing. Country inns and B&Bs have experienced explosive growth in the last two decades as patrons seek the personal charm, intimate scale, and bucolic settings offered by smaller facilities. In 1980 there were approximately 1,000 inns serving about a million guests in the US. Current industry estimates place the figures close to 25,000 inns serving 50 million guests. International figures are hard to find, but just one of the dozens of B&B-listing organizations claims 27,000 members worldwide. Many factors have contributed to this tremendous surge of new country inns and B&Bs, but it is the traditional qualities inherent in these facilities that remain central to their ever-expanding appeal. These qualities include generous hospitality, personal attention, owner involvement, architecturally interesting or historic structures, individually decorated rooms, comfortable ambiance, and unhurried surroundings.

Though endless variety exists with these inns, many guests envision a quaint country cottage or farmhouse with a wide front porch full of rocking chairs, a cozy fireplace, a floral-wallpapered bedroom with a four-poster bed, claw-footed bathtubs, and delicious country cooking all served up by a charming and gregarious couple. The personality of the innkeeper often is tantamount to the character of the inn itself and the quality of the stay. Some referral organizations actually suggest a phone chat with the prospective host to confirm personal compatibility before booking.

The trend towards high-quality personalized service is evident in many hotel segments and, as with the expanded development of luxury properties and the growth of boutique hotels in urban areas, is reasoned to be reaction to the impersonal service of the large corporate hotels. The friendly down-home appeal of country inns and B&Bs is often preferred over the grand impressions and commercial approaches followed by other types of lodging.

This new popularity has caused stiff competition in many high-profile locations where a virtual B&B glut has occurred. To compete, some inns have sweetened their amenity packages by offering gourmet meals, whirlpool baths, modem connections, and cooking classes. For the first time, country inns and B&Bs have begun marketing to mid-week business travelers and corporate retreat planners by providing fax machines, secretarial services, and meeting rooms. These inns have become popular with female business travelers who appreciate the added sense of security and high level of personal service offered by the owner/innkeepers. Many inns in more naturalistic settings have benefited by attracting birdwatchers, hikers, and ecotourists. The diversity of new inns is matched by the cultural diversity of their patrons as younger, more sophisticated, and more ethnically diverse travelers are changing the market.

Not since the 1950s, when chains overwhelmed the individual hotel owner, has the independent entrepreneur been able to enter a profitable segment of the hotel industry, free of prohibitive capital requirements or strong chain competition. The Internet has provided the means for small-scale operators to advertise their inns inexpensively without paying for a reservation system. There are thousands of homemade websites describing minute details of these inns, in many cases allowing the customer

The super-luxury country inn **Twin Farms, Barnard, Vermont.** With accommodations ranging from $700 to $1,500 per night, this elegant high-styled country estate demonstrates the rapid expansion and integration of the country inn concept with other hospitality segments including boutique and super-luxury (see p. C-19 for a further view).

The ecocountry inn **Yusuhara Visitors Center, Japan.** The pristine natural setting for this ultra-modern inn is nowhere more evident than in one of the communal baths with its stretched canvas roof and carefully framed Zen-view of brightly colored hillside foliage (see p. C-10 for a further view).

The futuristic country inn **Noto Monzen Family Inn, Ishikawa, Japan.** This hyper-modern manifestation of a country inn strings its copper-roofed guest cabins along an arching outdoor spine that encircles a sea-facing Japanese garden and culminates in a fanciful observation tower (see p. C-10 for a further view).

to view photographs and rates of every available guestroom for advance selection.

Often themed, individual guestroom designs have long been a feature of country inns and B&Bs. In fact, the appeal is greater if no two rooms are alike. The Artists Inn B&B in South Pasadena, California, decorated rooms inspired and named after famous artists including Gauguin, Matisse, and Degas. Another B&B close to a college town with a famous football team has rooms called Legends of the Game Room, the Trophy Room, and the Alma Mater Room. Accommodations at country inns cover a broad range of economic categories, from simple rooms for under $50 to the elegant luxury of the five-star Twin Farms Country Estate in Vermont where the Washington Room may be had for $950 per night or The Studio Cottage for $1,500.

The ever-broadening diversity of types of country inns and B&Bs has led the Professional Association of Innkeepers International (PAII) to codify the varieties of inns based on type of building, type of ownership and operation, size, location, services, and amenities. The PAII definitions range from 'homestay' to 'country inn' to 'bed and breakfast hotel' as detailed in the accompanying sidebar. The larger the property and the less involved the owner is in the day-to-day operations, the more it is perceived as a hotel instead of an inn by the traveler. Any facility with over 30 rooms is generally considered a B&B hotel.

One commonly thinks of country inns or B&Bs as restored historic buildings or renovated farmhouses where the charming characteristics and fine craftsmanship of past eras are essential values of the experience. Creating a B&B or country inn from an historic structure usually means carving out guestrooms and baths where none existed or adding wings. It is important when undergoing renovations of this kind to maintain the style and quality of workmanship original to the building. Housing of administration and back-of-house functions, such as laundry/housekeeping, food preparation, or repair shops is often accomplished in cellars, outbuildings, or away from the site.

There also are many examples of newly built country inns that range in style from traditional to ultra-modern. Many of the new country inns are designed to capture a sense of history and regional personality by employing the architectural styles, detailing, workmanship, materials, traditional furnishings, and artifacts of an earlier period. The Pitcher Inn, in Warren, Vermont, recently was built on the same site as the eighteenth-century original that had

Country Inn/B&B Categories

Homestay, Host Home

An owner-occupied private home where the business of paying guests is secondary to its use as a private residence. The hosts are primarily interested in meeting new people and making some additional income while continuing their present employment or retirement. Frequently located in residential areas, zoning or other government restrictions may prevent the use of signs, public advertising, etc. Usually between one and three rooms, these homes are often a member of, and usually inspected by a reservation service organization (RSO) but are rarely required to be licensed or inspected by local applicable governmental agencies. Breakfast is the only meal served. In some instances, it may be an unhosted apartment where breakfast is self-serve.

B&B (Bed and Breakfast)

Formerly a single family dwelling usually in the four- to five-room range, this owner-occupied establishment has an equally mixed use as home and lodging with lodging superseding home more often than not. It is located in a legally zoned area and meets all the tax, fire, building, and health requirements for this size and use of property. This establishment advertises publicly and can legally post a sign. Like the homestay or host home, because of its size, these B&Bs usually cannot support a family unit, so the B&B is often one partner's job and the other has outside income. Often the property is purchased specifically to be a B&B, but many are converted family homes. Reservations may be made directly with the property.

B&B Inn

Generally small, owner-operated businesses providing the primary financial support of the owner. Usually the owner lives on premises. The building's primary usage is for business. Inns advertise, have business licenses, produce their own brochures, comply with government ordinances, pay all appropriate taxes and post signs. Breakfast is the only meal served and only to overnight guests. The inn may host events such as weddings, small business meetings, etc. Room numbers range from four to 20 with a small, but increasing number up to 30. Reservations may be made directly with the property. Note that the distinction between a 'B&B' and a 'B&B inn' is not readily apparent, except with regard to building usage.

Country Inn

A business offering overnight lodging and meals where the owner is actively involved in daily operations, often living onsite. These establishments are, in fact, B&B inns which serve at least one meal in addition to breakfast, and operate as 'restaurants' as well as overnight lodging accommodations. Modified American plan (MAP) country inns serve dinner to overnight guests only, and the cost of dinner and breakfast is generally included in the room rate. A country inn with a full-service restaurant serves these additional meals to the general public. To be a country inn, a property does not have to be located in a rural area. Room numbers tend to range from six to 30.

B&B/Self-contained Cottage

A detached building affording privacy and seclusion to guests, with owner providing minimal services. Breakfast is either delivered to the room, taken with others in a central dining room or placed prior to arrival (or on daily cleaning) in the cottage kitchen facilities. Owner is usually available for questions, but generally guests choose this style of B&B when they want little help. The light, personal touch and memorable B&B décor further distinguish this genre from the vacation rental/condominium.

B&B Hotel

These are historic properties with over 30 rooms offering breakfast that can only be considered hotels. Only the historic structure, and perhaps some decorating components and breakfast provide the B&B feel.

(*Source: Professional Association of Innkeepers International*.)

been destroyed by fire. Painstaking care was used to follow the style of the original structure faithfully: a big, white colonial farmhouse with a red barn in the back. As a new-built structure, the inn was able to easily incorporate an efficient operational plan for both front- and back-of-house as well as equip its 14 stylish guestrooms with the modern amenities normally found in a first-class hotel. The Pitcher Inn provides another high-quality example of themed guestrooms, which include the Trout Room with its sculptured fly-tying table, the School Room with a vintage blackboard and an antique globe, and the Hayloft, located in the barn.

Contemporary approaches to the design of country inns have produced some dazzling new architecture and interiors. Babington House, situated on an eighteenth-century estate in Somerset, England, 12 miles (20 km) south of Bath, is a boutique country inn set in an antique manor house. Redecorated with brushed steel staircases and suede goose-down pillows, this country inn has a contemporary styling uncharacteristic of traditional English country houses. In stark contrast to the traditional notion of a country inn, the Noto Monzen Family Inn, sited in the Japanese countryside overlooking the Sea of Japan, represents a hypermodern evolution of the genre. Its futuristic architecture demonstrates a new and unique approach to lodging, with guestroom pods strung along a pedestrian deck that frames a carefully crafted garden overlooking the sea and leads to the lobby and a lookout tower.

Hotel du Saint James, in Bouliac, France, overlooking a small village and surrounded by a vineyard, represents a beautiful harmony of bucolic setting and contemporary architecture in a design befitting the traditional notion of country inn. Jean Nouvel designed this rustic, yet stunning, 18-room inn as four simple box houses clad in russet latticework, giving them the appearance of the traditional tobacco-drying sheds of the region. The façade's kinetic metallic louvers open mechanically revealing the spectacular panoramic view of the valley and the city of Bordeaux in the distance. At

The multiple segment urbane suburban hotel **Hyatt Regency La Jolla at Aventine, San Diego, California.** Serving several suburban markets including luxury, university, office park, spa, golf, mall, and conference center, the 400-room hotel shares the Aventine complex with a 225,000 ft^2 (20,900 m^2) office building, a 32,000 ft^2 (2,970 m^2) world-class fitness center, and a restaurant village that features five first-class restaurants.

The suburban hotel in an expanding urban area **The Manhattan Hotel, Makuhari, Chiba Prefecture, Japan.** Located halfway between Tokyo and Narita International Airport the hotel caters to the nearby Nippon convention center and to other regional business concerns. The gleaming 21-story alabaster tower with its green-tinted windows rises from center of Makuhari Messe, the corporate stronghold of the district.

the same time the rusty grilles conceal the austere luxury of plaster walls, polished concrete floors, bleached wood furnishings, and high, soft country beds of the guestroom interiors. The simple, yet elegant, forms derived from local vernacular architecture allows the inn to blend comfortably into the French countryside.

As the country inn continues to evolve as one of hospitality's most enduring forms, it will be the home-like atmosphere that continues to draw guests to the cozy hearth, pleasant conversation, and tranquil ambiance that it offers.

Hybrids and Other Suburban Inns

The explosive development and expansive diversity found in the suburbs has led to a wide variety of hybrid hotel types that cater to an even wider variety of markets. These hotels are characterized as accommodating a multitude of regional functions including shopping malls, universities, museums, amusement parks, medical centers, restaurant villages, and even small towns in addition to the larger audiences discussed above such as airports and office parks. Most suburban hotels accommodate more than one geographical market and so it would not be surprising to find a major chain hotel serving a small university town near an airport fly-in business park, a stone's throw from a major regional shopping center. In addition to satisfying price category requirements these hotels must provide a variety of amenities and facilities that satisfy all potential user types. Hilton Garden Inns have developed a management system referred to as focused service where the staff members are cross-trained to perform multiple tasks and to identify a guest's particular traveling needs on check-in and so provide tailored services while maintaining cost-effective operations.

Designed by architect Michael Graves, the Hyatt Regency La Jolla at Aventine, a 400-room luxury suburban hybrid located 5 minutes from the University of California–San Diego campus, was built as part of a complex that includes a 225,000 ft^2 (21,000 m^2) office building, five restaurants, and a 32,000 ft^2 (3,000 m^2) world-class fitness center and spa. The hotel features the 11,800 ft^2 (1,100 m^2) Aventine Ballroom and the 6,400 ft^2 (590 m^2), Barcino Pavilion glass-enclosed banquet facility for weddings, trade shows, receptions, and business meetings. The close-by University Towne Shopping Center and La Jolla Village Square Mall provide shopping opportunities and the world-famous Torrey Pines Golf Course is only a few miles down the road. With this multitude of facilities, this hotel could be considered a luxury/university/office park/spa/mall/golf retreat/restaurant village/conference center hotel.

Mall Hotels

Shopping malls reached their peak in the late 1970s with the natural growth of residential suburbs and served as a potent catalyst for further residential and business expansion. Suburban hotel development gravitated to these locations, lured to the crossroads by the same magnetic attraction that fueled residential, retail, and business growth. The area surrounding South Center Mall near Seattle, Washington, has attracted the development of

The small city hotel **Inn on the Biltmore Estate, Asheville, North Carolina.** Sited on the 8,000 acre (3,240 ha) historic Biltmore Estate, the 224-room hotel features spectacular views of the Blue Ridge mountain range and of the magnificent Beaux-Arts mansion designed by Richard Morris Hunt for Cornelius Vanderbilt.

more than a dozen brand-name hotels, ranging from economy to full service. Essentially hybrids, these hotels provide guests with proximity to the energetic shopping activity of the mall as well as neighboring Sea-Tac International Airport, several corporate business parks, and other suburban attractions.

Pyramid Company, a major east-coast shopping center developer, recently held a think-tank to investigate the feasibility of attaching a hotel directly to a large suburban shopping mall thereby offering guests the opportunity to come for a two- or three-day shopping-spree vacation. Design and planning considerations for such a hotel might naturally include larger rooms and more luggage handling and storage space. Full-length triple-leafed mirrors and a large dedicated dressing area with good lighting would certainly appeal to those who come shopping for a new wardrobe. A whirlpool bath or soaking tub would be inviting to those 'shop-'til-you-drop' guests. Other suitable amenities might include day care facilities, beauty salons, a health spa, and recreational facilities. The adjacency to a mall that has a variety of restaurants, entertainment, and recreation features may warrant a paring down of food and beverage and other functions within the hotel since these amenities are likely to be easily accessible in the mall. Collaboration between the hotel and the mall stores might provide for advertising displayed in the hotel's public spaces, current store catalogues in the rooms, or even coupons and store discounts offered with each night's stay.

Located directly across the street from the fashionable Short Hills Mall in New Jersey, the 300-room Hilton provides guest/shoppers with deluxe accommodations perfectly suited to the rigors of a shopping holiday. In addition to offering easy access to the malls, a large array of upmarket stores including Tiffany, Chanel, Hèrmes, and Saks Fifth Avenue, the hotel also houses an elaborate first-class fully equipped health spa with indoor and outdoor swimming pools, tennis courts, and a professional staff of physical trainers. The spa gives guests the opportunity to refresh themselves before another day of spending (see p. 305).

The 'museum-quality' hotel **Naoshima Contemporary Art Museum and Annex, Naoshima, Japan.** Located on Naoshima, a small island in the Sea of Japan near the port of Takamatsu, this museum was designed by architect Tadao Ando to include a small hotel as an annex that includes four twin rooms, two suites, a café, and a sheltered outdoor gallery. With most of its volume constructed underground to protect the natural park setting, the hotel wraps around an oval court with a sculpted water garden in the center.

University Hotels

Universities have always provided a profitable market for the hotel industry in accommodating visiting families and friends, invited lecturers, conference attendees, research-related business people, administrative functions, sporting event goers, and so on. Harrison Conference Centers, a Hilton Hotels brand and a premier conference and education center management company with executive education and training as the cornerstone of its mission, has developed several of its products in university settings. The Thomas Center is located on the campus of Duke University in the heart of North Carolina's Research Triangle and combines state-of-the-art meeting areas, high-tech support systems and a wide array of recreation and leisure options. The 111 guestrooms of the Thomas Center include a dedicated study area equipped with a large desk, retractable reading chair with ottoman, analog modem lines on an ethernet ring, and voicemail.

The university hotel **The Statler Hotel, Cornell University, Ithaca, New York.** The 150-room campus hotel and executive conference center serves the myriad university business, leisure, and group markets. It contains three restaurants and a variety of banquet and meeting rooms, including a 94-seat amphitheater used for university advanced-management programs.

The facility also includes 24-hour access to six guest lounges for informal meetings and study sessions, networked and Internet-linked PCs and laser printers, and fully stocked kitchenettes with complimentary snacks and beverages (see Chapter 6).

Small Town Hotels

Small town hotels represent perhaps the most cross-bred of all hybrids. Regarded by the large chains as a tertiary market, small town hotels can be found in the form of motels, budget to full-service suburban hotels, country inns, or small downtown hotels. Often staffed by local people, they lack the regimentation characteristic of less down-home accommodations. These hotels often take a role in community affairs as prominent as that of the local high school or town hall. They often are the setting for functions as varied as wedding receptions, high school reunions, local awards ceremonies, beauty pageants, bingo nights, Elks club meetings, seasonal festivals, and other town events. Swimming pools and health clubs often are open to local residents for a small admission or membership fee. Upmarket restaurants in these hotels often are the only ones in town and naturally become a social epicenter. Similarly, hotel discotheques and nightclubs sometimes provide the best nightlife.

Some small town hotels are miniature versions of the downtown hotels found in large cities. The seven-story Eola Hotel looms over the other two- and three-story buildings that make up the small downtown area of Natchez, Mississippi, a town built on the bluffs overlooking the river. For over half a century, the hotel, built in 1927, with its sumptuous lobby and restaurant and top-floor ballroom served as the center of social activity for the town until competition from newer roadside inns caused its closure. A renewed tourism industry, the introduction of riverboat gambling, and a program to revitalize the downtown area inspired developers to hire Charles Moore and Perez Associates to renovate the hotel in the mid-1980s. Balconies for river views were added, Peacock Alley was restored and the 'Top of the Town' was converted to the Moonflower Lounge as the hotel regained its stature as the social epicenter of Natchez.

The small town riverview hotel **Eola Hotel, Natchez, Mississippi.** Looming over the two- and three-story downtown buildings and visible for miles, the seven-story hotel historically served as a symbol of the town's prosperity and as its center of social activity. Through an extensive renovation that included the addition of balconies to enhance guestroom views of the mighty river, the hotel regained its former prominence.

Planning and Design Considerations

The design of suburban hotels, in many respects, is less challenging than that of their downtown counterparts. Lower real estate values and increased availability result in significantly larger building sites. Larger parcels of land and less restrictive zoning usually allow for more flexibility in massing and make functional layouts easier to achieve than on tight urban sites. The larger, less restrictive sites have many advantages. These include better vehicular arrival areas, convenient and plentiful parking, sensible lobby layouts based on optimum elevator core position and column spacing. These hotels also have the potential to locate circulation of service vehicles and loading facilities out of sight of the main guest entrance and outdoor areas and space enough for outdoor recreation including swimming pools and tennis courts.

Zoning regulations in the suburbs often mandate height and density restrictions appropriate to the regional architectural character. Airport hotels may have very strict height restrictions if near the approach or departure path of an active runway. Suburban hotels tend to be smaller in size than downtown hotels, usually under 300 rooms. The ability to spread out over the site lends itself to low- or mid-rise construction and, therefore, less expensive building methods, further reducing project costs. Less restrictive covenants governing the placement and configuration of the guestroom tower favors a more logical column grid and frees up long-span areas suitable for lobbies, ballrooms, and indoor pools. More flexible tower placement also permits locating guests and service elevator cores closer to their related functions and leads to a more effiicient back-of-house configuration.

Prominent visibility from surrounding roads continues to be a feature of successful suburban, airport, and roadside hotels. Drive-in customers without reservations account for over 15 percent of their occupancy, compared with less than 5 percent for downtown and resort hotels. Potential sites must be evaluated for their natural contours, visibility of building signage, or other alternatives for freestanding signs. For similar reasons, entrance approach patterns which provide easy auto access and flow for the traveler including adequate deceleration lanes, stacking space, and turning radii are equally essential.

The tradition of distinctive signage dates back to the European inns that opened in towns and along the Roman roadways serving the travelers of the day. As hotel owner René Hure recorded, each inn was known by 'the sight of its insignia, painted on a metal plaque, grating its rugged hinges in every wind, signifying the comfort of good lodging and bliss of good cuisine.' One can picture the traveler's smile on first spotting the sign being equal to that of today's weary traveler.

With almost total reliance on auto access, a suburban location's ability to develop its full potential for occupancy and outside business, including restaurant, lounge, and meeting use, is often governed by its ability to provide adequate onsite parking.

Suburban hotels generally require a minimum of 1.2 cars per room (see Chapter 17), or about 50 percent more parking than that of the average downtown or resort property. This reflects about 90 percent of guests with cars, including approximately 50 percent with rental cars at airport hotels, 75 percent of employees with cars, and one car for every 2.5 outside customers of food, beverage, and meeting facilities. Parking facilities should be sized to meet peak requirements, generally 8–10 p.m. on a Friday or Saturday night if the hotel has a major banquet facility or nightclub. At these peak times most guests have returned to the hotel and the restaurants and lounges are operating at full capacity. One of the advantages of a mixed-use development is that some of the parking space assigned to the office buildings can be used by the hotel during such peaks, reducing overall requirements by up to 15 percent. However, peak parking hours for apartments and shopping malls prevent overlapping or significant sharing by a hotel.

Guestroom sizes for most suburban and airport hotels are generally the standard 12.5 × 18 ft (3.8 × 5.5 m) with insignificant variations of no more than 5 percent in either direction due to minor differences imposed by various chains and/or owners. While the 12 × 16 ft (3.7 × 4.9 m) room, originally established by Holiday Inns and later increased to 12 × 18 ft (3.7 × 5.5 m) in more upmarket areas, became the standard in the motel industry. Further variations are being presented to the traveler to choose from on a price-value basis. By contrast, budget chains such as Ibis have maintained food and beverage facilities, but reduced room sizes to 12 × 14 ft (3.7 × 4.3 m). This more segmented market gives people a choice depending on what they want to spend and how they want to spend it and provides an opportunity for smaller entrepreneurs who have unlocked these marketing secrets to be able to compete successfully with the giant chains of the industry.

Increasing technical sophistication of business travelers and the explosion of information technology has produced a dramatic new emphasis in business hotels. Guestrooms made to function as office work spaces and high-tech business centers are becoming essential components of business hotels. Marriott, in a joint venture with AT&T and Steelcase, is developing a new concept for the business traveler called the 'room that works.' It includes a guestroom workstation with an ergonomic chair, a two-level desk, adjustable task lighting, and multiple power and data outlets.

Other new products that feature high-tech business guestrooms include Westin's 'guest office' and 'Room 2000,' Hyatt's 'business plan' and Hilton's 'Garden Inns.' New guestrooms in these facilities may also include flexible furniture such as a table that converts to a small conference table and in-room terminals for Internet video conferencing.

Club Hotels by Doubletree feature a 6,000 ft^2 (550 m^2) 'business clubroom' that includes a full-service business center, personal workspaces, small meeting rooms, and a café. Guestrooms at Club Hotels are designed with a residential office atmosphere. The Renaissance Hotel in Chicago is connected to a 24-hour Kinko's business center that has video conferencing, meeting rooms, fax, and computer rentals.

These examples indicate the extent to which suburban and airport hotels have added amenities approaching downtown hotels. At major airports or regional shopping or office centers hotels food and beverage facilities and retail areas are equivalent to those of the downtown hotel, while their meeting and function spaces average about 20 percent less and their lobbies and circulation spaces approximately 25 percent less.

Lobbies, circulation space, and retail areas in small town and roadside hotels and motels are generally 50 percent less than those same spaces in suburban and airport hotels. But due to the greater percentage of guests eating breakfast in the hotel, the roadside hotel requires about 5 percent more restaurant space to handle the breakfast peak. Since the restaurant space is not fully used for lunch or dinner, this results in inordinate operating costs as well as capital costs to provide adequate food and beverage service. But reducing service or lowering standards would risk guest satisfaction. To resolve this dilemma, some roadside hotels have eliminated this service entirely. If there are no restaurants close by, some motels lease portions of their sites to fast-food chains or free-standing restaurants to provide for guests' convenience as well as to attract sufficient outside business to support the restaurants on their own.

Roadside hotels require about 25 percent less meeting space than that of the average suburban or airport hotel, and their administrative and service areas are about 20 percent less than those of other types of hotels since fewer guest services are generally required. Space standards for small town hotels are similar to those of roadside hotels but usually with 15 percent more meeting space allowed for groups.

Trends

The expansion of the information highway and the explosive growth of digital technologies have everyone guessing where commerce in the new millennium will reside. Strategic uses of information technology are primary concerns in the development of new research-based science/technology parks such as Tsukuba Science City in Japan, Sophia-Antipolis Research Park on the French Riviera, Oulu Technopolis in Finland, and Hsinchu Science Park in Taiwan. Experiments are underway to promote cities linked and functioning independent of their particular location in an intricate information web called a multifunction polis (MFP). The question posed by the MFP experiment is: why, given global electronic communications, does commercial activity have to be gathered in one place like business parks or traditional cities? Can it not be a net of small nodes linked electronically all around the globe?

It is this trend toward worldwide digital communication that has the travel industry and hospitality companies concerned that the need for business travel may be lessening. By the same token, telecommuting using computers from a home office calls into question the very nature of suburban development and is thought to be at least partially responsible for a general population increase in rural areas.

- In many medium-sized US cities, more office space currently exists in outlying areas than in the central business district. History has shown that certain business functions must remain at the core of the city—those that require face-to-face contact in the daily conduct of business. Banking, law, finance, advertising broadcasting, publishing, entertainment, and selected corporate headquarters are among those where people still need to meet. Business travel related to these industries will endure. Even with the increasing sophistication of virtual officing, video conferencing, and perhaps even holographic conferencing, people will continue to travel for interpersonal interaction.
- An ironic trend reversal can be detected in places like Millennium Point in Birmingham, England. Here, low property values are attracting high-tech industries and energetic young companies, which are drawn from the suburbs to the vitality of the city and its transportation, shopping, cultural, and other advantages.
- In a return to the basic principles of Sir Ebenezer Howard and other traditional city planners, a growing movement called new urbanism seeks to address the sprawl and isolation caused by decades of poorly planned suburban growth. Seaside, Florida, is perhaps the best-known example of a traditionally styled new community with narrow streets, front porches, and back alleys designed to enhance the sense of neighborhood. According to Vincent Scully: 'Like the successful older neighborhoods and small towns where many of us grew up, the designs of the New Urbanists integrate housing, shops, workplaces, parks and civic facilities into close-knit communities that are both charming and functional.' Fundamental to this new urbanism is a reduced dependence on the auto and increased use of light rail and other forms of mass transit (see Chapter 12).
- Major hotel companies have come to learn that environmental responsibility, ecological design,

and sustainable architecture are good business. The trend will continue as global warming, ozone depletion, and the devastation of our environment continue to be sharp reminders of the delicate balance of our ecosystems. Suburban hotels will be designed to ensure minimum disruption of the surroundings during construction and preserve existing ecological resources.

- Short-break holidays will gain in popularity as the general public experiences continually decreasing leisure and vacation time. Urban and suburban residents will seek vacation spots closer to home where they can enjoy a quick escape and relax over a long weekend at a suburban resort. The Center Parcs Company has developed more than a dozen short-stay holiday villages throughout Europe, all in close proximity to major metropolitan areas. In recognizing that a short vacation could easily be rained out, especially in northern Europe, the company has developed its subtropical swimming paradise, a domed structure covering a tropical landscape of water recreation activities—a holiday experience the weather cannot spoil.
- Regional facilities management is a course that many of the larger hotel chains are employing in large metropolitan areas where anywhere from five to 25 properties are able to effectively share storage facilities and back-of-house functions in central facilities close by. Hilton Hotels recently built a central laundry operation for several of its properties covering New York City and northern New Jersey. The facility allows many of the hotels to recoup the area formerly dedicated to an in-house laundry for badly needed meeting spaces, health club, administration offices, or other service functions.
- Suburban hotels will continue to be a laboratory for new prototypes and hybrids. Just as the diversity reflected in suburban markets led to broad-reaching market segmentation and new products such as all-suite and extended-stay hotels, suburbia will continue to be fertile ground for new lodging innovations.

The seaside site contextual resort **The Westin Regina Golf and Beach Resort, Los Cabos, Mexico.** This example of the most modern resort genre bridges two hill tops to carve out a popular mountain-courtyard resort with perfectly framed sea views—the fruit of designing a resort in close collaboration with nature (see pp. C-20 and 66 for a further view).

Resorts 4

The first resorts were seaside spas in ancient Greece and Rome, a concept which soon advanced throughout the Roman Empire (see the list of Hotel Milestones in Chapter 1). After their decline in the Middle Ages, spas were revived along with the arts and sciences in the Renaissance, and returned to prominence throughout Europe. For example, the resort community of Bath, England, founded in Roman times, still flourishes today. And the most famous of ancient spas, Baden Baden, considered luxurious by the Emperor Caracalla, was recently restored with new marble around its pools and gold banding on its columns. Following similar origins, the earliest American resorts were spas, starting in the 1750s in White Sulphur Springs, West Virginia, and in the resort community of Saratoga Springs, New York, which reached its height of popularity as a national social center in the 1850s.

During the early years of the industrial revolution, resorts remained the province of the well-to-do. Fashionable hotels such as Mohonk Mountain House in upstate New York and the Hotel del Coronado in San Diego, California, prospered in diverse scenic mountain and seaside settings. But the twentieth century saw the resort become increasingly accessible to the middle class, through steadily rising disposable income and paid vacations, particularly following World War II. This included dramatic increases in leisure travel by Europeans and Asians, primarily Japanese, as well as Americans. Resorts experienced a sustained growth boom, eventually evolving, as did other hotels, into more customized categories serving different types of vacationers as will be discussed in this chapter.

Beyond type, location is a prime influence on resort development. In established resort regions such as Hawaii or the desert areas in southern California, resort amenities are provided in virtually all hotels for increased flexibility and because they are preferred and expected by most travelers in these regions. Also, resort amenities often are added to nonresort properties because of the continued growth of health consciousness and fitness megatrends (see p. 402). Resort programming, site layout, and hotel design are vitally influenced by such cultural and market trends.

Cultural and environmental considerations determine whether the resort buildings are low-rise structures sensitively blended with the traditional landscape, as at Costa Smeralda in Sardinia, or mid-rise towers, as at the Jumeirah Beach Resort, or the striking 'ultratels' as the Burj Al Arab Hotel, both in Dubai (see pp. 106–110).

While most vacation spots are places one travels to, frequently well off the beaten path, new types of resort-like city hotels are designed to advance weekend or other nontraveling vacations. Often located on the urban waterfront or in the upscale shopping district, and offering elaborate spa facilities, they function effectively as 'urban resorts,' designed for tourists as well as local guests preferring convenient nearby vacations that save on travel-time and expense.

Worldwide resort expansion ranging from spas to theme parks is organized into ten basic categories in this chapter, with such resort-like hotels as the entertainment hotel, mega-hotel and casino hotel types discussed separately in Chapters 2, 11, and 13, respectively.

Beach, Golf and Tennis Resorts

From the Sardinian coast to the Gulf of California, Capetown to the Canaries, and Key West to Kauai, most vacationers head for the coast, where seemingly endless beach-fronts continue to supply idyllic sites for most new resorts. Spectacular views, water sports, and imaginative accommodations keep the second oldest form of resort, after the health spa, the most popular of all. Major beach-front

The seaside site contextual resort **The Westin Regina Golf and Beach Resort, Los Cabos, Mexico.** The 238 guestrooms are in two single-loaded buildings with views of the sea, and low-rise terraced structures. Free-form pools are located near the beach and in the space behind the guestroom wall.

resorts provide top golf, tennis and spa facilities matching those of the scenic mountain and desert resorts that specialize in these activities. Such resort amenities also attract the typical business traveler who often chooses them, where available, over downtown or suburban hotels. And corporate groups increasingly prefer resorts for business gatherings, as their more relaxed atmosphere promotes teamwork and closer personal contacts. 'Even when people play a bad round of golf together, it brings them closer,' one manager observed. Corporate meeting planners feel that resorts:

- combine the most effective training atmosphere, with a touch of reward added as motivation
- are self-contained, with conference and recreational amenities closely integrated, making it easier to keep a group together in a more productive series of meetings
- go 'all out' to please aesthetically, with imaginative design, lush scenery, and recreational features that leave groups with a sense of reward for their working meetings.

But the above factors apply only if the resort provides the highest quality conferencing technology, uppermost in the meeting planners' requirements. Of equal importance, to attract both family and business groups, resorts must provide the widest and most imaginative array of sports and recreation activities, from golf to aerobics and teen activities, to ensure satisfying all guests in the group.

Planning Considerations

Although closeness to the water is the essential ingredient of the beach-front resort, environmental regulations in many areas, particularly for those lacking comprehensive master plans, mandate large setbacks of 200 ft (61 m) or more from the shoreline. While guestroom balconies and full exterior window walls help dramatize beach views, designers add such water features as canals and decorative pools to enhance the hotel's relationship to the shore and to compensate where the hotel is off the beach. This is done at the Kahala Mandarin Oriental Hotel in Honolulu, Hawaii, which has its own large lagoon and dolphin pond, and at the Camino Real in Cancun, Mexico, which is entirely surrounded by pools. Both the Mauna Kea Beach and Mauna Lani Bay resorts on The Big Island of Hawaii feature indoor canals with brightly colored reef fish, while an octopus provides hours of entertainment for children and adults at the Mauna Lani.

Shade structures, whether moveable, trellised, or landscape types, increase comfort along beaches, and are essential at swimming pools and other water sports facilities, whirlpools, bars, and food service areas. Siting the hotel at or close to the shoreline, or in a lagoon, becomes more interesting and exciting when environmentally compatible, such as at Club Med in Cancun, Mexico, and the Burj Al Arab Hotel in Dubai (see views on pp. 87 and C-24).

Hotels built into shoreline bluffs or cliffs can be strikingly effective, as at the Tahara on the Tahiti coast, Princeville on the Kauai coast, and the Amandari resort overlooking a river gorge in central Bali. Resorts provide water views for virtually all rooms. The more-efficient double-loaded corridor designs are oriented perpendicular to the shoreline, allowing interesting 90° views of both land and water. Single-loaded hotel wings provide the guest with a 180° water view, but the construction costs are about 15 percent higher, since they require twice the normal corridor space plus additional exterior walls with windows in the corridors and related air conditioning. Known as 'cost guzzlers,' they not only are wasteful of energy and land, but require additional staff due to the structure's increased servicing distances. But a small percentage of single-loaded spaces often can be most cost effective, particularly where it helps provide an economical solution to an otherwise unusable site or building orientation problem. However, where climates permit the single-loaded hotel to have an open air balcony corridor, it costs about the same as the double-loaded scheme, and may present a viable solution.

As with other types of lodging, architects can plan resorts in a variety of ways. Atriums with single-loaded interior balcony corridors may be justified in luxury resorts with the highest rates. For example, if the architect locates guestrooms on three sides of the major lobby space, all oriented toward the ocean, the guests are rewarded with views of the crashing surf. The total land area requirement for a luxury resort, however, depends on larger considerations than the coverage or bulk of its buildings. For example, a 500-room mid-rise beach-front hotel generally requires about 10 acres (4 ha), including a swimming pool and related landscaping, with most parking placed below grade. However, the total land development for the resort depends on the extent of major recreational components such as golf, tennis, and other such amenities. For instance, a tennis center with ten courts would require an additional 3 acres (1.2 ha) and an 18-hole golf course approximately 110–160 acres (45–64 ha).

The modern beachfront resort **Sandals Royal Bahamian Resort & Spa, Nassau, Bahamas.** (A) Beach resorts feature wave-pools, lagoons, falls, and extensive water features, in this case a huge surreal-themed pool surrounding the mid-rise resort tower. (B) This imaginative design and cove beach location of the whirlpool pleases guests as well as enhancing its stress-relieving benefits.

Design Considerations

Architect Marcel Breuer pointed out that the main visual features people focus on are the landscaping and the building finishes. But while building materials may vary in their appeal, proper landscaping always receives praise. And this is never more true than at a resort. It also relates the development to its natural environment, whether coastal, mountain, or desert. Outstanding examples include The Ritz-Carlton Kapalua and the Four Seasons Resort Hualalai in Hawaii, Atlantis on Paradise Island in the Bahamas, and Costa Smeralda in Sardinia.

Architects and interior designers appropriately draw on the beauty of the natural landscape as a vital theme of the resort's design. Since guests are drawn to their favorite environments, such as the Caribbean for the beach and sun, or mountain locations for scenery, such natural attractions are reinforced by both the architecture and interior design through color, form, and materials. For example, earth tones and rugged finishes often psychologically blend with mountain resorts, pastel colors more closely recall beach locations, green interior accents complement forest settings, and natural sandstone finishes harmonize with desert sites. In addition, local artwork and decorative motifs recall and inform the guest of the area's traditions.

Besides natural and traditional beauty, resorts emphasize comfort and luxury. Historically, most vacationers expect resorts to be more lavish in amenities and décor, even when informal in mood. Lobbies should be 30 percent larger than those of suburban or airport hotels and 10 percent greater than those of downtown hotels of comparable size. This also reflects the additional time guests spend lounging and socializing in lobbies at resorts. Since many guests like to shop on vacations, 50 percent larger retail space should be provided than in downtown or suburban hotels. Complete space requirements are provided in Chapter 22.

Since both the average length of stay and number of occupants per room is greater in resorts, guestrooms should be at least 10 percent larger. In areas with higher family occupancies such as in Orlando, near Walt Disney World Resort and Universal Studios theme parks, the guestroom length should be increased from the standard 18 to 21 ft (5.5 to 6.4 m) for ease in accommodating required roll-away beds and cribs. Closets should be at least 4.5 ft (1.4 m) long, since vacationers pack more clothing and sports equipment. Guests expect larger bathrooms, with dressing areas and additional amenities. Balconies should be at least 5 ft (1.5 m) deep, furnished with a table, chairs, and two chaises, essential for lounging and sun bathing, as well as enjoying views and relating to the outdoors.

A full height window wall may be provided at the balconies to enhance guestroom views, with interlocks recommended on the doors, so that if left open, the cooling system automatically shuts down. In addition to conserving energy, this avoids possible mildew from causing discomfort in the guestroom. Some otherwise fine resorts experience this condition, particularly where care is not taken to vent wall cavities that may cause in-room condensation.

Exterior back-of-house areas, particularly loading docks and service drives, should be concealed by retaining walls, trellises and landscaping. Truck docks must be roofed and enclosed to prevent unsightly views, noise, and odors. Where visible from upper levels, roofed areas should be terraced and decoratively landscaped to ensure pleasant exterior views from all guestrooms.

But no element sets the ambiance of the resort more than its pool area. Since guests spend more time there than in any public space, it affects their overall impression of the resort more than any other element and provides the same memorable experience as the main lobby in the downtown hotel.

Guests expect imaginative pool designs, which often provide a transition between the building and its surrounding natural land forms. Fanciful elements such as bridges, islands, grottos, and waterfalls as well as totally abstract free forms provide decorative photo backgrounds sought by guests at the pool. However, the overall pool size and shape must allow for swimming laps, group play, wading and, with today's accent on fitness, sports such as water polo. Nevertheless, diving boards should be avoided since they are a prime cause of accidents. The design also must maintain sight lines for lifeguard surveillance of all areas. A whirlpool at least 8 ft (2.4 m) in diameter should be located adjacent to the swimming pool, with a second whirlpool near the beach. Wave-pools, waterslides, and pools with spray fountains and related play equipment are particularly important for resorts with high family occupancy, but a separate adult pool must be provided in such cases. Children's wading pools, where desired, should be located close to the main pool for purposes of surveillance by parents. (Waterparks are discussed later in this chapter.)

However, pool design is subject to regional and cultural differences. For example, in China, a separate pool for younger children is generally not desirable because many believe that families should treasure swimming together and be encouraged to do so. In parts of the Middle East, communal bathing is not permitted in public. Local health and safety regulations also may vary. For example, ramped pools, allowing bathers to wade in from one end, as at a beach, while popular with many guests, are prohibited in some areas due to their lack of safeguards against entry by small children.

Pools must be located to obtain maximum sunlight exposure but, in equatorial climates, shading such as trellises must be designed over a part of the pool, for relief from the sun. For example, at a resort in Sharjah, along the Arabian Gulf, a tensile fabric structure is provided over the pool during the day, to reduce the intense sunlight, yet the pool must be heated at night.

And for one of the resort's most popular vacation sports, people-watching, for which more guests use the pool-deck than the pool, adequate chaise-longue space must be provided. More than any other area, the pool deck encourages socializing, and many guests make friends there. Therefore, provide area for at least 1.5 chaises per room. Often built into or contiguous with the pool, convenient outdoor snack, juice, marina, or *tiki* bars provide food and beverage service to virtually all outdoor areas.

Environmental Considerations

With rare exception, the hotel industry understands fully the folly of any lack in preservation of the environment if for no other reason than to avoid problems that could diminish the guest appeal of the region. As Scott Berman, partner in the hospitality and leisure group of PricewaterhouseCoopers warns: 'Limpid, turquoise seas sell. Polluted waters and destroyed reefs don't.'

Yet examples persist of inadequate protection, bureaucratic authorities, improper actions by developers and builders, and lapses in enforcement of standards posing potentially incremental as well as irreversible effects on total communities and business economies. For example, in an 80-mile (129-km) stretch along the east coast of Mexico's Yucatan Peninsula, extending from the fully developed Cancun area to the protected Mayan archeological sites of Tulum, is one of the largest resort construction programs in history. It started with over 9,000 resort rooms and condominiums to be followed by another scheduled 15,000 resort units over a 5-year period—expansion that took fast-growing Cancun 20 years to develop. Dubbed 'The Riviera Maya,' developers proceeded, in many cases, without approved permits, paving hundreds of acres of mangrove swamps, the crucial plant-life responsible for nourishing ocean reefs as well as wildlife. Such natural phenomena, properly protected, can preserve an ancient geographic area such as the Yucatan as a viable ecotourist paradise no matter how fragile it may be. But radical land use changes require adequate study and respect for sound technical judgment. Only through alert international news reporting was the condition exposed, publicly condemned, and corrected by the developers. Hopefully, such publicity encourages proper legal reforms in other delicate environmental areas.

Acapulco, former Mecca to the jet-set and popular resort, suffered serious long-term environmental damage from over-development which, along with severe crowding and related social problems, resulted in a major decline in its tourism. Not surprisingly, some of our most superb resort areas, those best able to attract natural and historic interest and favored by sunny climates and convenient airline connections, may be lured into developing unreasonable resort densities. Therefore, for any large new resort development, studies should include an assessment of the eventual total capacity and an analysis of alternative physical concepts. These need to offer the developer a fair return, provide the guest with a vacation experience, and protect and preserve the environment and community. Frequently, developers run into legal difficulty by not being familiar with the local requirements. It is important that developers work within the system to:

- prepare environmental and other analyses and keep clear documentation at each stage
- identify the government agency responsible for approving various aspects of the project
- acquire copies of all legal requirements, necessary permits, or technical standards applying to the project
- monitor construction and proactively seek government inspection and approval at each stage.

Significant Beach, Golf, and Tennis Resorts

Unique Site Context Resorts

The Boulders, one of the most exciting resorts of the southwest US, was developed in Carefree, Arizona, in the 1980s adjoining a natural rock formation (see p. 242). This early organic concept was sponsored by Rockresorts, the chain founded by environmentalist Laurence Rockefeller. These examples illustrate more recent projects of the new genre.

Westin Regina Golf and Beach Resort, Los Cabos, Mexico

For Sordo Madeleno, resort architects, the popular impressive Westin resort in Los Cabos personifies modern Mexico. Both organic and high-tech, the nine-story boldly curved tower fills a gap between two hill tops, forming a gutsy and colorful, yet intimate and natural resort with interiors enlivened by bright colors and softened by textured finishes, fabrics, residential furnishings, and palms. Guests enter the lobby and adjacent conference center to dramatic views of the Sea of Cortez, framed by giant pierced openings in the guestroom tower. Townhouses surround the base of the hotel. This unique 238-room view resort contains 753,500 ft^2 (70,000 m^2) and cost $138 million for a modern milestone with a natural twist (see pp. 64, 66 and C-20 of the color section).

Wyndham Buttes Resort, Tempe, Arizona

A butte formation of stone deposits resembling nearby Camelback Mountain, the barren rocky site was considered near unbuildable. However, this was overcome by an environmentally sensitive nestling of the structure into its suburban hillside site and by creating an exciting interior design. The resort seems like a natural outgrowth of the hill on which it is so gently set. The architect placed a natural pool within the confines of the butte and perched a striking redwood rooftop restaurant overlooking the local stone façade of the guestrooms. The resort's instant success permitted immediate expansion of the development, even though the economy was in a recession at the time (see p. C-20 of the color section).

Island Resorts

The benefits of clean environments to islands have not escaped savvy vacationers who, by the planeload, choose them as preferred getaways. Call it the 'island phenomenon,' but with economics amiable to leisure travel, land values of island resorts compared to those on other sites may soon exceed megatrend proportions.

Beginning at mid-twentieth century, the Big Island, one of Hawaii's most unique lava-based geological formations, began collecting the era's largest group of environmentally motivated, experimental, and ultimately successful resorts. Respected environmentalist, Laurence Rockefeller, founder of Rockresorts, and architect Nathaniel Owings, created the Mauna Kea Beach Hotel, one of the world's finest resorts, with Polynesian art displayed throughout and its residential wings elevated to permit the landscaped grounds to freely flow into its interior gardens and courtyards, further enhancing the resort experience. Far ahead of its time, the developers tested mock-ups of villa units which, decades later, became a popular environmental resort concept. Also, they made a noble effort to preserve the natural lava surface on the golf course; however, guests, wearing cleated golf shoes eventually required grassing over the slippery surface.

Four Seasons Resort Hualalai, Kona, The Big Island, Hawaii

Crashing Kona surf and lavish villas sited around the eighteenth hole mark this remarkably relaxing and refreshing luxury resort on the 'island of islands.' Its stunning 243 spacious villa units are arranged in four crescent-shaped formations to afford greater panoramic views of the sea. In line with architect Hill Glazier's dedicated environmental concept, no roof line is more than one story above the highest point of the site. The island's newest resort reflects airy Hawaiian detailing with unabashedly luxurious interiors, drawing their warm residential flavor from natural architectural materials such as slate floors, mahogany window and door frames, and louvered wood screens. For example, the original lighting fixtures not only recall Polynesian culture but are extremely effective in expressing the unit's residential feeling (see unit plans in Chapter 16).

For maximum views and enjoyment, all three restaurants are located on the beach. The overall low-rise, low-density design features a distinctly different pool experience at each villa cluster. These include a salt water beachside pool, another for laps near the fitness spa, a third with underwater trails recessed into the lava to minimize any undertow, and a large central pool for socializers—the guests who enjoy staking out positions on the pool's free-form peninsulas while watching their toddlers in an adjoining wading area. Less splashy and more meditative is an elegant, tiled rectangle of water, its calm reflective surface perfectly level with a teak border. One villa group boasts a small whirlpool, tucked away in a coconut palm grove, capturing the ultimate in relaxing design.

The Orchid at Mauna Lani, Big Island, Hawaii

The resort, carefully nestled on an intimate sand-beach swimming lagoon on the dramatic Kohala Coast shared with an ancient preserved fishpond, blends perfectly with its idyllic site. The hotel maintains the desired residential effect with broad roof overhangs and airy façade detailing, including deeply recessed balconies with outward-opening doors and windows. A grand outdoor stair featuring local koa wood banisters unifies the entrance. Public functions are located near the arrival area and guestroom wings are sited perpendicular to the sea, helping to maintain direct ocean views across the large central landscaped courtyard for all areas.

The efficient plan conserves maximum open space within the 32 acre site by concentrating the 542 guestrooms, seven restaurants, generous conference space, fitness center, 11 tennis courts, and an exhibition court in one area. The resort's 10,000 ft^2 (3,050 m^2) natural themed pool complex and surrounding hardscape surfaces link the courtyard to the beach. The current design represents a remodeling of the original interior spaces to a luxurious informal tropical island theme by architects WAT&G. A scenic 18-hole golf course, with panoramic ocean views, closely adjoins the hotel.

The island environmental resort **Four Seasons Resort Hualalai, Kona, The Big Island, Hawaii.** This breakthrough all-villa concept blends its low profile structures into the landscape in one of the island's most environmental resorts (see unit plans, p. 279).

The island ocean-view resort **The Orchid at Mauna Lani, The Big Island, Hawaii.** A model of efficient site planning and indigenous detailing, this luxurious resort provides the maximum open space and ocean views for each of the major elements of the resort.

The Lodge at Koele, Lana'i, Hawaii

As authentic a symbol of Lana'i as coffee is of Brazil, talented architect, artist, photographer and essayist Arnold C. Savrann skillfully 'painted' the idyllic island environment with his camera in a much admired book. The design and detailing of this resort proves the high value of his technique.

Set in Lana'i's central highlands, the 102-room lodge is a rare inland Hawaiian resort, reminiscent of a plantation owner's country estate, complete with fine Japanese and Hawaiian gardens. The lodge's central hall is dominated by stone fireplaces and heavy timber columns supporting a 35 ft (10.7 m) high beamed ceiling. The space showcases painting, sculpture, and other works by local artists and octagonal rooms designed at the hall's corners host frequent musical recitals. The Lodge's porch is the favorite spot for relaxing while watching spectacular sunsets. Other amenities include three themed restaurants, a music room with afternoon tea, an English Conservatory where gardeners cultivate orchids, and croquet and lawn bowling courts on the manicured grounds. The extremely popular Greg Norman and Ted Robinson-designed Experience at Koele Championship golf courses are onsite.

The island inland-view resort **The Lodge at Koele, Lana'i, Hawaii.** The Lodge's unique plantation manor setting combined with the perfect golf experience are among the rewards designed into this choice resort.

Manele Bay Hotel, Lana'i, Hawaii

Overlooking the pristine beaches of Hulopo'e Bay, framed by Lana'i Island's brilliant red cliffs, guests enjoy a spectacular view from the resort's lavish high grounds. Designed and developed by the same architect and owner of the Koele Lodge, The Manele Bay Hotel's 250 luxury guestrooms and suites, with their loggias and landscaped court-yards, comprise an elegant blend of Hawaiian and Mediterranean styles. The lobby area is devoted to lounging, browsing, and viewing regional artifacts. The resort displays the work of Lana'i artists throughout, including in the elegant boutique, library, veranda, adjacent private meeting rooms, and oceanview lounge providing evening entertainment. Guests choose from the gourmet cuisines of the Hawaiian-Mediterranean and French restaurants.

The central pool, sundeck and spa areas contain a series of murals by artist John Wullbrandt. The 12,000 ft^2 (1,115 m^2) conference center, accommodating banquets for 240 guests, boasts panoramic views of the Lana'i coastline and houses a permanent collection of Lana'i artifacts curated by the Bishop Museum. A marine preserve with tidal pools rich in aquatic life is maintained at the adjacent Hulopo'e Bay Beach. The resort features the Jack Nicklaus-designed 36-hole Challenge at Manele seaside course.

The eminent Castle & Cooke Hawaii Company limited development to only these two exclusive resorts as part of an overall plan to preserve the island's unique heritage and environment. The island has only one small town, miles of untouched beaches, and a spectacular mountain formation rising 3,400 ft (1,035 m) from the sea.

The Ritz-Carlton Kapalua, Maui, Hawaii

On a choice ocean-front site of a vast Hawaiian pineapple ranch, whose several generations of owners exercised remarkable environmental stewardship, architects WAT&G designed The Ritz-Carlton resort in the traditional Hawaiian plantation style balanced by luxurious interior hotel décor. To achieve visual intimacy with 550 guestrooms on a 38.5 acre (15.6 ha) site, the architects divided the resort's massing into half a dozen six-story guestroom buildings which step down with the site's natural contours toward the sea and are angled to maximize guestroom views. For similar reasons, the public areas were divided into the main lobby public spaces, with expansive ocean views, and a three-tiered pool area located in the building's courtyard, also open toward the ocean. Service facilities, to the greatest extent possible, were located below grade and built into the hillside. The hotel also includes 30,000 ft^2 (2,800 m^2) of meeting space, a 165-seat amphitheater, ten meeting rooms with ocean views (some with fireplaces), and ten ocean-front tennis courts. The site is totally surrounded by three championship golf courses and the ocean.

Local design elements incorporated into the resort include the deeply overhanging gray-blue roofs, the pineapple theme—a symbol of Hawaiian hospitality—used as a decorative element on the balcony railings, and floral motifs cast into the exterior concrete panels. The hotel frequently is toured by Hawaiian residents and foreign visitors seeking examples of local traditions.

The island coastal-view resort **Manele Bay Hotel, Lana'i, Hawaii.** With views overlooking idyllic beaches and lavish gardens, an artwork collection, tennis club, and a Jack Nicklaus championship golf course, its world-class amenities combine with an intimate courtyard design and residential atmosphere.

The island plantation resort **The Ritz-Carlton Kapalua, Maui, Hawaii.** This treasured resort by WAT&G Architects, on one of the best resort sites in the Pacific, rewards guests with its well-conceived organization, superb views, intimate scale, and a plantation setting that offers a true sense of place and history.

Europe's island convention resort **Gran Hotel Costa Meloneras, Canary Islands, Spain.** Combining island charm with high-tech conferencing and a touch of the fabled grand hotels of the 1920s, this major conference resort is well targeted toward its principal European corporate group market.

Gran Hotel Costa Meloneras, Canary Islands, Spain

This 1,700-room complex conjures up the unmistakable mood of the historic grand hotels of the 1920s era yet includes advanced technology to attract European corporate meetings to a major island convention resort. The adjoining 1,200- and 500-room hotels share appropriate amenities including casinos, nightclubs, and themed restaurants. The resort preserves the island's traditional character with such design details as Andalusian wooden balcony banisters and hand-formed clay tile rooftops framing landscaped courtyards and sun-drenched plazas, relieved by deeply shaded archways.

West Island Golf and Casino Hotel, Hainan, China

Hainan is China's southernmost province. With a sunny climate, natural resort characteristics, and a population of 6 million, it is the choice vacation destination for millions in China. New resort complexes and casino entertainment hotels are being

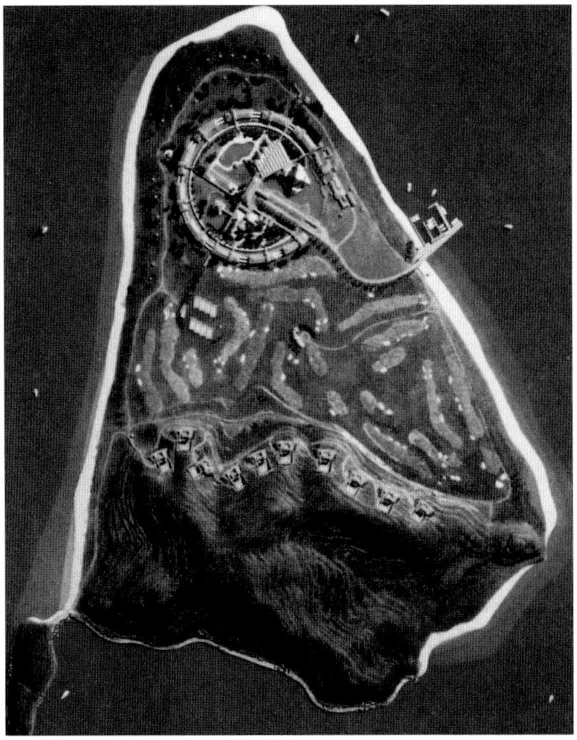

China's island gaming resort **West Island Golf and Casino Hotel, Hainan, China.** This breakthrough multiresort is designed for the developing Hainan resort area on the South China Sea. A unique trilevel circular guestroom structure encompasses a lavishly landscaped courtyard featuring lagoons, pools, sundecks, shops, restaurants and the casino. Dramatic hillside villas overlook the resort, its golf course, and beach pavilion with related seaside bungalows facing the surrounding surf. This world-class gaming casino is designed as one of the growing resort region's prime attractions. Sited near the arrival dock and resort's main entrance pavilion, the distinctive focal structure by KPF Architects unifies the design composition.

developed to attract both domestic and international guests, supported by a major airport at Sunya City.

The main 1,000-room, 600 acre (240 ha) West Island Golf and Casino Hotel complex is paired with a nearby 600-room resort hotel and marina. The project includes luxurious guestrooms and suites, and a casino of 49,500 ft^2 (4,600 m^2) encompassing the gaming floor, restaurants, bars, and lounges as well as service facilities. The unique circular arrangement of buildings spreads across the northern third of the island, surrounded by sand beaches and ocean views. The first phase is to build 940 guestrooms, the second phase an additional 36 villas, located on a mountain ridge rising on the southern third of the island, overlooking the casino. The program also includes 24 super-luxury suites and an 18-hole golf course on the middle third of the island.

Arriving guests are bussed from the airport to the resort marina, then proceed by high speed water transport to West Island, a distance of 5 miles (8 km), and the short ride through a lush landscape to the heart of the complex. Guests have dramatic views of the casino from the driveway and adjacent entrance pavilion. Expressed as a tiered multiroofed structure, resting on massive masonry bearing walls, the gold tile roofs distinguish the casino from the terra cotta tile used on the other structures. The area adjacent to the casino provides pools, sundecks, gardens, theme restaurants, and a large lake.

The innovative circular plan comprises ten three-story double-loaded guestroom buildings, with 94 super-luxury guestrooms in each. The elegantly furnished rooms have five-fixture bathrooms, including separate showers, and feature marble walls, floors, and vanities. Each floor includes a public lounge and connecting doors between guestrooms, allowing them to expand into two-room suites. On the top floor of each building, eight rooms overlooking the sea have oversized balconies.

The building rooflines are connected with trellises, covered by lush vines, framing the view between the buildings. The circular building form is further reinforced by a covered walkway and adjacent stream. Phase II adds a six-story all-suites tower within the circular courtyard area, plus 16 luxury double-key beach-front villa-units. Other recreational amenities located outside the circular area include a beach pavilion, tennis center, health club, and golf clubhouse.

The site plan requires no significant change in the natural topography. A central mechanical plant is included as part of the new structures; electric power and water will come from the mainland, with full capacity emergency back-up onsite. On the island, longer distances are covered by frequent jitney service while shorter distances are traversed by foot paths and covered walkways. In addition, guests will have high-priority access to the hotel's helicopter service. The program and site organization represent an imaginative breakthrough in casino resort design.

Red Sea Rim Resorts

Long a leader in tourism, Egypt is committing a good part of its national budget to an eight-fold expansion of its 70,000-room hotel supply with a goal of 618,000 rooms by 2017. Of these, 20,000 new rooms are underway, many to support the shift to a greater tourist economy. Happily, the views from most of the new hotels are now of the Red Sea, not only the traditional Nile.

With new resorts gingerly dotting the Red Sea's shorelines, four main resort cities are staking out new futures. Consequently, the following discussion compares four exemplary projects, one from each burgeoning resort community. Sharm el Sheikh, occupying a hillside site at the southern apex of the triangular Sinai Peninsula, retains its commanding position on the sea's northern coast, extending east and west to the Gulfs of Aqaba and Suez. Facing it from the Suez side is the newer tourist area of el Gouna. The area of Sharm el Sheikh, in common language, would be regarded as old money and el Gouna as new. A third resort subregion extending eastward along the Sinai Coast toward Aqaba may become an intercultural area, while a fourth growth

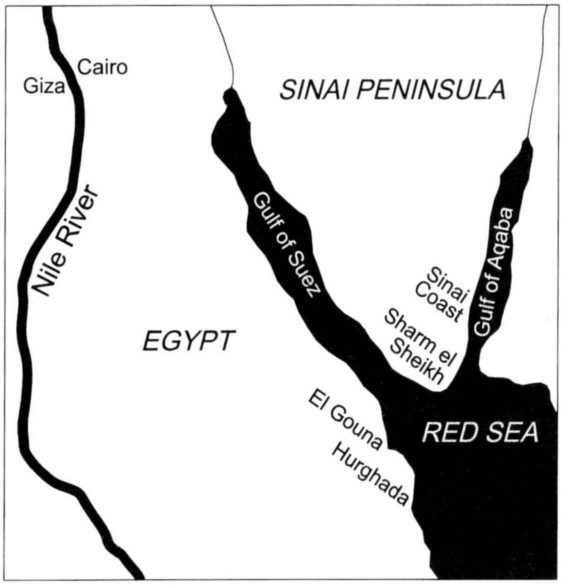

Egypt's well-conceived resort expansion program, more ambitious than the Pyramids **Red Sea rim resort map.** This map locates the resort case studies illustrating four newly energized multiresort communities selected by Egypt to spark the region's rapid rebirth.

vector heading south on the sea's western shoreline is centered on the historic town of Hurghada.

The government designated international consultants to establish strict environmental controls to preserve the Red Sea's scenic underwater trails and flourishing reefs. Working collaboratively, the developers, international resort chains, and architects are following the dedicated footsteps of the most influential Egyptian environmentalist/architect, Hassan Fathy, whose hand is evident in the response to the region's culture and ecology.

Sheraton Miramar Resort el Gouna, Egypt

Architect Michael Graves has succeeded in creating a most intimate and luxurious hotel through a welcome series of inventive 'scaled-down' design elements, including highly individualized private villa units. With the sea on the east, the developers added numerous lagoons and channels to create a 1,615,000 ft^2 (150,000 m^2) island site filled with intriguing waterways crossed by artful pedestrian bridges. In this manner, the concept for the 240-room Sheraton Miramar Resort provides a splendid variety of different experiences and an array of vacation units including those served by a corridor in the main building and others located in free-standing clusters. This approach creates the highest possible perception of choice and a wide selection of views, including those facing into handsome courtyards, preferred by families with young children.

Graves has designed a totally original architectural vocabulary for the unique resort, yet one which is completely at home with Pharaonic traditions. He has created exciting views from the public spaces including two restaurants and bar/lounges, recreational amenities including separate family, children's, and exercise pools, and efficient service systems throughout the hotel, That, and the guestrooms, with their varied shapes, textures, colors, orientations, window sizes, skylights and high-domed ceilings, serve to create the exciting and luxurious feeling that every guestroom is special.

Inter-Continental Taba Heights Resort, Sinai Coast, Egypt

It is more challenging to achieve the desired scaled-down effect and comfortable residential atmosphere for a larger, 500-room resort. However, Graves has accomplished this largely by subdividing the guestroom component into three differently shaped residential courts, open to the Aqaba Bay beach-front. On the entrance side, the natural constraints of the

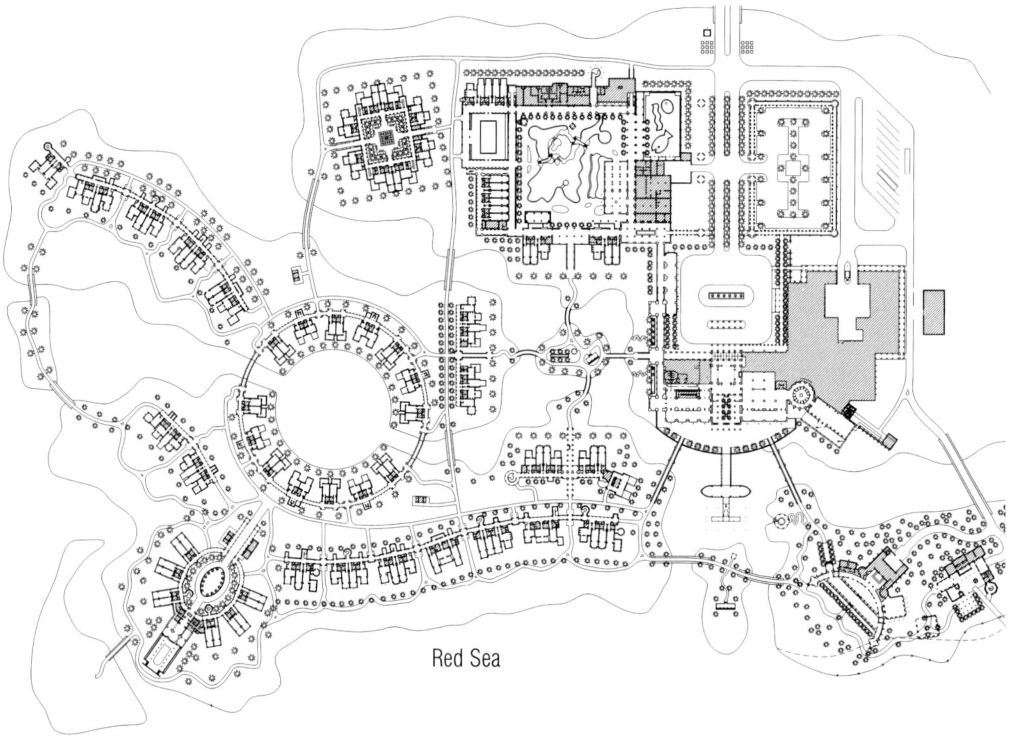

An original resort design vocabulary **Sheraton Miramar Resort el Gouna, Egypt.** This site plan outlines the main elements of the resort's bold and unique design displaying an unmistakable affinity with ancient Egyptian culture (see view on p. C-25).

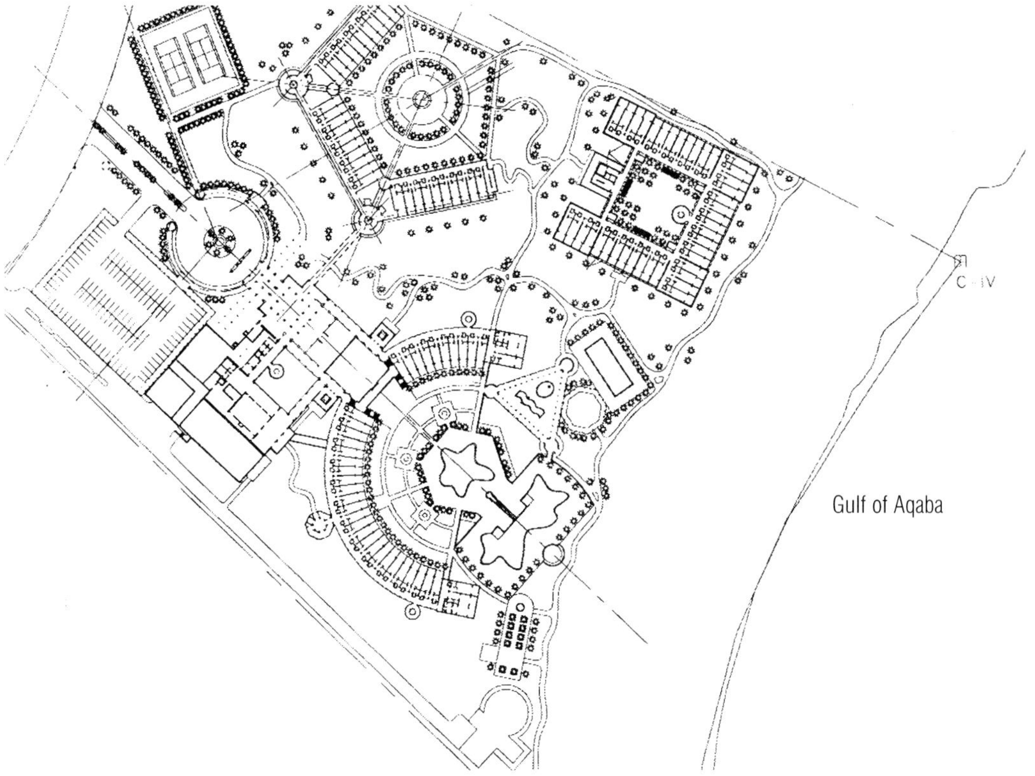

The multicourt resort design **Inter-Continental Taba Heights Resort, Sinai Coast, Egypt.** This site plan of the second of three resorts by Michael Graves within the Red Sea region exemplifies the architect's success in visually 'downscaling' large resorts through a variety of innovative methods referenced in the text.

steeply sloping land were turned to advantage by entering the three-story building at its top level, terracing down to the mid- or restaurant level, and then to the lower, or health club level, characteristic of how hillside villages follow their natural contours.

Graves faces the constraints of size, steep terrain, and need to provide diverse and interesting views with wisely direct as well as playful geometric solutions, expertly contrasting the alternative square, pentagonal, and crescent-shaped forms the way pyramids once were sited for more solemn responses. However, by the same token, the large resort is perceived as being smaller and much more enjoyable. And, while often not recognized by feasibility studies, such creative design improves the bottom line of the project's investment for its owners more than any other single item.

Four Seasons Resort, Sharm el Sheikh, Egypt

With dramatic sea views and appropriately luxurious villas at the region's most prestigious location, the Four Seasons Resort rises to its fullest promise. Entering under a shaded canopy of palms at the

The resort with the spectacular Red Sea views **Four Seasons Resort, Sharm el Sheikh, Egypt.** Responding to this most dramatic location, Hill Glazier Architects selected exactly the right priorities in maximizing views from the site's topmost elevation to the sea's sand-beach edge, while including in the design of the suites, the traditional residential domes and courts popular in Egyptian vacation homes.

apogee of an incline recalls the exciting hillside towns of the Middle East and Mediterranean regions. In a unique lobby, under a dome pierced with colored glass openings, arriving guests are introduced to the Red Sea's most dramatic views. Known for their environmental resorts, architects Hill Glazier keep the buildings to within one story above the site's highest point in cascading the guestrooms and public amenities down to the water's edge and its idyllic beaches. A funicular is planned to enhance the excitement (see p. 248).

While two specialty restaurants, a conference center, ballroom, and health spa provide views from the high point of the site, the casual themed restaurants and lounges relate to the beach. The 270 guestrooms and residences, including the Royal Presidential Villa, a few two-bedroom villas, 68 two-bedroom chalets, and 35 four-bedroom private villas, are shared by the Four Seasons hotel and its vacation ownership club program. Styled like North African and Egyptian homes, the luxury accommodations boast stone floors and color-washed plaster walls, divans built into bedroom niches featuring colored glass windows and casual, but sophisticated, fabrics and furnishings throughout.

With its Moorish domes and arches as well as roof gardens reminiscent of Cairo's famed Semiramis hotel, the resort is laced with traditional courtyards, cooling fountains, and tall palms. The guestrooms and suites, all with sea views, terraces, and windowed bathrooms, combine the best of the old with new technology.

Steigenberger Resort el Fanadir, Hurghada, Egypt

The resort radiates out from its playfully themed Adventure Island park, carved in the shoreline. The Island offers numerous recreational activities including separate pools for different age groups, sports, themed restaurants, and lounges. From their balconies overlooking the island and the sea, guests also can enjoy strolling performers during the day and concerts in the evenings. The guestrooms form a five-story single-loaded serpentine structure affording privacy on the entrance side as well as connections to the convention center, lobby, and parking. Other amenities include four restaurants, four lounges and space for 200 cars (see site plan in Chapter 14).

The channel forming the island moves the beach frontage closer to the guestrooms. Other cost-effective design strategies include: (1) open balcony corridors serving the guestroom tower compensate for the single-loaded design; (2) a villa enclave is

Table 4.1 Facilities program: Steigenberger Resort el Fanadir, Hurghada, Egypt

Guestroom programs	*No. of units*	*Net area/unit*		*Net area*	
Guestrooms and suites					
Standard guestrooms	245	409	(38)	100,176	(9,310)
Junior suites	8	592	(55)	3,551	(330)
Deluxe rooms	96	452	(42)	43,600	(4,032)
Suites (two bays)	15	807	(75)	12,105	(1,125)
Executive suites (three bays)	2	1,227	(114)	2,453	(228)
Presidential suite (seven bays)	1	2,044	(190)	2,044	(190)
Family apartments					
Two-room apartments	10	689	(64)	6,886	(640)
Three-room apartments	16	1,033	(96)	1,627	(154)
Four-room apartments	3	1,377	(128)	4,132	(384)
Total	396			195,150	(18,130)

Summary space program	*Net area*		*Percent*	*Gross factor*	*Gross area*	
Guestrooms	195,150	(18,130)	59.8%	1.20	234,095	(21,756)
Public areas	7,941	(738)	2.4%	1.30	10,308	(958)
Restaurants/lounges	20,315	(1,888)	8.2%	1.25	25,383	(2,359)
Convention center	24,425	(2,271)	7.5%	1.20	29,321	(2,725)
Sports/entertainment	25,351	(2,356)	7.8%	1.30	32,947	(3,062)
Service areas	33,840	(3,145)	10.4%	1.10	37,229	(3,460)
Administration	2,991	(278)	0.9%	1.20	3,594	(334)
Technical areas	16,140	(1,500)	4.9%	1.10	17,754	(1,650)
Total	326,153	(30,306)	100%	1.20	390,631	(36,304)

Areas are in ft^2 (m^2).

sited to utilize available views; (3) a separate waterpark is placed convenient to the guestrooms; and (4) a themed bazaar at the vortex of the complex further unifies the design.

California and Florida Resorts

From California's seminal Hotel del Coronado of 1873 to Florida's influential resort architect, Morris Lapidus, designer of the first resorts of the post-World War II era including the multicurved Fontainebleau Hotel in Miami Beach, and from California's Disneyland to Florida's Walt Disney World—no regions have influenced resort design more than the citrus states of California and Florida.

Hyatt Regency Coconut Point Resort, Naples, Florida

After purchasing a highly valued 17 acre (6.9 ha) site with adjoining golf course in this burgeoning resort community, the architect conducted research and value design techniques to blend a 20-story tower with its surrounding environment.

The research into local design traditions and selection of the popular architectural theme known as the 'Cracker style' led to combining wood walls with metal roofs as the most appropriate motif for the arrival level. Also, research found a high local regard for Bermuda, suggesting stepped structures as the ideal rooftop treatment. Design of the buildings and site included:

- vertical scaled-down techniques, including double-story floors to visually reduce the building's height
- enriched residential detailing, including balconies with decorative metal balusters
- coconut plantation landscaping determined to be most appropriate for the site and basis of the project's name
- an onsite environmental park
- proposed golf-cart transit system to nearby lagoon and ocean island.

A Cracker-style resort design **Hyatt Regency Coconut Point Resort, Naples, Florida.** The architects' effort in researching community preferences for architectural styles, major amenities, and detailing proved key to obtaining zoning approval for this highrise design.

The Ritz-Carlton Half Moon Bay, California

Overlooking the crashing surf on the preserved rugged northern California coast, the resort's authentic design exudes the grandeur of a nineteenth-century seaside lodge. Surrounded by the famed Ocean Colony Golf Course, it provides 256 guestrooms each with a dramatic view of the ocean, fairways, or neighboring mountain ranges. With French doors and terraces the guestrooms have a feeling of grandeur, inside and out, while separate showers and contemporary appointments ensure luxury and comfort. The intricate roofscape, with its bewildering barrage of dormers, gables, turrets, and chimneys silhouetted in the twilight provides adequate reason for re-creating the past.

Long Point Resort Hotel, Palos Verdes, California

As a peninsula jutting into the Pacific, Long Point provides perfect proximity to the surf as well as dramatic views of the southern California coastline, Catalina Island, and the Palos Verdes mountains. To preserve the area's historic Spanish American heritage, the resort is designed in the traditional hacienda style including variations of hand-formed and randomly

An ideal site-blended resort design **Long Point Resort Hotel, Palos Verdes, California.** On this perfect Pacific-front site, where ocean waves comb the beaches on three sides, the resort blends into the natural terrain by terracing its guestrooms down to the beach, pools, recreation, and sports areas from the highpoint of the arrival court, main lobby, and public entry spaces.

A nineteenth-century themed resort design **The Ritz-Carlton Half Moon Bay, California.** The historic era in which the surrounding resort community was created proved to be the most powerful influence on the design of this luxurious new resort overlooking the Pacific. (Photo: John Sutton.)

stacked barrel tiles on the roofs, artful towers, and Mexican artifacts displayed throughout the lavishly landscaped gardens and courtyards. Its spa complex, including outdoor massage courts, provides a model of effective and innovative planning.

The resort's welcoming court features a traditional cooling fountain shaded by a canopy of palms. Following the site's existing terrain, the guestrooms terrace down from a highpoint at the lobby, shops, and amenities area, with unobstructed views of the resort's coastal beaches, pool, spa complex, and championship golf course.

Golf Resorts

Introducing golf courses to new resorts can significantly improve their overall reputation and bottom line, beyond golf's own direct contribution. For example, while golf is preferred over other resort activities by one out of six vacation travelers, its value is far greater both in relation to the aura it brings to the resort and the increased occupancies through cross-marketing the hotel with the popular sport. The benefit of the 'golf touch' to the resort is analogous to what the 'boutique touch' is to the urban makeover.

Although golf may be virtually nonexistent in various global markets, it is omnipotent in many of the most lucrative ones. Invented by the Romans, named by the Dutch, and born of Scottish working classes, its dedicated enthusiasts span every level of skill and background, increasing the game's golf grip to megatrend status. While as vigorously practiced and played as any sport, for many it's more of an experience than a sport, which reinforces its role as a key element in the planning, marketing, and design of upscale and luxury resorts. Golf components increasingly attract extended-stay and limited-service hotel brands. Small wonder, given the over 16,000 golf courses in the US alone, plus 300 new ones built each year.

Research shows that many of the best links now are at luxury resorts. While the venerable early Scottish courses once boasted dormitories ('dormies') for their employees, few golf clubs provide guestrooms for members or guests and fewer public courses provide overnight lodging, an exception being one of the world's most admired courses, Torrey Pines in La Jolla, California, and its superb hotel resort. Therefore, it may be time to explore such potential applications to new golf developments especially in uncharted regions.

Typical development costs range are $7 to $12 million on average for an 18-hole resort course, including clubhouse (pro shop, grill, bar/lounge, banquet rooms, lockers, and showers) and service buildings (maintenance, golf cart, and storage facilities).

The growing US golf resort experience **Doral Golf Resort and Spa, Miami, Florida.** With its Greg Norman-designed Great White as a challenge this resort is red hot.

Doral Golf Resort and Spa, Miami, Florida

A full-service golf resort on 650 acres (263 ha), the Doral Resort features four championship courses, with the latest, 'The Great White,' designed by Greg Norman, boasting a triple green spreading over 25,000 ft^2 (2,300 m^2). The eighth hole is an island green and holes 9 and 18 are difficult finishing greens. On the older Raymond Floyd-designed course, aptly called 'The Blue Monster,' the fourth hole is one of the most difficult on the PGA Tour.

The resort includes 694 luxury rooms and suites in multiple double-loaded buildings bordering the golf courses and 48 suites at the spa. The oversized rooms offer private balconies and terraces, spacious bathrooms, and typical resort amenities. The public building includes 75,000 ft^2 (6,970 m^2) of conference space with over 40 meeting rooms ranging from boardrooms for ten to a grand ballroom accommodating 1,000, five restaurants and lounges offering a range of experiences from casually elegant to informal, and five boutique resort shops.

The Greenbrier at West Village Golf Resort, Fukushima, Japan

On a wooded, rolling site, an hour-and-a-half north of Tokyo by *Shinkansen*, two championship golf courses, with a clubhouse and world-class hotel, offer a unique approach to the golf experience. The building is organized as a series of pavilions surrounding a set of gardens and water features, with the clubhouse overlooking the eighteenth hole to the south, and a 100-room luxury hotel providing maximum mountain views to the north (see p. C-21 of the color section).

The grouping of the clubhouse areas, including a bell tower and pavilions for different activities surrounding the central garden space, combines western-style classic planning with a traditional form of Japanese masonry architecture exemplified by the Horyuji Temple complex in Nara, and Osaka Castle. The building's interior spaces focus on the lobby reflecting pool, creating an element of tranquility at the elevator core and entry to the banquet pavilion. Emulating the Zen gardens in Ryoanji, the pool provides a welcome spaciousness amid the busy circulation between activities.

The building's clear axial plan eases new hotel guests into all activities: an east–west axis connects the porte cochere, lobby, reflecting pool, and formal gardens and a north–south axis joins the lobby and hotel on the north to the golfing and banqueting facilities on the south. Elevator access to recreation facilities on the ground and first floors is simplified by the pavilion plan.

Pointe South Mountain, Phoenix, Arizona

Featuring a mountainside course at one of Phoenix's major desert resorts, the Pointe Phantom Horse

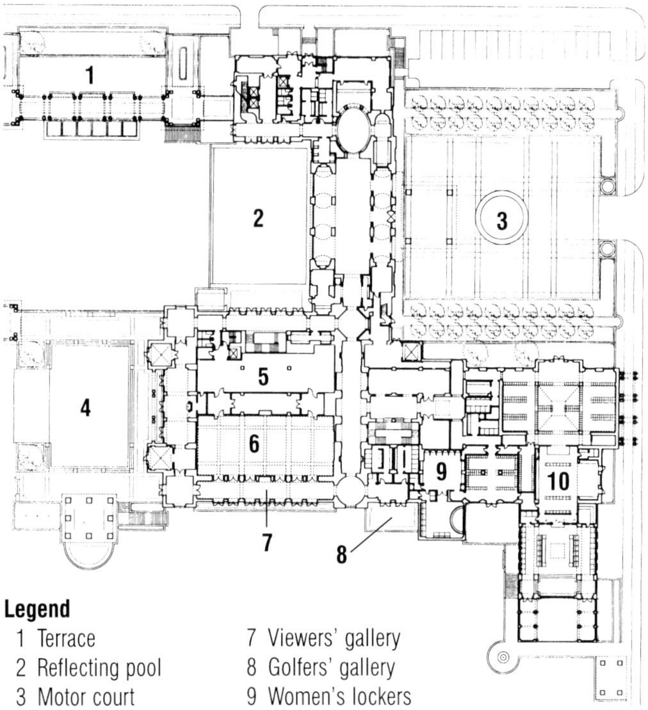

Legend
1 Terrace
2 Reflecting pool
3 Motor court
4 Dining lawn
5 Kitchen
6 Banquet hall
7 Viewers' gallery
8 Golfers' gallery
9 Women's lockers and spa
10 Men's lockers and spa

Lobby level

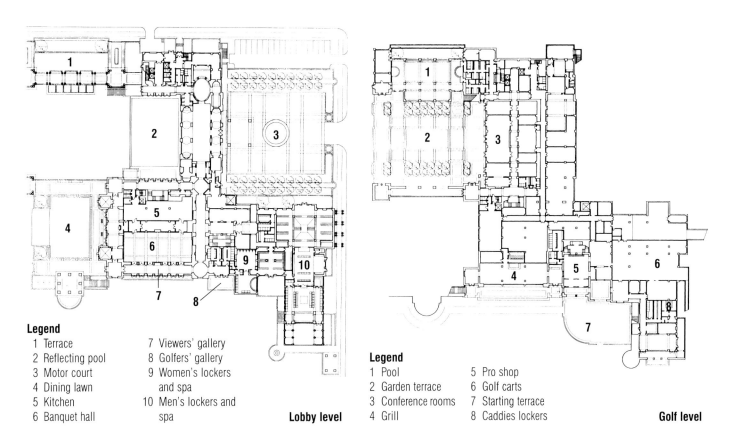

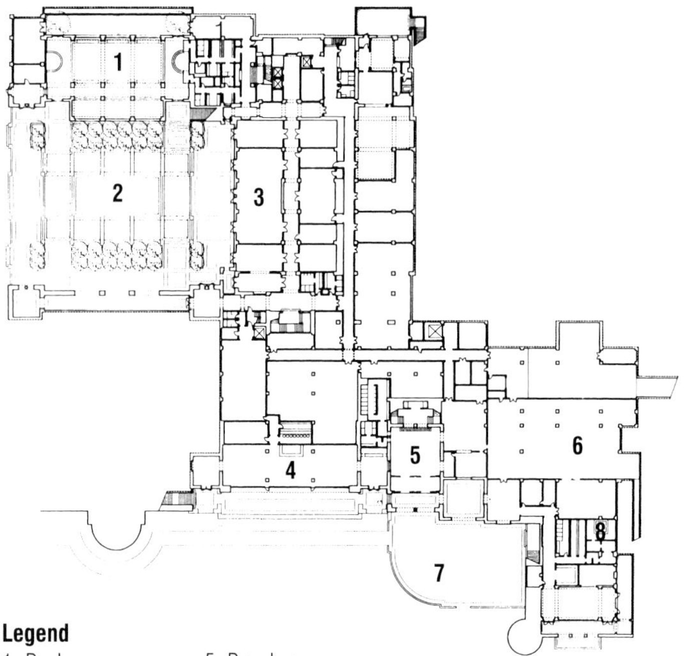

Legend
1 Pool
2 Garden terrace
3 Conference rooms
4 Grill
5 Pro shop
6 Golf carts
7 Starting terrace
8 Caddies lockers

Golf level

The growing global golf resort experience **The Greenbrier at West Village Golf Resort, Fukushima, Japan.** Japanese and American influences are combined in this outstanding popular resort and clubhouse designed by Robert A.M. Stern, Architect. The design of the golf club level provides spacious carpeted dressing areas and tiled wet facilities featuring personalized men's and women's spas. An extensive pro shop and spacious stone starting terrace as well as a fine grill room with a generous balcony overlooking the golf course heighten the experience (see view on p. C-21).

championship golf course is unique. Its name reflects the legendary stallion believed to roam the range that backdrops the 6,211-yard (5,660-m) course.

The architecture of the resort and its spacious hacienda-style golf clubhouse reflect the region's historic Spanish American tradition. The golf experience combines traditional links play with desert target golf that takes full view of the Sonoran desert's raw beauty. Nestled against the 16,000 acre (6,475 ha) South Mountain Preserve, few courses feature as dramatic mountainside elevated tees and greens. The scenic desert characteristics laced throughout its 90 acres (36.4 ha) are painstakingly designed to preserve the natural landscape for challenging and scenic play.

Golf course architect Forrest Richardson points out that the total golf experience, including legends, quality caddies, traditional course and hole names, graphics, and the course's relation to its resort is as absorbing as the game itself.

Spa Resorts

Researchers could have predicted the boom in cruise ships based on the increased purchasing power of the elderly, who have adopted cruises as their ideal getaways. But what about their children, the baby-boomers? They're doing as the Romans did—going to spas, which they strongly feel are essential to their well-being. Research shows that baby-boomers dominate 60 percent of the spa market; of these, 81 percent stay at the hotels and resorts that offer the top spas, causing many to expand. Another influence is the 20 percent increase in women using spas, as they move up in the workplace. But of most significance for the future, is the fastest growing group of spa-goers, the under 30 'X-generation,' who use spas on business trips. Research shows that, overall, half go to relieve their stresses and the other half go to indulge their fitness requirements and be pampered. But whatever they do, 70 percent report that they feel more relaxed when they come out.

While traditional spa treatments have varied in popularity through the ages, with the advent of antibiotic medicine in the twentieth century, sports, fitness, and hydrotherapy programs gradually replaced the use of mineral water in spas. For example, Palm Springs, California, originally a mineral spa, became a famous sports-oriented resort instead. With water as the medium, not the medicine, hydrotherapy uses jet-spray action, warm temperature, and buoyancy with plain tap water as an important ingredient of exercise, stress-relieving programs, and to treat joint and rheumatoid conditions.

But, regardless of changing techniques, the spas' overriding virtue of providing psychological environmental treatment is unquestioned. This has long been recognized, from the Baths of Caracalla to modern, carefree Palm Springs. In addition, many guests select spas because of their health education as well as behavioral and awareness programs, ranging from different forms of meditation and biofeedback (immune system response to gentle thoughts) to weight reduction diets, with tutoring by nutritional experts in the spa's restaurants and cafés. Behavioral health seminars usually include these topics:

- lifestyles
- art and soul
- parenting
- memory enhancement
- stress management
- smoking cessation
- food habit management
- alcohol and health
- illness and transition.

Development and Planning Considerations

Spas are recognized as part of the luxury market in which, notably, Four Seasons, Hyatt, and Ritz-Carlton are expanding their spa facilities on a grand scale in order to generate more bookings, not as in the past just to provide additional frills. Spa operators reacted by launching popular branch spas at other resorts. For example, many travelers have experienced the large 42,000 ft^2 (3,900 m^2) spa facility at The Peaks Resort & Golden Door Spa, operated by the famed California-based Golden Door Spa Resort, in Telluride, one of Colorado's major ski resorts. The spa offers 44 treatment rooms, ten types of massages, Zen touches such as ikebana flower arrangements, and a variety of spa cuisines and skin-care techniques. But where the spa resort is operated by a dedicated spa operator, offering a high degree of personal service, the resort generally is no larger than 100–200 rooms.

In addition to the health spa areas, the spa resort provides luxury accommodations including outdoor recreational features similar to beach, golf, and tennis resorts. But spa resorts serve outside memberships and visitors as well as hotel guests. Therefore, their reception facilities and parking areas may be up to twice the size of those at other resorts.

The spa resort requires a separate reception area for the health spa for local members, which should be easily accessible to guests from the hotel lobby. A special spa elevator may serve the guestroom floors and allow guests to move freely between their room and the spa without moving through the lobby. The luxurious reception area requires seating groups for guests waiting for friends, a clothing boutique, and an expanded pro shop concept. After signing in, storing valuables, and completing locker/key formalities, guests proceed to approximately mirror-image men's and women's spas. Other special amenities include a billiard and game room, library, and juice bar. Since health spas generally attract a more affluent clientele, their guestrooms normally are 20 percent larger, with about 20 percent of them suites. Where the climate allows, the rooms should include large guestroom balconies.

Design Considerations

The spa buildings are designed for multisybaritic experiences ranging from tension relieving massages to progressive-resistance exercising and beauty and fashion consultation. They are conducted in sumptuous tiled and skylit surroundings, according to individually prescribed 3–10-day programs supervised by medical, fitness, and behavioral experts. Dressing areas should be spacious, carpeted, generously mirrored, and luxurious, with back-up areas for storing and issuing robes, slippers, soaps, hair-dryers, and so on. The central wet areas containing hot and cold plunges and hydro-massage spa baths should be atrium-like in design, with full ceiling-retractable skylights, and surrounded by whirlpools, saunas, steam baths, loofah bath, and Scotch and Swiss showers. Nearby are the massage rooms and an outdoor massage terrace as well as outdoor whirlpools and a large exercise pool to accommodate active sports such as water polo.

Proper detailing of the finishes and equipment in the wet areas is essential, requiring expert consultation. Examples of these design details include:

- provision of steam rooms with internal shower and shaving facilities
- design of tiled ceilings at a slight slope to properly carry off condensate
- provision of terraces for outdoor massages, where weather permits, in addition to indoor massage rooms
- provision of a glass partition between the director's office and the wet area, to encourage establishing personal rapport with guests.

Spa resorts maintain five-star standards and are among the highest rated in service of any type of hotel, with the exception of the super-luxury hotel category.

Significant Spa Resorts

The most significant new spa resorts of this oldest resort type range from the modern glass sea landmark of Sir Rocco Forte's RF Hotels in the

The pristine waterfront spa design **The St. David's Hotel & Spa, Cardiff, Wales.** The welcoming registration desk celebrates its unique sculptural and functional position as focal point of the spa resort's bright and cheery arrival atrium, bathed in sun from its skylight roof. The upper level pool with its refreshing sun terrace overlooking the lively harbor provides an ideal setting for an invigorating massage hydrotherapy treatment while nestling in a relaxing pool recliner (see p. C-21 for a further view).

burgeoning harbor of Cardiff, Wales' (p. C-21 of the color section) to the sumptuous estate nestled in New England's rolling hills with the unlikely name of Canyon Ranch, and including its large branchspa at the 3,036-room Venetian hotel in Las Vegas.

The St. David's Hotel & Spa, Cardiff, Wales

Rising in pristine elegance over Cardiff Bay, this inviting glass tower personifies the modern spa era. Its transparent entrance and sunny atrium lobby are welcoming and cheery; the 136 guestrooms offer water views from cantilevered balconies; and the restaurant and lounge, nine meeting rooms, and business center provide additional amenities with water views. A special spa elevator allows guests to circulate directly between the guestroom and spa complex without crossing the hotel lobby.

The spa includes an indoor pool and outdoor sundeck overlooking the Bay. Staff expertly administer hydrotherapy massages using marine nutrients, swan-neck massage fountains, and submerged whirlpool napping recliners. The 14 treatment rooms on the spa's mezzanine level dispense a full menu of holistic, hands-on facials, massages, and body wraps using new skin-care lines of distilled organic and wild plants selected by guests based on their preferred aroma and designed to induce different reactions in the muscles. They dream of coming back. Such experimentation inspires spas to become self-laboratories, trying new treatments, and continually exchanging health ideas with other resorts.

The market 'value' of the spa experience **Canyon Ranch SpaClub, Las Vegas, Nevada.** At the heart of the Vegas strip, on some of the world's most valuable land, a 40 ft (12.2 m) high climbing exercise wall symbolizes the continuing strength of the fitness and health consciousness megatrend.

Canyon Ranch in the Berkshires, Lenox, Massachusetts

Suburban spa resorts traditionally blend into lavishly landscaped preserves with scenic views to balance the demanding fitness programs with the most attractive and relaxing settings. The Canyon Ranch, based in Tucson, Arizona, acquired a 120 acre (48.6 ha) wooded site in the Berkshires, with a palatial mansion set on beautifully manicured grounds. It comprises a central 100,000 ft^2 (9,290 m^2) spa pavilion and 127-room three-story inn, facing a unique architectural replica of Le Petit Trianon, Louis XVI's gift to Madame de Pompadour. This houses the guest dining rooms, lounges, conference rooms, library, computer center, and a two-story solarium. The buildings are connected with glass-enclosed corridors.

Sports amenities include indoor and outdoor tennis, racquetball, squash, indoor and outdoor pools, a suspended indoor running track, hiking, bicycling, canoeing, kayaking, sculling, cross-country, and nearby downhill skiing. This extensive, but intimate, campus caters to Canyon Ranch's guests mainly from the Boston and New York regions.

Canyon Ranch SpaClub, Las Vegas, Nevada

With a record area of 65,000 ft^2 (5,850 m^2), the spa is sized to serve the 3,036-room (planned for expansion to 6,000 rooms) Venetian Resort and Casino Hotel where guests may exercise between visiting the gaming tables (see Chapter 13). Themed as a Venetian garden, the spa adjoins the hotel's 5 acre (2 ha) pool deck and offers a menu of almost 100

Varied spa venues **Canyon Ranch in the Berkshires, Lenox, Massachusetts.** Built as a replica of a famous French chateau, the Spa's New York and Boston area devotees are welcomed by the palatial campus comprising a modern spa pavilion and comfortable inn on the chateau's grounds, with the spa's main dining, lounge, conference, solarium, and its other 'royal' amenities located in the sumptuous chateau.

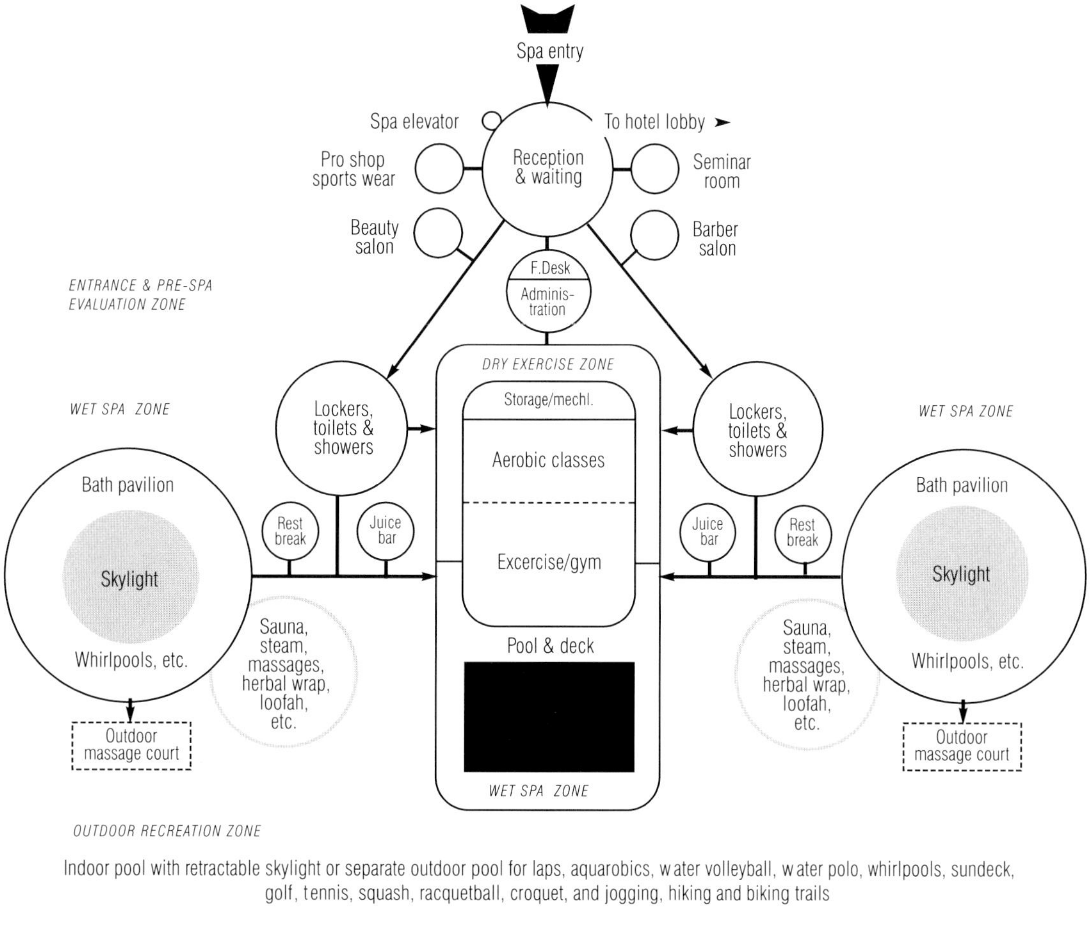

Effective spa planning standards **The spa circulation flow diagram.** This diagram outlines the modern spa's basic elements and functional relationships. While final plans vary based on the ultimate grandeur envisaged for the spa and its site, the adjacencies of the elements are vital to the spa's effective operation.

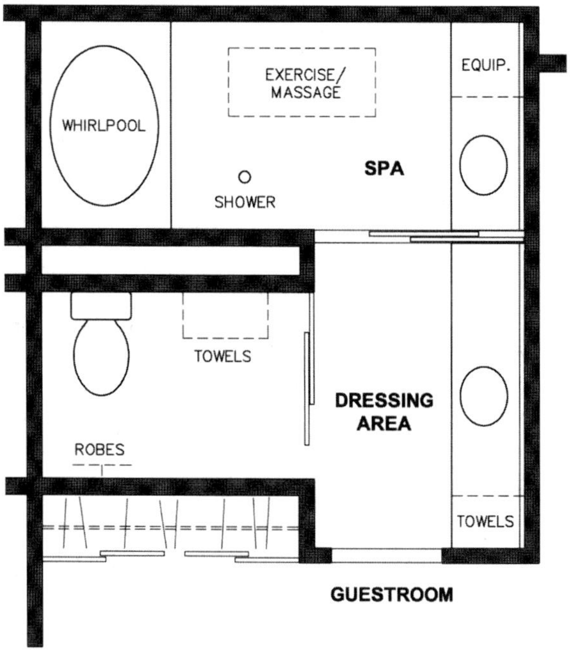

The guestroom spa **The In-Room Spa-tel Concept Plan.** Exciting concepts advancing in the spa resort field include an in-town resort with sophisticated spas in its guestrooms. Luxurious whirlpools and high-tech massaging showers are provided in a special spa room, offering a varied menu of personalized exercise programs and hydrotherapy massage treatments. While greatly enhancing the function, value, and attraction of the guestroom, the space required is equivalent to that of the bathroom in many luxury hotels. Combining elements now used on a piecemeal basis in conventional hotels, this integrated concept is designed to upgrade the guestroom to meet expanding consumer preferences thereby raising the hotel's attraction and rate as a spa resort. However, it is vital in introducing this new prototype concept, that the design and detailing of the in-room spa-tel be of the highest quality and the concept include such features as automated self-cleaning systems in the wet areas and retain wheelchair accessibility and maneuverability.

different services, massages, and treatments. After decades of research at its Tucson, Arizona, spa resort, Canyon Ranch now develops spa resorts to serve their national and international clientele at regional locations.

Trends

The continued influence of education, greater accountability in testing the effectiveness of spa procedures in improving fitness, and the growing variety of treatments will increase the popularity of spas. The most successful health spa techniques also will become available in guestroom spas as well as home spas:

- In-room spas adjacent to guestroom dressing and bathroom areas will become popular features of future spa-tels (see accompanying plan), possibly with universal Americans with Disabilities Act accessibility as well as automated self-cleaning systems.
- Natural health treatments such as hydramassages offered to complement medicine in the prevention and treatment of disease will continue expanding.
- The focus on relaxation, confirmed by most spagoers as their prime objective in spa usage, will ensure that spas concentrate on that direction.

Vacation Villages

One of the boldest and most influential concepts in resort history, the vacation village introduced a super-casual atmosphere reflecting the socioeconomic changes of the mid-twentieth century when Club Med introduced the concept with the following entreaties: 'an antidote for civilization . . . ,' 'a respite from the frantic pace . . . ,' 'an avenue to other civilizations,' and 'hotels offer you a room, Club Med gives you an entire villiage!' This influenced all hotel design, even outside the resort category. It captured the true dictionary meaning of vacation, a break in routine, which at a vacation village occurred on several levels:

- location and culture (far away, exotic local themes)
- design (unique, fanciful, themed)
- spirit of guests and staff (encourages group activities)
- spirit of entertainment (music, dance, mime, improv, and comedy)
- cuisine (gourmet café).

Development Considerations

By the turn of the century, vacation villages themselves were beset with the need for a respite from the frantic pace, due to major shifts in market demographics. These required updating and improved strategies to respond to changes in consumer preferences. Villages needed to cater to:

- more mature and affluent guests, desiring improved quality and more segmented types of design
- families and children, by providing educational programs including trained instructors, study materials, and classroom space
- new markets, by conducting research on potential new concepts including ecotourism, entertainment, and high fashion and by considering a greater diversity of locations.

Planning Considerations

Vacation villages are planned to focus views on exotic elements and to screen out distractions. Long walking distances, normally a source of guest complaints in spread-out low-rise hotels, can become an architecturally exciting, enjoyable experience in the context of a village. Staff take arriving guests by golf cart on a leisurely orientation tour of the entire village before arriving at their room. Rather than focusing on the distance from the lobby to their guestroom, guests are impressed by the best features of the resort and have quickly and pleasantly learned where everything is even before the vacation begins.

Planners have encouraged walking and made it a feature of the village by planning the facilities similar to the anchor stores in a shopping mall or the attractions in a theme park. For example, the entrance lobby may be at one end, and a campanile designed to create interest at the opposite end, with pools, snack bars, sports and other activity centers widely spaced through the resort. A central plaza is the meeting place and focal point with dual areas, one shaded with trellises for daytime use and another more open to the sky for the evenings. By breaking the village into several courtyards on different levels and with distinctive themes, even an 800-room resort easily can maintain a smaller-scale, more intimate atmosphere.

Spa enhancement through image design **Sandals Royal Bahamian Resort & Spa, Nassau, Bahamas.** The imaginative design of the spa's whirlpool area proves inviting to guests.

Design Considerations

To further enhance the walking experience, the design needs to provide more than beautiful vistas and lush indigenous landscaping. Since smooth walkways bear urban connotations, designers give surfaces varying textures appealing to the tactile senses. For ambient sound, cooling fountains are mounted on walls at turns in walkways or set freestanding in courtyards. Outside illumination is provided by wall sconces and path lighting, rather than high-intensity floodlights, to avoid harsh shadows. Earthy colors are used with bright accents that reflect local decorative themes and artwork. In these idyllic surroundings, guests are made more aware of their senses, becoming more responsive to aesthetic themes and detailing.

Cancun's popular prototypical vacation village **Club Med Cancun, Mexico.** Surrounded by lagoons and swimming pools, this extremely successful resort features extensive water sports instruction and group activities.

Significant Vacation Villages

Club Med Cancun, Mexico

Club Med encompasses 120 novel resort villages in 36 countries, segmented into four categories

Vacation village theming **Sandals St. Lucia Golf Resort & Spa, West Indies.** With floating restaurants and architectural columns rising from its idyllic pools, the resort's unique and surreal theming creates a much-desired carefree atmosphere. Villages such as Sandals St. Lucia provide extensive children's activities increasingly themed for families, while other villages cater to couples.

Entertainment at vacation villages **Sandals Antigua Resort & Spa.** Resorts featuring tasteful and intimate live entertainment are increasingly preferred worldwide. For example, amphitheater entertainment is a popular feature with some large resorts including three different types—at the beach, near the entrance, and in the resort's central court.

according to whether a family has children and their ages (infant, 2 years, 4 years, adult). This popular Club Med is virtually surrounded by pools and lagoons, with the 406 guestrooms raised above the pool deck area. The resort features a main buffet restaurant, three bar/lounges, a nightclub, and sports lessons in kayaking, wind surfing, and sailing.

Sandals St. Lucia Golf Resort & Spa, West Indies

Sandals International offers luxury villages throughout the Caribbean region created and designed for groups, families, couples, and singles. Themed on surreal, fanciful, luxurious design, this mid-sized Sandals resort boasts five themed restaurants, including a swim-up restaurant set in the pool, a nightclub, three bar/lounges, meeting space for 150, and an exotic spa and fitness center. Recreational areas include three pools and whirlpools, extensive sports and watersports, and a golf course on a lushly landscaped 155 acre (63 ha) beach-front site. Its 273 guestrooms include 60 suites, 30 with exotic plunge pools. An adjoining 56-villa deluxe enclave includes a 5,000 ft^2 (1,525 m^2) pool, an additional restaurant, and business center for the complex.

Sandals Royal Bahamian Resort & Spa, Nassau, Bahamas

This larger vacation village with 406 guestrooms and suites boasts eight themed restaurants, five bar/lounges, a theater, extensive meeting space, seven pools and whirlpools comprising 20,000 ft^2 (1,860 m^2).

Sandals Antigua Resort & Spa

The smaller Sandals resort sized at 191 guestrooms and suites offers four themed restaurants, a nightclub, three bar/lounges, an exotic spa and fitness center, five pools and whirlpools, ten sports, 11 watersports, and meeting space for 100 on a lavishly landscaped 155 acre (63 ha) site.

CuisinArt Resort & Spa, Rendezvous Bay, Anguilla, BWI

This unique ocean-front resort is designed as a village in the dictionary sense, comprising 25 buildings with 93 guestrooms, suites, and villas and a working hydroponic farm as well as orchards, herb gardens, playgrounds, tennis, croquet and bocce courts, watersports, spa, and art gallery.

The botanical hydroponic resort **CuisinArt Resort & Spa, Rendezvous Bay, Anguilla, BWI.** Ninety-three rooms and suites are housed in white-washed beachfront villas on a botanical oasis with more than 37,000 plants of more than 150 species of trees, flowers, and shrubs. Employing state-of-the-art principles of ecoscience, pesticide-free fruits and vegetables are produced on the resort's hydroponic farm and served in its three gourmet restaurants (see ecotourist resorts).

Trends

Villages adapting to potential new markets and product improvements will continue expanding in the Caribbean, Pacific Rim, Indian Ocean, South China Sea, Australian Gold Coast, Arabian Gulf, Red Sea Rim, and Gulf of Aqaba. Multiresort destination complexes increasingly will include appropriate village designs as essential elements to maintain variety and reduce density as required in large scale integrated beach-front developments.

Vacation Ownership and Condominium Resorts

Introduced in Europe in the 1960s, with its name taken from the computer industry, 'timesharing' was a simple, economical method of easing family vacation costs by sharing apartments in blocks of 2–4 weeks. But as the concept spread, it fell prey to unbusiness-like promotions, applying aggressive sales tactics, which disaffected consumers for years. Eventually, when regulated, marketed, redesigned, and managed by experienced hotel companies and renamed 'vacation ownership' in the 1990s, this truly beneficial financial breakthrough, and former 'rascal of the industry,' morphed to its 'booming self.'

Expanding four times faster than the hotel industry, vacation ownership has spread worldwide. With resort shares extremely strong, developers now are expanding into urban locations and yacht ownership. While the innovative system was almost an early casualty due to its poor management and unscrupulous marketing, the development of timesharing confirmed that brilliant financial concepts emerge from simple needs. But with Four Seasons, Hyatt, Ritz-Carlton, and other major operators developing

The themed vacation ownership resort **Hilton Grand Vacations Club at Hilton Seaworld International Center, Orlando, Florida.** This pioneering vacation club design was one of the first to introduce the latest theming techniques for the high-growth vacation ownership market.

The vacation ownership golf resort **Marriott Vacation Club International at Marriott's Grande Vista Resort, Orlando, Florida.** This resort was one of the earliest vacation club designs to feature golf cross-marketing combined with upscale St. Augustine-style theming.

sumptuous villas at their most posh resorts, the original timeshare members wonder who let the millionaires into the club.

By 2000, there were upward of 6,000 projects worldwide with over five million owners and $6 billion in yearly sales. The market was growing at 15 percent annually—the fastest rate of any resort segment—indicating many advantages for the typical product. These sell for between $8,000 and $18,000 per week at mid-price to upscale resorts, while the typical luxury vacation ownership product is sold in one month units:

- *Product*: 1/12 share of residence at a 40–80 unit 5-star resort.
- *Length of time purchased*: 1/12 of year (28 days) pre-reserved access.
- *Hotel services*: 'Four Carltons' (concierge, housekeeping, room service, and valet package).
- *Price*: (1–3 bedroom units): $90,000–330,000+ annual dues.

The primary advantage of the vacation ownership system is that the units enjoy significantly higher occupancies than other resorts. Therefore, hotel chains can improve revenues by converting units that have lower than normal occupancies to vacation ownership. Consequently, hotels consider vacation ownership as being complementary to their business rather than competing with it.

Different network groups such as RCI (a network of 3,500 affiliated resorts in 90 countries with over 2 million member families) or Interval International (1,800 affiliated resorts in 70 countries, over 1 million members) encourage vacation owners to stay at destinations in other locations by using their exchange privileges. Just as the name 'timesharing' came from the computer world, the exchange concept works like an Internet of Resorts, turning vacation ownership's potential disadvantage of being tied to one location into a plus. Virtually all members have an exchange affiliate that encourages them to try new destinations. Surveys show that fully 70 percent of owners want to take their next vacation at a location where they've never been before.

Design preferences include a full kitchen, balcony or terrace, and a whirlpool bath in the expansive master suite. The latest customized resort features are becoming more prevalent in vacation ownership resorts than in hotels. Some unusual projects are offered with the design feel of a farmhouse, but most common is a Mediterranean-style design.

Development financing is easier for vacation ownership projects, which are considered safer investments than hotels, since the loan is paid back by the development company from the sales of the units, generally before the property fully opens. Hotel debt service, on the other hand, is paid back over many years from the property's cash flow. Also, while hotel rooms must be sold every night, vacation units are sold only once or twice. Revenues and expenses are more predictable for vacation units while hotel occupancy is subject to greater variation, incurring many of the same costs whether occupied or empty.

Research indicates that vacation ownership is an increasingly popular option for families. While a second home remains one of society's most popular status symbols, vacation ownership retains much of the same aura for fully 27 percent of American households who believe that their likelihood of purchasing a recreational property during the next 10 years is 50–50 or better.

Other development considerations:

- 75 percent of leisure and business travelers prefer staying at branded locations. This trend is even more decisive in purchasing vacation ownership units, as most consumers do not have the time to independently research their purchase and feel safer choosing a well known brand.
- Typical owners are baby-boomers: 30 percent are in their 30s and 40 percent are in their 40s, with annual incomes above $75,000; 88 percent are married. These families recognize the importance of spending as much time as possible with their children. Family size averages 3.4 people: 29 percent are families of 4; 27 percent with 2; 21 percent with 3; and 19 percent with 5 people or more. Such demographic data are essential for developers and architects to properly plan new resorts.
- The customer satisfaction rate in the vacation ownership field is 85 percent—significantly higher than for hotels.

Vacation ownership developments are ideal for combining with mixed-use commercial project since their owners typically visit more often, bring family members or friends with them, stay longer, and spend more per unit than do guests at other resorts.

Significant Vacation Ownership Resorts

The following examples are among the most significant advanced design concepts responding to market trends and megatrends for future vacation ownership and condominium resorts.

The vacation ownership oasis resort **Hyatt Regency Lake Las Vegas Resort, Nevada.** Pioneering the first entry of a major chain into the outlying desert perimeter of the Las Vegas phenomenon, the Hyatt includes a Monte Carlo-themed casino, spacious vacation ownership units, and the latest Jack Nicklaus-designed desert golf course.

The vacation ownership ski lodge resort **Hyatt High Sierra Lodge, North Lake Tahoe, California.** These vacation ownership unit designs incorporate luxurious modern comforts with the highest ski lodge traditions and High Sierra views. They include such features as whirlpool spas, rugged stone fireplaces, and exterior timber balconies.

Hilton Grand Vacations Club at Hilton Seaworld International Center, Orlando, Florida

With a most sensitive stroke of theming, architects HHCP designed the 360-residence Hilton Grand Vacations Club to contrast the calm visual atmosphere of Bermuda's impeccable rain roofs against Florida's lush vegetation. A clock tower serves as the focal point of the complex of 12 six-story buildings set on a 33 acre (13.4 ha) undulating site. The amenities include a clubhouse complex with activities room, game room, fitness center, massage room, and a convenience deli and four spa areas, surrounding a waterfall pool with rock grotto, caverns, and a pool bar. The two main pools are rimmed with traditional Bermuda-style pyramid 'butterys' for sun shading, while a moon-love arched gateway frames the walkway to the adjoining lake with its surrounding gardens and jogging trails.

The vacation residences include 26 luxurious grand villa three-bedroom suites of 2,000 ft^2 (186 m^2) and 334 two-bedroom units with lock-out suites, private whirlpools, and outdoor dining terraces. Each building has its own personality in terms of a unique coat of arms, and colors representing a different Bermuda parish.

Marriott Vacation Club International at Marriott's Grande Vista Resort, Orlando, Florida

Convenient to Central Florida's major attractions, Marriott's Grande Vista Resort features golf, a spa and pool complex, and boating and fishing on its 25 acre (10.1 ha) lake. Its upscale St. Augustine-style architectural theme creates an appropriate residential atmosphere for the one-, two-, and three-bedroom vacation units overlooking the lake and golf course. The residences range from 885 to 1,710 ft^2 (82 to 159 m^2) with such features as double-size spa tubs. Recreational amenities include swimming pools for children, a lap pool, and an oversized family pool with a separate area devoted to water volleyball.

The spa includes weight and fitness exercise areas plus sauna and steam rooms. The golf club includes high-tech indoor driving ranges monitored by video cameras directed by the golf pros. A 2.5 acre (1 ha) putting green is designed with sand traps and water hazards to improve technique. The 160 acre (65 ha) site contains a rare plant preserve and related nature walking tours.

Hyatt Vacation Club at Hyatt Regency Lake Las Vegas Resort, Nevada

Overlooking an oasis-like lake, back-dropped with Nevada's desert mountains, the nine-story Hyatt Regency is one of the first major hotels to venture into the gaming capital's suburban perimeter. The 21 acre (8.5 ha) site offers guests inviting views of the Jack Nicklaus signature golf course. A lushly palmed entrance drive drops guests off at a formal court with a stunning double-story indoor/outdoor lobby and view of the watersports lake that is the focus of the resort site. Extending through the lobby's lower level are themed restaurants, a series of loggias, terraces, and the Monte Carlo Casino, leading to the resort's conference and function rooms, spa, and pool complex.

The Mediterranean façades are crafted in hand-finished terracotta with clay tile roofs and iron filigree to catch cooling breezes. The upper floors contain 496 guestrooms and 200 lavish two-bedroom vacation ownership residences with lake views and convenient access to water sports, golf, and gaming—now blossoming in the most remote suburbs far from the famed Strip.

Hyatt Vacation Club at Hyatt's High Sierra Lodge, North Lake Tahoe, California

The Hyatt resort's distinctive ski lodge architecture, including traditional rugged wood exteriors and massive stone fireplaces, overlooks Lake Tahoe's crystal clear waters with the majestic High Sierras in the background. Each of the six three-story buildings, sited to maximize the views, has ten spacious two-bedroom, two-bathroom vacation units with fireplaces, whirlpool baths, and sun balconies. The eco-tourist-like retreat excels in privacy and intimacy. The units are served by a central activities building, pool, whirlpool, terrace, and pond.

Four Seasons Resort Club Scottsdale at Troon North, Arizona

Pinnacle Peak, a towering rock formed eons ago when the Sonoran Desert was a rainforest, marks a new high in resort development. Adjoining it are two of the most scenic Tom Weiskopf and Jay Morrish-designed golf courses, as well as one of the most authentically detailed adobe hacienda resorts. Based on extensive research as well as design of other major southwestern-style resorts, luxurious vacation ownership residences are blended with the desert landscape by architects Hill Glazier.

The vacation ownership desert mountain resort **Four Seasons Resort Club, Scottsdale at Troon North, Arizona.** In the shadow of Pinnacle Peak, adjoining Tom Weiskopf and Jay Morrish scenic Sonoran golf courses, lavish vacation ownership units are offered in this choice hacienda-style resort.

The resort integrates hacienda restaurants, lounges, conference center, shops, a pool and spa complex and other sports amenities, with 210 casita units and 126 vacation ownership residences. Sited for dramatic views of the Valley of the Sun from its vantage point high above the lights of Phoenix, the luxuriously furnished two-bedroom units offer 1,670 ft^2 (155 m^2) with full kitchen, living room, two fireplaces, two-and-one-half baths, and two private balconies, along with all of the resort services.

The Ritz-Carlton Club and The Ritz-Carlton at Bachelor Gulch, Vail/Beaver Creek, Colorado

As centerpiece of the Vail/Beaver Creek resort area, this mountain-lodge design enhances the surrounding area by stretching the public spaces around the entry courtyard, thus concealing much of the traffic from the ski slopes. The court also provides sunlight deep into the ground floor public spaces and conceals 100,000 ft^2 (9,290 m^2) of service and parking on three floors below grade.

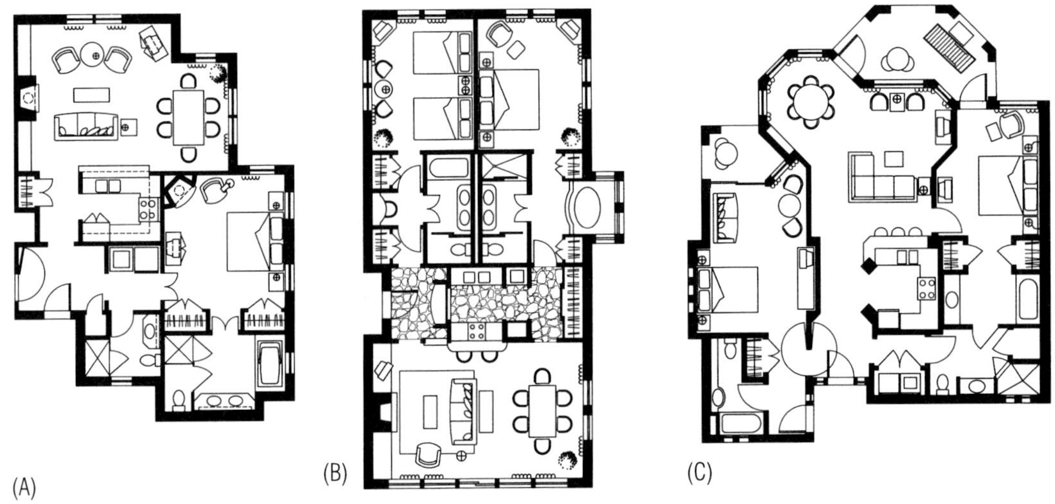

Vacation ownership unit design **Vacation Ownership Unit Plans.** (A) At the Four Seasons Vacation Club at The Four Seasons Resort, Troon North, Scottsdale, Arizona, spacious areas and luxurious furnishings accommodate family living and dining. Features include traditional corner fireplaces in king-size master bedrooms, gourmet kitchen appliances, roomy bathrooms with whirlpool spas, and dressing rooms with additional vanities and expert lighting. (B) At the Hyatt Vacation Club at Hyatt's High Sierra Lodge, North Lake Tahoe, California, in addition to traditional sun and view balconies and large stone fireplaces, these units feature king-size bedrooms, whirlpool spas, bathrooms with double vanities, separate showers, and stone floors in foyer and kitchen areas. (C) At Marriott's Desert Springs Villas II in Palm Desert, California, the popular villa unit features a large living room with a L-shaped sofa seating group and large TV, open to a dining room seating six and kitchen with gourmet appliances and serving counter for three. The master bedroom has a king bed and large-screen TV, and oversized bathroom with whirlpool, separate shower, and two vanities. The flexible lockout section includes a second bedroom with sofa seating group and access to second patio.

Spectacular views of the ski slopes are provided through large spectator balconies and ground floor terraces at the lobby, lounge, library bar, and health club. Architects Hill Glazier placed the 240 luxury guestrooms and suites as well as 25 exclusive penthouse condominiums on the upper floors of a linear lodge structure, with steeply pitched roof and dormers. The rooms also have magnificent views of the ski slopes and the valley, while the 50 signature vacation ownership units enjoy a special on-slope setting with premier views and convenient access to resort amenities.

Condominium Resorts

Condominiums, not based on the vacation ownership system, include individual living units with resort amenities, which are operated for the condominium owners as resorts. As in vacation ownership, the individual borrowing power of the owners may accrue tax benefits on interest expenses, real estate taxes, and depreciation. The site planning requirements and amenities generally are similar to beach, golf, and tennis resorts but the developer places greater emphasis on the residential quality of the individual villas and townhouse units, or low-rise apartment clusters. For hotel servicing purposes, adequate housekeeping and other service functions should be provided for each group of 12–20 units.

With landscaped balconies, irregular façades angled toward the views, and stepped building forms, both the condominium resort and vacation ownership systems emphasize the individuality and privacy of the units to an even greater extent than do other resort designs.

Cayman Grand Harbour, Grand Cayman, BWI

In the British West Indies, separate condominium and vacation ownership resorts are included in an ideal island setting along with a shopping village, marinas, and an exciting waterpark—the centerpiece of the 9.2 acre (3.7 ha) complex. The 114 condominium villas, located on a network of meandering canals amidst lush landscaping, are oriented to views of the ocean waterways, where owners dock their leisure watercraft. The villas benefit from immediate access to the impressive clubhouse with its full range of luxury amenities. Building façades are sculpted in the famed Key West architectural style with attention to detail reminiscent of the Victorian era.

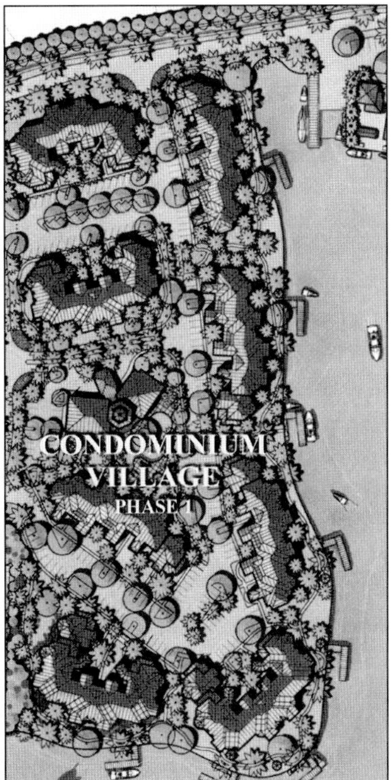

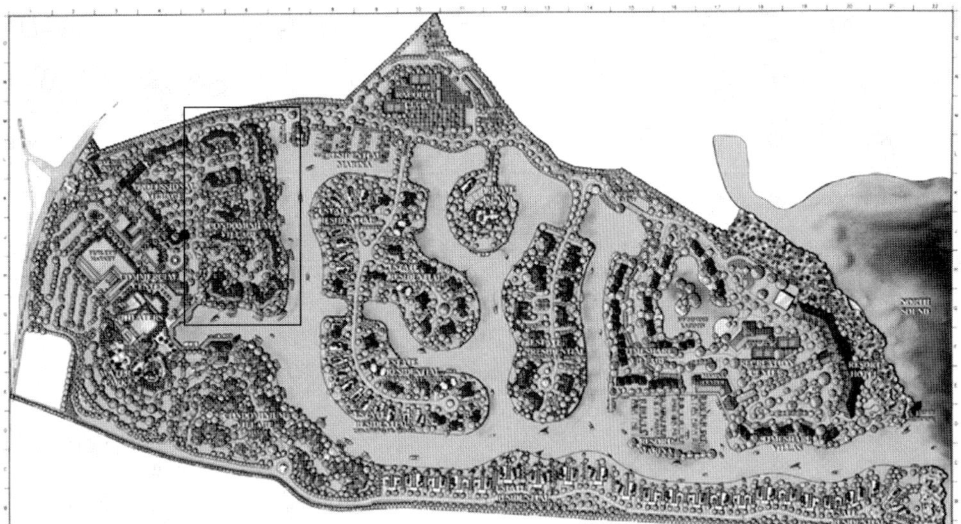

The island multiresort condominium **Cayman Grand Harbour, Grand Cayman, BWI.** This imaginative design of the harbor-front area and its public amenities are key to the development's idyllic atmosphere. The large-scale resort master plan maintains the use and favorable environment of the complex, thereby enhancing its long-term value.

Trends

Vacation ownership increasingly will pick up slack from resort home ownership and, eventually, prove to be the most efficient method and long-range vehicle for the management of all types of private residential property. This very well may extend to vacation, senior, and senior-assisted residences, as well as mixed-use, all-suite, and extended-stay hotels.

Marina Hotels

Since its debut in the early 1980s, the marina hotel has advanced greatly in technology and amenities. But interest in expanding knowledge of the oceans promises to be the key impetus to future development. 'Our marina teaches the guests and visitors valuable information about the oceans,' observes Steve Jewell, dockmaster of Atlantis, one of the world's premier marina hotels.

Case study examples envision resorts with marinas, marine habitats, and undersea marinetels, many of which may be booked through vacation ownership exchange privileges. Research indicates that yachts and second homes remain the leading status symbols for many people. The boom in luxury marinas is due to the increased number of yachters, just as the boom in vacation ownership, to a large extent, is aided by the symbolism of the second home.

Mid-market marina development is slowed by improved dry storage technology as well as by people moving up to larger boats, causing vacancies in slips 20–30 ft (6–9 m) long. But the larger boats are more efficient and provide greater satisfaction. As a solution, developers propose new waterfront hotels for places such as Marina del Rey in Los Angeles, and larger mixed-use projects combining marina, hotels, and additional recreational amenities for areas near the approaches to New York City's suspension bridges, which still await City approval.

Planning and Design Considerations

Developers try to closely integrate hotels with marinas wherever possible. This is important to ensure convenient access to the marina, provide efficient catering to boats, and better dramatize the marina and water themes in the hotel. Whether it is a boat rental facility and starting out point for sports sailors, stopover resort for inter-coastal boating excursions, or convenient vacation center for water sports enthusiasts, the marina hotel hosts local boaters from surrounding communities who sail or motor over to dine out or spend the weekend. Other guests dock boats permanently at the marina, driving to the resort to use the boatel for weekend sailing.

As a destination resort for yachters, the marina hotel is more luxurious than most beach-front developments as well as extended-stay hotels and some vacation ownership sites. This should be reflected by 25 percent more luxury suites and a higher standard of furnishings. In addition, marina hotel guestrooms should have balconies overlooking the water. The ultimate size of the dock is a function of the local boating market. For example, in a coastal resort area, with a tropical climate, the marina should contain at least two boat slips for every five guestrooms. Full access to golf and tennis is required to attract vacationers, satisfy all members of a group or family, and provide destination attractions for yachters. The marina facility must include retail shops for boating supplies, fishing and water sports gear, groceries, a clothing boutique, and self-service laundry, as well as fuel supply and repair shops. Large complexes may decide to include a major boat overhaul facility if none is available nearby.

The marina administration office provides navigational facilities and expert personnel to assist guests. Its docks are equipped with standard boat-servicing outlets for electricity, communications, water supply and waste, as well as general boat maintenance if not otherwise available in the vicinity. Some developers may test the feasibility of building a private yacht club adjacent to the hotel, to create another visual element and amenity for guests.

Significant Marina Resorts

The following projects are among the most significant advanced design concepts responding to market trends and megatrends in developing future marina resorts.

The Marina at Atlantis, Paradise Island, Bahamas

While the world's legendary yacht harbors form a highly selective club, none has more themed dockside restaurants, shops and boutiques, and superb marine habitats than does Atlantis. The Marina at Atlantis is a vital centerpiece of the resort and the first to be expanded at the luxury megahotel and entertainment complex.

The marina includes 63 oversized yacht slips, including 160 ft (49 m) finger piers with 37 ft (11 m) beam, accommodating yachts from 40 to 220 ft (12 to 67 m), in addition to lay-along-side berths with no beam restrictions. With a water depth of 11.5 ft (3.5 m) at low tide, the marina's key feature is its extremely spacious design with easy maneuverability for large vessels. Service is provided to guests, charter boats, and yachts as well as transient guests traveling by yacht or boat. Features include 24-hour security, tie-up and transfer assistance, sanitary sewer pump at each slip, trash pick-up, single and three-phase power, concierge services, two telephone lines, cable TV connection, and laundry and dry-cleaning service.

The unique natural aquarium, a favorite attraction for hotel guests and visiting boaters, has 11 special exhibit lagoons containing sharks, stingrays, turtles, and predators—thousands of sea animals from over 200 different species. Dramatic lighting shows offer the public views of vibrant tropical fish and coral in the evening.

The Porto Cervo Marina at Costa Smeralda, Sardinia, Italy

Among the most comfortable and well-equipped Mediterranean marina resorts in the world, the Porto Cervo Marina is part of a hotel complex flagged by The Luxury Collection of Starwood Hotels and Resorts. The four hotels offer 800 guestrooms with eight restaurants, a Robert Trent Jones golf course, tennis, fitness club, and conference center.

The project also includes 650 private slips ranging from 20 to 180 ft (6 to 55 m) in length and an additional 150 berths reserved for boats in transit, each with water, electricity, and plug-ins for phone and TV. The master plan proposes expansion for 200 additional boats. A dockside marina village provides entertaining shopping, restaurants, and bar/lounges as well as a supermarket with convenient shuttle service to Porto Cervo Village and the hotel.

A special service is provided at the marina by Marinasarda, to explore Costa Smeralda with its fleet of motor boats. These boats range in capacity from two to ten passengers and may be hired with or without a crew for any period of time.

Fisher Island Marina, Miami Beach, Florida

Fisher Island is steeped in yachting traditions, not only due to its 216 acre (87 ha) size and gateway position to Biscayne Bay harbor, but because it was founded in 1925 as the Vanderbilt Mediterranean-style winter estate, now artfully restored as a membership club and luxurious visitor's inn. In their family tradition, the Vanderbilts renamed the Island in honor of Florida's pioneering developer, Carl Fisher.

Two surge-proof deep water marinas with 131 slips accommodate vessels of virtually any size. All services including water, electric, telephone, cable TV, and ship's store are available. Yachts can reach the gulfstream within minutes of departing their slip at the Fisher Island Marina.

The Island, which is home to an international community of 500 family condominium residences,

The Caribbean marina resort **The Marina at Atlantis, Paradise Island, Bahamas.** Tops in dockside entertainment and educational amenities as well as its spacious mega-slip maneuverability, this complex 'floats' a variety of new directions in future marina development. Its extremely innovative marine habitat greatly attracts both marina buffs and theme park enthusiasts (see pp. C-29 and 194 for a further view).

The Mediterranean marina resort **The Porto Cervo Marina at Costa Smeralda, Sardinia, Italy.** The region's premier state-of-the-art marina resort features a special fleet of small motor boats with available guides for exploring the unique wonders of the ancient coastal inlets of the surrounding islands (see pp. C-25 and 106–108).

Florida's island marina resort **Fisher Island Marina, Miami Beach, Florida.** Founded by the legendary yachting Vanderbilt family, on an island convenient to the gulfstream, this highly equipped modern marina is surrounded by a posh international condominium community including its charmingly restored visitor's inn, part of the original estate.

including choice restored Vanderbilt-era villas, boasts one of America's top spas, a conference center, an aviary, tennis center with 18 courts of different types, beach and yacht club, seaside village, world famous yachting marina complex, and Pete Dye-designed island golf course and clubhouse. The residences range from 2,000 to 8,200 ft^2 (186 to 762 m^2) and are valued from $1 million to $5 million. The Island community has eight individually themed restaurants, clubs, and lounges.

Trends

While technical advances have reduced demand for boat slips under 30 ft (9 m), adversely affecting revenue at many marinas, long-range trends at marina hotels are toward larger boats due to their ease of maintenance and greater satisfaction. A form of 'shared-yacht' ownership paralleling vacation ownership may make yachting dramatically accessible to the vast number of middle class boaters, a dream that even capitalism's leading founder, Adam Smith, would not have imagined possible.

Ski Resorts

Following the development of efficient snow-making equipment and safe, user-friendly ski gear in the 1970s, interest in cross-country and downhill skiing has continued to climb each season. And with consistent demand, ski lodges matured into full-fledged, year-round hotels, complete with spas, gourmet food, entertainment, and conference centers. These, increasingly, were managed by upscale chains, happy to maintain the ski lodge's traditional ambiance. With the introduction of retail base camps needed at large-scale resorts, the original ski lodge has become a 'village resort for all seasons.' These newer ski resorts match the full range of comforts and services offered by other types of resorts including indoor-outdoor pools and whirlpool baths, tennis courts, trails for hiking, mountain biking, and scenic excursions. Also, they increasingly attract summer and shoulder-season tourists and conference attendees, as well as many nonskiing guests in the winter.

In addition, the major hotel companies are expanding in the vacation ownership arena, including at sites suited to the needs of skiers and their families, who are attracted to the timeshare concept. While the slopes and the larger resort environment generally are high quality, what attracts buyers most is the value of the residential unit along with the economic advantages and pride of ownership. Not surprisingly, the first of the new 'buttoned down' family vacation prototypes at ski areas were launched by Hyatt, Ritz-Carlton, and Four Seasons at the long-established Lake Tahoe, Vail, and Aspen ski resorts.

Development and Planning Considerations

Due to valid concerns regarding natural preservation in rapidly expanding ski areas, strict planning and environmental controls are the rule in new developments. At the same time, larger-scale ski resorts are needed to satisfy the increasing demands for recreation as well as to meet complex ecological requirements. But most agree that large-scale developments can be planned better to blend in with the natural landscape. Also, through phased development, authorities can more easily monitor the development against exceeding approved densities or ignoring environmental controls. For example, The Ritz-Carlton Highlands in Aspen requires no more than 20 acres (8 ha) to create a village setting including retail, dining, entertainment, and service facilities for guests and visitors.

As most guests travel by air to ski resorts, lodges should be located within a two-hour drive of a major airport and, better, close to a commuter airport. While the majority of guests arrive by van or tour bus, up to 40 percent drive or rent cars at the airport. Due to heavy snow conditions and to avoid the negative visual impact of unrestricted open parking, developers generally provide parking below the hotel, thereby preserving the views and contours of the natural terrain.

At ski resorts, as at an ecotourist retreat, vacation village, or country inn, one of the most inviting elements of the lodge's arrival experience is its natural unspoiled environment. Therefore, parked buses and building signage which intrude on the natural landscape should be avoided. As guests arrive, skis are checked outside the lodge and routed directly to a central ski storage area, often by a special outside ski elevator. The lodge generally is located on a sloped site, with its ski facilities, including storage, service, and ski shop areas on a lower level accessible to the ski run-out and remount area behind the lodge. A 200–300 ft (61–91 m) wide area at the base of the chairlift is needed to accommodate any waiting lines or assemble classes.

Ski slopes usually are located on the shaded side of the mountain for better retention of hardpack snow base, with the lodge oriented so that guestrooms have maximum sun exposure and views of the ski slopes. While balconies and roof terraces are popular at ski lodges, as they are at beach resorts, they are more costly to construct due to snow loads and the greater waterproofing required. Guests strongly prefer upper-floor rooms with panoramic views. Wherever possible, rooms with dormer windows and sloped ceilings should be designed into lodges, as market research indicates that such features are highly desired.

Design Considerations

The mountain location and ski focus help determine many details of the design solution. Developers and operators prefer fireplaces in the main public spaces and, as practical, in hotel suites and condominium and vacation ownership units. However, the number of fireplaces in some locations may be restricted by environmental regulations which might limit them, say, to a few specific suites. Air conditioning, on the other hand, may not be required if summer temperatures are comfortable, as is often the case at higher elevations. In the rooms and suites, showers might be substituted for bathtubs in some units. Durable-finish

The modern ski lodge with dramatic views **Amangani, Jackson Hole, Wyoming.** The two-story, high-windowed lounge celebrates breathtaking views of the Grand Teton range, framed by the lodge's rugged sandstone columns. Like its public spaces, the suites feature luxurious comforts, from fireplaces and balconies to slate-floored showers and soaking tubs with mountain views, and furnishings decorously harmonizing with the western mood (see p. C-23 for a further view).

materials must be used throughout the interiors to avoid the damaging effect of ski boots. Hard-surface stone flooring should be used at entrance areas due to heavy boot traffic and dampness. However, for acoustical reasons, dense carpet is required in other public areas, to cushion the boot steps.

Bar and lounge areas should be designed to enhance the unique camaraderie that occurs at ski lodges, among skiers of all ages. Multiple outlets may be necessary to meet the differing needs of diverse age groups. The main cocktail lounge or a lobby bar, offering a fireplace, comfortable furnishings, mountain views, and entertainment generally is for more affluent middle-aged guests. But another bar nearby may attract the more boisterous skiers. It has a dance floor, popular music, and doesn't absolutely require outside views. Finding ways to combine the diverse age groups, as they recall the day's ski runs, contributes to the lodge's pleasant atmosphere.

While lunch is at most a light snack, dinner at ski lodges is considered an important social occasion for more discussion of skiing experiences and re-energizing for the next day. Restaurants should have natural light, with outdoor decks for daytime use, and raised interior levels to enhance mountain views. An ideal restaurant mix includes an upscale dinner restaurant, a three-meal café, and an optional self-serve indoor/outdoor kiosk for light daytime snack service.

Significant Ski Resorts

Among the most significant advanced design concepts responding to vital trends in the growing ski lodge market are the following examples, as well as those included in the earlier section, Vacation Ownership and Condominium Resorts.

Amangani, Jackson Hole, Wyoming

In the Native American language of the Shoshone, *gani* means 'home,' whereas *aman* is Sanskrit for 'peaceful.' Any way you take it, this intimate 40-unit best-of-everything ski resort is designed for a variety of atmospheres in which to relax, play, concentrate on passions, or whatever the setting inspires. The resort could not be better suited to its location amidst the grandeur of the Teton Range in northwest Wyoming. Sited at an elevation of nearly 7,000 ft (2,135 m) on the crest of an undulating butte, all-weather swimming is ensured by the resort's 115 ft (35 m) long pool and nearby whirlpool, with magnificent views of meadows and snow-capped mountains.

Responding to its inspirational setting, the superb and novel architectural solution highlights rugged sandstone walls, combined with modern interior finishes. Most striking is the lounge, with its redwood ceiling and two-story-high windows framing dramatic views.

The luxurious suites feature balconies with mountain views, fireplaces, and furnishings reflecting the western mood—king-size platform beds, woven cowhide chairs, and pine stump occasional tables. The suites feature a private dressing room and spacious bathroom with a deep soaking tub with its own panoramic mountain view. In addition to the 29 standard suites, accommodations include eight upgraded suites and three deluxe suites.

The mood of the 65-seat grill is set by a large wood-burning fireplace and cinnamon and fruitwood table tops. A spacious library with natural daylight adjoins the lounge with a selection of books on western and Native American culture and regional flora and fauna, plus CDs, videos, and games. An adjacent room with a wood-burning fireplace is available for meetings and special-occasion dining. Thehealth spa features four treatment rooms, two exercise studios, steam rooms, and a space for individualized programs.

The Alpine resort area encompasses 2,500 acres (1,000 ha) of ski trails and snowboarding terrain. Extensive cross-country skiing begins a few minutes from the resort. Snowmobiling, dog-sledding, snowshoeing, sleigh-rides, horseback riding, mountain biking, fly fishing, river rafting, golf and tennis, as well as nature tours and scheduled ecotourist events are available year-round. The resort's ambiance is appropriately rooted in the Rocky Mountains of the American West and the cattle ranches nestled in the nearby valleys.

Sun Mountain Lodge, Winthrop, Washington

Like the ski industry itself, Sun Mountain Lodge reconstructed itself to meet significant changes in customer preferences. The resort's rugged timber log expression set the design character for the renovation of a nearby guestroom building. In the lodge, older public and service areas were updated and others, a library, meeting rooms, boardroom, restaurant, and retail shops were added, along with a new wing of 50 additional guestrooms.

Inspired by the magnificent mountain, lake, and river views as well as the culture of the Methow Valley artisans whose work graces the original and enhanced interior, the designers and craftspeople

The ski lodge renovation and addition **Sun Mountain Lodge, Winthrop, Washington.** In expanding this rugged stone and timber lodge, the traditional style of the original design was preserved and enhanced by local artisans crafting decorative elements ranging from fireplace screens and carved mantels, to split-log table tops and inventive lighting fixtures.

The Alpine ski lodge **The Ritz-Carlton Bachelor Gulch, Vail, Colorado.** The design of this premier ski resort incorporates a full range and variety of recreational amenities as well as different types of residential units. The views of the hotel are enhanced by recessing the arrival court to conceal its standing vehicles. Large spectator terraces at the lobby level and guestroom balconies have wide views of the ski slopes.

The mega-ski village second home resort community **WestRock Resort, Lake Cascade, Idaho.** Based on a master plan concept developed at the turn of the century, a 3,460-residence project is the first major US ski resort created in virtually three decades. Supported by the state, this all-season resort on the 7,672 ft (2,340 m) West Mountain, featuring fishing as well as skiing and snowboarding, is being developed by an international ski consortium. Environmental authorities and economic growth advocates are evaluating the proposal, containing 20 ski lifts and 850,000 ft^2 (79,000 m^2) of village commercial space.

collaborated on such decorative elements as lighting fixtures, fireplace screens, carved mantels, desk tops, custom fabrics, and artwork.

The Ritz-Carlton Aspen Highlands and The Ritz-Carlton Club Aspen Highlands, Colorado

Despite boasting some of the most expert ski terrain in North America and the greatest vertical drop in Colorado, the Aspen Highlands ski area fell behind the times. Inadequate lifts created long lines and the virtually undeveloped base area led to gradual decreases in the ski mountain's popularity. Eventually, Gerald Hines, a part-time Aspen resident and international developer, in partnership with the Aspen Ski Company, sparked the rebuilding of the ski trails and created a multiunit village at the base flanked by two residential neighborhoods including townhouses with direct ski access.

Its architecture draws on the American rustic design tradition exemplified by such admired structures as the Ahwahnee Inn in Yosemite Valley, Old Faithful Lodge in Yellowstone Park, Timberline Lodge at Mount Hood, and Paradise Lodge at Mount Rainier. Native stone, logs, and rough clapboards form solid walls and broad eaves which shed Aspen's powdery snow and protect guests and residents from the strong sunlight.

Trends

- Such different factors as fitness consciousness, and improved ski-learning techniques, and vacation ownership designs strongly appealing to the second-home phenomenon, will strongly stimulate growth of ski resorts.
- The increasing importance of summer resort activities will promote development of new resorts based on the site's year-round appeal.
- Ski resorts will add modest-sized conference and meeting centers to extend business into shoulder and off-season periods. Conferees enjoy multiple recreational opportunities which abound at ski resorts, even during the nonskiing months.
- Ski resorts will adopt elements of vacation ownership in their guestroom layouts to better accommodate longer stays and more frequent use in the off-season.
- Environmental concerns will be satisfied by planning and density controls as well as design techniques such as underground parking and clustering of ski lodge villages to better preserve major open spaces.

Ecotourist Resorts

Clearly the problem of man and nature is not one of providing a decorative background for the human play, or even ameliorating the grim city; it is the necessity of sustaining nature as source of life, milieu, teacher, sanctum, challenge and, most of all, of rediscovering nature's corollary of the unknown in the self, the source of meaning. (Ian McHarg, *Design with Nature*)

The world's heightened concern for the survival of the planet and a new awareness of the preciousness of threatened ecosystems and cultures has fueled the global emergence in the past decade of ecotourism as one of the strongest growth areas in the travel industry. Travelers range from passionate advocates of ecological responsibility to those wanting to experience unspoiled nature, its wildlife, and indigenous cultures up close. Most travelers are eager to escape their homogenized settings and experience the local environment or its people. Ecotourist resorts specialize in catering to these needs in varying degrees.

The ecotourist resort perched on water **Pangkor Laut Resort, Lumut, Malaysia.** Residing in the thatch-roofed over-water cabins strung along the winding wood pier, guests enjoy stimulating exposure to native culture and the wonders of nature while immersed in the comforts of a luxury resort (see p. C-16 for a further view).

Ecological Responsibility

Ecotourism, sustainable development, and green architecture in many ways are descendants of the environmental movement of the 1960s and 1970s when 'back to nature' was the call. Over 30 years ago, *The Whole Earth Catalog* provided a sourcebook of tools for living off the land for a generation who embraced the principles of ecological responsibility. It provided detailed technical information on alternative energy and fuel sources, recycling, organic agriculture, and other nonpolluting, ecofriendly technologies. Stanley Selengut, a civil engineer who has been called the godfather of ecotourism resort development, utilized many of the ecological principles of sustainable design in the creation of an experimental resort which he called Harmony, in the US Virgin Islands. Harmony was designed to run on solar and wind power and leave its hilly ocean-front site as undisturbed as possible. Floor tiles were made from slag and discarded glass, carpeting from last month's plastic bottles. Rooftop solar hot-water and photovoltaic collectors augmented by windmills provide power. Passive systems such as cross-ventilation, heat-resistant glazing, and a wind-scoop at the roof peak help to make the interiors comfortable. Gutters catch rainwater, which then is stored in cisterns built into the foundations, for later use. Interior wallpaper is made from recycled newsprint. Occupancy sensors detect lack of motion and turn off power in unoccupied rooms.

The ecotourist resort of solar, wind, and rainwater **Harmony Maho Bay Camps, US Virgin Islands.** Designed to run on solar and wind power and to leave its hilly oceanfront site as undisturbed as possible, the resort embraces fundamental issues of sustainable architecture and eco-friendly technologies while providing guests with a valuable and entertaining hospitality experience.

The eco-ethno-tourist resort **Amandari, Kedewatan, Bali, Indonesia.** Visitors to this Balinese resort are treated not only to luxurious service and the majestic natural setting but also to the richness of its people and the intricacies of their culture. Employees make daily offerings of food, flowers, and cloth to the Hindu shrines that are woven into the landscape. Native building materials, methods, and architecture reflect the indigenous spiritual and cultural cosmology (see p. C-16 for a further view).

The ecotourist resort at the rainforest's edge **Sheraton Timika Hotel, Irian Jaya, Indonesia.** The main lodge housing reception, lobby, restaurant, meeting rooms, and fitness center rests on an expressed base of local river stone while the guestroom bungalows are elevated on stilts above the rainforest floor, preserving the fragile ecosystem (see p. C-16 for a further view).

Selengut maintains that ecotourism has much to do with providing a valuable educational experience to the traveler. According to him, 'The qualities needed for successful ecotourism are more attuned to the entertainment industry than real estate development. Most resorts try to protect guests from experience, but we try our best to put them into the experience.'

Also referred to as 'soft-path tourism,' an important goal of ecotourism is to provide experience without disruption. There is a responsibility incumbent on both the developer and the tourist to prevent damage to fragile ecosystems and to avoid negative influence on indigenous cultures. For such conservation groups and trade organizations as the Ecotourist Society, the goal is to set the standards of ecotourism and to support responsible travel to natural areas where the environment and its wildlife is being conserved and the well-being of the local population is sustained. This usually means encouraging resorts that utilize recycled or locally produced building materials, employ solar or alternative energies, provide environmental education, design to blend in with their surroundings, donate part of their profits to local conservation efforts, recycle waste and wastewater, serve locally grown and produced food and beverages, and sell and display handicrafts of local artisans.

'Ethno-tourism' (or eco-ethno-tourism) is a term used to emphasize the cultural and spiritual dimensions of sustainable development and to promote the experience and conservation of regional culture and heritage. Consequently, archeologists and anthropologists have become important consultants of the eco-ethno-tourist resort's design and development team.

Amandari, Kedewatan, Bali, Indonesia

Amandari, a luxury resort in Central Bali, embodies many of the fundamental principles of ecotourism and ethno-tourism. It is sited on an escarpment perched above a river gorge and surrounded by terraced rice fields. According to owner Adrian Zecha, Amandari creates a platform for tourists to absorb the emotive, cultural context—the feeling of old Bali. Seeking to be at one with the village life, Amandari encourages the staff to practice their religion and folk art. Hindu shrines are woven into the resort's landscape where a Hindu priest may offer prayers to a replica of a Balinese tiger. Each day, employees make offerings of food, flowers, and cloth.

Bali, the sole Hindu island in Indonesia, mixes its Hinduism with powerful doses of animism and ancestor worship. Constructing a hotel in Bali is a very intricate science, often involving Balinese craftspeople who believe hotels are living things with a complex cosmological order. Consideration must be given to the arrangement of hotel uses so that the kitchen, the laundry, and the health club, for example, are facing in cosmologically correct directions. Trees are the homes of the spirits; therefore, when a tree trunk is used as a column the end where it was cut near the ground must always face downward.

The designers of Amandari were exacting in their use of local materials and building methods. Balinese masons rubbed stones together by hand in the traditional manner to produce perfect mortarless joints. Landscape architect Michael White designed the swimming pool to echo the form of the rice terraces on which the resort was built. The former rice terraces later were replanted with rice, fruit trees, and gardens in order to remedy erosion that was plaguing the gorge.

White transformed a deforested mountain area into a beautiful Balinese romantic courtyard and garden utilizing a design principle called site repair as delineated by Christopher Alexander in his pioneering book on design methodology, *A Pattern Language*. In proposing the concept of site repair, Alexander states: 'Buildings must always be built on those parts of the land which are in the worst condition, not the best. And, on no account place buildings in the places which are most beautiful. In fact, do the opposite. Consider the site and its buildings as a single living ecosystem. Leave those areas that are the most precious, beautiful, comfortable, and healthy as they are, and build new structures in those parts of the site which are least pleasant.'

Explora en Patagonia and Explora en Atacama, Chile

A special breed of ecotourist resorts are located in the most remote and extreme environments. These often are the most beautiful to visit for the more adventurous tourists. The Explora Patagonia is one such resort set in the wilds of the Andes amidst giant majestic horn-shaped peaks, glacier fed lakes and primordial forests. Weather in Patagonia can be quite intense with sustained winds sometimes reaching in excess of 70 mph. The hotel serves as a base camp for explorations into the spectacular surrounding wilderness.

To minimize damage to the terrain the hotel was designed as a series of small structures with no intermediate space between indoors and out. The pool house sits on the edge of Lake Pehoe and the main building has no porch, terrace, or yard. Buildings are connected by boardwalks raised above the ground to protect the native flora. Rather than blending into its surroundings, the hotel design purposely distinguishes between artificial and wilderness yet in a nonintrusive manner like a ship at sea.

The ecotourist wilderness resort **Hotel Explora en Patagonia, Lake Pehoe, Chile.** Poised on the water's edge and resembling a ship at sea, the architecture of this adventuresome resort is designed to endure sustained winds of over 70 mph that frequently whip across the surface of the lake (see p. C-17 for a further view).

Located in the Atacama Desert in northern Chile the Explora Atacama is a sister to the Patagonian resort. The desert is one of the driest places on earth, with relative humidity often as low as 2 percent and occasionally approaching 0 percent. As a result, the sky is remarkably clear and the sunlight very

The ecotourist desert resort **Hotel Explora en Atacama, San Pedro de Atacama, Chile.** Beneath the resort's expansive verandas and trellises guests take refuge from the intense sunlight caused by the desert's extreme low humidity while viewing llamas and alpacas that wander through the fields surrounding the complex (see p. C-17 for a further view).

strong. Wide verandas and expansive trellises are designed connecting parts of the complex to shield the guests from the intense sunlight. Even though the setting is extremely arid it has plenty of water from the runoff of the Andes Mountains and underground aquifers. The landscape design called for preserving the canals and aqueducts built by the ancient Inca and Tiahuaniaco tribes to irrigate their fields for thousands of years. To minimize disruption in wildlife, irrigated fields that surround the hotel are open to roaming packs of llamas and alpacas.

Main-line Ecotourism

The Grand Hyatt Bali, Pangkor Laut Resort, and other finely crafted resorts which practice good principles of ecosensitive construction and fulfill many of the credentials recommended by the Ecotourist Society are, nevertheless, primarily luxury resorts where the guest is pampered and there is little sense of roughing it with nature. Not all visitors to ecotourist resorts wish to be thrust into the teeming wilderness or to be immersed in the customs and rituals of a distant culture. Many want the stimulating and illuminating exposure to the wonders of nature without compromising the creature comforts of a luxury resort.

Built on the edge of an Indonesian rainforest, the Sheraton Timika Hotel celebrates environmental sensitivity. The main building is connected to a series of bungalows with bilevel walkways elevated on stilts so as not to disturb the flora and fauna of the rainforest floor. Visitors enjoy comfortable contact with the rainforest from covered porches while pampered with western amenities or, if they wish, avail themselves of a deeper experience on guided tours into the rough. Local tribal culture is evident throughout the resort with native artwork and handcarved artifacts integrated into the décor. The architects succeeded in designing a quiet building on the edge of a primitive forest, heavily influenced by the local tradition. They accomplished this by paying responsible attention to the surrounding ecosystems, incorporating principles of sustainable development and providing economic benefit and opportunities to the local citizenry.

Trends

The hotel industry will expand its long-term worldwide interest in advances in 'green' architecture and ecosciences such as hydroponics as exemplified by the CuisinArt Resort & Spa's hydroponic farm on the Caribbean island of Anguilla. The state-of-the-art hydroponic process produces pollutant- and-pesticide-free fruits, vegetables, and edible flowers used for preparing meals in the resort's restaurants.

There are still great realms of empty ocean, deserts reaching to the curvature of the earth, silent, ancient forests and rocky coasts, glaciers and volcanoes, but what will we do with them? In the quest for survival, success and fulfillment the ecological view offers an invaluable insight. It shows the way for the man who would be the enzyme of the biosphere—its steward, enhancing the creative fit of man–environment, realizing man's design with nature. (Ian McHarg, *Design with Nature*)

Multiresort Destination Complexes

The primary goal in developing new resorts is to ensure a sound future for the environment. This can be accomplished by designing large-scale master plans which preserve and enhance the regional ecology, maintain reasonable density standards, and mitigate vital concerns for traffic, utilities, clean air, pure water, and the natural landscape. Multiresort destinations can vary as much as any individual resort. The examples discussed below range from a sensitively blended multiresort in Sardinia to a towering beach-front center in Dubai, a gaming community in Nevada, and an entertainment community in Missouri. Such developments provide needed expansion of recreation amenities as well as benefits to local economies. They extend the existing social and physical infrastructure by contributing vital support to airport development, roads, and necessary services. However, sound guiding principles must be followed to avoid overcrowding, congestion, and cultural and environmental problems.

Costa Smeralda, Sardinia, Italy, The Luxury Collection, Starwood Hotels and Resorts

No major development has protected its environment so well and enriched its culture, while at the same time generating significant economic gains for the entire region, as has the Costa Smeralda multiresort in Sardinia. Begun by a group of owners, including His Highness The Aga Khan, who was dedicated to enhancing the island's idyllic natural advantages, it has become a brilliant model for future resort development.

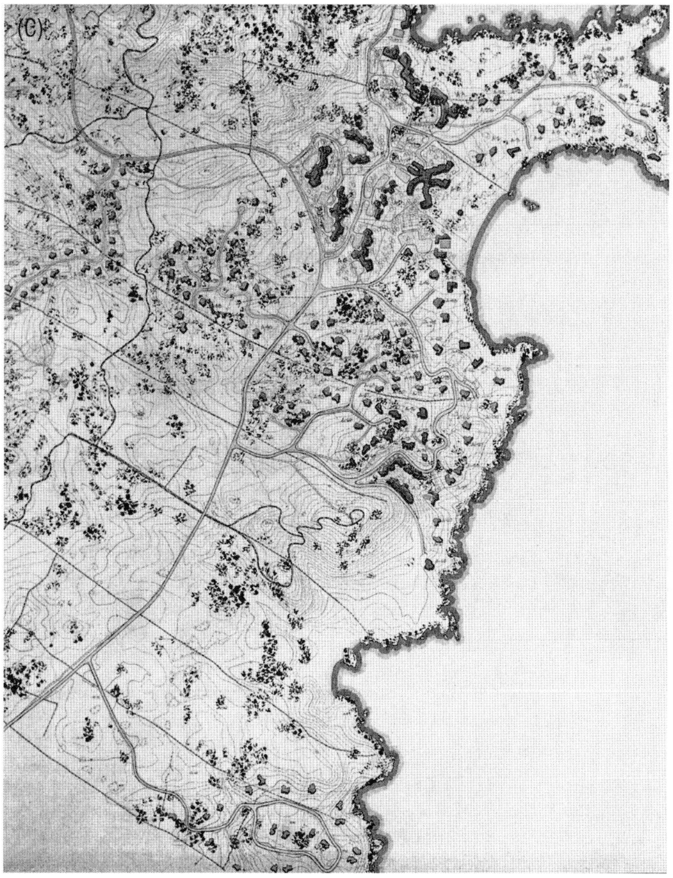

The island contextual multiresort **Costa Smeralda, Sardinia, Italy, The Luxury Collection, Starwood Hotels and Resorts.** (A) The modern fitness spa at the Cervo Conference Center, with views of Sardinia's sea and the shopping village of Porto Cervo, is one of the four major resorts of the Costa Smeralda complex. It features a tennis club and spa, with indoor and outdoor pools, as well as the resort's neighboring world-class marina. (B) The island's timeless indigenous detailing provides an elegant expression for its modern resort comforts as shown in this suite at the Cala Di Volpe Hotel, one of the four resorts. (C) Such sectional land use and master plan drawings and standards indicate areas being preserved and new installations proposed by the resorts as well as related limited-density community developments (see p. C-24 for a further view of Cala Di Volpe Hotel and p. 98 for Cervo Conference Center and Marina).

An international team of planners and local architects conceived four distinctive environments in the indigenous Sardinian design vernacular. The master land use plan created by Sasaki Associates proposed a long-term strategy of low-density luxury development to provide a homogeneous extension of the island's natural and built environment. This included maintaining sensitive relationships with the regional ecosystems by preserving the natural shoreline, from the smallest cove beaches to the most ancient sea walls, and integrating available historic objects and cultural sites into the development.

Planning Considerations

The owners and planners decided to subordinate the primary resort structures and amenities and give precedence to the natural land forms and other existing features. The varied relationships between the decentralized resorts and special amenities centers created an individual character for each resort and gave the architects the freedom to use different local architectural vocabularies.

Another highly sensible provision of the master plan is that virtually all buildings, whether single-story villas or low-rise hotels, are located inland, on Sardinia's undulating terrain, to enhance views to the sea. The planners conserved the stunning high ridge formations, too steep for development, which serve as handsome backdrops to the composition of buildings and landscape. Tables 4.2 and 4.3 list the main resort elements and their amenities, as well as new concepts for future development, including a Mediterranean golf center with five courses, all part of the original master plan.

A network of three villages, blending in with the resorts, further unifies the concept. Guests enjoy

Table 4.2 Master plan program: Costa Smeralda

Program element	*Completed*	*Proposed*	*Peripheral (by others)*
Land (ha)	600	2,400	1,000 (est.)
Hotels: five-star	3	8	–
Hotels: four-star	1	–	2
Condominiums	2,000	1,900	2,000 (est.)
Villas	600	2,000	2,000 (est.)
Vacation ownership	(in above)	(in above)	1,000 (est.)
Total condominiums	2,600	3,900	5,000 (est.)
Shops	250	100 (est.)	–
Supermarkets	4	8 (est.)	–
Restaurants	6 (outside resorts)	6 (est.)	–
Yacht club	1	–	–
Marina slips	800	250	–
Shipyard (class-A)	1	–	–
Tennis club and spa	1	–	–
Tennis courts	28	24	–
Golf club holes	18	72	–
Golf clubs	1	2	–
Golf academy	–	1	–
Population	12,000	20,000	6,000 (est.)

Table 4.3 Decentralized planning of resorts and amenities: Costa Smeralda

Hotel (star rating)	*Beds*	*Features and amenities*
Hotel Pitrizzia (5)	102	Views of the sea and stunning natural rock formations with guestrooms built into the landscape
Hotel Cervo (4)	216	Contains conference center, tennis center, central shopping village, and marina
Hotel Romazzino (5)	180	Adjoins golf course, tennis courts and spa center, panoramic sea views and watersports school
Hotel Cala Di Volpe (5)	235	Adjoins Robert Trent Jones-designed Pevero golf course, spa fitness center, and harbor village; contains an additional 12 special suites

Architects: Hotels Pitrizzia and Cervo, Luigi Vietti; Hotel Romazzino, Michele Busiri-Vici; Hotel Cala Di Volpe Jacques Couelle.

strolling in the villages, leaving the beaches less congested. Different than the French or Spanish Riviera, Acapulco or Cancun, Costa Smeralda offers a much sought after alternative to increasing overcrowding while also ensuring pristine waters, clean air, and an authentic historic experience. It continues to do more than fulfill its marketing target by strongly attracting getaways from major European cities. Additional vacation ownership units, condominiums, and resorts being built in the peripheral areas embrace the Costa Smeralda concept, although some exceed the recommended density limits of the original master plan. This impressive demand confirms the economic success of the development, not only as a luxury vacation destination, but also in terms of its increased land values.

Development Considerations

Flagged as The Luxury Collection by Starwood Hotels and Resorts, Costa Smeralda's continued success and that of peripheral developments that have adopted similar master plan concepts have renewed faith in the effectiveness of the master plan principles and confirmed these supporting corollaries:

- Private ownership can successfully manage long-term development by adopting a detailed prospectus as a guide to future planning decisions.
- Reliance on government can be minimized other than in building code matters and coordination with offsite transportation and utility infrastructures.

What differentiates Costa Smeralda from other large-scale developments is its having a single direction for the entire project. The alternative is to break large projects into numerous sites under different ownership, with no central strategy, design guidelines, or master land-use plan.

Design Considerations

The Costa Smeralda master plan confirms the sites of the resorts, limits their size, number, height (three stories), and the maximum volume of future developments. It also establishes a model system of architectural controls based on historic traditions and research, so that the project's design balance between architectural variety and contextual unity will continue in the new developments. The owners established strict design guidelines and a process of committee review including:

- *Architectural design*: drawings of architectural vocabularies and forms of the Sardinian design vernacular; list of indigenous construction materials and related methods; dimensions and profiles of wall openings, setbacks, and heights; samples of colors.
- *Landscape design*: descriptions of landscape techniques; list of indigenous plant materials.
- *Site planning design*: drawings of prototypical site planning solutions based on varied topographical situations, drainage conditions, wind directions, and view maximization.
- *Design review committee*: process to ensure that the guidelines are interpreted fairly and that the context for any exception is fully understood.

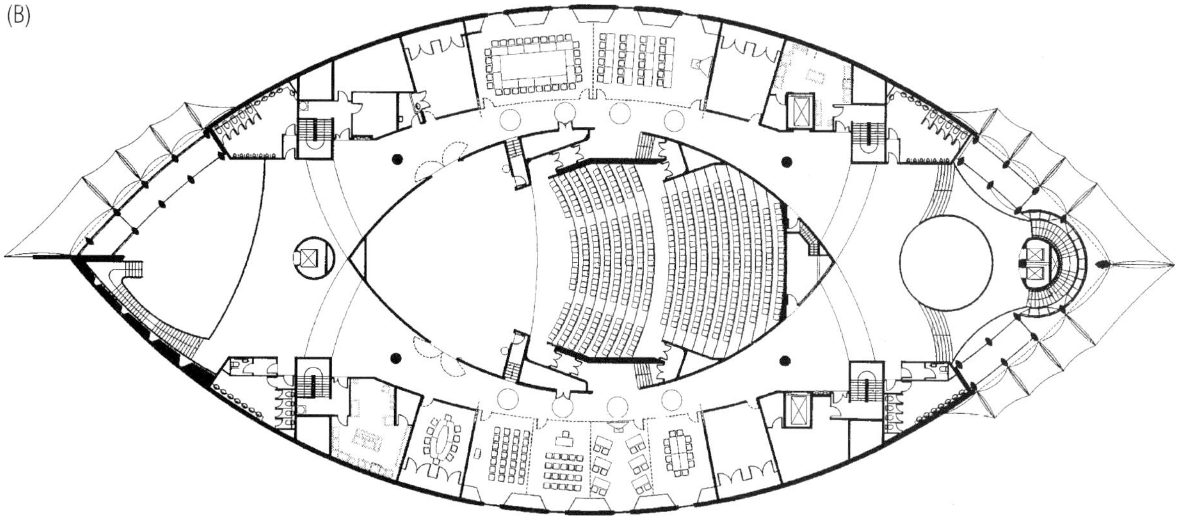

The multiresort 'nautical' conference center **Jumeirah Beach Resort Conference Center, Dubai, UAE.** (A) Completing this multiresort's tribute to an ancestral passion for the sea is a building in the form of a ship, adjoining the much larger sail and wave structures. (B) The ship form offers dramatic opportunities for special functions in the pointed 'bow' and 'stern', and space for larger assembly rooms 'amidships' (see p. C-25 for a further view).

Jumeirah Beach Resort and Burj Al Arab Hotel, Dubai, UAE

Among the seven members of the Emirates, Dubai is more inclined to grow its successful economy through varied types of land development rather than oil revenues. Among its sources of pride are a 35-story World Trade Center, innovative designer office and bank towers, major US-style retail malls, an exotic planned theme park, a bayside golf course and ultra-contemporary clubhouse, contemporary apartments and villas, and long stretches of beach. The most recent structures gaining world attention include an ultratel beach resort complex attracting European vacationers and a unique twin-tower business and tourist hotel and downtown office complex (see Chapter 12).

By combining local development funds, foreign management, and world-class design consultants, the bold aesthetic strategy created three individually

The multiresort booming gaming community **Laughlin, Nevada.** The strategic vision of Don Laughlin combines a natural Colorado River resort with family budget gaming, creating a multiresort with five million annual vacation visitors.

The multiresort booming entertainment community **Branson, Missouri.** No one person is responsible for Branson's boom as America's capital of country and western music which, combined with some of the world's best natural fishing, attracts upward of seven million annual family vacationers.

striking themed architectural statements. The world's tallest resort, the Burj Al Arab Hotel, located in the sea facing one of Dubai's primary beach-front sites near downtown, resembles a giant sail of clear glass rising from the turquoise sea (see p. C-25 in the color section).

In sharp contrast, the second highest, yet equally stunning, structure recalls a giant wave, as it is regarded throughout the Emirates, with its 20-story high crest glimmering in the sunlight as it seemingly glides across the sand beach. The third, an international conference and convention center, is designed as a traditional ship of state. The latter two seem rooted in the sand, while the taller structure seems to promise clear sailing ahead. Citizens and visitors are impressed by the imaginative architecture and high-tech engineering including environmental precautions to preserve the beach areas. The three buildings form a monument both to the nation's ancient seafaring heritage and to its future.

Laughlin, Nevada

Following Las Vegas' legendary rise, visionary developer Don Laughlin theorized that a niche-resort strategically positioned at the confluence of the two fastest growing resort states of Nevada and Arizona would attract everyone driving through the Mohave Desert, with no other stopover nearby. Searching from his private plane, he spotted a dilapidated resort at just the right point along the beautiful Colorado River, 90 miles from Las Vegas. He quickly acquired it and, as the only resident, gave his name to the area, as suggested by the post office, so as not to require sorting his mail.

Lured by the life-giving Colorado River, Laughlin sensed that the site was a textbook example of nature's ability to heal hundreds of thousands of years of environmental deterioration. To preserve the natural open space and to increase visibility, Laughlin built a tall 28-story tower, the 1,402-room Riverside Resort and Casino Hotel. A curiosity at first, the novel concept soon became a Mecca for low-stakes players on family vacations, preferring the advantages of a riverside oasis to the Vegas Strip. Laughlin, like such larger cities as Nashville, Anaheim, Orlando, and Branson, Missouri, keeps the family vacation alive and well, with a gaming twist.

But nothing remains pure, even with gaming resorts. With rising discretionary income, some visitors who were low-rollers became mid-rollers, joining high-roller families, to enjoy Laughlin-style hospitality. Ten top casino hotels followed suit, including the best known brand names such as Hilton, Harrah's, Golden Nugget, and Circus Circus. While Las Vegas shifted its image so that more visitors now come for other reasons than gaming, an upwardly mobile Laughlin still retains its handle as the capital of the low-roller family market, where it continues to differentiate itself from other gaming and entertainment centers through its unique and relaxing riverside ambiance. This includes a casino hotel that simulates a giant paddle-wheel steamboat and another that uses a steam-engine to shuttle guests around the hotel. Nearby, the most popular river-front casino is bordered by a Mediterranean-style sand beach.

The innovative multiresort town gives evidence of the advantages of combining skilled development with sound technical and environmental planning. Laughlin's hotels offer 11,000 resort and tourist rooms and operate at 83 percent occupancy. Now a significant multiresort community attracting five million visitors annually, it has continued to grow even in times of recession and plans for expansion in the next decade.

Branson, Missouri

The residents of Branson, a community of 5,000 in the rural Ozark Mountains of Missouri, are blessed with a passion for popular music and hundreds of miles of lake shoreline, spawning world-class fishing. Although Branson is not a large city, it functions as well as amy polished business entity capitalizing on its natural and business advantages.

In the 1970s, research identified Branson as lying within a 6-hour drive of a dozen of the country's largest cities and a third of the US population. Cars remain the primary means of leisure travel for families while tour busses fill this need for seniors. Surveys also confirmed a strong preference in the family vacation market for the natural setting and environmental amenities that Branson offers, as well as a growing interest in live musical entertainment.

Based on this knowledge, Branson community leaders convinced several singing stars, regular visitors to the Ozark resort town, to develop live theaters or 'show palaces' modeled on Nashville's famed Opryland. Now, with over 40 show palaces and 15 major resorts, Branson is among the country's most popular destinations. The lavish show palaces typically have a capacity of about 1,500 seats; the Grand Palace with 4,000 seats hosts the Radio City Rockettes, Miss USA Pageant, and other international events. As in Las Vegas, neon-signed theaters line the main highway, referred to as the Strip, but without gaming. Branson is a happy hybrid of the Las Vegas Strip and the Nashville entertainment concept, mixed with a strategic location and natural attractions, so vital to Laughlin, Nevada's success as well.

This unique combination of neon and nature draws seven million annual visitors, the majority family groups. Music includes pop, country, swing, rock n' roll and Broadway show tunes, in addition to magic and comedy. Fishing still prospers, blessed by a series of unique geological formations creating three lakes of widely differing depths, temperatures, and varieties of catch—a fishing enthusiast's dream. The Chamber of Commerce proudly proclaims Branson 'The Entertainment City.' However, resort success must not overwhelm concern for the environment; stewardship of its lakes and streams continues as the town's topmost priority.

Resort Theme Parks

One of the earliest examples of resort theming, inspired by the imagination of the nineteenth-century *fin de siècle* period, was at the seaside amusement park on Coney Island, New York. It featured a high-rise roller-coaster, the *Cyclone*, architecturally themed resorts of oriental and Queen Anne styles, and another hotel that expanded each season as news of the innovative concept spread. Further developments over the next half-century included remarkable technical advances in roller-coasters, a major breakthrough in World's Fair exhibitions, and the emergence of a uniquely enterprising tradition of small roadside theme parks. They ranged from alligator farms in Florida to such whimsical themes as the Gingerbread Castle, a park in Hamburg, New Jersey, costing over a quarter of a million dollars in 1928, according to a local newspaper account.

In the two decades between the world wars, a Golden Age of over 2,000 flourishing rollercoaster rides attracted crowds of enthusiasts to beaches, ocean piers, and amusement parks. But with the rationing of materials in World War II, most parks fell into disrepair, closed, and few ever reopened. In 1955 Disneyland launched an imaginative new age of themed attractions for the now more sophisticated consumers, who preferred the far faster Matterhorn and Space Mountain 'coasters. Knott's Berry Farm countered with the Corkscrew (360° loop) and adopted tubular steel tracks to enable even more daunting future versions. Today's *Guide to Rides* includes 300 major ones in North America, such as the Beast, with a 540° spiral (Cincinnati, Ohio), Magnum, combining nine 'coasters (Cedar Point, Ohio), and Le Monstre, featuring 18 crisscrosses (Montreal, Canada). As for the elaborate 1878 themed hotels and amusements on Coney Island, the buildings were replaced by new construction, while the Cyclone, declared a national landmark, stands in all its glory.

The 1939 the New York World's Fair burst on the scene with exhibit techniques that were difficult to improve on—even 43 years later at Disney's Epcot Center in Orlando, Florida. No one who experienced the General Motors *Futurama* exhibit, designed by Norman Bel Geddes, failed to be inspired by it, and it is still a standard reference of comparison for contemporary systems. It inspired exemplary expos at Montreal, Osaka, Vancouver, and Barcelona, further advancing theming technology.

The fantasy waterpark-based theme park **Caribbean Bay Waterpark, Seoul, South Korea.** The world's largest waterpark is expanding by adding a water-themed resort hotel, directly connected to the park (also see p. 121).

Theme Park and Resort Influences

Walt Disney's ingenious concept of Disneyland set the course for what would become a huge global industry, where a ride was no longer a mere mechanical aesthetic but, enhanced by movie-like props and dressings, created an atmosphere and storyline. And when grouped into theme zones such as Fantasyland, Adventureland, Frontierland, and Tomorrowland, it became 'The happiest place on earth.'

The added cost of theming rides and shows was significant, but proved a good investment, as the bottom line at Disneyland far exceeded expectations. Research comparing a theme park to a nonthemed amusement park of the same size and capacity shows that the theme park is superior in attracting visitors, generating revenue, and enhancing satisfaction. Theme parks exhibit these attributes:

- greater geographical attraction
- longer length of stay
- enhanced food and beverage sales (when themed)
- enhanced retail, logo, and themed merchandise sales
- improved overall experience and increased repeat business.

Spending on retail items and food and beverages, when appropriately themed, increases in proportion to the length of stay, with higher quality theming capable of significantly increased margins. Similarly, the number of days visitors spend at a park is proportional to the distance they travel for the unique experience. Not surprisingly, asset values of theme parks are positively affected by the quality of the themes. As leisure venues and vacation destinations, theme parks offer an escape from the routine. Thus, Universal Studios' multipark resort stated the obvious with its original name, 'Universal Escape.'

The early themed architecture of Walt Disney World's Polynesian Resort, including its interior design, landscaping, stonework, and water features, began the odyssey of creating resorts which redefined authenticity at a resort. The resort's restaurant menus, *luau* shows, and themed shopping set the stage; the staff's wardrobe, accessories, and *aloha* greetings further reinforced the Polynesian theme.

At Disneyland Paris Resort, six resort hotels representing distinctively American regional themes include the Disneyland Hotel, Cheyenne Hotel, Santa Fe Hotel, New York Hotel, The Newport Bay Club, and, representing the American national park system, the Sequoia Lodge. The number of hotel rooms built for the first phase of Disneyland Paris Resort exceeded initial demand. However, to meet increases in demand, the long-range master plan provides for future pedestrian connections from each resort to the park's main gate via a retail entertainment village. Dubbed Disney Village, it offers an ideal mix of themed restaurants, shops, and nightclubs within a neon super-graphic environment. The village provides the active nightlife desired by resort guests as well as visitors strolling to the park exits.

Portofino Bay Hotel, the initial themed resort at Universal Studios in Orlando, provides leisurely walks and water connections to City Walk, its entertainment and retail village adjoining the gated entries to the dual theme parks, Universal Studios Florida and Islands of Adventure. The convention resort, themed on the famous picturesque Italian seaside village, boasts charming mid-rise residential façades and a boat-filled harbor designed to humanize the large scale of the 750-room convention hotel with an ambiance of southern European relaxation and escape.

Themes for most leisure parks and resorts fall within one of the following four basic categories:

- *Historic places and cultures*: these parks are readily researched and widely appreciated. Depending on the theme, however, it can be costly to achieve quality and authenticity. Site conditions may require extensive area development of landscape, hardscape, topographical, and visual site control. Exemplary parks include World Showcase at Epcot in Florida, the original Knotts Berry Farm in California, Taiwan Folk Village, Universal Studios' Port Aventura in Spain, and the Polynesian Cultural Center in Hawaii.
- *Fantasy characters and places*: these provide flexibility to create a unique atmosphere for escape from reality. This theme and storyline approach can be used to manipulate design for cost benefits. The developers of a waterpark in China wove together a cartoon character (Hydro Hero) with a storyline, creating a strong concept for park promotion, retail merchandise, and specialty fast food. Some of the most prominent parks in the world that fit into this theme category are Disneyland, California, Islands of Adventure, Florida, Caribbean Bay waterpark, South Korea, and Parc Asterix, France.
- *Subject-focused themes*: these are strongest when well defined and clearly identified. The subject of the park establishes the architectural vocabulary and thematic atmosphere. It is important that the theme subject not be too trendy or quickly outdated. For example, parks with a 'future-theme often are out-of-date by the time the project gets off the drawing board and is constructed.

The focused entertainment and activity-based theme park **Tatilya Park, West Istanbul, Turkey**. A touchstone of the fast-growing new city, this indoor family entertainment park provides a principal amenity to the dynamic Bati Tourism Center (also see pp. 205–206).

The cultural/historic-based theme park **Taiwan Folk Village, Chang Hua, Taiwan.** The village concept blends displays of traditional Taiwan culture—such as history, folklore, education, and leisure—with modern technology to create a popular tourist attraction.

Prominent subject-focused theme parks include Universal Studios, California and Florida (films), SeaWorld (oceans), Lego Land, Denmark (toy blocks), and Disney's Animal Kingdom at Walt Disney World Resort, Florida (animals).

- *Activity-focused theme parks*: These often have a limited theme and, in those cases, it could be argued that activity alone does not justify the theme. However, the general media and public perceive most amusement parks and waterparks as a theme park. Certainly activity-focused parks can be themed as an enhancement for the activity. Particularly strong examples are Malibu Raceway,

A movie and islands themed resort **Universal Orlando, Florida.** Lagoons and water features highlight the arrival experiences at the dual theme park after visitors filter through the City Walk entertainment and shopping village. This village, the theme park, and the first two of three themed hotels are connected by a series of themed islands and waterways including a full-size replica of an Italian fishing village as a setting for its unique Portofino Bay Hotel. The water features include an inviting boat taxi system between these major elements (see views of Portofino Bay Hotel, pp. C-28 and 198, and Hard Rock Hotel, p. 388).

Table 4.4 Types of theme park experiences

Resort theme park hotels, convention centers, waterparks, and multitheme parks	Types of venue convergence exhibits
Multitheme parks (including thrill-rides)	Educational
Historic themes	Institutional
Animal habitats	Sports
Geographical themes	Historic
Marine habitats	Professional
Religious themes	Fraternal
Ecosystems and environmental themes	Museum
Music themes	Corporate
Science parks	Fair and expo exhibits
Art themes	Religious
Fantasy themes	Trade shows
Waterparks	Retail and food and beverage
Magic themes	
Sports parks	
Circus and acrobatic themes	
Fairs and expos	
Amusement parks (Including thrill-rides)	
Entertainment centers	

Texas (personal racing venues), Tatilya Park, Turkey (nature themed indoor amusement park), Wet 'n Wild, Florida (waterpark), and Game Works, Las Vegas (recreational/game arcade).

Within these four theme categories are a vast number of specialized theme parks and venue convergence exhibits which, when appropriately combined, can attract and even develop new targeted markets (see Table 4.4).

A park's overall theme normally is segmented into subthemes. For example, a park with an overall theme of music could have subtheme zones of jazz—New Orleans environment, Rock & Roll—American 1950s environment, classical—European environment, and Country Western—American Cowboy town. This mix of subthemes provides a more interesting guest experience because during a single day in the park visitors experience four different environments within one overall theme. Four different environments provide the guest variety in their memory-experience, help organize areas and places of interest in the park, establish a meaningful variety of cuisine and retail theme options, and establish a more particular theme segmentation for both ride and show attractions.

During the 1980s and 1990s the idea of theming environments reached new heights not only for parks and resorts but for independent free-standing restaurants, retail outlets, and residential developments. Over this period of time, theme has become more sophisticated and more easily constructed due to new materials and proven construction techniques. What some may have considered 'theme-mania' has clearly become a permanent segment of design for projects around the globe where creating unique escape environments is desired.

Resort Theme Park Planning Methodology

Ideation begins with a series of brainstorming sessions between the developer and the design and economic consultants specializing in themed entertainment experiences. Practiced interdisciplinary consultants explore the project's objectives and myriad of potential solutions, including details such as how to encourage different age groups to benefit from each other's presence. The above think-tank method is also used in developing trend analyses.

Once the concept is approved in sufficient detail, including a workable budget and source of financing, the full technical team of specialists turn the desired concept into reality. Throughout the design and planning process the key factor for success is to focus the product on the best guest experience within realistic budget parameters. To do this the design team must have a clear definition and understanding of the target markets including any seasonal shifts and related promotional and yield management systems. The park should be designed to allow flexibility in live shows and capacity levels as well as shifts in retail merchandise and food and beverage selections. The greater the ability to satisfy the market, the longer that market group will be in the park and the more they will spend.

The key to a positive guest experience is the attraction mix. The attractions, whether shows or rides, are measured in several ways beyond the expectation of it being a quality entertainment experience. The team considers the attraction's appeal to different age groups, and how many people per hour the attraction can accommodate, measured by its hourly 'entertainment capacity units' (ECU) (see the Park Attraction Matrix on p. 116).

The calculation of ECUs is easily understood by using a theater attraction as an example. A theater seating 500 people which can process the guest entry, seating, safety orientation, film presentation, and guest exit in a total of 20 minutes has an hourly ECU of 1,500 (500 people × 3 cycles/hour = 1,500 ECU). At times, planners need to modify new attraction concepts to achieve overall ECU demands because guests only will tolerate queues of a certain duration.

Queue time is an important aspect of park design since as much as 30 percent of a guest's park stay will be spent standing in line. Cultural tolerance for queue times varies dramatically around the world. Attractions which reputedly offer the best guest experience will generate longer queues balanced by a higher tolerance for a longer wait. Designers for new parks now provide theming and air-conditioning specifically for the queues.

Another measurement of overall park capacity is based on the average density of guests per acre or hectare. One rule-of-thumb is 700–1,000 guests per acre (0.4 ha) of actual park area, excluding parking. If park area densities fall too far below 400 guests per acre it may give an impression of being unsuccessful. Indoor theme parks normally are a unique challenge with economically driven demands for around 1,500 visitors per interior acre. The market in Japan has the record with popular Expo Parks reaching average attendance densities of up to 2,000 guests per acre.

Daily guest attendance is never consistent. Even in major year-round tourist destinations such as the parks in and near Orlando, Florida, attendance patterns fluctuate within seasonal markets. With the given fluctuation of daily attendance, parks are planned and designed based on the 'design day' and 'design hour.' The design day is neither the annual average daily attendance nor the peak day average attendance; rather, it is a more sophisticated figure based on an analysis of critical attendance days within the annual attendance pattern. Sometimes, a rule-of-thumb of the 10–15 busiest days can provide a preliminary design day number. The design day attendance then is used to establish the design hour which is a function of the park's operating hours and the visitor's average length of stay based on the park's overall ECUs. The tighter the margin between park operating hours and guest length of stay, the closer the design hour attendance is to the design day attendance.

Legend
- • Primary
- \+ Secondary
- – Tertiary

Component		Purpose								Age appeal				
No.	Description/name	Ride	Show	Gameplay	Special event/display	Food and beverage	Retail	Guest services	Operations	Young child (2–5)	Child (6–12)	Teen (13–20)	Adult (21–59)	Senior adult (60+)
69	Ferris wheel	•								–	•	•	•	•
70	Lagoon show amphitheater		•		+					+	•	•	•	•
71	Interactive live show		•	+						+	•	•	•	•
72	Buffeteria					•								
73	Chair swing	•								+	•	•	•	–
74	Sleeping beauty's castle			•						+	•	•	+	–
75	Puppet theater		•							•	+	–	+	+
76	Carousel	•								•	•	+	•	•
77	Canoe/paddle boat dock			•						+	+	+	•	•
78	Street entertainer		•							+	+	+	+	+
79	Fast food kiosk					•								
80	Retail cart (two total)						•							
81	Ticket and information booth							•						
82	Restrooms							•						
83	Theme retail (two total)						•							
84	Food cart					•								
	(•) Primary subtotals									2	6	5	6	5
	(+) Secondary subtotals									5	3	3	3	2
	(–) Tertiary subtotals									2	0	1	0	2
	Zone total	3	4	2	0	3	2	2		9	9	9	9	9

The Rosetta Stone of theme park design **Park Attraction Matrix.** Since the highest-performing parks hold their guests the longest, the optimum design is one which accommodates the most guests per acre (or hectare) and makes adequate provisions to satisfy demand at the park's newest and most popular attractions.

Attractions Per Hour

The design hour attendance is the primary park sizing guide. Everything from the more macro figures such as in-park density, total park ECUs, and restaurant and retail mix to such micro measures as restroom capacities and wheelchair/stroller rentals are sized based on the design hour attendance.

The park's size and attraction mix has the most to do with determining a guest's length of stay. Attractions with extremely high ECUs may process guests too quickly and reduce the length of stay, whereas attractions with too limiting an ECU will create congestion and result in such a negative guest experience that visitors may leave early out of frustration. Another rule-of-thumb is that guests should visit about 1.5 attraction experiences per hour; therefore, to generate an 8-hour length of stay, each guest should see about 12 attractions in addition to food and retail experiences. If the park's design hour is 10,000 people, then the overall park's hourly ECU would be 15,000–18,000 depending on the overlapping age appeal of the attraction mix.

Attraction Location Strategies

After the development and design team has established the major capacity and overall use characteristics, they proceed with the preliminary conceptual plan for the park. One of the most critical success factors is the placement of attractions within the park. Common strategies include:

- locating some of the most appealing 'must see' attractions on the extreme edges to draw guests through the park past impulse retail shops and less popular attractions
- offering within each subtheme area attractions which appeal to a variety of age groups
- placing the attractions so that the overall hourly ECU count is uniform to avoid congestion and ensure an uniform of guests throughout the park.

The physical layout of the park is strongly influenced by site conditions, theme parameters, operational policies, and cultural differences. There are several overall planning models commonly used in theme park design.

- *Hub-and-spoke plan*: developed by Walt Disney for Disneyland in Anaheim, California, and still considered today one of the best models for theme park planning. In its original form it had the entry/exit spoke flanked with appropriate retail shops. This spoke channeled all arriving guests to the center of the park where a visual icon punctuated the hub and became an orientation element seen from multiple vantage points in the park. At Disneyland, this is Cinderella's Castle. From the central hub, the other spokes are circulation gateways to the various subtheme zones of the park. The advantage of quickly bringing guests to a central location and then exposing multiple gateway options is excellent for swift and even distribution of guests into all subtheme areas. Often included with the hub-and-spoke plan is an outer loop connecting the subtheme zones.

- *Loop plan*: used at Universal's Islands of Adventure (IOA) in Orlando, Florida, where the loop surrounds a central water amenity. However, some loop plans place general service and maintenance functions in the center for ease of operations. A major challenge of loop parks is that once visitors establish a direction of travel there is no choice, whether they might want to revisit a favorite attraction or jump across the center. Where there is a single entry to the loop, attractions opposite the entry point (regardless of popularity) often do not operate at full capacity during the opening hour while, somewhat later, they have long queues because both circulation directions converge. Some parks with the loop layout try to move guests to subtheme zones beyond the entry point by using various modes of group transportation, but that is rarely as effective as a central pedestrian entry point to all subtheme zones.
- *Figure-eight plan:* essentially two loops, this plan has many of the attributes of the hub and spoke. Generally, designers make the entry point at the crossover of the figure eight, where the two loops connect, and where it acts as a central hub to distribute guests in four directions through the subtheme zones. A park planned for the Child and Nature Trust in Turkey places the crossover entry at one side of an artificial lake and directs one loop around an earthen dam. The dry side of the dam is used for a river rapids ride, always a popular high-capacity attraction for any park.
- *Random plan*: unconventional or random plan strategies are often a result of unusual site conditions or external planning forces which dictate an unusual approach to park planning design. An example of this is the Fantasy Island Water Park on Sentosa Island in Singapore where an irregular site was crossed by several utility easements. Planning was further complicated by the requirement for both a primary entry and a secondary gate for a future monorail station. Designers determined that the random plan could best integrate the lost-civilization theme and archeological dig storyline.

Resort Theme Park Development Considerations

According to latest trend research, the recommended rule-of-thumb to gauge the annual potential theme park attendance in mature economies is one visit per person each year. With 270 million annual visits, the US leads the way. The more innovative parks in western Europe have reached only a third of their potential and in countries such as China immense success awaits developers who can identify appropriate concepts and manage the development process.

The vital importance of understanding local customs was experienced at Disneyland Paris Resort where, for example, the initial operation dismayed both German and French guests who were unable to find beer or wine on the theme park menus. Also, operating hours must be adjusted to local customs; for example, parks in Spain need to stay open until at least 2:00 a.m. Other strategies developed at Disneyland Paris Resort involve adding more thrill attractions in relation to the size of the park, including an entire new area to strengthen the attraction mix for longer-staying visitors. This was needed to offset an unusually high percentage of one-day visits from nearby urban centers. Further shopping and restaurants, including a major anchor mall, are being added to help reposition the park as a primary destination rather than a secondary and short-term attraction.

Following the example of Walt Disney World Resort, major parks now provide hotels to enhance the visitor's total experience. Also, as was learned at Disneyland and applied at Walt Disney World, a major destination park needs a vast site with adequate space for future growth, including resort hotels, to protect itself from competitive businesses ringing the park. In addition to a variety of themed resorts, park developers add convention hotels to increase theme park visits, realizing that families often accompany meeting attendees if the destination is attractive, or the larger 'mega-hotel,' which serves the four major markets—convention attendees, business travelers, sports vacationers, and theme park visitors. In Orlando, the convention

The hub-and-spoke plan theme park **Magic Kingdom, Walt Disney World Resort, Orlando, Florida.** This exemplary park demonstrates the radial planning configuration first applied by Walt Disney at Disneyland in California.

market has filled the traditional low attendance periods at the major theme parks and operators have found that parents will take their children out of school for the opportunity of a family vacation.

The market needs a variety of resorts at major destination theme parks, reflecting the diversity of the park's visitors. Many people prefer the experience and convenience of staying within the park, offering easy access, longer hours, and package pricing. Walt Disney's original concept of providing the most desirable themed resort concepts inside the gate, to enhance, and be enhanced by the resorts, ultimately proved the most successful course both in Orlando and at Disneyland Paris Resort. Each theme park company needs to consider its strategy for developing lodging inside or outside the gate and whether to establish its own management company.

Significant Resort Theme Park Hotels

The decision on what type of resorts to build at a theme park, the number of rooms, rate class, and operational policies will vary depending on the market study for the resort as well as a separate analysis of the theme park elements. Familiarity with new hotel types will assist the developer in determining the most appropriate elements for a new theme park resort.

The random plan theme park **Fantasy Island Waterpark, Sentosa Island, Singapore.** Unique site constraints often dictate an unusual design. Here, multiple utility lines cross the site of Asia's largest waterpark, located in the center of Singapore's most popular attraction.

Disney's BoardWalk at Walt Disney World Resort, Orlando, Florida

Themed resorts have become destinations in and of themselves. In fact, some new themed resort concepts have theme park-like components within them. Disney's Epcot Resort district of Walt Disney World Resort contains three large resorts (BoardWalk, Yacht Club, and Beach Club) and a vacation ownership component themed as a seaside boardwalk resort. The resorts are linked by the bike cart and pedestrian boardwalk that encircles the central lake offering a nostalgic ambiance of shops, restaurants, skill games, and boat docks providing water taxi service to Epcot. This boardwalk environment is theming at its best, creating extensive cross visitation between resort guests and visitors experiencing the themed environment.

Hotel Cheyenne at Disneyland Paris Resort, France

This 1,000-room hotel is organized as a complex of two-story buildings conceived in the image of a nineteenth-century American western town, filtered through the lens of Hollywood. Unlike its original prototype, providing a single hotel along Main Street, USA, the Hotel Cheyenne is the town itself. The reception building and restaurant are placed at the principal crossroads, where a street leads across the creek to the Hotel Santa Fe.

While the streets of typical western towns ran in straight lines and opened to endless vistas of prairie and mountains, the streets of Hotel Cheyenne, like those of back-lot western towns built by the Hollywood studios, have vistas angled to screen out backstage areas from the cameramen and the actors who, in this case, are one in the same—the hotel guests.

Caribbean Bay Hotel, Seoul, South Korea

The master plan for this pioneering development in Seoul, Korea, presents a fully integrated resort theme park. Caribbean Bay, the world's largest indoor/ outdoor waterpark, is planned with direct access to

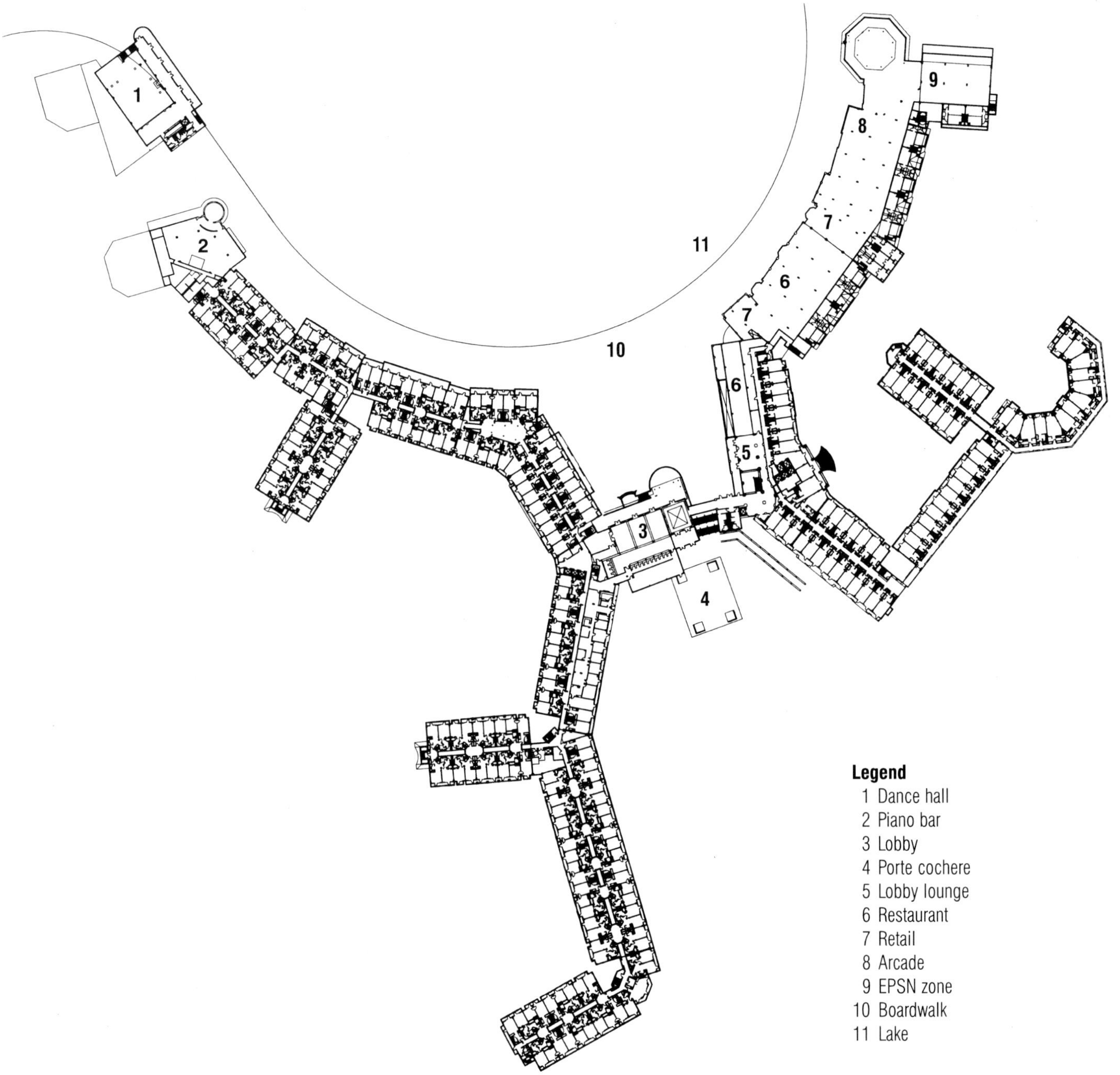

A nostalgic resort theme **Disney's BoardWalk at Walt Disney World® Resort, Orlando, Florida.** Evoking a varied 1890s resort town, its porches, awnings, shutters, dormers, lookout towers, and widow's walks create an intimate experience. Further enhancing the town-like quality, the era's bungalow style cottage design and Victorian-Gothic architecture are introduced in sections of the resort. Its 378 hotel rooms, 528 Disney Vacation Club suites, 15,000 ft^2 (1,400 m^2) of meeting space, and 49,000 ft^2 (4,550 m^2) of dining, lounge, and shopping amenities further unify the total lakeside complex.

the family resort hotel. During the cold winters guests change into swimming attire in their resort room and wear a robe/cover-up when walking in heated comfort to the indoor waterpark. The feel of a Caribbean village is created not only on the exterior but also with an interior street, which connects the resort and waterpark in a seamless warm, tropic environment. In this case, the resort and the indoor/outdoor waterpark serve as amenities to one another.

When resorts and theme parks are developed together, additional privileges can be provided as part of an accommodation package. This includes early park access, discounted entry fees, purchases charged to the room card, special queue lines, preferred seating in park restaurants, and delivery of park purchases to the guestroom. Many park privileges are designed to reinforce the themed experience of escape and relaxation for guests of all ages.

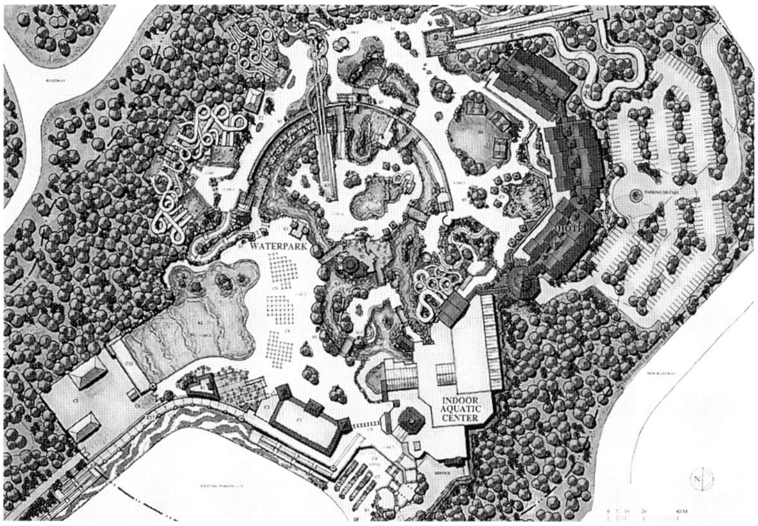

An integrated waterpark resort theme park **Caribbean Bay Hotel, Seoul, South Korea.** The maximum benefit of theming is obtained by integrating the waterpark and resort into a single complex.

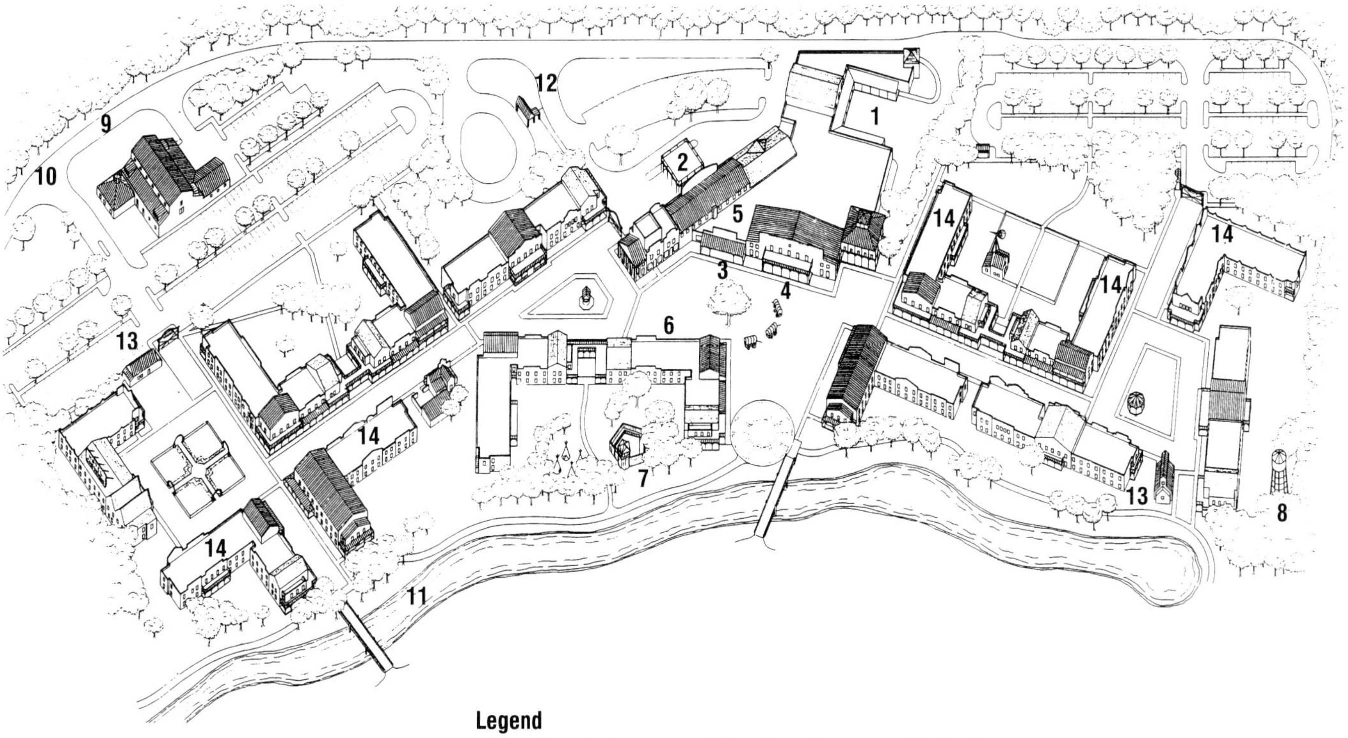

Legend

1 Loading dock
2 Porte cochere
3 Bar
4 Dining room
5 Lobby
6 Sundries shop
7 Playbround (fort)
8 Water tower
9 Grounds building
10 Entry road
11 Creek
12 Bus stop
13 Laundry and vending
14 Guestrooms

A wild-west resort theme **Hotel Cheyenne at Disneyland® Paris Resort, France.** One of six major themed hotels integrated into the park, this resort is based on the stage-set version of the hotel which appeared in western movies. The Hollywood version of the hotel, shown in this axonometric drawing, was found suitable for a resort because of its spread-out plan required for filming.

Ship of Dreams, Orlando, Florida

Possibly the best example of fully integrating the resort and park attractions is the pioneering Ship of Dreams resort planned on the edge of a 60 acre (24 ha) lake between Walt Disney World Resort and Universal Studios in Orlando, Florida. The 500-room resort takes on the form and exterior dimensions of the steamship *Titanic*. The interior replicates many of the familiar spaces seen in the movie yet the overall resort appropriately departs from the ship's plan by creating large suites, additional public amenities, and essential back-of-house areas to meet current four-star resort standards. The building, in the form of a ship, is 186 ft (97 m) high at the top of each of its signature smoke stacks. The experience includes an on-board *RMS Titanic* museum and a walking tour through major public areas of the resort-ship, designed with separate entry/exit and circulation routes for day visitors in order to maintain privacy and exclusivity for the hotel guests.

The ultimate themed experience is when the resort and park are one. This completely integrated effect provides immediate access to the park and to the guestrooms which look into the park, allowing guests to observe the simulated life, street performers, or fireworks at night. The hotel building also provides additional thematic massing for the park, with each element an asset to the other. Larry Ziebarth of HHCP Design International, observed: 'Escaping into a themed experience at a resort or park will be even far more exciting in the future than it is today.'

Trends

In a strong economy, hotel demand in Orlando and Las Vegas rises the most because, as the best known resorts of their type, they frequently are the first destinations a guest visits. The next major theme parks are expected to be developed in such international cities as Shanghai, Taipei, Singapore, Beirut, Jerusalem, and Warsaw, as well as on Native American reservations in New Mexico, Arizona, and Connecticut. While economic viability remains the key threshold factor, high-profile parks are a continuing megatrend in an industry where 40 percent of adults surveyed say that they will visit a theme park.

More specialty experience parks will provide a low-capacity, high-experience, high-cost ticket for an affluent special interest niche-market. Possible concepts include such ideas as ecotourism, archaeology, or a weightless weekend at a space park.

An integrated nautical/historic resort theme park **Ship of Dreams, Orlando, Florida.** When the resort guests and park visitors are together on board the giant replica of the ship, the themed experience reaches its peak.

- Urban entertainment parks, both horizontally and vertically tiered, will provide pay-as-you-go debit cards allowing busy residents to pay only for the attractions they use, encouraging many shorter repeat visits.
- Small niche-parks will be developed in suburban or multiblock urban renewal sites to compete with the major destinations, offering the precise experience the visitor is seeking, shorter lines, and more affordable prices.
- More resorts will be located within park gates, both to create greater guest convenience and to heighten the experience. Costumes will be encouraged on special occasions.
- Advanced theming techniques developed for parks will be extended to museums, airports, shopping malls, restaurants, and even hospitals, where their effectiveness in treating illnesses will be further explored.
- Roller-coasters and other thrill-rides will continue to stretch the engineer's skills and the body's ability to tolerate the sense of excitement. Greater thrills also will be developed through simulation methods.
- Interactive attractions where the guest participates with the entertainment experience will grow significantly, an evolution of today's video games.
- Holography will make almost anything simulatable, from walking through walls to wrestling with lions.
- Animal habitats will be upgraded to science-learning and ecosystem parks, and other themes and attractions similarly will continue to improve and upgrade to meet customer expectations for new experiences.
- Marine habitats will be advanced to live contact and communication sessions with dolphins, tame stingrays, tortoises, and schools of tropical fish.
- The next megaleap for entertainment parks, since the amusement park to theme park in 1955 by Walt Disney, will be 'partici-park,' where all attractions will integrate some form of guest participation. Guests might receive scores, making the experience competitive, either among friends or against set thresholds or records.

Cruise Ships

The golden age of luxury ocean liners came to an end in December 1967, when the Cunard Line's *Queen Mary* made its final docking in Long Beach, California, where it was converted, appropriately, into a hotel. The era of crossing the seas in elegant floating hotels where one dressed for dinner and spent long days relaxing on deck with a book became obsolete with improvements in air travel and changing attitudes toward leisure. Being there, not getting there, became more important.

The *Queen Elizabeth II*, which was launched in 1969 and refitted in 1999 at a cost of $312 million, is the only passenger ship that still crosses the Atlantic on a regular basis. It claims to be the only true ocean liner, although it, too, sets out on cruises in the off-season. Passenger ships today have become less a way of transportation and more destinations unto themselves. The old ocean liners were built as seafaring hotels. Today's cruise ships offer a whole array of additional activities on a grand scale that include tax-free shopping, casinos, diverse entertainment, and sports facilities. Many are modeled on the Las Vegas hotel, often with the same splashy interior design. Once offshore, cruise ships are not subject to laws prohibiting gambling. Also, freedom from taxes allows cruise lines to set lower prices for liquor and other goods than their onshore counterparts.

A major boost to cruise travel has been the great number of healthy, affluent, retired people who have time for leisure travel. Cruise ships allow one to check-in once to a room and dine in a familiar setting with assurances of consistent quality, a comfort particularly to people who are relatively new to travel. The ship can visit exotic ports without guests needing to move luggage, look for accommodations, find restaurants, or make transportation connections. For these same reasons, cruise ships are becoming very popular for families with children. Disney's cruise line, a leader in this category, offers a variety of packages that tie in with their theme parks, resorts, and urban entertainment centers.

The competition of cruise lines to out-do each other has exploded in recent years. In 1999 Royal Caribbean International launched its 142,000-ton *Voyager of the Seas*, which is 42 percent heftier than the largest vessel in the US Navy and accommodates 3,114 passengers. The interior features two giant atrium spaces, flanking a shopping arcade two-football fields long and four decks high, above which 138 staterooms overlook the activity. This is the first vessel that offers cabins with interior views into skylit public spaces, in addition to sea views. With more space than any other vessel at sea, the Voyager also includes a 1,350-seat theater modeled after Milan's La Scala, a driving range for golfers, rock-climbing wall, ice-skating rink, and wedding chapel in the sky.

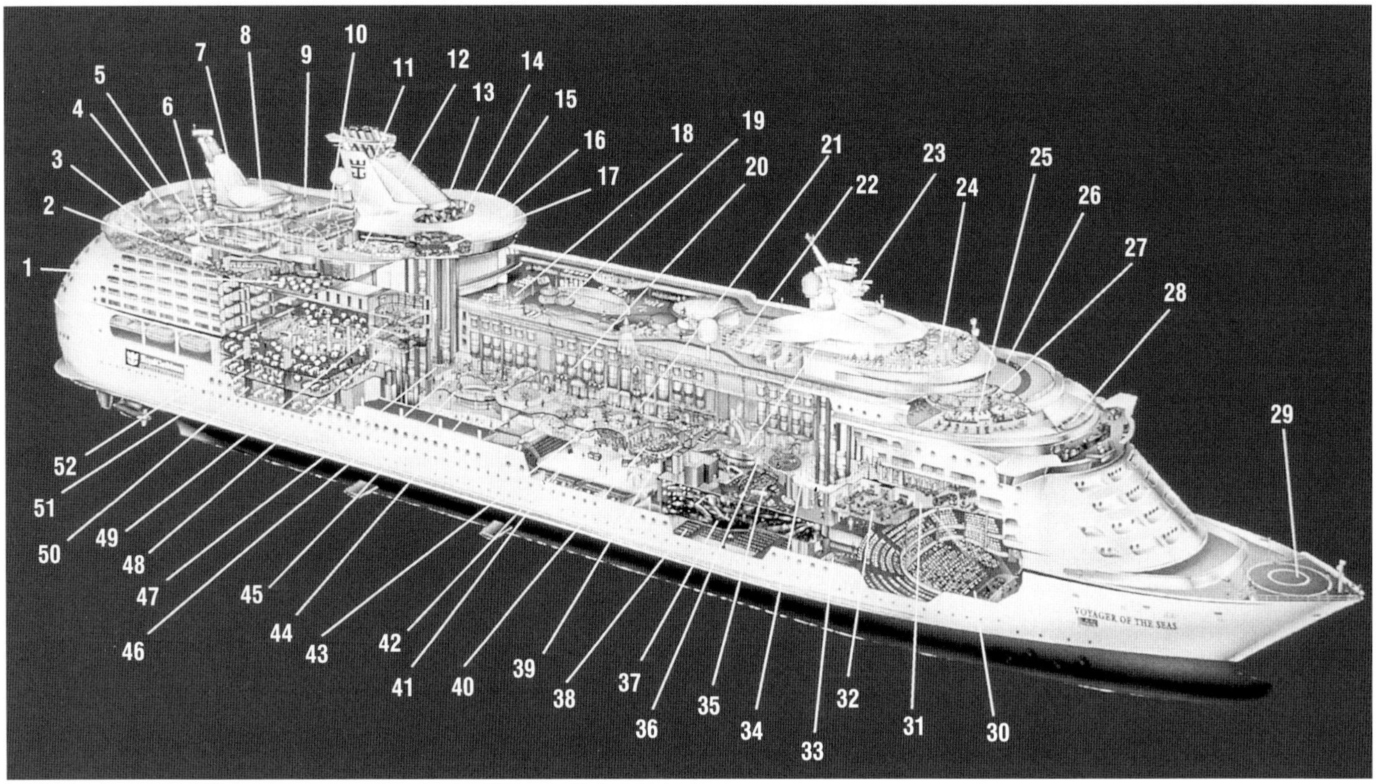

Legend

1 Portfino Italian Restaurant
2 Windjammar casual dining
3 Island Grill casual dining
4 Voyager Dunes golf course
5 Seaside Diner casual dining
6 Adventure beach outdoor family deck
7 Adventure ocean youth area
8 Golf simulator
9 In-line stating track
10 Sports court
11 Rock climbing wall
12 Nineteenth hole golf bar
13 Seven Hearts card room
14 Skylight chapel
15 Cloud Nine cocktail lounge
16 Crow's Nest observation lounge
17 High Notes jazz club
18 Cool zone
19 Pools/whirlpools
20 Atrium view staterooms
21 Boutiques duty-free shopping
22 Solarium
23 Sprinkles ice-cream bar
24 Sunbathing area
25 ShipShape® fitness center
26 Jogging track
27 ShipShape® spa
28 Peek-A-Boo bridge overlook
29 Observation point
30 La Scala theatre
31 Cleopatra's Needle dancing lounge
32 Connoisseur Club cigar club
33 Boardroom
34 Forward Centrum
35 Schooner bar
36 Café Promenade
37 The Vault nightclub
38 Conference center
39 Casino Royale
40 Spinners gaming arcade
41 Center Ice at Studio B
42 Studio B entertainment complex
43 Scoreboard sports bar
44 Aquarium bar
45 Champagne bar
46 Royal Promenade
47 Aft Centrum
48 Business Services
49 Library
50 Carmen dining room
51 La Bohème dining room
52 Magic Flute dining room

The cruise ship resort **Royal Caribbean, *Voyager of the Seas*.**

In 2000, Royal Caribbean International launched an identical ship, *Explorer of the Seas*.

Not to be outdone, America World City operating out of Port Canaveral, Florida, has plans to build a one-quarter-mile-long craft that will carry 6,200 passengers housed in three eight-deck-high hotel towers rising above the ship's hull. Proposed amenities include a theater for 2,000, a museum, and a 100,000-book library. It will be a veritable self-contained resort at sea.

With 70 percent of the earth's surface water, ships have access to a wide range of sites that are difficult to reach by other means. Many of the world's great cities, picturesque villages, and some of the oldest and most spectacular human settlements are on water and convenient for sea travelers to visit. Also, breathtaking natural landscape, often untouched by human occupation, can best be explored from seafaring vessels. Views of volcanic islands in the Hawaiian archipelago, South Pole penguins, Norwegian fjords, Alaskan glaciers, and even more remote and exotic locations are accessible to ships. The ability to travel during the night while enjoying restful sleep and without the hassle of airports, allows the sea passenger to visit a number of ports at ease.

Unlike resort hotels that weather low seasons, cruise ships have the freedom to navigate wherever the demand is greatest—winters in the Caribbean and Mediterranean, summers in Alaska and Scandinavia. In addition, for major events that will make local hotel rooms hard to come by and expensive, and air travel tight, ships can provide on board rooms for short periods. Several ships docked in Sydney, Australia's, great natural harbor to provide additional lodging for the 2000 Olympics.

Some of the most popular cruises are organized with a theme. Much like conventions, they require little physical modification of the facility to accommodate the particular group, which enjoys the freedom of being surrounded by others sharing the same outlook or interests. Packages are put together for both well-established groups and those assembled solely for the cruise. They range from frolicking on the high seas by singles, gays, and salsa aficionados to more sober groups who study the Bible, hear lectures on the environment, or remember Pearl Harbor by sailing into Honolulu's harbor.

Unlike most hotels, cruise ships provide their own utility infrastructure, including electricity, water, sewage and waste disposal. Another major distinction is that cruise ships have to provide accommodation, all meals, exercise facilities, and entertainment for its crew who do not mix socially with the passengers. Not only does this involve more space, but also, as in the case of the 2,600-passenger *Grand Princess*, a 'sub-crew' of 50 who are on board to clean the quarters, prepare meals, and handle payroll for the 1,150-member staff.

Trends

With a strong economy and an aging population, the popularity of cruise ships will continue. In 2000, 12 new cruise ships were planned for launch. Major hotel companies such as Radisson and Disney are becoming important players in the cruise-line industry. Not only is there the lucrative cruise business, but these ships also bring guests directly to resorts owned or managed by the same companies that own them.

The cruise ship resort **Royal Caribbean, *Voyager of the Seas*.** Following innovative trends of the hospitality industry, the cruise ship's luxurious atrium staterooms face onto the bustling streetscape of the Royal Promenade, cruising's first horizontal atrium. More than two football fields (200 m) long and four decks high, the space offers a wide selection of shops, restaurants and entertainment. Other features of this 142,000-ton, 3,800-berth floating entertainment hotel include a 1,350-seat theater, ice skating rink, aquarium, rock climbing wall, and multipurpose entertainment complex with state-of-the-art broadcasting and recording facilities.

Chicago's convention center/hotel complex **Hyatt Regency McCormick Place, Chicago, Illinois.** The 800-room Hyatt Regency is connected to North America's largest convention and exhibition center, McCormick Place, via the Grand Concourse, marked by its soaring arched roof. The hotel has relatively little meeting and banquet space of its own, but over 50 hospitality suites to support the convention activity.

Convention Hotels

5

Among the largest lodging properties are those hotels and resorts which are designed to host conventions and other national and international meetings. In North America, most of the larger cities have several hotels in the 750–1,500-guestroom range while surprisingly few international cities boast even one hotel of this size. In the US and Canada the foundation for group business is the large association meeting while in Europe, for example, the convention market focuses on the international trade shows held in such cities as Berlin and Milan. These major industry events often occupy more than 1 million ft^2 (92,800 m^2) of exhibition space and fill every hotel in the city—many of them older, relatively small properties—but do not require the kind of meeting and banquet space that is the essential characteristic of a major convention hotel.

The French philosopher Alexis de Tocqueville, among the first to identify America's appetite for group participation, would not be disappointed by the mass meeting activity held in today's convention-oriented hotels and conference centers. Cities such as New York and Las Vegas, for example, host several million convention guests every year and, worldwide, the number of people attending meetings and conventions is well in excess of 100 million. Even resort areas, such as Orlando or Palm Springs, have become major convention destinations. In addition, smaller resorts find that they need to cater to meeting and group business in order to fill guestrooms in the shoulder- and off-season. In major cities, on the other hand, the convention market extends throughout the year, with the few slow periods around major holidays.

Given the increasing importance of the group market, and the ability to attract meetings at a wide range of locations—downtown, suburban, airport, and resort, for example—the late 1990s saw the explosion of a variety of distinctly different convention hotel types. Smaller cities of up to 250,000 people may have a convention-oriented hotel in the 300–400-room range, with a ballroom for 800–1,000 people. Major cities push these numbers much higher, and most hoteliers would define a convention hotel as having a minimum of 500 rooms for regional and small national meetings, up to 1,500 or more rooms at major destinations or for headquarters hotels adjoining leading convention centers. With the development of airport hubs around the world, developers have built convention-oriented properties outside the major cities, to ease the burden on travel and because large sites are more available outside the downtown areas. And, increasingly, conventions are held at resort areas, where guests can take part in nonmeeting activities or where families can spend a day on vacation while one parent is busy.

There are many examples of convention hotels which combine these elements. For example, in Orlando, Florida, the Orange County Convention Center is immediately surrounded by three large hotels, all within a few minutes walk, each one alone which might host a substantial meeting but which, together, provide a sufficient base of overnight rooms for nearly any major convention. Disney World continues to expand its convention-oriented properties in order to attract groups which find it appealing to combine meetings with the Disney theme-park experience. Less than 10 miles (16 km) from the convention center, Universal Studios is developing three major resort hotels with a strong meetings orientation for exactly this same market. Table 5.1 suggests how large these major hotels may be, especially when the destination is widely favored.

As the table shows, the number of hotel rooms is only part of what defines today's convention hotel. In addition, the property requires a major ballroom and substantial amounts of exhibition and multipurpose meeting space, totaling some 50–100 ft^2/room (4.6–9.3 m^2), or about two to three times the amount of meeting space that is normal for suburban or business-oriented downtown hotels. In

Table 5.1 Orlando, Florida, selected convention hotels

Hotel	*Guestrooms*	*Meeting rooms*	*Ballroom area* ft^2	m^2
Hotels adjoining the Orange County Convention Center				
Rosen Centre Hotel	1,334	33	35,000	3,250
Peabody Hotel	950	32	26,700	2,480
Clarion Hotel	810	22	26,000	2,410
Convention hotels within Walt Disney World				
Walt Disney World Swan and Dolphin*	2,267	75	54,400	5,050
Disney Coronado Springs	1,967	45	60,200	5,585
Disney Yacht and Beach Club*	1,217	21	38,000	3,525
Disney Contemporary	1,041	33	44,800	4,160

*Two hotels marketed and operated together.

addition, these hotels offer multiple food and beverage outlets, expanded health and fitness facilities, and a much higher number of suites, typically 5 percent and sometimes approaching 8 percent of the total number of guestrooms.

A large convention hotel today requires a minimum of 1,000 rooms committed to the convention, without which large groups may not consider a hotel. In planning the facility another 200–400 rooms must be added to avoid turning away transient travelers during peak convention periods. Secondary cities may have convention-oriented hotels about half this size. The convention hotel's smaller counterpart, the conference center (see Chapter 6), caters to smaller groups who require only 50–200 guestrooms and who prefer single-purpose conference and training rooms. While the convention hotel can accommodate varied meetings of all sizes, it focuses primarily on larger groups, whereas the conference center provides a more intimate atmosphere and such dedicated spaces as an amphitheater and dozens of breakout rooms needed by smaller groups.

Many older convention hotels, unable to expand, have been made obsolete because of the growth in the size of association and other larger organizational meetings. Increasingly, higher attendance at conventions and trade shows—especially at the popular destinations—often spills over into several hotels clustered around a 'headquarters' hotel. This has created opportunities for larger capacity meeting and exhibit halls in such lead hotels, in some ways duplicating or replacing the older city convention centers and municipal auditoriums.

This interest in convention hotels is easy to understand. Group business, and especially the large meeting market, grew at over 5 percent a year in the late 1990s. Occupancy percentage and room revenue in large convention hotels generally outpaced those of smaller properties.

Table 5.2 Convention hotels operating data

Number of rooms	*<500*	*500–1,000*	*>1,000*
Average size (rooms)	281	733	1,511
Occupancy percentage	65.4	67.8	73.8
Revenue per room	$27,917	$31,267	$45,059

Source: PKF (2000), *Trends in the Hotel Industry*, USA edition.

Planning and Design Considerations

Convention hotels are among the most difficult building types to plan and design because the usual complex functional requirements are exacerbated by the size of the program—1,000 rooms or more, substantial public areas including a large clear-span ballroom, and increased back-of-house spaces. In downtown urban locations this is made even more difficult by small sites and restrictive zoning. In selecting a site, the development team needs to recognize the major planning considerations for a successful convention hotel and test the site against these key criteria:

- Test site for FAR (floor area ratio) to accommodate total hotel area at program ratios such as 850–900 ft^2 (80–84 m^2) per room.
- Separate hotel entrances including main lobby, ballroom and exhibit hall, restaurants, hotel receiving, employees, and exhibit unloading.
- Provide sufficient public arrival space for cars, taxis, and shuttle buses.
- Provide sufficient service space including for unloading of exhibits.
- Create a lobby space of sufficient size for the market and appropriate to the site.
- Allow sufficient clear-span for hotel ballroom, often as much as 125 ft (38 m) or more, outside the guestroom column structure.

Because of the scale of new convention hotels, these criteria, while similar to those for smaller downtown or airport hotels or for larger resorts, create new challenges for the development team. In addition to having many more guestrooms and suites, the total amount of public and support space, the size of the ballroom, and the number of elevators often are two to three times that of other major hotels which do not focus on the convention market.

Downtown Convention Hotels

The traditional convention hotel is a major chain-operated property in one of the large convention cities—New York, Chicago, New Orleans, San Francisco, and so forth—and may have 1,000–1,500 rooms or more. While it may be more convenient to the convention center, these projects are not usually directly adjacent to the city facility and do not depend only on that business, but market to mid-size groups (500–1,000 people) which need large amounts of meeting, dining, and breakout space. Based on the strength and projected continuing growth of the convention market, new convention hotels with 1,000 rooms and over 50,000 ft^2 (4,640 m^2) of meeting and exhibit space are being announced in major cities. If sites were not so difficult to acquire, operators would consider doubling their meeting space by providing a second major ballroom and additional breakout rooms. If still more area is available, many would add a major exhibit hall as well.

In Philadelphia, Marriott built a 1,410-room hotel one block from the convention center, which had opened in 1993. Because the center is undersized compared with other nearby east coast cities (in 1997 the city began plans for its expansion), Marriott decided to build a self-contained convention property, with its own exhibition space and multiple ballrooms. In addition, by 2000, Marriott had added three additional small hotels nearby, as satellite projects, bringing its total room count to over 2,200. Where possible, hotels of this type should devote about 40 percent of its function area to exhibition space, 40 percent for grand and junior ballrooms, and 20 percent for small meeting rooms.

In San Antonio, Texas, an increasingly popular convention destination, Marriott recently built on the popular Riverwalk, only half a block from the convention center. This highly successful hotel is used as a model for new convention hotels on constrained sites, in which the many ballroom subdivisions serve the need of smaller groups.

The urban destination convention hotel **San Antonio Marriott Rivercenter, Texas.** This 1,000-room convention hotel, overlooking the exciting Riverwalk, is connected to the Rivercenter Mall and is a short walk to the city convention center. It anchors San Antonio's growing convention and tourist business with a 38-story tower rising atop a soaring atrium lobby. Increasing numbers of cities are able to support hotels of this size because of the growing importance of major regional and national meetings.

Table 5.3 Philadelphia Marriott Hotel, 1,410 guestrooms (76 suites)

	Area available ft^2	m^2	*Percentage of total*
Exhibit hall	33,000	3,060	40%
Grand ballroom	33,000	3,060	40%
Other meeting rooms	16,000	1,485	20%

Table 5.4 San Antonio Marriott Rivercenter, 1,000 guestrooms (86 suites)

	Area available ft^2	m^2	*Percentage of total*
Grand ballroom (divides into 13 parts)	41,600	3,860	76%
Conference rooms (19)	12,900	1,200	24%

Downtown, Convention Center Headquarters Hotel

As the major destination cities build new convention centers or expand older ones (see Table 5.5), many at 1,000,000 ft^2 (92,900 m^2) or more, they often provide one or more sites for an adjacent 'headquarters' hotel, usually connected directly to the convention center. Because they operate at relatively high occupancies and rate, compared with other first-class hotels in the same market, these projects usually are awarded on a competitive basis. For example, Boston, which is planning to open a new $700 million convention center in 2003, went through a careful competitive process with three major hotel management groups, including conceptual design of the respective hotels, before selecting Starwood and its Sheraton brand for the new 1,120-room headquarters hotel.

These hotels, connected to the convention center, do not need as much dedicated function space, because they benefit from the symbiotic relationship with the public facility next door. In Atlantic City, New Jersey, the city provided a site for a new 500-room headquarters hotel adjacent to its new convention center. The Sheraton Hotel is designed to complement the exhibition and meeting facilities in the convention center and, therefore, has only 27,000 ft^2 (2,500 m^2) of its own ballroom, banquet, and breakout rooms, in addition to other amenities.

Some cities are partnering with hotel companies to build a hotel connected to the public convention center. The city of Chicago recently expanded its McCormick Place Convention Center to make it the largest facility in North America, with over 2 million ft^2 (185,800 m^2) of exhibition space and 110 meeting

The convention center headquarters hotel **Sheraton Atlantic City Convention Center Hotel, New Jersey.** Developers responded with competitive proposals for a convention headquarters hotel connected to the gaming destination's new convention center. The hotel public space serves as a connecting link between the convention center and new retail space that pulls meeting attendees toward the famous Boardwalk fronting the many casinos overlooking the Atlantic Ocean.

The convention center hotel **Hyatt Regency McCormick Place, Chicago, Illinois.** The 12,000 ft^2 (1,115 m^2) ballroom is graced by a soaring perforated-metal canopy in its prefunction space, helping to pull down the scale of the space at the ballroom doors.

Table 5.5 Largest convention and exhibition centers, North America

		Total area	
City	*Exposition center*	*ft²*	*m²*
Chicago	McCormick Place	2,200,000	204,000
Las Vegas	Las Vegas Convention Center	1,300,000	120,000
Atlanta	Georgia World Congress Center	1,180,000	110,000
Houston	Astrodome USA	1,130,000	105,000
Orlando	Orange County Convention Center	1,100,000	102,000
New Orleans	Ernest N. Morial Convention Center	1,100,000	102,000
Louisville	Kentucky Fair and Exposition Center	1,070,000	99,500
Las Vegas	Sands Expo & Convention Center and Venetian Resort Hotel Casino	1,000,000	93,000
Cleveland	International Exposition Center	900,000	83,500
Dallas	Dallas Convention Center	850,000	79,000

Source: *Tradeshow Week* 1998 Major Exhibit Hall Directory; Smith Travel Research, US Lodging Census (Top 25 Hotel Markets), 1999.

Table 5.6 Hyatt Regency McCormick Place, Chicago, 800 guestrooms (53 suites)

	Area available ft^2	m^2	*Percentage of total*
Ballroom	12,000	1,110	69%
Meeting and breakout rooms	5,500	510	31%

rooms. At the same time, the city built a hotel connected to the center, operated by Hyatt (see p. 126). Because of the great size of McCormick Place, the Hyatt Regency requires very little convention space of its own. While a convention hotel in every respect due to its market orientation, and with great demand for suites and breakout rooms, the hotel space program is much closer to that of a transient hotel.

Suburban or Resort Convention Hotels

Suburban, airport, and resort destinations also offer the opportunity to capture convention business. But, frequently, these projects are physically removed from nearby attractions and, as a result, need to be fully self-contained. The Hyatt Regency at O'Hare Airport, Chicago, one of the early John Portman-designed atrium hotels, has seen the market grow up around it, including the suburban Rosemont Convention Center, but originally it was a dedicated airport convention hotel. More descriptive of this type are resort projects in such cities as Palm Springs, California, and Orlando, Florida.

Among the largest and most successful is the Orlando World Center Marriott, which expanded in 2000 by adding 500 guestrooms and 50,000 ft^2 (4,640 m^2) of function space. It features an exhibit hall and two major ballrooms, as well as small meeting and breakout rooms and extensive prefunction areas, much of it outdoors. While both Orlando and Las Vegas offer continued opportunities for large convention hotels, many with themed designs, these projects can not be universally applied to other locations.

Development Considerations

The major hotel management companies all try to have a presence in each major market. While some chains traditionally may have been oriented more towards resort or downtown or airport locations, as they have grown the companies have become more similar in the distribution of their properties. That is, each of the major companies, Marriott, Sheraton, Hilton, Hyatt, Westin, and so forth, includes a blend of resort, business, and convention hotels and competes head to head in most locations, including for the convention market. In some cities they collaborate. In Boston, for example, the Sheraton (1,180 rooms) is the closest hotel to the Hynes Convention Center, but both Marriott (1,150 rooms) and Westin (800 rooms) operate major hotels within walking distance. These three hotels frequently collaborate to attract major city-wide conventions.

Downtown sites large enough to support major convention hotels of over 1,000 rooms are rare. Consider that the hotel requires a clear-span ballroom, and adjoining prefunction areas, placed where they do not fall beneath the guestroom structure.

The convention resort megahotel **Orlando World Center Marriott, Florida.** Now the largest Marriott hotel, following the opening in 2000 of a 500-room addition, the 28-story megahotel offers every resort amenity to the conventioneer and other guests. Sprawling over 200 landscaped acres (81 ha) and including a redesigned championship golf course and health spa, the convention complex covers 200,000 ft^2 (18,580 m^2), including two major ballrooms and an exhibition hall.

Table 5.7 Orlando World Center Marriott, 2,000 guestrooms (98 suites)

	Area available ft^2	m^2	*Percentage of total*
Exhibit hall	49,200	4,575	24%
Crystal ballroom	39,500	3,675	20%
Grand ballroom	37,400	3,475	18%
Meeting rooms	15,000	1,400	8%
Prefunction/foyer	61,000	5,675	30%

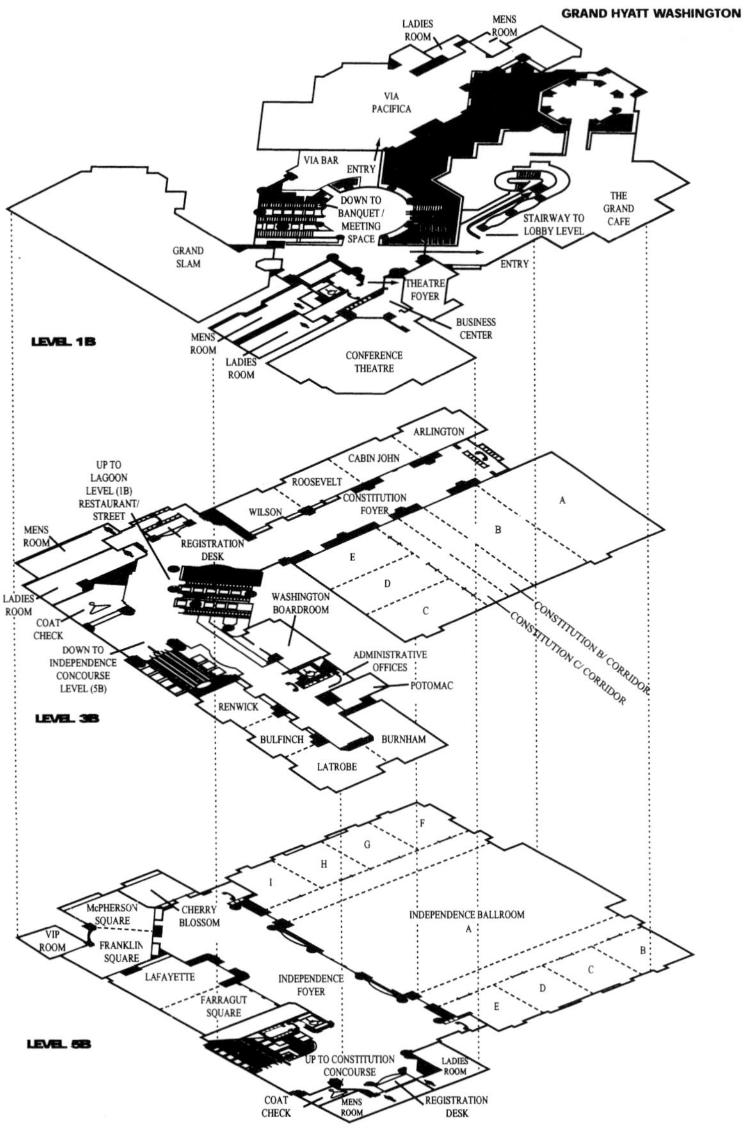

The compact urban convention hotel **Grand Hyatt, Washington, DC.** With building heights limited in Washington by city ordinance, architects struggle to organize the hotel elements in a compact mid-rise building. The exploded diagram illustrates how the 900-room Grand Hyatt's atrium lobby, with restaurants and lounges overlooking its central water feature, covers two floors of underground convention space, cleverly solving the structural tension between large-span meeting rooms and the guestroom structure. The smaller meeting rooms and support functions fill the zone around the ballrooms, where the structure does not permit a major column-free space.

Therefore, a site to accommodate a major ballroom of 120 × 250 ft (36 × 76 m) and public and service functions that surround it, in addition to the guestroom tower, may require a site of more than 60,000 ft^2 (5,500 m^2). In fact, a normal rule-of-thumb in urban locations is to seek a site that is at least 2.0–2.5 times the size of the largest ballroom. While careful planning at the schematic stage may allow the developer to build on a smaller site, this requires the architect to place the ballroom on an upper level, requiring additional elevators or escalators, and a junior ballroom on still another level. This stacking of the function rooms complicates the design of the vertical circulation, requires additional egress stairs, and forces duplication of back-of-house service areas.

Building in Washington, DC, is further hindered by strict height limitations. Many hotel developers, therefore, excavate two or three levels underground in order to provide enough floor space to make a project feasible. The Grand Hyatt Washington, with 900 guestrooms and 58 suites, has about 40,000 ft^2 (3,700 m^2) of function space including two mid-size ballrooms, reached by escalators leading down from the lobby entrance to basement floors. The hotel atrium essentially falls directly above the ballroom space, with guestrooms ringing it on three sides filling the city block.

Early convention hotels, such as the Willard in Washington, DC, and The St. Regis in New York, were able to provide open, column-free ballrooms only by placing them on the top floor. This approach was structurally efficient, and the rooftop ballrooms it produced are still much admired for their dramatic views. But with the increased capacities of today's meeting and banquet facilities and the extensive elevators and fire stairs that now are required, this solution is no longer practical. Cities wisely are considering special zoning or other means of assembling larger sites needed to satisfy the demand for major new convention-related hotels.

Ideally, convention hotels are better located on large sites where the function space spreads out over only one floor. Therefore, the goal at airport and suburban locations, or in major urban renewal sites, is to acquire a parcel four or more times the size of the largest ballroom. A compromise may be possible, for large projects, to put some smaller meeting rooms, as well as food and beverage outlets and back-of-house areas on another floor, but the major function space should be configured as compactly as possible.

Planning Public Areas

As with every hotel, planning the public space begins with the arrival sequence. At major convention hotels architects need to consider the volume of arrivals or departures likely at peak times, as well as the need to accommodate shuttle buses to the convention center or other attractions. Therefore, for a 1,000-room hotel it may be necessary to have as many

The casino hotel convention center addition **MGM Grand Conference Center, Las Vegas, Nevada**. Opened in 1998 as an addition to the 5,000-room MGM Grand Hotel, the 380,000 ft^2 (35,300 m^2) conference center offers one more substantial meeting venue to Las Vegas's incredible mix of huge facilities. The main focus is on two large subdivisible ballrooms, capable of seating over 8,000 people for a banquet; yet the facility can be flexibly rearranged to provide 42 individual meeting rooms. The 38,000 ft^2 (3,500 m^2) of pre-function space support the meeting activities and overlook the Grand Pool and Spa complex.

as four lanes at the porte cochere, in order to avoid congestion.

In fact, all spaces need to be somewhat oversized: lobbies must accommodate greater numbers of guests checking in or out, elevators must transport guests within confined periods of time, restaurants and lounges experience dramatic peaks around the convention schedule, and recreational facilities are taxed when sessions are not being held. Lobby planning guidelines of 15 ft^2 (1.4 m^2) per guestroom may be 1.5 times the norm for suburban or small city hotels, which do not generate substantial group business. Restaurant capacities increase because of high double-occupancy in the rooms and lounges are oversized to accommodate late afternoon and evening demand from meeting attendees. Guests are more likely to shop during a convention than they are on other business trips, so retail space may approach the amount found at resorts.

Of course, the main feature of convention hotels is the function space: exhibit hall, ballrooms, meeting and banquet rooms, and small breakout rooms must be designed to meet very particular needs of a wide range of business and social activities. Convention hotels do not do the same amount of social business that smaller city hotels do, so the rooms can be designed more fully for meetings. And, unlike conference centers which provide very purpose-specific meeting space for their guests, convention hotels generally provide more generic, multipurpose rooms, with a high number of subdivisible walls creating flexible arrangements of space.

While the program is different from other hotels, the planning principles are much the same: creating a sense of arrival, separating public and service activities, making spaces and functions easily locatable, and so forth. The interrelationship of the key convention spaces must encourage the flow of attendees mainly between the ballroom and the exhibit hall and between the ballroom and the meeting and breakout rooms. If any of these elements is on a different floor,

A versatile convention resort with a daylight ballroom **Loews Miami Beach Hotel, Florida.** The first major luxury hotel to be built in Miami Beach in more than 30 years, the 800-room property combines 100 rooms in the historic art deco St. Moritz Hotel with a new 18-story tower. The stylish resort offers services and amenities important to leisure, incentive, and convention markets. Unusual, but critical for resort destinations, the grand ballroom features floor-to-ceiling windows overlooking the landscaped gardens, pool, and Atlantic Ocean. Prefunction space seamlessly flows between the new building and the outdoors.

the architect must provide a grand stair or escalators and a visual connection between their prefunction areas. Where the climate offers the opportunity, foyer spaces must open onto plazas and pool decks, and small and mid-size rooms, especially, might have their own access to outdoor terraces. The new Westin Park Towers hotel in San Diego is designed with one side of the ballroom featuring a series of sliding panels that can open the space fully to the foyer, and to the terrace beyond.

The architects must incorporate a number of features in the schematic design of the ballroom to provide for future operations:

- *Extra-wide (9 ft or 2.7 m, minimum) service corridors*: the usable width of the corridors may be reduced by the partition storage areas, banquet service equipment, audiovisual equipment, egress requirements, structure, or mechanical and electrical provisions.
- *Prefunction area*: include support functions such as public toilets, coat rooms, telephone areas, grand stair or escalators, meeting registration, meeting planner's office, and business center.
- *Back-of-house support space*: space is required for furniture storage, audiovisual storage, pantry and prep areas, back-of-house staff space, partition storage, and so forth.
- *Two-story or higher space*: consider the impact of the high-ceilinged ballroom on window location and views, or related issues, on the next level. Allow for a deep roof structure, control rooms for translation, projection, and lighting with direct

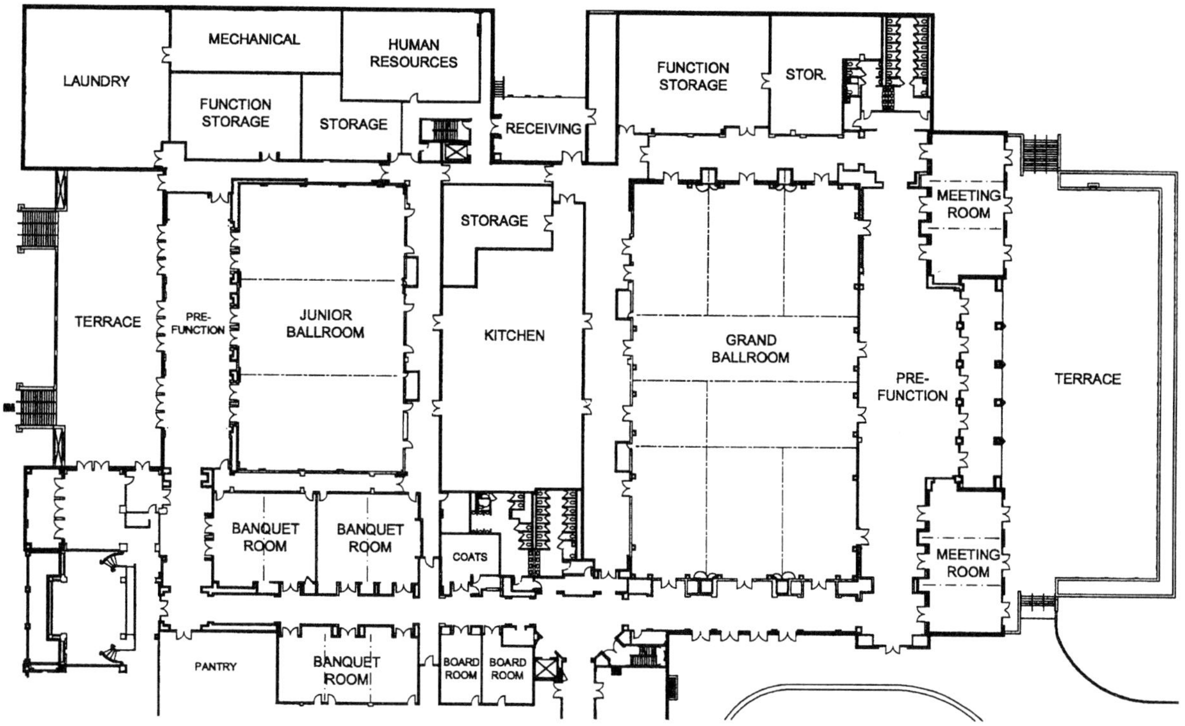

The efficient convention-resort hotel **Hyatt Regency Coconut Point Resort & Spa, Naples, Florida.** Larger resort sites permit architects to organize the convention space horizontally. The 450-room Hyatt Resort, overlooking the Gulf of Mexico, features 20,000 ft^2 (1,850 m^2) of function space including two ballrooms, each with its own dedicated prefunction terrace leading to manicured lawns and gardens. Outside guests can enter the Grand Ballroom from the arrival court without passing through the hotel lobby. The kitchen is located between the two rooms and other public and service support functions are conveniently placed nearby (see p. 79).

views to the ballroom, perhaps by using a mezzanine space above the prefunction area.

- *Additional freight elevators*: large functions place high demands on back-of-house flow and the service elevators supporting the guestroom tower are insufficient for banquet service.
- *Truck space for loading and unloading of exhibits*: use of the ballroom or meeting space for exhibits requires truck space far in excess of what usually is available at the hotel receiving area. Plan for easy display access and truck entry to the ballroom through full height doors.

Convention hotels require the latest in computer networking and audiovisual technology including teleconferencing capability throughout the function space, projection booths and equipment, sophisticated sound systems, flexible lighting, and soundproof movable partitions to subdivide function rooms. Where there is demonstrated demand, convention hotels may need to include such additional features as space and equipment for simultaneous translation and a movable stage in the ballroom.

Trends

- Cities continue to expand public convention centers, increasing the need for lodging close by. The top convention destinations worldwide should see further expansion and development opportunities for convention hotels.
- Increased travel generated by the European Union and the growth of professional associations should dramatically increase the need for convention hotels.
- Convention hotels traditionally maintain high levels of computer and technological innovation as conventions offer one of the first opportunities to introduce new products.
- Cities and private developers are creating downtown entertainment districts which further fuel convention activity. Sites near shopping, cultural attractions, or new entertainment districts offer alternative locations for convention-oriented hotels, despite their distance from the convention center.

The medical research conference center **Howard Hughes Medical Institute, Chevy Chase, Maryland.** The HHMI campus in suburban Washington, DC, combines the research center headquarters with dedicated conference facilities and guest accommodations in the main structure and in four 'cottages' nearby. The three functions all make use of paved courtyards and shaded lawns arranged around the storm-retention pond (see p. 150).

Conference Centers 6

One of the more confusing distinctions to the layperson is between the related terms 'convention' and 'conference.' But to a hotelier, a convention attracts several hundred to many thousands of attendees, while a conference caters to relatively small groups seeking a more intimate venue and close personal interaction. Although a few important conference properties existed since early in the twentieth century—Asilomar was founded on the northern California coast in 1913—it was not until the last half of the century that major universities and corporations saw the need for dedicated educational or training centers. Even then, the movement started slowly with the Arden House, operated by Columbia University in Harriman, New York (1950), among the earliest, followed by such notable examples as the Harrison Conference Center at Glen Cove, New York (1968), The Learning Center at Marlboro, Massachusetts (1974), and Doral Forrestal in Princeton, New Jersey (1979). Only in the 1980s did conference centers become truly competitive and demonstrate a successful product that was widely accepted and which offered promise for continued growth.

Distinct from other types of lodging properties that cater to groups, a conference center is designed, first and foremost, to provide an environment conducive to effective meetings, especially for groups of fewer than 50 people. The conference center provides a dedicated, distraction-free, comfortably furnished, and technologically equipped facility with, importantly, the added feature of a professional staff to provide a high level of service both to the meeting planner and the conference attendees. At such a center, all aspects of the facility design, conference support services, food and beverage program, and recreational amenities enhance and further the goals of a meeting.

The rapid development of conference properties paralleled a corresponding period of substantial growth in the number of (and attendance at) meetings, from the smallest workshops to the largest national conventions. Various studies by the trade press and independent research organizations show that while all segments of this market are increasing, the smaller corporate management, training, and sales meetings are growing the fastest. For example, while the number of association meetings—usually those with the largest attendance—actually decreased from 1995 to 1999, corporate meetings in the US increased by nearly 10 percent, to about 835,000 annually, with an attendance of over 50 million people and expenditures in excess of $10 billion.

The Small Meetings Market

The conference center industry is at a point where its specialized lodging product has gained wide acceptance; the positive experience of the 1980s and 1990s has educated both meeting planners and attendees. At the same time, the demand for venues for small conferences is rapidly increasing. Recent studies of the number of small corporate and association meetings estimate that there were 800,000 small conferences (those with less than 50 people) held in the USA in 2000, with an additional 50,000 held by US organizations overseas. In addition to these small meetings, which ideally are held in the more intimate, better-serviced conference centers, the properties frequently accommodate groups as large as 200–300 people. Most experts anticipate that the number of small conferences and training programs will continue to grow, even during periods of economic downturn, for several key reasons:

- Corporations are facing an increasingly competitive environment, and their employees are being challenged to understand new manufacturing, marketing, and financial techniques and concepts.
- The growing trend to consolidation in many industries requires that company management meet to meld cultures and business practices.
- Omnipresent legal and regulatory issues necessitate frequent educational seminars.

- Increasing reliance on technology and computerization make it necessary for businesses to continually train and update employees.

Conference and educational planners struggle to find the ideal meeting or training environment for their particular program. They increasingly find that dedicated conference centers offer a setting and services that cannot be matched by traditional multipurpose hotels and resorts. These new facilities must be programmed and designed to accommodate a particular mix of conference sessions.

Training programs are the most common type of small meeting, often incorporating a high level of audiovisual support. Some companies may feature fairly standard video presentations, while others involve the trainees in intensive role-playing exercises and group sessions, which may be videotaped and played back for critique and discussion. While these events average only a few days, many training programs can last several weeks. Although a typical class size is about 20, many training meetings include as many as 30–50 people. Depending on the degree of involvement of the corporate human resources and training staff from a particular company, the training site may be selected because of its proximity to the corporate headquarters. As companies in the 1990s recognized the increasing importance of training, many bypassed the proximity issue by building their own dedicated training center, complete with guestrooms and extensive classroom and meeting support areas.

Management meetings include executive conferences and management development sessions. These generally range from about 2–5 days and are designed for groups of 10–50. The meetings often are very intensive, and planners may schedule recreation and social activities to offer an opportunity for relaxation. As a result, organizers usually select resort or suburban conference centers with extensive recreational facilities.

Professional and technical meetings are similar to the training and management sessions in many ways but may only run 2–3 days. The size of the meeting depends largely upon the topic and sponsor. Many are held at universities, where the faculty of business, management, or engineering schools serve as seminar instructors; however, all types of conference centers attract at least some small number of technical meetings.

Regional and national sales meetings ideally are held at conference centers because of the need for highly sophisticated audiovisual presentations and the desire to keep the attendees focused on the session theme. These meetings generally last 3–4 days and vary in size, with national meetings reaching as large as several hundred attendees. Sales meetings have many objectives, among them increasing employee motivation and enthusiasm, familiarizing employees with new product lines or sales strategies, and reasserting corporate goals and philosophies. Many larger sales meetings are held in hotels and resorts, but the small and midsize regional meetings are ideal for conference centers.

Incentive trips and other types of meetings are also good candidates for using conference centers. Incentive trips, which usually last about a week, generally are held at major resort hotels or popular destinations. Companies that offer incentive trips as a reward to sales or management personnel tend to include business meetings during the event, although their intensity and rigor varies. Resort conference centers, especially those with onsite golf or skiing, and those properties near popular destinations are best positioned to attract this business. Product introductions, smaller association meetings, and other specialized types of conferences are a less important part of the conference center market—these often involve hundreds of people, may be fairly short in duration, and do not generate the food and beverage and rooms revenue essential to supporting the more expensive conference center operations.

Conference Center Types

Conference centers fall into distinct categories. These distinctions are based for the most part on the ownership, market orientation, and usual mix of facilities. Of course, many conference centers exhibit the characteristics of several different categories: the new Conference Center of the Americas on the grounds of The Biltmore Hotel in Florida is a joint venture of the historic resort with both the city of Coral Gables and the University of Florida system. And many of the corporate conference centers, for example, compete with executive properties by soliciting general meetings. Also, like other lodging properties, an older conference center may find that its market matures and may need to reposition itself to continue to attract business. Doral Arrowwood, for instance, north of New York City, was conceived as a corporate center by the financial giant Citicorp in the early 1980s. It then evolved into an executive facility (late 1980s),

Table 6.1 Conference center characteristics

Type of center	*Typical meeting uses*	*Facility characteristics*
Executive	Mid- and upper-level training and management development; management planning; sales meetings	Suburban locations; 200–300 mid-size to large guestrooms; multiple dining and beverage outlets; moderate number of mid-size conference rooms; large number of breakout rooms; moderate recreational facilities
Resort	Mid- and upper-level management meetings; incentive trips; sales meetings	Resort destination or suburban locations; 150–400 large guestrooms; multiple dining and beverage outlets; small to moderate number of conference rooms; additional banquet rooms; extensive recreational amenities (especially outdoors)
Corporate	Technical and sales training for low- and mid-level employees; management development meetings; outside conferences if company policy permits	Suburban or headquarters locations; 150–400 guestrooms (size varies); limited dining alternatives; extensive training or conference rooms to meet corporate objectives; specialized rooms; auditorium; moderate to extensive recreational amenities
University	Executive education for middle managers; scientific meetings and continuing education programs	On-campus location; 100–200 small to midsize rooms; limited dining and beverage options; small to moderate number of conference rooms; amphitheater; auditorium (at continuing education centers); recreation usually located elsewhere on campus
Not-for-profit	Religious, educational, and government staff training; association and foundation meetings	Often at remote location; 25–100 rooms; single dining room; small to moderate number of generic conference rooms; large multipurpose room; limited recreation (primarily outdoors)

added a strong resort orientation (early 1990s), and in 2000 opened new guestroom and meeting wings dedicated to the training needs of Pfizer, a leading pharmaceutical company, reverting to its corporate heritage. Table 6.1 identifies the principal types of conference centers, the typical meetings they attract, and their general physical characteristics. Tables 6.2 and 6.3 compare the space program and conference facilities among the four major conference center categories.

Executive Conference Centers

The executive conference center presents the most typical facility and usually falls either in the mid- or high-price category. Oriented toward corporate meetings, including both training and management development sessions, the executive centers feature a relatively large number of conference rooms—as many as 20–30 meeting rooms for 200–300 guestrooms. Most executive centers are located in the suburbs around the larger cities, such as New York, Washington, Atlanta, and Chicago, or close to a major airport hub. The late 1990s saw similar growth of executive conference facilities in the major business centers of the UK, Scandinavia, Japan, and Australia. With increasing competition and land costs, the main concern of both developers and operators should be whether a proposed facility has the potential to attract weekend conferences or social business, both of which are necessary to ensure profitability.

The 1990s saw growth in a hybrid conference center when several major urban convention hotels added a wing or renovated one or two floors to create the more intimate conference environment that their otherwise extensive function spaces failed to provide. The Sheraton New Orleans, with 1,100 rooms and 90,000 ft^2 (8,360 m^2) of function space, constructed a five-story addition in 1994 to house a new executive conference center. The facility offers eight additional high-quality meeting and board rooms totaling 17,000 ft^2 (1,580 m^2) with amenities typical of the best conference centers:

- flexible controls for lighting, power, audiovisual components, and climate
- comfortable ergonomic chairs and oversized tables
- state-of-the-art high-speed communications capabilities and multiple dataport outlets
- stackable walls and presentation railings
- permanent walls rather than divisible partitions for superior acoustics
- support functions including private group office space, conference concierge, refreshment kiosks, upgraded restrooms, and public telephones.

Table 6.2 Facilities comparison by conference center type

	Executive	*Resort*	*Corporate*	*University*
Guestrooms	Average- to large-size rooms; few suites; club floor	Large to very large rooms; 5–10% suites	Small- to average-size rooms; few or no suites; commons area on each floor	Small- to average-size rooms; few or no suites; case study or commons area on each floor
Public areas	Large lobby with lobby lounge; conference dining and specialty restaurant; entertainment lounge and game room	Average lobby with view over grounds; conference dining, specialty restaurant and recreation dining; entertainment lounge	Lobby size highly variable; lobby lounge if corporate policy permits; conference dining and private dining; game room	Small- to average-size lobby; reading room or quiet lounge; conference dining and private dining; cocktail lounge
Conference areas	Ballroom; large variety of conference rooms and many breakout rooms; boardroom	Large ballroom; moderate number of meeting and breakout rooms; amphitheater	Auditorium; large number of similar classrooms; computer or special-purpose rooms; offices for trainers	Executive education: amphitheaters, breakout rooms and faculty offices. Continuing education: auditorium and many classrooms
Recreation areas	Swimming pool; racquet courts; health club	Many outdoor facilities; pool; health club/spa	Gym or pool; racquet courts; health club	None

Table 6.3 Schematic design program by conference center type

	Executive	*Resort*	*Corporate*	*University*
Guestrooms				
Number of rooms	225–300	150–400	125–400	100–200
Typical net area*	300–350 (28–33)	325–375 (30–35)	275–325 (26–30)	250–300 (23–28)
Gross area*	470–525 (44–49)	525–625 (49–58)	450–55 (42–51)	400–525 (37–49)
Percent of total	50–55	45–55	35–45	40–55
Public areas				
Number of restaurants	2	3	1–2	1
Number of lounges	2	2–3	1	0–1
Gross area*	90–125 (8–12)	90–125 (8–12)	60–200 (6–19)	85–115 (8–11)
Percent of total	8–12	8–12	7–12	9–14
Conference areas				
Number of ballrooms	1	2	0	0
Number of auditoriums/ amphitheaters	0–1	1	1–4	2–3
Number of meeting rooms	10–20	6–15	6–40	3–10
Number of breakout rooms	6–20	4–8	4–20	6–15
Gross area*	175–225 (16–21)	125–190 (12–18)	250–400 (23–37)	175–300 (16–28)
Percent of total	16–22	8–20	20–35	20–35
Recreation areas				
Gross area*	15–50 (1–5)	50–200 (5–19)	35–90 (3–8)	0–20 (0–2)
Percent of total	2–6	4–15	3–5	0–2
Administration/service				
Gross area*	125–175 (12–16)	140–190 (13–18)	200–300 (19–28)	125–200 (12–19)
Percent of total	13–18	14–17	15–25	12–15
Total gross area*	950–1,100 (88–102)	1,050–1,200 (98–112)	1,150–1,500 (107–140)	800–1,100 (74–102)

*Floor area figures are in square feet (square meters).

Starwood completed a similar project at its Sheraton New York Hotel and Towers in 1999, when it totally refurbished its underutilized exhibit hall into dedicated conference space with high-quality meeting rooms surrounding a central registration and concierge area.

Resort Conference Centers

The resort conference center has grown in prominence in two distinct and opposite ways: many evolved from executive properties by marketing and promoting their expanded recreational facilities while other centers changed from a resort by adding a meeting complex to better fill low shoulder and off-season periods. The resort centers are designed for the same type of management meetings, as well as for sales and incentive groups. Resort conference centers vary in size: in the 1990s most new properties had approximately 300–400 rooms in order to support the recreational infrastructure, but more recent projects have only 150–200 traditional hotel guestrooms but include nearby timeshare rental units (see Chapter 4). The resort centers usually have somewhat less meeting space than do executive centers, but offer more food and beverage choices and substantially larger recreational facilities. New resort centers are being built in suburban locations where there is sufficient land and in the more traditional resort destinations, such as Arizona and California.

Corporate Conference Centers

The corporate conference and training center is the largest physically—in the 1980s a few corporations opened properties with more than 1,000 rooms. However, these became tremendously difficult to fill during recessionary periods and expensive to maintain; also, consolidations among major corporations made many of these obsolete. Although some corporations more recently have built facilities with 150–250 rooms, new projects tend to be in the 250–400-room range. Corporate centers contain much more conference space than do other types because of the need to meet very specific training needs. Many major corporations, especially those in telecommunications, insurance, pharmaceuticals, and financial services struggle with the decision of whether to build their own suburban residential center (or urban day center), or to rent space at executive centers or at another site. Fortunately, they all realize the importance of training and employee development to their success.

The convention hotel executive conference center **Sheraton New York Executive Conference Center**. Major convention hotels have responded to the small corporate groups that require a more intimate meeting venue by renovating one or more floors to create a dedicated executive conference area with upgraded meeting rooms, improved audiovisual technology, and additional business concierge services. The 1,750-room Sheraton now offers a separate facility with 13 small refurbished meeting rooms, meeting planner offices, and videoconference capability.

The major distinction among corporate centers is whether the facility will be used for training or for management development. Training centers may be very large, with many hundreds of guestrooms, or companies may build a series of smaller centers for different products or service needs. The training centers tend not to have a ballroom or even many large meeting rooms, perhaps only one room larger than 2,000 ft^2 (185 m^2). They do, however, feature a large number of mid- and small-size conference rooms: the Aberdeen Woods Conference Center in Georgia, operated by Pitney Bowes, has over 50 small training rooms for its 233 guestrooms. Management development centers, on the other hand, have more mid- and large-size rooms, fewer small conference rooms, a high number of breakout rooms, and one or more amphitheaters for special presentations, equipped with the latest audiovisual technology including distance-learning capabilities.

The environmentally focused not-for-profit conference center **Lied Conference Center, Arbor Day Farm, Nebraska City, Nebraska**. The Arbor Day Foundation's conference center supports environmental stewardship in its design, incorporating a wood-fuel heating and air-conditioning system, energy efficient lighting and plumbing systems, and recycled materials throughout the furnishings and operations.

University Conference Centers

The university conference center meets three different needs: the most luxurious are designed for dedicated business school executive education programs, some provide for campus visitors and educational conferences, and still others for growing continuing education programs. The university centers generally are no larger than 150–200 rooms and feature amphitheaters or a large auditorium as well as the more typical conference rooms. These centers exist because the large research universities realize that their reputations depend, in part, on the types of executive and adult education programs they run, and on their ability to bring business executives to campus on a regular basis.

Not-for-profit Conference Centers

The not-for-profit conference center is the most variable conference center category. It may be owned by a religious or educational organization, association or foundation, research center, or private humanitarian or arts group. The facilities reflect the particular mission of an organization and may offer the public or specific interest groups the opportunity to meet, for example, in a spectacular mountain setting or near a historic landmark.

Planning and Design Considerations

There are significant differences in the physical organization of conference centers and those of more traditional hotels and resorts. Many of these differences are related to the conference center's principal planning objective: to separate the conference and training areas from the other functions in order to eliminate distractions and intrusions during a meeting. Dining, lounge, banquet, and recreational areas usually are located away from the meeting wing, in connecting structures, or even in separate buildings. Other objectives include the architectural massing and careful siting of the facility to enhance the residential scale and create a feeling of closeness with the environment. Roadways, parking areas, and surrounding activity are screened. Moreover, the architects must design a particularly efficient building. Given the additional floor area programmed for meeting and recreational facilities, it is essential that architects keep non-essential space to a minimum.

Planning the Guestroom Areas

Because of the major focus on the public areas, and especially the conference core, the architect must deal with the guestroom areas in a straightforward manner. For example, the usual program for the guestrooms calls for fairly standard rooms of 300–350 ft^2 (28–32.5 m^2), typical three-fixture bathrooms, a small number of suites, and few additional amenities. The architect should attempt to organize the guestroom wings along double-loaded corridors to reduce the amount of public circulation space (see Chapter 15).

The rooms at the smaller end of the range are in facilities designed for single occupancy, generally at the more price-sensitive corporate and university centers, but this may be shortsighted in that they are less adaptable for more upscale markets in the future. These facilities also have few suites, certainly no more than two per 100 rooms, and no 'club floor' or executive level as do upmarket business hotels. On the other hand, the executive and resort centers, as well as the management-oriented corporate centers, provide rooms fully competitive with those in the best hotels, 350–400 ft^2 (32.5–37.2 m^2), include four-fixture bathrooms, allocate up to 5 percent suites (resorts as many as 10 percent), and feature additional amenities in order to meet the demands of the nonconference guests throughout the year. The layout of these guestrooms must recognize the need for meeting attendees to work on case studies or other training materials in their rooms, often involving group discussion. University centers may provide group study rooms on the upper floors, just for this reason, to accommodate the focus on group discussion and project work. Often, these rooms are treated similarly to suite living rooms, but with the focus on work space rather than lounge and entertainment activities.

Planning the Public Areas

In contrast to the fairly typical guestroom areas, conference centers are far from typical when it comes to planning the public areas and, especially, the function space. Like convention hotels, the conference facilities frequently provide two major entrances, one the lobby entrance for the overnight guests, the other the function entrance, here intended for the day conferee. Unlike many hotels, conference centers generally do not market or position their food and beverage operations to the general public but prefer to reserve them for the conference attendees, to support the learning objectives of the meeting. Beverage outlets are common, but understated. Many university and some corporate centers, as a general policy, do not provide any bar or lounge spaces, although these may be found as part of a game room or informal 'pub' operation.

The emphasis, of course, is on the meeting areas. The planning and design objectives specific to the conference core include the following:

- Locate the conference core, whether in the form of classrooms, breakout rooms, amphitheaters, or other special-purpose rooms away from other public functions to minimize distractions.
- Dedicate the conference core to the meeting functions; provide a separate area for such social activities as banquets and receptions in the general vicinity of the food and beverage operations.
- Provide a conference foyer with direct access from outside or from the main hotel lobby.
- Incorporate necessary public support functions including meeting registration, conference concierge, restrooms, and coat and phone areas.
- Design and equip each conference room to enhance the meeting purpose. In general, provide spacious, brightly daylit, high-ceilinged rooms which incorporate flexible lighting and audiovisual systems, comfortable furnishings, and individual climate control.
- Place assembly and refreshment areas throughout the conference core to provide opportunities for frequent informal gathering and to allow greater flexibility in scheduling breaks. Include outdoor terraces where site and weather permit.
- Locate service support functions such as conference services offices, pantry space, audiovisual equipment, and furniture and other storage rooms nearby.

Conference center operators demand that the architect design the other principal areas to support the meeting focus. For example, most facilities include a dedicated dining room for the conference attendees. This is designed to allow clusters of people coming out of a session, often groups as large as six to eight, to find a table and seat themselves, serve themselves from a lavish buffet, and leave as they are ready—in contrast to guests waiting for a host to seat them (usually at a number of small tables), then waiting for the server and the meal and the check. Larger conference centers,

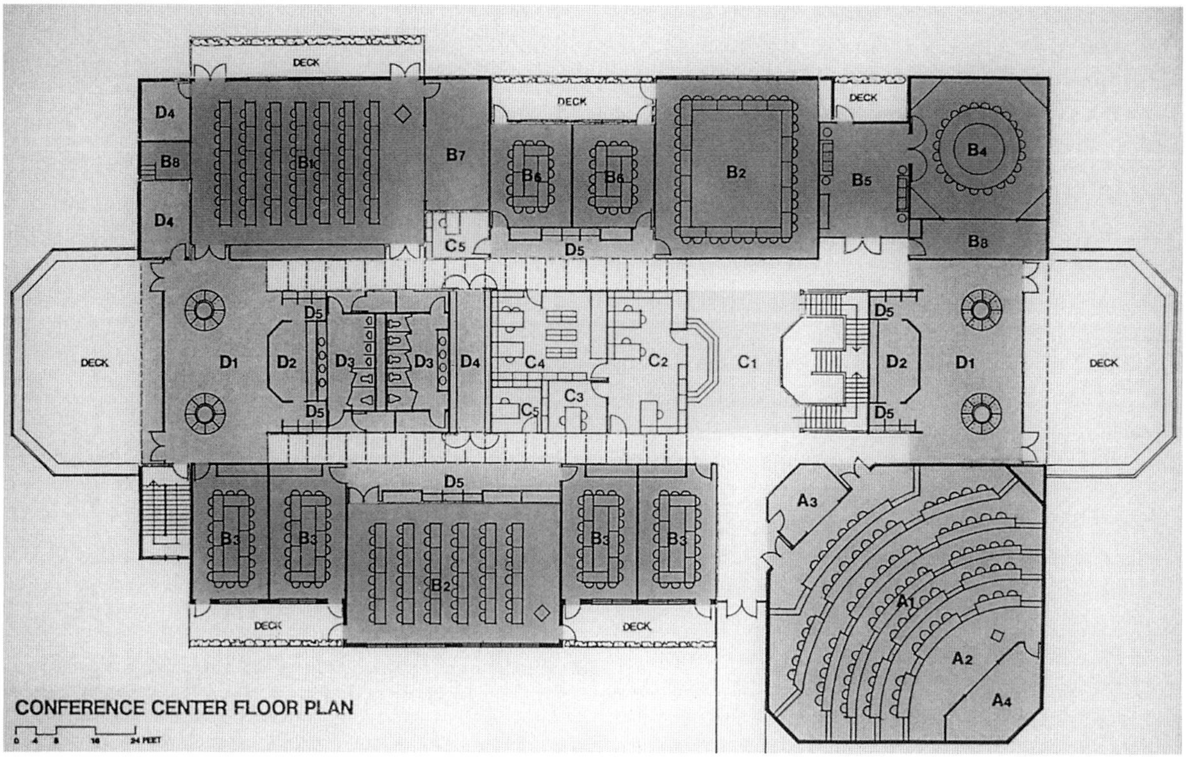

Accommodating the needs of the small meeting **Conference Center Prototype.** The plan illustrates the key relationships in the conference core: amphitheater, single-purpose meeting rooms of different sizes, and small breakout rooms all are clustered close to the conference service office, refreshment break lounges, and other public support areas (courtesy of The Hillier Group).

and most executive and resort properties, usually provide a more upscale specialty restaurant and, increasingly, an additional, more casual room with an informal snack menu.

The recreational areas are considerably more extensive than in most hotels: the typical conference center will include an indoor pool, health club with exercise and aerobics rooms, basic spa facilities, and, frequently, racquetball courts. University-based centers may have limited recreational amenities, given budgetary constraints and the knowledge that nearby on campus are myriad recreational facilities. Resort and some executive conference centers may have multiple golf courses, extensive tennis facilities, and other recreational amenities to rival the best in the country.

Planning for Operations

Equally important to the success of a conference or meeting are the types of services that the conference center provides: a conference coordinator assists the meeting planner with arrangements during the weeks leading up to the conference; the conference concierge provides the meeting participants with information, messages, and such business-center services as typing, faxing, copying, and express mail; audiovisual technicians not only provide and, if necessary, operate the audiovisual equipment, but they may even produce a custom videotape or CD-ROM for a particular session or as a record of the meeting; and many centers have their own closed-circuit television production studio, print shop, and photographic darkroom.

Most conference centers price their facilities based on the 'complete meeting package,' or CMP. This offers the meeting planner a single daily rate including lodging, three meals in the conference dining room, 24-hour use of conference rooms, refreshment breaks, and standard audiovisual support. The only extras are for special event dinners, such specific audiovisual requests as the production of a tape, and golf-green fees. The CMP also includes continuous refreshments, permitting the instructors increased flexibility in scheduling a break. The refreshment centers generally feature a wide selection of hot and cold beverages, pastries and fruit in the morning, and various snacks in the afternoon. This typical arrangement of the conference dining room and the continuous breaks necessitate fewer decisions by the meeting planner in terms of cost, schedule, and exact number of attendees. It also offers more flexibility and choice to the attendees themselves, and gives the operator greater certainty in planning staffing and food purchasing.

Significant Conference Centers

The end of the twentieth century saw the development of many fine conference centers representing the categories described in this chapter, which can be used as models for future development.

Palisades Executive Conference Center, Palisades, New York

The Palisades center sprawls over 100 acres (40.5 ha) on a wooded site north of New York City. It was built originally by IBM as a customer education center, a facility where the computer company could train and update users of major IBM systems. Now open to the public, its 50,000 ft^2 (4,650 m^2) of conference space include a main auditorium with rear-screen projection for up to 650 people, 24 additional meeting rooms, plus 34 breakout rooms. Major spaces include three multimedia amphitheaters for 65–95 people with touch-screen controls and response keypads, another dozen rooms with fixed tables for 20–60 people, two computer labs, and smaller flexible meeting rooms. Ten elegant, glass-enclosed refreshment pavilions overlook a large pond in the center of the site.

The 206 guestrooms are organized along wide, multistory galleries in a serpentine structure somewhat removed from the rest of the complex. The single-occupancy rooms feature a wood-grille divider between the bed area and the dressing room and all are equipped with personal computers. The Palisades Executive Conference Center is the largest such facility of its size, with 2,090 ft^2 (194 m^2) per guestroom, or double the total space of many conference-oriented properties and triple the space of many full-service hotels. The project is beautifully sited and detailed, with stone, metal, and wood trim throughout the lobby, dining and lounge areas, recreational center, conference and training core, and guestroom building.

The suburban executive conference center **Palisades Executive Conference Center, Palisades, New Jersey.** Originally constructed to house training programs for IBM corporate customers, the Palisades center features 13 amphitheater and dedicated case study rooms among its total of 59 meeting and breakout rooms. The sprawling U-shaped campus places guestrooms and recreational amenities in one wing, hotel services (lobby, food and beverage, administration) in a middle section, and conference and training spaces in the third, each focused outward to the landscaped grounds and pond. The meeting space includes ten refreshment pavilions, offering brightly sunlit spaces to counter the windowless meeting environments.

Resort at Squaw Creek, Squaw Valley, California

The year-round conference resort is located near the former Olympic site in Squaw Valley, California, with spectacular mountain views rising beyond the valley golf course. Other resort amenities include three swimming pools, a major tennis complex, executive fitness center, ice-skating rink, horseback riding, mountain biking, and cross-country skiing. In mid-2000 the resort opened a newly expanded 10,000 ft^2 (930 m^2) health club and luxury spa with an exercise area, new locker rooms with a private dry sauna, ten massage/treatment rooms, a variety of custom treatments including mud wraps and water therapy, and a lounge where spa guests may relax before and after their treatments.

The ski resort conference center **Resort at Squaw Creek Olympic Valley, California.** High in the Sierras near Lake Tahoe, the Squaw Creek resort overlooks the ski runs used for the 1960 Winter Olympics. These and other recreational amenities (golf, tennis, fitness center/spa) offer substantial benefits to conference attendees, who seek 'leisure' activities to complement the 'learning' and 'living' aspects of a several-day meeting. The guestroom suites, restaurants and lounges, and two floors of high-quality meeting space all are oriented towards the spectacular mountain views.

These recreational amenities support the resort's 403 guestrooms, more than half of which are suites, and 33,000 ft^2 (3,065 m^2) of conference space organized on two floors. The lobby level includes two major ballrooms and the lower level ten meeting rooms. The meeting facilities feature rear and front screen projection, audio conferencing, and state-of-the-art video production capabilities. Permanent refreshment kiosks and other conference support amenities are located throughout the two floors. Food and beverage operations include five outlets from the three-meal conference dining room to Italian, steakhouse, and deli offerings and lounges.

Guests arrive at a porte cochere tucked between the lobby and a sheer cliff and enter into a lobby featuring a massive stone fireplace and groups of overscaled clusters of soft seating. Conference attendees gather in the lobby, adjoining lounge, and nearby terraces which cascade in levels to the swimming pool and outdoor grill. The guestrooms, in a separate dark glass structure that reflects the Sierra Nevada peaks, are reached by an outdoor street of shops that feature resort clothing and souvenirs. The typical one-bedroom suites are creatively designed with an angled wall to make the most use of the 450 ft^2 (42 m^2) space, the living room becoming wider to accommodate seating and expanses of window overlooking the mountains, while the bedroom narrows from an oversized bathroom at the corridor to a small window seat on the outside wall.

The resort retreat conference center **Brasstown Valley Resort, Young Harris, Georgia.** Nestled in the Blue Ridge Mountains not far from Atlanta, the mountain-style resort is crafted from local stone and timber. The 106-room main lodge, containing meeting and banquet facilities and health club, is surrounded by eight four-bedroom cottages. Developers worked closely with environmental and Native American organizations and agencies to assure the minimum impact on the mountain site.

Brasstown Valley Resort, Young Harris, Georgia

Located high in the Blue Ridge Mountains of Georgia, Brasstown Valley is a 134-room conference resort dedicated to environmental preservation. The developers worked hand-in-hand with state and federal agencies as well as Indian alliances to preserve wetlands, archaeological sites, and animal habitats. The lodge architecture features a great room with a 72 ft (22 m) stone fireplace and vaulted ceilings exposing massive pine beams. Eight four-bedroom log cabins accentuate the mountain setting with fireplaces and porches. The resort includes 14,000 ft^2 (1,300 m^2) of flexible meeting space including a 300-person ballroom, a 75-seat tiered amphitheater with rear projection, six conference rooms and two boardrooms. Many meeting groups use the cabin 'great rooms' for small meetings or breakout sessions. Recreational amenities include a Scottish-links-style golf course, four illuminated tennis courts, and a complete fitness center with indoor/outdoor pool, along with such additional activities as hiking, rock climbing, mountain biking, white water rafting, and horseback riding. The mountain lodge perfectly fits the setting while the interior design, conference facilities, and services provide a sophisticated meeting environment.

Rough Creek Lodge, Glen Rose, Texas

Rough Creek Lodge opened in 1998 as an upscale Texas executive conference center retreat and resort. Sited on 11,000 acres (4,450 ha) of rolling hill and lake country 90 minutes from Dallas/Fort Worth airport, the working cattle ranch offers a remarkable setting for upper-level executive strategic meetings. Focus groups determined the need for comfortable conference rooms with state-of-the-art presentation technology in a secluded setting plus other amenities: myriad leisure and recreational choices, fine dining, and personal service.

The design evokes the natural feel of the surrounding terrain and incorporates native limestone, 60 ft (18 m) high beamed ceilings, and polished wood, wrought iron, and leather accents. Guestrooms and suites are furnished for the business executive with oversized desk, data connections, and three telephones. The deluxe rooms have balconies overlooking the lake and lavish four-fixture bathrooms. The four meeting and board rooms can accommodate groups up to 100 people, but generally attract smaller strategic planning meetings, team-building sessions, and executive retreats.

The luxury nature-retreat conference center **Rough Creek Lodge, Glen Rose, Texas.** With the tag-line 'executive conference center retreat and resort,' the developer positions the lodge to attract the highest-level of the corporate retreat market, in addition to sportspeople and leisure guests who appreciate nature—and every comfort. The exclusive 39-room retreat combines indigenous materials—native limestone, wood timbers, and leather—to create a finely detailed yet rustic setting (see C-19).

AT&T Learning Center, Basking Ridge, New Jersey

Set on a 35 acre (14 ha) campus in north-central New Jersey, the AT&T Learning Center offers a comfortable conference environment utilizing much of AT&T's advanced communications technology. The center was built to consolidate and replace several earlier training and conference facilities that AT&T had operated in the area but which had become obsolete and uneconomical to operate. The 171 guestrooms include 16 spacious suites and feature state-of-the-art systems for video and voice conferences and Internet connectivity. Ten business rooms are equipped with computers, printer/fax/copier, and entertainment systems.

The main conference complex is organized with prefunction spaces overlooking a central courtyard. The 24 conference rooms include a 4,600 ft^2 (425 m^2) ballroom and 84-seat tiered amphitheater, equipped with a $5 million audiovisual infrastructure and equipment inventory encompassing fiber-optic technology, interactive meeting capability, videoteleconferencing, and rear-screen projection. The learning center offers a 170-seat dining room with an exhibition kitchen, additional private dining rooms, and a relaxed lounge with billiards and Inter-

The corporate training center **AT&T Learning Center, Basking Ridge, New Jersey**. Communications, pharmaceutical, financial services, and other major industries with needs to continually retrain and develop staff favor developing their own corporate training centers. AT&T consolidated several New Jersey area facilities into a new high-tech center, fully equipped with the top video and data systems, and all the amenities of a first-class hotel. For efficient operation, automated service kiosks provide meals for groups in lounge seating areas convenient to their seminars.

net access. A complete sports complex includes tennis courts, fitness center, indoor pool and whirlpool, sun deck, and a sports court with basketball and volleyball.

Emory Conference Center Hotel, Emory University, Atlanta, Georgia

The new conference center at Emory University, with 198 guestrooms and 20,000 ft^2 (1,850 m^2) of conference space, was designed to meet the specific needs of the business school and continuing education needs of the medical school as well as nearby medical research organizations. Opened in 1995, the center is nestled into a forested hollow on the edge of the campus, where the dining and conference spaces on the lower floor easily flow out onto landscaped terraces. The meeting space itself is very compact, with amphitheaters for 70 and 230 surrounded by a ring

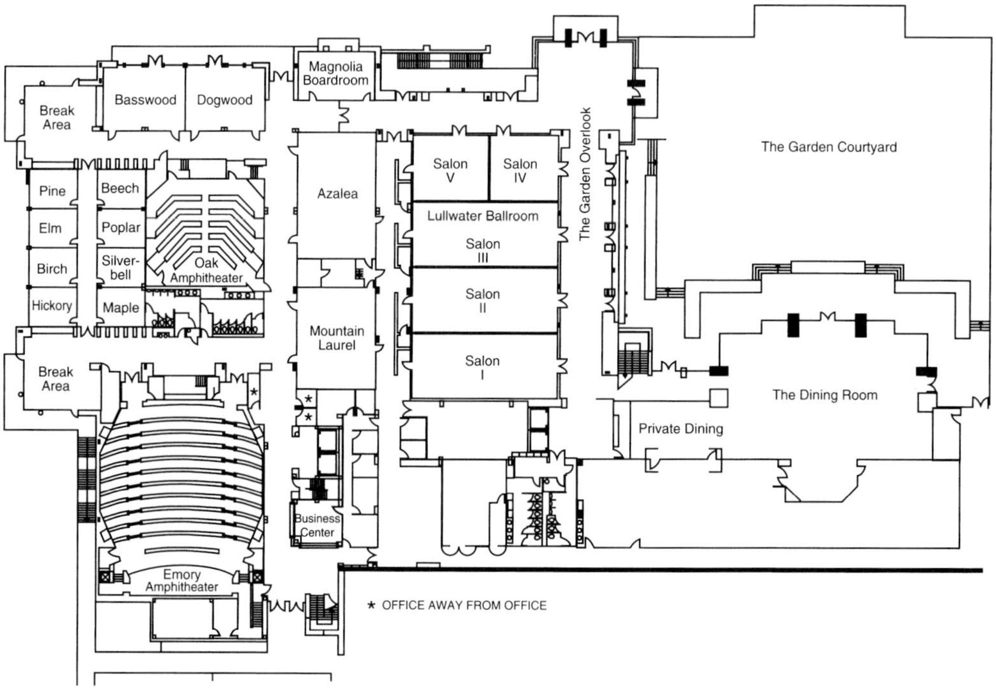

The university conference center **Emory Conference Center Hotel, Atlanta, Georgia.** Adjoining the Emory campus is the headquarters for the Centers for Disease Control, one impetus for a facility to cater not only to university conferences but to major medical research symposia. Accommodating university and corporate business, conference and training, and medical meetings, the center features a strong organization of the public levels with clear separation between the ballroom, conference, and food and beverage activities on the lower floor. Arts and crafts motifs appear consistently in the choice of furnishings and decorative details.

of 13 conference and breakout rooms. Refreshment break areas are located in glassy corner pavilions, which encourage casual conversation and networking.

The center is designed with a strong arts and crafts motif incorporating vaulted ceilings, flagstone floors, Stickley-style furnishings, and period lighting fixtures which give the property a comfortable and gracious character. Architecture, interiors, and landscape all contribute to provide a restful retreat atmosphere within the bustle of a world-class university.

Kingsgate Conference Center, University of Cincinnati, Ohio

The University of Cincinnati opened its 206-room conference center located between the medical and main academic campuses in 1999. Hotel guests arrive at a porte cochere located on a raised terrace overlooking a major landscaped campus space. The center is extremely well zoned, with the main lobby floor containing all the food and beverage functions, including a 5,350 ft^2 (500 m^2) subdivisible ballroom, and a lower level providing all the conference spaces. Day attendees enter directly into the conference foyer from either a separate car drop off or the parking garage or, alternatively, as would overnight guests, from the lobby by descending the grand stair or hotel elevators.

The project includes 23 conference rooms of different types—two-tiered amphitheaters, a range of large and small meeting rooms, board rooms and breakout rooms—each one carefully designed to enhance the meeting activities by providing high ceilings, flexible lighting, permanent audiovisual systems, comfortable furniture, and so forth. The conference rooms, many of which have natural light and views across the campus, are arranged around three different refreshment break areas to encourage networking and continued discussion by the meeting attendees. Additional conference support functions are located immediately adjacent to the meeting area. The Cincinnati center is a model for university projects: well-integrated with the campus; clear separation of hotel, banquet, and conference areas; well-equipped and detailed single-purpose meeting rooms including amphitheaters and flexible flat floored rooms; substantial amounts of both public- and service-oriented conference support; and study rooms on the residential floors.

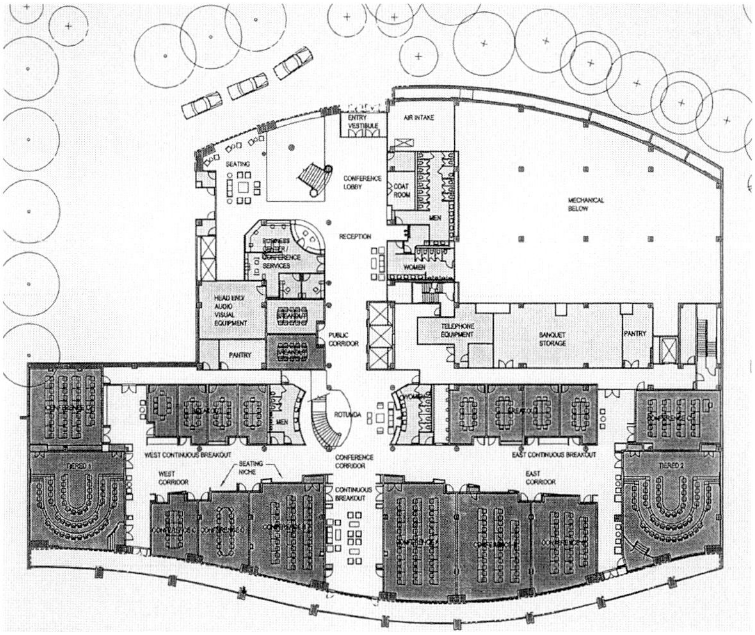

The blended campus conference center **Kingsgate Conference Center, University of Cincinnati, Ohio.** Cincinnati held a design competition for a three-building complex on a new site between the academic campus and several university-related hospitals. This solution shows the conference center organized along a pedestrian promenade connecting the two, with hotel activities on one level and the conference areas segregated to a lower level, free from distraction. The plan identifies the separate conference entrance for day-business and the full complement of support functions (audiovisual, storage, pantries, break areas, etc.) necessary for a successful center.

Howard Hughes Medical Institute, Chevy Chase, Maryland

This headquarters and conference center is located on 22 acres (9 ha) in a residential area outside Washington, DC. The handsome campus of interconnected brick and stone structures, designed to preserve much of the wooded character of the site, combines three main elements: office building, conference and dining wing, and residential houses. The conference program includes an auditorium, five meeting rooms, many lounge and reception rooms, and a dining room. The 75 guestrooms are organized both in the main building and in four separate guest houses, creating a strong residential scale and character. The office and conference wings incorporate a number of terraces for informal gathering and social functions (see p. 136).

Legend

6 Service
7 Dining room
8 Dining terrace
9 Garden
10 Main hall
11 Living room
12 Auditorium
13 Meeting room
14 Conference center entrance
15 House

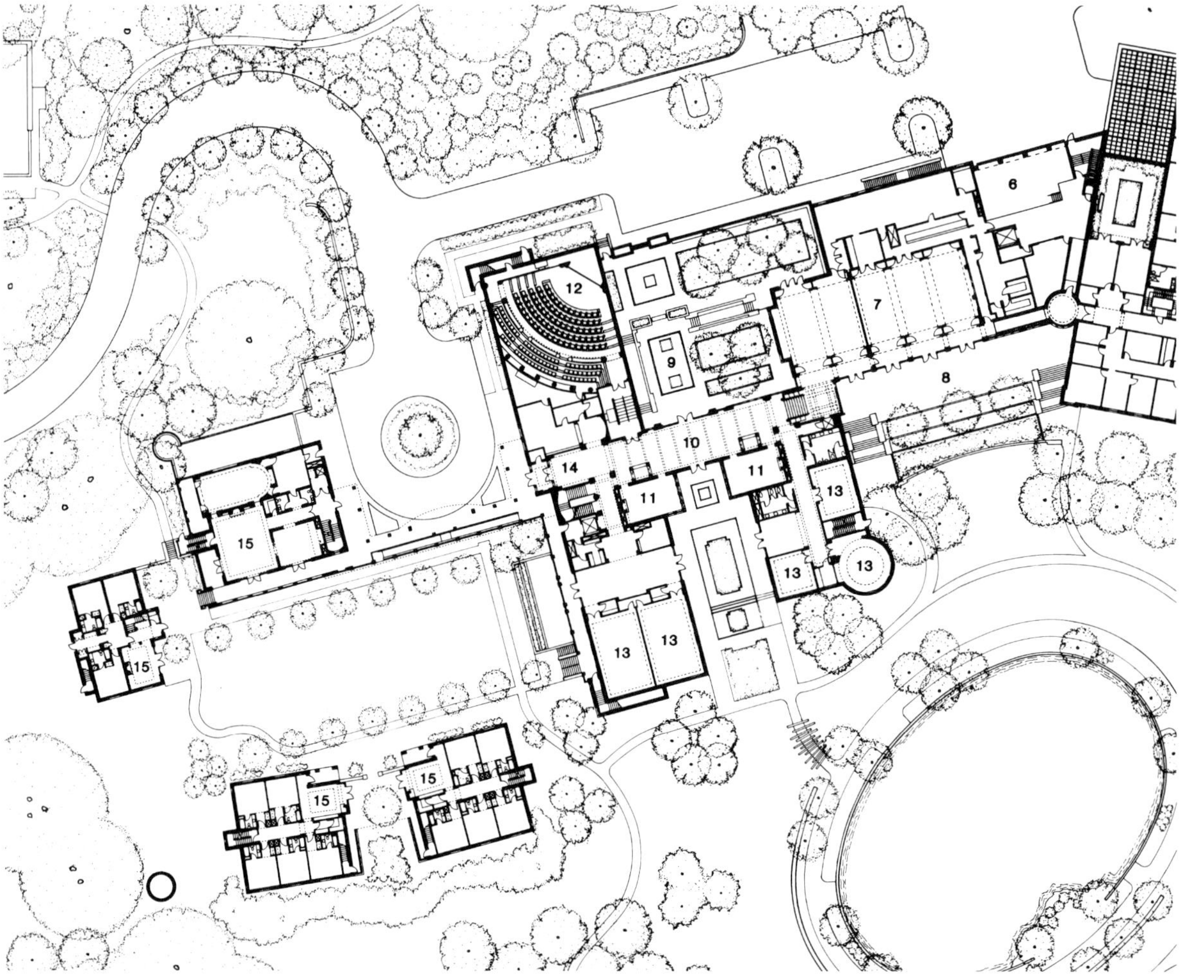

The medical research conference center **Howard Hughes Medical Institute, Chevy Chase, Maryland.** The HHMI provides a comfortable conference area adjoining its headquarters complex, including meeting rooms, amphitheater, and handsome lounges, library and other gathering spaces. Some guestrooms are on the second floor, but most are in cottages of 7–11 rooms located on a landscaped lawn. In creating a series of interconnecting low-rise buildings the architects carefully controlled the scale and architectural detailing of the center (see p. 136).

Trends

The conference center industry is undergoing changes as fast as any lodging segment largely because of the need to meet the dynamic demands of competitive business.

- *Joint-venture conference centers.* Hybrid centers should appear as corporations, government, and education look for collaborative opportunities. The historic Biltmore Hotel in Coral Gables, Florida, opened in mid-2000 a conference center on its resort grounds, in a joint venture with the city and University of Florida. It adds 40,000 ft^2 (3,700 m^2) of meeting space including two tiered amphitheaters and 15 other conference rooms. One emphasis is expected to be conferences focused on doing business in Latin America, in addition to Florida and regional government conferences, executive education programs, and degree and nondegree courses.
- *Not-for-profit centers.* The number of not-for-profit centers should continue to expand and will become more upscale. The relatively simple centers run by scouting or religious organizations, for example, are being surpassed by first-class properties developed by organizations with a range of educational, social, or other specific orientations. For example, the National Arbor Day Foundation in 1999 expanded its Lied Conference Center in Nebraska—dedicated to environmental stewardship—to 144 guestrooms and 14,000 ft^2 (1,300 m^2) of meeting space. The AH&MA has honored the center for 'a culture of integrating environmental management practices that improve everyday operations and the bottom line, while maintaining quality service and meeting guest expectations.' The center features a wood-burning plant for heating and cooling and is open as an educational demonstration site.
- *Convention hotels add dedicated conference centers.* In the 1990s several major convention hotels added or renovated space to create small higher-quality conference centers. This should continue with many more hotels and resorts segmenting their function space into larger convention areas with exhibit rooms, ballrooms, and multipurpose meeting rooms versus separate conference centers, in another floor or wing, dedicated to groups of 20–100.
- *University projects.* More and more universities are investing in conference centers to better control availability of rooms and the quality of the overnight and meeting experience. In addition to providing basic lodging, business and other professional schools need executive centers; public colleges and universities have the mission to offer continuing education programs to the community; and all institutions attempt to keep in touch with alumni and prospective donors. University projects should continue to grow in size: where most projects now are in the 100–200 room range, the next decade should see this increase up to 300 rooms at larger campuses.

The serviced condominium and luxury hotel overlooking New York Harbor **The Ritz-Carlton Battery Park, New York.** Designed by The Polshek Partnership with Gary Edward Handel & Associates, the 38-story tower rising at the southern tip of Manhattan with spectacular views of the harbor includes a 300-room hotel in the 13-story base and 215 residential units, with full luxury-hotel services, in the tower.

brated writers, artists, and performers: Thomas Wolfe, Dylan Thomas, Brendan Behan, Mark Twain, Tennessee Williams, Sarah Bernhardt, Arthur Miller, Jackson Pollock, Bob Dylan, Leonard Cohen, Tom Waits, and Sid Vicious. Many were said to have drawn a special inspiration while living at the Chelsea Hotel. Arthur C. Clark and Stanley Kubrick chose a room at the Chelsea as their workshop when writing the screenplay for *2001: A Space Odyssey*.

Residential hotels reached their peak of fashion in major US cities during the 1920s with affluent celebrities, artists, and others who could afford to savor hotel services. Examples in New York City include the St. Moritz, Hampshire House, Ritz Tower, New Netherland (now the Sherry Netherland), and Hotel des Artistes. With a few exceptions, such as the Pierre, these hotels had small exclusive lobbies and limited public space, setting themselves apart from the grand public rooms of hotels that primarily catered to transient guests. What these hotels lacked in their public spaces they made up for in the large, opulent private suites in the tower. Considered one of the last gasps of the Great Boom, The Car-

resemble the notable twin-tower residential buildings that line Central Park. However, it is actually a single tower that rises to a height of 625 ft (190 m) over the 25-story base of transient hotel rooms and sumptuous public spaces. Service elevators thread through the base to the hotel's vast system of kitchens and back-of-house areas bringing services to the suites. Famous former residents include General Douglas MacArthur, the Duke of Windsor, Henry Kissinger, and President Herbert Hoover who, in 1931, delivered a radio address from the hotel on opening night.

Development and Planning Considerations

Condominium ownership with hotel services is more successfully filling the markets previously served by older models of residential hotels by providing the buyer with tax advantages and more favorable financing. In this respect the downtown hotel condominium parallels the advantages of resort condominiums in vacation areas.

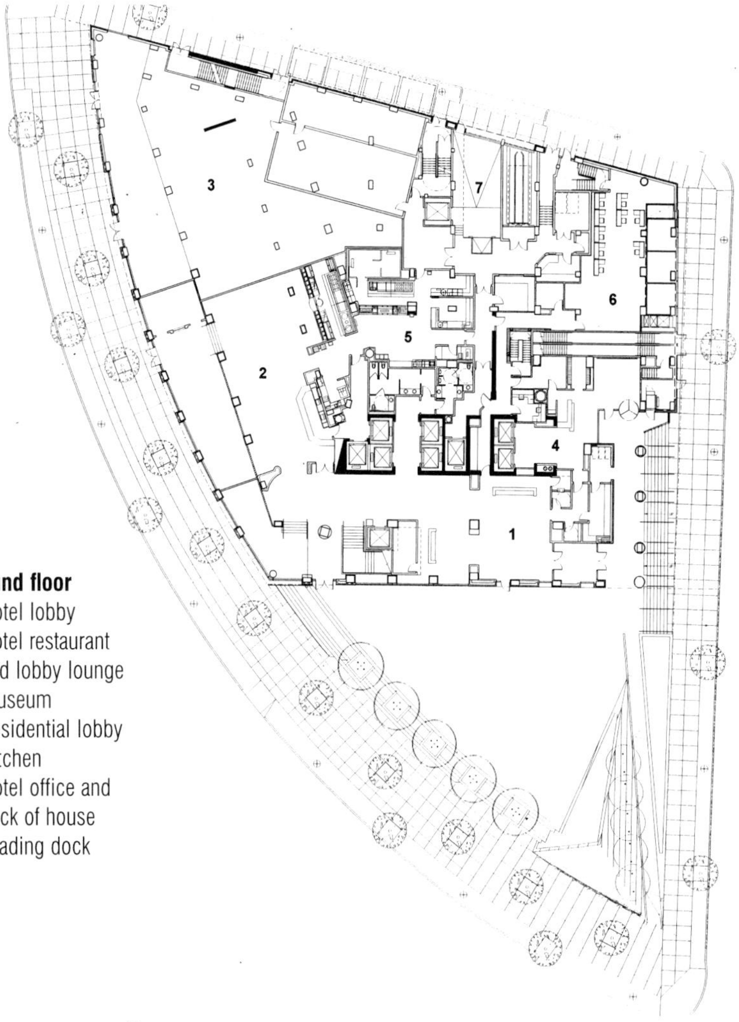

Ground floor
1 Hotel lobby
2 Hotel restaurant and lobby lounge
3 Museum
4 Residential lobby
5 Kitchen
6 Hotel office and back of house
7 Loading dock

(A)

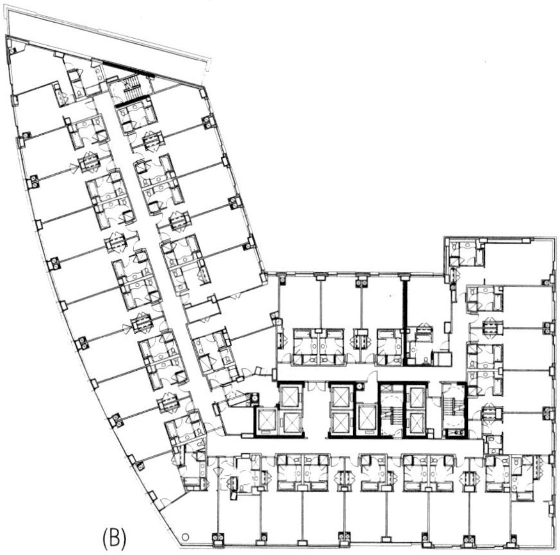

(B)

14th Floor
1 Fitness center
2 Spa
3 Changing room
4 Electrical room
5 Spa dining
6 Warming pantry
7 Serving pantry
8 Dining
9 Outdoor dining
10 Mechanical room

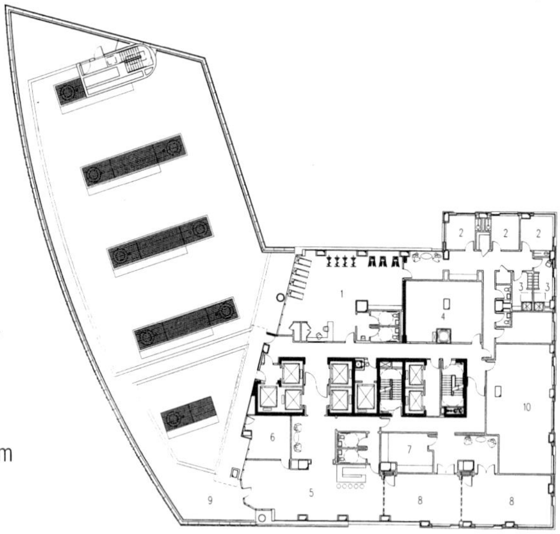

(C)

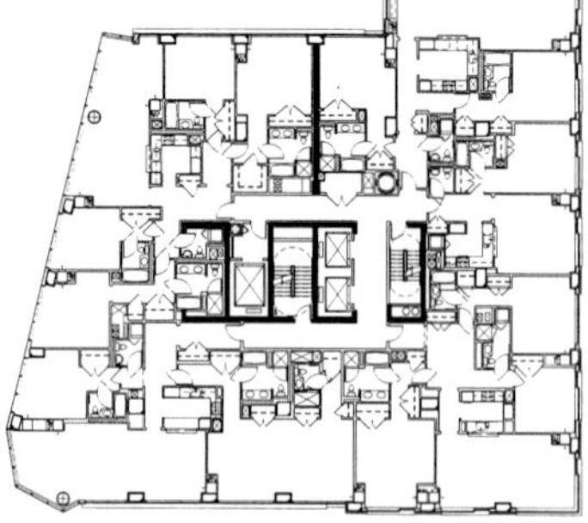

(D)

The integrated condominium and hotel tower **The Ritz-Carlton Battery Park, New York.** (A) The ground floor houses the new home of the Skyscraper Museum in addition to the hotel lobby, lounge and restaurant, and a small intimate residential lobby with a separate entrance. (B) The typical hotel levels include 35 keys laid out in a hybrid double-loaded slab and H-corridor tower configuration. (C) The fourteenth floor separates the hotel from the residential tower and includes a fitness center, restaurant, and outdoor dining terrace open to the public. (D) Residential tower floors, with units ranging from one to four bedrooms, share a common service elevator with the hotel (see p. 152).

But, most importantly, its financial structure will prove attractive to both residents and hotel owners for the following reasons: (1) the developers can help finance the hotel from the sale of the condominiums, thereby reducing the direct interest expense, including those during construction if the units are pre-sold; (2) condominium owners can take normal personal tax write-offs for interest and real estate taxes or depreciation on rental property; and (3) the hotel can manage the condominium portion more efficiently for the owners while gaining additional revenue for the hotel company.

Christopher Jeffries and Millennium Partners are developers in projects worth $2 billion that combine condominiums and hotels in mixed-use complexes in San Francisco, Washington, DC, Boston, New York, and Miami. Joining forces with the luxury chains Four Seasons and Ritz-Carlton on separate projects, the developers are taking advantage of a robust economy and a shortage of luxury housing in the largest US cities to reintroduce and expand on the 'hotel and towers' concept initiated by the Waldorf=Astoria 70 years ago. These mixed-use projects integrate high-end condominiums, retail/entertainment centers, exclusive sports clubs and, in the case of the Miami Four Seasons Hotel and Tower, timeshare units and commercial office space.

As with other mixed-use projects, the components of the complex benefit synergistically in their interaction with other components, each adding value to the project as a whole (see Chapter 12). But the key to the success of the development is the inclusion of a five-star hotel chain. For the Four Seasons Miami project the condominiums are expected to sell for a minimum of 25 percent premium over the top of the market because of their association with a luxury hotel and the services they provide. Condominium sales are further bolstered by the inclusion of a premier sports and fitness facility. The hotel gets incremental revenue from condominium users, sports club patrons, and office tenants. Hotel guests also have access to a 100,000 ft^2 (9,290 m^2) fitness facility and spa rather than the hotel having to provide its own facility. Office rents of 10 percent above market are projected because of both the image of the building and services provided.

Foreseeing the potential value of a residential component in the hotel, the developers of the RIHGA Royal Hotel in New York directed the design to accommodate a future conversion of the upper floors to residential service-apartments. For this purpose a 30 ft (9.1 m) rear yard was maintained as required by zoning for residential use and kitchen exhaust ducts were installed over the bar units so they could be converted to kitchenettes. A separate high-rise elevator bank served larger suites including two- and three-bedroom units. The popular success of the hotel as an all-suite property has made this conversion unnecessary.

The mixed-use condominium and hotel tower **Four Seasons Hotel and Tower, San Francisco, California.** Serving as an important link between the north and south of Market Street districts in downtown, the 40-story tower combines a luxury hotel, residential condominiums with hotel services, a state-of-the-art health club, and 160,000 ft^2 (16,720 m^2) of retail space. The project represents the first major introduction of luxury residences to the Yerba Buena Art District.

The luxury all-suite hotel unit **RIHGA Royal, New York.** This typical suite, featuring bay windows with their enhanced views and natural sunlight, as well as its spacious well-studied design layout, details, and décor, based on the expert advice of scores of consultants, proved to be well worth the concentrated studies (see suite plan, p. 164, and p. C-6 for a further view).

All-suite and Extended-stay Hotels

8

The final decades of the twentieth century saw rapid development of the overlapping all-suite and extended-stay concepts. Both initially featured one-bedroom suites but the extended-stay properties now add a full kitchenette to one- and two-bedroom configurations. These concepts continue to evolve, responding as quickly and efficiently as any hotel segment can to the era's major market megatrends:

- unquestioned preference for residential style and comfort
- increased demand for efficient two-room suites, with full height partitions between living and sleeping quarters and flexibility to accommodate families as well as business needs
- parallel popularity, depending on price points, of efficient mini-suites featuring full kitchen appliances without full separation between living and sleeping areas.

By the end of the twentieth century extended-stay hotels represented 4 percent of the US market. In the final 5 years they doubled their market share, customer demand fueling annual growth at a rate of 34 percent. In addition, extended-stay properties typically average 10 percent higher occupancy than the rest of the market, further benefiting from their below-average operating costs to generate even stronger returns. All-suite hotels also outperform the lodging market, although to a lesser degree than extended-stay properties, depending on the speed at which the extraordinary demand for extended-stay hotels is saturated.

But, even more importantly, the continued development of both the all-suite and extended-stay hotel concepts adds much needed flexibility to the residential housing inventory. Locations with rapid population and employment growth, high-tech industries, and high rates of inbound migration exhibit strong demand in the extended-stay segment because of industry retraining programs, extended business assignments, and corporate relocations—including family visits.

Planning and Design Considerations

Actually, the construction cost of the two-room suite often is only about 20 percent more than for a typical hotel guestroom. The larger suite has the same bathroom and single heating/cooling unit cost as does a guestroom; the main cost factor is the minor expense of the additional floor, walls, roof, and carpet. The additional capital cost is balanced, however, by reducing the public spaces to compensate for the more spacious suites and by a somewhat higher room rate, based on the highly enhanced suite product. The suite is popular with the business traveler as well as with families, who otherwise might need two separate guestrooms, costing considerably more.

All-suite hotels often are planned with the guest units on upper floors organized around an atrium. Generally, the bedrooms face outside and the living room faces the atrium corridor. It should have a large window, appropriately draped for privacy and double-glazed for soundproofing. Although most codes allow interior living rooms to be built without windows, this approach does not satisfy guests. Interior rooms along the atrium are popular and are considered safe in emergencies, with sprinklers placed on each side of the atrium window, often subdivided for a residential feel with mullions enclosed between the double glass to simplify cleaning.

The typical suite unit consists of a separate living/dining room, bedroom, and bathroom. The living/dining room often includes a wet-bar, mini-refrigerator, microwave, and coffee maker built into a wall unit or credenza in the dining area close to the plumbing riser for economy. Compared with a king-bedded guestroom with a hide-a-bed sofa, the two-room suite requires only a few additions: somewhat more lounge seating, a small conference/dining table, and a second television. The convertible sofa and 42 in. (1.05 m) diameter table seating four are essential in the living/dining room

Embassy Suites Hotel, Battery Park City, New York

The largest all-suite chain, Embassy Suites, recently opened a major hotel near Wall Street in lower Manhattan. Embassy Suites' original design concept, launched in the mid-1980s, attracted diverse markets from mid-scale to luxury and family to business. Its atrium design proves superbly suited to mixed-use developments such as this project by architects Perkins Eastman, a 463-unit suite hotel linked by a skylit 14-story atrium to a major entertainment and retail center. The complex boasts a 16-screen multiplex theater, 90,000 ft^2 (8,370 m^2) of retail shops, and a 30,000 ft^2 (2,790 m^2) spa, serving the World Financial Center area.

Variations

Developers and operators around the world are experimenting with a variety of all-suite and extended-stay projects. Radisson Hotels and Suites launched the Atrium Plaza, a 12-story, 456-suite property in the coastal resort area of Beirut, Lebanon. It offers a 200-store mall with restaurants, lounges, a movie multiplex, and global business center. Remington Suites in North Dallas, Texas, incorporates an array of lively atrium amenities including an adjoining pool and health spa in its new 250-suite prototype. Peter Blyth, President of Radisson Development, observes: 'Having an atrium under the same roof as the suite guestrooms is unbeatable in attracting four of the most lucrative markets for suites: corporate executives, weekenders, extended-stay families, and business flex-office guests.' (See Appendix C, Hotel Classifications, for major all-suite and extended-stay chains.)

Residential Trends

Along with other residential markets, such as the vacation ownership and condominium resorts discussed in Chapters 4 and 7, the new extended-stay hotels mark the entry of hospitality management into virtually every residential sphere from day-care to senior assisted residences, villas to high-rise mixed-use ultratels, and super-luxury to budget markets. In the 1980s researchers felt that historic circumstances may have created pent-up demand for all-suite and extended-stay developments. Prior to the advent of hotels, the earliest travelers received their first impressions of the 'room at the inn' from monastic inns. While improvements were made as hotels evolved, the minimal guestroom remained more like a monastery than a residence. In fact, the single-room concept was never really challenged until the 1980s, even for hotels that catered to families or the most affluent guests. This major anomaly might never have surfaced if not for the following serendipitous event: during a recession, unsold condominiums were rented in desperation, as hotel suites. They were expected to appeal mainly to long-term guests, but with living, dining, bedrooms, and full kitchen, not surprisingly, these economically priced suites attracted all types of travelers, including many overnight walk-ins knowing a good buy when they saw one.

From that chance beginning, over the next two decades the all-suite and extended-stay sectors enjoyed one of the highest growth rates in the industry. Also, with some hotels introducing weekly and monthly rates and more expansive villa units, offshoots of the original extended-stay hotels created more sumptuous variations far beyond their far-sighted roots. Among the most significant examples are Staybridge Suites, with full kitchenettes in studio units of 355 ft^2 (33 m^2), one-bedroom suites of 502 ft^2 (46.7 m^2) and two bedroom suites of 775 ft^2 (72.1 m^2), and Summerfield Suites, with an ingenious two-bedroom configuration which easily subdivides into a one-bedroom-plus-studio unit, in the upscale category.

The greater average length of stay—for some suite hotels more than double that of competing nearby properties—indicates the success of the concept. When asked by a guest for the number of monthly customers, one frontdesk agent was overheard to sigh, 'Many of our guests who checked in at the opening over a year ago are still with us.'

The most unique example of the trend is the super-luxury Trump International Tower in New York, designed as a partial extended-stay hotel, with impeccably furnished units, views over Central Park, and every conceivable service. At the opposite end of the spectrum, flush with its hard won position as king of the cost-effective operators, French-owned Accor's Motel 6 brand launched Studio 6, a super-budget extended-stay prototype. It features a room of 290 ft^2 (27 m^2), a fully equipped kitchen including utensils and cookware, phones with data ports, and other amenities desired by both family and price-sensitive business travelers. Accor's target is the 'five-night super-budget' guest; with three of the world's most economical brands—Formule I, Motel 6, and Studio 6—Accor does more than any other operator to serve the moderate wage-earner.

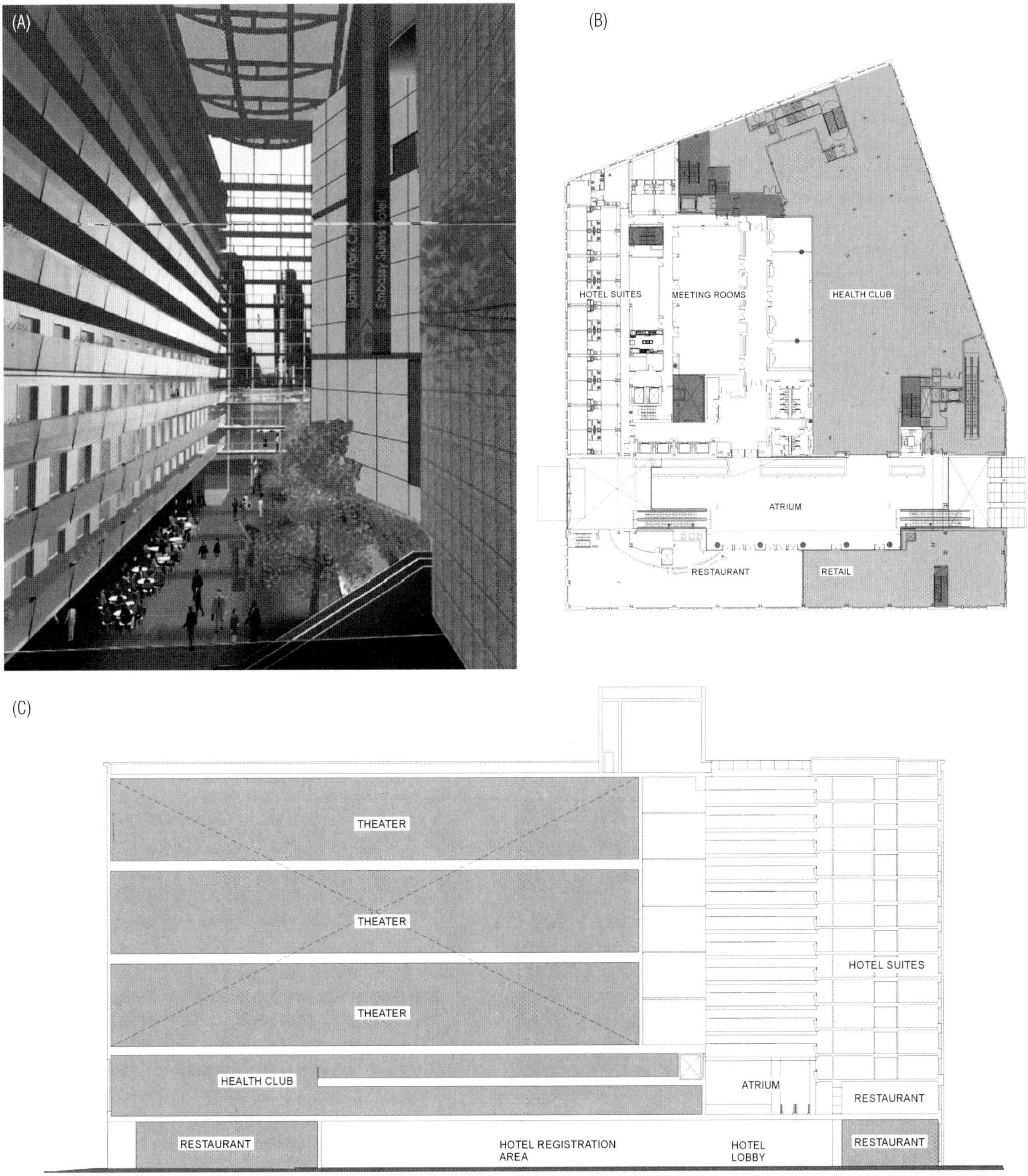

The community all-suite hotel **Embassy Suites Hotel, Battery Park City, New York.** (A) While all-suite hotels absorb short-term demand for residential living accommodations based on such leading megatrends as frequent career shifts and longer family and senior stays, they boast the potential outreach of their lobby atriums to link them to public services and amenities. In this example, a multilevel through-block arcade conveniently links the affluent neighborhood with a major private health club, a high-end shopping mall, three levels of multiplex theaters, and an off-Broadway playhouse within or attached to the hotel structure. (B) Plan showing links among community, hotel, and commercial areas. (C) Section identifying the neighborhood entertainment and shopping areas in the hotel structure.

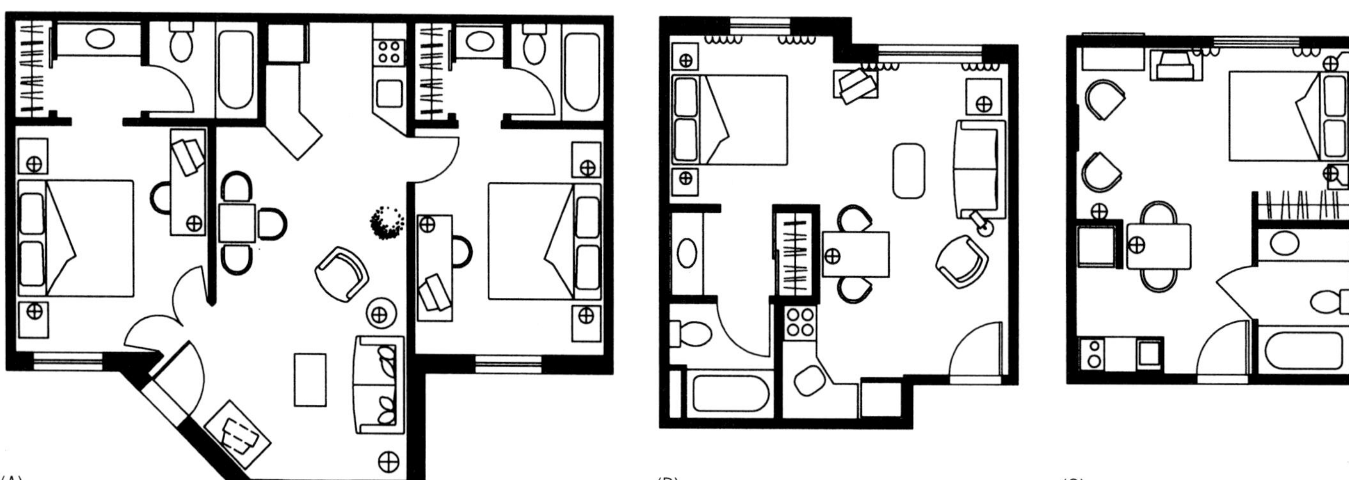

(A) (B) (C)

The extended-stay hotel unit **Extended-stay prototype plans.** (A) Summerfield Suites typical upscale suite provides an ingeniously efficient plan with full-height partitioning of bedrooms. The two-bedroom plan with separate bathrooms, desks, and TVs can be shared by two different guests with significant savings. (B) Extended StayAmerica typical mid-rate extended-stay suite offers a variety of plans, typically without enclosed bedrooms. (C) Studio 6 typical budget unit is the most economical and efficient plan, with less floor area than most economy-hotel studio rooms, yet providing full kitchen appliances and creating the leading perception of value in the field.

- Developers of extended-stay hotels may dispute whether their product is more like an apartment or a hotel. But for those who live there it's 'home suite home'!

- The merging of Embassy Suites, the leading all-suite chain, into the more internationally positioned Hilton brand, should launch the largest export of a US lodging concept, primarily to Europe and the Middle East, where the early Hilton International hotels were built in the 1950s and 1960s.

- New brands, recognizing the popularity of the concept, will continue to explore ever-smaller prototype units, less than 300 ft^2 (27.9 m^2), carefully designed to provide additional amenities in a minimum space.

- Urban areas worldwide should see new luxury mixed-use residential all-suite hotels, individually designed for the market, offering the business traveler spectacular rooms with every comfort and technological amenity.

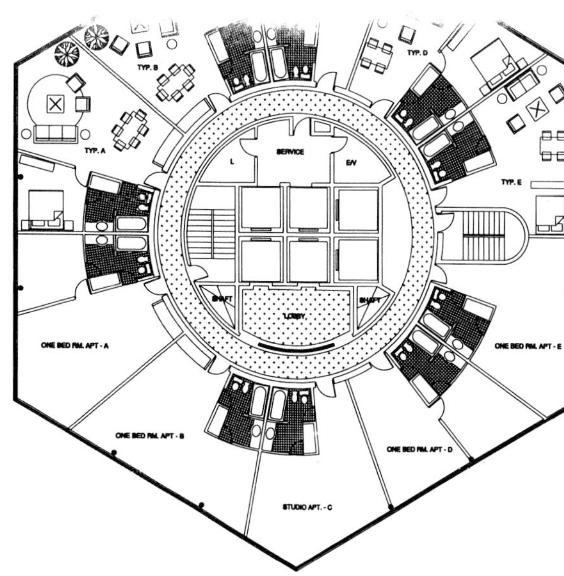

The all-suite high-rise hotel central core floor plan **Al Ain Center, Abu Dhabi, UAE**. To reduce land requirements this high-rise all-suite prototype by Ahuja Priya Architects reduces the amount of perimeter walls as well as structural and mechanical costs. The suites are more varied and appealing by breaking out of the typical box mold of other hotels (see pp. 2, 238 and 358 for conceptual views of the public areas).

The royal suite at the super-luxury hotel **The Lanesborough, London, England.** The Royal Suite, with three bedrooms, a drawing room, a dining room, and its own kitchen, is decorated in Regency-era furnishings and décor recalling a nineteenth-century London townhouse. With floor-to-ceiling windows offering superb views of Buckingham Palace across the street, the suite is a favorite of celebrities and heads of state.

Super-luxury Hotels 9

At The Lanesborough in London a gentleman arrived not long ago, having forgotten some important personal items at his previous destination in Paris. The guest discovered this before he was due to leave on a flight that evening. He declared that these items had to be retrieved before he left, so management dispatched the personal butler—provided by the hotel—to Paris, who returned with the precious cargo with time to spare.

Impeccable service, urbane management, sumptuous décor, and elegant architecture are the hallmarks of a rare breed of small super-luxury hotels that uniquely cater to royalty, foreign dignitaries, captains of industry, celebrities, and cultural leaders. The most prestigious major chains have endeavored for decades to emulate, but have rarely been able to accomplish, the sophisticated charm and posh accommodations of the world's most exclusive closely managed hotels. Such hotels provide a private world of rare and refined beauty where the art of personal service is practiced with efficiency and aplomb.

As with any hotel that provides a high level of personalized service, the virtues and reputation of super-luxury hotels largely are dependent on the management style of the hotel owner and staff. The owner often is very well known to the hotel's elite clientele and a copy of the managing director's impressive resume sometimes can be found in the literature describing the most important features of the property. But, most often, the leading force on which the style of service is defined is by the ever-resourceful concierge. Erudite and multilingual, the concierge commands a carefully selected, highly trained professional staff to fulfill any guest requirement, no matter how capricious, with verve and flare. For example, a concierge in one deluxe hotel was called on to shop for and deliver an elaborate stereo system to the room of a famous conductor, who needed to rehearse for an upcoming performance.

It is not uncommon to find the staff at these hotels outnumbering guests by three to one. Some super-luxury hotels provide 24-hour personal butlers who, in addition to the more mundane duties of packing and unpacking or drawing baths, might be called on to hand deliver an important document across town, have a suit tailored for an important meeting, iron newspapers to prevent ink from rubbing off, or provide a stenographer for dictation at 2:00 in the morning. In addition to a personal butler, one European hotel provides its guests with a chauffeured Bentley.

Of course, the management staff must keep a detailed dossier on the predilections and idiosyncrasies of all repeat guests to know, for instance, that one guest sleeps until noon and must have a very quiet room shielded from morning sunlight or that another requires a special brand of pet food for her temperamental cat.

Perhaps the most important aspect of super-luxury accommodation is the privacy, discretion, high-level security, and inconspicuous service sought by its most distinguished and prestigious clientele. 'Our staff knows when it's appropriate to introduce two heads of state, or when they should blend into the Aubusson rugs,' says Dan Camp, president and managing director of The Carlyle in New York City.

Design Considerations

Most super-luxury hotels derive much of their opulent character from the superb historical buildings they occupy. In fact, many such as the Hotel de Crillon in Paris and Hotel Danieli in Venice inhabit national landmarks. Built in the eighteenth century on the Place de Concorde, Hotel de Crillon recently underwent an extravagant makeover orchestrated by celebrated French fashion designer Sonia Rykiel and architect Jean Lou Roubert under the auspices of the French National Landmark Commission. As a testament to Hotel de Crillon's magnificent origins, a replica of the Salon Duc de Crillon complete with a 19.7 ft (6 m) high ceiling, traditional hand-painted wooden paneling and marble and

The exemplary London super-luxury hotel **The Lanesborough, London, England.** The Withdrawing Room, a delightful sitting room with full-bar service, exhibits the elegant residential style and atmosphere of the hotel (see p. 166).

wood bathroom, remains on permanent exhibition at New York's Metropolitan Museum of Art. Rykiel redecorated all 45 suites, referred to as 'grand apartments,' in Louis XV style with chandelier-lit living rooms, baby grand pianos, gold-colored furniture upholstered in ruby red velvets, and trompe l'oeil ceilings and introduced a contemporary touch with major paintings by Dali, Miro, and Braque. She used as her inspiration for the décor of the magnificent presidential suites the stones of garnet, ruby, sapphire, and pearl, while maintaining the original traditional French atmosphere of these suites with Louis XV and Louis XVI style furniture, Aubusson carpets, and Baccarat chandeliers.

In the case of The Lanesborough, across from Buckingham Palace, a hotel was designed into a national landmark that formerly was a prominent hospital. Originally built as a private home for the Viscount Lanesborough in 1719, this property later was converted to St. George's Hospital by William Wilkins, architect of London's National Gallery, and only recently was transformed into a super-luxury hotel. The current developers of the hotel can thank nurse Florence Nightingale who in 1859 insisted on the addition of a new wing and a third floor because the hospital beds were too close together. Under the auspices of four esteemed historic preservation organizations extensive interior reconstruction was required to create the new facility and to impart the luster of a luxury hotel. A highly accurate recreation of the original Regency-era façade was accomplished and the original entrance foyer, first-floor gallery, main corridors, and graceful stairways were restored intact. Regency period furnishings and décor recall a nineteenth-century London townhouse and contribute to the residential-style service and atmosphere of the hotel. In addition to the assiduous attention to historic detail, the designers of The Lanesborough incorporated cutting-edge high-tech features cloaked behind wood casework and plaster, including sophisticated security surveillance and locking systems, state-of-the-art control panels for air conditioning and lighting, and heat and motion sensors in the room so that the guest's personal butler can know when guests are in their room and are not to be disturbed.

Far more rare, however, than historic restorations or adaptive renovations are hotels of this high stature designed as new buildings. The Four Seasons Hotel New York, originally designed as the New York Regent Hotel, is a magnificent example of the latter. Developer William Zeckendorf Jr. and chairman of Regent International, Robert Burns, saw the opportunity to build on 57th Street near Park Avenue the grandest new hotel that New York had seen since the Waldorf=Astoria. Architects I.M. Pei and Frank Williams were instructed to design the hotel along the lines of the luxuriously serviced properties that Regent operated throughout Asia where service is paramount, as evidenced by a far higher staff-to-guest ratio than is found in the US or Europe. But the vision for this hotel was not to call on classical motifs of the past to elicit a sense of historic luxury but, rather, a challenge to achieve a level of supreme luxury as a contemporary architectural masterpiece. This was accomplished not by ornate moldings, gilded cornices, or crystal chandeliers, but through exquisitely proportioned volumes and richly composed materials in a decidedly modern approach.

The tower of the Four Seasons Hotel New York was masterfully crafted within the strict limitations of a complicated zoning envelope as a series of cascading setbacks reminiscent of many of New York's great early twentieth-century skyscrapers. The setbacks are punctuated by custom-designed decorative lanterns that give New York's tallest hotel a sparkling presence on the night skyline.

While hotels in the super-luxury category are usually located in the world's most sophisticated cities such as New York, Paris, London, and Venice, there are a handful of resort properties that fulfill the high standards of this category. Sun International spent $8 million renovating the Ocean Club on Paradise Island, returning it to its former status as one of the most exclusive and premier resorts in the world. Situated on 35 acres (14.2 ha) of lushly manicured Versailles gardens, the estate features fountained courtyards, a magnificent twelfth-century Augustinian cloister, and beautiful marble sculptures located throughout seven terraces. Equally magnificent, Sun's Zimbali Forest Lodge in South Africa is set against the natural beauty and wildlife of surrounding lakes, wetlands, and subtropical forest. The main complex is enclosed by a cluster of eight opulent Zulu-styled lodges, each with its own butler.

The exemplary Paris super-luxury hotel **Hotel de Crillon, Paris, France.** A French National Landmark, the hotel draws international recognition for its magnificent opulence as evidenced by a full-scale reproduction of the Salon Duc de Crillon (original shown here) on permanent display at the Metropolitan Museum of Art in New York City (see p. C-15).

Public Spaces

Entrance lobbies most often are elegantly small and distinctly residential in character. Registration may occur at a small front desk or, sometimes, at private desks where the guest is invited to be seated. At The Carlyle, located in New York City's most exclusive residential area and for many years the only five-star hotel in that city, a quiet side entrance away from the hustle and bustle of Madison Avenue leads visitors into a luxuriously intimate lobby that feels more like the entry hall of a stately home than the center of a busy hotel. From the understated elegance of the hotel lobby guests may enter the gallery for afternoon tea, have drinks in the renowned Bemelmans Bar, with its 1940s murals by Ludwig Bemelmans, or find top-name entertainment served up at Café Carlyle, well known among New York's elite as the premier cabaret room in the country.

The Four Seasons Hotel New York, the first major chain hotel to achieve super-luxury status, represents an exception to the rule with regard to the scale of the lobby. In fact, the lobby is quite grand and features a backlit onyx-coffered ceiling over an imposing central rotunda clad in French limestone. With 360 rooms on 54 floors the hotel is larger and taller than most in this category and requires 1,400 ft/min, high-speed elevators to whisk its prestigious guests to and from their rooms.

The design of the Four Seasons called for staff to take the guest's luggage on arrival into a special luggage elevator adjacent to the entrance, carry it to a room in the subcellar where it was tagged and logged into the computer, and then transport it by high-speed service elevator to the guestroom before the guest entered the room. Three separate desks were designed for the lobby—reception, concierge, and cashier—where the style of operation called for additional staff to separate the sometimes inharmonious check-in and check-out functions.

Guestrooms and Suites

Luxury was designed into every corner of the Four Seasons Hotel New York. Over a million dollars were expended on the construction of fully detailed guestroom mockups that were torn apart and rebuilt several times in perfecting the design. A decision was made early during this process to extend the floor-to-floor height of the building to yield 10.5 ft (3.2 m) ceiling heights for every room, and to bear the exponential construction cost increase to achieve this grand scale. The rooms were equipped with bedside controls allowing the guest to open and close the drapes, turn on a discreet privacy sign, or call for maid service at the push of a button.

Bathrooms in many luxury properties now exceed one-third of the overall room size. The recent renovation of The Beverly Hills Hotel in California reduced the number of guestrooms from 253 to 184,

Four Seasons Hotel New York, Luxury on 57th Street

I.M. Pei, Architect, New York

The commanding location of the Four Seasons Hotel on East 57th Street, on one of the few prominent sites remaining in the heart of New York, required a building of classic elegance to transcend time and fashion.

We used fine honey-colored limestone from France. The tower's tapering vertical thrust is expressed by a series of setbacks that cascade down 682 ft from the cruciform top to the sidewalk below. The setbacks are signaled by pairs of 12 ft high lanterns that bathe the hotel in a silhouette of soft light, giving it a festive glow distinct from the many tall office buildings on the skyline.

The hotel is entered under a translucent glass canopy that fans out above the sidewalk, almost to the curb, in order to dramatize the hotel's mid-block presence. Inside, a richly detailed lobby court conveys an air of both grandeur and intimacy. The Grand Foyer is surrounded by a multiterraced waiting, seating and light-dining area where hotel guests and New Yorkers alike may enjoy tea, drinks and conversation in a salon-like setting. It is a public space in which to see and be seen. Grand hotels have an element of theater. By emphasizing this quality and by providing a stage for gracious social exchange we have revived the grand tradition of a former time when visiting a hotel was a memorable event.

primarily to increase the size of the bathrooms. Ultra-luxury bathroom design now includes multiple head showers with ten-button controls and automatic temperature settings, marble vanity with two porcelain basins and brass fittings, heated fog-free mirrors, deep cast-iron soaking tub with adjustable hand spray, three-stage mood lighting including a reading light over the tub and toilet, remote control TV with steam-free screen, 'hands-free' two-line speaker phone with special digital processing circuits that minimize the sound of running water and automatically lower the volume of the radio or TV when a call comes in, toilet in separate chamber with privacy door, heated marble floors, heated towel bars, heated toilet seats, and bidets with hot-air drying functions. Specialty suites offer deep whirlpool baths with windows facing out onto a spectacular view. But for all the bells and whistles the most prized luxury item—and sometimes the most expensive to build—is good water pressure, a feature that is harder to achieve in new build projects because of new regulations on water-saving devices and low flow requirements. Not a problem for the Four Seasons Hotel New York which warns its new guests that the deep soaking tub fills in less than 60 seconds.

Back-of-house Areas

The Four Seasons Hotel New York went through over 50,000 resumes and selected only one staff member for every ten that were invited to be interviewed. Highly prized as they are, facilities for the staff in super-luxury hotels most often are on a level well above employee facilities in other hotel types. Super-luxury hotels pamper their employees not only to foster a sense of loyalty but to create a feeling of high esteem commensurate with the behavior and attitude required in delivering first-class service. Employee lockers, showers, dining rooms, and lounges are often 1.5 to 2 times larger than those of less luxurious establishments and are treated as part of the hotel's basic décor rather than given the usual sterile finishes found in these facilities.

Development and Planning Considerations

Urban super-luxury hotels such The Carlyle, Hotel de Crillon, The Lanesborough, and the Four Seasons Hotel New York usually are located near luxury shopping, theater, and entertainment centers. However, the Mansion on Turtle Creek in Dallas and the

➤ *The exemplary New York super-luxury hotel* **Four Seasons Hotel, New York.** (A) Having obtained the commanding site at 57th Street between Madison and Park Avenues, the developers seized the opportunity to build the grandest hotel in the City since the Waldorf=Astoria. New York's tallest hotel is also its most elegant. The tapering 54-story tower is clad in Magny, the same French Burgundian limestone specified by I.M. Pei for the reconstruction of the Louvre. (B) With distinctive modern styling, the standard 610 ft^2 (56.7 m^2) guestroom has over one-third of its area devoted to the bath and dressing room. All rooms have 10 ft 4 in ceilings (3.1 m) providing a scale of luxury rarely found in newly constructed hotels. Fiddleback English Sycamore, the same wood used to make Stradivarius violins, was used for all cabinetwork, doors and furniture. (C) Marking the trend in luxury hotels toward larger more elaborate bathrooms, the specialty suite bathtubs are provided with spectacular views of Central Park and the sparkling lights of the city below (see p. C-2).

(A)

(C)

(B)

The super-luxury resort **Ocean Club, Paradise Island, Bahamas.** Fifty new guestrooms and a new restaurant were added to this exclusive Caribbean compound that offers the ambiance of a small private club. In the traditional style of British colonial architecture, long verandas with deep overhangs, cooled by fans and ocean breezes, open wide to views of the white sandy beaches of the Bahamian coastline.

The exotic super-luxury lodge **Zimbali Lodge, KwaZulu-Natal, Africa.** The *foyer du public* with its high-peaked roof presents a luxurious colonial-style setting for informal gathering and refreshments. Sited on a hillside, the main lodge overlooks a formal swimming pool with vistas across a lake and championship golf course to the distant Indian Ocean. Other facilities in the 72-room, four-suite boutique resort include an exclusive beach club and spa.

Remington in Houston, among the newly constructed super-luxury Texas hotels, selected suburban locations close to luxury stores on the edge of exclusive residential areas. The porte cochere should be relatively inconspicuous, an enclosed courtyard, or thoroughly screened with landscaping to assure its distinguished clientele privacy. Exterior signage should be kept understated and discreet.

While traditionally located in or near major cosmopolitan cities, a few of these super-luxury properties may be found at the world's most exclusive resort areas. Begawan Giri, built in the emerald hills of central Bali, offers lavish service and breathtaking natural beauty in an Indonesian jungle garden. The guest's full-time personal butler, dressed in a white Nehru jacket, will prepare an exotic meal and serve it in the outdoor dining room of a private villa surrounded by a wrap-around private pool, open fire pits, Javanese sculpture, and jasmine meditation garden. The resort has five residences with a total of 22 suites ranging from $475 to $4,400 per night.

Heydar Ghiai & Sons is an architectural firm that specializes in high-security resorts for political figures, monarchs and their entourages, and guests who seek the ultimate in privacy and security. Based on an ancient Persian architectural principle, the design of these resorts often calls for a series of pavilions laid out with layers of privacy, with access through a succession of guarded arcades, foyers, and antechambers.

Trends

- Security and privacy will continue to be essential features of super-luxury hotels and technological advances will produce ever more sophisticated systems. Such high-tech systems as electronic door locks that alert security on entry to a room, surveillance cameras, and window sensors add to the guest's peace of mind.
- Ultimate service and choice amenities will continue to be a goal as hotel chains pursue their quest to develop super-luxury brands. Guests of The Lanesborough receive personalized business cards and stationery bearing the individual phone and fax numbers for the two phone lines and fax machine in their rooms. State-of-the-art electronic heat and motion sensors are wired from each room into the 'butler's pantry'—a space somewhat closer to mission control. The butler knows if guests are in their room so he won't disturb their privacy, but is always close at hand to answer a call. In addition, the electronic key systems permit the butler to coordinate with housekeeping, engineering, and other hotel services to prevent guests from being disturbed.
- Demand will grow for high-tech rooms with emphasis on business components that permit the guestroom to become both office and home for those busy guests whose enterprises take them to the financial and business capitals of the world.

The exotic super-luxury lodge **Zimbali Lodge, KwaZulu-Natal, Africa.** The interior detailing of the resort's eight luxury lodges reflects classical African colonial architecture with natural timber roof trusses, ivory stucco walls, untreated leather, and ochre-tinted concrete floors.

The elegant addition to a Grande Dame **The Peninsula, Hong Kong, China.** A major expansion to the 1928 neoclassic masterpiece took the form of a modern 30-story tower, increasing the number of guestrooms from 168 to 300. In contrast to the colonial character of Hong Kong's most renowned hotel, the sleek new tower signals a marriage of the past with the future. While many original interior details of the hotel were faithfully restored, the project's goal of saluting the future was achieved with Philippe Starck's dramatic design of the two-story penthouse restaurant, Felix.

Updating Existing Hotels

10

Hotels continually are being updated. Renovation work and refurbishing are necessary for the financial health of hotels and, each year, more money is spent on these activities than for the construction of new hotels. About every 5 years there is the need to replace worn-out soft goods, such as wall coverings, carpets, and drapery. Case goods, including beds, furniture, and some equipment, require replacement every 10 years. Modernized mechanical systems, up-to-date lighting, new plumbing fittings, and other extensive changes are called for every 15–25 years.

In addition, hotels frequently alter existing spaces, such as enlarging a successful restaurant, adding an exercise facility or business center, or converting an underutilized discotheque to another use. In cases where there is no available space, owners might consider constructing an addition to the existing hotel in order to meet market demands and realize greater profits. Over time hotels lose their luster and styles need to be updated to reflect current tastes. A fresh look to an existing hotel often is essential in order to compete with a new or recently renovated hotel nearby. Targeting a growing segment of the public interested in ecology leads to renovations that make a hotel more environmentally friendly. Improvements in operational efficiency, and to back-of-house facilities to provide better services and to boost staff morale, are also reasons to renovate.

Such work typically is performed while the hotel carries on business as usual and with as little disruption to service as possible. All efforts should be made to keep noise, debris, and general inconvenience to guests at a minimum. Construction projects undertaken in an operating hotel are more costly than those when the hotel shuts down. This is due to limited hours the crew can work, partitions required to block off areas under construction, complimentary goods and services provided to guests, and temporary facilities set up for those that are out of service. However, closing a hotel, or even a portion of operations, can also have drawbacks, including loss of revenue and valued employees, and making regular guests seek out competitors. Planning must be done carefully. Often, the renovation of guestrooms is scheduled in stages with blocks of rooms or floors done in sequence while the rest remain in service.

Renovations of a major scale involve the complete overhaul of an existing hotel or the conversion of another building type for use as a hotel. The main factors favoring total renovation over new construction are savings in construction expenses ('gut' renovations generally cost 30 percent less than building from the ground up), the lack of prime and spacious sites (particularly in urban areas), time savings, and continuing appreciation for historic architecture by the public.

Renovations

In periods of economic downturn, hotels often postpone renovation work and sometimes defer maintenance. When good times return, cash is available to do things that have been put off or owners take advantage of having money on hand as an incentive to upgrade facilities. In order to change the look of a hotel substantially, or to undertake a major renovation that requires that the building be totally emptied, a liquidation sale can generate income by selling off furniture, equipment, lighting fixtures, and other items that still have some life, but will not be used in the renovated hotel.

The existing building places serious constraints on most renovation projects and these must be addressed during the design process. While initial building surveys are as complete as possible, contractors or others on the team inevitably discover unknown existing conditions. Sometimes the builders uncover magnificent details which the owner or designer wants to incorporate into the finished project. At other times, serious deterioration is only

The adaptive modern high-rise office landmark hotel **Loews Philadelphia Hotel, Pennsylvania.** Built in 1932, America's first modern skyscraper was designed in the International Style by William Lescaze and George Howe. The 36-story PSFS Building is a National Historic Landmark, easily recognized on the city skyline by its 27 ft (8.25 m) high stainless steel letters on the roof. After lying vacant for 8 years, Jonathan Tisch and the Loews Corporation undertook a comprehensive historic restoration project in transforming the former office building to a 583-room hotel. Unaltered since opening day, the original main banking floor, located on the second level with 30 ft (9 m) ceilings and vast windows facing the street, has been converted to the 9,800 ft^2 (910 m^2) Millennium Hall ballroom.

evident after demolition. As a result, both the budget and schedule for a renovation project can be substantially off their initial projections due to these unforeseen conditions. This is a gamble for all renovation projects and contingencies must be built into the design, documentation, and construction budgets to cover these possible costs.

Hotels reflect the economic circumstance of their communities. Prosperity in the industrialized nations at the end of the twentieth century, especially in the US, has transformed a few rural towns into very affluent ones. On eastern Long Island, one-time potato farms now sprout extravagant leisure homes for New York's super-rich. In the past, there was little need for hotels in the Hamptons and the few that served these towns were motels built at modest cost and scale. In many cases operations did not keep up with the demands of the market, which became driven by a strong desire for quality accommodation by a public not worried about spending money. Because local zoning laws discourage new hotel and motel construction, in order to maintain the scale of the residental neighborhoods, many of the older motels have been purchased by developers who seek to reposition them in this new market. One hotel in Southampton raised the daily rate for standard guestrooms from $29 to $300 per night over only a few years. However, for hotels that were originally of low-quality design and construction, significant upgrades are needed in order to justify such rate hikes.

In an effort to spur development in a certain area or to protect an historic building, governments may offer tax credits for private developers to renovate an existing building. These subsidies help to attract offset risk and financing. Such sites should be pursued for possible hotel development. Loews Hotels converted the historic PSFS (Philadelphia Savings Fund Society) building into a 583-room hotel. This project, which opened in 2000, was substantially financed with public money in an effort by the City of Philadelphia to increase business for its downtown convention center. Another Loews project, to renovate the art deco St. Moritz Hotel in Miami Beach and construct an addition also received municipal money in that city's plan to spur convention business. Being part of a public redevelopment scheme from the beginning also may have the advantage of saving time as these projects often have an easier time gaining necessary approvals from city agencies.

Table 10.1 Renovation cycle of existing hotel

Stage	*Cost/room*	*Scope*
5-year refurbishment	$6,000–15,000+	Replace carpet, fabrics (upholstery, bedspreads, drapery), vinyl wall covering, repaint
10-year major overhaul	$25,000–40,000+	Repeat above, replace case goods, plus upgrade systems and equipment (computers, life safety, kitchen, laundry)
50-year 'gut-renovation'	$60,000+	Repeat above plus change functions, circulations, etc.; consider exterior renovation

The individual business traveler and groups are the primary markets for most hotels today. Many hotels are turning over more space for meeting rooms and business centers. In addition, guestrooms are being modified to be business-friendly, with two phone lines, large desks, task lighting, and flexible layouts that allow rooms to be used for small business meetings. Couples who travel often include one who uses the room to work and the other who uses the room for leisure. Converting two small rooms into a suite or providing a separate dressing area between the sleeping area and bathroom are ways that hotels find to balance the needs of couples staying for mixed purposes.

Hotels which need to complete the renovation or remodeling in time to meet the high season, to set new rates, or to accommodate a special event bringing in many guests, now can get turnkey packages from companies that bundle together design, purchasing, and consulting services. These firms provide all items for a standard guestroom at a lower cost and in less time than can be accomplished with the traditional design process. While this might not be an option for hotel owners who take a personal interest in every detail, it does answer to those who are satisfied with a good look that is completed quickly and saves money. Working from basic choices set up in showrooms, the owner has limited options for customization. These are cosmetic renovations that do not involve mechanical, plumbing, or electrical modifications or spatial changes that require services of engineers and architects.

The international style of architecture was truly that. It even made its mark on the Scottish countryside, where the original St. Andrew's Old Course Hotel was constructed in the 1960s as a stark modern building reflecting current taste. The 1998 renovation of the hotel sought to give the entire building, both interior and exterior, a 'past.' The original concrete box was re-clad in a traditional local material called 'harl' and a pitched slate roof, wrought-iron balconies, glazing with historic Scottish detailing, and cast stone cornices were added. The quality of the materials and their skillful application give St. Andrew's Old Course Hotel an authenticity that is frequently lacking in projects that superficially apply historic details. Today the hotel is more in harmony with the golf course that gave rise to the sport five centuries ago. It also is on par with current public taste.

Built in 1912, The Beverly Hills Hotel in California re-opened in 1995 after a 3-year, $100 million renovation. Rather than restore the building to its original Mission Revival Style, the most recent art deco renovation seeks to recreate the glamour of 1940s Hollywood, befitting the lifestyles of famous stars who used to frequent this hotel. Guests swim in the same pool as did Katherine Hepburn; check-in to bungalows where Marlene Dietrich stayed and Elizabeth Taylor honeymooned; have cocktails in the Polo Lounge where one almost expects Carol

The golf inn renovation **Old Course Hotel, St. Andrew's, Scotland.** The original bland modern façade was re-clad in a traditional exterior finish material and expanded with historic Scottish detailing including pitched slate roof, cast stone cornices and wrought iron balconies. The renovation successfully transformed the 125-key hotel into one of elegance and grace befitting the birthplace of golf five centuries ago.

The 'hotel of the stars' renovation **The Beverly Hills Hotel, California.** Reopened after a 3-year, $100 million renovation, the hotel's new décor recalls the glamorous Hollywood era of the 1940s when movie stars and celebrities populated the swimming pool, Polo Lounge, and Crystal Ballroom.

The convention hotel restoration **Hilton Chicago & Towers, Illinois.** The delicate balance of authentic historic preservation and practical marketing goals were met in the restoration of the 1927 hotel's grand public spaces. Inspired by the Versailles Palace, the 20,000 ft^2 (1,860 m^2) grand ballroom was returned to its original grandeur with the reapplication of 22-karat gold leaf to the ornate walls and carvings and the reconstruction of the room's 280,000-piece crystal chandeliers.

Lombard and Clark Gable to sweep through the door, and dance in the Crystal Ballroom like Fred Astaire and Ginger Rogers. The owners sought to recreate a specific period of time in the history of The Beverly Hills Hotel that would reflect its most charismatic guests. This fantasy of Hollywood even appeals to today's movie stars, moguls, and other celebrities, who see the hotel as part of their legacy and as a place to run into others in the film industry, just as in the past. To the general public it has more of a theme aspect, albeit one with some authenticity.

Hotels are part of today's business climate of mergers and acquisitions; they frequently change in ownership. Parent companies no longer demand a single standard to which all their hotels must conform when they add hotels of different styles and categories. Still, while a recently acquired hotel might not require renovation, it may need modifications that announce a change of flag and reassure the new owners' regular guests of the quality they expect.

Restorations

Restoration is a special category of renovation in which the objective is to re-create the original structure. Original building elements are retained and, when this is not possible, replicated. Most legislation for landmark structures stipulates that building exteriors be restored, but allows the owner discretion with respect to the interior. Restoration work usually involves the expertise of preservation architects who prepare documentation regarding the original design, along with proper materials and methodologies needed for cleaning and restoring historic buildings. Piecing together the design of a building long after its completion can be a difficult task. In most instances the drawings of the original architect are no longer available—and while these are most useful, they reflect the intention of the architect and not necessarily what actually was built. Old photographs are helpful, but they usually document only a portion of the building and do not positively identify materials. Probes of the actual structure to uncover elements hidden by subsequent renovations are a major source of discovery—even a fragment of an original element can reveal a great deal. Still, there frequently are gaps where there is no positive evidence or clue of the original component. In these

The atrium hotel restoration **Brown Palace Hotel, Denver, Colorado.** Open for business every minute of every day since 1892, the Brown Palace has never closed for renovation. The most recent renovation took 5 years and included redecoration and new lighting for the famed eight-story atrium and lobby and remodeling of 33 executive staterooms and numerous upscale suites on the top two floors. It introduced state-of-the-art heating and air-conditioning systems bringing individual climate control for the first time to each guestroom.

Table 10.2 Existing hotel checklist

Engineering systems

Heating, ventilating, and air-conditioning systems
Temperature and humidity control
Fresh air control and filtration
Mechanical noise and vibration control
Energy efficiency
Zone control
Environmental systems

Life safety systems (review updated local codes)
Sprinklers, standpipes, hose racks, fire extinguishers
Smoke detection, fire alarm, voice annunciation, fire command station
Emergency power generator, lighting, fire pumps, elevator recall
Kitchen hood protection (dry foam), computer room (halon)
Smokeproof exit stairs
Fire-resistive walls around guestrooms and stairs; fire-rated doors and closers
Fail-safe locking systems
Corridor smoke purge

Energy conservation
Computerized energy management systems
Heat recovery systems (kitchen and laundry hot water and exhaust)
Air purifying systems (exhaust recirculation)
Insulating windows (double and solar glazing)
Life cycle energy analysis
Motion sensors, lighting controls in guestrooms
Vestibule and revolving doors
Alternative energy sources (solar, wind, photo voltaic)
Variable air volume system
Long life, energy conserving light bulbs

Vertical transportation systems
Passenger elevators
Service and freight elevators
Escalators

Telephone and communications systems
Computerized least-cost routing, accounting, wake-up call
House and public phones, telex and fax service, cable and satellite dish, closed-circuit TV, HDTV
High-speed Internet connections

Light dimming systems
Meeting and banquet spaces
Restaurants and lounges
Lobbies
Guestrooms

Management systems

Computerized hotel management systems
Room status, guest histories
Accounting, auditing, inventories
Data storage
Billing, point-of-sale charging
Automatic bar code reader
Reservations
Time stamps

Security systems
Card-locking systems, door peepholes, security latches, motion detection
TV surveillance of entrances, service dock, elevators, escalators
Wireless communication
Alarms for exit stairs, cashier, F&B storage
Cashier vault, safe deposit boxes (front desk)
In-room safes
Security lighting

Entertainment systems
In-room movies, closed circuit TV
Satellite TV, AM/FM bedside control, CD, HDTV, video players
Cable

Health club equipment
Exercise equipment
Sauna, steambath, whirlpool
Swimming pool
Lockers, showers, plumbing fixtures

Guest bathroom accessories
Pulsating shower heads
Lighted make-up mirrors
Towel warmers
Heat lamps
Whirlpools and steam-baths

Audiovisual systems
Projection
Sound
Translation

Movable partitions
Meeting rooms
Ballroom

Soundproofing
Guestroom door gaskets
Windows
Meeting room partitions and doors

Parking systems
Control gates
Car elevators and ramps
Directional signs
Paving surfaces, landscaping, lighting

General
Interior fixed decor
Signage
Interior furnishings
Kitchen and bar equipment
Laundry and dry cleaning equipment, laundry chute
Waste disposal systems, compactor

Rate the existing condition of each item on a scale from 0 to 3, estimating the cost of new additions or upgrades as required to meet current standards.

instances the preservation architect relies on knowledge of other similar buildings in order to make educated assumptions.

Once the historic building is understood and documented, the painstaking reconstruction work begins. In the past, buildings, especially those meant to last, were built by craftsmen, many of whose expert skills are no longer part of today's building industry. While the growing movement to restore historic structures has brought a revitalization of many building crafts, it still is difficult to find qualified artisans. Because of their specialized skill and the labor-intensive nature of their work, restoration projects usually are more expensive and take more time than new construction. In some cases, the designers go to great extremes to find replacements for original materials, often custom making some items or fabricating special molds from surviving original building elements. While much depends on the condition of the existing structure and the elaboration of its architecture, these projects call for a strong commitment by the owner. Such undertakings have great

(A)

(B)

(C)

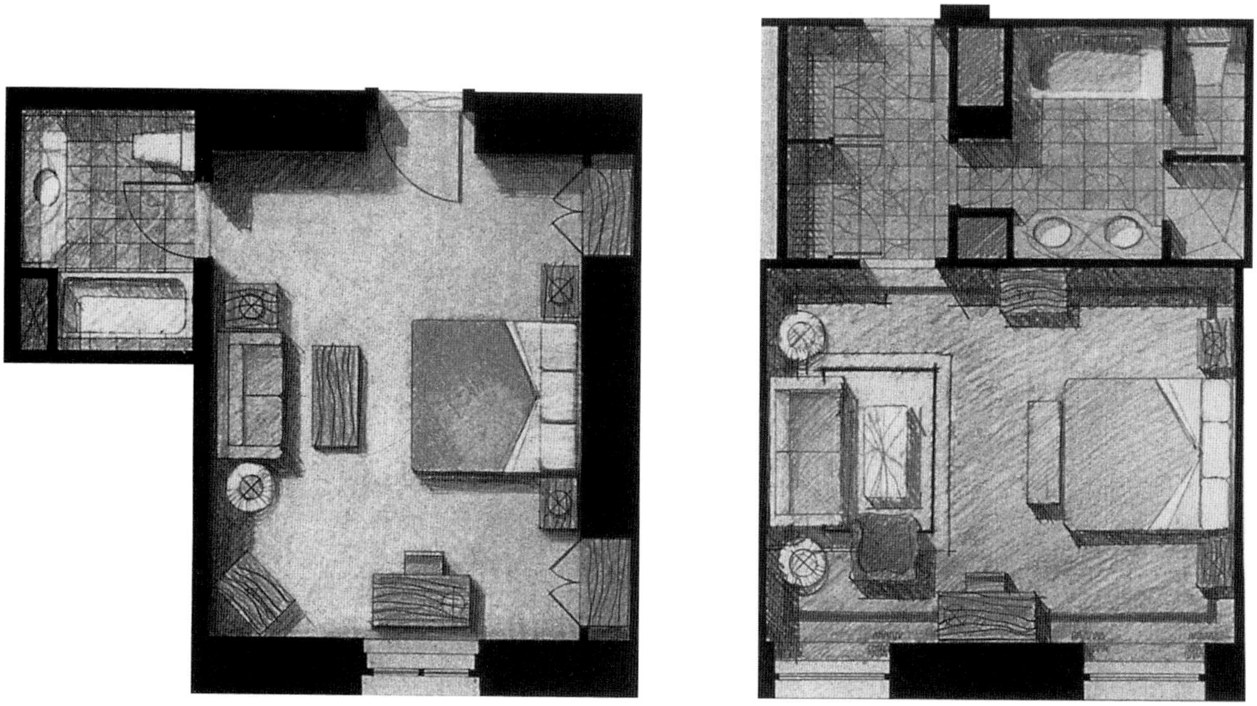

The high-rise landmark hotel restoration **The St. Regis, New York.** (A) The St. Regis Roof ballroom, historically the pinnacle of society events in the city, has been recreated in its original form, with all new mechanical, electrical, and lighting carefully blended into its arched ceiling. (B) In cooperation with New York's Landmarks Preservation Commission, ITT Sheraton undertook a massive exterior and interior renovation of John Jacob Astor's 1901 Beaux-Art masterpiece. Exterior work included the restoration of the building's original bronze and glass revolving entrance doors and the famed freestanding doorman's sentry which stands under the marquee. (C) The renovation combined and enlarged rooms, reducing the hotel key count from 436 to 363 while increasing the standard room size to 450 ft^2 (41.8 m^2). The plans illustrate typical 'before' and 'after' layouts.

prestige and are much appreciated by today's public who has come to highly value historic architecture.

By strict definition terms, totally restoring a hotel to its original condition is rarely possible or even desired. No matter how significant the architecture, no guest wants to be without the latest amenities and, additionally, hotels must provide different facilities to meet present-day demands. The recent $40 million renovation of the Hotel del Coronado, a seaside hotel constructed in 1888 near San Diego, California, successfully turned back the clock so that guests could relive a bygone period. However, guestrooms cooled only by ceiling fans lack air-conditioning and the hotel's wire-cage elevator is very slow. These are authentic restorations, but they do not reflect current lifestyles or expectations of comfort, and are not fully appreciated by some guests.

After decades of neglect and abandonment, cities are undergoing a renaissance and hotels are playing a major role in this transformation. They offer sophistication and formality that the suburbs lack. Most old cities have prominent hotels that played a significant role in shaping the political, social, and business life of the community. Restoring those that were not razed during urban renewal schemes in the 1960s and 1970s brings back a vital aspect of a city's history and is the source of great civic pride. Such hotels are at a premium and usually very profitable for owners who are able to capitalize not only on the valuable historic architecture but also on a name that resonates strongly within the community. Photographs of the hotel in its heyday and a roster of famous people who once were guests can be incorporated into promotional brochures. They also can be displayed in the hotel to give present-day guests the feeling that they are reliving history by seeing themselves in the same spaces as existed a century ago.

One aspect of luxury hotels constructed prior to World War II is that they were built to last. Materials were substantial and details often integral to the structure of the building itself. The cost of removing this work was prohibitively expensive. Renovations to these hotels in the mid-twentieth century tended to conceal any elaborate decoration. For example, in an era that valued neither historic architecture nor high ceilings, designs often included dropped ceilings to permit the installation of modern mechanical systems, totally concealing the interior detail. Columns, moldings, and other elements were encased in easily maintained materials. In peeling back these later renovations architects often discover unknown original details. The Pfister Hotel in Milwaukee, completed in 1893, underwent a restoration in 1993. Among the surprise discoveries were an original lobby fireplace hidden by a metal awning and marble pillars covered in suede. In many instances, such treasures are damaged beyond repair. However, in the past 20 years manufacturers have introduced reproductions of many historic building elements, fittings, and fixtures that have been made according to original specifications or in newer materials. The construction industry also has become more familiar in working on historic structures and there are now, in almost every community, builders who specialize in this field.

In 1988, The St. Regis Hotel on Fifth Avenue in mid-town Manhattan underwent a 3-year $100 million reconstruction. Built in 1901 by John Jacob Astor to the design of Trowbridge and Livingston, The St. Regis established a standard for luxury hotels around the world. Opulent building materials worked by master craftsmen, central air-conditioning and heating systems (the first of its kind for a hotel), magnificent public spaces, commodious well-appointed guestrooms, and a prime location made this New York's premier hotel. A 1927 addition was less grand than the original building and, over the decades, the hotel lost its claim for quality. The recent renovation included a full restoration of the exterior and the original public rooms and demolition and reconfiguration of most other public spaces, along with all guestrooms. Some of the smaller guestrooms from the 1927 addition were combined, reducing the number of keys from 436 to 363, in order to meet today's luxury standards. Where three rooms, each with a single window, were combined to make two new rooms, the middle window was glazed with spandrel glass in order to maintain the exterior façade. All building systems were replaced with state-of-the-art systems. The St. Regis Hotel became a trophy in the extensive ITT Sheraton holdings, much as the original hotel was for John Jacob Astor. In fact, the Sheraton luxury brand is now called 'St. Regis.'

Even more costly than The St. Regis restoration was that of the Hilton Chicago & Towers. Built in 1927 as the Stevens Hotel, it boasted 3,000 rooms and grand public spaces inspired by the Palace of Versailles. Its furnishings and equipment were auctioned off during World War II when the hotel served as an army barracks, after which Conrad Hilton acquired it. The $185 million renovation began in 1985 with the goal to lure lucrative convention business. A complete restoration of public spaces—one that would most please preservation aficionados—was decided against in favor of a selective restoration combined with lots of glass, brass, and highly polished

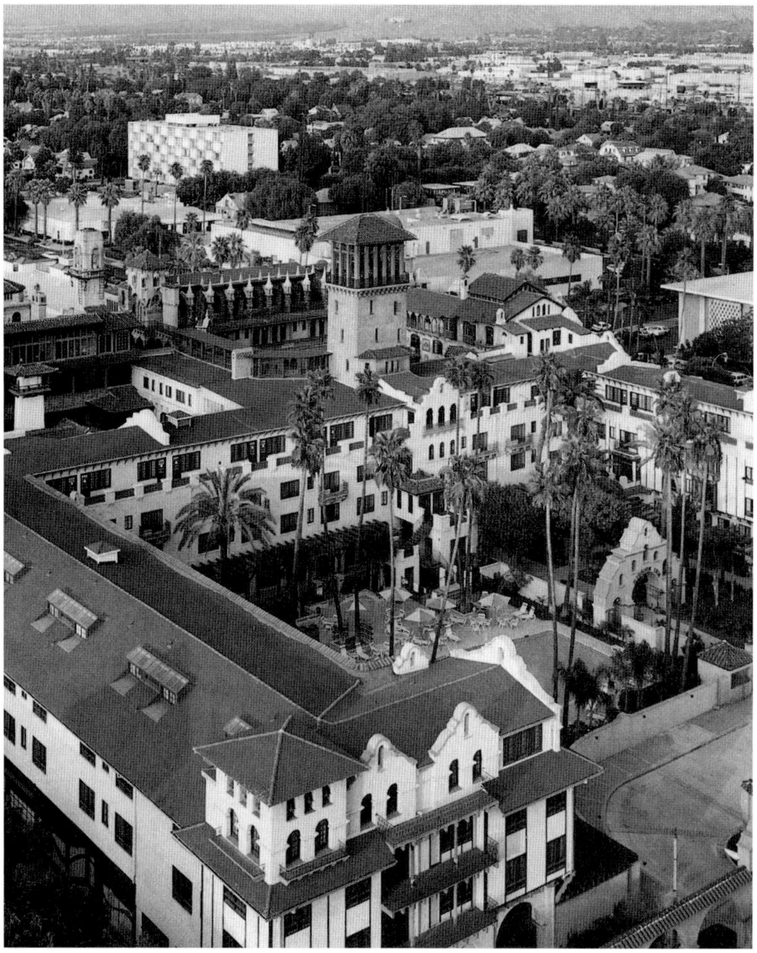

marble that would appeal to more guests. Hilton determined that their guests would think of a restoration as stodgy. The resulting hybrid recognizes the value of historic architecture but, at the same time, incorporates the taste of today's public. In opting against an historic recreation of the public spaces, the hotel designers had more flexibility in reworking public circulation in order to make an interior link to the newly constructed parking facility.

It is difficult for a new hotel to compete with a nearby rival with an impressive lineage. Owners planning to convert the former Knickerbocker Hotel in New York's Times Square from its current office building use are banking on the connection that the public will make to the Knickerbocker name, directly linked to New York's gilded age. Among several new hotels nearby, this is the only one that could claim a past with a well-recognized name. The Knickerbocker Hotel, built by John Jacob Astor in 1906, ceased operation in 1918, at the onset of Prohibition—a reminder of how legislation can affect a hotel's operation.

While it takes longer for a hotel with a name long synonymous with quality to lose its reputation, it does happen. A lax attitude toward new demands and to the quality of the interiors is a serious detriment to the financial operation of the hotel. Many nineteenth and early twentieth century luxury hotels were built to serve the wealthy, leisured class. These guests have given way to today's business traveler

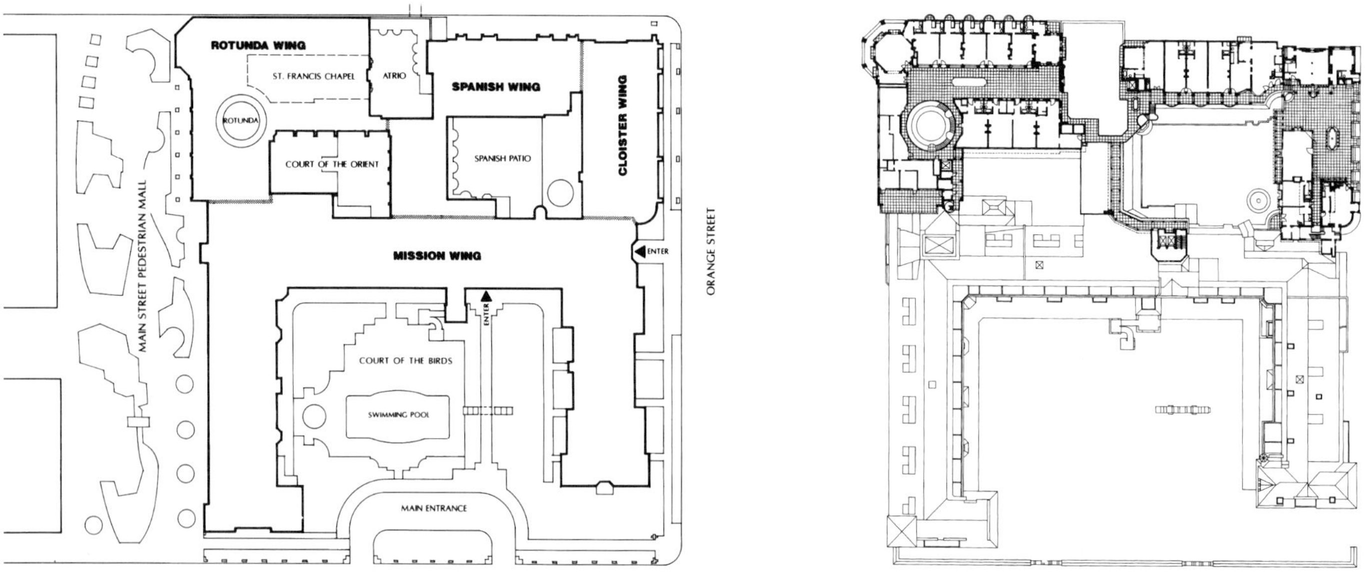

Hotel restoration in a seismic zone **Mission Inn, Riverside, California.** Occupying an entire block in the center of town, the restoration was the focus of a major urban redevelopment program. To restore the decaying national landmark to its original splendor and to meet the rigorous California seismic codes, the architects and engineers had to creatively solve pervasive structural problems.

who has different requirements—but who may still be willing to pay a premium for quality accommodations and service. American hotels have catered to this class of traveler for some time and, now, hotels everywhere are making this adjustment. In London, the Savoy, Connaught, Berkeley, and Claridge's are undergoing major revitalization. While travelers of yesteryear might have appreciated the patina of faded interiors, today's travelers are not so inclined. The meaning of luxury is redefined—it is flashier. The Savoy group's renovations include expanding the lobby space, providing air-conditioning in all rooms, installing digital phone lines, creating new meeting rooms and spas, updating plumbing and bathroom fittings, and offering other modernizations to attract a new class of traveler.

There are a few successful hotels with a dedicated clientele who do not want to see too much change. New York's Algonquin Hotel has a unique character which the owners do not wish to tamper with. The 1997 renovation of the lobby and more efficient space planning was carried out in a most discreet way so that guests would hardly notice. The refurbishment focused on the charm that gave the original hotel its reputation from the early decades of the twentieth century when New York's literary elite used to gather at the Algonquin's 'Round Table.'

Many existing buildings, even some that were originally hotels, have serious drawbacks in meeting the needs of present-day hotels. In the case of historic buildings it makes good sense to build a sound working relationship with government authorities in charge of landmark issues. Meeting the requirements of landmark agencies involves much negotiation and many compromises. Their mission is to protect the historic integrity of the building and they can often help to secure waivers from the building department that might allow for an overhanging canopy, curb cut for a loading dock, or other need.

Building codes and legislation affect all renovation work. It is a challenge in a restoration to incorporate new code requirements so that they do not distract from the interior design. Life-safety and accessibility codes are of foremost importance. In the US, the Hotel and Motel Fire Safety Act of 1990 prohibits federal employees from staying in hotels which lack sprinklers and smoke detectors. For hotels with federal employees as frequent guests, this was a strong incentive to install such devices. Special provisions for the disabled have extended well beyond providing accessibility for people bound to wheelchairs. The Americans with Disabilities Act of 1990 broadens the definition to include individuals with such disabilities as sight and hearing impairments, arthritis, heart conditions, emphysema, amputated limbs, and AIDS. Wide ranges of modifications are necessary to meet their requirements. While most codes only come into effect when new or renovation work is undertaken, some require that buildings comply by a certain date.

For buildings in earthquake zones, seismic upgrades are a major factor in renovation work. The Mission Inn in Riverside, California, was constructed in four stages from 1903 to 1931. For decades it flourished as a prominent destination, but its stature started to decline by the 1950s and despite being declared a national landmark in 1977, it closed in 1985. The magnificent structure occupied an entire downtown block and the city wanted it to become the focus of urban redevelopment. After several changes in ownership, both public and private, the Mission Inn re-opened in 1991 with its original splendor. The restoration architects had to contend with unreinforced brick, wood walls, non-aligned corridors with sagging floors, insufficiently sized wall framing, unbolted cast iron columns, and a host of other structural deficiencies that now had to meet California's stringent seismic codes. All structural work, plus the installation of up-to-date plumbing, mechanical, and electrical systems had to be concealed behind finishes that matched the original ones. It takes careful planning and effort to retrofit such systems into an architecture that remains faithful to its original appearance.

Additions

Small-scale additions allow hotels to meet changing demands and increase profits. The requirement for supplementary guestrooms, a conference facility, fitness center, or countless other needs can be met by additional construction. The addition must complement the hotel's layout and organization—new public areas connected to the lobby, guestroom floors located close to existing elevators, or service areas adjoining the current back-of-house on lower floors. On urban sites, where there is the impetus to add extra floors on top of a building, one must consider the carrying loads of the existing structure, plus the capability of elevators to be extended and their adequacy to serve more guests. For landmark buildings, one must appraise the appropriateness of an addition to the original structure and secure the necessary permits. All additions required zoning, building department, and other government approvals.

Table 10.3 Hotel addition checklist

Evaluate capacity of existing areas to accommodate added traffic
Entrance drives and parking
Lobby and front desk
Food and beverage outlets
Guest circulation (including elevators)
Service circulation (including elevators)
Kitchen, laundry, loading dock, employees' facilities
Recreation facilities (including health club)
Internet service capacity

Obtain data on existing conditions
As-built drawings
Site surveys including existing utilities and landscaping
Legal and zoning restrictions
Soil tests
Detailed inspection of existing structural and mechanical conditions

Evaluate engineering systems to be used
Connections to existing structure and foundations
Structural constraints of site
Energy analysis including existing mechanical and electrical systems and capacity of plant and utilities services

Re-evaluate renovation needs of existing hotel in terms of matching higher standards of new addition
Architectural upgrading of the exterior (for example, entrance canopy, balconies, façade materials, windows, roof treatment, signage, paving, landscaping)
Interior upgrading (furniture, furnishings, finishes, fixtures, equipment, lighting, graphics)
Guestroom amenities
Public space interiors
Life safety, security, communications, audiovisual, and computerized hotel management systems

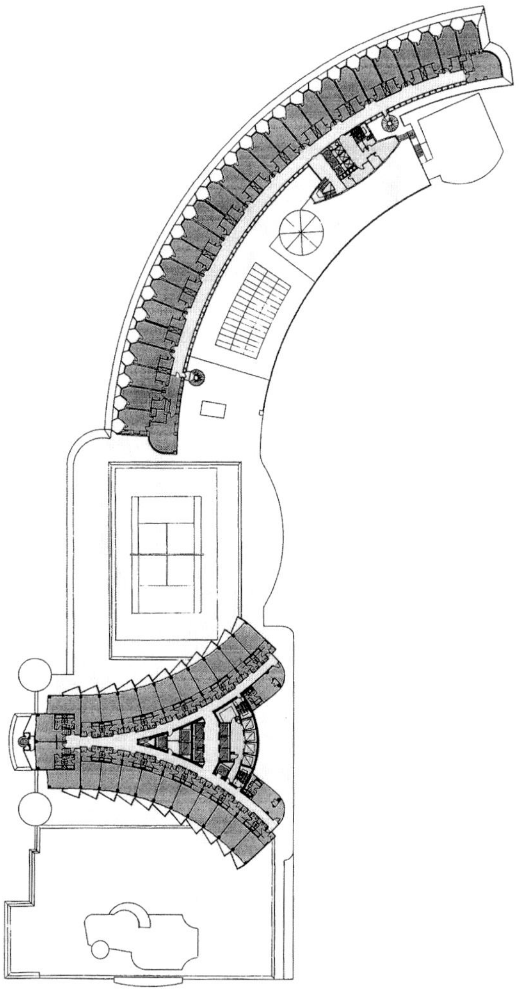

The hotel tower addition **Le Meridien Cairo, Egypt.** Located on Roda Island in the middle of the Nile River, the 40-story addition to the existing landmark hotel adds 870 rooms, a health club, ballrooms and meeting spaces, a nightclub, and a 100 ft (30 m) diameter revolving restaurant on top offering views of the Pyramids in the distance. The innovative curved Y-shaped tower plan provides all guestrooms with spectacular views of Cairo and the Nile.

There are natural sites so spectacular that they are irresistible to hotel developers. Such a place is the northwest tip of Puerto Rico where the Atlantic Ocean and Caribbean Sea converge. The large resort covering 265 acres (107 ha) on this site closed in 1980. After extensive renovations to the original complex and a program to build new facilities, it re-opened under new ownership as El Conquistador Resort and Country Club. The additions needed to complement the existing buildings but, also, to look up-to-date and provide a strong new image and central focus for the resort. Along with the renovations that introduce themes to original areas, they announce that this is a new enterprise.

Some hotels expand in stages. The Arizona Biltmore, designed by Albert Chase McArthur, a former apprentice of Frank Lloyd Wright, opened in 1929 in the desert near Phoenix. The fine resort and spa was developed by William Wrigley, Jr., who carefully maintained the identity of the original design until his death 1973. Often mistakenly thought to be the architect, Wright was, in fact, consulted on several issues during construction. A succession of new owners have maintained McArthur's design, including retaining Taliesin West, Wright's school and studio close to Phoenix, to plan several additions. The latest construction, in 1998, added a spa, fitness center, and wing of guestrooms, bringing the total to 730 rooms. Commitment of a new owner to the original architect's vision is rare in hotels, especially in the US, where marketing interests may suggest following the latest trends. Certainly, in the case of the Arizona Biltmore, Wright's architectural style, which has not always been valued by the general public, is much in vogue today, and serves as the preeminent characteristic of the 'jewel of the desert.'

In 1986 the owners of The Peninsula decided to renovate Hong Kong's renowned hotel, which had decidedly faded, and to construct a major addition. A sleek 30-story tower was built just behind the original 1928 neoclassical structure increasing the number of guestrooms from 168 to 300. The exterior contrast between the two buildings is distinct—the modern tower does not make stylistic concessions to the original hotel. While the two contrasting structures fit into the mix of scales and styles that define Hong Kong's urban landscape, its resolution on the interior was more challenging. While most details from the 1928 hotel were restored, the owners and architects did not want to recreate the past but, instead, to combine the past with modern elements. This makes a smooth transition to the addition, which reaches its sensational climax in the dramatic two-story penthouse restaurant and lounge designed by Philippe Starck. The integration between the old and the new calls for compromise with respect to historic authenticity, but it gracefully expands the hotel into one integrated whole.

In Egypt, a 40-story tower is being constructed as an addition to Le Meridien Cairo, a late 1960s luxury property prominently located at the north end of Roda Island in the Nile. The vertical thrust of the new tower, capped by a revolving restaurant offering spectacular views of Cairo and the pyramids beyond, complements the horizontal expanse of the original hotel. They share impressive modern façades, although they are not matched. The new 870-guestroom convention tower is almost three times the size of the original building, to which it is linked by a three-story gallery shopping mall. While the two towers share back-of-house and administrative facilities, the addition to Le Meridien Cairo is planned to function as a stand-alone hotel. At present they are under the same ownership. However, it would be possible for them to be divided and run as separate enterprises without major modification.

Adaptive Re-use

For centuries buildings constructed for other purposes have been converted into hotels. Irish castles, English country manor houses, French chateaux, and Rajput palaces in Rajasthan, India, have all been adapted as hotels. These largely residential uses lent themselves well to conversion. In fact, the intent was not to stray too far from the original. Part of the appeal of this transformation was that guests found themselves welcomed into the homes of aristocrats, gentry, maharajas, and other persons of high social rank whom they would not likely visit under other circumstances. This helped to compensate for shared bathrooms, no air-conditioning, and the lack of other amenities generally available at more typical hotels. Guests could take meals in the dining room, lounge in the drawing rooms, read in the library, and stroll in the private grounds just as the original residents did. Guests could think of themselves as members of a privileged class enjoying themselves at home. Some hosts continued to live on the premises and established these elaborate bed-and-breakfast accommodations in order to earn the monies needed to maintain their stately properties, while others ran them purely as businesses. Ownership often passed into the hands of other individuals bearing no relationship to the original owners but, mostly, they still were run as relatively small-scale operations.

The landmark adaptive reuse **The Ritz-Carlton San Francisco, California.** Heralded as the 'Temple of Commerce' when it opened in 1909 as the Metropolitan Life Insurance Company's Pacific Coast headquarters, this neoclassic landmark on Nob Hill was transformed with 336 guest-rooms and suites into one of the city's most luxurious hotels.

Today, with a high demand for accommodation, especially in urban areas, and a dwindling number of new sites on which to build or existing hotels to renovate, a vast array of building types are being converted into hotels. Many of these have little or no relation to lodging and some were not intended for human occupancy at all. They range greatly in scale, category, and location.

Office buildings are frequently considered likely candidates for hotel conversion. The soft market for office space in many cities compared with the tight market for hotels makes such transformations especially attractive to developers. The most sought-after are buildings of historic value. The Marriott Courtyard in the City Hall Annex in Philadelphia, The Ritz-Carlton adapted from the original Metropolitan Life Insurance Company in San Francisco, and the new boutique hotel in Raymond Hood's Radiator Building

The urban infill adaptive reuse hotel **Courtyard by Marriott at Scott Circle, Washington, DC.** The nondescript National Rifle Association headquarters building was given a new façade and a new life in its transformation to a hotel. The interior of the 1959 office building was stripped and gutted in creating the 158-key property.

in New York are such examples. The quality of materials and craftsmanship of these early twentieth-century landmark buildings cannot be equaled today and the grand scale of their public spaces lend themselves to dramatic entrances and lobbies. Such features give these hotels a monumental presence. The lavish budgets that owners apply to these hotel renovations, especially for properties in prime locations, allow for sensitive adaptations that please the city authorities who oversee landmark issues.

Few office buildings of landmark status come on the market today. Most are 1950s and 1960s structures in need of major overhaul, but not economically or functionally feasible to remain as office buildings. These structures often have footplates too small and ceiling heights too low to allow for renovation into office space that meets today's market demands. Yet these buildings sometimes are suitable as hotels. They often have a high proportion of windows to floor area—ideal for guestroom layouts—and a relatively low ceiling height for offices, yet entirely suitable for rooms. With cost savings over new construction, an obsolete office building can be the beginning of a new hotel.

Unlike landmark buildings, whose pedigree the hotel owners wish to promote, the owners of hotels converted from nondescript, post-war office buildings seek to conceal the use of the original building. A case in point is Marriott's conversion of the former National Rifle Association 1959 headquarters in Washington, DC, into The Courtyard Hotel. In addition to totally gutting the interior, the exterior was given a handsome facelift in order to change its image. Such conversions so far have been limited to mid-level accommodation, unlike the five-star option that landmark buildings can offer.

Often inherent in many buildings not originally planned as hotels is a disparity between existing conditions and optimal or, in some cases, even minimal hotel standards. The guestroom is most critical. In New York, where demand for new hotels greatly exceeds sites available for new construction and few existing hotels remain for upscale renovations, many buildings which do not obviously lend themselves to hotel conversion are being considered. A former jewelry manufacturing building in the newly gentrified Times Square district could only be configured into long, narrow guestrooms. To deal with this awkward arrangement, the architects creatively designed a spa room featuring an area with exercise equipment in the center of each guestroom.

The innovative adaptive reuse hotel **Hotel im Wasserturm, Cologne, Germany.** The exterior of Europe's largest historic water tower was protected by landmark status but the interior of this huge cylindrical structure with its massive masonry supports was fair game for designer Andrée Putman to create a uniquely elegant 88-key boutique hotel.

Today, landmark structures of all types are being converted into hotels. The rapidly expanding boutique segment is propelling a huge variety of building types for conversion (see Chapter 2). Some were never habitable buildings at all, like Cologne's water tower, the largest of its kind in Europe, which became the Hotel im Wasserturm in 1990. Limits imposed by the landmark status of this nineteenth-century structure included not removing a single exterior or interior brick. French designer Andrée Putman's signature modern, elegant interiors fit gently into the historic fabric of the water tower. The hotel's unusual circular form gives it a memorable presence and distinguishes it from most other business hotels. This appeal helps it to overcome its location, outside Cologne's central business district.

One of modern architecture's iconic industrial buildings, Fiat's Lingotto Factory in Turin, Italy, has recently been converted into a multipurpose complex, including Le Meridien hotel. Designed by Giacomo Mattè Trucco in the 1920s, the Lingotto factory was admired by Le Corbusier, who featured it prominently in *Vers une Architecture*. The great French-Swiss architect referred to the building as 'a guideline for town planning.' In its current adaptation with a convention center, business center, concert hall, exhibition area, art galleries, shopping mall, and hotel, Lingotto becomes a city within the city.

To ensure an ongoing appreciation of this remarkable structure, architect Renzo Piano, on the whole, defers to the fabric of the original building. He removes later ancillary structures, replicates the original fenestration grid, recreates stucco with a higher sand content, and restores the memorable and astonishing 1-kilometer long Fiat rooftop test track, now used as a jogging track. The client's desire was that the complex not just maintain the existing elements, but also invigorate the spirit of the old building, which was forward looking in its time. To this end Piano has left his mark by creating a dramatic conference room in a glass onion dome and helipad that provide a new silhouette for this historic complex, now oriented to the twenty-first century.

Le Meridien Lingotto is located around a courtyard in two three-story wings of the former factory. A glass-enclosed passageway through the courtyard, lush with Mediterranean vegetation, connects the reception area to the elevators serving the 240 guestrooms. On the sides are a restaurant and bar, which link to the business center and concert hall. Guestroom interiors are decidedly modern yet warm in a way that does not give way to the industrial nature of the renovated exterior. The ambiance of the hotel is distinct unto itself while part of a larger whole.

Buildings of all types have undergone changes in use over time. This includes buildings originally constructed as hotels and later adapted for other uses. Built in Washington, DC, in 1921, the Hamilton Hotel was converted into an office building when the demand for downtown hotels declined. In 1996 it reopened as The Crowne Plaza Hotel. The grandeur of the original entrance and lobby was restored and guestroom layouts were a straightforward recreation of the original plan. The difficult task for the architects was to add meeting rooms, a restaurant, and other requirements for a four-star hotel. Also, two additional floors were constructed within a mansard roof in order to make the hotel economically feasible.

The 1897 Norman-style castle in the lower Hudson Valley in New York, built for General Carroll, was bought in 1941 by an investment firm for use as its office. In 1997, it opened as a special events facility and inn. The first task was to remove all intrusions from its use as an office. The imposing public areas of the original house were readily transformed into the public rooms of the new enterprise and seven guestrooms were created from the family sleeping quarters. On the 10 acre (4 ha) site, architects found it easy to locate a new wing with 24 guestrooms, a fitness center, and meeting rooms off to the side of the original mansion.

In Europe, there still exists a surfeit of obsolete monasteries and convents. Monks' and nuns' cells typically are small and, in many of these abbeys, there are not enough rooms to convert them into profitable hotels without compromising their integrity. Yet there is an interest in adapting these buildings by governments which are less motivated by a high return on financial investment and more concerned with keeping this valuable part of their national cultural heritage alive. Since 1942 the Portuguese state has taken ownership of disused monasteries and convents, along with abandoned castles and palaces, and transformed them into 22 luxury hotels. In 1998, the 30-room Cistercian monastery in Bouro opened as a hotel. Architect Eduardo Souto de Moura was highly respectful of the former structure, wanting to keep the memory of the monastery alive in its new use. The rooms, decorated in a minimalist style, are highly popular with the sophisticated clientele and harmonize beautifully with the monastic ambiance.

Almost in a category of its own is the 310-room Grand Bay Hotel planned for Chicago. Its main façade will be clad with 4,000 pieces of carved limestone, cast stone, and pink granite removed from the 1929 art deco McGraw-Hill tower that occupied the site before its demolition in 1998. The cost to dismantle and re-erect the 16-story facade is $9 million, making it unlikely to start a trend. Only a few locations could justify such an expense. What it does point to is the lengths that developers sometimes have to go to find an appropriate central site for a grand hotel in a major urban area.

During decades of urban neglect, many hotels were converted into SRO (single room occupancy)

The adaptive 'mixed-use-reuse' hotel **Le Meridien Lingotto, Turin, Italy.** Featured in Le Corbusier's treatise, *Vers une Architecture*, the Fiat automobile factory's 1-kilometer long rooftop test track is now reused as a jogging track for the hotel's fitness center, poetically maintaining the spirit of its original use (see pp. C-14 and 300 for a further view).

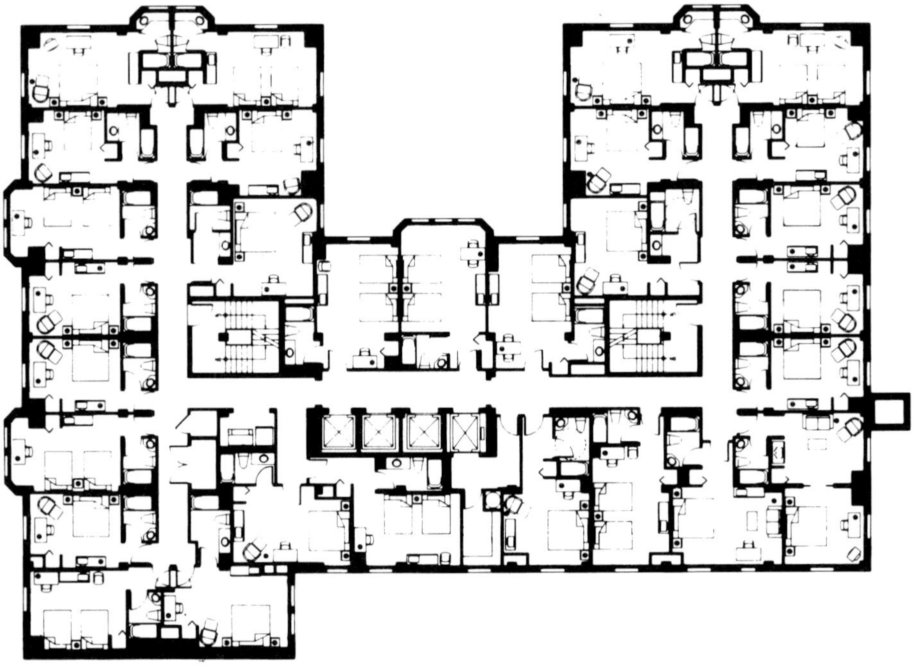

The 'unadaptive' reuse hotel **The Crowne Plaza Hotel, Washington, DC.** The original Hamilton Hotel, converted to an office building, was transformed back into a four-star hotel with traditional interiors. The guestroom level floor plans had to be recreated to accommodate the 318 new guestrooms (see p. C-15).

Table 10.4 Adaptive reuse: examples of structures converted to hotels

Type of structure	
Commercial	
Office building	Marriott Courtyard, Washington, DC
	St. Martin's Lane, London
	Shoreham II, New York
	W Union Square, New York
	Loews Philadelphia Hotel (PSFS Building)
	Hotel Burnham, Chicago
	Hotel Le Germain, Montreal
	Hyatt Regency, Buffalo, New York
	Landmark Hotel, San Antonio, Texas
	The Capital Hotel, Little Rock, Arkansas
Shipping headquarters	Hotel New York, Rotterdam, The Netherlands
Bank	Le Meridien Hotel, Boston
Department store or retail shop	The Chateau Sonesta Hotel, New Orleans
	Point Hotel, Edinburg, Scotland
	Canal Street Marriott, New Orleans
	Gran Hotel Cuidad de Mexico City, Mexico City
	Planters Inn, Charleston, South Carolina
Parking garage	Brookshire Hotel, Baltimore, Maryland
Manufacturing	
Automobile factory	Le Meridien Lingotto, Turin, Italy
Warehouse	The Mercer, New York City
	Adelphi Hotel, Melbourne
Flour mill	Art'otel, Potsdam, Germany
Fountain pen factory	Seidler Hotel Pelikan, Hanover, Germany
Ship engine plant	Bla Hallen Hotel 11, The Netherlands
Public	
College	The Ritz Carlton, San Francisco
Prison	Four Seasons Hotel, Istanbul, Turkey
Customs house	Marriott Customs House, Boston
Pub	The Prince of Wales, Melbourne
City hall	Hotel de Ville, Binghamton, New York
Fire station	Sheraton Greensboro, North Carolina
	Hilton Hotel, Columbus, Georgia
Lighthouse	East Brother Lighthouse Inn, Point Richmond, California
Railway terminal	Radisson Lackawanna Station, Scranton, Pennsylvania
	Choo Choo Holiday Inn, Chattanooga, Tennessee
	Hyatt Regency St. Louis, Missouri
Treasury building	Hotel Inter-Continental, Sydney, Australia
Residential	
Apartment house	The Mondrian, Los Angeles
	Sheraton Rittenhouse, Philadelphia
	Bleibtreu Hotel, Berlin
	Hotel Widder, Zurich, Switzerland
	Hotel Lancaster, Paris
	Regents Court, Sydney, Australia
	Stanford Court Hotel, San Francisco
	Marriott Essex House, New York
	Tremont Hotel, Baltimore, Maryland
	Sheraton Winnipeg, Canada
Townhouse	The Hempel, London
	Blakes, London
	Hotel Eden, Rome
Elderly home	The Standard, Los Angeles
Company housing	American Club, Kohler, Wisconsin
Dormitory	L'Hotel, Paris
Farmhouse	Inn at Chester, Chester, Connecticut
Harem	Shepheards Hotel, Cairo, Egypt
Hunting lodge	Oberoi Mena House, Giza, Egypt
	Ajit Bhavan, Jodhpur, India
Palace	Kempinski Hotel Taschenbergpalais, Dresden, Germany
	Marriott Cairo, Egypt
	Palace Hotel, Bussaco, Portugal
	Villa d'Este, Lake Como, Italy
	Udaipur Lake Palace, Rajasthan, India
	Villa Vista Hermosa, Mexico (Cortez's palace)
Private home	New York Palace, New York City
	Tarrytown House Conference Center, Tarrytown, New York
	Schlosshotel Vier Jahreszeiten, Berlin
	Seven One Seven, Amsterdam
	Hotel Qufo, China (Confucius's home)
	Hotel D'Angleterre Remmen, Copenhagen, Denmark
	Holiday Inn Chateau Le Moyne, New Orleans, Louisiana
	Roxborough Hotel, Ottawa, Canada
	Queen Victoria Inn, Cape May, New Jersey
	Numerous bed-and-breakfast inns
Antebellum mansion	Monmouth, Natchez, Mississippi
Maritime flophouse	Ace Hotel, Seattle
Adobe house	Hotel Terrantai, San Pedro de Atecama, Chile
Religious	
Church	Hilton International Budapest, Hungary
Convent	Milan Four Seasons, Milan, Italy
	El Convento Hotel, San Juan, Puerto Rico
Monastery	Pousada Santa Maria de Flor da Rosa, Crato, Portugal
	Geneva-on-the-Lake, Geneva, New York
Priory	Hotel at Bath, England
Other	
Castle	Schloss Ekberg, Dresden, Germany
	Chateau de Creissels, France (built 801)
	Chateau de Meyrargues, France (built 970)
	Numerous castle hotels throughout Europe
Water tower	Hotel im Wasserturm, Cologne,Germany
Grain silos	Hilton Quaker Square, Akron, Ohio
Historic fortress	Mandawa Castle, Rajasthan, India
	Namrana, Rajasthan, India
Granary	Copenhagen Admiral Hotel, Copenhagen, Denmark
Pirate hideaway	Sam Lord Castle, Barbados, West Indies
Ship	Queen Mary, Long Beach, California
Stable	Das Triest, Vienna
Social club	Dylan Hotel, New York

establishments to house people with low income, on public assistance, or with disabilities. Many of these marginal buildings, mostly in urban areas and often privately owned, are being emptied of these tenants in order to realize more revenue. With the high demand for urban hotels, a large number of SROs are being converted into hotels. While these buildings, many of which were built originally as hotels, might be physically opportune for such transformation, they often carry a negative association in the mind of the public, one that is aggravated by landlords who sometimes harass tenants to vacate the building. This is a matter of civic concern and advocacy groups often are successful in bringing these instances to the attention of the media.

The Regent Wall Street, New York, originally the Merchant's Exchange built in 1842 to the design of Isaiah Rogers (famous for his earlier Tremont House, Boston, and Astor House, New York), reopened in 2000 as a luxury 144-room boutique hotel. The imposing Greek revival structure, with massive monolithic Ionic columns, had earlier been renovated by architects McKim, Mead & White in 1908. The present adaptive use of this palace of commerce as a hotel maintains interior spaces of colossal scale. The oversized guestrooms range in size from 525 to 900 ft^2 (48.8 to 83.6 m^2). Suites are substantially larger. The banking hall is now the 34,000 ft^2 (3,160 m^2) grand ballroom with an 80 ft (24.4 m) high coffered ceiling. The furnishings, in Italian Renaissance style, will provide opulence befitting the magnificent scale of the interior spaces. This is the first hotel in the heart of the financial district and it attracts guests who are accumulating enormous wealth on the nearby New York Stock Exchange. It recalls the architecture that robber barons favored in the nineteenth century at a time when comparable fortunes are being amassed today.

Trends

- The unbeatable formula of historic architecture combined with present-day comforts and facilities will continue. However, as quality historic buildings and sites for new hotels become scarcer, especially in cities, buildings of all types and styles will be potential targets for redevelopment as hotels.

- The popularity of postmodern architecture has crested and the modern look once again is holding sway. International style buildings no longer will be adorned with decorative elements that recall the past. While authorities still stipulate that the exteriors of landmark buildings be restored to their original guise, hotel owners no longer will feel obliged to follow through in the same design with the interiors, where landmark regulations do not hold. The juxtaposition of sleek modern interiors within historic buildings will prove most popular, especially among young affluent guests, an increasing portion of travelers.

- Hotels can gain publicity from selecting a celebrity architect for a renovation, even if only to design a particular facility, like a restaurant or nightclub, such as Felix, the smashing multioutlet rooftop restaurant of Philippe Starck at The Peninsula, Hong Kong.

- Modern technology, which enables daring structural feats, will be enlisted for renovations and additions to incorporate a tour de force, such as the spectacular swimming pool cantilevered over a sidewalk in the Adelphi Hotel in Melbourne, Australia. A bold, dramatic gesture gives a strong identity to a hotel, and can be used to make a splash in changing the image of a hotel in attracting more upscale guests.

- More and more business travelers will be using their rooms for work as well as for rest and sleep. Updating existing hotels will require installing new technologies in the guestrooms (and other areas) including two phone lines, private fax machines, high-tech lighting, and other technologies and systems in order to be competitive.

- As the public continues to show an increased interest in personal health, hotels will offer more facilities for fitness, including exercise rooms, spas, massage and other health-related activities. In this same mode, renovations will favor environmentally friendly natural materials and building systems.

- Hotels in need of space for additional revenue-producing facilities, such as a business center, bar, or more guestrooms, may consider moving such back-of-house facilities as laundry or accounting to satellite locations. This can be an attractive option particularly for hotels in urban areas where constructing a building addition might not be feasible. This also can allow hotel companies that have several regional hotels to consolidate these activities.

Table 10.5 Prominent older hotels

Hotels over 100 years old
Three Kings Hotel, Basle, Switzerland
Cour St. Georges, Ghent, Belgium
Hotel Krone, Solothurn, Switzerland
Hotel d'Angleterre, Copenhagen, Denmark
Grand Hotel Sauerhof, Baden bei Wein, Germany
Hotel de Crillon, Paris
The Continental, Paris
Hotel des Trois Couronnes, Vevey, Switzerland
Royal Crescent, Bath, England
The Palace Hotel, San Francisco
The Strater Hotel, Dorango, Colorado
Le Chateau Frontenac, Quebec City, Canada
Banff Springs, Alberta, Canada
Chateau Lake Louise, Alberta, Canada
St Louis Hotel, New Orleans, Louisiana
The Chelsea Hotel, New York City
The Cincinnatian, Cincinnati, Ohio
Mohonk Mountain House, New Paltz, New York City
Grand Hotel, Point Clear, Alabama
Grand Hotel, Mackinac Island, Michigan
Hotel Del Monte, Monterey, California
The Capital Hotel, Little Rock, Arkansas
The Jefferson Hotel, Richmond, Virginia
Mission Inn, Riverside, California
The Brown Palace Hotel, Denver, Colorado
The Savoy, London
The Tovar Hotel, Grand Canyon
Hotel del Coronado, San Diego, California
Claridges, London
The Connaught, London
The Willard, Washington, DC
The Ritz, Paris
Oberoi Grand, Calcutta, India

Hotels over 75 years old
The Ritz, London
The Greenbrier, White Sulphur Springs, West Virginia
The Broadmoor, Colorado Springs, Colorado
The Copley Plaza Hotel, Boston
The Plaza, New York City
Old Faithful Inn, Yosemite National Park, Wyoming
The Fairmont, San Francisco
Huntington House, Pasadena, California
The Ritz, London
The Shelton Hotel, New York City
The Biltmore, Los Angeles
The Hotel Taj Mahal, Bombay, India
The Hermitage, Nashville, Tennessee
The Bellevue-Stratford, Philadelphia, Pennsylvania
The St. Regis, New York City
The Seelbach, Louisville, Kentucky
Mount Washington Hotel, Bretton Woods, New Hampshire
The Sagamore, Lake George, New York
The Breakers, Palm Beach, Florida
The Drake, Chicago
The Chicago Hilton and Towers

The multifaceted mega-hotel **Atlantis, Paradise Island, Bahamas.** With more major market segments than any other resort, ranging from gaming to visitors to marine habitats, Atlantis stimulates the widest variety of guest interests (see p. C-29 for a further view).

Mega-hotels

11

In an era of segmentation, the mega-hotel has emerged as the grand dame of the new century. While seemingly unsegmented, such hotels are designed to strongly attract each market, from tourist to business, and conventions to family theme parks, through a form of internal segmentation which so perfectly responds to the needs of each different guest, that they feel like the hotel was designed for them.

Pleasantly surprising the theme park industry, the first mega-hotels were launched in Orlando, Florida, in the mid-1980s as destination sports and convention resorts, as well as major headquarters hotels for family sight-seers and business travelers. They included the 750-room Hyatt Regency Grand Cypress and the 1,500-room Orlando World Center Marriott serving four major mainstream markets. But within a decade, Las Vegas' casino hotels added theme parks, raising their coverage to five major markets, while Atlantis, with a major casino, marine habitat, and marina, reached an even half-dozen markets. And so, the grand mega-hotel grew grander!

The planning and design of the mega-hotel differentiates the activities of each segment while, at the same time, bringing them together where appropriate, such as at the themed shopping and entertainment atrium or food fair. For example, these hotels may locate the children's pool in a landscaped courtyard surrounded by the family guestroom wing and a second, quieter, more relaxed pool on the penthouse level, offering dramatic views as well as a fully equipped health club. Each market segment benefits.

Mega-hotels may combine a superb marine habitat, virtual offices, and a lively atrium, complete with water features, lavish planting, and exciting art, in a more subtle and sophisticated concept than is possible with typical segmentation, attracting guests to such diverse locations as Atlantis in the Bahamas and the burgeoning Mohegan casino hotel and entertainment complex in Connecticut.

Perfecting internal segmentation extends to room locations. For example, at the Orlando World Center Marriott, guests or meeting planners may select their guestroom based on such preferences as:

- in the family wings near activity centers and parking (families)
- in the tower suites (business travelers)
- near the main lobby (tour groups)
- close to desired sports activities or the spa (special vacationers).

Although the Hyatt Regency Grand Cypress was one of the first grand mega-hotels to cater so effectively to many different guest markets within the hotel, ironically, it was Marriott, well known for its successful segmented brands, to first coin the term 'mega-hotel' for its grand resort in Orlando.

Planning and Design Considerations

Mega-hotels of 1,000–3,000 rooms, with extensive convention facilities and amenities, are uniquely located at resort sites of about 50 acres (22 ha). These large sites require comprehensive environmental studies to address community concerns ranging from flood control to archeology (see Appendix A). Such studies establish the project's cost and feasibility as well as identify necessary government approvals. In the case of the Walt Disney World Dolphin and Swan Hotels and Loews Portofino Bay Resort, planned as part of Walt Disney World Resort and Universal Escape, respectively, such approvals were taken into account in the initial master environmental studies when the land was acquired. This avoided piecemeal planning and expedited the rapid development of hotels integrated with tourist attractions based on predetermined standards for transit, utilities, landscaping, building massing, and density. Years of additional lead time would have been required if such previous approvals had not been obtained. Master planned hotel sites such as those created at Walt Disney World

Resort, Epcot, and Universal Orlando are key factors in the success of these developments.

Access into the site by at least three approach roads is required to provide adequate car queuing space. Because of the resort's entertainment function, huge parking areas, with vast amounts of landscape treatment are needed, for which a multi-million dollar budget would not be unusual. Planners should provide space for a minimum of 1.5 cars and 0.01 tour buses per room. The mega-hotel requires several entrances to accommodate people arriving at such varied functions as:

- main lobby
- convention/exhibit area
- tour group reception
- various sports centers and spa
- restaurants, lounges, and entertainment areas.

Land planners generally include large ponds, even lakes, to retain water run-off from the parking and other hard-surface areas; landscape designers add waterfalls, streams, and reflecting pools to blend the building with the land forms and to provide visual amenities for the main views from restaurants and guestrooms. Hotels of this scale often include their own special transit systems (for example, decorative trolleys, electric golf carts, boats and, where justified, monorail trains) to provide convenient access to the more distant guestrooms and recreational facilities and to generally enhance the guest's experience.

The basic outdoor amenities include separate swimming pools, one specially designed for children with water slides, waves, and other features, tennis courts (one for each 100 rooms), and an 18-hole golf course, if the hotel doesn't adjoin an existing one. Mega-hotels provide nurseries for different age groups, play areas with one dormitory bed per 75 rooms (which has proven safer and more efficient than hiring in-room baby-sitters), and a teenage classroom with computerized educational games. Larger guestrooms—minimum net living area of 13 × 21 ft (4 × 6.4 m)—are required to allow for the rollaway beds and cribs needed to accommodate families. The elevator capacity must be increased by 10 percent due to the greater number of occupants (average of 3.4 per room), the higher use of passenger elevators by children, and the greater demand for room service by families when on vacation.

To attract business travelers, the towers rooms, serviced by a private elevator bank, must be a minimum of 13 × 21 ft (4 × 6.4 m) plus balconies, compared with 13 × 18 ft (4 × 5.5 m) for standard guestrooms. The hotel provides guests on the towers floors with extra services and amenities including a rooftop lounge and outdoor terrace for continental breakfast, cocktails, and small meetings. Due to the hotel's large scale, architects should consider mini-atriums on the upper floors to integrate daylighting into the elevator lobbies.

Significant Mega-hotels

Atlantis, Paradise Island, Bahamas

With its extremely popular and superbly conceived marine habitat, yachting marina, sports, business, and convention center, as well as a premier casino in the Caribbean, Atlantis is intended as an ideal resort city, exciting its guests with the chemistry of its public spaces as well as the quality of its attractions.

The legend inspiring the design of the 1,200-room Royal Towers and Palace on Paradise Island is ascribed to Plato's original reference to a vast ocean empire built in a fortress of concentric rings of land and water, until a massive earthquake sent it to the bottom of the sea. Guests may view an imaginative display of the ruins of Atlantis, 'The Dig,' in giant picture windows, including deep-water life ranging from piranhas and sharks to jellyfish and eels. Visitors also may explore the legendary inventions of the ancient civilization, including their hieroglyphic alphabet.

Atlantis contains 2,300 rooms on an 826 acre (334 ha) site on Paradise Island, Bahamas, near both downtown Nassau and the airport. The resort's unique 100,000 ft^2 (9,290 m^2) entertainment center boasts one of the Caribbean's largest casinos, which sets new standards as one of the first to bring natural light to the gaming floor. The resort includes 38 restaurants and lounges and extensive meeting facilities, among them the largest ballroom in the Caribbean. The architects, WAT&G, also designed The Palace of the Lost City in Sun City, South Africa, for the same owner, Sun International, led by South African hotelier Sol Kerzner. EDSA designed the landscape and sitework; Wilson & Associates designed the interiors.

Recreational and landscape features include a water activities and attraction complex with slides, rides, swimming lagoons and three pools, 40 waterfalls, fountains, snorkeling and one of the region's best beaches. At the center is a six-story themed Mayan Temple enclosing four major waterslides, leading through a shark-filled tank to a seemingly steamy jungle swamp. But the focal point of this 34 acre (13.8 ha) Atlantis waterscape is the world's largest tropical marine habitat and aquarium, displaying 50,000 fish and sea animals from around the world.

Walt Disney World Dolphin and Walt Disney World Swan Hotels, Orlando, Florida

The Walt Disney World Dolphin and Swan Hotels are organized around a crescent-shaped lake and connected by a covered pedestrian causeway and trams traversing the lake crossing. The structures follow a consistent character and highly architectural thematic intent.

A wide range of facilities was designed to appeal to the several different types of guests ranging from tourists and business and convention groups, to family theme park visitors and sports vacationers. One of the main objectives of the hotel complex was to support the major international convention and conference center at Walt Disney World Resort and Epcot, which features three ballrooms and more than 250,000 ft^2 (23,225 m^2) of combined meeting space. The hotels offer 2,267 guestrooms including 191 suites, many themed to Italian, Egyptian, Japanese, and southwest US décor.

The character of the design and its colors, décor, and surroundings are in the tradition of native Florida resorts, with a thematic context consistent with Disney's program for entertainment architecture. The lakeside façades of the hotels are uniquely painted with large-scale banana leaf patterns on the Walt Disney World Dolphin and abstract wave patterns on the Walt Disney World Swan. Giant statues of dolphins and swans are placed at either end of the buildings' rooftops, announcing the themes of their hotels from a distance. Architect Michael Graves' use of whimsical super-sculpture as an important architectural element adds to the significant contributions of this convention resort and early grand mega-hotel.

Mohegan Sun Casino Resort, Uncasville, Connecticut

After the flowering of the first mega-hotels in the mid-1980s, it was axiomatic that the trend would bear new niche prototypes such as this culturally-focused mega-resort. Thorough research of Mohegan folklore by the designers inspired the interiors, from the variety of popular themed amenities to the entertaining and educational planetarium and the historic information 'time piles' located throughout the complex. The expansion of the casino continues the ingenious functional layout of the gaming areas based on Indian legend (see p. 234). This new mega-resort reinforces the five principal hotel markets targeted in the area—conventions, gaming, sports, themed attractions, and business travel.

The culturally-themed lobby **Mohegan Sun Casino Resort, Uncasville, Connecticut.** Large abstract representations of the Mohegans' favorite red cedar trees throughout the lobby create a spacious outdoor atmosphere for guests arriving at this first Native American-themed mega-hotel (see pp. 224 and 234–235.)

The themed site context resort **Portofino Bay Hotel at Universal Orlando, a Loews Hotel, Florida.** The massing of large convention resorts can be effectively reduced by visual downsizing methods, here in the scale of the fishing village. The main five-story façade faces the harbor; other guestroom wings enclose a secluded pool and spa courtyard and landscaped gardens (see p. C-28 for a further view).

Loews Portofino Bay Resort, Universal Escape, Orlando, Florida

The resort's unique exterior exactly replicates the harbor-line façades of the village of Portofino in Italy, complete with varying window patterns, residents' brightly colored walls, and decorative columns, pilasters, and moldings. It provides guests with the relaxed ambiance of a charming European harbor by day and a romantic setting for meals and casual strolling at night. Tumbled granite cobblestones and plaster wall finishes with marble mosaics add character and the desired aged look. 'Our hotel guests and visitors feel a real sense of place here,' observed Michael Sansbury, regional vice-president for Loews Hotels.

Forty percent of adult travelers say they want to take vacations at resort theme parks. With its extensive convention facilities and corporate conference center, Portofino is positioned to cater to diverse markets ranging from families visiting the major theme parks to convention groups, business visitors, and sports vacationers. Eight restaurants, bars, and other outlets are placed at various locations around the lake and piazza. The walkways and paving follow surveys of the Italian town which were used as a model for the hotel design. The 750 guestrooms feature worn wood furnishings including four-poster beds against a neutral color palette, and decorated with reproductions of northern Italian artwork.

The architectural concept succeeds in down-scaling the large structural requirements to a human scale, and by blending it into the water-theme scheme of the adjoining park, using the relaxing motif of the European boat-filled harbor to create one of the most endearing resort settings of any major hotel of the era. WAT&G were the design architects and Morris Architects were architects of record for the documentation.

With a second hotel, the 650-room Hard Rock Café Hotel opposite the Portofino Bay, the two Loews hotels together serve exactly the same function and market as the Dolphin and Swan mega-hotels at Walt Disney World Resort.

Trends

New hotels and resorts will continue growing in size, for economy of operation and market penetration. They also will continue to expand their in-house segmentation, by featuring new and hybrid niches depending on location and a creative mix of business and recreational amenities.

The community mega-hotel **The Westin Kierland Resort of Phoenix/Scottsdale, Arizona.** The centerpiece of the Kierland planned community, the new Westin resort is designed to attract multiple markets. The design orients 60,000 ft^2 (5,575 m^2) of meeting and seminar space, several restaurants and lounges, a 27-hole championship golf course, and spa amenities to surrounding mountain views (see pp. 216 and 392).

A democratically planned complex **AOL Time Warner Center and Mandarin Hotel, New York.** Located at the pivotal southwest corner of Central Park, Columbus Circle has long been among the most controversial development areas in New York City. Spurred by dedicated civic groups and public officials, talented development teams throughout the 1990s submitted competing schemes to anchor a much-needed westward expansion of the vital Fifth Avenue luxury hotel, shopping, and tourist district. The joint public–private effort produced several quality proposals illustrating different uses—this one incorporating a 250-room Mandarin Hotel—in a design that reduces the bulk facing the park and incorporates a series of traditional New York setbacks (see p. 208).

Mixed-use Developments

12

Each element of the mixed-use complex, including its hotel, office building, condominiums, and shopping mall, benefits from integration with a larger, more prestigious project. With its higher visibility and more ambitious overall planning concept, the impact of the entire development is far greater than the sum of its parts. In addition to its more efficient methods of land use, assembly, construction, and financing, the mixed-use complex encourages innovative design, often overriding outdated zoning regulations, improving traffic circulation patterns, and initiating planning variances beneficial to both the community and the developer.

The Exchange Coffee House Hotel, built in Boston in 1809, was one of the earliest hotels to provide ample public spaces that ushered in a new era of hotels as downtown social and political epicenters. In addition, it is one of the earliest examples of a mixed-use hotel building. The Merchants' Exchange, located under the giant sky-lit rotunda of the hotel's main floor, provided a market not only for the 200 guestrooms but also for the ballroom, coffeehouse, and dining rooms that were the very public spaces that defined this new genre. It set an early example for the synergistic advantages that result from combining diverse functions into mixed-use developments, especially when the hotel is a central component of the mix.

The end of the nineteenth century saw tremendous building development around major railway stations, including hotels, office buildings, retail, and other uses. The large and lavish hotels offered so many special amenities and public functions that they often were spoken of as 'cities within cities.' In Chicago one of the most spectacular of these developments was the Auditorium Building that combined three types of public use. Designed by Adler & Sullivan, it combined an office block, a luxurious 400-room hotel on Michigan Avenue, and an acoustically perfect 4,300-seat theater, the world's largest when it opened in 1889. Except for the entrance, the theater was almost completely enclosed away from the street by the hotel. Created to provide a permanent home for Chicago's opera, symphony, and other performing organizations, the multiuse commercial components—the hotel and office space—were included in order to offset possible losses from the operation of the theater. The complex rose 16 stories, the tallest in Chicago at the time, in part by adapting innovative structural systems to allow the hotel ballroom to span over the theater. More than a century later, mixed-use projects continue to be in the forefront of structural innovation and the competition to develop the tallest building.

Mixed-use Complexes

Pioneer of the modern downtown hotel, Ellsworth M. Statler constructed the Boston Statler Hotel, the first major mixed-use development combining hotel and office building, covering a full block in Boston in 1927. Two years later, on the day before the stock market crash in 1929, a $42 million dollar construction contract was signed for the Waldorf=Astoria, a monumental hotel/residential complex that represented the last major hotel project to be built until after World War II. Major mixed-use projects that contained hotels did not appear again until the government-sponsored urban renewal efforts of the 1960s prompted such huge developments as Place Bonaventure in Montreal and Boston's impressive Prudential Center. These key projects set the pace for downtown revitalization by attracting both regional and international clientele to their large convention facilities, office structures, and elaborate malls and by providing the latest in recreation and entertainment amenities for the city. The Prudential development, the largest complex of its kind up to that time, included a 50-story office tower with a popular visitors' observation center at its top, a 5,000-seat civic auditorium, a 1,500-room twin tower Sheraton hotel, two apartment towers, and a 3,000-car underground garage.

In the 1970s John Portman's designs for Embarcadero Center in San Francisco and Renaissance Center in Detroit demonstrated the use of huge atriums to provide the focus and organizing elements of mixed-use developments which included offices, retail, and hotels. Other significant complexes facing more stringent site limitations relied on the stacking of functions vertically such as Water Tower Place in Chicago, with its Ritz-Carlton Hotel topping a multistory shopping mall and Araldo Cossutta's cylindrical hotel occupying the upper floors of the Credit Lyonnaise office building in Lyon, France.

Two major mixed-use projects, the Houston Galleria and Boston's Copley Place, highlighted the public's infatuation with shopping malls where the hotels supplied potential shoppers while the malls provided hotel guests with a wealth of additional amenities. In these pioneering developments, which included office buildings and convention facilities, corporate travelers and executives could bring their families on business trips to enjoy the array of shops and recreational facilities, while many tourists may be drawn to the hotel-in-mall concept, providing instant activity for their vacations.

Two major mixed-use developments of the early 1980s signified the explosive business growth and rapid expansion of tourism in Singapore during that period. Raffles City, designed by I.M. Pei and taking its name from the world-famous Raffles Hotel, borders on downtown Singapore and contains two major hotels and an office tower connected by a seven-story podium containing retail and restaurants. Both hotels are operated by Westin Hotels and Resorts and, therefore, benefit from certain shared back-of-house and administrative functions. The Westin Stamford Singapore, at 71 stories, was the tallest hotel in the world when completed. The second project, John Portman's Marina Square convention complex, included an even higher ratio of hotel offering three major hotels each focused around a major atrium area with restaurants, cinemas, shopping, office, and recreational facilities clustered at their bases.

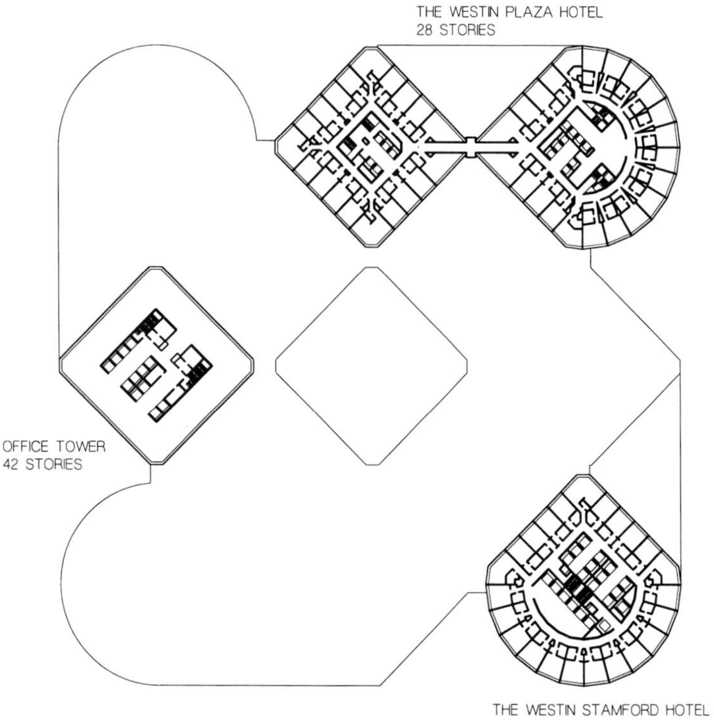

Typical floors of a seminal ultratel **The Westin Stamford and Westin Plaza towers, Singapore.** Taking its name from the venerable neighboring Raffles Hotel, this modern mixed-use complex pioneered two innovative hotel towers: the ultra-high-rise Westin Stamford (71 stories) and high-rise Plaza (28 stories) set the trend for the wave of efficient multiuse hotels and future ultratels. Their plans reflect research on resistance to wind and seismic forces.

Development and Planning Considerations

Because of their size and complexity and their potential impact on surrounding communities, large mixed-use projects very often are part of a comprehensive urban master plan and, therefore, are subject to the goals and guidelines set forth by the local planning authority. For the same reasons, these large projects often are subjected to intense scrutiny by local communities and civic groups and can be the source of heated debates over the economic, social, and environmental benefits and drawbacks. Many projects, such as the AOL Time Warner Center development at Columbus Circle in New York City, require huge capital commitments and can drag on for decades until a consensus is reached with regard to the scale and composition of the project. Because of the beneficial influences that a hotel provides, the city may offer zoning variances and bonuses, tax abatements, and other economic incentives to encourage developers to include hotels in their schemes. Hotels often act as catalysts, promoting other more lucrative surrounding development, and are as essential as residential development for a balanced community.

The key goal to a successful mixed-use development must be for each component of the development to benefit from its inclusion with the overall project and to draw significant advantages from its interaction with other components. For that to happen, a synergy must exist between its various uses—such as hotel, office, retail, residential, and entertainment—to produce a positive confluence where the entire development becomes far greater than the sum of its parts. Advantages of mixed-use projects include:

- higher visibility as a result of being part of a larger, more prestigious project
- more efficient methods of land use, assembly, construction, and financing
- greater built-in market demand
- adjacency to a captive audience
- certain shared operating costs
- combined efficiency of a central energy plant serving the entire complex
- combined loading facilities
- better control over and improved traffic circulation patterns
- combined comfort and security of an enclosed development
- shared parking where different peak business hours allow for a reduction in spaces
- insulation against market fluctuations of any one component.

Just as a hotel's success is based on the right mix of facilities, the viability of a mixed-use development depends on the optimum combination of uses it offers. A market analysis and feasibility study may provide a rational evaluation of the proposed uses and indicate the profitability of the overall project as well as each component by itself. It is difficult to find building types or uses that are not on some level compatible with hotels or for which some historic precedent cannot be found. One might think of factories or prisons, but it does not take much imagination to realize that a hospitality market could exist even for these functions.

Design Considerations

Whether connected through a mall, atrium, central lobby, or some other pedestrian circulation element common to the other primary functions in the mixed-use development, the hotel lobby should be designed as an extension of the overall development. In most cases, because of greater circulation resulting from traffic of adjacent uses, the hotel lobby should be 20 percent larger than those of other downtown hotels with comparable guestroom capacity. Hotel restaurants and lounges should have entrances directly on the common space, where possible, with open cafés on the center's atriums. Their restaurant and bar seating should be 30 percent more than in conventional downtown or suburban hotels, reflecting the greater built-in demand for lunch and dinner, drawing from the center's retail, entertainment, residential, and office areas.

In high-rise mixed-use complexes where uses are divided vertically and hotel guestroom levels are located on upper floors, above office, retail, or residential levels, a hotel 'sky lobby' may be required if adequate space is not available in the building's podium. A porte cochere and a well-defined street-level hotel entrance lobby must be provided that is separate and distinct from the office, residential, or retail entrances. The entrance lobby must be staffed by doormen and a reception desk where guests are greeted and directed to express elevators that take them directly to the sky lobby floor, which should contain all of the ingredients normally found in a downtown hotel lobby: reception desk, lobby lounge, restaurants and bar, and access to function rooms and health clubs. From the upper lobby guests gain access to a separate set of elevators connecting to the guestroom floors. Sky lobbies have the potential for great drama as they may open up to a panoramic view or be part of a 'sky-atrium' as is the case with the Grand Hyatt Shanghai, China, part of the Jin Mao Tower.

To determine the number of parking spaces required in a mixed-use complex, a study of peak hour business of all major uses should be conducted to determine the peaks and valleys of parking requirements for each use at different times during the day. For example, since the peak business hours of retail malls and hotels overlap, additional parking is normally required to accommodate both functions. A specific parking area should be set aside for hotel use to ensure space for its guests. With underground garages, a separate shuttle elevator between the garage and the lobby is preferable for security purposes, rather than extending the central elevator bank down to the garage levels.

Service entrances may be combined for all facilities in the complex and located underground on tight urban sites. Special security practices must be provided at the loading docks and receiving offices in this type of shared arrangement.

The lively mixed-use entertainment hotel center **Grand Hyatt Fukuoka, Canal City Hakata, Japan.** With 450 rooms and suites at the heart of this vibrant $1.4 billion entertainment and commercial mega-complex on the Naka River, the five-level hotel podium connects with the shops and venues of Canal City by a network of pedestrian bridges and pathways.

Significant Mixed-use Complexes

Grand Hyatt at Canal City Hakata, Fukuoka, Japan

No mixed-use complex represents the transnational trend towards the merging of entertainment and multiple commercial uses including hotels better than the Canal City Hakata project in Fukuoka, Japan. On 9 acres (3.7 ha) of riverfront property, the 2.5 million ft^2 (232,250 m^2), $1.4 billion mega-complex was designed by The Jerde Partnership International, world renowned for their designs of mixed-use retail and entertainment projects. The Canal City development contains a mix of entertainment, retail, business, and hotel as signified respectively by its four destination anchors: Fukuoka City Theater, Daiei's Mega

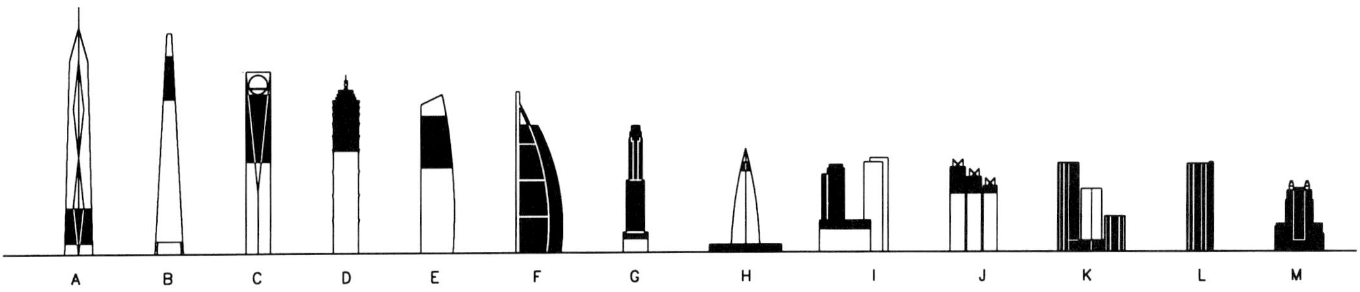

	PROJECT/HOTEL NAME	LOCATION	ARCHITECT	STORIES	HEIGHT
A	KOWLOON TOWER	HONG KONG, CHINA	SOM	102	1,883 FT (574 MTS)
B	GROLLO TOWER	MELBOURNE, AUSTRALIA	DENTON CORKER MARSHALL	113	1,836 FT (560 MTS)
C	WORLD FINANCIAL CENTER	SHANGHAI, CHINA	KPF	94	1,509 FT (460 MTS)
D	GRAND HYATT	SHANGHAI, CHINA	SOM	88	1,380 FT (421 MTS)
E	DAEWO MARINA CITY 21	PUSAN, SOUTH KOREA	KPF	102	1,312 FT (400 MTS)
F	BURJ AL ARAB	DUBAI, UAE	WS ATKINS & PARTNERS	60	1,053 FT (321 MTS)
G	BAIYOKE SKY	BANGKOK, THAILAND	PLAN ARCHITECTS CO	94	1.050 FT (320 MTS)
H	AL FAISALIAH HOTEL	RIYADH, SAUDI ARABIA	FOSTER & PARTNERS	30	853 FT (260 MTS)
I	JR CENTRAL TOWERS	NAGOYA, JAPAN	KPF	59	774 FT (236 MTS)
J	PARK HYATT	TOKYO, JAPAN	KENZO TANGE	52	771 FT (235 MTS)
K	WESTIN PLAZA & STAMFORD	SINGAPORE	I.M. PEI	72	733 FT (223 MTS)
L	WESTIN PEACHTREE PLAZA	ATLANTA, USA	J. PORTMAN	73	723 FT (221 MTS)
M	WALDORF=ASTORIA	NEW YORK, USA	SCHULTZE & WEAVER	42	566 FT (173 MTS)

Modern high-rises reach new heights **High-rise hotels and ultratel towers.** New high-rise mixed-use projects generally place the hotel functions high in the tower (shaded portions) but developers increasingly study the revenue potential of different planning strategies.

Vandle Department Store, Canal City Business Center and, the centerpiece of the project, the Grand Hyatt Hotel. Eight years in the making, Japan's largest privately-developed project transformed an abandoned, industrialized waterfront on the Naka River by integrating multiple uses into the urban fabric and revitalizing the commercial district to become a value creator and catalyst for nearby real estate.

The complex is laid out around five themed outdoor environments as a series of special districts that surround an artificial canal that serves as the interior circulation spine and organizing spatial element of the project. Rendered with contrasting geometrical forms these five districts represent five basic cosmic elements: the *Earth* Walk, the *Moon* Walk, the *Star* Court, the Red *Sun* Plaza, and the *Sea* Life Playground. The arc shaped canal provides a 700 ft (215 m) long pedestrian promenade along its banks with multiple bridges connecting the shopping, entertainment, culture, hotel, education, and office uses. A wedding chapel designed as a bridge spans the interior canal at the third level so that the wedding party floats over the water. The fourth level roof deck contains a Japanese garden and spa overlooking the interior of the complex.

The placement of the hotel at the center ideally establishes it as the 24-hour fulcrum of activity. When checking in, hotel guests are given a choice of rooms in the hotel tower: those facing west view the Naka River and the city of Fukuoka beyond, those on the east overlook the teeming activity of the canal. The hotel entrance serves as one of the front doors to the whole project, encouraging visitors to pass through the lobby thus linking it with the circulation system of the entire project and extending the hotel's boundaries. The hotel's five-level podium is connected with other shops and entertainment venues of Canal City by a network of pedestrian bridges and pathways. The canal-side façade of the podium showcases the hotel lobby and the hotel's entertainment and banquet facilities through huge glass windows, exposing the nerve center of the hotel and continuously infusing energy and activity to the center of the project.

Bati Tourism Center, West Istanbul, Turkey

Bati Tourism Center is a planned multiuse commercial center situated in a rapidly developing suburban

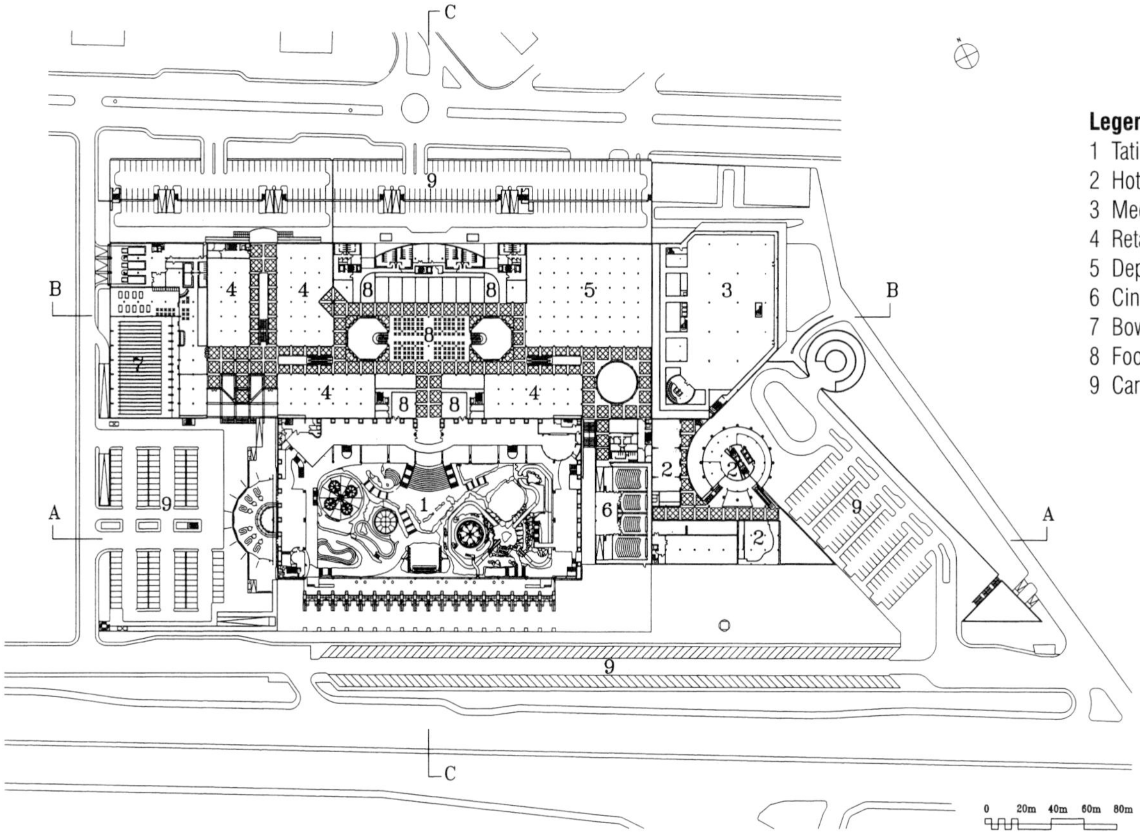

Legend
1 Tatilya
2 Hotel complex
3 Medical center
4 Retail
5 Department store
6 Cinemas
7 Bowling
8 Food court
9 Car park

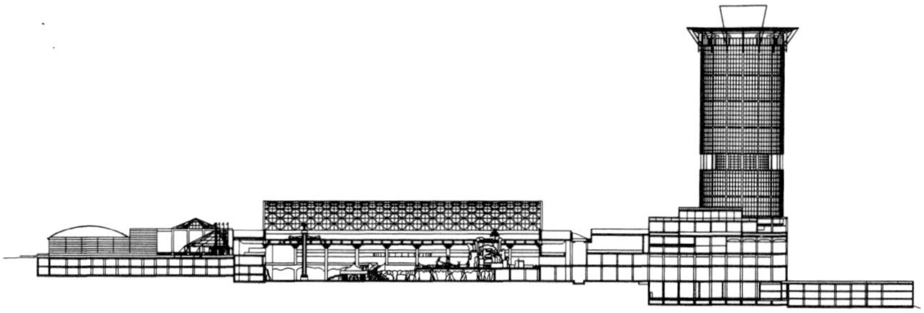

The entertainment mixed-use complex **Bati Tourism Center, West Istanbul, Turkey.** The 2 million ft^2 (186,000 m^2) retail and tourism complex emphasizes recreation and health care. In addition to the 250-room hotel and 200,000 ft^2 (18,600 m^2) medical center, it contains a shopping mall, multiplex cinema, bowling hall, supermarket, food court, and an innovative indoor theme park named Tatilya, meaning 'Holiday Land' (see Chapter 4).

area to the west of central Istanbul (*bati* means 'western'). Growth projections for the near future are for a new suburban city with a population exceeding two million people, larger than many major European cities. At approximately 2 million ft^2 (185,800 m^2), Bati Tourism Center will be the largest commercial center of this new city, containing a covered theme park (currently in operation under the name *Tatilya*, or 'Holiday Land'), a shopping mall, department stores, a multiplex cinema, recreational facilities, supermarket and food court, and 250-room hotel complex and a 200,000 ft^2 (18,580 m^2) medical center. It is a retail and tourism center with an emphasis on recreation and health care.

Instead of the classic linear diagram of North American shopping malls that stretch between two major chain department store magnets, the layout of this scheme calls for the various spatial and functional groups to be interconnected with a circulation grid arranged as a series of streets and squares. A coordinated system of skylights introduces daylight into the complex, enhancing the sense of place. The aim is to focus and accentuate the urban pattern of the surrounding residential areas in a more tightly knit spatial fabric and to create an urban center containing a multitude of functions and spaces instead of one large building.

The initial investment for the complex was for the construction of the highly successful indoor theme park. Tatilya is a rare, covered park that carries as its main theme 'entertainment in nature.' Suited to this earthquake-prone region, an innovative structural system of diagonal steel trusses was employed to span over the soccer field-size courtyard containing the primary entertainment activities.

The circular hotel tower rises 25 floors above the complex and echoes the ribbed vaulted dome of Tatilya, presenting a dramatic composition of forms. Uses within the hotel complex that are complementary to the overall project and integrated with the circulation grid at the base include a ballroom and meeting spaces for 1,500 people, two restaurants, a pastry shop, and a well-equipped fitness center. The center contains an indoor swimming pool, squash courts, and gym that provide important shared health related facilities to the medical center.

Al Faisaliah Center, Riyadh, Saudi Arabia

Designed by Sir Norman Foster & Partners, Al Faisaliah Center has been referred to as the Eiffel Tower of Riyadh. The 875 ft (267 m) high multi-use office tower is the tallest building in Saudi Arabia and its 78 ft (24 m) diameter gold-glass geodesic globe near the top is visible from miles into the desert beyond the city limits. Cantilevered solar-shade devices will project from the curtain wall system of the tower—an energy-saving feature designed to control glare and to allow the use of nonreflective, energy-efficient glass (see p. 384).

The project is unusual in composition since the luxury hotel and residential complexes are clustered at the base of the office tower rather than placed at the top like so many contemporary examples. The very top of the 30-story tower is reserved for a three-story restaurant encased in a giant glass sphere and a steel spire housing satellite connections to the world. The hotel and residential components, both of which will be operated by Rosewood Hotels as super-luxury properties, are connected to the office building and retail mall by the 'link building,' a six-story atrium at the base of the tower that boasts the largest stained-glass art wall in the world. The main entrance to the tower is approached via a plaza landscaped with water features and palm trees and flanked by the eight-story hotel and residence wings. The link building spans the entire width of the plaza and houses the huge entrance lobby and main reception space to the tower. A 3,000-seat banquet hall designed to host royal functions and large Islamic weddings occupies the subterranean section of the plaza.

The 2.4 million ft^2 (223,000 m^2), $320 million complex is being developed by the King Faisal Foundation, which will use the profits for its cultural, educational, research, and philanthropic projects worldwide.

AOL Time Warner Center, New York City

Typically, boldness, determination, and imagination by a dedicated group of developers and community leaders are needed to spearhead projects of such size and complexity, requiring extensive government and citizens' approvals, huge capital commitments, and a decade of planning and construction. In high-density urban areas, even assembling a few acres well served by rapid transit and in the path of commercial growth is often a miraculous accomplishment.

There may be no more embattled site for a mixed-use urban development project than the one on Columbus Circle in New York City, where Broadway intersects the southwest corner of Central Park. In 1985 the city and the Triborough Bridge and Tunnel

The Big Apple's reward for public/private teamwork **AOL Time Warner Center and Mandarin Hotel, New York.** The massive 2.8 million ft^2 (260,120 m^2) 55-story mixed-use development will include the home of Jazz at Lincoln Center with a 1,300 theater and performance atrium facing the park, headquarters for AOL Time Warner, CNN Studios, 540,000 ft^2 (50,170 m^2) of retail, 203 luxury condominiums and a 250-room five-star hotel (see p. 200 for a further view).

Authority issued a 'request for proposal' to replace the New York Coliseum, an early mixed-use exhibition center and office building complex dating from the late 1950s. The initial winning design included two mammoth office towers that would have cast deep shadows into Central Park and exacerbated the tangle of traffic at this node in the Broadway corridor. In a dramatic demonstration of the negative effect of the towers, protesters holding black umbrellas traced the shape of the vast shadow that would be cast over the park. Years of public debate followed until the pull-out of a key tenant and a lawsuit brought by civic groups against the city and planning authority eventually caused the project to stall.

A new proposal for a scaled-back development responding to many of the earlier issues of scale, massing, traffic, and public amenities is being advanced by developers The Related Companies and designed by architects Skidmore, Owings & Merrill (SOM). The new design includes lower profile twin towers drawing from historic references of traditional apartment buildings along Central Park West, pulled back from the circle to reduce their impact on Central Park. The mixed-use development includes the new AOL Time Warner world headquarters, CNN live broadcast production studios, luxury retail, entertainment, restaurant, office, and residential components, as well as a new 135,000 ft^2 (12,540 m^2) world-class performance hall named Jazz at Lincoln Center. The 2.5 million ft^2 (232,250 m^2) complex also will include the new Mandarin Oriental New York Hotel with 250 guestrooms and suites overlooking Central Park. In addition, the hotel will provide luxury services to the 203 residential apartments in the towers of the complex.

A 100 ft (30 m) rotunda functions as the main public space and organizing element for the building's base, serving as the entrance to the office building and the heart of a four-story retail mall, following the subtle curve of Columbus Circle. As with the residential lobby, a separate hotel entrance lobby is entered from a private through-block street from which shuttle elevators carry guests to the dramatic sky lobby 250 ft (76 m) above ground. From here the hotel's public spaces fan out to include a restaurant, lobby lounge, cocktail bar, and a state-of-the-art conference facility for up to 750 people, including a 5,500 ft^2 (510 m^2) ballroom with its own views of Central Park.

Palladium Center and Lincoln Square, Bellevue, Washington

The city of Bellevue, across Lake Washington from downtown Seattle, is located in the heart of the technology corridor just 4 miles (6 km) from the world headquarters of Microsoft Corporation—one of the greatest sources of room-night demand in Washington State. Plans for a new downtown mixed-use project, Palladium Center, will feature two hotels, a 241,000 ft^2 (22,390 m^2) retail/multiplex cinema complex, several upscale restaurants, and a 2,200-space underground parking garage. The project is being developed in conjunction with a major city-sponsored expansion of the Meydenbauer Convention Center, adjacent to the project, and with significant financial participation by Marriott International who will operate both hotels: the 550-room Marriott Bellevue Hotel and the 300-room Ritz-Carlton Bellevue Hotel.

Through 'strategic complexing,' the dual-hotel concept represents a unique example of how mixed-use developments can result in cost-effective construction, development, and operating efficiencies. Marriott will operate the hotels with shared back-of-house areas (housekeeping, property maintenance, and laundry) and such shared administrative functions as accounting, purchasing, and onsite reservations. In addition, the pairing allows for a unified marketing approach and source of overflow demand since the Marriott Hotel serves the corporate transient and group hotel market while the more luxurious Ritz-Carlton hotel will be the only five-star hotel east of Lake Washington. Together they will contain the largest concentration of upscale rooms in the region.

Two blocks to the west, adjacent to the new Bellevue Art Museum, another mixed-use project named Lincoln Square is being developed with a 304-room hotel. The Westin Bellevue is part of a complex that will include a 27-floor office tower, 182 residential units above the hotel, 150,000 ft^2 (13,935 m^2) of retail, five restaurants, an athletic club, an 18-screen AMC Megaplex theater, a 12,000 ft^2 (1,115 m^2) child-care facility, and five levels of underground parking. Microsoft Consulting Services has taken a key role in the project and will provide all essential system integration and software design management, as technology is one of the main focuses of the Lincoln Square development. The hotel will utilize the latest advances in communication technology and design, allowing guests to experience the ultimate personalization, integration, and recognition services, delivered via a high-speed technology infrastructure. Guestrooms will feature an integrated state-of-the-art 'information appliance,' serving as a central access point for all types of entertainment, voice, data, and video services.

Shanghai World Financial Center, China

The developers of the Shanghai World Financial Center (SWFC) are enthusiastic contenders in the race to build the tallest building in the world. Designed by Kohn Pederson Fox Architects to rise 1,520 ft (460 m), it would top the Petronas Towers in Kuala Lumpur by 26 ft (8 m). However, the project stalled because of financial problems and the overbuilt office market in Shanghai. With the delay, the SWFC lost claim to the title when the Skidmore, Owings & Merrill (SOM) design for 7 South Dearborn in Chicago was announced at 1,537 ft (468.5 m) tall. Not to be outdone, the SWFC's developer announced on the same day that construction would resume and that the design for SWFC would be enlarged so that it will once again be the tallest in the world when complete. The developer also stated, 'We can't announce [the height] yet, because some people might want to surpass it again.' But several other projects are already hot on their heels, including SOM's Kowloon MTR Tower in Hong Kong at 1,550 ft (472 m) and the Grollo Tower in Melbourne at 1,838 ft (560 m). Like the SWFC, both these towers are mixed-use projects with hotels as a primary component (see p. 205).

SWFC is located in the Lujiazui Financial and Trade district of Shanghai, a massive development zone designated by the Chinese government to be an Asian center for international banking and trading. Another major mixed-use project, the 88-story Jin Mao Tower (world's second tallest building at completion), stands only one block away.

Ancient Chinese conceived of the earth as a square and the sky as a circle. The interaction of these two geometric forms gives rise to the physical form and structure of this tower. The primary shape is devised as an extruded square intersected by two sweeping arcs, tapering to a single line at its top. (William Pederson, Joshua Chaiken)

The 164 ft (50 m) cylindrical void at the top of the tower forms an observation deck, called the 'moon gate,' and is equal in diameter to the pearl sphere of the Oriental Pearl TV Tower, purposely creating a solid-void dialogue with the district's most important landmark structure. The simplicity of the tower design is contrasted by a complex geometry at the base podium reflecting the multitude of activities and interactions at street level.

Three sets of elevators provide access from the podium. The office lobby is at ground level where office floors are accessed by double-deck elevators; observation deck elevators also depart from the podium. Hotel guests ride escalators to the second floor where they take shuttle elevators to the 49th floor reception area. Guestrooms and a hotel restaurant on floors 81 through 90 are accessed by designated elevators which depart from the mid-tower hotel reception floor.

The continuously tapering geometry of the tower presents the hotel layout with a difficult design challenge since each floor plate is slightly different, growing smaller the higher the floor, while the core dimensions remain constant. While this fluctuation of floor plate size can be easily accommodated in office planning, the geometry significantly increases the number of room types for the hotel and adds to the complexity of operation (see preface, p. x).

The 'pagoda-like' ultratel tower **Grand Hyatt at Jin Mao Tower, Shanghai, China.** The top 32 floors of this 88-story tower house the 555-keys of the hotel wrapped around a dramatic cylindrical sky-atrium. The rhythmic pattern of setbacks in the tower is intended to recall the form of ancient Chinese pagodas.

Grand Hyatt at Jin Mao Tower, Shanghai, China

One block away from the site of the Shanghai World Financial Center, Jin Mao Tower rises 88 stories and was the first major mixed-use project completed in the Lujiazui district. The 555-key Grand Hyatt Shanghai occupies 32 floors at the top of the building and includes the tallest atrium ever built. The lower 50 floors of Jin Mao Tower are used for offices. In addition to the hotel and office uses, a six-story podium building contains a shopping mall, cinema, auditorium, food court, and conference facilities for the hotel. Three levels below grade include parking for 993 cars and 1,000 bicycles. The hotel's sky lobby links multiple public space functions on three levels including reception, lobby lounge, several restaurants, hotel administration offices, and a health club with a swimming pool at the 57th floor. There are nine restaurants in the building including two on floors just below the 88th floor observation deck. While others claim to be the tallest hotel in the world, the Grand Hyatt Shanghai can claim to be the highest hotel in the world, at least until the SWFC next door is complete.

Daewoo Marina City 21, Pusan, Korea

The stunning 102-story Daewoo tower is part of a master plan for a major city center development at Suyoung Bay on the waterfront in Pusan, Korea. The proposed 2.7 million ft^2 (250,830 m^2) mixed-use project is to include office, hotel, service apartments, retail, performing arts center, museum, ballroom, and convention center uses. The elegant sail-shaped tower, reminiscent of the yacht races that occurred on this site during the 1988 Olympic Games, offers a monolithic simplicity much like that of the Shanghai World Financial Center, also designed by architects Kohn Pederson Fox.

The slender taper of the tower reflects its subtly different uses; the building's larger lower levels provide flexible office space while the smaller upper floors, hollowed by a huge north-facing atrium, are efficient for hotel use. The functions are expressed on the exterior by subtle horizontal bands that delineate the juncture of offices, residential, and hotel. The tower terminates with a large glass-enclosed void for gallery functions and an observation deck.

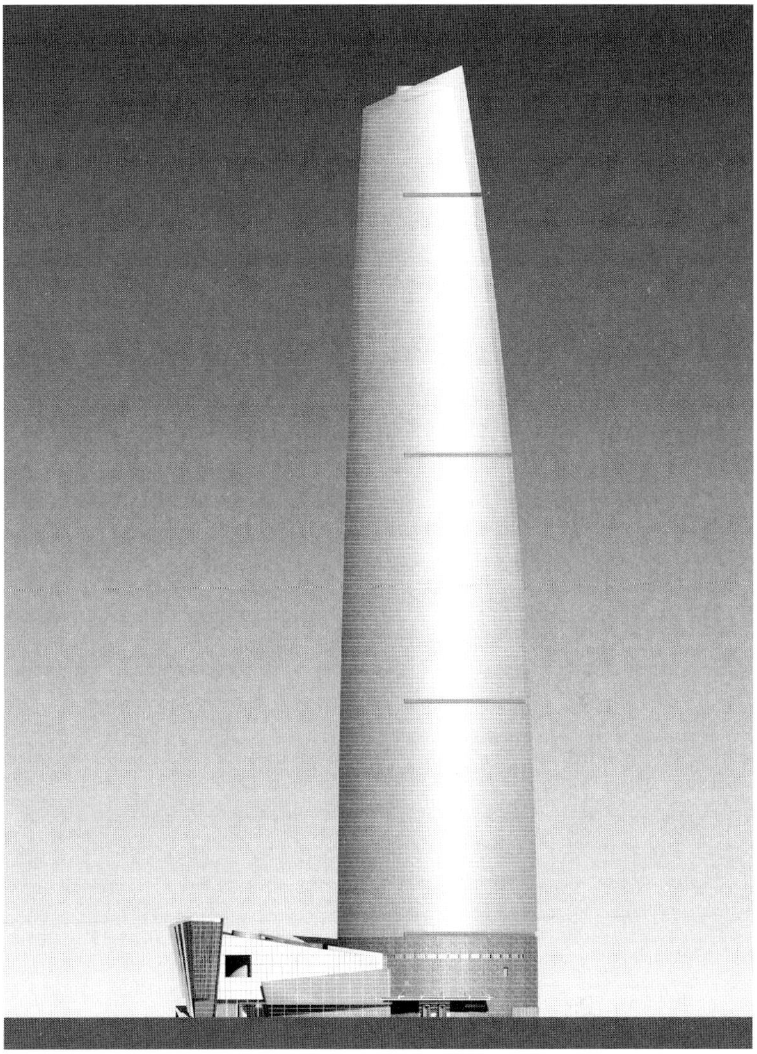

The Korean cultural ultratel **Daewoo Marina City 21, Pusan, South Korea.** The architects of the 102-story tower drew inspiration from artifacts of Korean culture where an elegantly curving line often expresses the dialogue between man and nature. The tower and podium house 2.7 million ft^2 (250,830 m^2) of hotel, office, service apartments, retail, performing arts center, museum, ballroom, and convention center uses.

JR Central Towers & Station, Nagoya, Japan

Developed by Japan Central Railways and also designed by Kohn Pederson Fox Architects, no new mixed-use development expresses the variety of functions it contains better than the JR Central Towers & Station in Nagoya, Japan's third largest city. The vertical elements of the 59-story hotel tower and the 55-story office tower intersect the horizontal banding of the 20-story retail podium which spans over a major transportation complex. The horizontal ribs of the podium emphasize the rail lines below that serve the high-speed bullet train (*Shinkansen*), the national railway network, several commuter trains, and the city subway and bus lines. In the future, a nearby station will serve as a stop for the magnetic levitation train, now in development. Helicopter-pads are located on the roofs of both towers, adding to the transportation web.

The design addresses the structural challenge of creating a large mixed-use building on top of an existing transportation hub, in addition to integrating the many thousands of people who daily use the terminal with those needing to access the mixed-use building. Construction was sequenced carefully to allow active transportation networks to maintain operations.

Circulation patterns of vehicles and pedestrians are clearly defined. Distinct and separate circulation paths for people using different aspects of the building are expressed in the 15th floor Skystreet, transforming the building into a vertical city, where the major uses of the hotel, office, and retail are linked. Such a configuration encourages diversity and integrity of uses and fosters future applications such as virtual officing where hotel guests may lease office space and services on a daily basis, in addition to their guestroom.

Park Hyatt at Shinjuku Tower, Tokyo, Japan

The Shinjuku Tower in Tokyo is a massive mixed-use complex of 2.8 million ft^2 (260,120 m^2) designed by

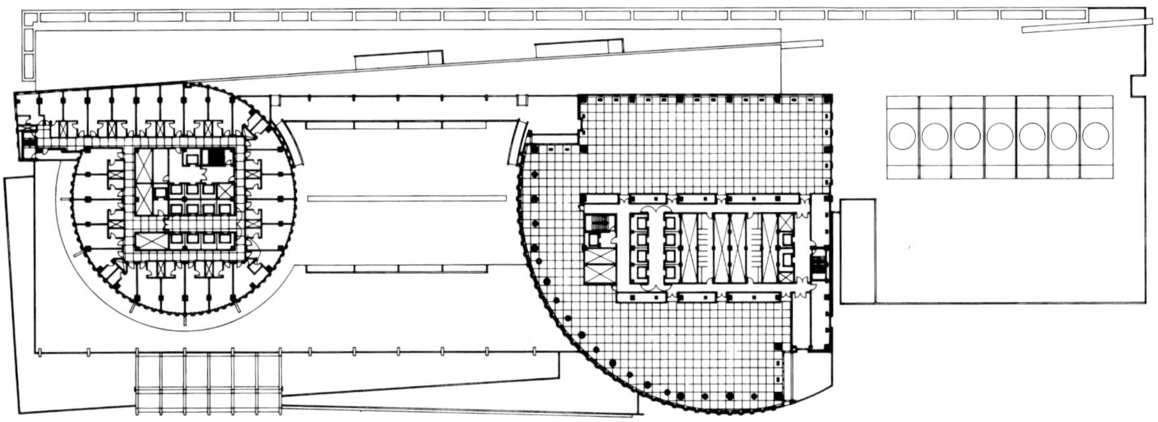

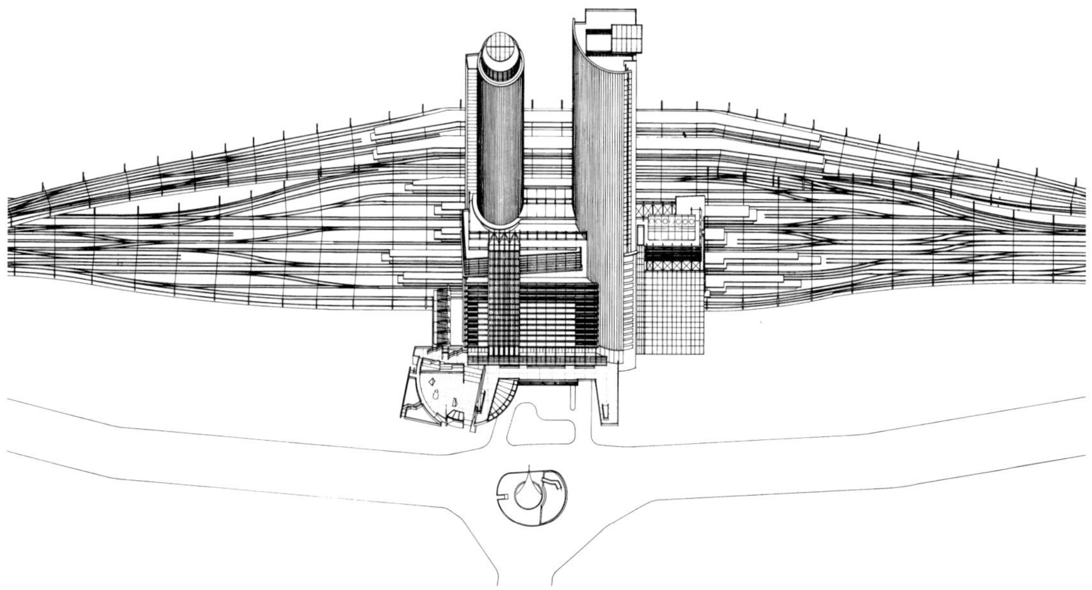

The ultratel transit hub **JR Central Towers & Station, Nagoya, Japan.** The *Shinkansen*, Japan's high-speed bullet train, passes through the middle of this futuristic complex situated on top of the city's primary regional transportation hub that serves the national railway network, several commuter rails, the city subway, and bus lines. Designers of the 4.8 million ft^2 (446,000 m^2) development masterfully solved the high-density pedestrian circulation between the station and other major components of the project that include a 59-story hotel tower, a 55-story office tower, and a 20-story retail podium (see p. C-5 for a further view).

Kenzo Tange, consisting of three intersecting glass towers, the tallest at 52 stories. Representing less than 15 percent of the total building floor area, the 178-room Park Hyatt occupies the top 14 floors. The remainder of the triple towers is devoted to office use; retail, showrooms, and restaurants are clustered in the building's podium levels. Tange was one an early proponent of the Metabolist movement in architecture that established a theory of urban mega-scale mixed-use structures as living growing organisms.

From the second-floor porte cochere and hotel entrance lobby, express elevators carry guests to the dramatic glass-roofed Sky Lobby and Sky Lounge on the forty-first floor. Here, the unusually large floor plate of over 54,000 ft^2 (5,015 m^2) permits the public spaces to spread out and allows a flexibility in the massing of the top of the building normally characteristic of large suburban sites. The tripartite tower culminates at three progressive levels, each covered by an asymmetrical polyhedron-shaped skylight structure. The lowest of the three towers features an indoor bamboo garden, the middle step houses the swimming pool of the Club in the Park fitness center, and the highest of the trio, the New York Grill restaurant, with spectacular panoramic views of Tokyo. The towers shrink inward slightly at the fourty-first floor expressing a break between the office levels and the hotel above. The only disadvantage of the building's creative massing is the distance that guests have to walk from the Sky Lounge express elevators to the guest floor elevators, placed to reach the top floors, at the opposite end of the lobby floor, nearly 400 ft (122 m) away (see color section, p. C-4).

Trends

- The sky is the limit, figuratively, in terms of the types of new mixed-use combinations that will succeed. The Pan Pacific Vancouver combines a hotel with a cruise ship terminal. The Naoshima Museum Hotel combines a contemporary art museum in a suburban resort setting attached to a guestroom wing. The Skydome in Toronto includes an in-stadium hotel where the guestroom windows face directly onto the playing field. Mixed-use developments will continue to explore new recipes of unexpected and diverse blends with hotels as the key ingredient yielding delicious results for its developers and guests.

- The sky is the limit, literally, in terms of mixed-use 'ultratels,' high-rise projects over 70 stories. Developers seek an icon on the skyline; architects and engineers eagerly explore innovative systems that make ultra-high-rise projects economically and practically feasible. Multiple uses—office, retail, hotel, residential—complement each other, making a larger project feasible than if it were a single use. Also, the different functions reduce the pressure on many building systems, such as elevators, by their having different peaks during the day.

The twin-towered ultratel **Emirates Towers Hotel, Dubai, UAE.** The two 51-story towers, one office and one 400-room hotel, are located in the city's central business district as a highly visible symbol of the region's corporate success. The design is composed of two opposing equilateral triangular towers linked at the podium level by an elaborate retail arcade which features spacious walkways with sky-lit courtyards, exclusive shops and theme restaurants. The office tower, at 1,150 ft (350 m) claims to be the tallest building in the Middle East and Europe, while at 1,000 ft (305 m), the hotel tower is the third tallest in the world.

- The mixed-use concept perhaps reached its most exaggerated form at the hands of architectural visionary Paolo Soleri with his proposal for a highly integrated urban form, which he named 'arcology.' An arcology literally is an entire city within a single building shell. Meant as a salve to urban and suburban sprawl, its highly compact form would leave the natural landscape relatively undisturbed while deriving benefits from shared energy sources, reduced transportation needs, effective recycling of waste, and reduction of pollution. With the growing interest in green architecture and environmental responsibility as evidenced by the tremendous expansion of ecotourism, future mixed-use projects may exploit the inherent environmental advantages and efficiencies where architecture fuses with ecology.

Planned Community Developments

Distinct from the more concentrated urban commercial/residential mixed-use complexes, planned community developments expand to embrace the demands of an entire living community. In addition to office, hotel, retail, entertainment, residential, and related uses, these developments also may include schools, parks, museums, a farmers' market, and town hall. When such developments are resort oriented, such as at Costa Smeralda or Laughlin, Nevada, they are considered 'multiresort complexes' (see Chapter 4). Planned community developments discussed here are those that provide the essential elements of a residential community and feature hospitality facilities.

As discussed in Chapter 3, New Urbanism is a growing movement among today's community planners. This movement, when applied to a new planned community, seeks to return to the principles of traditionally styled neighborhoods and downtowns in creating close-knit communities that are both charming and functional while reducing dependence on the automobile.

Seaside, Florida

No development has advanced the principles of the New Urbanism movement as completely as has Seaside. The 80 acre (32 ha) planned community on Florida's panhandle breaks sharply from orthodox planning notions and delivers innovative concepts that have sparked a broad rethinking of the design of new communities. For a half-mile stretch of beachfront property owned by his grandfather and considered a worthless tract of sand, Robert Davis engaged architects Andres Duany and Elizabeth Plater-Zyberk to devise a master plan that would incorporate Gulf Coast vernacular architecture in fostering a strong sense of place that characterizes seaside towns such as Charleston, Savannah, Nantucket, and Cape May. With a projected population of 2,000, Seaside includes plans for 350 houses plus 300 other dwelling units including apartments and hotel rooms.

Initial planning included a study of small towns in Florida and other parts of the southeast US that documented street widths, distances between structures, sidewalks, street trees, lighting, building forms, and their materials. As a result, wood-framed cottages with deep roof overhangs, ample windows, and cross-ventilation in all rooms, so well adapted to the climate that they enhanced the sensual pleasure of life by the sea, became the dominant building type for Seaside. The Seaside Urban Code sets forth a common vocabulary of building forms and materials while encouraging and promoting the opportunity for individual architectural expression. Each house is unique with designs spanning a wide variety of architectural expression as represented by their names: Blue Belle, Natchez, Lagniappe, Seven Oaks, Tiger's Paw, Dreamside, Jack's Beanstalk, Sand Castle, and Pelican Perch.

Based on patterns found in small southern towns, the master plan generated an immense variety of spatial experiences. The principal public spaces include the town hall and square, an open-air market, the school site, a tented amphitheater, a tennis club, a tiny post office, as well as shops and offices. The semi-octagonal form of the town center faces the Gulf of Mexico across the main road that passes through town. The street layout creates axial relationships among special structures and public spaces that contribute significantly to the sense of orientation and optimize waterfront access and views.

The master plan and code dictate a moderate level of density; the relatively close spacing of the houses and mandated front porches built out to the street line contribute to the sense of a close-knit neighborhood. The size and layout of Seaside is appropriate to the '5-minute walk' principle, which is the time it takes most people to walk a quarter of a mile. With all of the daily needs inside that distance, the town becomes a more pedestrian-riendly place, reduces dependence on cars, and promotes casual social encounters among residents.

Seaside offers a wide variety of overnight accommodations ranging from luxury full-service to modest limited-service lodging spread throughout the town. Many of the cottages themselves may be rented on a daily, weekly, or monthly basis. Others include the Honeymoon Cottages, full-service duplex units tucked behind the dune and facing the Gulf; Dreamland Heights, luxury penthouses overlooking the Town Square, and Seaside Motor Courts, providing old fashion motel-like accommodations.

Celebration, Florida

A second Florida community offers an interesting contrast to Seaside. The new town of Celebration, 30 minutes from downtown Orlando, is an innovative development conceived as a small southeastern town with pre-1940s architecture. Plans call for for 12,000–15,000 residents on 4,900 acres (1,980 ha) surrounded by an equal-sized protective greenbelt.

The planned community on the Gulf **Seaside, Florida.** Advancing the innovative principles of the New Urbanism movement, the planners sought to instill a strong sense of place and neighborhood by mandating regional vernacular architecture with houses close together, front porches, and an emphasis on pedestrian circulation. The semi-octagonal town center faces out to the Gulf of Mexico while the street layout creates axial relationships between special structures and public spaces and optimizes waterfront access and views.

Developed by The Celebration Company, a subsidiary of The Walt Disney Company, Celebration was designed by an all-star roster of architects that included Cooper, Robertson & Partners and Robert A.M. Stern Architects as master architects and land planners for the town. Other well-known architects who designed prominent buildings for the development include Cesar Pelli, Michael Graves, Philip Johnson, Charles Moore, Aldo Rossi, and Venturi, Scott Brown & Associates.

The developer's goal was to adapt ideas from the most successful American small towns of yesteryear to a community of the future. The development includes homes with front porches, community parks, a vibrant downtown business district, a magnet public school, a signature golf course, tennis courts, acres of parks, ponds, and open spaces, miles of nature trails and bike trails, a community swimming pool, a state-of-the-art fitness center, and a first-class hospital.

The planned community lakeside resort **The Celebration Hotel, Celebration, Florida.** The heart and soul of a planned community is its downtown, often including a hotel. In addition to generating a charming ambiance and instilling downtown with lively activity, the 115-room Victorian-styled lakeside lodge provides important amenities for the community, including a restaurant and bar, meeting spaces and a lakeside terrace, a perfect spot for informal gatherings and special events.

The planned community desert resort **The Westin Kierland Resort of Phoenix/Scottsdale, Arizona.** The Kierland Community, covering 730 acres (295 ha) outside Phoenix, integrates residential neighborhoods, elementary schools, offices, and specialty retail with a 750-room destination resort and 27-hole championship golf course. The hotel features a series of arcaded courtyards, each reflecting a distinct character, unified by indigenous southwest colors and materials and shaded by deep roof overhangs (see pp. 199 and 392).

The most important feature that promotes the hometown atmosphere and is visually and psychologically the heart of Celebration is its downtown. Restaurants, movie theaters, a farmers' market, shops, grocery store, post office, bank, and town hall combine with 123 apartments with front- or side-facing porches in providing an enchanting and lively village center along a scenic lake-front. A key element to the success of the downtown ambiance and activity is the Graham Gund-designed Celebration Hotel, a 115-room Victorian-styled lodge remindful of Florida's turn-of-the-century tourist trade when Henry Flagler developed his elegant resorts. With 5,000 ft^2 (465 m^2) of flexible event space, the hotel is able to attract corporate retreats and cater to special local functions much as would a small town hotel (see Chapter 3). The hotel's lakeside terrace provides an attractive outdoor gathering spot for guests and residents alike.

The successful downtown or village center sets planned communities such as Celebration apart from other suburban residential developments and gated communities like those that surround the Greater Orlando area. Well-designed planned communities will attract homebuyers to a real and viable family-oriented community.

Senior and Assisted-living Residences

Our society is aging—it's a demographic fact. As the baby boom generation rapidly approaches retirement, the demand for senior residential care facilities is rising steeply. People over the age of 85, the ones most likely to need chronic care programs, represent the fastest growing age group. In 2000, there were over 1.2 million people in assisted-living facilities and communities in the US and that number is ballooning dramatically. In the early 1980s there were only two basic choices for seniors in need of long-term care: minimum care retirement homes or medically intensive nursing homes. Today, reflective of increasing sophistication in consumer preferences, there is a vast array of service facilities to choose from, ranging from independent living complexes and assisted-living residences to special care units and 24-hour skilled-nursing facilities.

The senior and assisted-living residence on the Gulf **Bentley Village, a Classic Residence by Hyatt, Naples, Florida.** Gulf Coast vernacular architecture set adjacent to a wetlands nature preserve provides a country club-like setting for this 155 acre (63 ha) community that includes 500 independent living apartments, 48 assisted-living suites, 36 Alzheimer's suites and 93 skilled nursing beds.

Assisted-living Residences

The Assisted Living Federation of America (ALFA) defines an assisted-living residence as 'a special combination of housing, personalized supportive services, and health care designed to meet the needs—both scheduled and unscheduled—of

The lakeside senior and assisted-living residence **Lakeside Village, a Classic Residence by Hyatt, Lantana, Florida.** The traditional colonial architecture and interior décor of the Grand Lobby supports the goals of the Continuing-Care Retirement Community (CCRC) by providing a home-like atmosphere where residents feel both secure and independent. The Billiard Lounge located across from the main dining room fosters continued social interaction.

those who need help with activities of daily living.' The senior-living industry refers to 'activities of daily living' (ADLs) to represent the basic functional abilities (eating, bathing, dressing, toileting, and walking) that people need to care for themselves without assistance. Assisted-living facilities are designed for residents who generally need help with just two or three ADLs, but are relatively self-sufficient and who want to maintain a high level of independence. Designed for those who don't require full-time nursing care yet cannot live completely independently, assisted living provides a less institutional and more economical alternative to nursing homes that, on average, cost twice as much. The professed goals of most of these facilities are to provide quality personal care tailored to the individual's needs in a home-like setting and to promote independent living, choice of lifestyle, and to protect the right to privacy. Many offer service menus that allow the residents to choose what assistance they want and, just as importantly, what services they don't want. Basic service packages often are billed in increments of time so that those who need less assistance pay a lower fee.

In addition to assistance with ADLs, other services provided in assisted-living residences usually include:

- three meals a day served in a common dining area
- housekeeping services
- transportation
- access to health and medical services
- 24-hour security and staff availability
- emergency call systems for each living unit
- health promotion and exercise programs
- medication management
- personal laundry services
- social and recreational activities.

The full-service retirement community **TidePointe, a Classic Residence by Hyatt, Hilton Head, South Carolina.** Fitness programs for seniors are emphasized with a state-of-the-art spa and fitness center that includes a 25-m indoor lap pool along with a full range of exercise equipment and treatment rooms. Outdoor amenities include a putting green, swimming pool, and 1.5 miles (7.5 km) of meandering exercise trails (see p. C-18 for a further view).

A growing number of families bring a parent back from a retirement community, where services may be limited to housing and meals, and place him or her in an assisted-living facility nearby. A medical emergency or loss of a spouse often prompts the move. A warm, dignified, community setting, therefore, is of utmost therapeutic importance for those making the transition.

The level of services offered varies from facility to facility. While many assisted-living programs set basic entry standards requiring that residents must be able to get around their apartment without help and be able to communicate their needs, others provide more extensive assistance and services for frailer residents. Programs for those residents suffering from Alzheimer's disease or other memory disorders are increasingly provided within special units as new research points to treatment programs encouraging continuing independence for these patients. Facilities with units that specialize in treatment programs for residents with cognitive disorders are referred to as special-care units.

Continuing-care Retirement Communities

The flaw with many early stand-alone assisted-living facilities is that they provided no continuing-care programs for residents who became more disabled and had to relocate to receive the higher level of health care that they required. Today, most assisted-living facilities are being built as part of larger senior-housing communities to allow residents to 'age in place,' a concept that dominates the entire senior-living industry, accommodating the changing needs of residents as they grow more frail or decline in health. Continuing-care retirement communities (CCRCs) offer a complete range of housing and health care accommodations, from independent living to 24-hour skilled nursing care. They provide housing and health-related services for their residents under a legal agreement effective for the life of the resident or for a specific period of time. Many stand-alone assisted-living facilities are transforming themselves into CCRCs that often combine, on a beautifully landscaped campus-like setting, apartments for independent living, an assisted-living facility, skilled nursing beds, and special-care units for residents who have such medical conditions as Alzheimer's disease.

Also called full-service retirement communities and life-care communities, most offer a wide variety of activities and services that provide a rich selection of recreational, educational, and other activities of interest to residents. Communities offer such amenities as a bank, beauty/barber shop, exercise room, and garden plots. Most residents enter a CCRC when they are in good health and want the security of knowing that as they age, most of their long-term health care needs will be met within the retirement community without the need to relocate. An obvious advantage for married couples and all residents is that if the need arises for health care services they are not separated from their spouse or friends. Health care services delivered within or near the community are at the heart of the continuing care concept. Health-related services include a wide variety of accommodations such as nursing care, emergency response systems, dental services, and therapy. Residents with Alzheimer's disease are integrated onsite into a special assisted-care environment, allowing them to maintain independence and self-esteem while receiving 24-hour supervision.

Bentley Village, a Classic Residence by Hyatt in Naples, Florida, provides a campus of continuing care in a country club-style setting. The gated community is situated on 155 landscaped acres (63 ha) that feature stocked lakes, an 18-hole executive golf course with two clubhouses, and expansive natural areas. The campus also includes a 400-seat auditorium and a community center. In addition to a monthly service fee, residents pay an entrance fee that guarantees them a full continuum of care, including assisted living and skilled nursing care, at the on-site Bentley Care Center. Bentley Village features 500 independent living apartments, 48 assisted-living suites, 36 Alzheimer's suites, and 93 skilled nursing beds. Golf carts are the primary mode of transportation, so each residential unit has its own golf cart garage.

Andrus Retirement Community in Hastings-on-Hudson, New York, originally was built in 1953 and, until recently, was operated as a nursing home for elderly women who lived in hotel-like rooms in a single nine-story building. The new CCRC facility on the site includes six new buildings, 200 independent living apartments, 24 assisted-living suites, 48 skilled nursing beds, and a café, computer room, wellness center, and convenience store. Westchester Meadows, in Valhalla, New York is a new upscale lifecare community with 20 assisted-living beds, 10 skilled nursing beds, and 120 one- and two-bedroom independent living apartments.

Development and Planning Considerations

There is a misconception that older people want to live off in a serene pastoral setting by a pond. Most want to be smack in the middle of the action, connected to their communities near the familiar services that prolong independence and maintain their ties with their past. Heritage Assisted Living Residence in Framingham, Massachusetts, located next to an elementary school and across from a small shopping center, accommodates 95 residents in a three-story building with a wide front porch.

There is no single blueprint, because consumers' preferences and needs vary widely. Assisted-living residences that are not part of a CCRC can range from a new high-rise apartment complex to a converted Victorian home. Most facilities have between 25 and 120 units. Individual resident units may vary in size from one room to a full apartment.

Many facilities try to position themselves on the age spectrum when marketing their services. Some purposely appeal to the older, frailer market by offering a higher level of medical services and compete with nursing homes. Others market to younger healthier seniors who are less costly to care for and who may stay for a decade or longer.

Design Considerations

The primary design concern with assisted-living residences is for them not to look like a nursing home and to avoid all trappings of institutional care. Americans have such a deep-grained fear of nursing homes that a recent survey found that 30 percent of people 65 and older would rather die than live in one. Avoid at all cost fluorescent lights, plastic furniture, long corridors, and uniforms. Most successful assisted-living facilities are modeled after a beautiful retirement home and take on the appearance of a country inn or a large Victorian house with a grand piano in the living room, warm incandescent lighting, soft upholstered furniture, lace curtains, and oriental rugs. The overwhelming preference of the users, though not always affordable, is for larger living quarters in smaller, more homelike buildings.

Even though meals are served in a central dining room, individual suites should be equipped with kitchenettes, to enhance the resident's sense of independence. The center of activity is the dining room where residents gather three times a day for meals served on china and linen. A cafeteria would, of course, be too institutional.

One large chain, Sunrise Assisted Living, through research has developed many innovative approaches to the delivery of services and accommodations for their elderly residents. Recognizing that many residents are of a generation not accustomed to living communally with strangers, their facilities include preview windows that allow a person standing in the hall to see who is in the public living room or the café before deciding whether to enter. Even though many of their residents are in wheelchairs or use walkers, Sunrise residences usually include a grand stair at the entrance, both as a device to avoid institutional stigma and to signify to the residents that they still have choices and challenges.

Every Sunrise community has pets including dogs, cats, birds, guinea pigs, rabbits, and fish. The pets give everyone companionship, comfort, calm, and unconditional love and are very effective in stimulating memories and responses in residents with memory impairments. Residents in Sunrise are also permitted to bring their own pet. Another Sunrise trademark is the use of Victorian-style architecture that is aimed at baby-boomer family members who are instrumental in selecting the facility for their parent and who may be familiar with the design from trips to San Francisco, Nantucket, or Cape May.

It is important to provide staff supervision and to infuse vitality and robust activity in the public spaces of the facility. Unstaffed lounges at the ends of corridors are rarely used while spaces in the center of action are popular. Outdoor areas without shade trees or canopies likewise are rarely used, no matter how beautifully landscaped. The principles of barrier-free design for wheelchair accessibility is of prime concern throughout the public and private areas of the facility.

Requirements for Alzheimer's patients present many unique environmental design challenges. 'Safe wandering' should be encouraged in contained areas to permit residents to move about with dignity without endangering themselves or others. Cues built in to stimulate memory and contained indoor and outdoor areas should be provided for wandering activity and for interacting with family members. A discreet staff entrance limits resident agitation at shift changes, sometimes referred to as 'sundowning' behavior.

Trends

There are 75 million baby-boomers in the US who will begin to reach retirement age by the end of the decade. From 2010 to 2030 the population of elderly people aged 65–84 is expected to grow 80 percent, while the population aged 85 and over, representing those most likely to have chronic care needs, will grow 48 percent. In contrast, the population under age 65 will increase only 7 percent. With advances in medical science, the average life expectancy continues to increase. All signs point to continued expansion, innovation, and investment in senior and assisted-living residences by the major hotel chains and others.

Medical Hotel Complexes

During the early twentieth century, with the dawn of advanced medical services, the citizens of Rochester, Minnesota, were solving a community-wide problem. Annually, the Mayo Clinic medical phenomenon was attracting more than 60,000 patients to a city with a population of 15,000. Hospital waiting lists were long, and hotel accommodations were in short supply. To serve the growing demand, in 1907 John H. Kahler built his first hotel, with 60 guestrooms. Part convalescent hotel and part hospital unit, it contained an upper-floor surgical and obstetrical suite and nursing school. It soon became totally inadequate and, after numerous additions, reopened in 1921 as the Kahler Grand Hotel with 700 rooms and 16,000 ft^2 (1,485 m^2) of meeting space. Today, 50 hotels with over 5,000 rooms now serve the Mayo Clinic with occupancy rates approaching 80 percent.

The market for hotels adjacent to medical centers and hospitals is strong and diverse. Primarily catering to guests who are family members or friends visiting patients, some hotels are specially equipped to provide lodging to outpatients undergoing medical tests or recuperating from medical procedures who require after-care treatment. Medical practices at hospitals and clinics are expanding the scope of outpatient care, increasing the need for comfortable, convenient, and affordable accommodations. Diagnostic examinations, ambulatory surgery, physical therapy, or rehabilitation at the hospital or associated clinics create the need for hotels equipped to provide custom diet meals, limited nursing service, and pre-exam preparation. Hospital-related hotel complexes also may accommodate the local medical community including visiting doctors, nurses, students, trainees, consultants, lecturers, vendors, and other business guests of the hospital.

Following his heart transplant at New York Presbyterian Hospital in upper Manhattan, Paul Broadhead, an international real estate developer, required four months of convalescence. But the closest hotel to the hospital was across the Hudson River in New Jersey. He not only needed lodging for himself and his private nurse, but for his family and business associates when they wanted to visit. He also needed to be close to cardiovascular equipment to assist in his recuperation. Following his recovery and realizing this dire need, Broadhead, with partners and the cooperation of the hospital, is currently developing a new $200 million, mixed-use hotel complex on a 4.5 acre (1.8 ha) parking lot adjacent to the hospital. The project will have panoramic views over the Hudson River and downtown Manhattan and include a 350-suite DoubleTree Hotel, conference space, restaurants, a cinema, and retail. Two 20-story towers rising from a four-story base will include doctor's offices, staff housing, and an underground parking garage for 3,200 cars. Total usable area would be about 1 million ft^2 (92,900 m^2). The complex will be linked directly to the hospital by both a skywalk and an underground tunnel. Each suite will have a kitchenette, a sitting room, and a bedroom suitable to the longer-term needs of many occupants.

Med-Inn Centers of America

While the major hotel companies, including Inter-Continental and Marriott, operate properties near hospitals, none has developed a product that is uniquely tailored to this specialized market. The creators of Med-Inn Centers of America, a new chain devoted specifically to this very stable high-occupancy market, were attracted to the many advantages compared with other hotels including lack of seasonal fluctuations in business, strong 7-day occupancy, and low marketing costs due to referrals from doctors and hospitals. The Pillars Hotel, built between the Roswell Park Cancer Institute and Buffalo General Hospital in New York, is Med-Inn's first property. Others are planned, including one in Dallas-Fort Worth, Texas, that would service a cluster of hospitals, and another including conference facilities on the campus of the State University Center at Stony Brook, New York, to serve its hospital.

The medical campus hotel **Mologne Guest House at Walter Reed Army Hospital, Washington, DC.** The four-story, 200-room facility is designed in Georgian revival style to blend in with the predominant campus architecture. The warm residential character is a comfort to guests who are often in stressful situations.

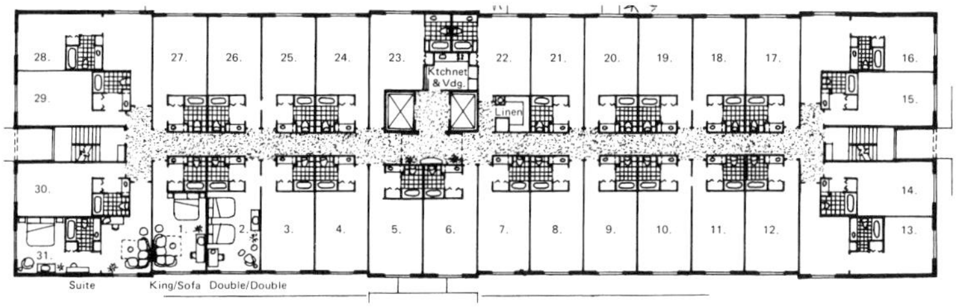

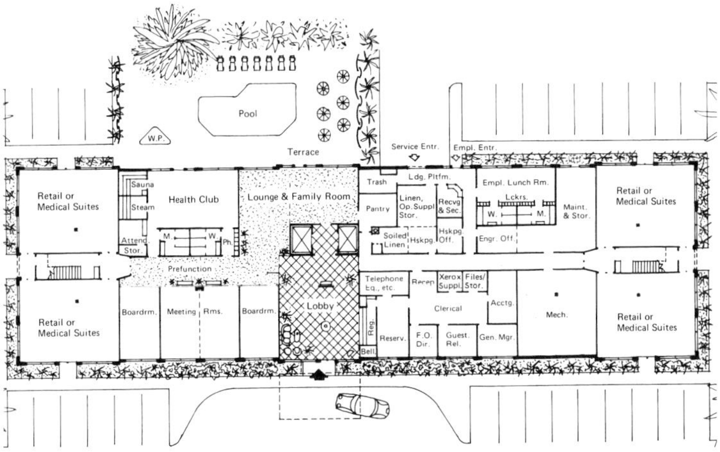

Medical stays at a fraction of hospital costs **Healthtel Prototype.** New 'healthtel' hotels efficiently serve the needs of outpatients and hospital patient visitors with, for example, a self-service kitchen on each level, where patients and families can prepare meals during the recovery period.

To help keep costs to patients at less than $100 per night, Med-Inns typically are built on land leased from the hospital corporation at below market values. Standard amenities include an enclosed connection to the adjacent medical building, extra wide hallways and doors for easy wheelchair access, shower stalls in each bathroom, medical waste disposals in each room, large easy chairs for daytime lounging, and an emergency response system monitored 24 hours a day by medical personnel. A Patient Center provides facilities where guests can use an exercise room, medical library, lounge, card and video room, or catch up on work at a complimentary business center.

Healthtel

A prototype hotel was developed by Walter Rutes for Healthtel Corporation to provide accommodations at major medical centers to serve the specialized needs of visitors or outpatients with room rates at a small fraction of hospital daily rates. Healthtel projects that its market includes 65 percent visitors of patients, 30 percent outpatients, and 5 percent business visitors. Research indicates the need for 12 rooms per 100 hospital beds for visitors and, depending on the type of specialized medical services, the outpatient component could add another six rooms per 100 so that an 800-bed hos-

The medical hotel **Rotary House International, Anderson Cancer Center, University of Texas, Houston.** The 200-key hotel, connected directly to the Cancer Center by a sky-bridge, provides support facilities, special programs, and lodging for patients and families. The elevators, hallways, and each of the guestrooms are designed to accommodate wheelchairs, stretchers, and other medical equipment.

pital would need a 150-key Healthtel. In developing the room mix it is important to recognize the phases of recovery that many patients may experience as they relate to guestroom needs. When first discharged from the hospital the patient may need to be attended by a private nurse or family member. The patient will not be mobile and may not feel presentable enough to mix with other guests. A full kitchenette is required as well as adjacent accommodations for attending family or nurse. Once patients become ambulatory, they may enjoy moving about on the floor and may be able to use a central kitchen area with a small dining room, TV lounge, or sunroom. The guest at this stage may require a room with only a microwave oven in lieu of a kitchenette. Patients near the end of their stay may enjoy the public lobby, restaurant, and exercise facilities or use the pool terrace.

Rotary House International at Anderson Cancer Center, Houston, Texas

The University of Texas M.D. Anderson Cancer Center in Houston provides long-term stay accommodations for patients and families. Directly connected by sky-bridge to the hospital, Rotary House provides support facilities and programs to create a hotel-like environment in a home-away-from-home for patients and their families, often during extended stays under stressful circumstances. The 200-key facility is divided into two sections with the lower two levels functioning as a traditional hotel and the upper floors devoted to residential-style accommodations intended to provide a more soothing and restful ambiance. The interior design of the facility was carefully planned to respect the psychological condition of the patients: a color palette of green and pink was used for its appetite enhancing qualities and complexion flattering effect and mirrored surfaces were used sparingly. Guestrooms include a combination of suites and single rooms, each with a kitchenette. The double, queen, and king-bedded rooms are fully equipped for long-term living with video-player, microwave ovens, refrigerator, dishwashers, and tableware. Elevators, hallways, and guestrooms are oversized to accommodate stretchers and wheelchairs. Public amenities include a restaurant, a deli/convenience store, gift shop with a section for special needs items, and beauty and barber shops. An important aspect of the facility is the inclusion of a patient/guest relations program, which provides accommodations for counseling and other special services for Rotary House's unique guests. Special consultation and private meeting spaces are provided for group and individual counseling.

Cleveland Clinic Inter-Continental Hotel, Ohio

Two Inter-Continental Hotels under development at the Cleveland Clinic demonstrate that the market for medical hotels has grown in diversity to the extent of warranting subsegments. One hotel will cater to the patient/visitor subsegment while the other will provide facilities for the business/education market. The first phase will be an eight-story 161-key Inter-Continental all-suite hotel intended primarily for family members and friends who require an extended stay to be close to a patient or for other visitors who prefer a more home-like setting. It will include a fitness center, restaurant, and lounge.

In order to maintain adequate accommodations for the clinic, following completion of the first hotel, an existing hotel will be demolished to be replaced with a 16-story Inter-Continental Hotel and Conference Center. The second hotel will include 291 rooms but only 28 suites, catering more to guests engaged with educational and business interests of the clinic. It will include two restaurants, a lounge, a fitness center, and offices for the Cleveland Clinic International Center, whose mission is to provide high-quality service and care to all foreign patients and to promote educational exchanges throughout the world. The conference center will feature a 500-seat auditorium, an exhibition center, 3,000 ft^2 (280 m^2) of breakout conference space, an audio-visual studio, and a state-of-the-art communication center with capabilities for teleconferencing to other clinics around the world. This super-high-tech facility will be ideal for hosting simulcast international medical seminars and conferences advancing the cause of medical science and education.

The billion dollar Native American casino hotel **Mohegan Sun Casino Resort, Uncasville, Connecticut.** With a major resort and entertainment program of 1,200 guestrooms and related public and service facilities, the resort guestroom tower is designed with extensive landscaping and water features to blend into the rolling countryside. The Mohegan Sun is indicative of new stand-alone casino-resort projects being developed close to major urban centers in the US by its original citizens on their ancestral homelands.

Casino Hotels 13

While the Broadmoor Resort in Colorado Springs, Colorado, briefly experimented with gaming at the turn of the nineteenth century, it wasn't until 1947 that the first major successful casino hotel, the Flamingo, was built in Las Vegas. Reputed to be owned by the underworld, from this dubious start, gaming developed into one of the most popular segments of the US hotel industry.

From the middle to the close of the twentieth century, the US's casino hotel industry transformed the Las Vegas desert into the world's largest multifaceted resort. It conceived theme parks laced with hotels and tied to convention centers, shops, and shows by a variety of arcades, skyways, and people-movers, traversing geographic themes from New York to Paris, Rome, Venice, Egypt, North Africa, and Mandalay. More visitors now are attracted to Las Vegas than are tourists to any of the actual foreign destinations it celebrates. (For more on the value added to properties by high-quality theming, see Chapter 4.)

No other market change compared with Las Vegas' rapid attraction of the family market in the early 1990s with themes such as Treasure Island and The Mirage hotel, complete with pirates and volcanoes performing nightly on The Strip—until the even larger makeover that followed later in the decade.

In its second shift, Las Vegas added numerous outlets representing the world's most elite restaurants, ranging from New York's Le Cirque and Lutece to Wolfgang Puck's Trattoria del Lupo; the planet's most prestigious shops from Tiffany and Hérmes to Armani; the globe's most sophisticated entertainment, including Broadway theater, the House of Blues, and Cirque de Soleil's '0' show; and a taste of civilization's top art treasures. The long sought-after super-luxury market finally succumbed by the planeload to a group of super-luxury properties, including the Four Seasons Hotel, Bellagio, and The Venetian.

By adding scores of luxurious attractions to reach a pinnacle of 130,000 rooms, the still growing Vegas phenomenon generates upward of $5.5 billion a year in betting by an estimated 30 million visitors.

At the same time, significant design developments occurred internationally as other casino resorts combined fantasy themes with exotic venues and inspired the era's most imaginative individual projects. Two widely separated casino hotels, involving the talents of architects WAT&G, raised the art of conceiving themes and authentic detailing and blended design with the natural and cultural environment: the Palace of the Lost City, in South Africa (see p. C-31 of the color section), and Atlantis, in the Bahamas (see p. C-29 of the color section and Chapter 11).

In addition, Native Americans have rapidly developed a number of casino projects across the country. Leading examples are an inspiring museum built by Connecticut's Pequot tribe, funded by casino revenue and two nearby Mohegan Nation mixed-use casino developments valued at $1 billion. The contextual Hyatt Regency Tamaya, New Mexico, exemplifies new casino resorts from New England to California representing investments of well over $1 billion.

But the gaming industry's most quixotic new feature undoubtedly is the art museum at the heart of the Las Vegas Strip, where countless visitors queue up to absorb a selection of the world's most admired masterpieces. As Ada Louise Huxtable, architectural critic for the *Wall Street Journal*, philosophized on the themed design of the city's mega-resorts, 'The real fake reaches its apogee in places like Las Vegas, where it has been developed into an art form.'

Development Considerations

Market research indicates that 30 percent of vacation travelers prefer participating in gaming compared, for example, to only 16 percent who prefer golf. But with casino hotels under pressure to deliver their economic benefits to more communities, this statistic highlights the classic dilemma facing gaming. If casino gaming were to expand everywhere rapidly as has golf, for example, without control, some of our basic social interests might be diminished. This reinforces the case for maintaining a framework of strict sanction and control of gaming as is done by the individual states in the US.

Not surprisingly, lucrative gaming revenues often enable casino hotels to offer guestrooms—casino regulations require that they operate a given minimum number of rooms—at highly competitive rates, thereby attracting not only more gaming customers but a variety of other guests as well. Elaborate entertainment and some of the world's finest resort facilities act as magnets to international tourists and convention groups and provide attractive discounted vacations for families. This became evident early on and was used effectively to promote tourist travel in the Caribbean, Nevada, and other gaming locations. Casino hotels expanded worldwide, primarily in South America and Africa, the latter boasting one regional territory whose entire economy is based on casino hotel revenue.

The airy casino gaming floor **Atlantis, Paradise Island, Bahamas.** With innovative natural lighting and lively layouts, the gaming areas create a festive international flavor.

Due to competition with management groups specializing in casino hotels, conventional hotel chains entered the gaming field through acquisition and development, substantially increasing their earnings on lucrative properties in Nevada, Lake Tahoe, and Atlantic City. But over time, most relinquished their interests to more specialized casino hotel groups at handsome premiums.

Planning and Design Considerations

Because casino hotels provide many additional amenities to serve the gaming operation, they contain a greater ratio of nonrevenue-producing space than any other hotel type. This includes elaborate 'high-roller' suites and villas traditionally furnished free to high-stake players, star suites for big-name entertainers, and gourmet 'hold tables' permanently reserved in restaurants on or near the gaming floor for quick service to high-rollers who want to spend the maximum time at the tables. Therefore, casino hotels must be models of functional efficiency, designed to minimize initial and operating costs in back-of-house as well as public areas. Here, quality themed concepts, and their authentic detailing, play a vital role in the hotel's success.

The Casino Gaming Floor

No other type of building contains a greater amount of unrecorded currency than a huge casino hotel. Cash and negotiable chips on the floor at one time may run into tens of millions of dollars. This influences various aspects of the design. A maximum security 'money path' must be provided to and from the cashier's cage on the gaming floor. All cash and chips from the gaming tables are deposited at the cage, where access is protected by a 'man-trap' vestibule in which all people have to be let through two separate security doors. Due to the complexity of its security provisions, a single cage generally is preferred, regardless of the size of the gaming floor. Coins from the slot machines are transported by electric carts. For this reason, floors must be structurally reinforced to support live loads of 300 lb (136 kg), or three times the requirements of normal public assembly spaces.

The money path leads from the cage to 'hard' and 'soft' count rooms—for coins and paper money. Machines are used for counting except in certain regions, such as Atlantic City, where soft currency is required to be counted manually on transparent Lucite tables under TV surveillance. The money then proceeds to a special money truck loading dock. Since this usually is on another level, a separate money elevator with a 5,000 lb (2,270 kg) load capacity must be provided, operated from the cage and observed by TV surveillance cameras.

No other building contains security monitoring systems equal to a casino. Called the 'live peek' in Atlantic City and the 'eye-in-the-sky' in Las Vegas, the system of pan-and-tilt cameras concealed in glazed ceiling bubbles is monitored by security guards in special screening rooms. It also records the gaming action at each table on time-stamped videotape. Films can be closely reexamined if any complaints or other suspicions of cheating arise. In addition, the layout of the gaming tables is carefully designed to facilitate surveillance of the dealers and players by nonuniformed security guards or 'floaters,' generally positioned at the ends of each line of tables. Smaller European-style casino hotels often are less security conscious, with less extensive TV surveillance, and prefer a more casual arrangement of tables rather than the straight-line layout favored by American gaming operators. Gaming tables in large casinos generally are laid out in groups of 12, with each group centered around a supervisor, or 'pit boss.'

Overall security usually is maintained jointly by a government agency and the casino management, with control offices located in the cage and a room filled with TV monitors. Since one of their functions is to detain suspects, a security cell must be provided on the premises. Another requirement is for special facilities for the dealers, who generally are on 40-minute shifts, which includes men's and women's lounges, dressing facilities, and a self-contained private dining room adjacent to the gaming area.

The number and type of games varies with the location. But in a US casino hotel, a ratio of about five blackjack tables to each roulette and craps table is average. Typically, a baccarat and high-stakes blackjack table are provided in a high limit, baccarat or salon privée separate room, with more added at a ratio of about one for every 50 other gaming tables. While blackjack and roulette tables may be combined in any grouping, the other gaming tables are located in separate groups. In addition, separate areas are required for one big six wheel-type game, with others added at a ratio of about one for every 120 gaming tables. Based on the above ratios, the area required for the gaming floor will average approximately 250 ft^2 (23.2 m^2) per table. Hotel casinos planned with more widely spaced table layouts have, with few exceptions, proven less inviting to gaming customers, who generally prefer a more crowded atmosphere. As a rule, not only is it more pleasing for the guest to keep the space tight, but it also saves construction and operating cost.

The elegant casino gaming room **The Ritz-Carlton, San Juan Hotel, Spa & Casino, Isla Verde, Puerto Rico.** Decorative chandeliers and column sconces create a touch of international charm in this popular island casino gaming space.

Since some guests prefer to play slot machines alongside the gaming floor and others prefer them in separate areas, they usually are located about evenly in both places. A coin cashier's cage is required for about every 50 machines. Slot machine areas should have ceiling heights of 12–16 ft (3.7–4.9 m). Carousels with circular groups of slot machines are increasingly popular, occupying about 20 ft^2 (1.9 m^2) per machine as opposed to 10 ft^2 (0.9 m^2) for conventional lineal layouts. In some areas, including Las Vegas, additional space must also be provided for poker tables, keno, bingo, and sports book betting operations.

In European-style hotel casinos the ratio of types of games changes, with the number of roulette and baccarat tables generally doubling, and craps games cut by half.

Amenities and Entertainment Facilities

Bars and lounges should be integrated directly with the gaming floor to enhance the ambiance of both areas, and stimulate business from one to the other. This also simplifies bar service to the gaming tables. Restaurants also should be convenient to the gaming area and, if on a different level, accessible by escalator, with good visibility from the gaming and entrance lobbies. Cafés and buffet dining areas should be open to the main public spaces, with entrances to the signature and specialty restaurants directly off the main lobby and circulation concourses. Elaborate dinner shows and famous entertainers are expected in large-scale casino hotels but, due to their high cost, major show rooms usually are impractical for small or medium-size casino hotels. Those with gaming areas under 10,000 ft^2 (929 m^2) generally provide cabaret entertainment lounges rather than more costly dinner shows.

Convention Facilities

With the trend toward combining large trade shows with related corporate and association conventions, today's 1,000-room and larger casino hotels more than meet the requirements of the convention market. These groups, including family incentive groups, increasingly look to meet at resort locations. Therefore, the casino hotels' additions of theme parks, mega-health spas, small luxury signature restaurants (as many as 20 in the new wave of mega-casino hotels), and several more sophisticated, rather than merely larger, entertainment programs position casino hotels to increase their penetration of the convention market.

New York hoteliers used to be concerned at losing convention business to the expansion of the Atlantic City casino hotels. This has been replaced by a dream of hydrofoil service between New York waterfront hotels and New Jersey: welcoming sightseers from Atlantic City conventions as well as sending guests to the Jersey shores. Both entrepreneurs and community groups are eager to develop hotels and related attractions along the city's rivers. Such regional planning concepts would transform vastly underutilized shorelines into budding parks, marinas, ice-skating rinks, concert amphitheaters, jogging and bicycle trails, as well as other visitor attractions. A branch of the Guggenheim Museum is proposed for the Hudson River waterfront. The viability of such proposals is indicated by the oversubscribed bookings of the city's expanded convention center as well as market data on the existing hotel infrastructure. Visitors would enjoy sightseeing in the 'Big Apple' in conjunction with attending a convention in Atlantic City. In addition, attendees of New York City conventions would enjoy visiting New Jersey's casino hotels, beaches, golf courses, and generally overlooked vast nature preserves.

This symbiotic relationship between New York and Atlantic City can be as mutually beneficial as that of Los Angeles and Las Vegas or San Francisco and Lake Tahoe. Therefore, it would be of great benefit for an imaginative developer to consider master planning the coast of Atlantic City and, in the process, transforming New York's rivers into a Thames or Seine.

Guestrooms

Casino hotel rooms are larger and more luxuriously planned and appointed than suburban or downtown hotels. Typically, inside room dimensions range from 13 × 18 ft (4 × 5.5 m) to 14.5 × 20 ft (4.4 × 6.1 m). However, the most upscale properties, such as Bellagio, provide more of everything. One stunning choice is the 850 ft^2 (259 m^2) Salone studio room, with its king-sized bed projecting from one corner of the window wall diagonally into the room, and a large, six-fixture spa bathroom. Four completely different choices of one-bedroom suites range from 1,020 to 1,540 ft^2 (311 to 469 m^2). A unique model is located at the ends of the guestroom tower floors, semicircular in plan, offering a panoramic bay window view from the sunny living room. This again reflects both the ability of a casino hotel, because of its gaming revenue, to provide greater luxury while attracting resort and convention business in addition to their gaming customers.

Steve Wynn, the developer of Bellagio, does it with large sybaritic Roman-style spa baths, while Stan Addelson of Venetian Grand Canal fame, doubles the ante with the largest typical guestroom in hotel history. And the Mandalay Bay shares its guestroom tower with the luxury Four Seasons Hotel, together offering the largest array of suites under one roof. The 2,916-room Paris Las Vegas appropriately features armoires and impeccable charm, the 'complete Parisian experience.'

Significant Casino Hotels

The Palace of the Lost City, Sun City, South Africa

To create a memorable international destination, developer Sun International and architects WAT&G developed a strong fantasy theme based on the idea of a simulated archeological discovery of an exotic ancient city. The centerpiece of the project is the palace, an exciting rococo invention borrowing its design from several exuberant sources to convey the blending of cultures into a new society. The storyline literally shaped the opulent structure as a palace, first, and hotel, second. For example, to create a breathtaking scale the architects designed the entrance lobby in the form of an 85 ft (26 m) high rotunda, and treated the rich honey-colored masonry façades with a special patina to express its age. A themed lounge exhibiting exotic artifacts and local art is adjacent to the rotunda, in a special elephant walk atrium. The grand stair descends to the Crystal Court, on axis to a thematic restaurant and lounge located in a glass-walled quatrefoil pavilion, surrounded by a reflecting pool, with vistas of the palace and the valley below.

The eight-story stepped structure contains 672,750 ft^2 (62,500 m^2) of floor area, offers 328 regal guestrooms and 21 suites approached through a five-story skylit atrium. The decorative elements throughout the hotel were gathered from its home region of southern Africa.

Developed on an 80 acre (32.4 ha) site, the hotel creatively blends into the natural environment and is surrounded by lakes, lush gardens, its golf course and clubhouse, and the country's largest wild game preserve. The building's own wildly imaginative towers, topped by open air domes fashioned out of simulated elephant tusks and palm fronds, stand as elements of one of the most innovative hotels of the modern era.

Bellagio, Las Vegas, Nevada

Built on a large 122 acre (49.4 ha) site in the heart of the Las Vegas Strip, the Bellagio complex takes its name and inspiration from the Italian village on Lake Como in Tuscany, famed for its super-luxury resort. The entrance is marked by a recreated village bell-tower concealing the latest high-tech sound equipment, which beams sonorous bell chimes and opera arias. The 36-story, 3025-room hotel frames an 8 acre (3.2 ha) lake with a spectacular fountain sequence and light show watched nightly by

(A)

(B)

A rare 'ancient fantasy themed' casino hotel **The Palace of the Lost City, Sun City, South Africa.** (A) Recalling the stage set of a Cecil B. De Mille-directed movie, the expert sweep of imagination created by WAT&G Architects is unmistakable. (B) The resort exhibits throughout its buildings and grounds indigenous museum quality artifacts, including tusks and sculptural displays in the Elephant Court, Tusk Lounge, and other public areas (see p. C-31 for a further view).

And the luxury market followed **Bellagio, Las Vegas, Nevada.** Having attracted the middle-class market with a combination of worldwide monuments and popular family theme parks and inspired by this major luxury hotel, Las Vegas has captured the super-luxury market with a new wave of exclusive themed hotels offering an impressive array of upscale shops, restaurants, and entertainment amenities (see p. C-26 for a further view).

thousands of vacationers. The sumptuous interiors include many Italian touches from grand pedestrian arcades to artwork and decorative pieces. The resort is famous for its 20 restaurant, lounge, and entertainment venues, ranging from the casual to the formal, each with panoramic views and outdoor terraces. The 45,000 ft^2 (4,180 m^2) ballroom allows Bellagio to compete for high-end group business. Among its most celebrated spaces is the Conservatory, a three-story, glass-domed botanical garden filled with seasonal flowers and plants (see p. C-26 in the color section).

The Venetian, Las Vegas, Nevada

More visitors now come to Las Vegas than to Venice or any of the other great cities represented by Vegas casino hotels. But can a copy compete with an

The high-Renaissance casino hotel **The Venetian Resort Hotel Casino, Las Vegas, Nevada.** Attracted by its lavish theming, convention facilities, and super-large guestrooms, this unique hotel confidently provides for future expansion to double its current 3,036-rooms (see typical guestroom layout, p. 268, and p. C-26 for a further view).

original, no matter how authentically detailed? For many, no. Yet for others, given the travails and expense of travel, for sure! If the quality of the simulation is a factor, The Venetian draws them in by its painstaking attention to detail of numerous icons selected to capture the essence of one of the most important cities in political and artistic history, most readily adapted to hotel functions and activities.

Icons recreated at The Venetian	*Function performed in hotel*
Campanile with 15 ft (4.6 m) statue of biblical archangel Gabriel on top	Identify site and street entrance
Grand Canal system and gondolas	On-site transit and popular ride
Rialto Bridge	Cross canal at street entrance
Bridge of Sighs	Major canal crossing
Sixteenth-century clock tower	Hotel identification signage
Cobblestone St. Mark's Plaza	Open space and retail sales
Doge's Palace	Arcades, shops, and restaurants
Frescoed ceilings and galleria	Ideal art display and space for retail sales, restaurants, lounges, and impressive lobby

The $1.4 billion cost is only exceeded by Bellagio at $1.8 billion, but neither project cut corners, and it is impossible to compare canals and frescos with a lake and conservatory—or a $260 million collection of real Renoirs, Picassos, and Cezannes. Many other factors affect the economics. Bellagio's management has more experience in attracting high-rollers, while The Venetian adjoins the Sands Expo Center and is more experienced at drawing the group market. The fact that the two hotels are only blocks apart on The Strip should simplify the comparison by customers as well as consultants tracking financial results for the best answers to guide future development.

The Venetian may have one clear advantage. Its owners plan to double its current 3,036 rooms, at which time the hotel will become one of the largest on record. The Venetian's typical guestrooms, 665 ft^2 (61.8 m^2) including 110 ft^2 (10.2 m^2) guest bathrooms, are the largest of any hotel and among the most impressive. A marble foyer leads to the sleeping area, featuring a canopy bed, and to the sunken living room beyond, overlooking 24-hour activity on The Strip (see p. C-26 in the color section).

Mandalay Bay Resort & Casino and Four Seasons Hotel, Las Vegas, Nevada

The Four Seasons luxury chain pioneered a unique winning strategy by locating its 424 lavish guestrooms on the upper floors of the 3,700-room Mandalay Bay tower, flagship casino hotel of the Mandalay Resort Group. In designing the first major dual hotel structure, Klai-Juba Architects brilliantly solved a number of complex problems including providing distinct environments and separate circulation paths for the guests and staff of each hotel. For example, the guests arrive on separate levels and opposite sides of the building; the lobbies are distinct—Four Seasons has a sky lobby perfectly suited to their successful marketing approach to attract the guest who wants to stay above the crowd; each has gigantic pools, spas, restaurants, and lounges outside the tower and on different levels and sides of the building; and guests have a greater choice of amenities in that they enjoy visiting the other hotel (particularly those staying at the Four Seasons, who have convenient access to the gaming at the Mandalay casino). A 1.2 million ft^2 (111,480 m^2) shopping mall, anchored by a Nordstrom department store, connects to the Mandalay Bay.

Mohegan Sun Casino Resort, Uncasville, Connecticut

Rising from the Mohegan Nation's homeland overlooking Connecticut's Thames River is one of the world's most influential casino resorts. The project features an innovative gaming floor, themed as a curved organic form, appropriate to the Tribal Nation's natural culture. Named the 'Casino of the Sky,' it is domed by the world's largest planetarium, on which is projected a 24-hour star show of the heavens. At the gaming floor's vortex stands a replica of the Mohegan's most enduring memory—Wombi Rock—expressed by designer David Rockwell and his team as a soaring, translucent, illuminated alabaster and onyx outcropping, signifying the journey of the spirit.

As is the case of many Native American lands, the Mohegans' 240 acre (97 ha) site is located in the dense northeast corridor between New York and Boston. Therefore, it became prime real estate for a casino hotel and mixed-use development. To complement the scenic arrival experience, a towering tree of life celebrates the tribe's creation and future progeny. Their historic journey from the west is documented in the rock-like 'memory piles' used as interactive customer information stations in the 175,000 ft^2 (162,260 m^2) shopping mall. Nine

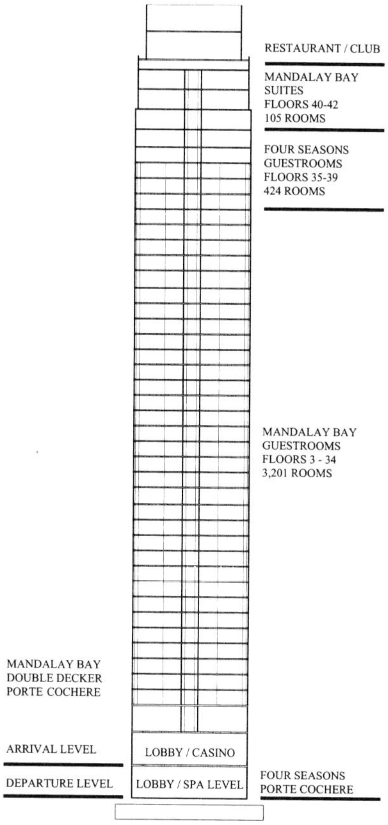

The dual casino hotel **Mandalay Bay Resort & Casino** and **Four Seasons Hotel, Las Vegas, Nevada.** This breakthrough concept of two different hotels sharing a single tower features separate public and service entrances and dual pools, spas, convention, and other major luxury facilities. The two hotels are marketed and operated as though they were individual properties on different sites. With this super-elegant Presidential Suite, the city's major noncasino hotel reinforces its differentiation from the gaming hotels, attracting affluent guests to the Las Vegas phenomenon.

restaurants, including four themed on the seasons, feature such elements as a cascading waterfall and a 40 ft (12.2 m) globe, depicting the 13 lunar phases of the tribal calendar.

The 34-story hotel, designed by Kohn Pederson Fox as a sleekly understated tower, features a striking lobby, designed by The Rockwell Group, representing a forest of the Mohegans' sacred red cedar trees surrounding a calm, reflecting pool. Hirsch Bedner Associates is creating the interior design for the luxurious 450 ft^2 (41.8 m^2) guestrooms and suites.

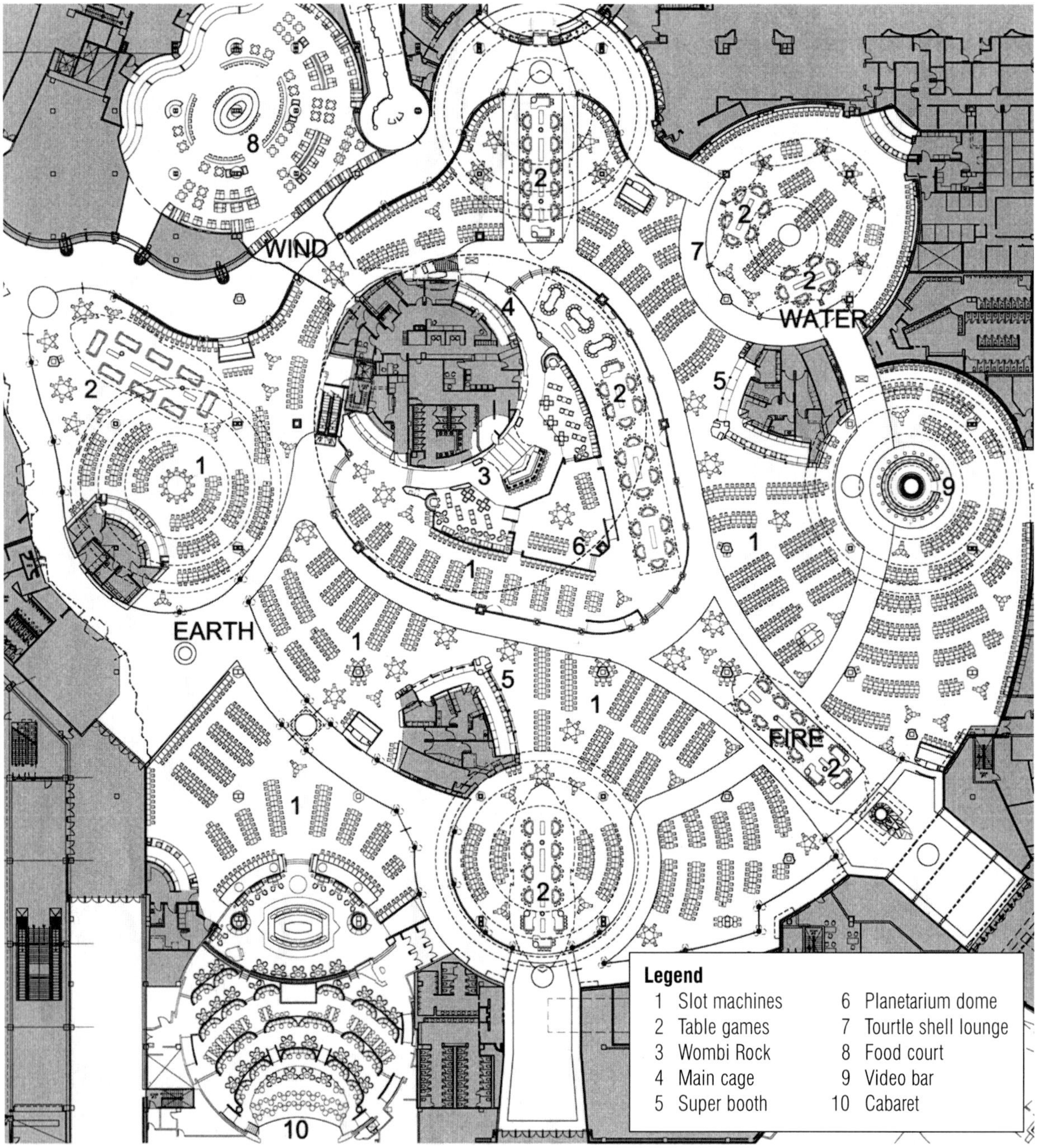

The natural-themed casino resort **Mohegan Sun Casino Resort, Uncasville, Connecticut.** The revolutionary casino plan ignores the standard straight-line gaming layout used by major operators for over half a century. Based on the Mohegan's cultural preference for natural curved forms, the designers conceived the casino as an organic shape rather than a box, and the circulation aisles as undulating trails. Other traditions incorporated in the plan include the significance of the compass points as primal forces of earth, wind, fire, and water, defining the locations and themes of each entrance lobby; further legends provide themes for the food court, video bar, and lounges.

The celebration of heritage in the Native American casino resort **Mohegan Sun Casino Resort, Uncasville, Connecticut.** Mohegan culture inspires a celebration of the legend of the Wombi Rock, ancestral meeting place of Western tribal councilors. The three-level back-lit onyx formation is featured at the vortex of the casino as a striking restaurant, lounge, and nightclub, while natural lighting refracts from crystals and woven multicolor beaded panels to set the daytime mood.

Other major hotel elements include the convention center with 60,000 ft^2 (5,570 m^2) of meeting space and the large 40,000 ft^2 (3,720 m^2) ballroom; the world-class spa complex featuring 20 treatment rooms and an indoor pool; the cabaret theater seating 300; and the 10,000-seat arena for major sports events and trade exhibitions.

Hyatt Regency Tamaya, New Mexico

The people living around the landmark 400-year-old Santa Anna Pueblo take special pride in maintaining the character of their community on the Rio Grande River. The Native American leadership selected Hyatt Hotels and architects Hill Glazier to capture the architecture of the Pueblo and local adobe detailing in the design of a new resort and casino.

The resort's arrival court is framed with timeless adobe walls with a deep portal for a mesquite-burning fireplace near the entry point. The 350 spacious and luxuriously appointed guestrooms occupy the resort's two main wings—called the turquoise and the pumpkin—its colors symbolizing the two clans of the Pueblo Nation. The interior design is inspired by research on Pueblo history: features include a story telling area off the lobby living room, traditional *hornos* for baking bread displayed in the restaurant; and reproductions of historic Pendleton blankets in the guestrooms.

Trends

- Casino hotels in major gaming cities will increase in size to 3,000–6,000 rooms for efficiency and to accommodate larger convention groups. Both convention facilities and casino gaming space commonly will reach 150,000 ft^2 (13,935 m^2) and recreational amenities will expand significantly. Experts expect to see gaming programmed from casinos into the guestrooms and potential two-way electronic gaming channeled into noncasino hotels.
- To reduce travel time as well as help relieve congestion, private companies will offer hydrofoil commuter systems between Atlantic City and New York, using people-movers from transfer terminals to waterfront hotels and convention areas. Some gaming hotel groups will develop downtown entertainment hotels as feeder-routes from major cities to their destination, for example, to New York/Atlantic City, Los Angeles/Las Vegas or San Francisco/Lake Tahoe.
- More cities will chase the golden grail of gaming that revitalized Atlantic City and was adopted by Detroit. In recession periods, casino hotels will be even more pressured to expand.
- Even now that it is one of the top tourist destinations globally, continued expansion seems certain

The design sensitivity of the Native American casino resort **Hyatt Regency Tamaya Resort & Spa, New Mexico.** Through authentic adobe design and construction this casino hotel blends with the indigenous materials, traditions, and architecture of the neighboring restored Santa Anna Pueblo.

for Las Vegas. Few cities have accomplished a comparable rise in barely a half-century. As it now is positioned, only a fractional rise in discretionary income can trigger demand for thousands of hotel rooms. Also, due to worldwide interest focused on Las Vegas, it will continue to be the industry's capital and laboratory for new prototypes and resort theme park venues. While the Eiffel Tower replica does not particularly attract Parisians, nor the Statue of Liberty bring in New Yorkers, many visitors enjoy seeing replicas of international landmarks in Las Vegas. Polling confirms that the majority come for reasons other than gaming. As one Frenchman guiding his family down The Strip confessed: 'We go to all the theme parks but, if we take a vote, the kids vote for Vegas.'

The blended urban casino hotel **Star City, Sydney Harbor Casino Hotel, Australia.**

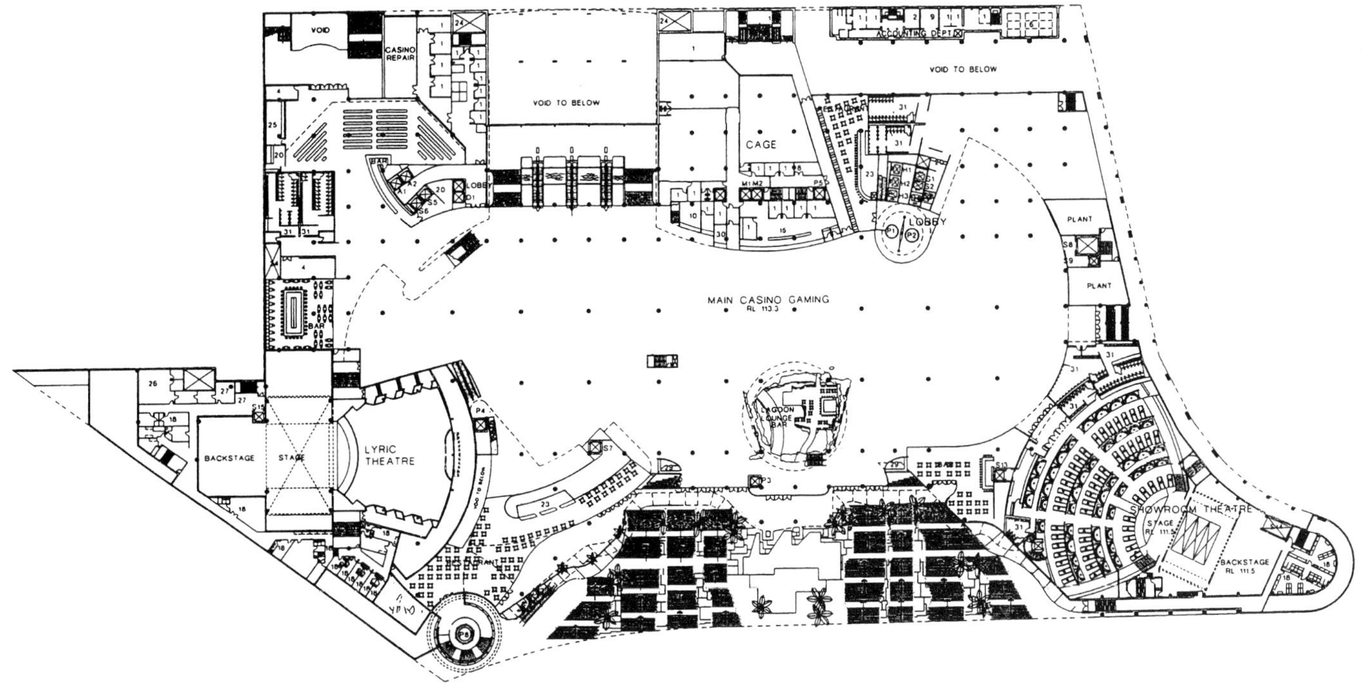

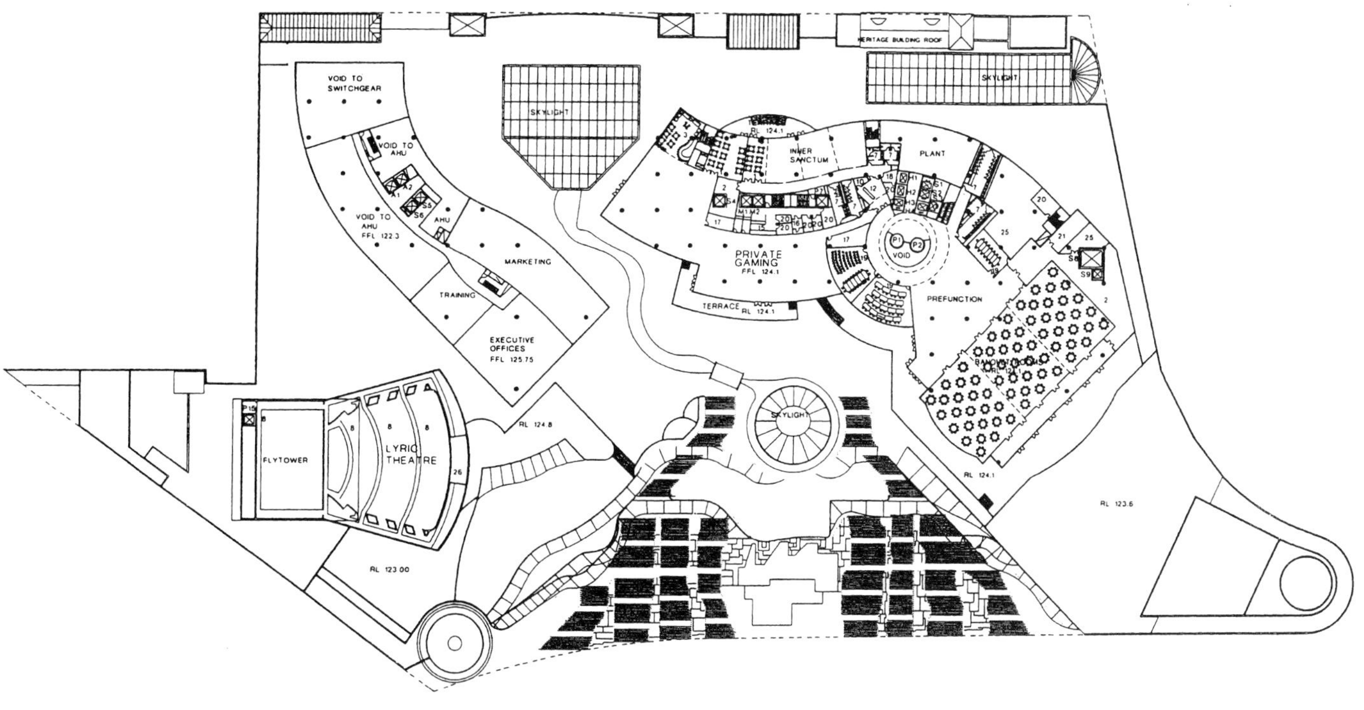

The blended urban casino hotel **Star City, Sydney Harbor Casino Hotel, Australia.** This popular multiuse casino hotel and entertainment complex blends its development with the city's needs including 'give backs' such as a 2,000-seat performing arts theater, a public landmark restoration, residential apartments, convenience shopping, and a major mall. Visual blending includes unique landscaping, water features, and street furnishings. The 2.2 million ft^2 (204,380 m^2) complex features a rooftop restaurant and lounge with panoramic views of the harbor from its 20-story, 350-room luxury hotel tower. In addition to the 30,000 ft^2 (2,790 m^2) of ballroom, banquet, and meeting space installed above the 116,250 ft^2 (10,800 m^2) main casino floor, amenities include an 800-seat dinner theater, luxury boutiques, and a 19,000 ft^2 (1,770 m^2) private gaming area. The popular center draws tourists and downtown residents as well as suburbanites to its lively attractions including a total of 14 themed restaurants and 12 lounges connected to a convenient commuter terminal and enclosed parking for 2,500 cars.

Part 2

Amenities

Design Guide

Hotels and resorts—in fact the full complement of lodging types described in Part 1—are particularly complex and difficult building types. The Design Guide focuses on the program, planning, and design issues critical to creating a successful lodging property and, in addition, highlights the types of operational and financial decisions that affect and influence the architectural and interior design. The first chapter in this part introduces site and master planning, perhaps the most important design issue for many resort properties. Succeeding chapters detail the key design guidelines for the functional areas in hotels: guestrooms and suites; lobby, food and beverage, meeting, and recreational areas; and administration and back-of-house areas. The Design Guide concludes with a discussion of special building systems and construction methods important to the whole range of hotel properties.

The vitality of high-quality resort landscape design **Seven Seas Resort, Side, Turkey.** Site improvements to this Mediterranean seaside resort included a new water park, new entrance and main terrace, a new amphitheater, pool and landscape planting, and a high-tech light rail transit system providing effortless access throughout the 21 acre (8.5 ha) complex.

Site and Master Planning 14

A hotel project becomes real once the site is selected. Up until that point, the developer and architect may have an idea of the hotel that they plan to construct, but conceiving the physical design cannot really begin until the property is known. Most hotels are developed on one of the following types of sites:

- rural and undeveloped sites (usually for resort hotels or retreats)
- suburban, small town, and roadside sites
- urban sites.

Each type requires special and particular criteria, both for its selection and the design for the buildings and grounds.

Resort Sites

Modern modes of transportation and longer vacation times, especially for Europeans, have made it possible for people to travel farther for their holidays. In fact, getting far away from home can be a strong attraction. Exotic landscapes with pristine beaches and warm weather continue to prove popular with today's travelers, especially during the cold winter months.

Resorts closer to home, especially those easily accessible by automobile, also are attractive. While they might not be as glamorous as the exotic resort, they still offer guests a rich variety of amenities in an environment close to nature. A nearby attraction such as a lake, trails for cross-country skiing, or even a top-notch restaurant can entice guests during the day, especially on weekends. Local residents also can offer important support for a project during its early planning stages.

For all resorts, the site selection is of paramount importance. Because rural resort developments often involve large sites, in part to provide protection from neighboring development, a good deal of attention must go into planning the relationship among lodging, public spaces, recreational areas, and services. Resorts in developing regions present a special group of issues for the development team, including:

- *Transportation and accessibility*. Select a site within 2 hours of an international airport and readily accessible by road. Construction of new roads is expensive and permission to cross over property not owned by the hotel may be difficult to secure. In more remote locations where local roads might prove difficult for coaches, jeeps and sport utility vehicles provide an alternative for shuttling guests from the airport to the hotel. Road access also influences the ease of handling construction equipment and delivery trucks once the hotel is operational.

- *Political climate*. Consider international attitudes toward the destination. Nothing keeps guests away like the possibility of political unrest. Even after it subsides and home countries no longer restrict travel to these regions, the vast number of vacation alternatives makes these countries unlikely destinations. In Sri Lanka, the protracted civil war, mostly on the northern tip of the country and in the capital, Colombo, has had a devastating effect on tourism, even on the resorts outside the area of conflict.

- *Ownership*. Investigate local laws influencing real estate development. For example, some countries do not permit foreign nationals to own property. Such legal restrictions can make it difficult for hotel companies wishing to operate abroad. Where this is the case a joint venture with local entities may be an alternative.

- *Community relations*. Establish good public relations with the local community. Tourism is a major industry and hotels bring in substantial amounts of hard currency. Often the developer needs to demonstrate to government officials the financial and social benefits that the hotel will bring to the local population. They may require the developer to improve some aspect of the local community infrastructure, such as providing a sewage system or constructing a new school.

In large resorts guest and visitor parking should be separated, with the guest spaces closest to the reception and guestroom buildings. Where visitors come to use a specific amenity, parking should be located near that particular feature and away from the hotel guest arrival area. In both cases provide a landscaped and shaded walkway between the parking area and the hotel.

An exemplary resort landscape design **Las Ventanas al Paraiso, Los Cabos, Mexico.** The multilevel landscape of traditional Mediterranean-Mexican architecture features adobe structures with thatched roofs which terrace down to a serpentine network of swimming pools, a swim-up bar, patios overlooking the sea, cactus gardens, and an infinity pool by the white sands of Mexico's Baja coastline.

The exciting new site contextual resort design **The Boulders, Carefree, Arizona.** Sculpted into the prehistoric landscape of volcanic rock formations in the Valley of the Sun desert, this resort provides a dramatic example of site integration where architecture and landscape become one expression.

Most resort guests are first-time users who are there to enjoy and experience the environment. It is important that they be able to grasp the overall layout of the property in order to get around fairly easily. If possible, the main pubic facilities should be located prominently on or near the highest point of the site, easily visible to guests as they approach the property. From here, guests can gain an overall orientation to the resort and staff can point out particular features. The site organization should allow views of the resort's main attractions, such as the beach, golf course, or ski lift, from the main lobby. While all of the features of a site need not be evident at once, facilities should not be difficult or confusing to access.

Large resort sites can be organized with such devices as a bell tower, fountains, sculptures, or flagpoles that stand out in the landscape as points of reference. Where major resort elements such as the public areas, guestrooms and suites, and recreational amenities are separated by more than a 5–10-minute walk, the property may require a transit system to move guests, as is done with decorative trolleys at the Hyatt Regency Grand Cypress in Orlando.

A major consideration in planning the landscape is its maintenance. Lushly planted gardens give pleasure to all and, especially in tropical climates, offer an opportunity to exhibit local specimens that interest visitors with their exotic character. However, manicured gardens and lawns are labor intensive. In regions where maintenance costs are low this is not a major factor and the designer can create an impressive landscape display, which is a wonderful way to embellish a special spot. But small gardens can have a strong visual presence as well and are part of most landscape schemes. Also, it is important for designers to consider water conservation, especially in climates where rain is scarce. A viable way to deal with this challenge is by recycling wastewater and building retainage reservoirs to supply the resort's irrigation requirements.

Both gardens and natural landscape encourage a contemplative mood. People come to resorts to get 'away from it all,' at least for part of the time. All resorts should have quiet outdoor places where one can be alone with nature. A simple bench with a tranquil view can be highly restorative to the soul. Water, too, has a calming and cooling effect, part of the reason for the popularity of ocean- and lake-front resorts. Watching the surf rush up the sand or the moonlight glisten on the water's surface is relaxing.

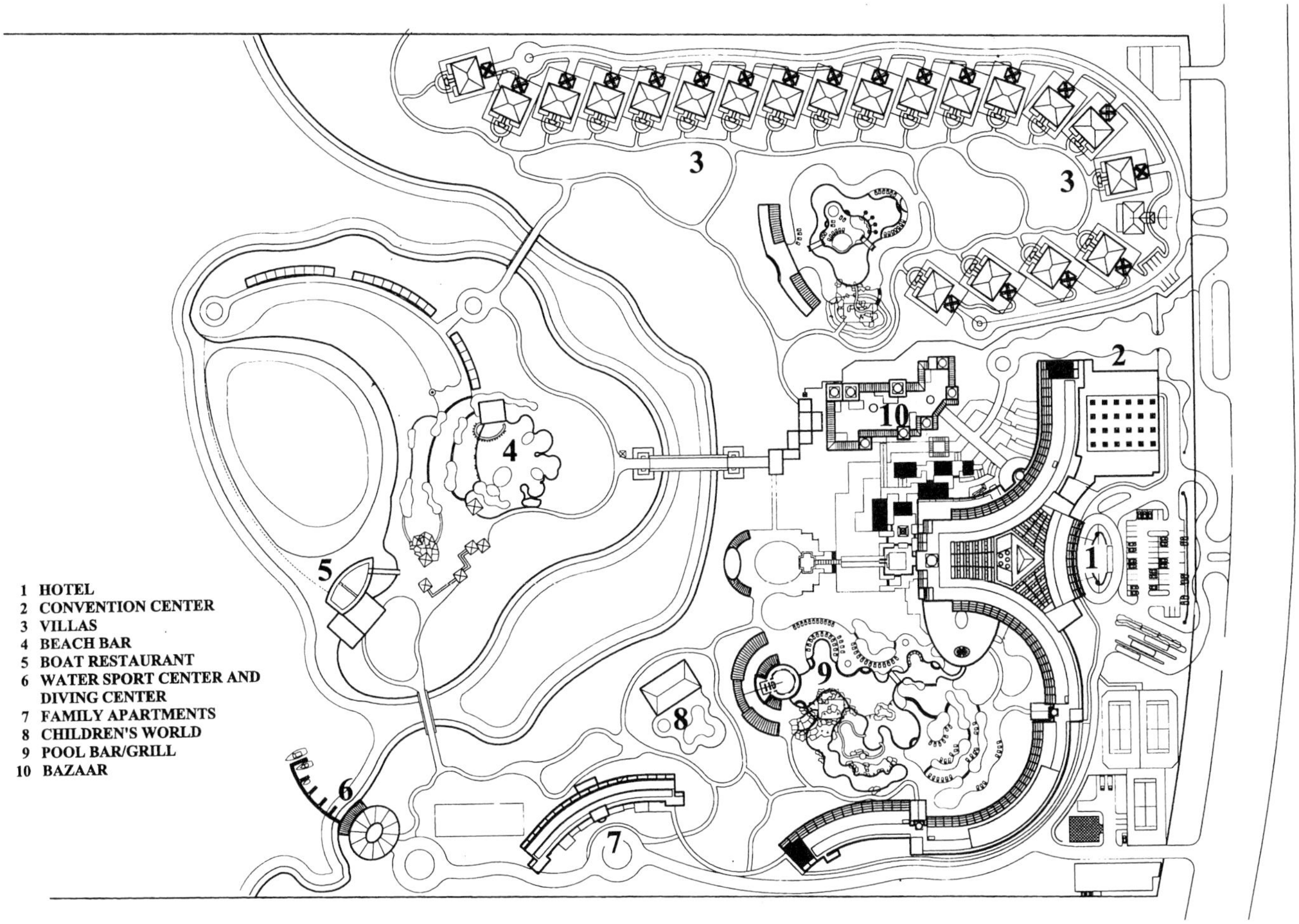

The seaside resort featuring a themed entertainment island **Steigenberger Resort el Fanadir, Hurghada, Egypt.** The Red Sea's pristine coastline, coral reefs, and shimmering seascapes provide ample motive to forgo the more efficient double-loaded guest level plans in favor of a single-loaded spine orienting as many of the 450 guestrooms as possible toward the spectacular view. The layout of this 50 acre (20 ha) resort focuses on a large, organically shaped rock-pool water feature and Adventure Island accessible by footbridge and including theme restaurants and grilles, shopping, and a disco illuminated by glass aquariums.

On sites lacking major bodies of water, ponds can be constructed or enlarged to create visual interest as well as to collect surface and subsurface waters.

Sporting activities, a major component of most resorts, require relatively large expanses of land. Table 14.1 provides general space guidelines for different recreational features. In calculating the actual space required, add 30 percent for landscaping treatment and circulation.

The natural landscape is an increasingly scarce and valuable resource and resort and hotel organizations must take a leadership role in helping to protect it. Many jurisdictions have strict laws regulating construction and other activity on designated sites. Resort development usually exceeds any minimum requirements since the lure of a resort comes from its natural setting and its continued success is highly dependent on the quality of the environment.

Senior travelers are a growing proportion of resort guests. With time available for extended stays, not limited to peak periods, affluent retirees are a major source of revenue for resorts. The design needs to meet their particular desires and provide less intensive activities such as card rooms, deck games, quiet swimming pools, golf pitch, walking paths, and similar amenities.

In order to attract employees, resorts remote from an available labor pool often provide staff with housing, recreational amenities, and other services separate from the guest areas. Large-scale resort destinations may need to build a community for staff close by, but outside the confines of the resort property, including space for family members, to establish a stable employee base.

In more remote regions, the indigenous population often lives in remarkable harmony with the

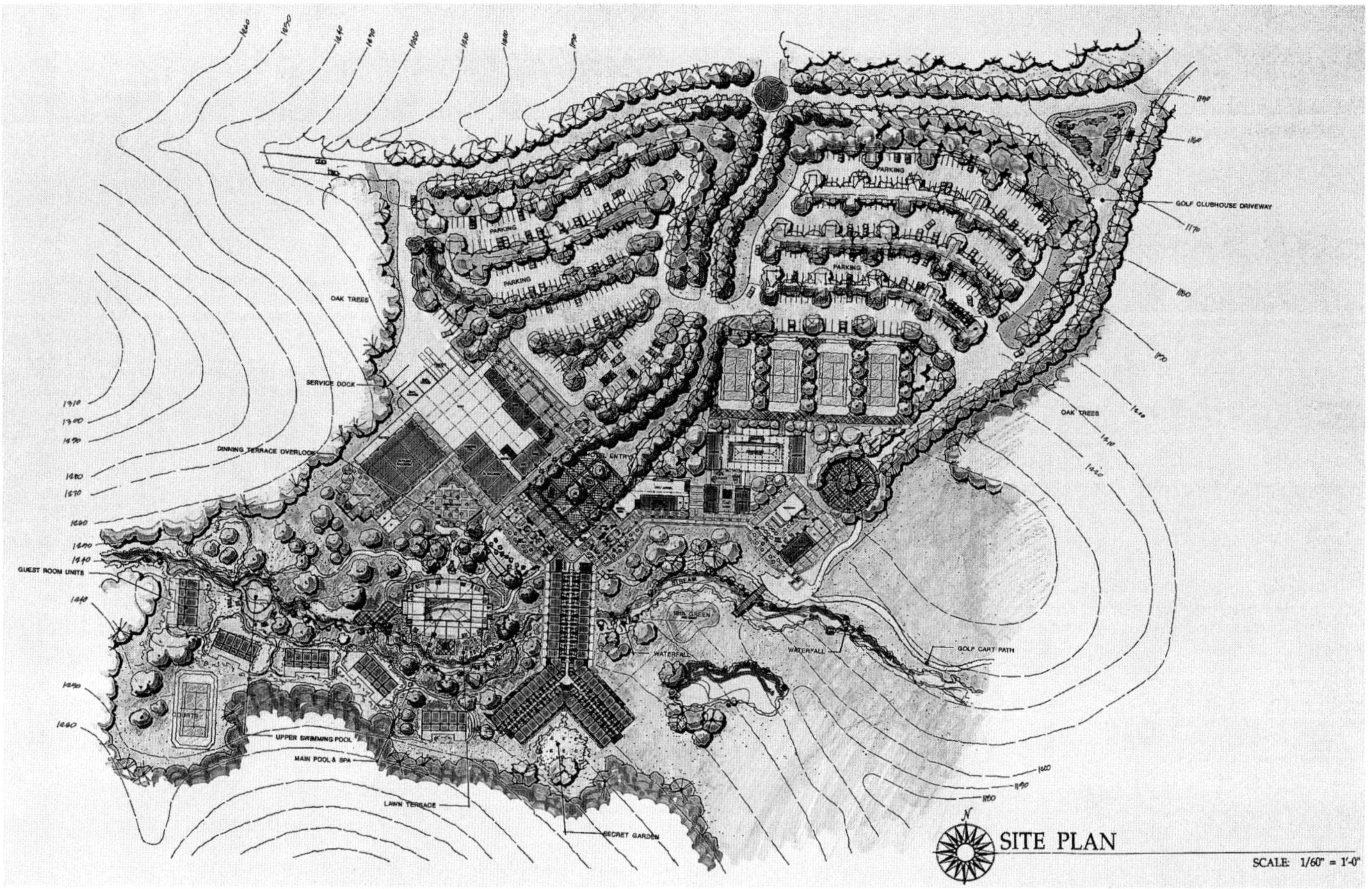

A well-sited urban resort **The Ritz-Carlton, San Antonio, Texas.** The architect and landscape architect worked closely to optimize the placement of buildings, recreational facilities such as swimming pools and tennis courts, and parking and to emphasize the natural landscape's inherent qualities, while minimizing views of service areas.

environment and, over centuries, has developed a language to shape their surroundings, making use of local materials, adding unique details and embellishments, and adapting simple technologies to their structures. Designers may consider features learned from this vernacular architecture to enhance a modern resort. For example, In Ubud, on the Indonesian island of Bali, Australian architect Peter Muller designed the Amandari resort with an appreciation for the local context. Many guestrooms, actually individual villas, are modeled after traditional homes, each with an enclosed private garden. The entrance to the hotel complex incorporates a temple gateway that is used once a year for ceremonial purposes by a Hindu priest and nearby residents. The swimming pool is a reflective plane of water that cleanly drops at one end to form a visual link to the surrounding rice paddies, sacred land to the Balinese. Such gestures make Amandari seem part of the local culture and give the guest a very special glimpse into local traditions (see p. 104).

In tropical climates the distinction between inside and outside is less rigid. The spilling out of interior functions onto adjacent exterior spaces is appealing and can occur through most of the year with terraces forming the link between the hotel structures and the landscape. Additionally, functions that normally occur indoors are held outside, away from the main buildings, as the exotic landscape makes for special guest occasions. The grounds may contain a small pavilion and service pantry for food and beverage service. Setups away from the main reception areas of the hotel offer privacy and can be used by outside groups such as local businesses and wedding parties without disturbing the resort guests.

Resorts and large hotel complexes often are planned in phases to gradually absorb room demand before building additional facilities. The designers must anticipate how the resort might grow

Table 14.1 Recreational facilities space requirements

Children's play area	1,000–3,000 ft^2 (93–280 m^2); varies by age group, play equipment, etc.
Swimming pool	40 × 82 ft (12 × 25 m); approximately 5 lanes
Racquetball	20 × 40 ft (6 × 12 m); add 10 ft (3 m) at backwall
Basketball	50 × 94 ft (15 × 28.7 m)
Volleyball	30 × 60 ft (9 × 18 m); add 8 ft (2.4 m) around all sides
Tennis	36 × 78 ft (11 × 23.8 m); add minimum of 12 ft (3.7 m) around all sides of court
Soccer	225 × 360 ft (68.6 × 109.7 m); championship field
Golf	160–180 acres (65–73 ha); 18 holes, including clubhouse, parking and practice areas

Confirm precise dimensions with local sports authority.

while planning for a range of future modifications and additions, for example, new guestroom villas or more function space or recreational amenities. For example, the master plan should locate the swimming pool or other major amenities, in the first phase, where they will not interfere with the future construction of additional facilities. The early phases provide the engineering infrastructure to enable later tie-ins. Generally, the most profitable additions are guestrooms, which cost the least to build providing that the plan contains sufficient amenities and supporting services.

The scale of a new resort hotel may be overwhelming, especially where it is located in a developing region with an indigenous architecture. One way to mitigate this contrast is to situate the hotel adjacent to a prominent landscape feature that can help integrate the building with its setting. In Sri Lanka, architect Geoffrey Bawa placed the Kandalama Hotel against a rocky cliff facing the Dambulla tank, or lake, and with views of nearby Sigiriya, the medieval rock fortress and one of the country's leading tourist sites. The new hotel hugs the rough edge of the cliff and incorporates massive boulders, too large to move, as sculptures in the public spaces, offering a reminder of the hotel's natural setting.

The Boulders resort in Carefree, Arizona, is sculpted into the dramatic volcanic rock formations in the Valley of the Sun desert. The prehistoric natural landscape provides a spectacular setting for the resort's vast array of activities, including two 18-hole golf courses, tennis, swimming, hot air balloon rides, and desert jeep and helicopter tours. Guests stay in individual villas that give a sense of intimacy with the environment.

A flawed master plan can be the source of problems in the future. For example, some designs may spread the resort over too much land, not taking full advantage of the site or anticipating likely additional phases. Modifications to the concept for the 50 acre (20 ha) Steigenberger Resort el Fanadir in Hurghada, Egypt, on the Red Sea, create an extremely efficient organization with guestrooms oriented toward the sea in sweeping single-loaded buildings. The plan by William B. Tabler Architects gives greater focus to the landscape, with a themed Adventure Island carved into the shoreline (see p. 243).

Suburban Sites

When selecting a suburban site, developers carefully consider the impact of adjacent properties on their hotel. While zoning places some restrictions, largely on use (e.g. residential, commercial, industrial, etc.), too many communities are lax in their regulation of commercial strip developments, where hotels and motels might best be located. And in some communities there are no zoning ordinances. Obviously, certain ventures are less compatible than others: manufacturing business are surrounded by storage yards, automobile service stations may have abandoned vehicles on their sites, and nightclubs and bars generate late night activity that may disturb guests. Before selecting a particular site the developer needs to consider the positive benefits and negative impacts of the surrounding area. Some businesses may generate additional room or food and beverage revenues; others may detract from the experience by their appearance or create congestion. The hotel site plan can help minimize these impacts; often, suburban hotels focus both public spaces and guestrooms onto a landscaped courtyard and place the parking areas around the hotel in order to provide a buffer zone to adjacent properties.

In addition, landscape devices may help to block out incompatible neighbors. A wall places a hard confining edge at the hotel property but may be necessary in some situations. Trees are a better solution. They contribute to a positive perception of the property, provide shade, protect from winds, muffle sound, and filter the air. Trees help to conceal, shade, and soften the parking areas of the site. They block out car headlights that can disturb ground floor guestrooms. The careful placement of trees can create a sense of greater space and privacy, especially if selected and planted with consideration of foreground, middle ground, and background.

Hotels in suburban and roadside areas, especially those not near a major tourist attraction, cater to a mix of business and tourist guests visiting nearby. The hotel should reflect the best features of its surrounding community. The image of a hotel can be greatly enhanced by landscape design. Even a small well-planted entrance court gives an essential favorable first impression and an alley of trees offers a sense of importance.

The traffic generated by the hotel must be properly managed. Traffic is a concern to the hotel's neighbors, especially where the hotel is on the edge of a residential district. Understandably, homeowners do not want the noise and pollution from guests' cars and delivery trucks. These are strong arguments often used to stop a hotel project. It is essential that early in the project an experienced traffic consultant develop a clear strategy for handling vehicles to help deflect reservations that the community might have. This is indispensable for a town center hotel as well. Economy and mid-priced roadside hotels that attract guests with highway billboards should design the signage to reinforce the image of the hotel and respect the environment, while complying with local restrictions.

With the dependence on guests arriving by automobile, the best sites often are those near a major highway intersection. However, busy intersections can be confusing to travelers and make access more difficult, not only for guests but service vehicles. It is unlikely that the developer can change existing road alignments to accommodate the hotel, so one needs to understand traffic patterns before selecting a suburban site.

Finding an adequate labor force near the site often is difficult. Many staff for suburban hotels may drive to work but others may depend on public transportation. Therefore, finding a site close to bus or train lines is an advantage—as it is for hotel guests as well. In some locations, management organizes car pools, provides bussing from outlying areas, or builds or rents staff housing.

One of the most interesting hotel sites occurs at a major transportation interchange. The high-speed TGV rail link from central Paris to Terminal 2 at the Charles de Gaulle Airport in Roissy makes the connection one of the most convenient in the world. Sheraton took advantage of this link to build the Sheraton Paris Airport Hotel directly atop the train station. At nearly all major airports hotels are located amid the road systems surrounding the complex, making them sometimes difficult to reach. In the case of the Sheraton Roissy, however, guests can take a rapid train from the station located just below the hotel's lobby and be in Paris within 20 minutes. This hotel is not so much an extension of the airport, but a true Parisian hotel, replete with sophisticated interiors by renowned designer Andrée Putman (see p. 48).

Urban Sites

In the denser urban areas the hotel building covers virtually the entire site; the hotel is a closed container for all its functions. The limited open space at ground level is reserved for a porte cochere, fountain or artwork, and incidental plantings that soften the building's edge. It is possible, in addition, to take advantage of areas where the building steps back, creating terraces for outdoor amenities. In tropical locations the hotel may offer a roof deck for relaxation or dining—or the swimming pool—all commanding breathtaking views. Al fresco dining on an upper floor terrace, with lush plantings and separation from the street noise can be a valuable asset and differentiate a hotel's lounge or restaurant from its competitors.

In many industrialized nations, the rural and suburban areas are relatively homogenous with respect to income levels, while urban areas offer a greater contrast. The range of hotel types reflects this difference with upscale hotels vying for the most prominent sites, close to expensive shops, museums, concert halls, business centers, parks, and other major attractions. Their guests have access to private cars and taxis. The cities also offer a market for budget accommodations, which may be located in fringe areas close to such public transportation centers as the train or bus station, or local transit stops.

Parking in cities increasingly is restricted to limit traffic congestion, especially in the central business cores. For hotels, valet parking, using a nearby parking garage, may be an option. Parking beneath the hotel requires a heavy capital investment, 5–10 times that of surface parking for a roadside or suburban hotel. But the garage provides both safety and convenience to guests. Mid-range hotels, which have the highest required ratio of cars to guestrooms, are most challenged by the need for and expense of providing parking on site.

Loading docks are a necessary component of hotels and should be located well away from public entrances, ideally on a different street where delivery and other trucks are well separated from guest vehicles. Security demands often mean that VIP and celebrity guests, including heads of state and their entourage, enter a hotel by a back entrance, all to often via the loading dock area. Therefore, where this may occur they should be well protected from view and designed for secondary access to the public areas.

Analyzing the Project Site

Once the development team understands the larger issues that make a site suitable for a hotel or resort, they must study more fully the individual characteristics of the property (e.g. its terrain, soil conditions, utility availability, governmental regulations). The site information, along with the hotel program and market demand data, are the major elements that form the basis for the project design.

Site Characteristics

A first step is the topographical survey that establishes a base map for the site. From the survey the designer may immediately identify several design opportunities as well as a number of constraints. For example, the grade or slope of the land influences the eventual building location and its entrances, both public and service, including handicapped accessibility, baggage handling, and truck access to the loading areas. On a larger scale, the architect plans the roads and walkways for access to various site components, sites recreational amenities, and establishes 'view corridors.' Accuracy is essential. An inaccurate survey can create innumerable problems in every aspect of the development: utilities, parking, landscaping, recreational areas, entrances, structure, zoning and building codes, and so forth. Finally, there are major cost implications in determining cut and fill, or the amount of excavation and grading necessary.

The survey also maps the boundary and locates features such as existing buildings, trees, and fences. War stories abound regarding lawsuits between neighbors who, accidentally or unknowingly, build a fence or building on an adjoining site. Even

The arrival design for a versatile downtown luxury hotel and serviced condominium **Trump International Hotel & Tower, New York.** Site planning on congested urban sites focuses on the process of guests entering and departing the hotel. In the case of this hotel on Central Park West, an expansive marquee clearly announces the identity of the property to passers by and provides ample room to unload luggage and wait for taxis and limousines.

government planning documents should be taken as guidelines and carefully confirmed.

The initial site survey generally does not provide information on soil characteristics or subsurface conditions such as the height of the water table or the ground's bearing capacity. These are important considerations that also have serious financial implications. Early in the project a geotechnical engineering firm should take a set of soil borings to answer a range of questions: is the ground generally rock or loose soil? Is it uniform throughout the site? Is it relatively wet or dry? What are the natural drainage patterns? What types of foundations are most suitable to the soil conditions? In rural sites, which might need both wells for water and a septic system, the type of soil can have a great impact on the budget. Also, good topsoil should be saved and shifted to be reused later in the landscaping phase. The geotechnical report will help the architect and structural engineers make appropriate and cost effective design decisions.

Government Regulations

A second major element affecting the site and building design is the set of government land-use and building regulations in place. Prior to acquiring the site, the owner should be familiar with the pertinent regulations and how they influence the project including the number of rooms and floors, parking spaces, and environmental conditions. However, the regulations also serve to protect the owner from inappropriate development on adjoining properties in the future, and establish a baseline for a quality project. Typical regulations include the following general categories:

- zoning and land use codes
- building, planning, and health standards
- historic preservation laws
- environmental conservation requirements
- community interests.

Zoning, which establishes the overriding parameters of what and how much can be constructed, is based on the desire of the community to control the type of development and to separate incompatible uses from each other. The city (or other jurisdiction) is divided into 'use' zones (residential, commercial, industrial, etc.) with specific regulations for each. The several commercial zones identified on the map, for instance, will have different requirements for setbacks (distance between the building and the property lines), height (number of floors), density (number of units), parking and loading spaces, and so forth. Zoning restrictions vary widely; in rural sites construction may be limited to two or three stories or it may not even be regulated. Urban zones may vary from a maximum height of three to six floors in residential districts to no limit in downtown business areas. In some cases, land parcels may be combined and air rights purchased to enable a larger development than would be permitted on one site alone. The city may award a zoning bonus in exchange for amenities such as increased public access or public open space.

The expanding Red Sea resorts **Four Seasons Resort, Sharm el Sheikh, Egypt.** The planned funicular between the 270-room Moorish-style hotel and the beach provides guests with dramatic views of cascading roof terraces and more distant vistas of the curving shoreline, boat pier, and sea beyond (see p. 77).

The lack of availability of public services may limit those projects that impose special demands on the fire department, schools, libraries, road capacity, and utilities—particularly water supply and sewage. In smaller cities, developers have purchased new fire equipment such as a ladder truck, which, in turn, removed the municipality's objection to the project and facilitated its approval.

Meeting early with the local city planning agency or the building department is essential. They are the source of up-to-date information, will render preliminary interpretations of the zoning and building codes, and help identify other requirements imposed by additional regulatory agencies. Some communities require consideration by a regional planning office or ocean-front towns may defer to a coastal commission. Projects in sensitive areas may be required to complete a lengthy Environmental Impact Study, leading to modifications to the development plan. Sites may include wetlands and flood zones, requiring consultation with the US Army Corps of Engineers. As the project moves forward, other agencies become involved, looking at such details as utility connections, waste removal, signs, lighting, and building elements overhanging public property such as canopies.

The developer should research the interests of the local community and draw them into the planning process, to both better understand and address their concerns. The developer, then, can more easily apply for needed variances or exceptions, or can request special FAR bonuses to improve the project if the city is so inclined.

A most imaginative themed design **The Palace of the Lost City, Sun City, South Africa.** The design and placement of all buildings and landscape elements support the fictional theme of the Lost City including the Palace (hotel), which is sited on the highest point of the 68 acre (27.5 ha) resort and surrounded by water, as if rising from a volcanic lake. To gain access to the complex, guests must traverse a legendary bridge that is struck by a simulated earthquake every half-hour. The Valley of Waves features 17 acres (7 ha) of artificial lakes and rivers including an Olympic-size pool and a water adventure park that produces 6 ft (2 m) waves (see p. C-31 for a further view).

Developing the Master Plan

In establishing the concept for the site it is critical that the owner prioritize the program and goals. Are views from the public areas or guestrooms most important? Is it necessary or desirable to provide alternate amenities for different guest segments, say families and business travelers? How important is conserving a portion of the site for future development? Is the budget adequate?

Who has this responsibility? The developer must provide a program statement of criteria and objectives, which becomes the guiding document for the entire project. The architect and other consultants should refer back to the program regularly as, over many months, they make the countless design recommendations that, together, create the 'big idea' that the guest experiences. It is the site plan that offers one of the greatest opportunities to enhance the project, its functional design, budget, customer appeal, and eventual success. Consider that a resort or other lodging type can have a variety of characteristics, depending on the location, qualities of the site, owner's objectives, and market segments. Luxury retreats can be grand or imposing or, just as easily, homey and comfortable; resorts can be designed in the local vernacular or in a more international style; business hotels more often may have a corporate feel but, in Orlando, for example, as in other locations, many of the most successful ones carry a theme. While other important operational aspects can be changed, the basic design is for the long term.

In addition to the character of the design, the architect and others need to integrate a range of practical functional objectives. The best designs accommodate these functional and operational aspects while they also create a special ambiance, appropriate to the site and market. That balance is essential.

Accessibility and Circulation

Two key issues important to the guests' arrival at the site are visibility of the entrances and appropriate signage. This can be enhanced by any of several means, including sight lines, road widening, lighting, divided highways, planting, and graphics. But the entrance to the site and, specifically, the location and number of curb cuts must be coordinated with the city or highway department. Larger projects and those in congested areas benefit from the analysis of a traffic consultant who may lead negotiations with the local authorities to obtain highway modifications for the benefit of the project. These might include a new highway exit, turning lanes, traffic lights, or pedestrian or vehicular bridges and under-passes.

Once the guest has arrived onsite, the major objectives are to separate vehicular and pedestrian routes and to conceal service circulation. Suburban sites may have limited pedestrian circulation except for movement across the parking lot, but resorts require careful study and design to protect the site from being overwhelmed by vehicles. All projects need to plan access to the service areas (loading, trash, and employee entrance), for maximum efficiency while avoiding cross circulation or inconvenience to guests. During the conceptual design

The ecofriendly resort **Grand Hyatt Bali, Nusa Dua, Indonesia.** Employing environmental principles of ecotourism, onsite botanical research is performed at the resort to help sustain traditional Balinese culture, including landscaping programs that incorporate native jungle plants. The lily ponds and pools that permeate the complex are naturally cleansed with a biological filtering process using fish instead of chemicals (see p. 287 for a further view).

the traffic consultant should study the plan and indicate possible problems caused by the location of roadways, parking, and public and service entrances.

Surface parking often is the single largest site component of a hotel development. Of course, tight urban sites may have no onsite parking, yet alternative arrangements must be considered, including valet service, and expensive onsite underground parking may be necessary. In several European cities automated high-density parking systems reduce the space requirements. In North America, about 200 ft^2 (18.5 m^2) per car typically is allotted for valet parking and up to 350 ft^2 (32.5 m^2) is needed for guest self-parking, including aisles and ramps. The developer needs to consider the importance of proximity of parking to the lobby and guestrooms and the how often guests may use their cars, ranging from several trips per day in rural and suburban sites to infrequent use in urban locations (see Tables 17.12 and 17.13).

Sackett Lake Resort, a project in the foothills of the Catskill Mountains in New York State, demonstrates a variety of conditions for traffic, parking, and transit. The program for the resort includes a hotel, tennis courts, swimming pool, amphitheater, hiking trail and cabins, 18-hole golf course and clubhouse, and condominiums. Each of the elements has been located on the site to its best advantage in terms of appropriateness and development cost. A two-lane county road bisects the site. In order to slow the traffic and provide a more gracious entry sequence, the landscape architect proposed to reconfigure the road as it passes through the site into an undulating curve and to split the traffic with a wide, landscaped median. The design also includes restoring an old underpass for pedestrian access between the hotel and the condominiums. Vehicular access always is screened from view and pedestrian and vehicular traffic is separated as much as possible. The extensive outdoor parking that supports the amphitheater is masterfully concealed in a natural depression behind rows of trees.

View

Once guests arrive in their hotel room, among the first things that they do is check the view. Guestroom views often are crucial in selecting the site, orienting the buildings, developing the building form, and designing the fenestration. Not every building is a high-rise; not every site is blessed with 360° views, but various enhancements can be added. The site designer may create interesting features or treat the terrain in ways to improve the views. These may be as simple as designing small gardens or pleasant landscape vistas or directing views across the swimming pool or tennis courts or into an interior atrium. Where there is a truly special view, of mountains or the beach, for instance, and if project budget and orientation permit, the guestrooms may be constructed as a single-loaded corridor building with rooms only on the view side.

The Palace of the Lost City in South Africa deals with the local topography in a dramatic and powerful way. The program called for a large, massive building to take advantage of service efficiencies. From the aerial photograph (p. C-31), one can see that the architect varied the massing, in part to complement the distant mountain range. It leads visually to the grandeur of the range without competing or detracting from it. The irregular aspects of the site are used to create a variety of levels and a rich, textural montage of plateaus and pools, beach and island, waterfalls and streams, bridges and buildings (see Chapter 13).

Utilities

Another vital aspect of site development that must be determined early on is the availability of such utilities as electricity, telephone, water, and sewer. In urban locations these all are assumed to be readily available, as are natural gas and high-speed data lines. Smaller cities may assess impact fees for new construction to support necessary additions to the sewage plant, roadway widening, and other improvements related to the project. Rural locations and sites on small islands may have a limited utility infrastructure. What is the source of these services? What are the factors that govern their acquisition? Are they available in the quantity required onsite or does existing service have to be upgraded or new service brought in completely? After an analysis of the costs from the local utility company, the developer may determine that it is better to have an onsite plant to take care of the project's needs. In some locations utility deregulation has forced utility companies to compete for rates and even to purchase excess power from private users.

The cost of these services can be a major component of the operating expense of the hotel or resort, generally falling between 3 and 5 percent of total revenues. Early investigation into the local cost of electricity, gas, fuel oil, and even solar or wind power as the predominant fuel source is necessary. Recently, and into the foreseeable future, a procedure called 'peak shaving' will have an increasing impact on the bottom line. During peak rate periods for electricity, the system automatically cycles certain equipment off and on to lower demand or shifts power to alternative sources such as gas or solar power.

Natural Landscape

Understanding how to use the natural landscape to benefit the site and building designs is important in increasing guest appreciation of the project and reducing construction and operating costs. The topographical plan identifies areas where excessive slope might mandate expensive grading and the construction of retaining walls. But, also, these areas may offer among the best views and, with proper landscaping, can become the most memorable features of a property.

Plants of all types—trees, shrubs, grasses, gardens, and so forth—provide obvious yet significant

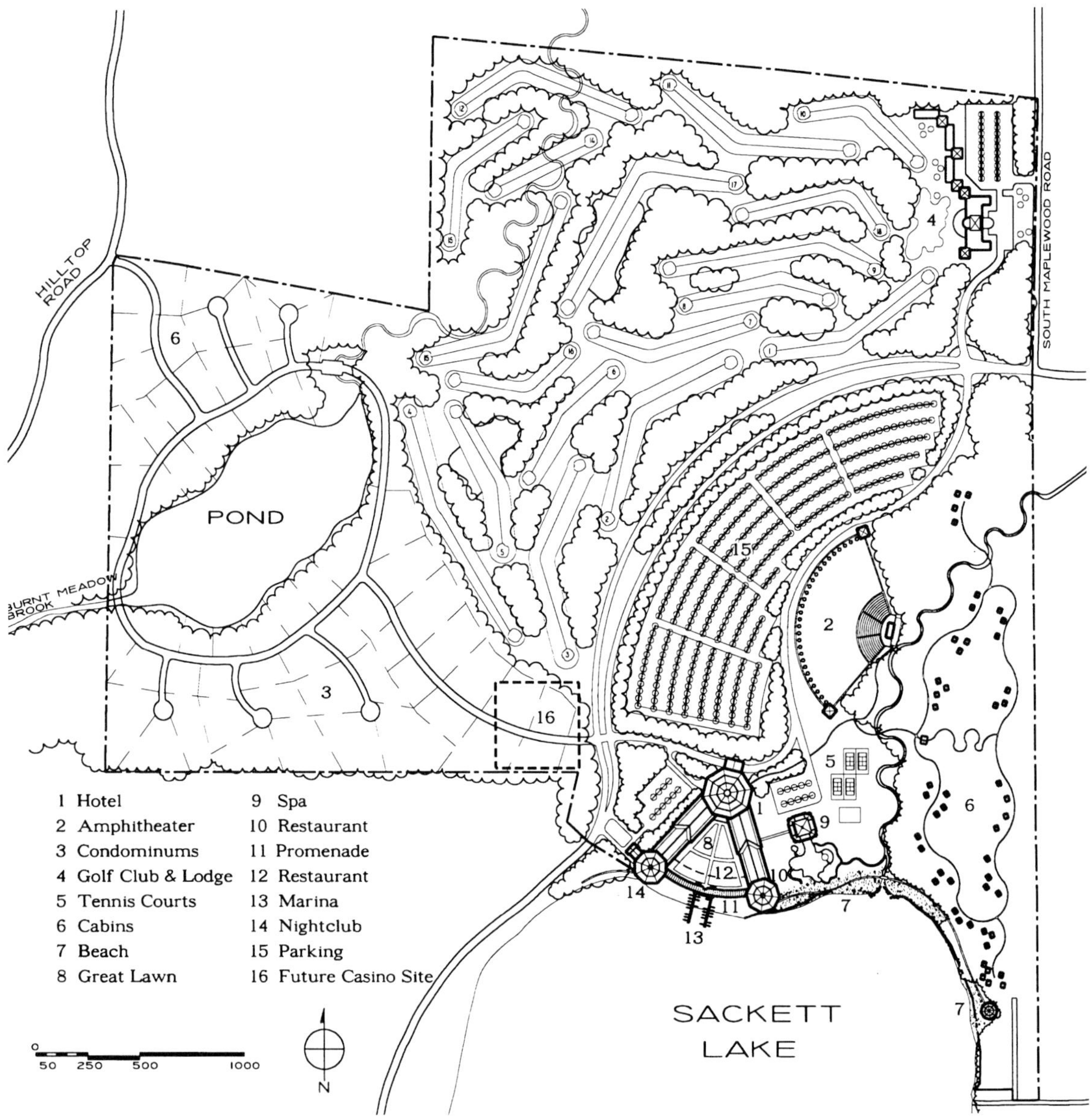

The redeveloped lakefront resort **Sackett Lake Resort, Monticello, New York.** On the 315 acre (128 ha) grounds of the former borscht belt resort, The Laurels, which was destroyed by fire, developers are planning a 500-room conference retreat hotel with a retail arcade along a lakefront promenade and beach, 50 wooded cabins, 60 condominium sites surrounding a wetlands pond, a 15,000-seat amphitheater sited in shallow valley and a restored 18-hole golf course. Parking and vehicular circulation are carefully planned to protect view corridors toward the lake.

Table 14.2 Site and outdoor furnishings checklist

Seating	Permanent, moveable
Lighting	Overhead, in-ground flush, ornamental, directional, architectural
Trees and plantings	Grates, guards, planter units
Bollards	Illuminated, vehicular
Fencing	Ornamental, territorial, security
Signage	Directional, building identification
Gazebos, kiosks	Custom, prefabricated; shuttle bus shelter
Shade structures	Trellises, fabric structures
Artwork	Sculptures, artifacts; ground- or building-mounted
Hardscape	Terraces, walkways, amphitheater
Water features	Fountains, ornamental pools, water walls
Accessory items	Flag poles, clocks, bike racks, waste receptacles, utility connections/site drains

benefits to a site. Trees and large plants offer cooling shade and protection from glare. They define views, provide sheltering canopy and flowering buds, and screen unwanted elements. Deciduous trees change with the season, offering a variety of effects, while the conifers and evergreens provide year-round shelter as wind breaks or snow barriers; all trees contribute to retaining soil and ground moisture.

The soil on the site can readily support the indigenous vegetation but the landscape architect determines if it is suitable for the new landscape plan and how well it is likely to survive the rigors of construction. Major trees on the site should be protected. The designer might decide to make special efforts to save unique plant specimens; otherwise suitable replacements will have to be selected. There is an art to arranging the landscape environment, to selecting plants for particular aesthetic and functional requirements, just as for planning the circulation and building functional elements of the site.

A related element is the design of any accessory structures and the selection of complementary site furnishings. These items, listed in Table 14.2, are best when they seem to blend into the landscape, whether by color, material, or placement, yet appropriately serve a variety of guest functional needs.

The Grand Hyatt Bali illustrates the goal of blending indigenous architecture with lush tropical vegetation to obtain a distinctive look. In the design the outdoors is brought inside through the use of the pagoda as an intermediate device, a place for repose and contemplation. The pathway edges are carefully defined with a flat central paver, rougher hewn edge stones, and a grass strip before the low foliage begins. Sculpture and water are integrated with the space to create a memorable image of beauty and repose.

The exquisite gardens of the Menele Bay Resort in Hawaii are another example of the sophisticated integration of many forms of local tropical plants. Rich foliage provides stark contrasts in color between the deep greens of the foliage and bright reds of the flowers. The pond, with its floating lily pads, is accessible from a solid platform or grassy path. The palm trees draw the eye toward the distinctive profile of the architecture. The guest is provided with a variety of visual cues and spatial choices (see pp. 72–73).

The Sackett Lake Resort illustrates site optimization because of its varied program and highly differentiated site. The architect and landscape architects incorporated and enhanced the many natural features by adapting them to the program. An existing low lying pond and marsh area is to be deepened and enlarged to capture runoff from the golf course and to become the central feature of a planned unit development. This pond will enhance the value of the property by creating waterfront sites. Also, north of the subdivision, an 18-hole golf course utilizes the rolling terrain (less suitable for housing), incorporates a preexisting nine-hole course, and adds new fairways, traps, and greens. The high point of the site, off the highway, is a natural location for the clubhouse and restaurant taking advantage of a sweeping vista of the course, hotel, and lake. The program includes an amphitheater for various-size crowds. A natural depression is moderately reshaped to direct sound away from the lake where it

Table 14.3 Security systems checklist

- Emergency command station near entrances and loading dock, connected with security office
- Alarm and annunciator panels located at command station with backup panel in security office
- Security guard staff
- Staff trained in security awareness
- Trained voluntary fire protection team
- Fire annunciation system (activated by floors and controlled by telephone switchboard)
- Fire protection system (sprinklers, standpipe, special kitchen and computer room systems)
- Design of site and buildings to include good surveillance and architectural barriers
- Site lighting
- Electronic surveillance
- Staff ID procedures
- Roadways with clearance for emergency vehicles
- Security alarms on walk-in refrigerators and freezers, liquor, golf, silver and china storage; corridor and fire stair ground floor egress doors

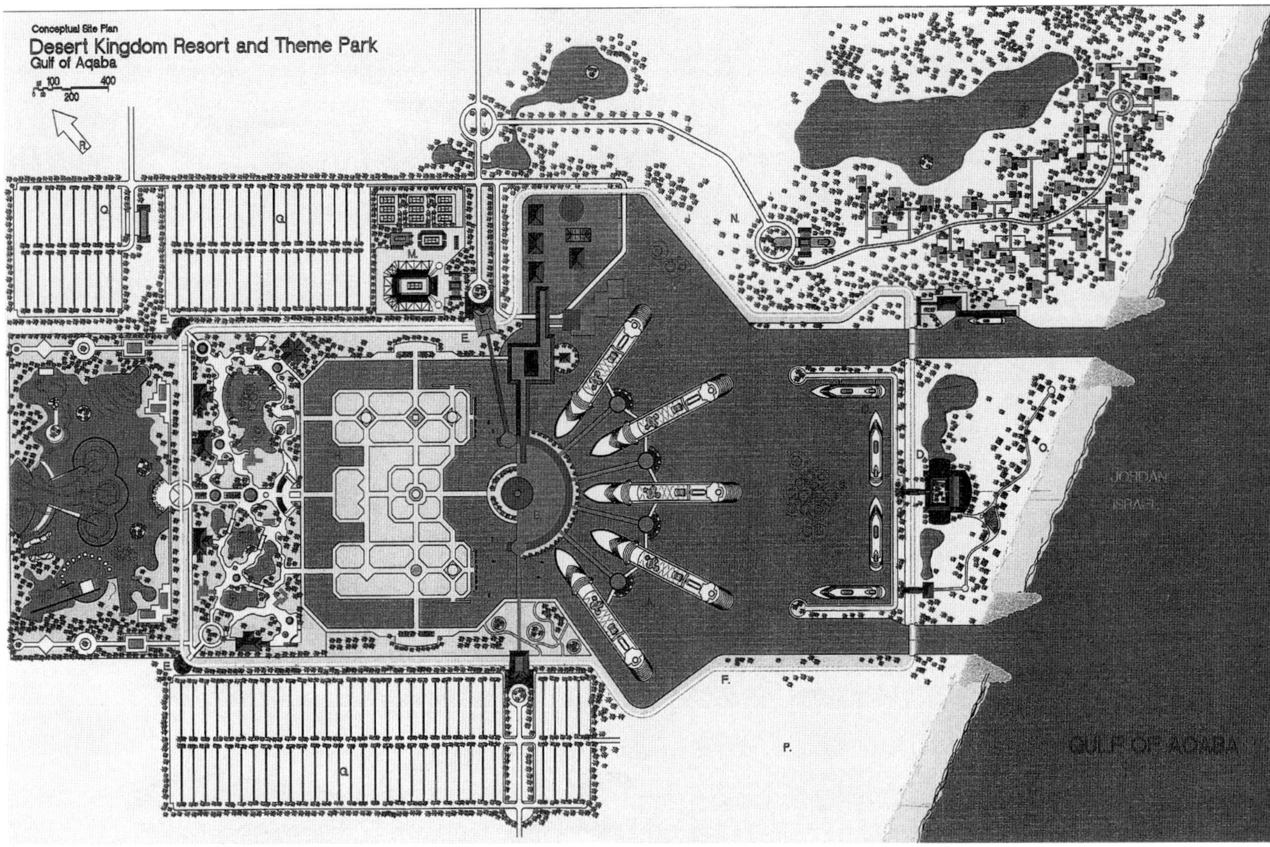

The partial Floatel **Desert Kingdom Resort Theme Park, Aqaba/Eilat, Jordan/Israel.** Maximizing the use of international waters, this 450 acre (182 ha) development in the Aqaba/Eliat area of Jordan and Israel is planned for 3,000 upscale and luxury rooms, themed entertainment attractions, extensive gardens, a major medical clinic, and a super-luxury villa enclave on territory straddling both countries. While available techniques used for floatel structures include lightweight concrete and steel, the architects will use a variety of methods including barges, fixed structures, and cruise ships calling on other ports (see Chapter 24). New forms of international cooperation support the growing tourism industry of the region. Nine floating structures will be moored in a protective lagoon dredged to the Gulf of Aqaba. Under a joint-nation agreement, guests will follow the rules of the country from which they enter, showing their identity by a high-tech palm-reading device.

may disturb neighbors and into a shallow depression where sound is dispersed by lawn seating. In addition, the rocky high area, otherwise virtually unbuildable, is turned into an asset as a hiking path with occasional cabins and the narrow lakefront becomes the site of the beach, boat pier, and hotel. The shape of the hotel maximizes the lake views.

Security

Security concerns are on the increase throughout the hotel industry worldwide. Operators strive to create an environment in which the guest feels safe and secure. The developer needs to give early thought to establishing a security plan for the site and may seek the advise of a consultant to identify threats and devise strategies for protection. Among the security and safety issues that the team must address are overall guest and employee security and safety, crime reduction, fire and life safety, and emergency medical response. Table 14.3 lists many of the specific ways in which security may be achieved. Strategies include monitoring access to the site and buildings and minimizing the number of entry points. The perimeter areas should be designed by using the natural characteristics of the site landscaping supplemented by walls, fences, TV surveillance, and motion detectors to discourage intruders.

Professional Documentation

The site development aspects of a typical suburban hotel, conference center, or resort play a major role in the design studies and eventual building plans and construction documents. The previous discussion touched on some of the special consultants who might be called on for their expertise in contributing to the site design and documentation, including:

- site plan showing all required features
- grading plans and existing contours
- utility layouts
- planting schemes
- lighting plan
- construction details
- plans of vehicular and pedestrian circulation systems.

Trends

- Resorts will continue to grow, particularly in remote exotic locations. With the ease of arranging travel, especially when organized as packages by travel agents or on the Internet, more and more people will seek out new destinations. More flexible work schedules are likely to create demand for shorter, niche vacations. Resorts need to consider what recreational amenities might be introduced to appeal to new market segments.
- While resorts with extensive sports facilities will attract the more physically-active guest, competition will be intense to provide innovative new facilities in order to attract future guests. Therefore, resorts should set aside land for future development as the market needs evolve.
- Concern for the environment has penetrated into the psychology of most travelers as evidenced by the great success of ecotourism. The resort industry is taking a more active role in the community with respect to its environmental responsibility and, especially, in terms of particular resort properties, many incorporating sustainable elements. High-quality site design reinforces this theme, with strong appeal to all guest segments.
- With the ubiquity of sport utility vehicles and cars with four-wheel drive, developers will find it more possible to situate their hotels farther into rugged territory away from cities and suburban sprawl. Guests' fears of traveling on country roads, especially during winter months, have been assuaged considerably by these vehicles and cellular phones, resulting in a confident and adventurous spirit and willingness to forge into untamed regions.

The crisp atrium geometry **Hotel Rey Juan Carlos I, Barcelona, Spain.** This highly sophisticated luxury hotel, timed for the Barcelona Olympics, places its 370 guestrooms in two opposing wings, whose spontaneous orientations are playfully expressed in its 14-story-high atrium curtain-wall.

The Guestroom Floor

15

The planning of the typical guestroom floor presents one of the greatest challenges in hotel design. Because the guestrooms and suites generally represent between 65 and 85 percent of the total floor area in a hotel or resort, any savings in the planning of a single level is multiplied many times. Therefore, a major planning goal in every lodging project should be to maximize the amount of salable guestroom space and keep to a minimum the vertical core, horizontal circulation, and necessary support areas.

In addition, there are several important architectural objectives. The architect should select a particular plan configuration and orient the building to enhance the appearance and visibility of the structure, to reduce energy costs, and to better accommodate possible future expansion. As lodging demand increases the owner may want to add rooms, either by extending the guestroom wings, adding additional floors, or constructing a new tower structure. For many projects, depending on the location, the architect needs to consider a configuration and orientation to take advantage of views from the guestrooms. In developing the plan itself, the designer should reduce as much as possible the walking distances for both the guest and the housekeeping staff, provide the support functions, and seek ways to reduce construction cost and nonsalable space. Table 15.1 lists the principal guestroom floor planning objectives.

The program requirements for the guestroom floors are relatively few: a designated number of guestrooms or suites, conveniently located public and service elevators, exit stairways to meet the building code and provide safe egress, adequate linen storage and vending areas, and small electrical and telephone equipment rooms.

The analysis of alternate plan configurations for the guestroom structure is one of the earliest design studies for a hotel, even before the exact guestroom mix is confirmed. The conceptual program may call for, say, 300 rooms including 15 suites, at a typical size of 350 ft^2 (32.5 m^2). The architect starts with the objective of providing a specific number of guestroom bays of a particular size and, taking into account constraints and opportunities of a particular site, may initially select a double-loaded corridor configuration, or a more compact vertical tower, or a spacious atrium structure—each with its myriad variations. Low-rise properties generally are planned using a double-loaded corridor and may be shaped into an 'L', 'T', square, or another configuration. High-rise buildings may follow similar patterns, can be terraced into pyramid-like forms, or can adjoin a large lobby space so that some of the rooms look into the hotel interior. The tower plan, where the guestrooms surround a central core, can be rectangular, circular, or practically any shape. And the atrium configuration, in early hotels such as the Hyatt Regency Atlanta a basic rectangular plan, in more recent projects has taken on numerous complex shapes. These various configurations are illustrated

Table 15.1 Guestroom floor planning objectives

Siting and orientation
Site the guestroom structure to be visible from the road
Orient guestrooms to enhance views
Assess the relative visual impact and construction cost of various guestroom plan configurations
Position the guestroom structure to limit its structural impact on the ballroom and other major public spaces
Consider solar gain; generally N/S is preferable to E/W exposures
Floor layout
Organize the plan so that the guestrooms occupy at least 70 percent of gross floor area
Locate elevators and stairs at interior locations to use maximum of outside wall for guestrooms
Develop the corridor plan to facilitate guest and staff circulation
Place the elevator lobby in middle-third of the structure
Provide service elevator, linen storage, and vending in a central location
Plan corridor width at a minimum of 5 ft (1.5 m), 5.5 ft (1.65 m) optional
Design guest bathrooms back-to-back for plumbing economies
Locate handicapped guestrooms on lower floors and near elevators

with selected plans throughout this chapter; a fuller discussion of the design of individual guestrooms and suites appears in the next chapter and, for particular hotel types, throughout Part 1.

What is the most appropriate configuration for the guestrooms? In densely populated urban areas, where land costs are high and the site may be relatively small, the ideal arrangement of public and support spaces on the lower floors may be the most critical consideration. Two major planning requirements, the preferred location of the public and service elevators and of the column-free ballroom, often dictate both the placement of the guestroom structure on the site and its shape. At resort properties, on the other hand, the opposite is true: the internal functional organization of the hotel elements is secondary to the careful siting of the buildings to minimize their impact on the site and to provide views of the surrounding landscape or beach. Many newer resorts feature not a single building but, instead, provide a number of villa structures that greatly reduce the perceived scale of the project, give the guest a greater connection to the site and the recreational amenities, and enhance the sense of privacy. At airport sites, height limitations often dictate the choice of a specific plan, one that packages the rooms into a relatively low and spread-out structure. Part 1 illustrates scores of hotels and resorts and makes clear the great variety of possible guestroom floor configurations.

While the choice of a plan type is the result of a balanced consideration of site, environment, and program requirements, the architect must realize that a particular configuration will shape the economics of the project. In addition to these budgetary issues—the initial construction and furniture, fixtures, and equipment (FF&E) costs as well as ongoing energy and payroll expenses—plan type also influences the more subtle aspects of guest satisfaction. The most economical design may not provide the best design solution. Thus, a less efficient plan type may offer more variety in room types, a more interesting spatial sequence, shorter walking distances, and other advantages that affect the guest's perception of the value of the hotel experience.

Analyzing Alternative Plan Configurations

In order for the operator to realize profits, the design team must maximize the percentage of floor area devoted to guestrooms and keep to a minimum the amount of circulation and service space (service elevator lobby, linen storage, vending, and other minor support spaces). Although the architect and developer must not ignore aesthetic and functional issues, a simple comparison among alternative plans of the percentage of space allocated to guestrooms versus nonrevenue-producing space can suggest more efficient solutions. The major alternatives among plan types are described in Table 15.2.

An analysis of the plans of hundreds of different guestroom floors shows that some patterns yield more cost effective solutions than others. The choice of one configuration over another can mean a saving of 20 percent in gross floor area of the guestroom structure and of nearly 15 percent in the total building. For example, the three principal plan alternatives—the double-loaded slab, the rectangular tower, and the atrium—when designed with identical guestrooms of 350 net ft^2 (32.5 m^2), yield final designs that vary from about 470 to 580 gross ft^2 (44 to 54 m^2) per room.

The study also indicates the effect of subsequent minor decisions on the efficiency of the plan—pairing two guestrooms back-to-back, choosing a double- or single-loaded corridor, grouping of public and service elevators, and planning efficient access to end or comer rooms. Because guestrooms account for such a major part of the total hotel area, the architect should establish a series of quantitative benchmarks for the efficient design of the guestroom floors.

The relative efficiency of typical hotel floors can be compared most directly by calculating the percentage of the total floor area devoted to guestrooms. This varies from below 60 percent in an inefficient atrium plan to more than 75 percent in the most tightly designed double-loaded slab. Clearly, the higher this percentage the lower the construction cost per room, which, in turn, offers the developer a range of options: build additional guestrooms, provide larger guestrooms for the same capital investment, improve the quality of the furnishings or of particular building systems, expand other functional areas such as meeting space or recreational facilities, or lower the construction cost and project budget.

The following sections describe, for each of the basic guestroom configurations, the planning decisions that have the most influence on creating an economical plan. In some plans, it is the number of rooms per floor, in others it is the location of the elevator core, or in another it may be the shape of the building that is most critical. In general, the most efficient configurations to construct and to operate are

Table 15.2 Guestroom floor analysis

Configuration	*Rooms per floor*	*Dimensions*	*Guestrooms (percent)*	*Corridor ft² (m²) per room*	*Comments*
Single-loaded slab 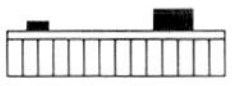	Varies 12–30+	32 ft (10 m) × any length	65%	80 ft² (7.5 m²)	Vertical core usually not affected by room module
Double-loaded slab 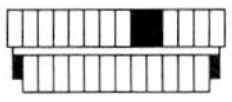	Varies 16–40+	60 ft (18 m) × any length	70%	45 ft² (4.2 m²)	Economical length limited by egress stair placement to meet building code
Offset slab 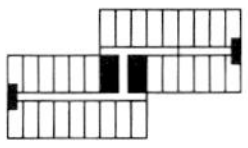	Varies 24–40+	80 ft (24 m) × any length	72%	50 ft² (4.6 m²)	Core is buried, creating less perimeter wall per room; more corridor because of elevator lobby
Rectangular tower 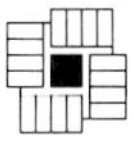	16–24	110 × 110 ft (34 × 34 m)	65%	60 ft² (5.6 m²)	Planning issues focus on access to corner rooms; fewer rooms per floor make core layout difficult
Circular tower 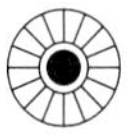	16–24	90–130 ft diameter (27–40 m)	67%	45–65 ft² (4.2–6 m²)	High amounts of exterior wall per room; difficult to plan guest bathroom
Triangular tower 	24–30	Varies	64%	65–85 ft² (6–7.9 m²)	Central core inefficient due to shape; corner rooms easier to plan than with square tower
Atrium 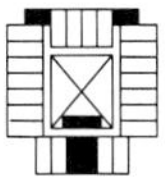	24+	90 ft + (27 m)	62%	95 ft² (8.8 m²)	Open volume creates spectacular space, open corridors, opportunity for glass elevators; requires careful engineering for HVAC and smoke evacuation

Each guestroom floor configuration has certain characteristics that affect its potential planning efficiency. The table shows the basic building dimensions, the usual percentage of floor area devoted to guestrooms, and the amount of area per room needed for corridors. For example, the table shows that the offset double-loaded slab is the most efficient in terms of guestroom area percentage and that the atrium configuration is the least economical, largely because of the high amount of corridor area required per room.

those where circulation space is kept to a minimum—either the double-loaded corridor slab or the compact center-core tower.

Slab Configuration

The slab configuration includes those plans that are primarily horizontal, including both single- and double-loaded corridor schemes (see accompanying plans). The few planning variables are concerned primarily with the building's shape (straight, 'L'-shaped, or other), the layout of the core, and the position of the fire stairs. The architect must consider the following questions:

- *Corridor loading*: given site conditions, are any single-loaded rooms appropriate?
- *Shape*: which particular shape (straight, 'offset,' 'L,' 'knuckle,' courtyard, or other configuration) best meets site and building constraints?
- *Core location*: should the public and the service cores be combined or separated and where in the tower should they be positioned?
- *Core layout*: what is the best way to organize public and service elevators, linen storage, vending, and other support areas?
- *Stair location*: how can the egress stairs best be integrated into the plan?

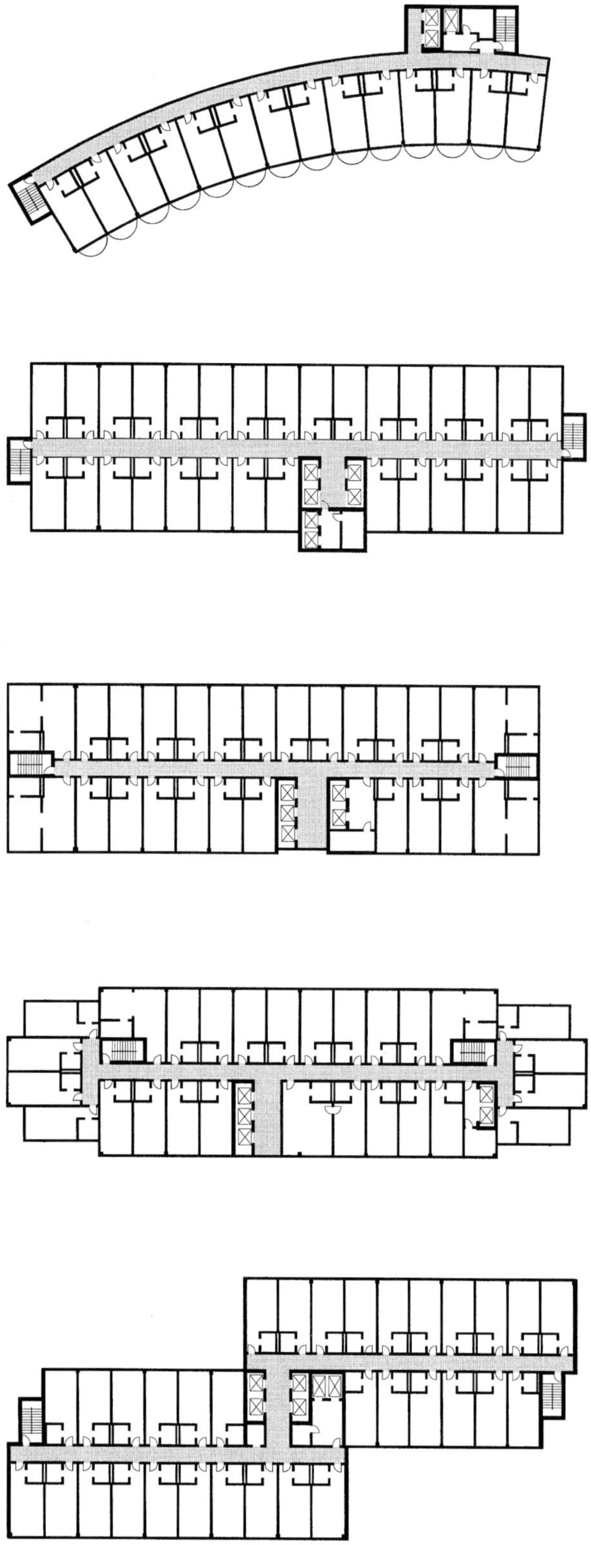

(A)

(B)

(C)

(D)

(E)

Efficient guestroom floor plans **Slab configurations.** (A) Single-loaded plans, while more costly, are sometimes necessary for narrow sites or to take advantage of views. (B–D) Double-loaded plans show paired back-to-back bathrooms, and most efficient options for elevator cores, egress stairs, and service functions. (E) Offset slab plan offers efficiency of interior core and as well as more variety in the façades.

The high degree of efficiency of the slab plan is based primarily on the double loading of the corridors; single-loaded schemes require 5–8 percent more floor area for the same number of rooms. Therefore, only where external factors are present—a narrow site dimension or spectacular views in one direction—should single-loading be considered.

While slab plans as a category are the most efficient, various approaches can tighten the layout of the typical floor. Configurations that bury the elevator and service cores in interior corners have several advantages: they reduce the nonguestroom area, reduce the amount of building perimeter, and increase the opportunities for creating architecturally interesting buildings. The offset slab plan, for example, is especially economical because the public and service elevator cores share one area and, in addition, they do not displace any guestrooms from the building perimeter. The 'knuckle' configuration, which bends at angles, creates the potential for interestingly shaped elevator lobbies, provides compact service areas, and breaks up the slab's long corridors.

The core design is complicated by the need to connect the public elevators to the lobby and the service elevators to the housekeeping and other back-of-house areas. This often necessitates two distinct core areas at some distance from each other, although in many hotels they are located side-by-side. One common objective is to position the elevator core in the middle-third of a floor in order to reduce the walking distances to the farthest rooms. Most often the vertical core is fully integrated into the body of the tower but, occasionally, the designer may, for planning reasons, add the core to the end of a compact room block or extend it out from the face of the façade.

The actual layout of the core is another determining factor of efficiency in the typical plan. In most slab-plan hotels, the vertical cores require space equivalent to two to four guestroom modules. If one goal is to keep the core to a minimum then the efficiency of the plan is improved when the core displaces the fewest number of guestroom bays. The comparison of many projects shows that the vertical core displaces fewer guestroom bays when the service areas are located behind the public elevators rather than beside them or at some distance. Many of the more efficient configurations also feature a distinct elevator lobby. Such a foyer space helps to isolate the noise and congestion of waiting people from nearby guestrooms. Also, those plans which incorporate an elevator lobby tend to have fewer awkwardly shaped rooms, thereby providing a more uniform guestroom product.

Building codes generally require egress stairs at opposite ends of the building. Each stair tower might simply replace the last guestroom on the corridor. But, instead, the architect may be able to integrate the stairs within the building, as part of an elevator core, at an 'inside corner' where the building turns, or within the usual bathroom zone of a guestroom bay (where it is part of an oversized room or suite). Careful placement of the stairs provides one more opportunity to create a more efficient overall plan by reducing gross floor area, compared with simply attaching the stair tower to the end of the building.

One limiting factor to the number of rooms on the guestroom floor is the typical building code requirement for hotels with automatic sprinklers that there be no more than, say, 300 ft (91 m) between egress stairs. Therefore, another goal in planning the repetitive guestroom floor is to create a layout that does not require a third fire stair. Experienced hotel architects have established techniques for maximizing the number of rooms per floor and manipulating the stairs and corridors to increase the building's overall efficiency.

Tower Configuration

A second major category of guestroom floor plans are 'tower' plans, generally organized with a central core surrounded by a single-loaded corridor and guestrooms (see accompanying plans). The exterior architectural treatment of the tower can vary widely as the geometric shape of the plan changes from square to cross-shaped, circular to triangular. The tower plan exhibits very different characteristics than the slab, but raises a similar series of questions for the designer:

- *Number of rooms*: how many guestrooms economically fit a particular layout?
- *Shape*: which shape is most efficient and permits the desired mix of rooms?
- *Corridor*: how is hallway access to corner rooms arranged?
- *Core layout*: how are the elevators, linen storage, and stairs organized?

Unlike the other plan configurations, selection of the tower shape creates specific limitations on the number of rooms per floor. For the most part, towers contain between 16 and 24 rooms, depending on the guestroom dimensions, the number of floors, and thc optimum core size. With only 16 rooms, the core is barely large enough for two or three elevators, two egress stairs, and minimum amounts of storage. On the other hand, designs with more than 24 rooms become so inflated and the core so large that the layout becomes highly inefficient.

For most guestroom configurations, the efficiency is improved by increasing the number of rooms on a floor, with little or no increase in the core or building services. With the tower plan, the opposite is true. The analysis of a large sample of hotel designs shows that, surprisingly, the fewer rooms per floor,

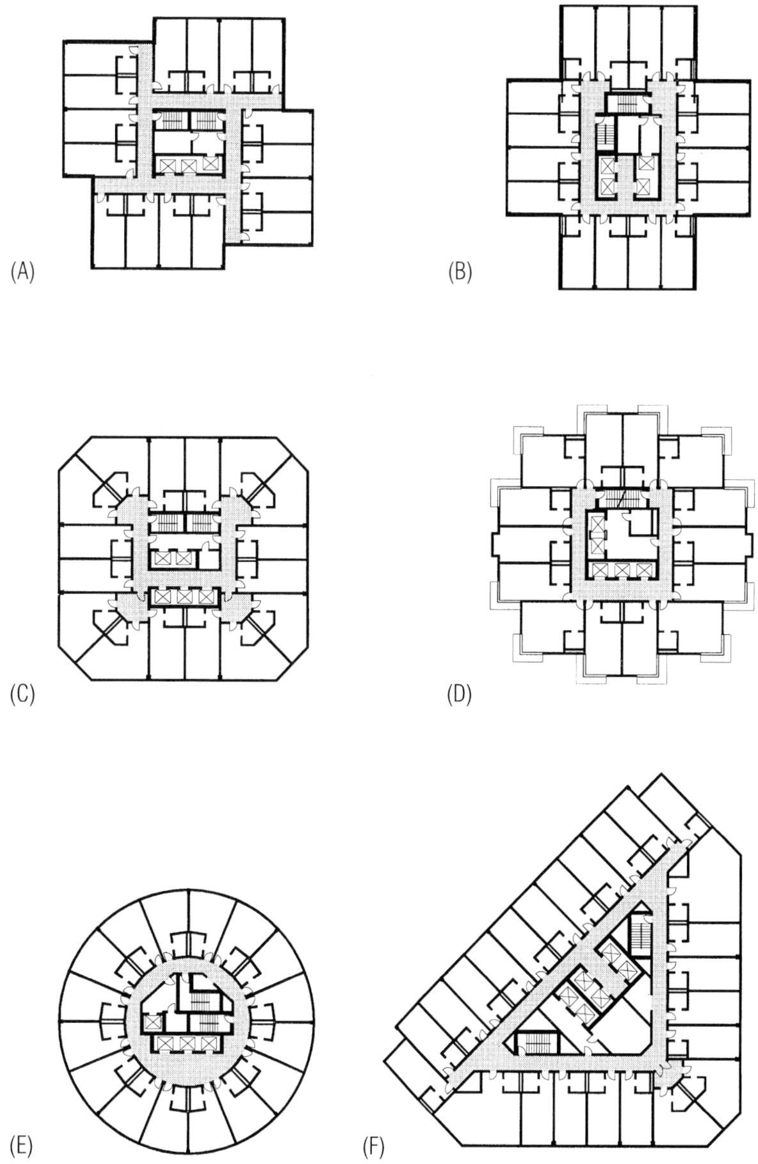

Compact guestroom floor plans **Tower configurations.** (A) Pinwheel plan accommodates all typical rooms but requires extra corridor. (B) Cross-shape plan reduces corridor but increases building perimeter. (C) Square tower features efficient circulation, back-to-back bathrooms. (D) Square tower provides most corner guestrooms and minimal circulation. (E) Circular tower offers minimum area and perimeter but substantially smaller bathrooms. (F) Triangular tower has less efficient core, but added variety of room shape.

the more efficient the layout becomes because the core, by necessity, must be extremely compact and, as a result, the amount of corridor area is kept to a bare minimum. The more *in*efficient layouts often result from *adding* rooms and from extending single-loaded corridors into each of the building comers.

The shape of the tower has a direct effect on the appearance of the structure and on its perceived scale. The efficiency of the plan, also, is a direct result of the shape because of the critical nature of the corridor access to the corner rooms in the rectangular towers and because of the design of the wedge-shaped guestroom and bathroom in the circular towers. Those plans that minimize the amount of circulation and, in addition, create unusual corner rooms exemplify the best in both architectural planning and interior layout.

For circular tower plans, the measures of efficiency are judged by the layout of the room as well as the core design. Typically, the perimeter of the wedge-shaped guestrooms is about 16 ft (4.9 m), whereas the corridor dimension may be less than 8 ft (2.4 m), thus challenging the designer's skill to plan the bathroom, entry vestibule, and closet.

While the design of the core in both rectangular and circular towers is less critical than the arrangement of guestrooms, certain specific issues have to be resolved. Generally, the core is centrally located, and the vertical elements are tightly grouped. The smaller hotels, those with only 16 rooms per floor, usually do not feature an elevator lobby, and the guests in rooms opposite the elevators must tolerate noise from waiting guests. In a few cases, the core is split into two parts, creating roughly an H-shaped circulation zone, effectively providing an elevator lobby on each floor. The two fire stairs can be efficiently arranged in a scissors configuration (if permitted by code) to conserve space.

In the larger tower plans, with 24 or more rooms per floor, the central core becomes excessively large. Some hotel architects introduce a series of multistory 'sky lobbies' to make this space a positive feature, or add conference rooms on every guest floor. The efficient design of hotel towers requires the simultaneous study of the core and the imaginative layout of guestrooms to meet the demand for ultra-high-rise mixed-use structures around the world.

Atrium Configuration

A third major category of guestroom floor plans is the atrium design, which was reintroduced by architect John Portman for the Hyatt Regency Atlanta hotel in 1967. The atrium prototype had been used successfully late in the nineteenth century in both Denver's Brown Palace, still in operation (see p. 178), and San Francisco's Palace Hotel, destroyed in the 1906 earthquake and fire. The generic atrium configuration has the guestrooms arranged along single-loaded corridors, much like open balconies overlooking the lobby space (see accompanying plans on p. 263). The following issues must be addressed by the architect:

- *Shape*: what configuration of rooms best fits the site and can be integrated with both public and back-of-house area needs? Should any guestrooms look into the lobby volume?
- *Public elevators*: how are scenic or standard elevators best arranged?
- *Corridor*: how can the amount of single-loaded corridor effectively be reduced?
- *Service core and stairs*: where are these best located and integrated into the overall building design?

Practically all atrium hotels feature glass-enclosed elevators that provide the guest with an ever-changing perspective of the lobby activity as well as add animation to the space itself. In some cases, scenic elevators are placed opposite conventional ones, creating two very different experiences for the guest. The location of the service elevators, housekeeping support functions, and egress stairs, while needing to be integrated into the plan and the lower service levels, are not particularly critical to the efficiency of the guestroom floor.

In addition to the open lobby volume, each atrium hotel is distinguished by the plan of the guestroom floors. While the basic prototype is square, many of the more recent atrium designs are irregularly shaped to respond to varying site constraints. This sculpting of the building contributes to creating a unique image for the hotel, a primary goal in selecting the atrium configuration, although by far the least efficient of the plan types. Recently, architects have sought ways to gain the prestige benefits of the atrium while increasing its efficiency. One technique that has been successful in several hotels is to combine a central atrium with extended double-loaded wings as was done at the Hyatt Regency hotels in Cambridge, Massachusetts, and Dallas, Texas. This effectively draws together the architectural excitement of the atrium space on a smaller and more personal scale than in the larger atrium volumes with the desirable economies of the double-loaded plan. However, many developers and architects believe that the atrium design has become a cliché—and also recognize its tremendous cost premium—and seek other means to create a memorable building and guest experience.

Defining the Guestroom and Suite Program

After the architect establishes the conceptual design, including a basic configuration for the guestroom floors, the team needs to refine and modify the earlier thumbnail guestroom program to fit the architectural concept—or shape the building to accommodate the nuances of the program. The room mix is based on the initial market study and, more importantly, on the advice and experience of the hotel operating company. The guestroom program defines the typical room module (key dimensions and bathroom configuration); the number of rooms furnished with a king bed, with two double or queen beds, or with other bed types; and the variety of suites. The proposed room mix is intended to reflect the estimated demand from the individual business, group, and leisure market segments. The details of guestroom and suite design are discussed in the next chapter.

Design development of the guestroom floors to meet the specific requirements of the program is among the earliest steps in refining the conceptual design. The design team studies a wide range of possible modifications including changing the width of the guestroom module, the number of bays per floor, the location and layout of the elevator and service cores, and the arrangement of suites. To avoid misunderstandings, the following definitions should be used:

- *Key*: a separate, rentable unit.
- *Guestroom bay*: the typical guestroom module.
- *Structural bay*: the dimension between two structural columns, typically equal to the width of one or two guestrooms.
- *Suite*: combination of living room and one or more bedrooms.

Generally, the hotel management thinks in terms of 'keys,' which represent the total number of individual guestroom units available to sell. A suite containing a living room that connects to two bedrooms totals three keys if the parlor has a full bathroom and convertible sofa and if the bedrooms can be locked off, only two keys if the living room and one bedroom must be sold together. Large suites often are described in terms of the number of guestroom bays they equal so a hotelier may refer to a four-bay suite containing a two-bay living room

(A)

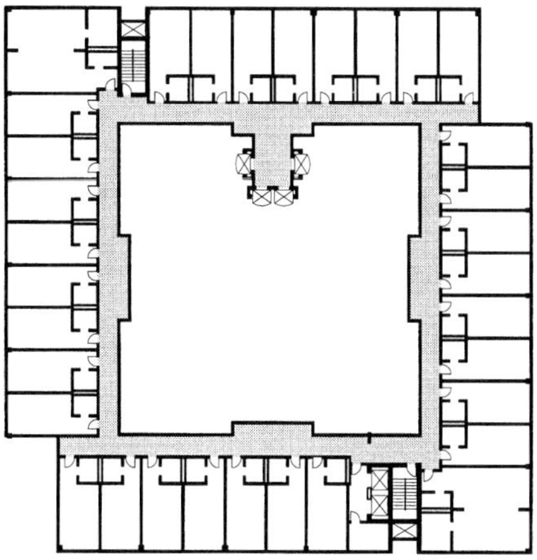

(B)

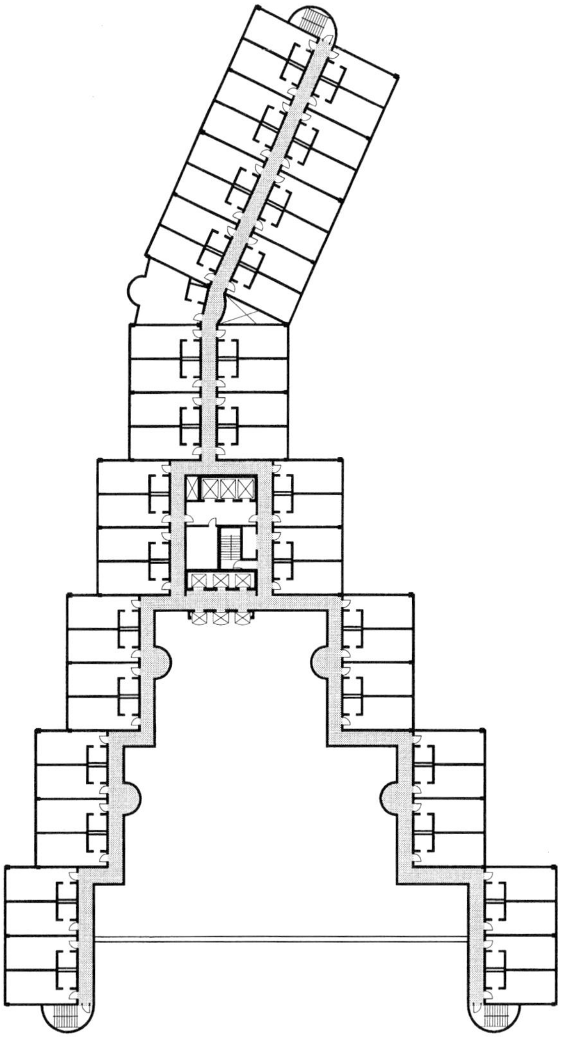

Dramatic guestroom floor plans **Atrium configurations.** (A) Typical atrium features scenic elevators and single-loaded balcony corridors. (B) Hybrid atrium plan combines visual excitement of atrium space with more efficient double-loaded slab extension (Hyatt Regency Dallas, Welton Becket Associates).

Table 15.3 Typical guestroom program for 300-room hotel

Room type	*Unit area**	*Keys*	*Bays*	*Total bays*	*Total net area**	*Comment*
King	350 (32.5)	120	1	120	42,000 (3,900)	
Double-double	350 (32.5)	160	1	160	56,000 (5,200)	
Parlor	350 (32.5)	6	1	6	2,100 (195)	Wet bar; connects to K and DD
Hospitality suite	700 (65)	6	2	12	4,200 (390)	Kitchen; connects to K and DD
Conference suite	700 (65)	4	2	8	2,800 (260)	Boardroom; connects to K and DD
Deluxe suite	1,050 (97.5)	3	3	9	3,150 (295)	Connects to K and DD
Presidential suite	1,400 (130)	1	4	4	1,400 (130)	Connects to dedicated K and DD
Concierge club	1,400 (130)	0	4	4	1,400 (130)	Include pantry and conference room
		300		323	113,050 (10,500)	

*Floor area in ft^2 (m^2).

and two connecting bedrooms. Architects, on the other hand, often refer to the individual rooms and to structural bays, the former being the basis of the contract documents and the latter a chief component of cost estimates for the guestroom portion of the hotel.

During the development phases, the feasibility consultants project revenues and expenses, occupancy percentages, and average room rates based on the number and type of guestroom keys. In addition, both parking requirements and zoning ordinances (used to control project size and density) are usually based on the key count. However, clarification is essential in order to avoid possible misunderstandings and delays. Table 15.3 illustrates an example of a typical guestroom and suite program and the use of the terms 'key' and 'bay.'

Documenting the Guestroom Mix

Throughout the later design phases the architect and other design team members continually modify details of the guestroom structure, in response to the owner's or operator's input or as the result of changes in the public and service areas on the lower floors. But often it is the result of the impact of a fuller design of the building's mechanical and electrical distribution systems, elevator cores, or stair towers. Because it is important that the team be able to keep an accurate count of the total bays and keys the architect or interior designer should prepare and regularly update a 'guestroom mix analysis.'

Table 15.4 illustrates one typical approach for documenting the guestroom mix. This technique forces the architect or interior designer to make a number of conscious decisions:

- *Architectural shape*: identify each room that has a different shape or configuration.
- *Bed type*: label each room by its bed type (king, queen, double-double, etc.).
- *Connecting rooms*: indicate adjoining guestrooms.
- *Suite locations*: position and label any suites.
- *Guestroom numbers*: assign final room numbers.
- *Key and bay analysis*: develop and maintain a summary table of keys and bays by architectural shape or bed type.

There are many advantages for documenting the room count. One, at the earliest conceptual design phase the design team can test the schematic design against the major element in the space program—the required number of guestrooms—and initiate any necessary changes. Two, a format is established so that, as the project proceeds through the later design phases, the designers can readily analyze the guestroom mix and maintain a precise record of the guestroom count. Three, details of the repetitive guestroom block can be considered at a relatively early phase. For example, the architect can study possible pairing of rooms to increase the number of back-to-back bathrooms and to establish a repetitive pattern of setbacks at the guestroom doors. Four, the interior designer can identify any potential problems such as unusually shaped rooms that might not easily accommodate the necessary furnishings and amenities. In addition, other members of the team can offer better input when changes to the guestroom tower are fully documented through the different phases. For instance, the engineering consultants can review the major systems in the guestroom tower—the elevators, HVAC, and communications systems, for example—in the same context as the rest of the design team.

Table 15.4 Guestroom mix analysis

The guestroom floor plans illustrate the procedure for analyzing the architectural planning and room layout for a hypothetical hotel. The plans show the typical and suite floors, the latter with five different room types–not unusual as the standard room bay is modified to fit around elevators, stairs, or support areas. The number of different room types is increased further by handicapped accessible rooms and by various suites. The following discussion describes the necessary steps including key plans for each floor, labeled with room shape (I, II, etc.), bed type (K, DD, etc.), room number, and connecting doors, and a comprehensive tally of the guestroom mix.

- *Architectural shape*: identify each room of a different shape or configuration (primarily different dimensions or bathroom layout) and assign it a number. Different room types are identified by a Roman numeral in the top half of the circular code in each room. Room I is the most typical; room II is similar but has a different configuration at the entry vestibule; room III is the corner guestroom with a wider bay and different bathroom; room IV is a two-bay conference suite (only one key); and room V is a two-bay living room that connects to two standard guestrooms.
- *Bed type*: label each room by its bed type (king, queen, double-double, twin, king-studio, parlor, handicapped room, etc.) and place a simple abbreviation (K, Q, DD, etc.) on the plan. Note that the standard room type may be furnished in a variety of ways.
- *Connecting rooms*: mark interconnecting rooms with an open circle, for example between rooms 15 and 17. Operating companies seek a specific number of connecting pairs of particular types (for example, half the pairs connect K to DD).
- *Suites*: position all suites, combinations of a living room and one or more adjoining bedrooms, within the typical room configuration. Two suites are shown in the example: a conference suite in the corner that connects to a standard double-double room, and a VIP suite that connects to two bedrooms. The VIP suite also counts as a 'key,' or rentable unit, because it has a full bathroom and a convertible sofa. Often, the suites are grouped together on the top guestroom floors.
- *Room numbers*: assign room numbers to the bays to meet the management company's eventual operating requirements. Doing this in schematic design greatly aids communication among the various design professionals and reduces later confusion if the operator were to modify the room numbering. Determine room numbers to simplify directional and destination signage; maintain corresponding numbers on different floors.
- *Key and bay analysis*: develop a summary table to tally the number of rentable 'keys' and room modules for each floor by architectural shape or bed type. The table next to each plan cross-references the number of room types (I–V) and the bed types for each floor. Frequently, a larger chart is developed for the entire hotel showing the stacking of typical and suite floors and providing totals of the number of rooms for each type.

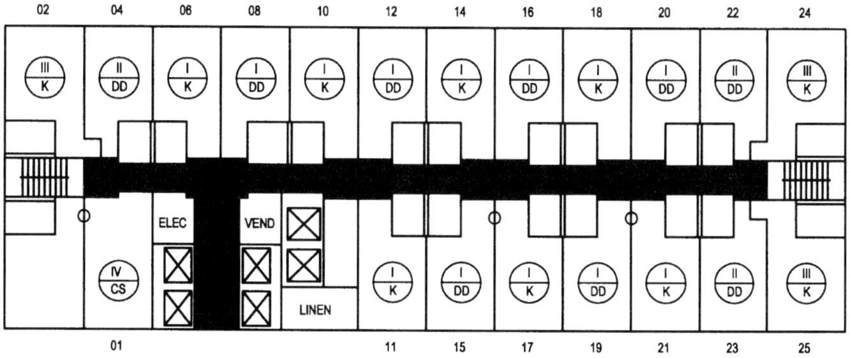

TYPICAL FLOOR

TYPE	BED	No.	BAYS
I	K	7	7
	DD	6	6
II	DD	3	3
III	K	3	3
IV	CS	1	2
		20	21

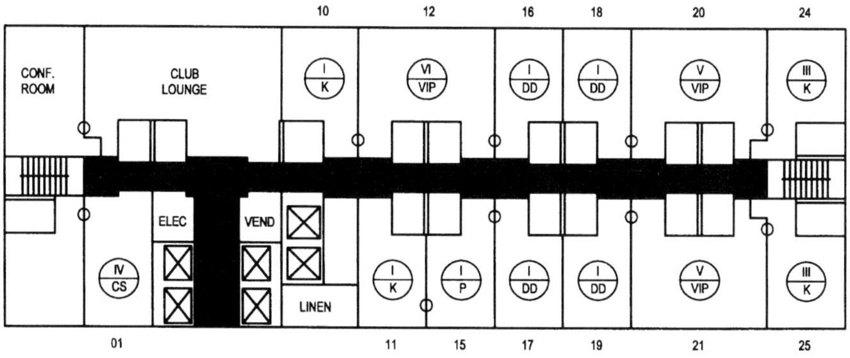

SUITE FLOOR

TYPE	BED	No.	BAYS
I	K	2	2
	DD	4	4
	P	1	1
III	K	2	2
IV	CS	1	2
V	VIP	2	4
VI	VIP	1	2
CL		0	4
		13	21

The Modernist guestroom and bath interior **Hyatt Regency Mainz, Germany.** The striking modern accommodations feature high-tech communications equipment in each of the 268 rooms and suites. The typical guest bathrooms incorporate a generous dressing area with a make-up bar and vanity, a separate toilet compartment, and a wet zone with a deep soaking tub and ceiling deluge shower.

Guestroom and Suite Design

16

Many hotel operators believe that the guestroom and guest bathroom make a more lasting impression on the lodging guest than does the exterior architecture or the lobby or any other single interior space. Design of the individual guestrooms and suites, while clearly more an interior layout problem than an architectural one, is still an important part of the architect's responsibility. Along with design of the public spaces, it is also one of the two major areas of focus for the interior designer. Because of the guestroom's residential character, such irritating deficiencies in layout or equipment as a nonworking light-switch at the room entry, inadequate mirror or counter area in the bathroom, or chair arms that won't fit under the desk, are especially obvious to the traveler. These design details call for the coordinated attention of the entire team: architect, engineer, interior designer, other design consultants, building contractor, and hotel manager.

The evolution of the hotel guestroom over the past two centuries shows how design and management professionals collaborated to design a better room. Until the Tremont House opened in Boston in 1829, no major hotels with private rooms existed; guests were content to share rooms—even beds—with whatever other travelers were staying in a particular inn. The Tremont House's innovative use of private and lockable guestrooms became an overnight success and set the standard for a burgeoning industry.

Throughout the nineteenth century, in order to remain competitive, the industry quickly introduced technological advances: gas—then electric—lights, voice annunciators—then telephones, and eventually elevators, central heating, and running water. These innovations culminated in the construction of the pioneering Hotel Statler in Buffalo, New York, in 1908 where, for the first time in a major hotel, all the guestrooms included private baths. 'A room and a bath for a dollar and a half,' the ads proudly proclaimed. Other design innovations of the Statler included bathrooms designed back-to-back for economy of plumbing, and such features in each room as circulating ice-water, a full-length mirror, a light switch inside the entry door, a bedside telephone, a built-in radio, and the 'servidor'—a shallow compartment within the guestroom door to facilitate delivery of laundered clothes.

Establishing Design Criteria

The layout of the hotel guestroom is intertwined with decisions that the design team makes during the schematic design, when they establish the dimensions of the guestroom module and the structural bay, accept a variety of nontypical room configurations, and approve a final room mix (see the previous chapter). These decisions provide the interior designer with the framework to creatively plan the individual spaces and give the guestrooms a character consistent with the public areas.

Guestroom design entails a series of steps confirming the following:

- major target market segments
- typical guestroom dimensions
- room mix including number and type of suites
- typical guestroom layout
- suite and special room layout (handicapped, etc.)
- proposed furniture, fixture, and equipment (FF&E) budget for guestrooms, suites, and corridors.

Designers recognize the specific needs of the target markets and identify features and amenities that these groups most want and expect. In general terms, the transient business person looks for single accommodations, the convention and group markets need double rooms, and the leisure market requires rooms to sleep two or more guests. For example, many of the hotel rooms around Walt Disney World Resort and Universal Escape in Orlando are designed with two queen beds and a

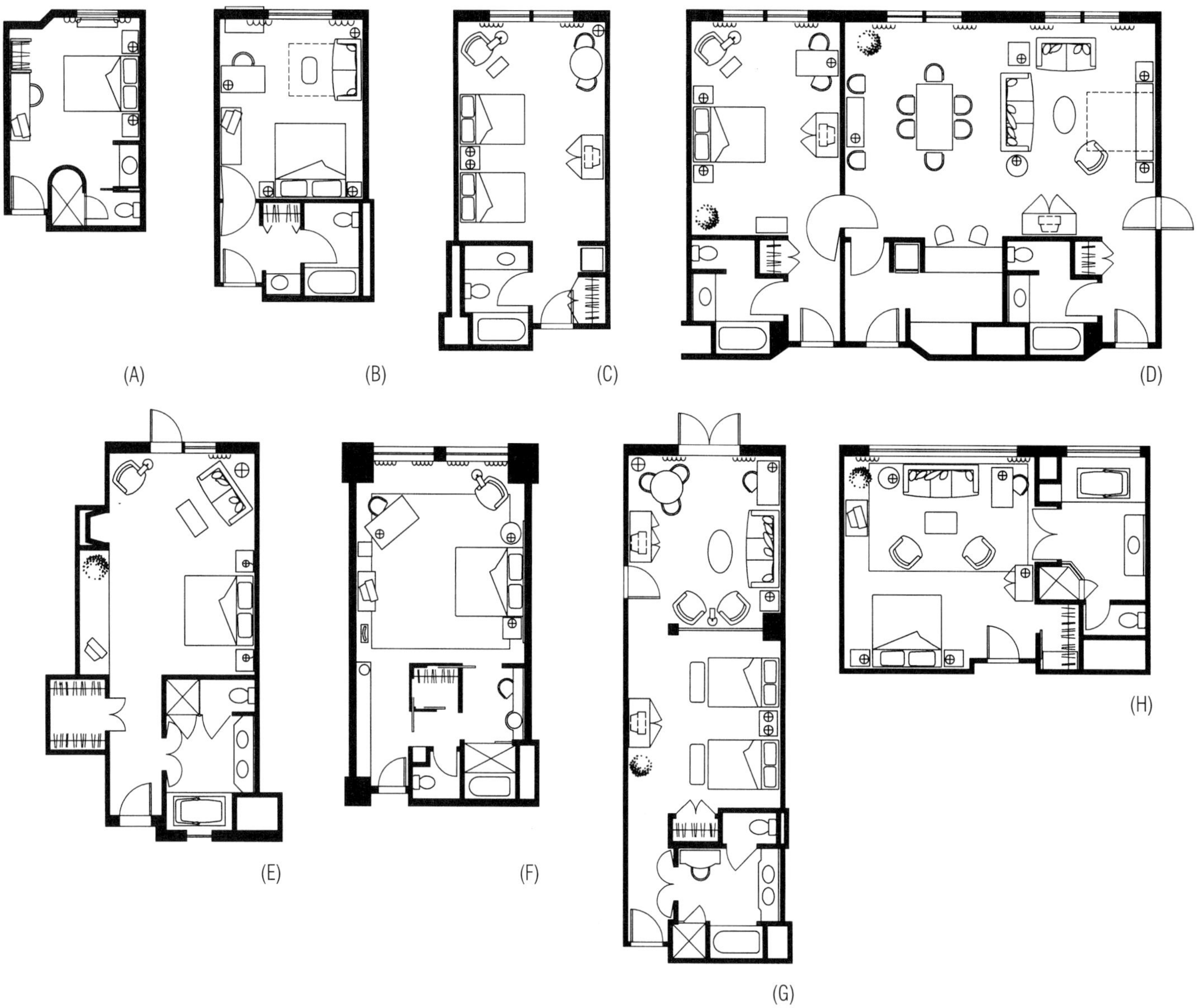

Typical and unique guestroom layouts **Guestroom plans.** (A) Economy queen room, 220 ft^2 (20.5 m^2) saves space with sink/vanity outside bathroom and one bed. (B) Mid-scale king room, 320 ft^2 (30 m^2) shows how placing the bed against the bathroom wall increases useable space. (C) First-class double-double room, 365 ft^2 (34 m^2) with typical furnishings. (D) Three-bay conference suite, 1,160 ft^2 (108 m^2) combines a two-bay public area with wall-bed, lounge seating, work area, full bathroom, and wet bar with a typical guestroom, and second connecting room. (E) Luxury resort room 550 ft^2 (51 m^2) introduces five-fixture bathroom and fireplace (Four Seasons, Scottsdale). (F) International luxury guestroom, 530 ft^2 (49 m^2) features carefully detailed built-in storage, sliding doors, and glass partitions for an open effect (Park Hyatt, Hamburg). (G) Luxury casino-hotel room, 665 ft^2 (62 m^2) features large bathroom, queen-queen beds, and separate living area (The Venetian, Las Vegas). (H) Rotated room configuration, 530 ft^2 (49 m^2) places whirlpool tub on the exterior wall of spacious bathroom and features unusually wide guestroom space (The Ritz-Carlton Millenia, Singapore). (For vacation ownership, all-suite, and extended-stay units see Chapters 4 and 8.)

convertible sofa to accommodate a vacationing family of four to six. Also, because each of these market groups uses the room differently, the designer must consider work and meeting functions in one case and family activities in another. The principal market characteristics that influence the layout and furnishing of hotel and resort guestrooms are identified in Table 16.1.

Room Dimensions and Configurations

The guestroom design decision which most influences the room layouts and much of the guest reaction to a hotel is the choice of three critical room dimensions: the inside or net width, the length of the room from the exterior wall to the bathroom wall, and

Table 16.1 Hotel guest characteristics

Market	*Guest characteristics*	*Purpose for travel*	*Guestroom design factors*
Business			
Group	Single or double occupancy; 2–4 -night stay; 55% men, 45% women; somewhat price insensitive	Conventions, conferences, professional associations, sales and training meetings	King or double-double; bathroom with dressing area; lounge seating with good work area
Individual	Single occupancy; 1–2-night stay; 50% men, 50% women; price insensitive	Corporate business, sales, conventions, conferences	King; bathroom with separate stall shower; lounge seating with good work area
Leisure			
Family	Double-plus occupancy (includes children); 1–4-night stay, longer in resort areas; budget or mid-price	Family vacations, sightseeing, sports, family activity	Double-double, queen-queen, or adjoining rooms; lounge seating and television; large compartmentalized bathroom; balcony, outside access
Couples	Double occupancy; 1–7-night stay; mid-price to upscale and luxury	Tours, clubs, associations, sightseeing; theater, sports, weekend packages, shopping, vacation	King; dining area, writing surface; moderate storage; large compartmentalized bathroom
Singles	Single occupancy; young professionals to seniors; mid-price to upscale	Tours, clubs, associations; culture, arts, theater, sports/recreation, shopping	King or queen; lounge/entertaining area; standard bathroom

the size of the bathroom. The net width establishes the structural module throughout the building (equal either to the width of one room or two rooms), which carries through to the public and service areas on the lower floors. The most common room width for the past several decades has been 12 ft (3.7 m), initially adopted as a standard in the mid-1950s by the Holiday Inn chain for all of their roadside properties. It was sufficient to comfortably accommodate two double beds against one wall and a desk/dresser/luggage stand and television on the opposite wall, with an adequate aisle between. While the typical room layout has evolved slowly over the last half-century, the industry's standard guestroom layout today is little different from the one pioneered in 1953 by Kemmons Wilson, the founder of Holiday Inns. Though, to be sure, style, comfort, and guestroom technology have seen major advances.

Until then, even the newest and largest convention hotels built in the post-World War II period incorporated a variety of room sizes, including a large percentage that were narrower than the new 12 ft wide standard. These hotels, many of them still operating and competing with properties 30–50 years newer, are greatly limited by the smallness of their guestrooms. In the US and Canada, no first class or chain-affiliated hotels (except for the budget inns) are built today with rooms less than 12 ft wide. Occasionally, when older downtown or resort properties are acquired and fully renovated, the size of some rooms may be smaller where they are limited by unavoidable architectural constraints. (See the discussion on updating older hotels in Chapter 10.)

In the past few years guestroom dimensions have become generally standardized for different quality levels of hotels or resorts (Table 16.2). While a few hotel operators have tried to provide noticeably larger rooms than their direct competitors, the guestroom size, quality of furnishings and finishes, and room rate remain closely linked because of the overriding influence of the initial cost of construction and furnishings.

The guestroom layouts in this chapter illustrate typical room design alternatives as well as a number of more innovative and luxurious layouts. The budget chains have reduced slightly the size of the 12 × 18 ft (3.7 × 5.5 m) mid-price room in order to lower construction costs, shortening it to between 14 and 16 ft (4.3–4.9 m), still sufficient to accommodate two double beds, and reducing the width by 4–6 in (10–15 cm)—although a few operators are building even smaller units. On the other hand, companies which are selling a more luxurious room have experimented with larger guestroom spaces and, especially, have created innovative bathroom layouts. Increasing the width of the room module to

13–13.5 ft (4.0–4.1 m) permits one major change in the room layout: a king-size bed can be positioned against the bathroom wall instead of the side wall, allowing for a variety of other furnishing arrangements.

Generally, there is little advantage to increasing the guestroom width beyond 13.5 ft (4.1 m). Even this slightly larger space does not improve the interior arrangement, and construction costs increase dramatically because of additional corridor and exterior wall area. However, at a room width of 16 ft (4.9 m) or more a new set of design alternatives arises: the bed or beds can be positioned against one side wall and the lounge and work area against the opposite wall. Also, the greater width permits unusually luxurious bathroom arrangements, often with four or five fixtures, as well as a larger entry vestibule.

The wedge-shaped rooms characteristic of circular towers present their own design problem in the layout of the guest bathroom. The smaller towers have a corridor frontage of only 6–8 ft (1.8–2.4 m), the larger diameter tower a more reasonable 10 ft (3 m). Although many of these room plans show such positive features as compartmentalized bathrooms (out of necessity), compact foyer space, a large lounge area, and expansive window wall, today's increasing competition in room size and upscale furnishings has made the smaller cylindrical towers virtually obsolete.

Designing the Individual Guestroom

The definition of the market determines not only the most appropriate bed combinations but also the other guestroom furnishings for a particular hotel. But the bed is the primary defining characteristic. Generally, hotels include a mix of rooms with one oversized bed (most often a king), two beds (generally double or queen beds), and suites of various types. Table 16.3 shows the more common alternatives. The selection of a proper room mix is important because it influences the hotel's ability to rent 100 percent of its rooms and to generate the maximum revenue. For this reason, rooms which offer more flexibility are popular with the management companies. A room with two double beds is more flexible than a king (one to four people); a king-size bed plus a convertible sofa is attractive to a single business person but can be converted to family use. Table 16.4 illustrates typical room mix percentages for the different types of hotels and resorts.

Typical King and Double-double Rooms

The full list of furnishings can be determined by analyzing the guestroom functions—sleeping, relaxing, working, entertaining, dressing—and their space requirements. The plan of the typical hotel room clearly shows these several zones: the bathroom and areas for dressing and clothes storage are grouped next to the entrance vestibule; the sleeping area is in the center of the guestroom space; and the seating and work areas are located near the window. New layouts combine the several functions in different ways or find techniques for separating them more fully. For example, the designer can provide suite-like characteristics in a standard room by adding a screen to separate the sleeping and sitting portions of the space. Or the designer may create a compartmentalized bathroom by isolating the tub/shower and toilet area from the sink and dressing function. The plan on p. 271 shows how the functional zones in a room may overlap.

Table 16.2 Minimum guest room dimensions

	*Living area**		*Bathroom*		*Total guestroom*	
	dimensions ft (m)	*area ft² (m²)*	*dimensions ft (m)*	*area ft² (m²)*	*dimensions ft (m)*	*area ft² (m²)*
Budget	11.5 × 15 (3.5 × 4.5)	172 (16)	5 × 5 (1.5 × 1.5)	25† (2.3)	11.5 × 20.5 (3.5 × 6.2)	236 (21.9)
Mid-price	12 × 18 (3.6 × 5.5)	216 (20.1)	5 × 7.5 (1.5 × 2.3)	37 (3.4)	12 × 26 (3.6 × 6.6)	312 (29)
Upscale	13.5 × 19 (4.1 × 5.8)	256 (23.8)	5.5 × 8.5 (1.7 × 2.6)	47 (4.4)	13.5 × 28.5 (4.1 × 8.6)	378 (35.2)
Luxury	15 × 20 (4.5 × 6.1)	300 (27.9)	7.5 × 9 (2.3 × 2.7)	71 (6.6)	15 × 30 (4.5 × 9.1)	450 (41.8)

*Living area does not include the bathroom, closet, or entry.

†Budget guestroom bath includes tub/shower and toilet but the sink is part of the dressing area.

Table 16.3 Guestroom bed types

Room type	*Bed types and sizes*	
Twin	Two twin beds	39 × 80 in. (1 × 2 m)*
Double-double	Two double beds	54 × 80 in. (1.35 × 2 m)
Queen	One queen bed	60 × 80 in. (1.5 × 2 m)
King	One king bed	78 × 80 in. (2 × 2 m)
California king	One king bed	72 × 80 in. (1.8 × 2 m)
Oversized twin	Two twin beds	45 × 80 in. (1.15 × 2 m)
Queen-queen	Two queen beds	
Double-studio	One double bed and convertible sofa	
Queen-studio	One queen bed and convertible sofa	
King-studio	One king bed and convertible sofa	
Parlor	One convertible sofa	
Wall bed	One wall bed ('Sico room')	

*Metric bed sizes.

With the continuing increase in construction and furnishing costs, it becomes more important to develop innovative layouts for guestrooms—designs that combine function and comfort within realistic budgets. Basic approaches include using fewer individual pieces of furniture, sometimes combining several functions, or scaling them down to give the perception of a larger and more luxurious room. The designer might include the following:

- *Queen or 72 in (1.8 m) king-size bed*: beds smaller than the 78 in (2 m) king creates more open space.
- *Convertible sofa or wall bed*: these provide more open space and flexibility, either as the second bed in a queen or king room, or as the only bed in a parlor.
- *Adequate luggage and clothes space*: sufficient drawers, luggage rack; and closet space reduce the clutter of clothing and personal items throughout the room.

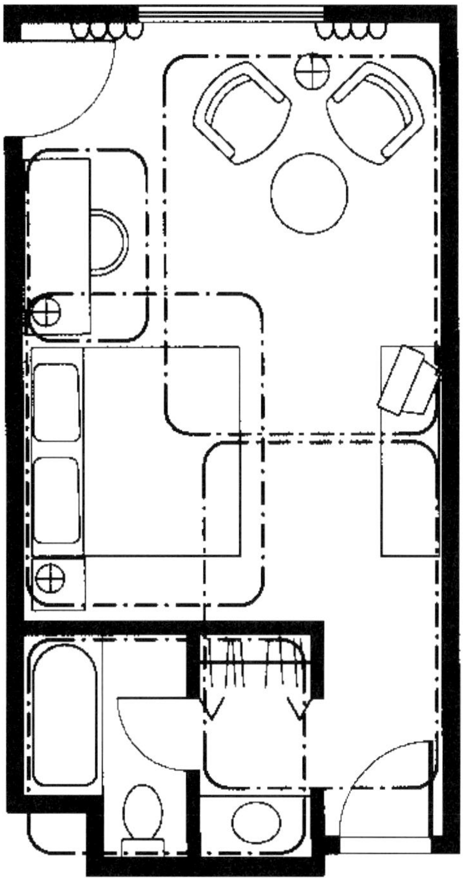

Planning the guestrooms for the market **Guestroom activity zones.** The hotel guestroom accommodates one to four or more people, sometimes with several activities occurring at one time (for example, bathing and dressing, sleeping, and watching TV). The designer needs to be aware of techniques for separating some while combining others, in both cases increasing the flexibility and adaptability of the room to different users. The plan illustrates the five principal guestroom activity zones.

Table 16.4 Guestroom mix for different hotel types

Type of hotel	*Percent of total guestrooms* Double-double	King	King-studio	Suites	*Comments*
Business (downtown)	30	60	3	7	Limited double occupancy
Boutique hotel	10	75	3	12	Suites depend on market and building configuration
Suburban/airport hotel	50	40	5	5	Full range of potential market segments; needs flexibility
Roadside inn	60	35	5	0	Trend away from all double-double
Budget inn	80	20	0	0	Usually queen instead of king bed
Resort/family	75	10	10	5	Some queen-queen; provide room for cots
Resort/couples	20	70	5	5	Increasing emphasis on suites
Convention hotel	55	35	0	10	Continuing reliance on double-double
Conference center	30	60	5	5	Single occupancy, except for weekend social business
All-suite hotel	30	70	0	0	All keys include living room with dedicated bedroom
Super-luxury	20	70	0	10	Double-double replaced with oversize twins
Mega-hotel	50	40	5	5	Double-double flexible for family/group/business markets
Casino hotel	50	40	0	10	D-D or Q-Q count depends on strength of tour market

The guestroom/suite variations **Guestroom and suite interior views.** (A) Pangkor Laut Resort, Malaysia. In this romantic island hideaway where the guests are pampered beyond complaint, the guest suites are arranged along the shore and mountains. (B) The Four Seasons Resort, Troon North, Scottsdale. The oversized guestrooms, each with large terrace or balcony, features a fireplace for cool desert evenings. (C) The Venetian, Las Vegas. The standard queen-queen room is nearly twice the size of most first-class guestrooms, and includes an oversized five-fixture bathroom and lower sitting area at the window (see plan on p. 268). (D) Pan Pacific, Yokohama. This suite guestroom, placed opposite the entry foyer, mimics many of the finishes and design motifs of the hotel's public areas. (E) Hyatt Regency McCormick Place, Chicago. The typical room for the business and convention market uses bold geometric patterns, including the veneer on the TV armoire. (F) Boeing Leadership Center, Florissant, Missouri. The guestroom, designed for single occupancy, features comfortable reading and working areas.

- *Armoire*: combine drawer space with a television cabinet and possibly a pullout writing ledge in a single unit to eliminate the need for two or three separate pieces.
- *Desk*: wheeled computer stand that rolls under the main desk offers a better height for a guest's computer and provides additional work surface.
- *Lounge and desk chairs*: lounge chairs designed at a height appropriate for the work desk may eliminate the need for desk chair.
- *Mirrors*: mirrors enlarge the space visually.
- *Wall-mounted bedside lamps*: these permit a smaller bedside night table.
- *Bathroom*: designs should increase lighting and enlarge the countertop and mirror surfaces; compartmentalize the toilet and/or tub/shower.

Several details in the room arrangement and furnishing do not have any best solution although there are more common ones for different types or categories of hotels. For example, many operators of economy properties insist that the telephone should be located next to the beds whereas others prefer that it be placed at the work area. Most first-class hotels solved the question in the 1990s by providing two phones—or three, with an additional one in the bathroom. In the future, designers will specify a cordless phone—with the base unit a speakerphone—which will enable guests to roam around their room while talking. Similarly, the lower priced inns often prefer drapes which combine the decorative drapery and blackout into a single unit to reduce the number of drapery tracks, whereas others insist on separate sheer, blackout, and overdrape to allow easy cleaning and maintenance. Guests in upscale hotels can control the drapes with a push of a button at the bedside. Throughout the room, the designer must balance the conflicting needs of function, safety, maintenance, comfort, aesthetics, and budget and, at the same time, consider the varying requirements of the several different guest markets that a single hotel tries to attract.

Not every operator is trying to provide the smallest possible room, or find ways to combine functions with multipurpose furnishings. The 3,000-room Venetian Hotel in Las Vegas opened in 1999 with standard guestrooms of 665 ft^2 (61.8 m^2) including a five-fixture guest bathroom of 110 ft^2 (10.2 m^2). In floor area this room is larger than many hotel suites, yet the room is only one bay wide. It features, in addition to the generous bathroom, clearly separated sleeping and living areas.

Suites

The principal way that a hotel provides different qualities of accommodations is to include a variety of guestroom suites in the room mix. A suite is defined simply as a living room connected to one or more bedrooms. Larger hotels frequently provide a hierarchy of suites, from single-bay living rooms with a sleeping alcove to multiple-bay living rooms with connecting rooms, including dining/conference rooms and one or two bedrooms (Table 16.5). Some management companies have earned a reputation for the overall quality of their suites. Four Seasons, the Canadian-based luxury hotel chain, offers a standard two-bay suite consisting of a one-bay living room with powder room connecting through double French doors to a bedroom with an oversized guest bathroom.

The number or percentage of suites varies among hotel types. Most hotels have no more than 2–5 percent of their keys allocated to suites. First-class and convention hotels, on the other hand, provide up to 10 percent of the total guestroom count in suites. These most likely are positioned on the upper floors of the tower where the rooms have better views, but may be stacked vertically where unusual conditions occur. For example, suites may be used to fill any larger structural bays on the typical floor, grow into additional area behind stairs or elevators, or are located where the building form provides uniquely shaped rooms.

Table 16.5 Suite types

Suite type	*Living room*	*Bedrooms*	*Keys*	*Bays*	*Percent**	*Comment*
Mini-suite	One bay	Alcove	1	1.5	0–1	Fits behinds stairs or elevators
Junior suite	One bay	1	2	2	1–2	Parlor plus single bedroom
VIP suite	One bay	2	3	3	2–3	Parlor plus two bedrooms
Conference suite	Two bays	2	3	4	1-2	Boardroom table and lounge area
Hospitality suite	Two bays	2	3	4	1–2	Expansive lounge seating, pantry
Executive suite	Two bays	2	3	5	0.25	Dining room and lounge area, oversized bedroom
Presidential suite	Three bays	2	2	6	0.25	One oversized, dedicated bedroom

*Percent of total rooms; that is, one to two junior suites per 100 rooms. (Approximate standard for mid-size downtown business hotel.)

Boutique style in guestroom/suite design **Boutique hotel guestrooms.** (A) The Delano, Miami Beach. The all-white guestroom décor sacrifices housekeeping efficiency to stylistic bravado. (B) W New York. The first hotel of Starwood's new brand, the guestroom features a 'floating bed' anchored to a peek-a-boo screen-wall at the room entry. Built-in elements help accommodate guest needs in a small space.

In the late 1970s several hotel companies in the US recognized the growing need of the extended-stay market and established chains of all-suite hotels. But the operators found that these small suites held great appeal to the traveling businessperson and family, both of whom appreciated the separate living and bedrooms and the provision of a small kitchen. At the time, operators such as Residence Inn, Embassy Suites, and Guest Quarters were successfully converting apartment buildings or building new structures with suites of approximately 450 ft^2 (42 m^2). In the late twentieth century a number of innovative franchise companies established new all-suite brands, many of them with entries in the 'economy suite' segment, with 'suites' no larger than a conventional hotel guestroom, but with a small kitchenette. (These and other suite products are fully described in Chapter 8.)

Many hotels now offer concierge or club floor levels to offer a higher quality room and additional amenities at a premium price. Usually representing 10–20 percent of the total room count, the club floor rooms are identical in size to the normal ones, but feature better quality finishes, furnishings, and bathroom amenities. More important to most guests are the additional services available in the club floor lounge, including express check-in and check-out, complimentary breakfast, tea, cocktails, and evening snacks, and the more personal services of a concierge on the guest floors. The lounge space usually is equal in size to at least three guestrooms and, in major convention hotels, with private conference rooms and additional business services, may displace as many as six to eight rooms (see plan on next page).

Accessible Guestroom/Universal Design

All hotel operators must provide accommodation and other services for guests with physical disabilities. In the US, the federal government in 1992 passed the Americans with Disabilities Act (ADA) which mandates equal access to public accommodations—not only in lodging properties but retail stores, restaurants, theaters, museums, and transportation services. Hotels before this time had made some token efforts to provide rooms for disabled guests, most frequently those in wheelchairs. But the ADA broadens the definition to those with other disabilities such as arthritis, or those who are hearing or sight impaired. All areas of the hotel or resort must meet the guidelines of the ADA, not only the public areas and guestrooms, but the employee areas as well.

However, one area where accessible design is most evident is in the 'handicapped guestrooms,' a small number of rooms which feature larger bathrooms with somewhat different fixtures—roll-in shower stall, for example—and a number of features intended to make the room better accommodate a person with specific disabilities. Interestingly, many of these features are helpful to all guests: lever handles on doors and faucets, a hand-held shower, grab bars in the bath/shower, large buttons on the telephone, and more accessible outlets and switches—that is, design features which have 'universal' appeal. Hotel interior designers have begun to realize the value of universal design and are adopting as many of these features as make economic and functional sense.

The franchise company, Microtel Inns & Suites, in 1997 surveyed some of the 20 million people with disabilities in the US who travel to ask them what they most want from their hotel. The respondents (73% wheelchair users, 5% sight or hearing impaired, and 22% 'other'), in particular, listed many characteristics of the guestrooms (along with other comments about the hotel providing accurate information, helpful staff, and accessible parking):

- accessible showers
- large bathrooms
- enough space for easy maneuverability
- suitable beds
- aesthetically pleasing guestroom
- refrigerator in guestroom
- easy access to guestroom controls.

Guest Bathrooms

Nowhere in the room is planning and design more important that in the guest bathroom. In the mid-twentieth century, with the great surge in the development of chain properties along the new interstate highways, bathrooms grew from about 30 ft^2 (2.8 m^2)—hardly big enough for the standard three fixtures—to 40 ft^2 (3.7 m^2). This growth in the bathroom paralleled the huge expansion in roadside inns to serve the family market. This bathroom is still used today, and the 5 × 8 ft (1.5 × 2.4 m) dimensions still accommodate comfortably the standard three fixtures. But competitive pressure, and marketing, and guests' eagerness for something better than they have at home, has pushed the first-class and luxury operators to add fixtures and other amenities. By 2000 it was common for downtown hotels, catering to a single business traveler, to offer a bathroom with a large sink/counter, bathtub, separate shower stall, and compartmentalized toilet. All for one person. Resort and super-luxury properties do this one better, adding a second sink, and plenty of open floor space.

Designers need to study the market data to understand what features and amenities will be most desirable. Is the market mostly men or women? Single travelers or couples or families? What are their demographics and do they expect unusual levels of luxury in the bathroom? One of the limited service brands, Sleep Inn, took to heart the research that showed that nearly 90 percent of travelers staying in their properties preferred showers and, as a result, in newer inns they have replaced the tub/shower combination with an oversized stall shower. In the late 1990s Hyatt International opened several hotels in Germany and Japan with unusual bathrooms, featuring a 'wet room'—a space about 5 × 5 ft (1.5 m × 1.5 m) with a normal tub plus open shower, a compartmentalized toilet, and a spacious sink counter and make-up area. The bathroom is separated from the bedroom by sliding panels or a glass partition. The accompanying photographs suggest how designers can use the guest bathroom to give the guest a truly memorable overnight experience.

Guestroom Equipment and Technology

The end of the twentieth century was a period of incredible innovation in hotel technology, much of it appearing in the guestrooms. Because nationwide nearly 60 percent of all roomnights were generated by business travelers, companies such as Marriott announced that they would install high-speed Internet access in all their hotel guestrooms, in addition to the meeting rooms and business centers. These ethernet-based systems offered connection speeds of 50 times faster than normal phone lines and, further, do not interfere with telephone use. Computer use by guests reportedly doubled between 1995 and 2000, with nearly two of three business travelers carrying laptops with them on trips, the great majority to stay in e-mail contact with their office or family. A side benefit is that adoption of the high-speed cable networks frees up the existing PBX (telephone) trunk lines, lessening the burden on another essential piece of the communications network.

Some luxury hotels look for every way to pamper their guest, and technology plays a role here, too. At The Peninsula in Hong Kong, a bedside panel controls lighting, heat and air-conditioning, television and radio, and the draperies. A small digital panel continuously displays the outdoor temperature and humidity. The Peninsula is studying how to install new ultra-thin televisions, which would eliminate the

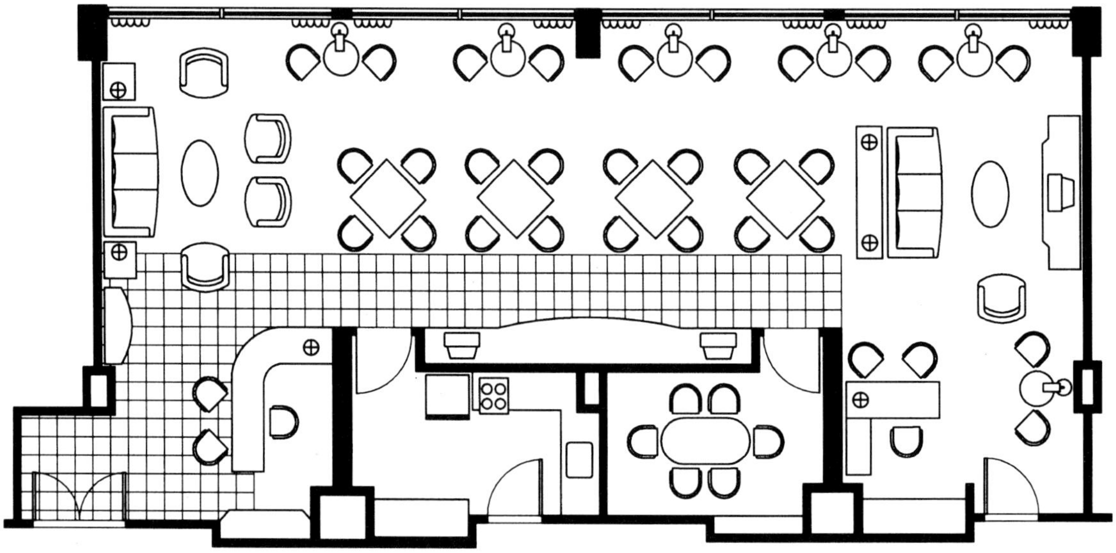

Planning for business and convention markets **Concierge floor lounge plan.** Luxury and convention-oriented hotels often provide a concierge or executive lounge covering three to eight bays on an upper floor, providing VIP services, Continental breakfast, all-day beverage service, and evening cocktails and snacks. This four-bay example includes a reception desk, large permanent buffet with adjoining pantry, small guest conference room, and guest work area (Marriott Hotels).

Table 16.6 Elements required for complete guestroom design

Furnishings	
Casepieces	Desk, dresser, tables, chairs, nightstands, headboard, and TV
Soft goods	Bedspreads, drapes, and upholstery fabrics; carpet sometimes included
Lighting	Lamps at the bedside, desk, and lounge seating areas
Accessories	Framed mirrors, art, planters, other amenities. (Wastebaskets, coffee maker, iron and ironing board, and other miscellaneous items are provided by the hotel operator.)
Guestroom finishes	
Floor	Generally carpet over padding although resorts might have tile (warm climates) and suites may have wood parquet with area rugs
Wall	Vinyl wall covering preferred, or paint; baseboard and moldings if budget permits
Ceiling	Acoustical treatment
Doors	Wood, pre-finished, or painted—all solid core
Door frames	Painted to match doors, walls, or accent color
Bathroom finishes	
Floor	Ceramic or marble tile
Walls	Ceramic or marble tile around tub; vinyl wall-covering or paint elsewhere
Ceiling	Paint
Electrical/mechanical	
Outlets	Minimum of five duplex outlets: two at the beds, one each at desk, dresser, and lounge area; require outlets convenient for guest computer and for housekeeper
Cable	Television, dual telephone lines, internet, fire alarm, or other communications system
Mechanical	HVAC integrated with room layout; bathroom exhaust
Fire protection	Minimum of one heat or smoke detector and one sprinkler in each guestroom; some areas require additional sprinklers in foyer, closet, and bathroom. All interior furnishings should be carefully checked for fire retardant and nontoxic finish

need for the armoire, thereby changing the whole appearance of the room. Such a high-tech television might become integrated with the video-telephone, offering a larger than life-size visual link to home or office. Additional innovation is likely in guestroom door locks, which can be programmed to recognize a guest's voice or thumbprint.

Proposing the Guestroom FF&E Budget

Early in the process, after preparing the initial guestroom mix, the interior designer proposes a budget for the guestroom furniture, fixtures, and equipment (FF&E). This represents approximately half of the total interior design budget. Generally, the designer accomplishes this in several stages, each one more focused and detailed, as the design becomes more specific:

- *Concept design*: budget based on cost per guestroom, per suite, and per key for corridor.
- *Preliminary design*: budget based on an allowance for each furniture item (cost per bedset, armoire, desk, etc.) prior to selecting the individual item.
- *Design development*: Budget with cost for each specified FF&E item with some allowances (artwork, signage, accessories).
- *Contract documents*: figure for each item including input from purchasing agent and some competitive pricing from vendors.

By 2000, costs for guestroom interior, FF&E ranged from $3,000 to more than $10,000 per room, depending primarily on the quality level of the property. While the size of the room is a factor, it has relatively minor significance. The lower priced rooms have extremely basic furnishings: base-grade carpet and fabrics, painted walls, inexpensive light fixtures, and casegoods with plastic laminate finish. The higher priced rooms have a sumptuous feel with luxurious fabrics, wood veneer casepieces, overstuffed furnishings, triple-matted and framed artwork, and extra lighting to enhance the visual effect. Each individual item may be at least twice as expensive, and designers include a number of additional accessories or extra amenities.

The sheer number of guestrooms requires that the designer be particularly conscious of seeking economies in the layout of the rooms and the selection of the furnishings and finishes. Because of their importance in influencing the guest's perception of the hotel as well as these cost factors, developers usually build a full-scale mock-up to test the design before purchasing the furnishings. This model room provides the perfect setting for final co-ordination of the many furnishing, room finish, and engineering-system decisions that affect the room design and guest comfort. In addition, the model room is used as a promotional tool to interest business or convention groups in the hotel and to provide them with assurances of the quality of the final room product.

Trends

Innovation in the guestroom and guest bath may be more obvious because the spaces are so personal. We are well aware of how design, whether texture or technology, affects our satisfaction with the environment. Also, we are sure to measure our overnight accommodation against our own home, whether it be heated towel bars or unusual lighting or some idiosyncratic feature that each one of us particularly cares about. Therefore, we will marvel at many of the trends in guestroom design that should appear in the next few years:

- Communications systems will continue to evolve at an incredible rate and hotels must develop a flexible infrastructure based, most likely, on the TV-cable distribution system. High-speed Internet access will become a standard amenity.

Designing the bathroom for dramatic effect **Bathroom interior views.** (A) Royalton Hotel, New York. The boutique design uses stone walls and floor, glass vanity counter and toiletries shelf, stainless steel fixtures, and subdued lighting to create a subtle mood. (B) Far Eastern Plaza, Taipei. The marble bathroom features an oversized whirlpool tub overlooking the city and such luxury amenities as separate shower cubicle, telephone, and mini-television. (C) Park Hyatt Hamburg. Dressing area and Japanese-style bathroom. The spacious spa-like dressing and bathing areas include ceiling-mounted shower heads and floor drainage for showering in the bathroom, soaking tub, and glass partitioning between the bathroom and dressing area, creating a luxurious spa atmosphere.

- Entertainment systems will multiply as well but will be less critical in business-oriented hotels. Flat screen TVs should become standard freeing them dimensionally from the armoire. Eventually, entertainment and computer will become fully integrated, allowing guests to interweave sports programming with movies with office work.
- Designers will continue to explore alternatives to the traditional desk offering more work surface, computer cart, better lighting, and ergonomic seating.
- Exercise equipment may find its way into rooms in business-oriented hotels (see Chapter 4, Spa-tel).
- Guest bathrooms will increase in size as guests demand more spa-like features including whirlpool bath, multihead shower, and exercise equipment. The bathroom will become more physically and visually integrated with the hotel room with privacy being provided by polarized glass partitions or sliding panels.
- The remainder of the room will *not* increase in size. Developers will attempt to hold down overall increases in floor area and construction costs by maintaining overall room dimensions close to the current size.

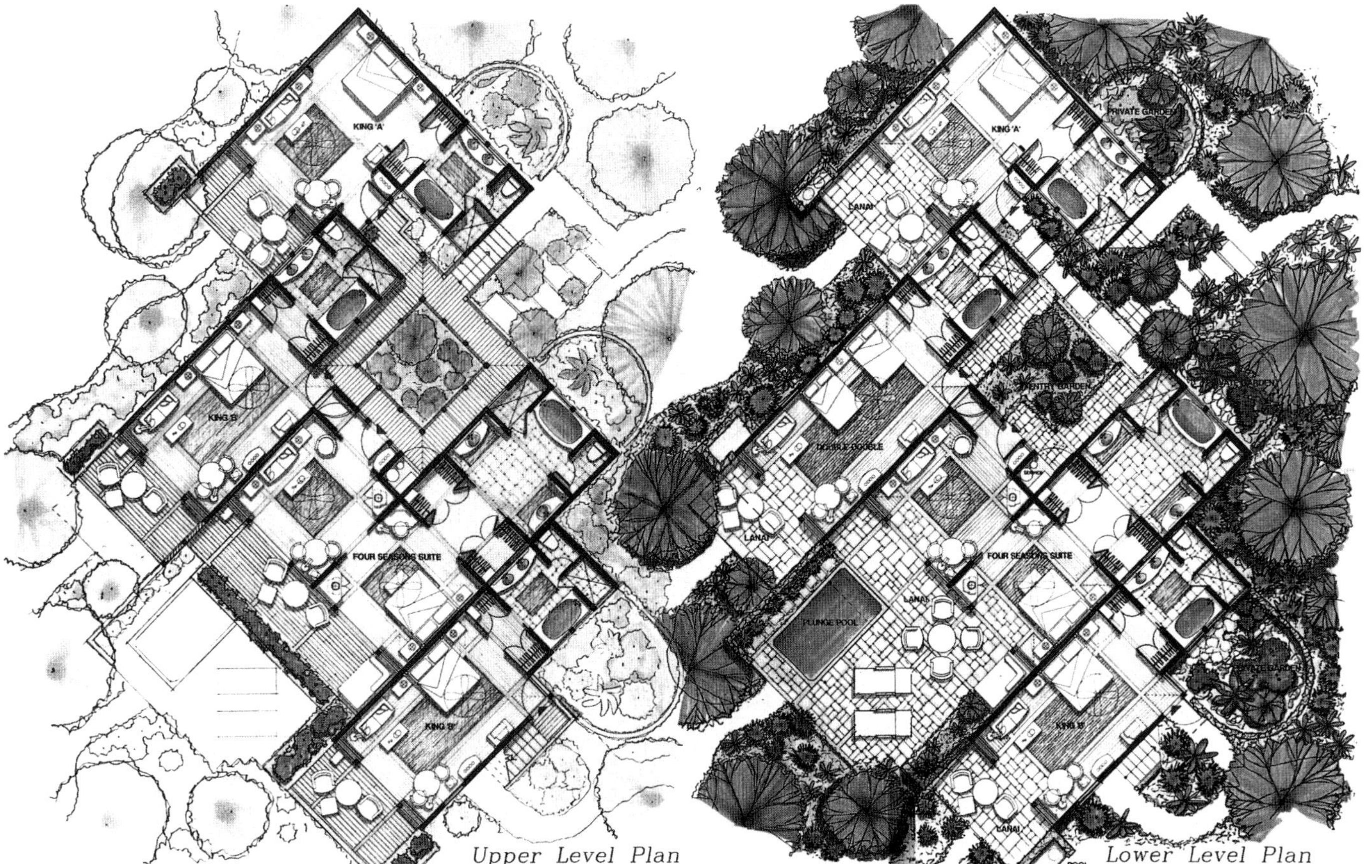

The beachfront luxury 'villa' unit **Four Seasons Resort Hualalai, Kona, The Big Island, Hawaii.** The luxury resort locates its rooms and suites in spacious intimate upper and lower beachfront and golf club villa units. The upper floor has balconies extending over the lanai terraces but, otherwise, features the same sumptuous oversized rooms with a granite and slate five-fixture bathroom. The executive suites separate the bedroom from the living room with sliding wood doors and include outdoor lava rock showers adjacent to the bathroom (see p. 71).

The themed luxury resort lobby **The Palace of the Lost City, Sun City, South Africa**. Conceived as the architecture of a lost civilization, the luxury resort hotel features a soaring reception atrium, lighted through clerestory windows, and further enhanced by a six-story-high hand-frescoed dome (see p. C-31).

Public Space Design 17

While the hotel guestrooms make up the majority of the floor area in virtually all hotels, it is the public space that defines the differences among the various types. Because the lobby, restaurants and lounges, meeting and banquet space, and recreation facilities vary so greatly (from only 5 percent in a budget motel to 25 percent at a conference center), understanding the distinctions among the different hotel types is crucial to programming and designing a successful project.

Table 17.1 identifies the key differences in the public spaces for the various hotel types. Convention hotels and conference centers, for example, need extensive meeting and banquet space; resorts and, more recently, conference centers include major recreational components; and downtown and luxury hotels, among others, have generally high-quality restaurants.

In addition to providing the appropriate mix of facilities for each type of hotel, the architect must create a plan that meets the functional requirements and market objectives as defined by the developer and the hotel management company. The budget and mid-price companies insist on tight and economical layouts for the limited but multipurpose public areas. The first class and deluxe operators, too, strive for efficiency, while they are more concerned with the visual qualities of the building and in providing a level of amenity; these companies frequently will accept a less economical layout in order to accommodate more appealing and saleable architectural and interior design features.

Whatever the type of hotel, an overall objective for the planning and design of the public areas is that they be clustered around the lobby. This arrangement assures that the hotel guests can find the various facilities with a minimum of difficulty and provides the opportunity for functions to overlap. Hotel atrium lobbies, especially, exhibit such characteristics, where the guest registration area, multiple restaurants and lounges, meeting prefunction space, guest elevators, and upper floor corridors, all occupy the same volume.

A second major objective in highrise projects is to organize the public areas with an understanding of their location in relation to the guestroom structure. This is important for two reasons: One, the architect needs to plan the lobby floor so that the major guest circulation from the entrance to the front desk to the elevators is convenient and logical. Two, the designer must position any long-span spaces, primarily the ballroom and other larger meeting rooms, so that they are not directly under the guestroom tower, in order to simplify the structural design of the hotel and reduce construction costs.

Arrival

The architectural aspects of the building, of course, are best observed on the approach to the hotel entrance, and the details of the site and exterior design—the landscaping, the night illumination, the entry drive and canopy—all contribute to the guests' anticipation of their stay. Larger hotels may develop a number of different entrances to help separate overnight guests and visitors, to reduce the amount of unnecessary traffic through the lobby, to establish a distinct identity for a restaurant or other facility, or to provide increased security. The designers should assess the relative need for the following entrances:

- main hotel entrance
- ballroom/banquet entrance
- restaurant/bar/nightclub/casino entrance
- health club/spa entrance
- tour bus/airport bus drop-off
- suite or condominium entrance.

Each entrance needs to be clearly identified according to its function with a canopy, signage,

Table 17.1 Public space matrix

Hotel Type	*Lobby*	*F&B areas*	*Function spaces*	*Recreation*	*Retail*	*Parking*
Business (downtown)	Moderate	Small	Varies	Moderate	Moderate	Small
Boutique hotel	Moderate	Small	Small	Small	Small	Small
Suburban hotel	Moderate	Moderate	Moderate	Moderate	Small	Large
Airport hotel	Moderate	Moderate	Large	Small	Small	Moderate
Roadside inn	Small	Moderate	Small	Small	Small	Moderate
Resort (golf/beach/tennis)	Moderate	Large	Moderate	Large	Large	Large
Resort (other)	Small	Moderate	Small	Large	Large	Moderate
Convention hotel	Large	Large	Large	Moderate	Large	Moderate
Conference center	Moderate	Moderate	Large	Large	Small	Large
Condominium hotel	Small	Small	Small	Moderate	Small	Moderate
All-suite hotel	Moderate	Moderate	Moderate	Moderate	Small	Moderate
Super-luxury hotel	Small	Moderate	Small	Small	Moderate	Moderate
Mega-hotel	Large	Large	Large	Large	Large	Moderate
Mixed-use hotel	Large	Large	Large	Moderate	Large	Moderate
Casino hotel	Moderate	Large	Large	Large (casino)	Moderate	Moderate

'Small' means lobby <6 ft^2/room; food and beverage areas <0.7 seat/room; function spaces <2 seats/room; recreation area = small pool or health club plus limited other facilities; parking <0.7 car/room. 'Moderate' stands for lobby 6–10 ft^2/room; food and beverage areas 0.7–1.2 seats/room; function spaces 2–4 seats/room; recreation area = pool and health club plus other facilities; parking for 0.7–1.2 cars/room. 'Large' indicates lobby >10 ft^2/room; food and beverage areas >1.2 seats/room; function areas >4 seats/room; recreation areas = extensive facilities; parking >1.2 cars/room. Some types of hotels require additional parking for buses.

The dramatic porte cochere **The Beverly Hills Hotel, California**. The low sweeping lines of the candy-striped entry canopy of the landmark hotel greets movie stars, business travellers, and vacationers alike. The canopy is essential for offering weather protection and creating a positive impression on arriving guests.

special illumination, or other architectural treatment. Some entrances require space for waiting taxis or buses, others require temporary luggage storage, and the condominium entrance requires special security. Some city hotels may succeed with no more than a drop-off at the curb but, in destinations such as Orlando or Las Vegas, the largest hotels often have four to six lanes at the porte cochere to handle the heavy volume of arrivals and departures. The design requirements for the hotel entrances can be summarized briefly:

- *Canopy*: provide a porte cochere or covered drop-off at the main entrance and principal secondary entrances (ballroom or restaurant) to protect guests from inclement weather; include lighting, signage, and heat, if necessary; ensure sufficient height for buses and emergency vehicles.
- *Driveways*: predict the amount of traffic and provide a sufficient number of aisles and queuing space for waiting taxis, loading and unloading of passengers and luggage, and short-term standing including valet-delivered cars and tour or airport buses.
- *Parking*: make garage access convenient to and from the main hotel entrance; if there is valet parking, establish a location for the valet office near the main entrance.

- *Sidewalks*: design pedestrian areas sufficiently wide for handling baggage, storing baggage carts, and providing doorman or bellman station; at bus locations provide space for groups to assemble.
- *Doors and vestibules*: develop a weather vestibule with revolving or automatic doors to limit temperature differences; include access into luggage storage room from curb; provide ramps if necessary for both disabled guests and luggage.

Lobby

Among the many public areas of the hotel, the lobby makes the single greatest impact on the guest and on visitors to the hotel. Its design—whether intimate or expansive, formal or casual—sets the tone for the hotel or resort. Therefore, the planning of the major lobby elements and the design of the details are crucial to making a positive and lasting impression on the guest. The most successful designs carefully balance two key factors: visual impact and function.

For most of the past century, until the Hyatt Regency Hotel opened in Atlanta, Georgia, in 1967, most hotel lobbies were relatively small, designed along the same economical principles as the rest of the hotel. However, in the 1970s emphasis shifted toward larger lobbies, not only in convention hotels and mixed-used complexes, but also in smaller hotels built in suburban areas and at airports. The end of the twentieth century, with its increase in hotel specialization, showed evidence of a return to more intimate interior spaces, especially in the super-luxury, all-suite, and conference center categories. Thus, among the initial questions facing the developer and architect is to decide the scale, atmosphere, and image of the lobby.

Program and Planning Objectives

The space program for the lobby must recognize the type of hotel and the amount of circulation within the public areas. Larger hotels, such as convention properties and those located within mixed-use projects, require a great amount of space to accommodate the number of guests and visitors drawn to the variety of facilities. Mid-price hotels and those that cater to few outsiders require relatively little public area. Most hotels provide between 6 and 10 ft^2 (0.6–0.9 m^2) of floor area per guestroom in the lobby, not including circulation to remote functions (see Chapter 22). Convention and mega-hotels and those developed as part of a mixed-use project may require 10–15 ft^2 (0.9–1.4 m^2) per room.

Locating bars, restaurants, and retail kiosks within the lobby is one way to increase the apparent size of the space without adding additional gross area. Atlanta architect John Portman refers to this concept as 'shared space.' Additional lobby functions create variety not only in scale but in relative level of activity, with fluctuating usage throughout the day. In order to accomplish this diversity successfully, the best plans provide a clear definition of the several functions that occur within the lobby and make their organization obvious to the guest.

Hotel Public Space

John C. Portman, Jr., Chairman, John Portman & Associates

At the end of the nineteenth century, the world experienced a transition from an agrarian to an industrial society. Now, at the dawn of the twenty-first century, the world again is in the throes of transition, rapidly evolving into an age of technology.

Design in this period will continue to reflect changing social views and evolving technology. We have only begun to sense the impact of technology and innovation on human endeavor and its effect on work, play, travel, and perceptions of 'place.'

These perceptions are influenced by the art and architecture of the environment, the natural surroundings and the times. It is the architect's responsibility to integrate these elements to create an enhanced human experience. In hotels, for example, the resurgence of the hotel lobby as an active place to see, be seen, and participate has returned from a time where it had become less multidimensional. Public space is a happening place. Lounges and restaurants, shops and libraries, and special seating groups participate and interact to create comfortable and convenient environments.

Public space today is a space where people linger as well as move in, out and through. The challenge to designers is to create architecture that by its expression gives acknowledgment to many varied usages.

The architect must integrate public spaces, indoors and outdoors, in a way that people are drawn to the space. Today you must immerse people in an evolving diversified world. Whether the desired effect is to calm or excite, the architect must sequence a person through the hotel. From approaching the building, to entering the front door, and through to their room, the guest must sense a build up of the experience which is often created by the lure of anticipation established in the design.

The planning requirements of most hotel lobbies are similar regardless of the type of hotel (see Table 17.2). In addition to establishing the image of the hotel, the lobby serves as the main circulation space, directing guests to the front desk, elevators, food and beverage outlets, meeting and banquet facilities, health club, and other public areas; as guests linger, it serves as an informal gathering space. It also functions as a security control point, where the staff is able to visually supervise access to the building. The several planning objectives for the lobby include:

- *Entrances*: consider additional exterior entrances for the main lobby, banquet facilities, restaurants, health club, or other high traffic areas.
- *Front desk location*: locate the desk so that it is immediately visible to the entering hotel guest and so that desk personnel can visually oversee access to the passenger elevators.
- *Office access*: provide entrances to the front office, safe deposit area, executive offices, and sales and catering offices.
- *Guest elevators*: locate elevators close to the front desk and the main entrance and provide sufficient elevator lobby space for handling luggage.
- *Seating area*: provide a seating area near the desk and entrance including some private seating groups; locate additional seating contiguous with the lobby bar.
- *Circulation*: establish clear paths to the front desk, elevators, restaurants and bars, meeting and banquet areas; where possible, separate hotel guest traffic from convention-oriented visitors.
- *Retail areas*: provide lease space convenient to the guest circulation areas or with exterior frontage.
- *Bellman/luggage*: position bellman station near the front desk, elevators, and front entrance; locate luggage storage nearby.
- *Support functions*: locate such accessory functions as toilets, coats, house phones, public phones, meeting directory, and assistant manager's desk conveniently in relation to other areas.

Table 17.2 Lobby planning checklist

Front desk area
Stations for registration, cashier, information
Assistant manager's desk
Bellman station, luggage cart storage
Luggage storage
House and pay phones

Seating area
Seating capacity and type
Food or beverage service
Water feature or other focus

Circulation
Access to public elevators
Access to restaurants and lounges
Access to function rooms
Access to recreation facilities
Access to retail shops and other public areas
Access to parking garage

Retail area
Sundries shop (newsstand, toiletries, souvenirs)
Travel services (city tours, airlines, rental cars)
Clothing (men, women, specialty shops)
Gifts (jeweler, florist, toys, books)
Other services (bank, copy center)

Design Objectives

The written design objectives for the lobby should provide a detailed description of the front desk, seating area, circulation, and secondary functions. To a large extent, the architect and interior designer must first study each area individually, solving a multitude of design and functional issues, and then put them together. Some issues are more related to the back-of-house (front desk), others to food and beverage (lobby bar), and others to organizing the public flow. The design of the front desk and related activities, just one aspect of the lobby, requires making conscious decisions on each of the following features:

- *Size of desk*: provide individual work stations each 6 ft (1.8 m) long for registration and cashier; assume two stations for first 150 rooms, one more for each additional 100 rooms.
- *Queuing space*: provide sufficient space in front of the desk for guests to line up; for convention hotels provide at least 20 ft (6.1 m) clear of circulation.
- *Assistant manager's desk*: if required, provide a desk, seating, and storage near the front desk for a concierge or assistant manager; consider making the desk a major decorative feature within the lobby.
- *Bellman station*: provide a bellman station near the front desk and main entrance.
- *Luggage storage*: provide a lockable storage area adjoining the bellman station with shelving for checked luggage; provide direct access to the curb.
- *Telephones*: include house phones close to the front desk and public phones convenient to the lobby, approximately 1 per 100 rooms.

- *Furniture and fixtures*: establish ambience of lobby area by providing special millwork detailing and finishes, front desk, bellman station, assistant manager's desk, and furnishings (lounge seating, decorative fighting, artwork) to establish the image of the hotel.

The design of the other areas of the lobby deals with fewer functional elements but requires more manipulation of the space. The definition of circulation, seating, and retail areas usually is advanced by such standard design techniques as level changes, floor materials, varying ceiling heights, special light-

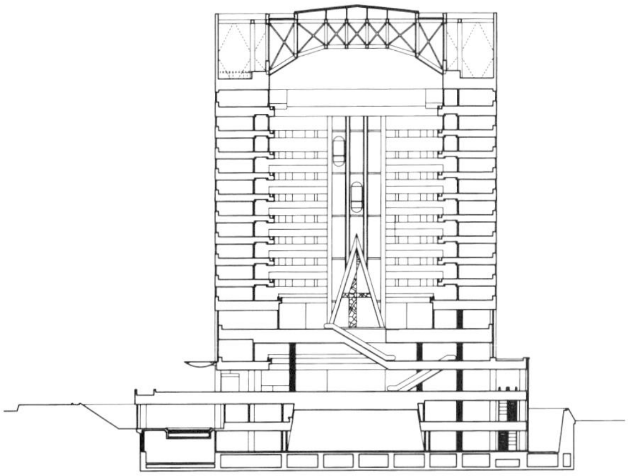

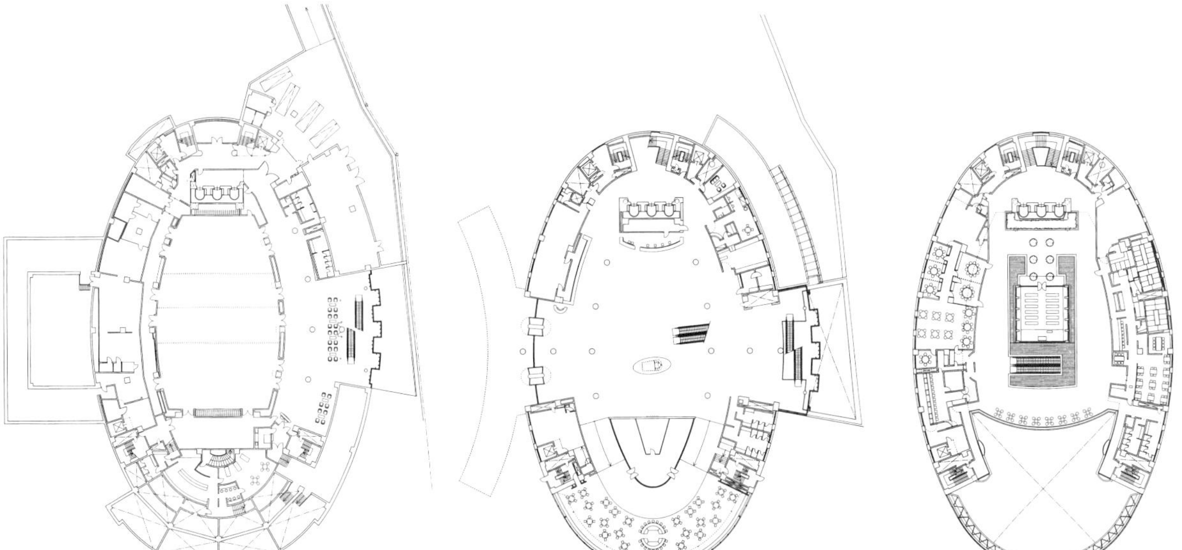

Basement level **Ground level** **Mezzanine level**

Planning the multifunction urban hotel **Hotel Kyocera, Kagoshima, Japan.** This transparent, highly geometric form encloses a 200 ft (60 m) high atrium space, offering views over Kinko Bay. The hotel's public and support functions include: the ballroom below grade covered by the lobby, dining rooms, lounges, wedding chapel, and private function rooms on upper floors, and the lounge, bar, and boardroom on the top floor (see p. C-8).

ing, signage programs, articulation of decorative details, and custom millwork. Many of these are evident in the Illustrations of hotel and resort lobbies throughout Part 1.

Food and Beverage Outlets

The hotel's restaurants and lounges offer the potential to differentiate the property and to make a business or vacation trip memorable. Generally, at least one restaurant and one cocktail lounge are placed close to the hotel lobby. These and other more specialized types of food and beverage (F&B) outlets—specialty or theme restaurants, deli and coffee/pastry shops, lobby bar and entertainment or sports lounges—form a second more complex category of public spaces. However, these vary so widely in quality and character that the program and design of each outlet must be developed individually based on a survey of the total market and the existing competition.

Hotel food service has gone through frequent cycles of popularity with the public. Until late in the twentieth century, and then only in the better hotels, most American hotel restaurants had a reputation for poor food and uninspired design. Their mediocrity may have been due to the fact that hotel restaurants often were only profitable at breakfast, when overnight guests could be depended on to fill the more casual outlet; guests scarcely used them at lunch and hardly more at dinner. In the 1970s, in a climate of increased competition, the industry began to recognize the marketing opportunities of improved restaurant and lounge operations. They found that well-conceived food and beverage outlets increased the demand for guestrooms and

Creating a distinct mood **W San Francisco, California.** The dramatic W Hotel, adjacent to the San Francisco Museum of Modern Art and directly across from Moscone Convention Center, features a two-story 'living room' lobby, distinct from the registration area, with comfortable seating areas convenient to the lobby lounge and restaurant (see pp. 12 and 17).

Multiple functions occupy shared space **Hyatt Regency Paris—Charles de Gaulle, Roissy, France.** Guests use the sunlight-filled atrium space for meeting prefunction, dining, lounge, or general gathering. Guestrooms overlook the lobby, especially appropriate at airport locations where noise and limited views may make rooms facing outward less desirable.

The open-air resort lobby **Grand Hyatt Bali, Nusa Dua, Indonesia.** The understated resort lobby creates a restful sense of place. The open-air space, with its exposed beamed ceiling, stone floor, handmade area rugs, ethnic-style furnishings, and local artifacts, welcomes the arriving guest (p. 250).

meetings, attracted the general public, especially at the low volume lunch and dinner periods, and had the potential to generate additional profits. But the cyclic nature of the industry and resultant downsizing of staff at many hotels in the 1990s forced a new series of economies and challenged designers and operators again to seek creative solutions.

Some companies decided, instead, to outsource their food and beverage operations, selecting a local or national brand to occupy space in the hotel, rather than run the outlet themselves. Such branding became a major theme in the 1990s and should continue to flourish. However, it does have some downsides. Leased operations remove the hotel operator from direct control over the product quality, introduce nonhotel staff into the property, and greatly complicate, for example, room service and back-of-house functions such as receiving and storage. Where it works it can be a great success: Heartbeat, the restaurant in the W New York, serves 180 dinners and about 300 room-service meals each day.

Designing successful restaurant and bar operations must recognize the public's changing attitudes toward food. For example, more people now eat outside conventional meal times, foregoing breakfast but taking a larger morning coffee break or putting off dinner for a late-evening meal or snack. Travelers appreciate restaurants that provide self-service elements—an elaborate buffet set up or more traditional salad bar—from which they can select items and portion size and where they can better control the time spent dining. These considerations should be part of the market analysis, which defines both the hotel guest and the local customer, so that the hotel's food and beverage facilities can enjoy the largest possible audience.

Ground Floor
1 Lobby
2 Front desk
3 Lobby lounge
4 Restaurant
5 Health club
6 Kitchen
7 Back-of-house
8 Receiving

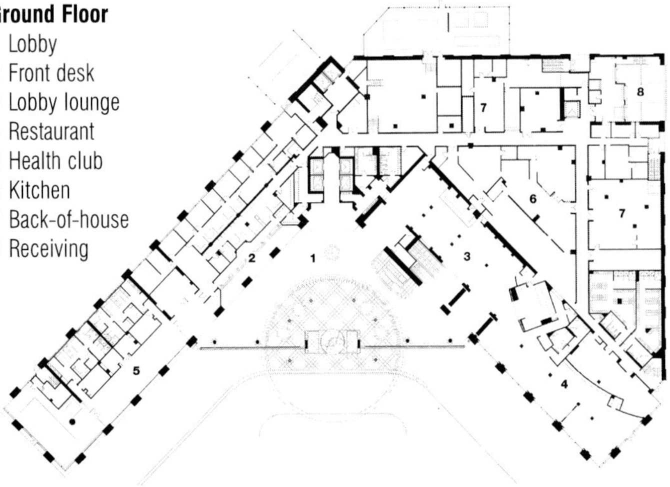

Second Floor
1 Atrium
2 Ballrooms
3 Prefunction
4 Meeting rooms
5 Banquet rooms
6 Back-of-house

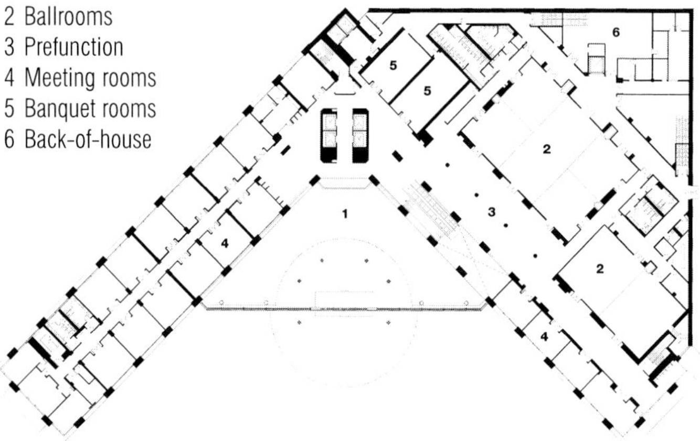

Separating major functions depending on structure **Hilton Boston Logan Airport, Massachusetts.** The new airport Hilton illustrates the clear zoning of the public space: guests enter into a multistory lobby in front of the L-shaped guestroom structure with food and beverage outlets immediately accessible within and around its perimeter; meeting space is somewhat separate (here, on the second floor); and the fitness center is differentiated from the main public areas. The smaller meeting/breakout rooms, offices, and support spaces are placed in the short-span areas under the guestroom tower.

Food and Beverage Concept Development

The high visibility of hotel restaurants suggests that both management and designers should think through their detailed operations early in the development phase. However, in smaller and mid-scale hotels, restaurant menus often are not developed until a few months before the hotel opens. As a result, the restaurant may not be designed until well after the building shell is complete, when modifications to the public area or kitchen access or the addition of level changes, display features, or special ceiling treatments are impossible. The result, too often, is an unexceptional restaurant.

Experienced hotel management companies evolve food and beverage concepts in two ways. Some, like Marriott and Hyatt International, define the operations early in the development process and establish the type of food and service, the hours of operation, the theme and general atmosphere including even the outlet's name and logo. The architect and interior designer then develop a schematic building design that accommodates these themes. Before considering the detailed planning and design issues of hotel restaurants and lounges, designers should become familiar with such operational aspects of food service as marketing, menu planning, service, and food preparation techniques. This enables them to communicate better with the managers who establish detailed restaurant and lounge criteria:

- market characteristics
- concept (type of menu, style of service, entertainment)
- design elements (atmosphere, tabletop, display elements)
- operations (hours open, staffing, seating mix)
- financial projections.

The designer should address the components of restaurant or lounge design identified in the food and beverage concept checklist (Table 17.3).

The other procedure is to establish only rough space requirements at the program phase and, after the architect has conceived the organization of the hotel, to develop the food and beverage concepts in light of the actual location and type of space provided. For example, the three-meal restaurant might have one theme if it is within an atrium space, another if it overlooks the pool or a garden courtyard. This was carried even further at the Seaport Hotel in Boston, where the developer decided to delay establishing any restaurant concept until 6 months before the hotel opened. He reasoned that many hotel restaurants are redesigned every 3–5 years in order to remain current. Therefore, the hotel plan included a generic kitchen and restaurant space that was not finally designed or detailed until the hotel was nearly complete and about ready to open.

A recent approach to hotel food service has been

Table 17.3 Food and beverage concept checklist

General
Name of outlet
Location
Capacity
Operating hours
Market description
Financial projections
Staffing

Food or beverage concept
Menu
Style of service
Food/wine display
Bar/lounge emphasis
Exhibition cooking
Atmosphere
Entertainment

Layout (general)
Entry sequence
Seating mix
Orientation (interior display, exterior views)
Level changes
Entertainment area
Kitchen or back-of-house access

Layout (food outlets)
Host/maitre d'
Cashier
Self-service buffet
Service stations
Food/wine display
Exhibition cooking
Service bar

Layout (beverage outlets)
Bar
Bar storage
Stage
Dance floor
Special entertainment

Design/decor
Atmosphere
Finishes
Seating types
Feature elements
Window treatment
Lighting
Tabletop
Artwork
Uniforms
Uniform design

Special equipment
Exhibition cooking area
Bar equipment
Tableside carts
Point-of-sale computers
TV/video and sound system

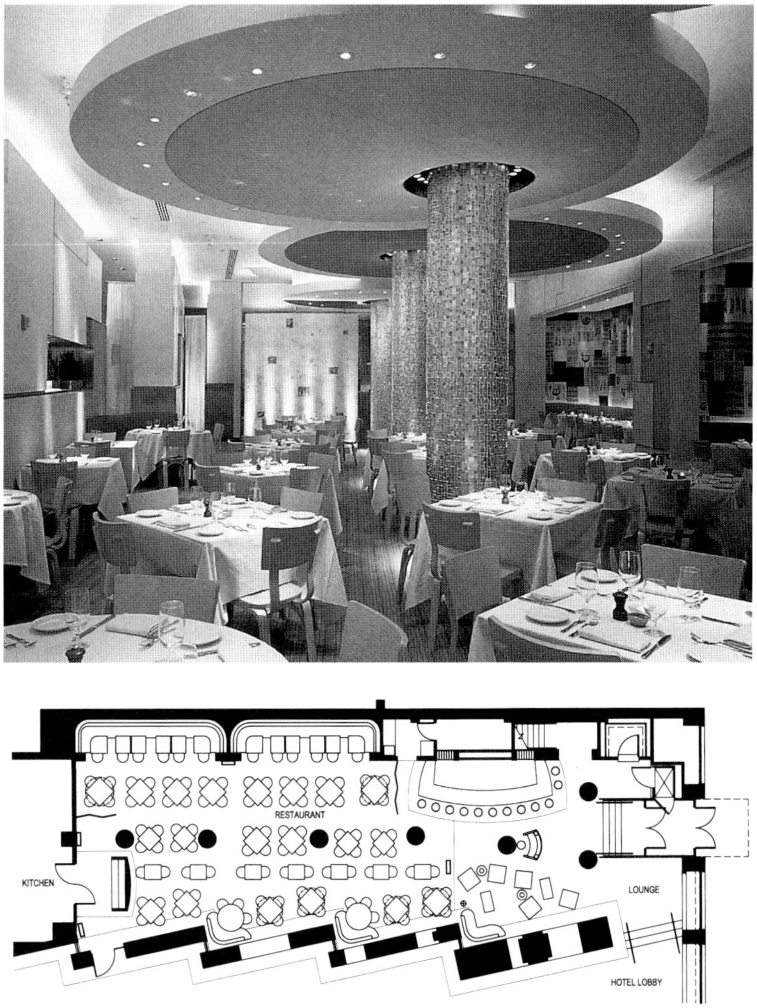

The efficient urban restaurant **W New York.** The Heartbeat restaurant, immediately off the hotel lobby and with its own outside entrance, features a popular health menu. Smaller restaurants often incorporate tight seating layouts including banquettes and fewer tables for large groups.

to develop a single restaurant with several distinct moods that are appropriate to the different meal periods and levels of informality. This is especially appropriate in smaller properties where one three-meal restaurant must have a bright and airy feel and include a buffet setup at breakfast, a balanced casual yet business atmosphere at lunch, and an intimate or formal mood at dinner time. This can be accomplished partly by the larger design elements: placing some seating near windows, some around the buffet, some on hard flooring, some in an adjoining semi-private alcove, and so forth. In addition, the operator may adjust the atmosphere from one meal to the next by closing window blinds or dimming the room lights, modifying the use of food displays, adding music, changing the tabletop, or dressing the staff in different uniforms.

However, larger hotels and resorts still have several restaurants requiring individual and distinctive themes. If a property includes only two outlets, they usually are a three-meal restaurant (the former 'coffee shop')—and a specialty restaurant. A third operation might be a casual deli or a coffee/pastry outlet. Few hotels today attempt to compete with local restaurateurs with a fine dining room. Each restaurant has its own image and, while attracting hotel guests, attempts to compete for different groups of outside diners.

Many food and beverage concepts include conscious attempts to merchandise the food in novel ways such as through an elaborate display or an exhibition kitchen. Increasing the visibility of the food choices and developing unusual food combinations can greatly increase revenues. Some of the many opportunities for better food merchandising are shown in Table 17.4.

Table 17.4 Opportunities for food merchandising

Restaurant outlets	
Multiple themes	Several small restaurants, size 30–80 seats, with distinct ethnic or other themes operating from a single commissary (English pub, French bistro, Italian trattoria, etc.)
Exhibition cooking	Food is prepared in the restaurant or at an area visible from the seating areas and is used as the source for many menu items (pizza oven, grill, bakery, pasta making, rotisserie, or Chinese wok)
Food display	A display area either at the entrance or located near the center of the outlet serves either as a source for food or as decoration (appetizers, carved roasts, desserts, wines, and special coffees)
Buffet	Display area is used for guest self-service.
Tableside service	Service carts are rolled to each table with the presentation or preparation of individual entrees (specialty appetizers, Caesar's salad, desserts, and liqueurs)
Takeout	In downtown hotels, especially in shopping and tourist areas, fast service and informal outlets with takeout counter (ice cream, pastries, deli sandwiches, coffee, and other specialty foods)
Lobby breakfast	Temporary cart or kiosk service in the lobby to sell coffee, juices, and pastries during peak breakfast hours
Atrium restaurant	Exposed and visible food outlet, such as a sidewalk cafe in the lobby, increases awareness of the restaurant and encourages guest use, whatever the theme

Bar operations are similarly varied. While nearly every type of property except budget inns and the smallest hotels (under 50 rooms) includes a small lounge of some type, larger hotels offer a lobby bar, a sports bar or entertainment facility, and, occasionally, a rooftop lounge, where the view warrants it. Additional small outlets for food and beverage may complement and support a hotel's recreation facilities, such as the pool bar, marina bar, or the grill room at the resort's golf or tennis clubhouse.

Program and Planning Objectives

The optimal number of restaurant and bar outlets varies with the size, type, and location of the hotel and with the relative emphasis that the operator gives to that part of the operation. Convention hotels, at which the breakfast meal creates the largest peak demand, usually have a large three-meal restaurant, at least one specialty restaurant, and substantial demand for room service. Remote destination resorts, where the typical length-of-stay is longer and all the guests must be served three meals, plan for the flexible use of outdoor areas—breakfast terraces and pool snack bars, for instance—in addition to the two or more outlets. Cruise ships (the ultimate destination resort) plan the capacity of the main dining room to accommodate all passengers in two sittings for the formal 'captain's dinner,' but include several additional theme outlets for the bulk of the dining. At extended-stay hotels, where many guests stay several weeks or longer and where they often prepare their own breakfast and dine out in the evening, only minimal food and bar service is needed.

In Asia, where the tradition is to dine out at hotels more than at independent restaurants, the hotel F&B operations become a major revenue generator. A hotel with 300–400 rooms may have a dozen or more different themed dining rooms and lounges. Table 17.5 illustrates the variety of ethnic or other distinctive outlets that are common in business hotels such as the Westin Taipei (288 guestrooms) and the Grand Hyatt Fukuoka (370 rooms).

Experienced hotel operators approach the food and beverage program with an instinct about the relative size of the several outlets. A good starting rule-of-thumb in North America and Europe is to provide restaurant seats equal to 0.6 times the number of guestrooms and lounge seats equal to 0.3 times the number of rooms. This initial program objective can be increased or decreased according to the consultants' market study and the hotel operator's further financial analysis. Thus, a 400-room hotel might feature, instead of a 240-seat restaurant (0.6 times the number of guestrooms), a moderate-priced food outlet for 160 people and a specialty restaurant with about 80 seats. Table 17.6 gives guidelines on restaurant and bar capacities for different size hotels; however, these generally need to be modified to recognize site and local market conditions as well as regional attitudes toward hotel dining—such as just described in Asia.

The planning requirements for restaurants and lounges are as critical as for the other public areas, but, to a large extent, each outlet is independent of the others. Nevertheless, the following points are essential to an effective organization:

- Provide each food outlet with direct, convenient access to the kitchen; those outlets with minor food service may be served from pantries.
- Provide each beverage outlet with service backup, either from the kitchen or bar storage area.
- Locate each outlet accessible from public flow areas; make the café visible from the lobby.
- Pair each food outlet with a nearby bar or include a small holding lounge.
- Plan larger restaurants and bars so that sections can be closed during slow periods.
- Locate restaurants and bars where appropriate with exterior frontage and direct outside access.

Restaurant Design Objectives

Design objectives follow directly from a clear and well-researched operational and marketing concept. Based on the menu and such operational aspects as the type of service, method of beverage service, check handling, and use of entertainment, designers create the desired mood, function, layout, finishes, lighting, and furnishings.

Each restaurant outlet, depending on its type and quality level, must have a different design treatment.

The bi-coastal designer restaurant **Boutique hotel restaurants.** (A) Royalton Hotel, New York. In Restaurant 44 the banquettes save floor space and the strip mirror at eye-level allows visual eavesdropping on nearby tables. (B) Mondrian, Hollywood. The acclaimed 'Asia de Cuba' restaurant offers framed views of the Los Angeles skyline.

Table 17.5 International hotel F&B outlets

Westin Taipei, Taiwan (288 rooms)	
Chinese (four outlets)	Separate theme outlets featuring cuisines from Shanghai, Peking, Canton, and local regions; includes private rooms
Japanese	Includes Sushi bar, Teppanyaki table, and private western and tatami rooms
Italian	Includes antipasto bar area
Buffet	Main three-meal outlet open breakfast, lunch and dinner
New York deli	Offers coffee, sandwiches, snack items
Cappuccino bar	Lobby location with coffee and pastries
Tea lounge	Offers tea and cocktails
Entertainment lounge	Live music
Irish pub	Live music
Juice and snack bar	Swimming pool/health club location
Grand Hyatt Fukuoka, Japan (370 rooms)	
European	Features both buffet and à la carte
Cantonese	Offers fresh seafood; private rooms
Japanese	Rooftop restaurant with traditional cuisine
Sushi bar	Adjoins rooftop outlet; set within authentic tatami room
International food court	Open plan food court featuring seven international cuisines: Italian trattoria, German beer house, Chinese noodle shop, Mongolian BBQ, different Japanese themes, bakery and wine shop; also casual bar
Lobby bar	Offers tea cakes, teas and coffees, all drinks
Dark bar	Private hotel bar with limited food; cigar theme

For example, the hotel's main three-meal restaurant needs a theme that will permit the mood to vary from light and casual at breakfast to more formal at dinner. This may be accomplished by providing variable lighting, changing the tabletop from placemats to table linen, closing the counter seating, presenting a food display, or extending room dividers to make smaller and more intimate dining areas. The design of a three-meal restaurant should include the following considerations:

- *Cashier/hostess station*: provide a combined station to control access to all sections of the room, handle guest checks, and supervise coat check area.
- *Separate sections*: divide the restaurant into two or more areas so that sections can be closed during periods of low occupancy.
- *Flexible arrangement of tables*: provide paired deuces, flip-top fours (table leaves convert a square table into a larger circular one) to provide for large parties.
- *Counter seating*: provide about 10 percent of total seats at counter for singles.
- *Buffet/display areas*: provide an area for self-service buffet or food display.
- *Service stations*: provide wet service stations for every 80+ seats to supply water and coffee, store linen and cutlery, and hold soiled dishes.
- *Adaptable lighting*: provide dimmable lighting to change the mood from breakfast to lunch to dinner.
- *Background music*: consider including soft music.
- *Uniforms, tabletop, graphics, and signage*: design the accessory elements to complement the outlet or hotel theme.

Table 17.6 Restaurant and bar capacities for different size hotels

	Number of guestrooms					
	200	*300*	*400*	*500*	*750*	*1000*
Three-meal restaurant	120	180	160	180	225	250
Specialty restaurant			80	80	100	150
Theme restaurant					75	125
Deli/pastry shop				40	50	75
Lobby bar	60	30	40	50	60	60
Cocktail lounge		60	80			80
Restaurant holding bar					20	20
Entertainment lounge/ sports bar				100	140	140

Food and beverage capacities in number of seats.

Similarly, design objectives can be established for a hypothetical higher-priced restaurant. The specialty or signature restaurant may be open daily only for dinner, although lunch service is profitable in urban locations and Sunday brunch in the suburbs. Its mood and décor may reflect a theme developed, primarily, around the menu or style of service. Decorative touches in materials, detailing furnishings, planting, artifacts, artwork, and tabletop design further reinforce the theme. The design objectives, modified and refined by analyzing the market and developing a unique food concept, include the following:

- *Entry sequence*: establish a foyer space to set the mood for the restaurant.
- *Maitre d'*: provide a host station at the entrance to the restaurant.
- *Focal point*: organize all seats to take advantage of some focal point, either inside (food display, fountain, and entertainment) or outside, the dining room.
- *Seating areas*: incorporate screens or level changes to create more intimate, semi-private groups of tables.
- *Table seating*: provide clear definition to the seating areas, separating them from the aisles, service,

buffet, and host areas. Each table should have some privacy from other tables.

- *Food display*: arrange a food display either near the entrance or central to the seating.
- *Exhibition cooking*: based on the food concept, consider providing an open area for food preparation such as a wood-fired oven, grill, or Japanese Teppanyaki feature.
- *Entertainment*: provide a small stage and dance floor or consider how the plan might be modified to accommodate entertainment in the future; tables should be organized with views toward this focal point.
- *Service stations*: develop inconspicuous wet and dry service stations to improve staff efficiency.
- *Bar or holding bar*: provide beverage service from an adjacent cocktail lounge or a separate holding bar designated for the specialty restaurant, or from a kitchen service bar.
- *Intimate lighting*: design the variable lighting to create a more intimate mood at dinner; allow for brighter levels at lunch and for cleaning (fluorescent lights should not be used in any area).
- *Uniforms, tabletop, graphics, and signage*: select all design accessories to complement and reinforce the specialty theme of the room.

Most other restaurant outlets feature aspects of these two dining types. The more casual theme restaurants may combine the counter seating and cashier functions—a 'diner' outlet, for example—or introduce some variation on a native cuisine. A deli operation might be open 24 hours in an urban hotel and feature imaginatively designed display cases

The themed lobby lounge **The Palace of the Lost City, Sun City, South Africa.** The elephant tusks carry out the myth of the lost city, with its own architectural order based on native African motifs. The lounge is a center-piece of the dining and entertainment areas, with jazz piano accompaniment in the evenings (see p. C-31).

The local dining variations **Luxury hotel restaurants.** (A) At The Ritz-Carlton, Millenia Singapore, the airy three-meal restaurant separates the 242 seats with screens and dividers to create intimacy. The open kitchen features pizza ovens and bakery specialties. (B) At the Great Wall Sheraton Hotel, Beijing, the formal restaurant, one of five dining outlets in the 850-room hotel, offers a quiet refuge from the bustle of the open atrium lobby.

with pastries and other specialty items, sandwich preparation areas, high lighting levels, and easily maintained finishes.

Restaurant designers need to understand the influence of different types of seating on creating efficient layouts. Booth and banquette configurations, which reduce the amount of flow space around a table, are more efficient but are not always popular with customers. Larger tables, say for six diners, are more efficient overall than are deuces (tables for two), which need to be spaced for a modicum of privacy. In addition, the type of service and general quality level influences the space programming which, in general, requires 15–20 ft^2 (1.40–1.85 m^2) per person, or up to 25 ft^2 (2.3 m^2) for formal settings (see Table 17.7).

Lounge and Bar Design Objectives

Similar to how the design team conceives restaurants, the hotel operating company establishes bar and lounge concepts, the architect prepares preliminary plans to accommodate these requirements, and the interior designer more fully develops these themes including their furnishings and fixtures. Even more than the restaurants, the lounge areas vary extensively among different types of hotels. In a small downtown property, the primary beverage outlet may be a quiet and luxuriously furnished lobby bar, whereas in a convention, casino or resort property, it may be an action-oriented sports bar or entertainment lounge, adding a major nighttime focus for the hotel. Variation among these active bars and lounges is usually based on the opportunities of the local market and on the expected hotel clientele. Therefore, it is especially important that the designer be given a clear set of design objectives for each outlet.

Table 17.7 Restaurant and bar area requirements

Outlet type	*Casual*	*Formal*
Three-meal restaurant	16 (1.50)	18 (1.70)
Specialty restaurant	18 (1.70)	20 (1.85)
Fine dining	–	25 (2.30)
Chinese-theme restaurant	20 (1.85)	25 (2.30)
Deli/take-out restaurant	16 (1.50)	–
Ice cream/fast food	12 (1.10)	–
Lobby bar	20 (1.85)	25 (2.30)
Sports bar	15 (1.40)	–
Cocktail lounge	16 (1.50)	20 (1.85)

Approximate area requirements per seat in square feet (square meters).

The lobby bar developed in the 1970s as a way to create activity and excitement in the open atrium spaces in large hotels. After it proved itself as a popular meeting place and revenue generator, the lobby bar became standard in most types of hotels and locations. Fully open to the lobby space, separated only by planters, railings, a water feature, or level change, the lobby bar offers additional public seating when it isn't used as a beverage outlet. Operators discovered, too, that they also could utilize the space for continental breakfast or for merchandising late evening snacks. The designer should attempt to include the following features in the lobby bar:

- *Visibility*: provide an open area that is obvious to hotel guests and visitors.
- *Seating*: furnish the bar primarily with lounge seating—sofas, lounge chairs, end tables—or with a combination of lounge and bar seating; provide a few seats at a service bar.
- *Bar*: feature a small bar for beverage service with nearby storage or backup from the kitchen.
- *Entertainment*: specify a location for a piano or other entertainment.
- *Food service*: consider back-of-house access for limited food service, especially continental breakfast, hors d'oeuvres, and snack service.

The second beverage outlet often is some type of active bar or lounge, usually featuring a sports/video theme or entertainment, sometimes with dancing. Quite different from the more subdued lobby bar, the entertainment lounge is completely enclosed to reduce high noise levels and features lower light levels and more closely spaced seating. The designer, in developing the layout and design of entertainment lounges, should consider the following:

- *Entry sequence*: develop an enclosed entrance to maintain acoustic and visual separation between the lounge and the hotel circulation areas.
- *Separate sections*: establish distinct zones for the bar, the video/games area or entertainment/dancing area, and quieter lounge area.
- *Bar (about 10–25 percent of the lounge area)*: provide a large bar that is visible from the entrance and is situated so that guests can view the video screens or entertainers; provide pick-up stations for the staff, provide close-by bar storage.
- *Entertainment area (50–65 percent)*: develop an integrated section to accommodate at least half of the guests—provide multiple video screens and display of sports paraphernalia or create stage and dance floor area; add platforms to provide better sight lines throughout the space.

The flexible open lobby lounge **The Ritz-Carlton, Millenia Singapore.** The lounge, enclosed under the hotel's trademark barrel-vault lobby skylights, offers a typical mix of comfortable soft seating arranged with side and coffee tables for beverage and light food service, or incidental business meetings (see p. 14).

- *Lounge area (20–30 percent)*: design a separate lounge area where guests can sit outside but within reach of the active zone; consider soft lounge seating.
- *Lighting*: install flexible lighting, controlled at the bar, including stage and dance floor lighting as appropriate.
- *Video and sound system*: provide control of all video screens at the host stand or bar; or provide integrated sound system with speakers focused on the dance floor area.

Developing the restaurant and lounge concepts and establishing design goals are only part of the process. Often, the constraints of the building's schematic design greatly influence, for better or worse, the success of the food and beverage areas. The designer needs to combine the programmatic requirements with the operational standards to create a workable scheme. Hotel restaurants and bars, because they face such severe outside competition, create the greatest of all interior design challenges. While guestrooms and meeting spaces include their own important pragmatic requirements, the dining experience—combining food, service, and design elements—or the bar scene—with its new focus on entertainment—requires more imagination.

Function Space

The third principal category of public space includes the meeting, banquet, reception, and exhibit spaces, which form a major core in many medium and large hotels and in conference centers. Variously referred to as 'function space,' 'meeting and banquet area,' or 'convention complex,' the cluster of individual spaces generally includes a large ballroom, intermediate-size banquet rooms, and smaller meeting and breakout rooms. In fact, the principal distinctions among types of hotels often focus on the size and mix of the function space.

Introduced in the late nineteenth century to accommodate important civic and social gatherings, hotel function space more recently has been designed to meet the needs of corporations and professional associations. The two create very different demands. The corporate group market mainly requires a variety of relatively small but high-quality spaces for sales and management meetings, launching new products, and continuing-education programs for executives. The association market primarily needs facilities for large group meetings, smaller general-purpose rooms for seminars and workshops, and extensive exhibition space. In addition, local organizations use hotel meeting space for a variety of meetings, banquets, and reception functions.

The men's cigar bar **The Ritz-Carlton, San Juan Hotel, Spa & Casino, Isla Verde, Puerto Rico.** Hotel operators match the dining and lounge operations to the market. At the 414-room beachfront hotel, with one of the largest casinos in Puerto Rico, among seven outlets is 'The Bar,' serving late afternoon and evening cocktails and cigars.

Program and Planning Objectives

Generally, the hotel feasibility study recommends a mix of function space that is based on an analysis of the demand for different types of business and social uses. Small town hotels and chain franchise properties, for example, commonly offer a single multipurpose ballroom, simply decorated, which is intended to accommodate the full range of small meetings, civic lunches, wedding receptions, and local product displays. It usually is not intended to attract business to fill the hotel guestrooms. On the other hand, convention hotels and conference centers provide a wide range of facilities—large and small, simple and elegant, with and without high-tech audiovisual equipment—as the principal attraction to the hotel. Meeting planners select the hotel, to a large extent, for its ability to provide complete meeting facilities, which, in turn, sells large blocks of guestrooms.

At resort hotels where seasonal fluctuations in demand create low periods for several months of the year, properties have added conference wings to increase the demand for guestrooms throughout the shoulder and off-season periods. In super-luxury hotels, which have relatively fewer rooms and which place an important emphasis on intimacy and exclusivity, developers include small but elegantly finished meeting and function rooms; these areas tend to be used for receptions and banquets and to cater to the surrounding community rather than to hotel guests.

In all but the smallest properties, function space is an essential ingredient of the successful hotel. The earlier chapters on convention hotels (Chapter 5) and conference centers (Chapter 6) illustrate a number of successful properties of those types. But for each type of hotel or resort, not just these, the development team must carefully establish the appropriate mix of function space, and detail the equipment and features needed to meet the expectations of the market. Table 17.8 identifies the typical size for different function spaces and highlights many of the key features which the designer must incorporate into the design.

Once the program is established, the architect, interior designer, consulting engineers, and operator must cooperate in planning the function space in order to create a salable property. The success of meeting and banquet sales depends on a number of functional planning considerations—which meeting planners have learned to seek out—as well as interior décor, proper lighting, acoustical and mechanical engineering, and other technical requirements. The key planning requirements include:

- Group all function areas together (in major convention hotels some separation may be desirable).
- Provide a separate function entrance from the street or parking area.
- Locate the function space close to and easily accessible from the hotel lobby.
- Locate additional function areas such as an exhibit hall or audiovisual theater convenient but not adjacent to the ballroom foyer.
- Include adjacent public support areas: toilets, coatrooms, telephones, and a convention services office.
- Provide direct food service access to the ballroom and all banquet rooms; locate the banquet pantry on the ballroom level.
- Include essential meeting and banquet storage adjacent to the ballroom.
- Design the ballroom and other larger rooms to be independent of the guestroom tower so as to simplify the building structure.

Table 17.8 Function room characteristics

Space and uses	*Principal planning requirements*	*Program (capacity) for hotel types*	
Ballroom			
Meetings, banquets, receptions, exhibits	Divisibility, high ceiling, direct food access, no columns	Typical, most types:	2 × GR
		Resort:	0.5–1.5 × GR
		Convention:	2–4 × GR
Ballroom foyer			
Reception, meeting registration, flow	Access to all ballroom sections and support, functions access to terraces	Typical:	0.2 × BR
		Resort:	0.3 × BR
		Convention:	0.25–3 × BR
Banquet rooms			
Banquets, meetings, receptions	Divisibility, direct food access, natural light	Typical:	0.2–0.6 × BR
		Convention:	0.4–0.6 × BR
Meeting rooms			
Meetings, limited banquets	Built-in audiovisual, limited divisions	Typical:	0.2–0.4 × BR
		Convention:	0.4–0.6 × BR
		Conference center:	0.5–0.8 × BR
Boardroom			
High level meeting	Separate from other meeting rooms, built-in audiovisual, superior finishes	All hotel types:	12–20 people
Exhibit hall			
Exhibition	Display access, floor loading, high ceiling, high lighting level	Convention:	Number of booths varies
Auditorium or amphitheater			
Lectures, audiovisual presentation, case discussion	Sloped floor or tiered levels, fixed theater seats or permanent work-counter, built-in audiovisual	Convention:	0.2–0.4 × GR
		Conference center:	0.4–0.8 × GR

Key: GR = number of guestrooms; BR = capacity of ballroom.

The first item in this list identifies the need to decide on the relative clustering of the function areas. Convention hotels, especially those which serve as the headquarters for a major meeting, may attract one major group or as many as four or five smaller groups at one time. For the occasions when a single major convention is in the hotel, it is convenient to have the ballroom, junior ballroom, and several meeting rooms immediately adjacent to each other, perhaps sharing a foyer or prefunction area. This is the usual and preferred arrangement in small and midsize hotels of 250–400 guestrooms.

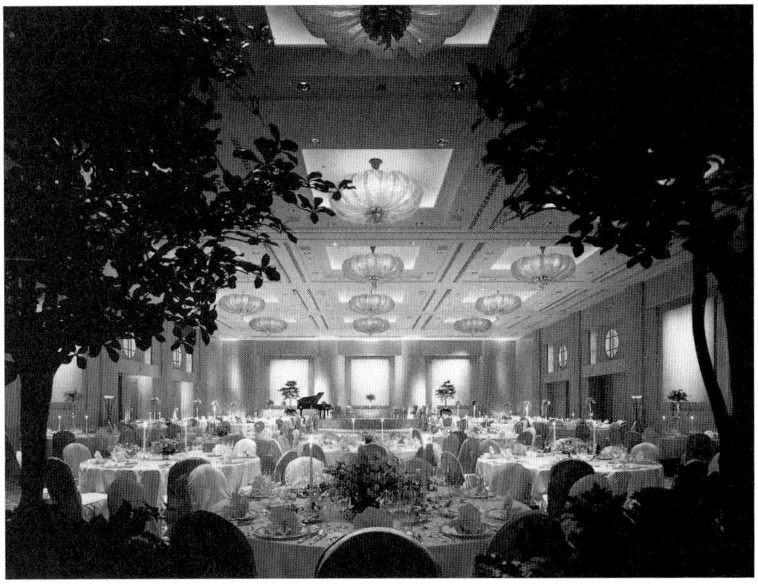

An upscale social ballroom **The Pan Pacific Hotel, Vancouver, Canada.** Many successful hotel ballrooms tend to be oriented either towards meetings and conventions or to social functions. The elegant ceiling and wood-veneer wall panels, enhanced with dramatic lighting, provide an impressive setting for banquets and receptions.

The modern renovated convention ballroom **Hyatt Regency Atlanta, Georgia.** The first modern atrium hotel, opened in 1967, has seen several major expansion and renovation projects, the latest to remake the Centennial Ballroom into a unique convention space, whose suspended ceiling panels hide the painted-out mechanical and electrical systems, from which engineers can drop electrical service flexibly to exhibit booths.

When multiple functions need to be accommodated, it may be preferable to separate the principal meeting and banquet areas so that several groups can assemble simultaneously without interference or distraction. The 900-room Grand Hyatt Washington has function space arrayed over three levels (see p. 132): the main ballroom (17,000 ft^2; 1,580 m^2) and junior ballroom (8,500 ft^2; 790 m^2) are on separate levels below grade and the 90-seat conference theater (5,000 ft^2; 465 m^2) is on the lobby floor. At the 1,400-room Sheraton Centre in Toronto, the largest convention hotel in Canada, the main ballroom and exhibition hall are on a basement floor, whereas two junior ballrooms are in separate areas on a mezzanine level; three different organizations easily can meet without interference or direct contact with the others. For the same reason, although at a very different scale, small conference centers arrange their meeting rooms and breakout areas in several clusters so that each group is assured privacy.

Design Criteria

The coordination among the design team is especially important in the evolution of the details for the function space. The architectural aspects (proportions, divisibility, and access), the interior design considerations (finishes, furnishings, and lighting), and the engineering requirements (ventilation, sound system, and fire protection) are clearly related and heavily influence each other.

Connecting these facts are several overall issues. One is the relative specificity of the various function areas, that is, the degree to which each is designed as a multipurpose room or, instead, is intended particularly for a single purpose, say a board meeting or film presentation. The principal considerations include size, divisibility, complexity of services, and quality of finishes. The better defined the use of a particular room, the more specific the interior design can be. Larger hotels, and those with a clear market orientation such as luxury properties and conference centers, can afford to provide very specific meeting and banquet rooms and further assure their use by groups with individual needs. The suburban hotel, however, must use its single ballroom for so many different functions that, too often, none is particularly well served. Table 17.9 identifies the type of architectural, decorative, and

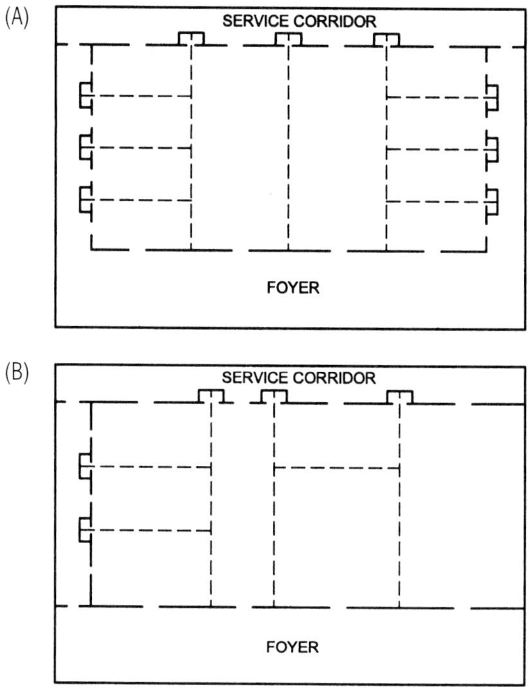

The luxury of flexibility **Ballroom schematic.** Added functionality is accomplished by a subdivisible ballroom. (A) Small rooms at the ends of the ballroom are reached by a combined public/service corridor outside the ballroom. (B) Larger rooms require dedicated service access, with the public reaching the spaces through the ballroom itself.

engineering decisions that the design team must make to create a successful large function room such as the hotel ballroom. Many similar issues arise in designing the smaller rooms, as well.

A second consideration is planning the divisibility of ballroom and larger function rooms. Practically all hotel ballrooms are divided into several sections so that a smaller group is in an appropriately-sized space, two or more groups can use the room simultaneously, or a group can use one part for a meeting and the adjoining section for meals. Two typical approaches for subdividing the ballroom are illustrated in the accompanying diagram.

A third aspect of function room design is matching the room layout to the space. The larger multipurpose rooms usually are furnished either banquet- or theater-style—or are essentially unfurnished when used for an exhibition or reception. But the mid-size and smaller rooms will be furnished and equipped in a variety of ways to meet the particular needs of a group. The designers must test the actual capacity of each room under different furnishing configurations. Table 17.10 illustrates typical area requirements for different seating configurations over a range of large and small function rooms.

Many designers and hotel operators have found that one critical element in the function rooms is the design of the ballroom ceiling. When a hotel

Table 17.9 Design criteria for large function space

Architectural	
Divisibility	Number of subdivisions and proportions of each, storage of dividing walls, acoustic rating of dividing walls
Proportions	Location of and views to head table stage
Structure	Full span, no columns
Ceiling height	Projection booth, use for exhibitions, chandeliers, cost of divisible walls, implications for second floor
Floor load	Use for displays and exhibits
Access/egress	Public and service access to each subsection, storage, display access, emergency exits
Windows	Desirability, blackout requirement
Interior design	
Floor	Carpet, patterned to assist furniture placement; portable dance floor
Walls	Various finishes (paint, vinyl, fabric panels), chair rail, folding wall material to match other walls
Ceiling	Downlights, chandeliers, track lighting, emergency lighting, HVAC diffusers and air return, sprinklers, smoke detectors, sound system, wall tracks in integrated pattern
Windows	Full blackout capability
Lighting	Combination of functional, decorative, display, and accent lighting
Furniture	Round banquet and rectangular meeting tables, stacking chairs, risers, lectern, audiovisual equipment, foyer seating
Mechanical/electrical	
All	Fully separate controls in each room and subdivisions of larger rooms
Lighting	Fully dimmable, control at podium, flexible track lighting where required
Electrical	208 volts available in ballroom and exhibition areas
Sound	Television, telephone, microphone jacks in each area, control from sound and light booth
Mechanical	Full air-conditioning, fire protection
Plumbing	Wet utilities available near ballroom and exhibition areas

The cache of unique board rooms **Le Meridien Lingotto, Turin, Italy.** Among the globe's most spectacular meeting rooms, the convention space in the former Fiat automobile factory in Turin features the 'Bolla' room, within a glass dome atop the mixed-use project. The room is perfectly conceived, with a central oversized board table, surrounded by seating for associates, and with necessary support services provided in freestanding modules (see pp. C-14 and 189).

ballroom is set up for a banquet or meeting, the tables and attendees obscure most of the floor and the lower part of the walls. The ceiling, though, is totally visible and contains downlights, chandeliers, and track lighting, as well as mechanical diffusers and return grills, sprinklers, sound system speakers, smoke detectors, and movable wall tracks. All must be integrated into a single, cohesive, organized, and attractive pattern.

Another design aspect that too often is ignored during design development is provision for sufficient electrical and communication services to the ballroom, meeting rooms, and, especially, the exhibit hall. Not only electrical outlets, but telephone, television, and microphone jacks, controls for various projectors, projection screen, and lights, and, in some cases, a wet utility panel must be provided. Exhibit halls, for example, should contain electrical outlets every 10 ft (3 m) in the floor, ceiling-mounted spotlight tracks 30 ft (9 m) on centers, and convenient water and drain connections for exhibitors.

Table 17.10 Area requirements for hotel function rooms

		Reception	*Theater*	*Banquet*	*Classroom*	*Boardroom*
Ballroom	>10,000 ft^2 (930 m^2)	7 (0.6)	8 (0.7)	10 (0.9)	–	–
Ballroom	>3,000 ft^2 (280 m^2)	8 (0.7)	8 (0.7)	11 (1.0)	12 (1.1)	–
Banquet room	<3,000 ft^2 (280 m^2)	9 (0.8)	10 (0.9)	12 (1.1)	14 (1.3)	–
Meeting room		9 (0.8)	10 (0.9)	12 (1.1)	14 (1.3)	16–20 (1.5–1.9)
Boardroom		12 (1.1)	–	15 (1.4)	–	20–25 (1.9–2.3)
Auditorium		–	8–10 (0.7–0.9)	–	–	–
Amphitheater	–	–	–	15–20 (1.4–1.9)	–	

The approximate area requirement per seat in square feet (square meters). Conference centers generally provide much more generous spacing, increasing these figures by 30–50%.

Legend

1 Main entrance porte cochere
2 Hotel registration
3 Lobby bar/water feature
4 Mechnical/electrical/ telecommunications mezzanine
5 Public elevator lobby
6 Restaurant
7 Snack bar
8 Kitchen
9 Indoor lap pool
10 Meeting room
11 Ballroom
12 Prefunction
13 Ballroom porte cochere
14 Ballroom registration
15 Ballroom offices
16 Outdoor terrace
17 Outdoor pool
18 Swim-up/walk-up bar
19 Truck dock
20 Gift shop
21 Dress shop
22 Smoking balcony
23 Rotunda to existing conference center
24 Equipment yard

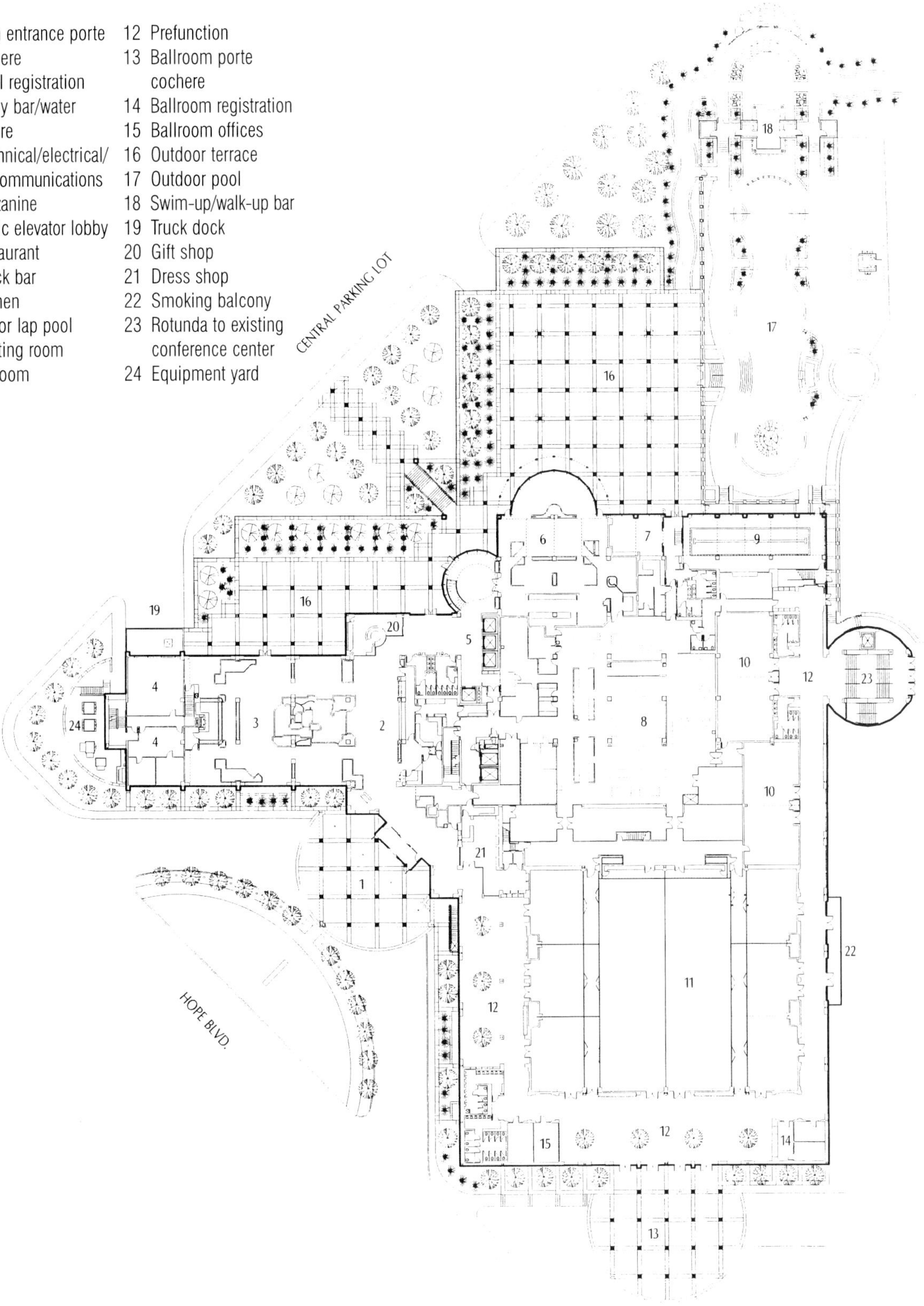

Planning the hotel for service **Moody Gardens Hotel, Galveston, Texas.** The ground floor plan illustrates the clear separation of major functions. From the entrance the function spaces are to the right, the lobby and lounge areas immediately to the left, with dining and recreational amenities beyond. The public areas totally surround the kitchen, which is supported by back-of-house activities easily accessible in the basement below (see p. 37).

Recreation Facilities

Increasingly, hotels provide recreational facilities, ranging from an outdoor pool at a roadside inn, to major health clubs in downtown hotels, to extensive golf, tennis, marina, or ski complexes at destination resorts. While surveys show that relatively few guests actually use the swimming pool and other recreational facilities at most hotels, nonetheless, many guests expect them and it is essential that the developer provide these amenities in some form.

To counter low use, some operators expand rather than minimize their recreational features and profitably promote them to the community, in addition to the hotel guest. In a highly competitive market, this is one more area in which a hotel can gain an edge over other properties. The developers of a downtown hotel, for example, may include a full-size health club to complement the property's other business-oriented facilities; for a suburban hotel provide an enclosed pool and related amenities as a swim club for the community; or for a conference center add extensive outdoor jogging, tennis, or golf facilities to attract the high-level executive retreat.

Table 17.11 Fitness facilities checklist

Activity	*Minimum overall size ft² (m²)*
Swimming pool	
Pool surface	800 (75)
Total including deck area	2,400 (225)
Health club	
Reception	300 (28)
Hair salon	300 (28)
Lockers and toilets	20/person (1.9)
Whirlpool/hot tub (single)	50/person (4.7)
Whirlpool/hot tub (group)	20/person (1.9)
Sauna	20/person (1.9)
Exercise room	
Exercise room	600 (56)
Nautilus circuit	400 (37)
Exercise equipment	50/unit (4.7)
Aerobic classroom	
Aerobics room	800 (75)
Gym	2,400 (225)
Steam bath	20/person (1.9)
Loofah bath	100/person (9.3)
Herbal wrap	100/person (9.3)
Massage	100/person (9.3)
Barber/hairdresser	70/person (6.5)

The accompanying checklist (Table 17.11) shows the principal types of recreational facilities that a developer or operator might program into a property.

The hotels discussed in Part 1 of this book illustrate the kinds of recreational facilities that are commonly found at different types of properties. Generally, the smaller, budget, and mid-priced motels and hotels, those which attract a large number of price-conscious family travelers, include little more than an outdoor swimming pool and a game room or small fitness center. Larger hotels and especially those with a business market frequently add extensive health clubs, including exercise rooms, saunas, and, perhaps, racquetball. Resorts and other lodging types, catering to longer-staying guests, and hotels in outlying areas, where land costs are less, feature additional outdoor facilities.

Swimming Pool

Nearly all hotel management companies require the developer to include a swimming pool, although minimum sizes vary. The pool area should be separated from other public spaces so that guests dressed in bathing suits need not pass through the hotel lobby. Other key planning considerations include:

- *Location*: place the pool so that guests can reach it from guestroom elevators without passing through the lobby; provide some guestrooms with views of the pool; screen any exterior views toward the pool.
- *Orientation*: position the pool so that it receives unobstructed sunlight from mid-morning to late afternoon.
- *Size*: provide a pool of sufficient size to accommodate the swimming and sunbathing needs of the guests, but no smaller than about 20 × 40 ft (6 × 12 m) with at least 10 ft (3 m) of deck space on all sides.
- *Support functions*: provide toilets and lockers where required, towel issue area, snack bar or vending, equipment room, and furniture storage.
- *Safety*: do *not* provide a diving board; include slip-free deck surface, depth markings, underwater fighting, safety or 'pool rules' signage.
- *Wading pool, whirlpool*: include additional pools within view of the swimming pool but slightly separated.
- *Indoor pool*: design either an operable roof or glass walls to provide direct sunlight and ventilation.

The luxury urban swimming pool **Four Seasons Hotel, Tokyo at Chinzan-so, Japan.** Urban hotels increasingly feature such resort amenities as a full spa and fitness center. Here, the pool with its vaulted skylight and sensuous curves serves as the focal point, with sauna, steam rooms, whirlpools, gym, and beauty salon close by.

Health Club

A second major component of hotel recreational facilities is the health club, a feature that for many types of hotel has become more central than the pool. The focus of the health club is a combination of exercise equipment (such as Nautilus or Universal machines) and such specialized facilities as steam rooms, whirlpool baths, and saunas. Larger complexes may add a unisex hair salon, multipurpose room for aerobic exercise, and racquetball or squash courts. The health center at the Hilton Short Hills in New Jersey is representative of how a medium-size, upscale property can cater to guests and the local community. (See the further discussion of spa facilities in Chapter 4.) The following items should be considered during the planning phase:

- *Location*: plan the club so that guests can reach it directly from the guestroom elevators and members from the street or parking area without passing through the hotel lobby.
- *Program*: include reception area with attendant; hair salon; lockers, showers, and toilets; exercise room; sauna, steam room, and whirlpool; massage rooms; and lounge, depending on the market.
- *Adjacencies*: plan the complex with the control area and lounge most visible and with the private functions either shared (exercise room) or back-to-back (saunas).

The splendor of the marble spa **Manila Diamond Hotel, Philippines.** The exclusive Diamond Spa evokes a feel of classic luxury, with opulent white marble walls and black granite flooring. It features high-tech cardiovascular and exercise equipment, aerobics classes, and the full complement of skin and body therapies (see C-6).

Parking

The provision of sufficient parking can be a crucial element, in both the budgeting and conceptual planning for a hotel or motel. And its design often influences the guest's first and last impressions of the property. Roadside inn developers know they must provide one space per room; full-service hotels need additional spaces for employees and for any public areas—restaurants, bars, meeting space, or recreational facilities—that attract guests from the community. An otherwise successful hotel can be seriously affected—especially its ability to attract local banquet business—by insufficient or inconvenient parking.

The key objective should be to provide optimum but not excessive amounts of parking. Unless unusual conditions (sports complex, large banquet facility, retail center) exist, the parking provision for different types of lodging properties falls within the ranges shown in Table 17.12. Land cost is an increasing problem in suburban and rural locations, where parking usually is on grade, covering more land than the building itself, making it necessary for developers to program their parking requirements more carefully. However, the more critical concern is at downtown hotels and other properties where high land costs preclude extensive amounts of surface parking or require the construction of a garage, often below the hotel. It is not uncommon

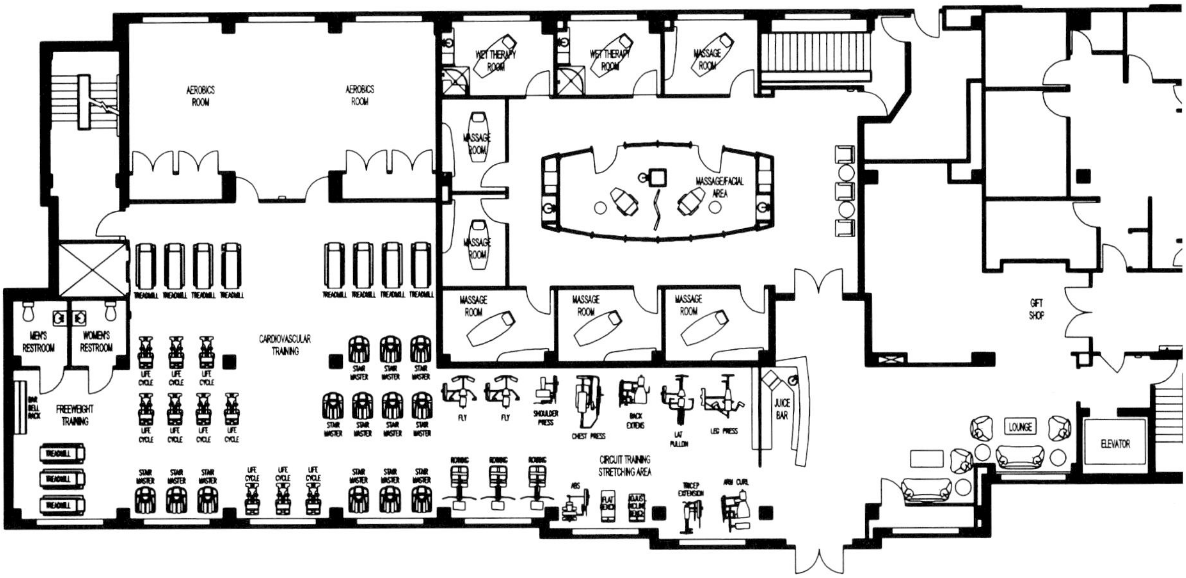

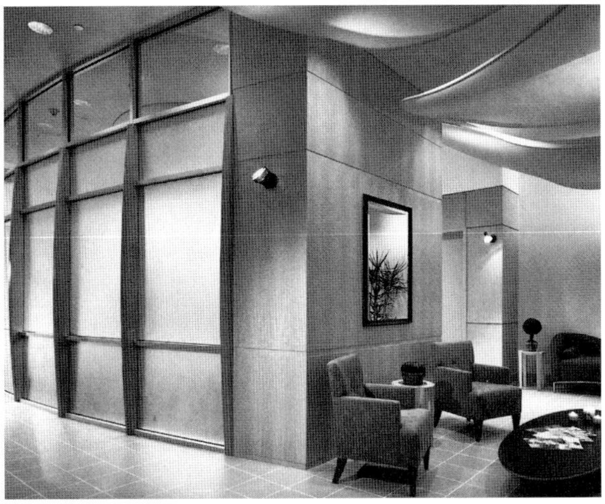

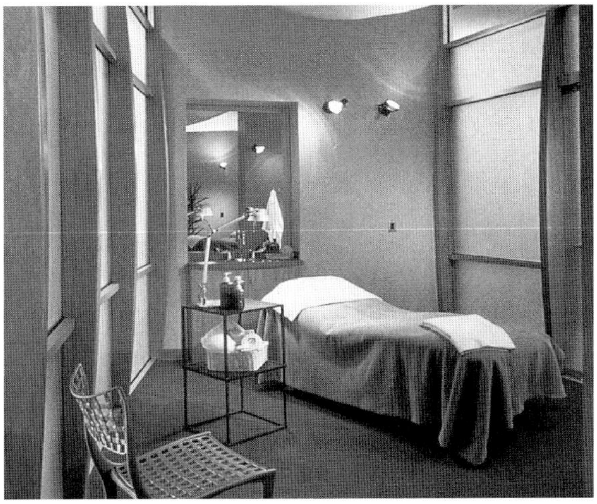

The suburban spa/exercise complex **Hilton Short Hills Spa, New Jersey.** Recent renovations of the five-diamond suburban hotel include a 16,000 ft^2 (150 m^2) boutique spa including cardiovascular and strength equipment, aerobics rooms, nine individual spa treatment rooms, and a reception area/juice bar. The high quality interior finishes enhance the luxury experience.

for the developer and architect to appeal zoning regulations, if justified, based on an analysis by traffic experts. One technique is to project hourly parking requirements, recognizing that the hotel guest, conferee, banquet guest, and employees create peak demands on parking at different periods of the day (see example, Table 17.13).

In addition to programming the parking, the design team must consider the impact it makes on the guest's lasting impression of the hotel. Designers need to address concerns about convenience, safety, and possible claustrophobia:

- *Garage entrance*: locate the entrance so that it is readily accessible to the guest drop-off area.
- *Hotel access*: provide a secure and convenient interior route, usually an elevator, from the garage to the hotel lobby.
- *Safety and security*: design the garage to be visually open with wide aisles; provide security cameras to scan area.
- *Guest comfort*: find solutions to reduce feelings of claustrophobia, by increasing lighting levels, raising ceiling height, painting surfaces light colors; provide art, murals, or music.
- *Signage*: provide clear signage both for drivers (to exit) and pedestrians (to lobby or street).

Table 17.12 Parking needed for different types of hotels

Hotel type	*No. of spaces/room*	*Comment*
Business (downtown)	0.4–0.8	Assumes limited function space
Boutique hotel	0.3–0.8	Higher factor in resort areas
Suburban hotel	1.2–1.4	Heavy local meeting and banquet use
Airport hotel	0.6–1.0	Moderate rental car use
Roadside inn	1.0–1.2	Very limited local banquet and F&B use
Resort (all types)	0.2–1.4	Varies by market, location, and proximity to urban centers or major attractions
Convention hotel	0.8–1.4	Regional convention hotels need higher provision
Conference center	1.0–1.3	If full house, minimum local use
Condominium hotel	1.2–2.0	May need two spaces/condominium
All-suite hotel	0.8–1.2	Limited F&B and function areas
Super-luxury hotel	1.0–1.2	Limited function areas
Mega-hotel	1.0–1.2	Limited local business; high rental car use
Mixed-use hotel	0.6–1.2	Highly variable depending on other activities
Casino hotel	0.8–2.0	Varies by location (for example, Atlantic City requires extensive bus parking)

In mixed-use projects, the hotel should negotiate its own parking spaces, perhaps behind an access gate, to assure that parking is available to hotel guests. Also, this permits the hotel to set up security for that dedicated portion of the garage. Many hotels choose to offer valet parking as a guest amenity. Equally as often, though, this decision is made because of space and budget limitations: hotel staff can park many more cars in the same amount of space and do not require the wide aisles or other design features that guests expect.

Signage and Iconographics

The perception of a hotel goes well beyond its architecture and interior design. Such small yet critical details as signage, graphics, tabletop items, and uniform design complete and reinforce the desired image and marketing goals of a hotel. These elements, which should be conceived of as an integral part of the design process, require the collaborative effort of the architect, interior designer, lighting designer, and such specialists as a graphic consultant or uniform designer.

The themed cultural/historic decor **The Beverly Hills Hotel, California.** (A) Reproductions of the original banana leaf wallpaper are used throughout the fully refurbished hotel, continuing the pink and green theme from the exterior and the grounds to the interiors. (B) Designer Hirsch Bedner and Associates repeats the same motif in the printed materials, from gift bags to the guestroom portfolio and other specialty items.

Table 17.13 Parking analysis

The following steps describe an approach to calculating parking requirements based on the changing needs of the guestrooms and other hotel facilities throughout the day. The maximum parking demand in most properties is created not by the rooms but by the meeting and banquet space. The provision of parking must recognize the sum of the various components and the interrelationship of the peaks and valleys over a 24-hour period.

1 Determine the components of the parking requirement: overnight guests, restaurant and bar patrons, meeting attendees, and other visitors (see Step 3).

2 Calculate the maximum number of cars that might be reasonably anticipated, planning to accommodate full demand on 80–85 percent of all days, but not peak demand for each component. The overnight guest calculation is illustrated by the following example:

Number of rooms	400
Percent occupancy	85
People per room	1.4
Percent arriving by car	40
People per car	1.5

The equation for calculating the guests' parking requirement is as follows:

$$\frac{(\text{Rooms}) \times (\%\ \text{occupancy}) \times (\text{people/room}) \times (\%\ \text{by car})}{(\text{People/car})}$$

Example: $\frac{400 \times .85 \times 1.4 \times .40}{1.5} = 127$ cars

The calculation for the other components includes similar factors as appropriate, such as food and beverage covers, percentage of diners arriving by car, and number of employees by shift.

3 Develop a table showing hourly parking use factors (example shows 4-hour periods). For example, the parking facility needs to accommodate all (100 percent or 1) overnight guest cars from midnight to 4:00 a.m. but, because of checkouts, only 60 percent (0.6) during the midday periods.

User	*Midnight 4:00*	*4:00 8:00*	*8:00 Noon*	*Noon 16:00*	*16:00 20:00*	*20:00 Midnight*
Hotel guests	1	0.95	0.6	0.6	0.9	0.95
Restaurant and bar patrons	0.05	0.1	0.1	0.1	0.2	0.25
Meeting/banquet attendees	0.05	–	0.1	0.1	0.4	0.4
Health club members	–	0.2	0.1	0.2	0.2	0.05
Visitors	–	0.1	0.2	0.1	0.2	0.4
Employees	0.25	0.25	0.4	0.4	0.35	0.35

4 Combine the parking requirements for each component (Step 2) with the use table (Step 3) to calculate the total amount of parking necessary during each time period. In this example, hotel guests would require 127 parking spaces (1 × 127) at midnight but only 76 spaces (0.6 × 127) at noon. Recognize that high evening demand, for example, might be partially met by available parking nearby.

Signage and Graphics

The signage and graphics program not only provides guests with immediate information and orients them to the project, but it also may help to reinforce the branding of a particular hotel. The major components include directional and destination signage and printed graphics. The corporate or property identity, which later may be embedded in the signage throughout the hotel or resort, often is introduced to the public in the advertising and promotional literature prior to the opening. Hyatt revised its corporate logo in the mid-1990s and frequently uses elements of the design not only in the printed graphics but in much of the interior signage throughout the hotel. Starwood Hotel's W brand successfully incorporates the logotype into both signage and graphical images throughout its hotels. The elements most commonly included in a signage and graphics program are listed in Table 17.14.

Architects and designers often have challenges in creating a meaningful image for the property. For example, frequently, the first identification that a guest may see, the building's exterior signage, is restricted in its placement, size, color, and lighting by local ordinances. At more expansive resorts, especially, arriving guests depend on directional signs to guide them to the hotel lobby, or to restaurant or banquet entrances. Signs identify staff and receiving areas or highlight handicapped routes or parking spaces.

Table 17.14 Signage and graphics

Exterior signage	
Brand and building identification	
Vehicular directional signs	Guest entrance and exit, receiving area, employee entrance; guest parking, handicapped parking, staff parking; taxi and public transportation
Pedestrian directional signs	Lobby entrance, restaurant entrance, ballroom and meeting room access; outdoor amenities including beach, pool, spa, tennis, golf, and boating
Interior signage	
Event directory	
Directional signage	Lobby, retail shops, food and beverage outlets, ballroom and meeting rooms, recreational amenities; floor identification and room direction, emergency exiting
Destination signage	Front desk, guestroom numbers, function rooms, toilets, coats, elevator identification, F&B outlet logos
Print graphics	
Marketing materials	All hotel advertising, marketing, sales brochures and related items
Guestroom amenities	Room service and guest information books; bathroom soap/shampoo and related packaging; robe and towel logos; stationery items such as note pads, letterhead, envelopes, and pencils; guestroom card-keys
Menus and restaurant/bar supplies	All food and beverage menus, wine lists, tabletop merchandising, etc.; related paper products such as matchbooks, coasters, napkins, etc.
Front office and accounting forms	Registration materials, guest receipts, invoices, etc.

These all may be subject to local regulations. Once inside the hotel, guests rely on signage to find their way from the lobby to guestrooms, F&B outlets, function space, recreational amenities, and so forth. Some architects at the schematic design phase test the hotel organization by imagining the future signage—if it is difficult to conceive how directional signage can orient guests and lead them through the property then the entire architectural organization needs to be rethought and clarified.

Both the hotel's exterior and interior signage should be integrated with the architecture and interior design so that the design elements reinforce the theme and style of the property. This commonly is achieved through the consistent use of color, shape, or pattern, and by repeating the same typeface and materials that are found in the architecture and hotel interiors. At the Beverly Hills Hotel the signage and graphics package draws from the lush banana plants that permeate the grounds around the hotel. This banana leaf motif is repeated throughout the interior decoration on wallpaper, drapery and upholstery fabrics, and even on printed items, consistently applying the theme through a multitude of visual elements.

The American Hotel and Motel Association (AH&MA) has approved over one hundred universal symbols to represent such common hotel areas or services as check-in, information, restrooms, and luggage check. These standard graphics are a good starting point for the design of signage, since the symbols are easily recognized internationally, but most operators wish to make their signage and graphics programs unique and more reflective of the character of their property. The destination signage throughout the hotel—at individual guestrooms as well as at each function room—or the identity graphics at each restaurant or lounge are especially important.

Uniforms and Tabletop Design

Uniforms and restaurant tabletop design are two additional visual elements to which guests are directly and constantly exposed. For many years the hotel management company, to reflect the corporate image, designed and specified uniforms for the front-of-house staff. Increasingly, today, for first class and luxury hotels and resorts, companies retain an independent uniform designer to complement and reinforce the hotel theme, service style, and local customs in the design of the uniforms. Once again, the designers creatively manipulate color, pattern, and shape to coordinate the uniforms—or 'costumes'—with the hotel's architectural and design style. The uniforms may vary as much as does the style of the property, ranging from formal attire—even top hat and tails at luxury properties—to beachwear at resorts. The operators of urban boutique hotels have established uniform design as a statement of high fashion—doormen clad in black Armani suits instantly identify the genre.

Table 17.15 Uniforms and tabletop design

Uniforms	
Front-of-house	Doorman, bellman, concierge, front desk staff
Food and beverage	Hostess, wait staff, bartender, bus staff, room service
Back-of-house	Food and beverage, security, housekeeping, maintenance, parking
Tabletop	
Linen	Tablecloths, table runner or placemats, napkins
Place setting	China, glassware, tableware
Tabletop accessories	Flower or bud vases, salt and pepper cellars, tea service, cream and sugar, wine buckets, ashtrays, etc.

Tabletop design is another integral part of the guest's experience that should be conceived as part of the overall theme of the property. The tabletop items appear in many areas outside the normal F&B outlets—the several restaurants, lobby lounge, sports bar, and so forth. Consider that food and beverage sales occur in the lobby itself, in function rooms and prefunction areas, around the pool, and in the guestrooms and suites. The style and complexity of the tabletop often is reflective of the design and formality of the hotel. For example, Greek antiquity is the expressed theme in the table settings at the Hyatt Regency Thessaloniki (see p. C-22). Some of the tabletop items are standard within one hotel company. However, designers or corporate management, or occasionally the executive chef or the food and beverage manager, may custom design individual pieces for the particular hotel and its setting. Table 17.15 identifies the most common items included in the hotel tabletop program.

Art and Artifacts

Art plays a growing role in the styling of a hotel. The development of an art program is a service frequently provided by the interior designer or an independent art consultant and should be conceived as an integral thread throughout the design. Art, artifacts, and antiques can create the 'feeling of home' for the business traveler or the 'element of fantasy' for the leisure traveler.

Artwork appears in nearly every hotel. Budget properties include framed prints in the guestrooms and in the hotel lobby, if nowhere else. Midscale hotels introduce art and artifacts into the food and beverage outlets and the meeting prefunction areas, and may place a framed mirror in each guestroom-floor elevator lobby. These mid-market hotels may be able to incorporate original art fairly economically by commissioning a local artist to create pieces, which they then reproduce in quantity for the guestrooms or other areas.

Among the most lavish art programs—which sometimes approach museum quality—are those found in traditionally styled luxury properties. The Ritz-Carlton chain, as an example, has collected eighteenth and nineteenth century European and American art and antiques—paintings by renowned artists, sculptures, tapestries, decorative accessories, oriental carpets, and a variety of unique furniture pieces—which they display throughout the

The unified design concept **Manila Diamond Hotel, Philippines.** (A) Interior designers often extend their unified concept through restaurant table top, uniforms, signage, logos, floral displays, print menus and other appropriate elements. The hotel's guest bathroom amenities coordinate with the interiors throughout, adding one more touch to the design vision. (B) The color board illustrates the designers' early concept communication to the owner and management company.

hotel public areas. The Ritz-Carlton hotel in San Francisco keeps a fine-arts advisor and curator on staff to document, maintain, and conserve their art and antiques collection. In addition, they train their staff to answer the most common questions that guests have regarding the collections.

The traditional art and antiques program has expanded to include new and creative uses for art, and the term 'antiques' has been redefined to include twentieth century decorative objects, furniture, and art from many cultures. Once just the accents which completed the feel or look of a property, art and antiques often are used now to create the overarching theme of a hotel and have become integral to the marketing of a property. The boutique Claris Hotel in Barcelona displays on the lobby mezzanine the hotel owner's private collection of Greek and Roman antiquities; the guestroom art program features additional ancient artifacts placed in carefully lighted niches which are a dramatic contrast with the hotel's strikingly original and very contem-

Fine art as landmark décor **The Ritz-Carlton, San Francisco, California.** Creatively reconstructed within the 1909 former west coast headquarters for Metropolitan Life Insurance, The Ritz-Carlton publicly displays its private collection of fine art, oriental rugs, antiques and artifacts, enhancing the total guest experience at the landmark building.

Art exhibitions as lobby décor **Chambers, New York.** The new West-Side hotel celebrates the surrounding arts community talent by incorporating a system within its lobby to display artwork.

The soft touch in design **Uniforms.** Staff uniforms are among the important design accessories which must be fully coordinated with the market concept, architecture, and interior design of the hotel. Larger hotels and resorts may require over 50 different uniform styles to help unify and reinforce theming (Angelica Image Apparel).

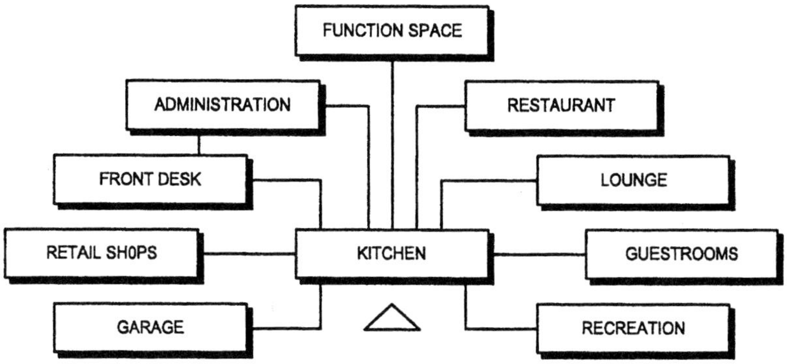

LOBBY SCHEMATIC

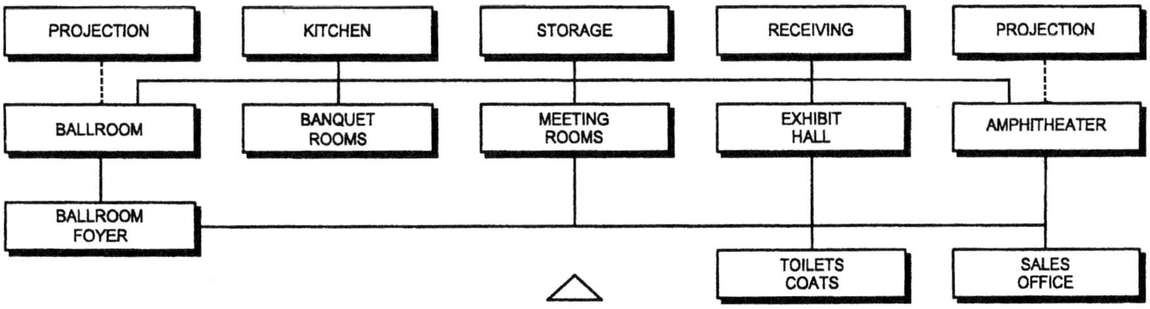

FUNCTION SPACE SCHEMATIC

Assuring the image **Lobby and function space schematics.** The lobby diagram illustrates the principal objective that designers should locate the public facilities close to and visible from the main lobby. Many problems in the hotel planning are resolved when guests can find their way easily around the public areas. The second diagram illustrates the sparate public and back-of-house circulation to the many types of function rooms.

porary interiors. Drawing from the neighborhood context of New York City's many fine art galleries along 57th Street and Fifth Avenue, the boutique Chambers hotel features *Art Walls* in its public space. The entire hotel theme is expressed by the paintings, prints, and etchings set in a custom system of horizontal tracks of blackened steel that exhibits constantly changing artwork.

The designer may need to consider how the art will be installed in order to prepare the space. Even small and mid-size pieces require structural support, lighting, security, water, or other preparation:

- *sculpture*: an additional structural support (floor or ceiling) and coordinate accent lighting
- *water feature*: provide an additional structural support, plumbing connections, and power for underwater lighting
- *paintings and mirror*: provide a blocking inside walls for support and power connections to security systems; coordinate accent lighting.

New uses for art are everywhere. In addition to incorporating a museum within the property as an amenity or celebrating art through changing exhibitions, designers have used over-scaled art as headboards and museum postcards as guestroom art. Today, we find art even in elevators, restrooms, exercise rooms, and parking garages. A growing number of cities require the developer to invest one percent of the construction cost in public art. This has resulted in the commissioning of major exterior sculptures for the hotel's arrival courtyard to large-scale murals, water features, or other art for the hotel lobby.

The welcoming interface **Park Hyatt Johannesburg, South Africa.** Each management and service function contributes to the guest's positive reaction to the hotel. In this luxury property staff work behind a traditionally styled front desk, under part of the hotel's extensive collection of native art and artifacts, helping to establish a 'sense of place.'

Administration and Back-of-house Design 18

The planning and design of the administration offices and other back-of-house or service areas of the hotel, most of which the hotel guest rarely sees, are equally critical to the eventual success of the hotel. Generally comprising between about 10 and 15 percent of the total floor area in all lodging types—somewhat less in motels and budget inns, the organization of the offices and service areas greatly influences the staff's ability to meet overall administrative needs and to provide efficient food and beverage, housekeeping, repair, and engineering services to the hotel. The main functional areas include the following:

- administration offices
- food preparation and storage areas
- receiving, trash, and general storage areas
- employee areas
- laundry and housekeeping areas
- engineering and mechanical areas.

These spaces vary considerably from property to property, depending on the type of hotel or resort and on its size and location. Larger hotels and resorts have extensive administrative staffs and require substantial office suites to accommodate the complex office functions whereas small properties may be run out of little more than a single office. Resorts in remote areas may need to provide their own engineering services, including electricity and fresh water, as well as employee housing. In contrast, motels that don't include a restaurant or meeting space need only limited service areas—no more than sufficient storage for guestroom linen, operating supplies, and maintenance equipment.

It is essential not only to provide adequate back-of-house areas but also to plan them appropriately so that staff, for example, can reach all areas of the hotel without passing through the lobby and other public spaces. Basic planning objectives include clustering the major service functions around the receiving area and employee entrance or along a major service corridor, and grouping the food outlets close to the kitchen or at satellite pantries, where required. The following sections discuss the operational characteristics and planning and design criteria for each area.

Administration Offices

The effective layout of the front desk and administration offices influences the guest's impression of the hotel. While all guests have contact with the front desk, many other visitors each day meet with the sales and catering staff or with assistant managers. Therefore, the proper planning, design, and equipping of the hotel's office space deserves no less attention than that given to the guestrooms and public areas. The planning and interior design of the workplace and its equipment are essential not only to the morale and productivity of the staff but also to the public's perception of the quality of the hotel.

The offices areas generally are divided into four clusters (other office components, such as the human resources and purchasing functions, typically are placed in the back-of-house close to related service areas):

- front desk and front office
- executive office
- sales and catering office
- accounting office.

While there are substantial advantages—shared reception and support areas, closer communication among the staff, and better visibility to the guest—in having offices located together, most hotels of over a few hundred rooms separate the administrative offices into two or three clusters. This is done, in part, in order to locate the sales and catering offices near the ballroom and other function space. More than anything else, though, such arrangements should not be the result of unclear programming and hastily conceived schematic designs. Often, space near the front desk that initially was designated for offices must be reallocated for other support functions that had not been sufficiently recognized in the program and early design phases. Where office suites are located on separate levels the architect should consider adding a dedicated stairway connecting the floors.

Front Desk and Front Office

The front office, which supports the guest registration and cashier functions at the front desk, is the largest of the four clusters and the one with which the casual guest is most familiar. The key elements in terms of layout are the front desk itself and the work area behind it, around which most of the other offices are clustered. It includes the following areas:

- *Front desk*: provide dual-function registration and cashier stations.
- *Front office work area (includes mail, copy, fax, etc.)*: provide work area immediately adjacent to the front desk, with built-in work counter and files.
- *Front office manager*: provide private office convenient to the work area.
- *Reservations and telephone*: provide space with counter work area and acoustic partitions for telephone operators and reservations staff, convenient to the front desk; include security and alarm monitoring systems. In large hotels reservations and telephone are usually separate functions.
- *Reservations manager*: provide semi-private office adjoining reservations work area.

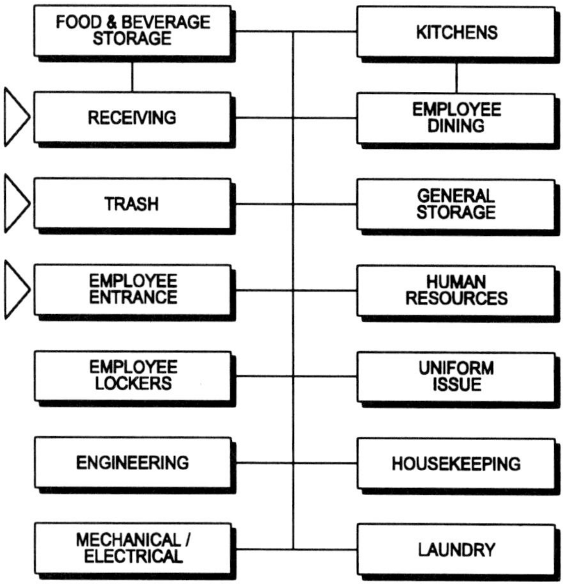

The hotel's hidden heart **Back-of-house schematic.** The organization of the service functions is critical to the efficient planning and staffing of the hotel. Key is to arrange the back-of-house into several clusters, organized along a wide spine or service corridor, with easy access to the receiving area and to service and freight elevators.

- *Safe deposit area*: provide secure space with safe deposit boxes and, adjoining, a small guest view room with counter and chair.
- *Counting room*: provide secure space where F&B outlet and retail managers count receipts and place the deposit in a drop-safe or pass directly to cashier.
- *Fire control room*: provide space next to front entrance with dedicated alarm panels for use by the fire and police in responding to fire and other emergency situations.
- *Support functions*: provide for such accessory needs as toilets, storage, coats, and pantry.

In smaller hotels, where employees may be cross-trained to perform a variety of duties, such functions as telephone and reservations need to be convenient to the front desk because on the night shift only one person may be on duty. Increasing payroll costs in all types of hotels and resorts have made it more important for management to rethink how they staff departments. Smaller hotels, for example, may locate a modest sundries shop immediately adjacent to the reception area so that the desk clerk can double as the shop cashier. Also, instead of locating a business center at some distance from the lobby, and needing to staff it throughout the day, companies

Table 18.1 Front office planning

Program

Provide 3 to 5 ft^2 (0.3 to 0.5 m^2) per guestroom for the front desk and related front office functions

Allow 6 linear feet (1.8 m) per workstation; provide two stations for the first 150 rooms plus additional ones for each 100 rooms

Planning

Locate the desk so that it is visible from the entrance

Locate the desk in sight of the guest elevators

Position the luggage storage and bellman near the desk

Provide fire control room near the front desk or main hotel entrance

Position the front desk plan where it is not constrained by structural columns

Plan the front office so that both reservations and telephone operators are near the guest registration area

Place the safe deposit room so that a cashier can handle guest requests

Design

Design the front desk so that the cashier and registration functions can be staffed flexibly

Screen guests' views into office work areas

Recognize requirements for support functions: house phones, brochure display, concierge or assistant manager, and bell station close to front desk

Provide decorative focus at the desk: counter material, lighting, treatment of backwall, and signage

(A)

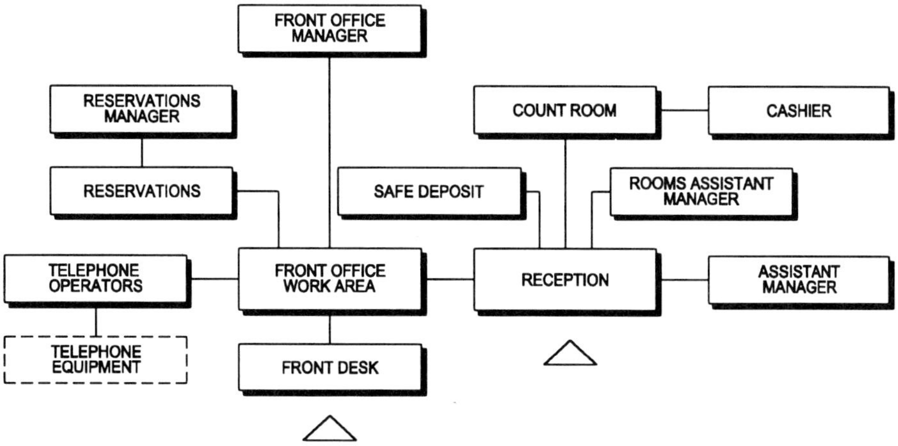

FRONT OFFICE SCHEMATIC

(B)

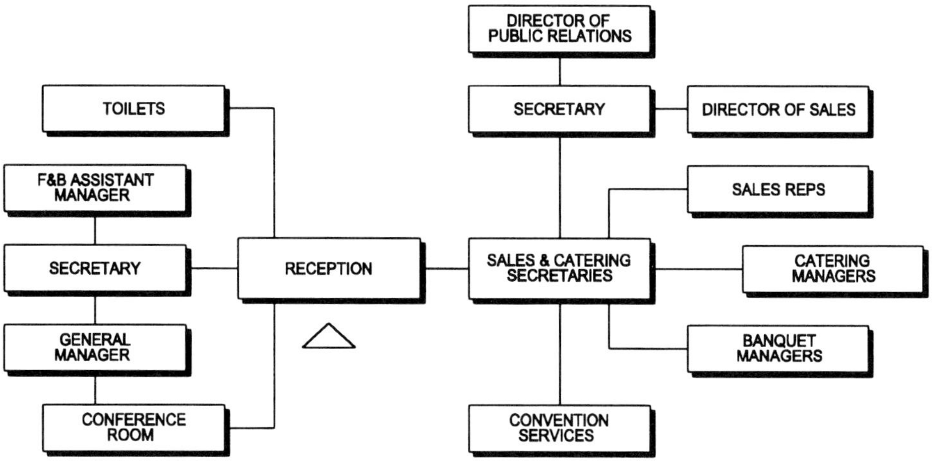

EXECUTIVE AND SALES OFFICE SCHEMATIC

(C)

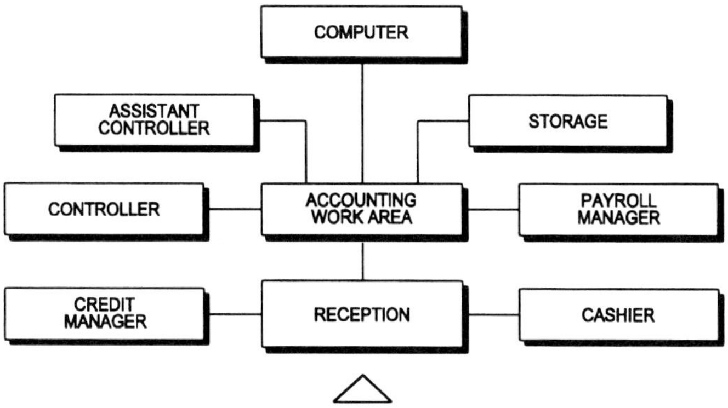

ACCOUNTING OFFICE SCHEMATIC

The efficient details **Administration office schematics.** (A) Front office schematic, (B) executive and sales office schematic, (C) accounting office schematic. Hotel administration offices are organized in four clusters, often separated by some distance, one related to the front desk and the registration and check-out processes, two others for the general manager and sales activities, which often are combined, and the last for the accounting function.

increasingly place it next to the front desk, enabling further sharing of staff duties.

In planning the front desk, as with many other areas in the hotel, collaboration among the members of the design team is necessary. One, the architect establishes the general location of the desk and the offices; two, the interior designer may modify the details of the plan for design or functional reasons and propose a series of finishes and lighting; three, the technical staff from the management company specifies and places the computers and other equipment in the workspace.

Executive Office

The executive office is the smallest of the four administration clusters. In smaller hotels, the operator may choose to combine it with the front office, the general manager assuming the duties of rooms division manager. In larger hotels, the executive office includes the following:

- *Reception area*: provide reception/waiting area for visitors; include receptionist desk, visitor seating, and appropriate display.
- *General manager*: provide large private office for the GM, appropriate to the size of the hotel.
- *Executive assistant managers*: provide private offices for the senior staff, including the resident manager, food and beverage director, marketing director, etc.
- *Secretary*: include space for one or more administrative assistants with necessary support functions (copying, fax, etc.).
- *Conference room*: include private conference room for 8–12 people for use by the senior staff or for meetings with visitors; include small pantry for coffee/refreshment service.
- *Support functions*: provide space for toilets, coats, coffee area, etc.

The general manager in large hotels may be highly visible, greeting dignitaries and hosting special visitors. Thus, his office and conference area may begin to resemble public reception and lounge areas. Where this is the case, the offices need to be larger and should be located where guests can readily find them and where security can be assured. Some senior managers prefer that their office is located near the receptionist, whereas others insist on it being more remote, even on another level, away from the distractions of the office routine. The resident and food and beverage managers, who share in policy decisions, usually are clustered with the general manager rather than with their respective departments.

Sales and Catering Office

The third group, the sales and catering office, is responsible for attracting conventions and group business and for servicing the meetings and banquets once they are in the hotel. The sales and catering staff deal with many outside visitors and the offices should be designed to present the best public image of the hotel. The cluster includes the following:

- *Reception:* provide separate reception/greeting function or combine with executive office reception.
- *Director of sales:* provide large private office.
- *Sales representatives:* provide semi-private cubicles for additional sales staff adjacent to files and work counter.
- *Catering manager:* provide private office for staff person responsible for arranging details of banquet functions.
- *Banquet manager:* provide small office for supervisor of banquet staff; this may be located in back-of-house.
- *Convention services manager:* provide private office for person who serves as liaison for all non-banquet functions; this may be combined with 'conference concierge' service in larger convention properties or conference centers.
- *Conference room:* provide dedicated conference room (may be combined with executive office) for sales and catering meetings.
- *Secretary:* provide space for several administrative assistants for the senior staff and for all sales, catering, and banquet representatives.
- *Support functions:* provide necessary space to accommodate usual support functions.

Since the sales staff show prospective guests the available meeting and banquet facilities, the office suite frequently is located near the function area rather than off the lobby. As with the other clusters, the most common arrangement is to group the private offices around a secretarial work area. The sales and catering office becomes fairly large in convention and other properties that cater extensively to group rather than individual guests. The space requirements, which vary depending on the type of hotel, usually fall between 2 and 4 ft^2 (0.2–0.4 m^2) per guestroom.

Accounting Office

The accounting office, while best located as part of the main complex near the front desk, can operate satisfactorily at some distance. Its main connection to the front office is the need to coordinate the counting room and general cashier functions.

The accounting cluster includes the following requirements:

- *Controller:* provide private office for the hotel's senior financial officer.
- *Assistant controller/auditor:* provide a semi-private office for the assistant controller who is the day-to-day manager of the accounting activities.
- *Cashier:* provide secure room with pass-through window similar to bank teller; provide large floor safe and alarm system.
- *Accounting staff offices:* provide work areas for payroll, accounts receivable, and accounts payable managers.
- *Accounting work area:* provide cubicle workspace for accounting secretary and any additional staff, depending on the size of the hotel. Include work counter with files and space for copying, fax, etc.
- *Other: toilets, storage, pantry:* provide for accessory functions, especially if the accounting area is remote from other office suites.

The layout of the accounting area is not complicated by special operating requirements or technical equipment other than the standard office computer systems. The architect should allocate approximately 3 ft^2 (0.3 m^2) per room for the accounting offices.

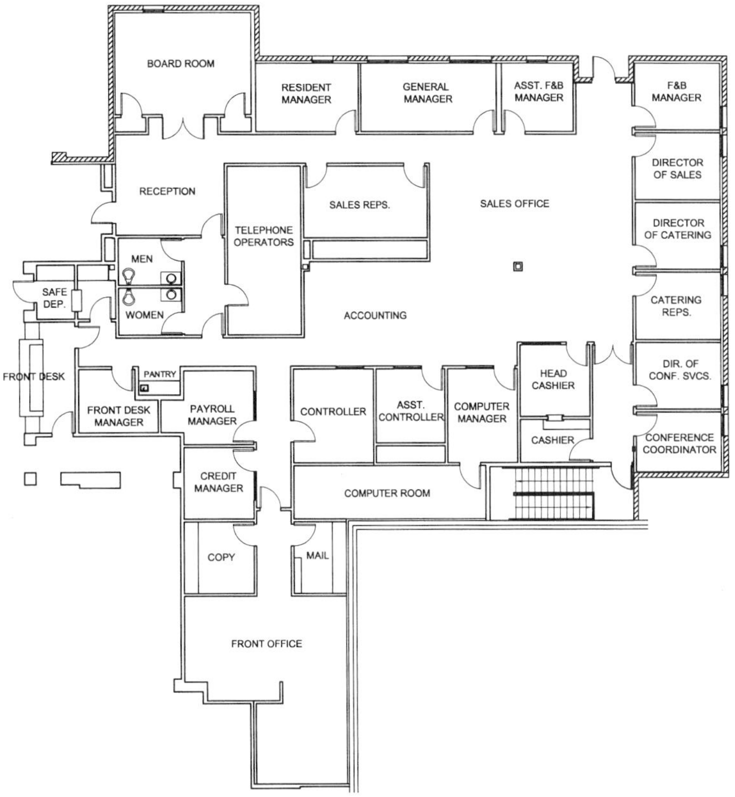

The bunker **Administration office plan.** The office plan illustrates how the discrete functions may be separated. Here front office, accounting, and executive and sales offices each occupies their own office cluster (Four Seasons Resort Scottsdale).

Food Preparation and Storage Areas

Of all the service areas in a hotel, the kitchens and related food preparation areas require the most design attention, in part because of the integration of the mechanical, electrical, and plumbing systems with the layout of the kitchen equipment. More important, though, the design of the kitchen and related areas critically influences labor costs for the life of the building. The design team must plan the kitchens so that all food-related activities are located close together, distances between the kitchen and the several outlets are as short as possible, and the individual layouts are flexible in order to accommodate changes in the future. Therefore, the planning and design aspects of the kitchens require the coordinated attention of a variety of specialized kitchen and engineering consultants.

Program and Planning Objectives

The amount of floor space required in the kitchen and food and beverage storage areas depends on the number of meals served, the complexity of the menu, and the delivery schedule. One goal, because of the high cost of equipment, energy, and labor, should be to design the smallest kitchen that meets the operational objectives. For example, many downtown hotels, where space is at a premium because of high land costs and where most foods are readily available, operate with a minimum food storage area. Yet, while some small kitchens function well because of close proximity of these elements, the layout of larger hotels must compensate for the separation of storage, preparation, cooking, serving, and washing areas.

Rules-of-thumb for space allocation vary depending on the quality level of the hotel. However, a typical starting point is to base the kitchen size on the number of restaurant and banquet seats and hotel guestrooms and to refine it as the food and beverage concepts are better defined. The accuracy of these rules-of-thumb is affected by the size of the hotel; smaller hotels (fewer than 200 rooms) and satellite restaurant pantries require a larger allocation per seat in order to equip even a minimum kitchen. Food preparation areas for representative types of hotels are included in the sample space programs in Chapter 22. Table 18.2 provides the initial space

Table 18.2 Kitchen planning

Program (kitchen)	Design
6 ft^2 (0.6 m^2)/restaurant seat 2 ft^2 (0.2 m^2)/ballroom and banquet seat 1 ft^2 (0.1 m^2)/lounge seat 1 ft^2 (0.1 m^2)/hotel guestroom **Program (F&B storage)** 30–50% of main kitchen area **Planning** Provide straight-line flow of food from storage to serving; eliminate cross-traffic and backtracking Minimize distance between kitchen serving area and restaurant seating Arrange compact work centers Locate secondary storage near each station, as required Place shared facilities centrally Plan for the efficient use of utilities Group all walk-in refrigerators and freezers together to share common walls and compressors	Provide automatic fire protection systems throughout, especially over cooking equipment Provide the minimum of heat-generating equipment Locate the soiled dish drop-off immediately inside the doors from each restaurant, feeding a single dishwashing area Provide service vestibules between the kitchen and all outlets, banquet pantry and ballroom; baffles between service corridors and banquet rooms Depress floor slabs for refrigerated storage so that the refrigerator floor is even with the kitchen floor Consider sanitation and employee safety Provide for security at the kitchen service bar Plan aisles at a minimum of 3.5 ft (1.05 m)

requirements for hotel kitchens and lists overall planning and design objectives.

Among the many planning requirements that the architect should address during conceptual design, the most important is to locate the receiving area, food storage, kitchen, and all outlets (restaurants and banquet areas) on a single floor. When this goal is not possible, usually the case in downtown hotels and other properties over 400 rooms, the designer must assess the relative merits of alternate groupings of service and public functions. Table 18.3 identifies the critical adjacencies in the food-service areas.

Main Kitchen

Once the kitchen area program is established and the architect has established its location and general plan in the schematic design phase, the food service consultant tests the appropriateness of the space and proposes a preliminary equipment layout. If major planning criteria are met, such as providing a single main kitchen close to the restaurants and function outlets, the overall design is greatly simplified and the duplication of equipment eliminated. While the food-facilities consultant is responsible for preparing the detailed kitchen plan, the architect must understand in general the flow of food and personnel through the kitchen and related support areas. Table 18.4 identifies the individual kitchen areas that must be integrated into a workable layout, and includes the area breakdown of F&B storage areas.

Table 18.3 Food-service adjacencies

Essential
Food storage to main kitchen
Main kitchen to restaurants
Room service area to service elevators
Banquet pantry to ballroom
Desirable
Receiving to food storage
Main kitchen to banquet pantry
Banquet pantry to smaller banquet rooms
Banquet pantry to prefunction area
Coffee shop pantry to room service area
Kitchen to cocktail lounges
Kitchen to garbage/trash holding
Kitchen to employee dining

The kitchen planner usually approaches the design in two opposing ways: one, to locate each department (such as the bakery or the dishwashing area) within the larger kitchen space and, two, to develop each work station by selecting and arranging the specific pieces of equipment. The food service consultant also must incorporate a wide range of details—some mechanical, electrical, or plumbing; some related to precise dimensions; others to particular finishes or features of the kitchen space—coordinating them with the architect so that the kitchen can accommodate the equipment as designed and specified.

F&B Storage Areas

The food and beverage storage areas in most cases are located adjacent either to the receiving area or to the kitchen, the latter being preferable. The storage

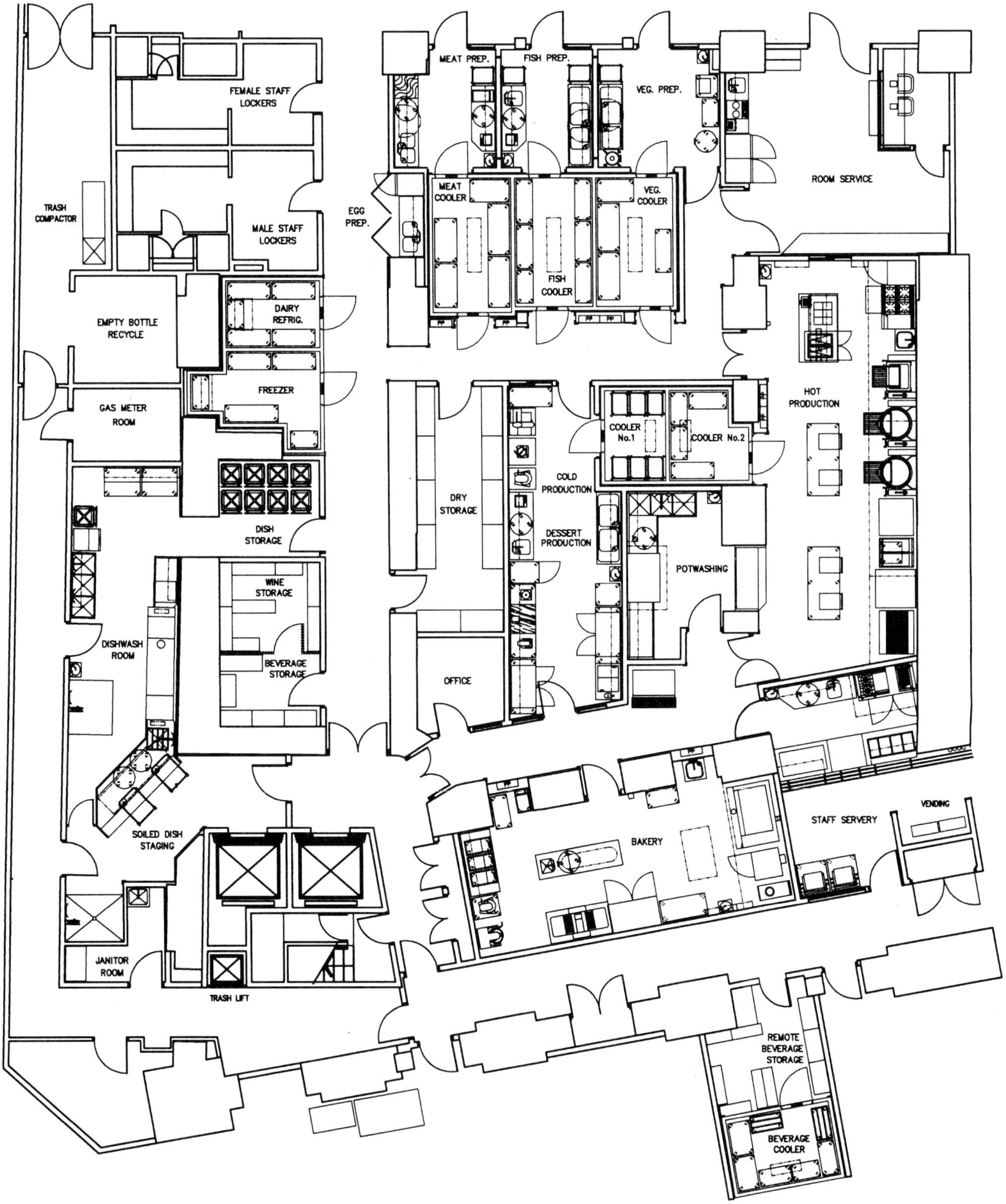

An appetizer **Kitchen plan.** The food-service operations are among the most difficult to coordinate, combining major technical requirements for cooking, refrigeration, and ventilation with functional needs for efficient service flow. The plan shows how many hotel kitchens are divided into such discrete work areas as storage, hot production, cold production, room service, and dishwashing (Four Seasons Hotel, Budapest).

Table 18.4 Kitchen checklist

Receiving and storage	
Dry food storage, 30%	
Refrigerated food storage, 25%	
Frozen food storage, 10%	
Beverage storage, 15%	
Refrigerated beverage storage, 5%	
Nonfood storage (china, silver, paper), 15%	
Preparation areas	
Butcher shop	
Bake shop	
Vegetable preparation area	
Meat preparation area	
Salad and dessert preparation area	
Cooking areas	
Restaurant cooking line	
Banquet cooking line	
Short order cooking line	
Sanitation	
Dishwashing	
Potwashing	
Garbage and trash removal	
Serving areas	
Restaurant(s) pickup	
Banquet pickup	
Room service area	
Other	
Chef's office	
Service bar	
Staff toilets	

and control requirements for hotels require that supervision and security be available at all times. A key feature in planning kitchen storage areas is to cluster all the refrigerated storage together. Walk-in refrigerators and freezers require a depressed floor slab (to accommodate floor insulation) and share common insulated walls and a compressor system, best located slightly away from the storage. The closely grouped storage areas are clearly designated in the accompanying kitchen plan.

Receiving, Trash, and General Storage Areas

The hotel's receiving and trash areas, while sharing the loading dock, require clear separation of incoming and outgoing goods. Only in smaller hotels and motels are the two functions actually combined into a single area. The receiving area connects directly to the main back-of-house corridor and, eventually, to each major service area. In some properties the receiving area is immediately adjacent to the kitchen. This is a great boon to the F&B department but may necessitate an unusually long route to move goods to the laundry, housekeeping, maintenance, or general storage areas. The security of any incoming items is controlled at the receiving dock.

Equally important to the layout of the receiving and trash area is its integration with the site plan so that it accommodates the necessary movement of trucks without disrupting guest parking, yet is hidden from the hotel guestrooms and such public areas as restaurants, lounges, and recreational areas. An otherwise well-designed hotel can be severely downgraded by the poor location of its receiving and trash areas. The overall planning requirements are listed in Table 18.5.

The receiving and trash areas require between 2 and 3 ft^2 (0.2 and 0.3 m^2) per guestroom, but the size of the area is determined only in part by the number of guestrooms. More important is the relative amount of restaurant, lounge, and function space—reflecting the volume of food and beverage operations—and the quality level of the hotel.

Hotels require considerable amounts of storage area. Most of this space is associated with specific activities: food storage near the kitchen, function storage near the ballroom and banquet rooms, linen storage on each floor and with housekeeping, and records storage close to administration offices. However, in addition, two categories of storage often are

Table 18.5 Receiving and trash area planning

Receiving
Provide an elevated loading dock large enough to accommodate two trucks at one time (three trucks if 400 rooms); provide roof overhead; confirm size of trucks and height clearance
Provide enclosed receiving area for inspection and temporary holding of incoming goods
Include windows between the loading dock, receiving area, and receiving office
Arrange access to the area to avoid cross-traffic between incoming goods and outgoing items
Trash, garbage, and holding area
Separate the trash/garbage holding area from receiving and provide space for one vehicle
Provide refrigerated area for garbage and a space for can washing, if needed
Enclose compactor area, yet allow staff accessibility at all times
Provide adequate space for storage and recycling of paper, cardboard, glass, and other items
Provide additional space for temporary holding of soiled and clean linen if the hotel uses an outside laundry service

(A)

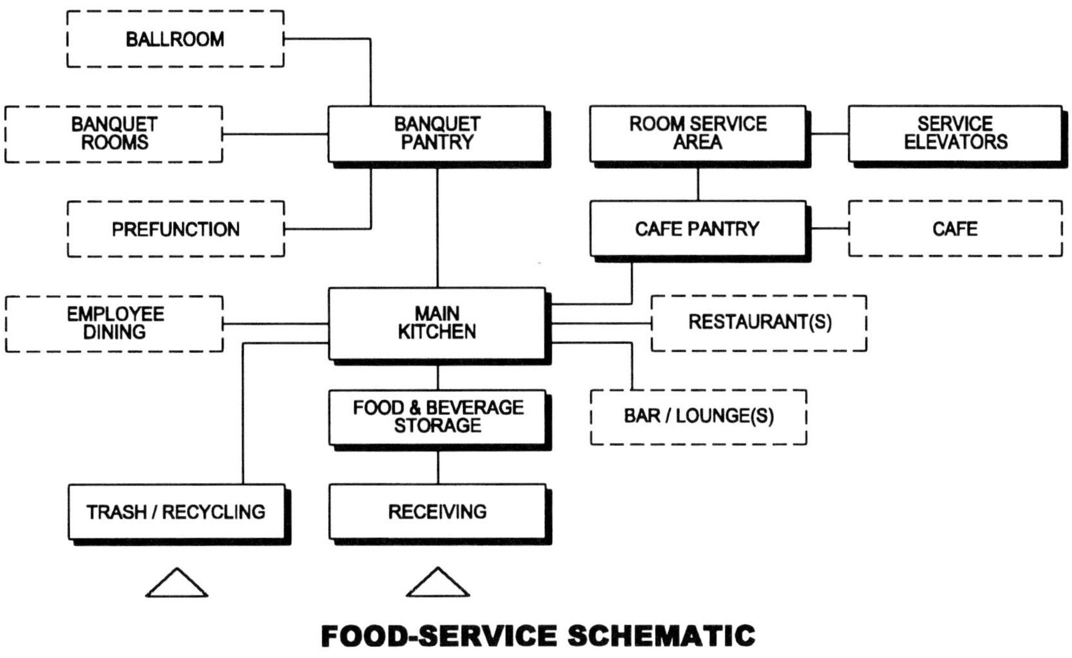

(B)

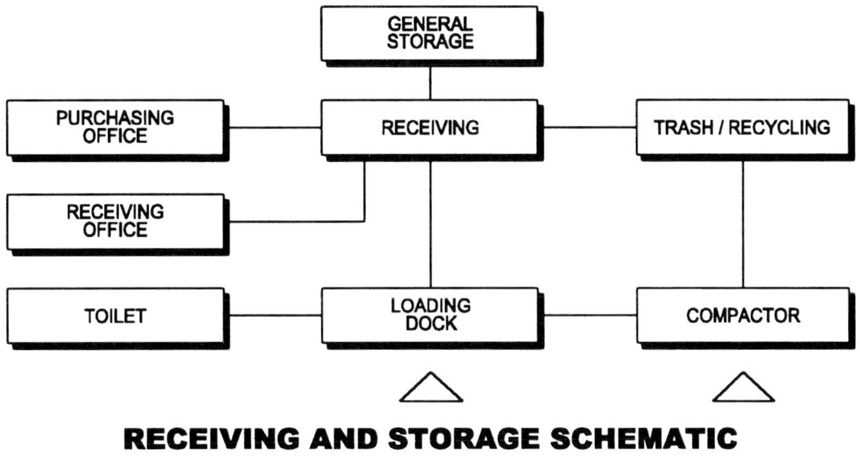

The efficient flow **Back-of-house schematics.** (A) Food-service schematic, (B) receiving and storage schematic. The food production areas are closely related to receiving and storage. While they may be somewhat separated, even on different levels, providing a direct connection between the two is a key planning requirement.

located near the receiving area: outdoors equipment and general storage. The first, generally requiring a few hundred square feet (except in resorts), is for building and grounds maintenance equipment and outdoor furniture. The second, often occupying an area as large as the entire receiving and trash area, is for extra furnishings and equipment, archived financial records, printed material, and various unassigned items.

While they must be near receiving, these storage areas have different requirements. Often omitted from the program, space for outdoor equipment such as for lawn care or snow removal should be located at grade level. The general storage area needs to be secure, perhaps comprising several distinct areas separated by wire fences, so that different operating departments control particular sections of the room. Although the general storage area is necessary for a variety of miscellaneous items, it does not replace the need for adequate storage at each of the back-of-house functions discussed previously.

Employee Areas

The staff areas form a third major part of the hotel's back-of-house areas. While in smaller and economy properties these areas may be limited, adequate space for the hotel staff is essential to a full-service hotel. (In a few cases, primarily resorts and overseas hotels, the developer may even include large-scale staff housing.) The usual components—personnel offices, men's and women's lockers, and employee dining—are somewhat independent from each other and relate to other back-of-house areas as much as they do to each other. For example, the personnel function is related closely to the employee entrance, the lockers to the uniform issue area and to the timekeeper, and the employee cafeteria to the main kitchen. The adjacency requirements are described in the accompanying schematic diagram.

The area requirements total between 6 and 10 ft^2 (0.55 and 0.9 m^2) per room. Security, circulation, and equipment requirements for the employee areas are less rigid than for other back-of-house functions, allowing greater flexibility in their location within the service block. The architect, nevertheless, must incorporate important operational features into the planning and design of the employee areas (see Table 18.6).

Many major hotel chains require that their general manager live in the hotel. Often, this unit is the equivalent of a five-bay suite, including a two-bay living room, one-bay dining room and kitchen, and two bedrooms. In destination and some highly seasonal resorts, as well as hotels in many developing regions, where no community is close enough to provide housing for the full staff, hotel developers must build their own employee housing. For example, in much of the Middle East, where virtually all hotel employees are from other countries, the developer must construct a major housing complex—effectively a second hotel. While entailing substantial capital cost, such housing complexes can be justified in terms of lower payroll costs and such operating advantages as reduced absenteeism, lower turnover, and greater employee productivity and promptness. It may be necessary, in Muslim and some other countries, to provide prayer rooms or other accommodation for religious practice.

Laundry and Housekeeping

The laundry and housekeeping areas create the fourth key element of the service facilities of a major hotel. Even the smallest roadside property provides some space for storage and control of guestroom linen. In larger hotels the amount of space required for linen storage is substantial and, in addition, most developers invest in a full in-house commercial laundry. This is different from smaller properties, say up to 150 rooms, where a recurring question is whether or not to include an in-house laundry. In small inns, the cost to build and equip the laundry, plus its ongoing operating expenses, causes many operators to either rent linen or send the hotel's laundry to a commercial service. On the other hand, virtually all mid-price and better hotels operate their own laundry in order to control quality and assure the availability of linens—as well as to reduce overall laundry expense.

The laundry and housekeeping areas are closely related and should be adjacent, even though they are managed separately. But when the laundry space is omitted, extensive areas still are required for collecting and loading soiled laundry and receiving and storing clean linen. The main function,

Table 18.6 Employee area planning

Human resources office
Provide office suite for HR director, assistant director, and administrative support with sufficient space for job applicants
Include additional private office for interviewing and counseling employees.
Provide a training room for staff meetings and education
Provide small first aid room

Employee entrance, timekeeper, and security
Provide employee entrance separate from receiving area
Locate timekeeper and security office immediately inside the employee entrance with visual control of the main service corridor

Employee lockers and toilets
Provide separate facilities sized according to the staff program and shift schedules; estimate staffing at 60% male, 40% female unless local experience differs
Consider separate lockers for banquet staff
Plan separate access to toilets without passing through lockers

Employee dining
Plan cafeteria near kitchen or, if on different floor, near employee locker rooms
Design cafeteria to contain service line, seating, and soiled-dish holding area; include snack vending machines
Provide sufficient capacity for peak periods; consider numbers at shift change

Employee housing/other
Provide manager's apartment as part of guestroom program
Where necessary, include two-bedroom apartments for senior management and one-bedroom apartments for junior staff; plan dormitory units for other employees
Provide appropriate commons areas such as recreation room, self-service laundry, pool, and lounges
Provide religious facilities in international locations where local custom dictates

(A)

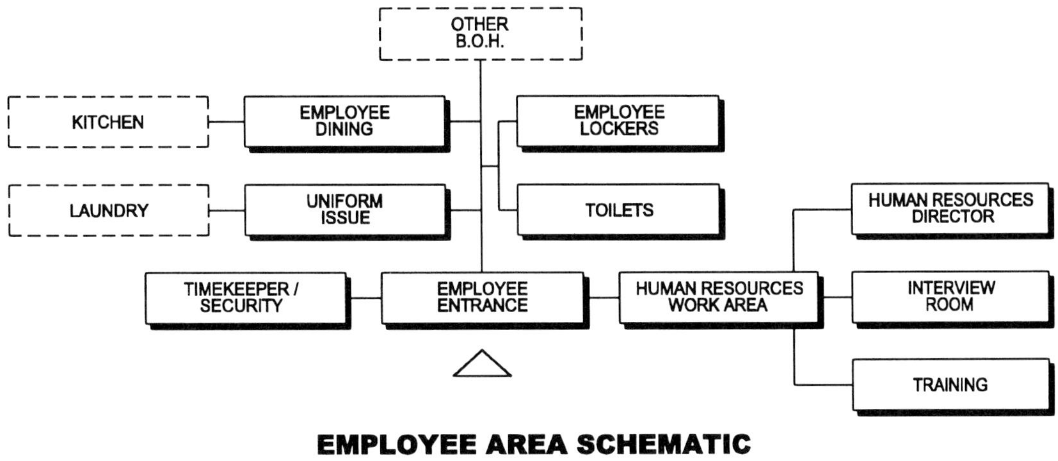

(B)

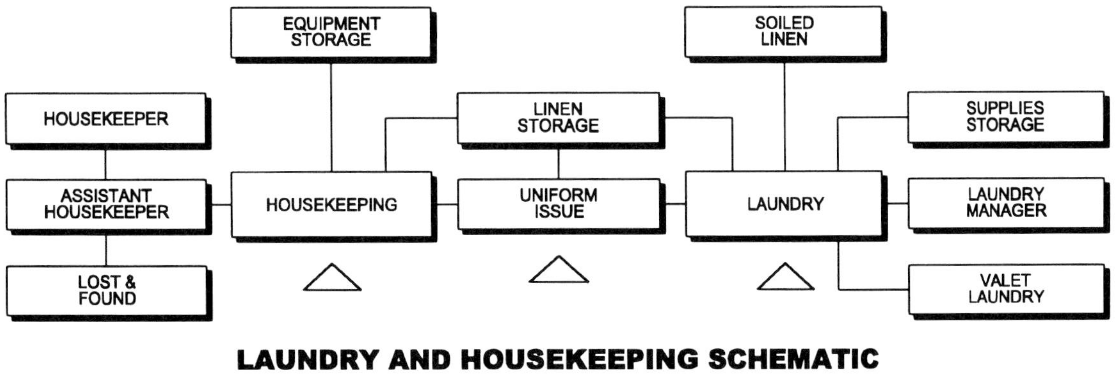

(C)

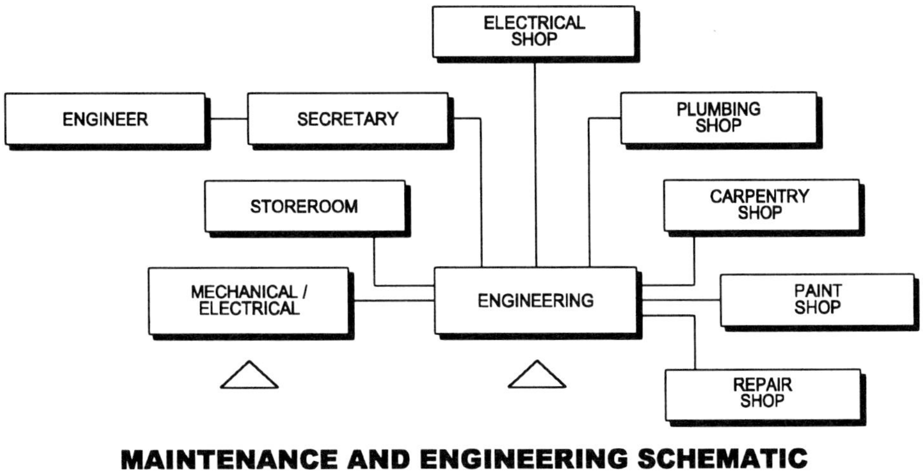

The effective service **Back-of-house schematics.** (A) Employee area schematic, (B) laundry and housekeeping schematic, (C) maintenance and engineering schematic. The efficient planning of these service areas is important to reducing staff numbers and payroll and providing a high level of guest service.

Legend

1 Receiving
2 Purchasing
3 Security
4 Human resources
5 Employee dining
6 Employee lockers
7 Laundry
8 Housekeeping
9 Engineering office
10 Mechanical and electrical
11 General storage
12 F&B storage
13 Bakery
14 Function storage
15 Administration offices

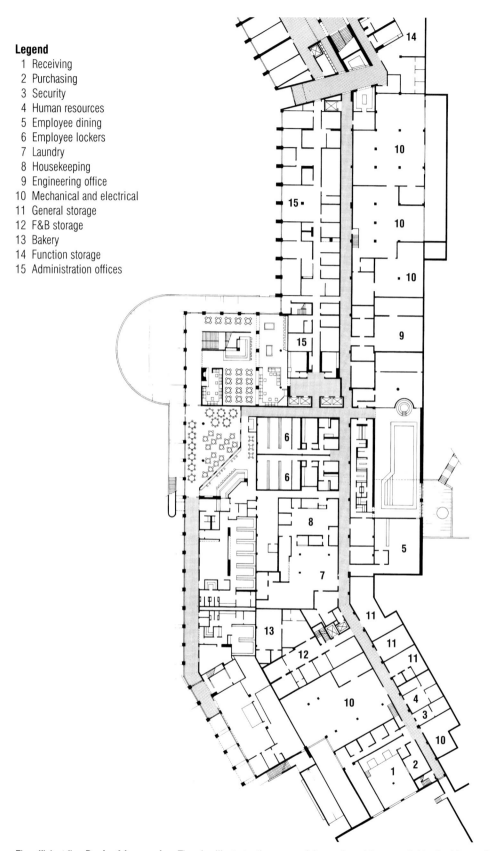

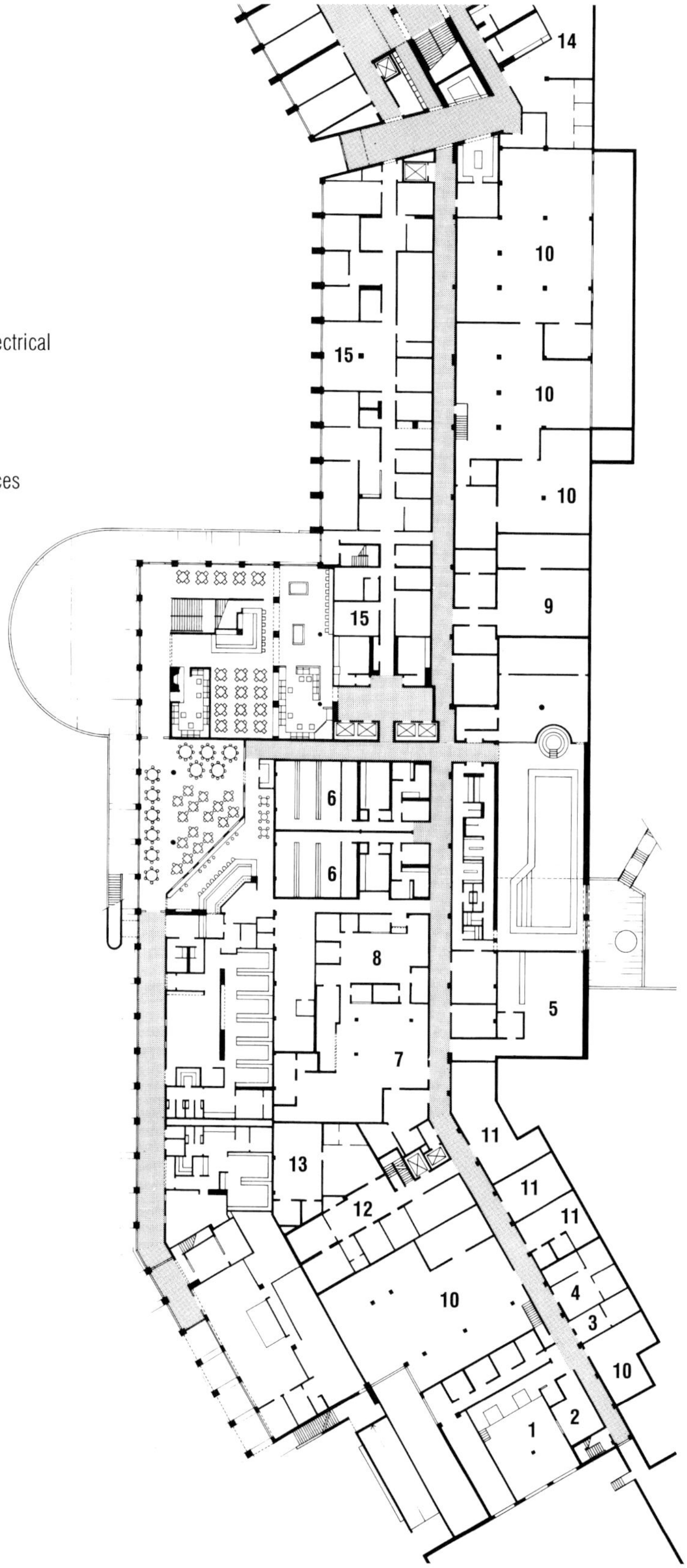

The efficient flow **Back-of-house plan.** The plan illustrates the successful grouping of the essential back-of-house functions as clusters of related activities, all accessible along a major service spine or corridor (Inverness Hotel and Golf Club, Denver).

of course, is to clean and distribute guestroom (bed and bath) linen, restaurant and banquet table linens, uniforms, kitchen linens, and guest clothing. Resort hotels may have additional laundry demands, such as for towels at the swimming pools. The laundry and housekeeping areas have key adjacency requirements, related to servicing the guestrooms and providing staff uniforms and other linen.

The area requirements are fairly standard—from 10 to 14 ft^2 (0.9 to 1.3 m^2) per room—because the great majority of laundry demand is generated by the guestrooms. Two very different types of hotels, smaller roadside inns and larger transient business hotels (over 600 rooms), are at the low end of the range. On the other hand, resort hotels, properties with extensive food and beverage or function facilities, and first-class and luxury properties reach toward the high extreme. The necessary space is about equally divided between the laundry and housekeeping areas, including their respective support spaces.

The laundry layout often is designed by the technical services staff of the hotel management company or by a laundry design consultant, sometimes associated with a major commercial equipment manufacturer. The hotel laundry preferably should be located at the hotel's lowest floor to lessen the chance that noise and vibration from the laundry might interfere with any public or guestroom areas. Table 18.7 identifies the principal planning requirements for the two areas.

Engineering and Mechanical Areas

The final back-of-house area contains three related functions supervised by the hotel's chief engineer: engineering offices, repair and maintenance shops, and mechanical and electrical areas. Too often these activities are given insufficient space. While the architects and engineering consultants provide more than enough space in the mechanical and electrical areas, they may allocate only leftover space to the offices and shops.

The mechanical equipment areas do not need to be immediately adjacent to the other service areas, although they should be close to the laundry, kitchen, and other high-energy-use areas for most economical operation. In fact, the equipment rooms can be organized along a separate service corridor for better control and supervision. However, the maintenance and engineering function operates 24 hours a day and, therefore, must directly connect to back-of-house areas and to the service elevators. It should be convenient to the loading area in order to receive equipment and materials needed for engineering activities. The schematic plan shows the organization of the department with various repair and maintenance areas clustered around the offices.

The offices and shops require between 3 and 5 ft^2 (0.3 and 0.5 m^2) per room; the area requirements for the mechanical and electrical areas vary considerably, depending on such factors as climate, size of hotel, type of construction, orientation, and operational objectives. Most often the architect and engineers together determine the necessary space requirements for the building systems. Plans for the engineering spaces should accommodate the basic planning requirements identified in Table 18.8.

Table 18.7 Laundry and housekeeping planning

Laundry
Provide a linen chute including provisions for smoke control, venting, and locked access
Plan continuous flow of linen and uniforms through the laundry cycle
Consider energy conservation approaches such as heat recovery for all equipment
Provide dry-cleaning services in upscale and luxury hotels
Provided locked storage for laundry chemicals

Housekeeping
Locate offices where they visually control the laundry and housekeeping areas
Locate uniform issue area off main service corridor, convenient to locker rooms
Establish separate locked linen storage for particular departments, such as food and beverage or health club
Provide locked room for guestroom amenities; provide lost-and-found storage room
Create separate area for night shift to access cleaning equipment and supplies

Table 18.8 Engineering and mechanical area planning

Engineering offices
Locate the secretarial area to control all access to the shops and mechanical areas
Group engineer, assistants' offices, and record and drawing storage around central work area
Provide energy management computer room as required

Maintenance shops
Position the carpentry, upholstery, and paint shops adjacent to each other.
Provide exhaust system from paint shop (fumes) and carpentry shop (airborne sawdust)
Provide additional electrical service to all shops
Connect TV antenna system to television repair shop
Locate grounds maintenance space convenient to the outdoors

Mechanical, electrical, and plumbing equipment areas
Locate mechanical areas in high-ceiling space (16 ft or 5 m) where noise and vibration will not disturb guests or public activities
Provide secure rooms for telephone switch and for television antenna system and associated video/movie functions
Locate rooms where large equipment can be replaced reasonably easily

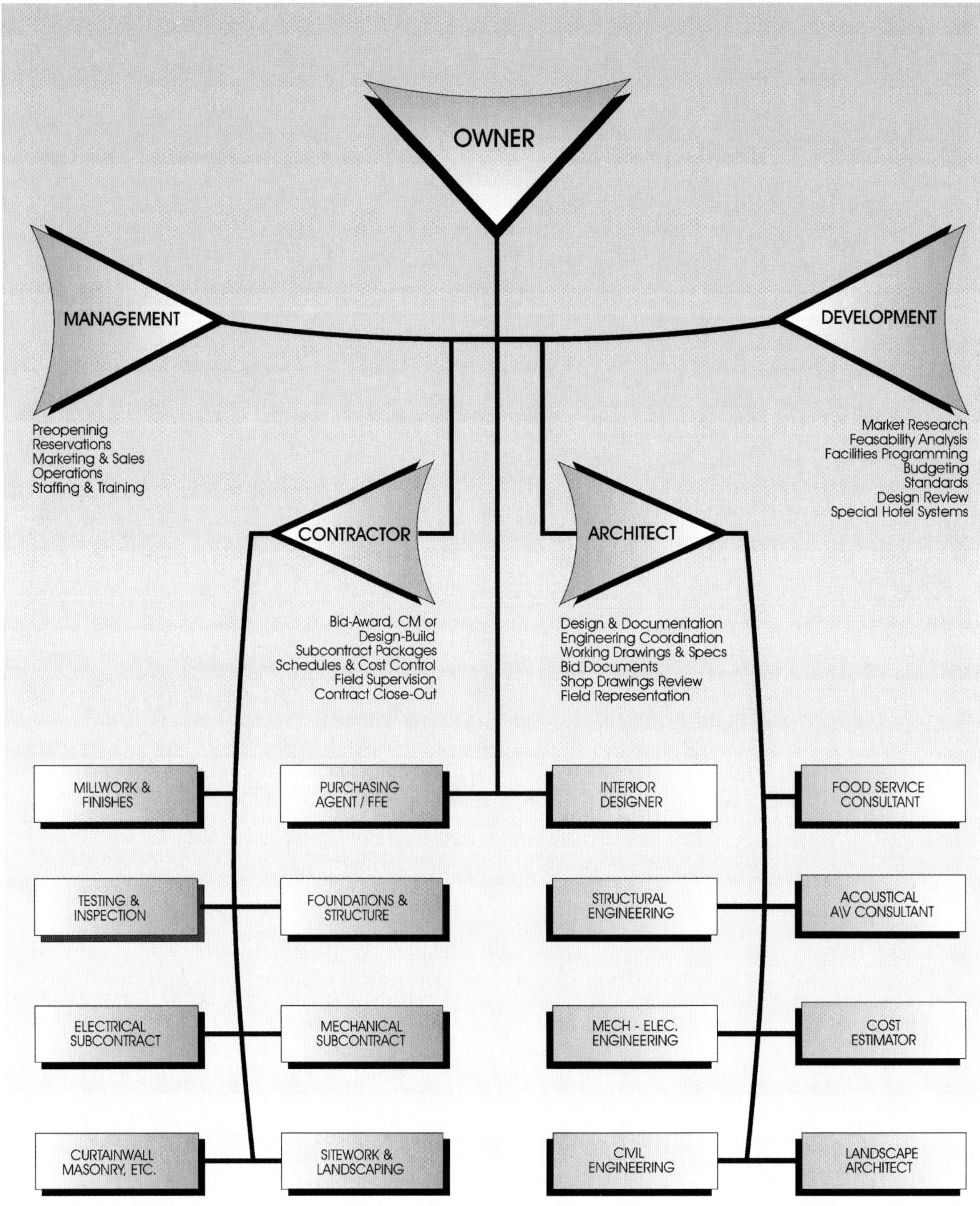

The coordination **Development Team Flow Chart.** This diagram delineates the essential disciplines required to create a successful hotel from the 'big idea' to welcoming the first guest.

Technical Coordination

19

The mid-point of the twentieth century marked the beginning of the most dramatic increase in worldwide education and mass travel in history. William B. Tabler and Richard E. Smith, two young architects at the famed Chicago firm of Holabird and Root, planned the first new group of hotels to be built in two decades of depression and war. They developed studies demonstrating that advanced technology would make hotels more viable. Thus began a new era for one of the most complex building types, led by pioneering hotel operators such as Statler-Hilton, the largest chain of its day, and Inter-Continental, the first major chain created by an airline (PanAm). A system of teamwork was developed at this time, between hotel companies, architects, interior designers, and consultants, which continues to flourish today (see Tables 19.1 and 19.2).

The process begins at the project level with the initial guidance by the developer and operator to ensure that the hotel will comply with the latest standards. To this end, hotel companies offer their technical data and assistance by providing specialized hotel information, design, review and new prototype concepts, if desired. As market strategies are developed, feedback from the operator is essential in areas ranging from trend research to detailed space requirements, special hotel systems, food and beverage service requirements, and typical layouts of back-of-house and other areas. As hotel operators have an important stake in the project's success, they participate in the design process.

A developer compared the coordination required on major hotel projects to other building types as follows: 'it is like developing apartments, offices, and a mall, rolled into one, with all the tenant trimmings.' The procedures outlined below are intended to maximize efficiency on such major complex developments, based on their applicability to the requirements of the specific project. To this end, the key consultants and a synopsis of their typical agreements, containing special hotel provisions, are discussed in this chapter. For example, one of the main procedures on hotel projects is to organize the consulting agreements so that:

- all necessary services are covered
- duplication and overlapping of responsibilities is avoided
- primary cost responsibility for each budgeted item is assigned by mutual agreement.

Methods of organization vary with the size and complexity of the project, required schedule, and construction contract system selected (see Table 21.1) as well as existing procedures of the various team members.

Types of Professional Services Agreements

Hotels include more consultants than most building types because of the variety of special operational and technical requirements (e.g. kitchens, laundry, audiovisual, water features, etc.) that are a part of most lodging. Among the first contracts the owner signs, before the architect or interior designer or construction agreements, is the technical services agreement with the future hotel operator, who provides continuing advice and input throughout the planning and construction phases. The types of agreement discussed in this book are not intended to provide legal advice and no such material should be used without consultation with an attorney

Technical Services Agreement

Through technical services agreements, hotel companies provide such additional design information and guidance as agreed including, facilities and area programs (number, size, and type of guestrooms and suites; seating capacities for food, beverage, banquet, and meeting areas; recreation; retail; parking; and other special requirements); technical guidelines; circulation flows; special systems layouts (communications and computer equipment, back-of-house service areas, kitchens, laundries, front desk); operating and design themes for food and

Table 19.1 Typical development and design team

Owner	The owning company which also may be the developer, an equity investor, operator, government, or a combined joint-venture of any of the above
Developer	The entity actively managing the overall development process for the owner
Operator	The hotel company that holds a management agreement and, normally, a technical services agreement with the owner. The operator also may be an owner or joint-venture partner or developer
Franchiser	The hotel company that holds a franchise agreement with the owner, as franchisee
Lender or funding source	Institution or entity providing primary debt financing; may also be an owner or joint-venture partner
Construction lender	Institution providing temporary financing until construction is complete
Feasibility consultant or appraiser	Independent accounting, appraisal, or similar professional firm recognized in the field of hotel development and finance
Design consultants	Architect, engineers, and additional specialty consultants such as interior design, food-service, landscape, etc
Lender's architect	Architect independently reviewing design and construction for the lender
Contractor	General construction contractor experienced in hotels, who holds agreement with owner to build the project as described in the program for a stipulated sum (lump sum) or on a guaranteed maximum price basis
Construction manager	Consultant employed by the owner to manage the construction and equipping of the hotel when not managed directly by the owner

beverage areas; staffing requirements (offices and employee back-of-house areas); required office layouts and equipment; signage and room numbering; and other detailed hotel requirements affecting the design and budget.

Coordination review is provided in all phases of design from initial program and concept to final documentation, field inspection, and acceptance, to ensure that the operator's and owner/developer's needs are fully met. The Budget Coordination Checklist (Appendix B) indicates the stages at which facilities programming information and other hotel technical data are incorporated into the architectural and interior design documents as well as their review and approval by the owner/developer, operator, and city.

Technical services fees vary by chain and are often based on a fixed amount per room with a minimum total sum per hotel.

Table 19.2 Types of consultants and contractors

Consultants to Owner/Developer	Cost estimator
Architect	Building code consultant
Interior designer	
Food-service consultant	**Consultants to Interior Designer**
Theming consultant	Lighting consultant
Golf course architect	Graphics consultant
Site surveyor	Art consultant
Geotechnical engineer	
Construction manager (CM)	**Contractors and Specialty Suppliers**
Project manager	General contractor (or CM)
	Separate trades contractors
Consultants to Architect	Purchasing agent (for FF&E)
Structural engineer	FF&E installer
Mechanical engineer	Landscape contractor
Electrical engineer	Artwork supplier
Life-safety consultant	Sign contractor
Landscape architect	Printed materials supplier
Water-feature consultant	Uniform supplier
Traffic/parking consultant	Inventory suppliers (china, linen, misc. supplies, etc.)
Acoustical consultant	
Audiovisual consultant	Systems suppliers (computer, data, phones, audiovisual)
Elevator consultant	
Laundry consultant	Field representative

Architect's Agreement

The architect shall perform the following professional services pertaining to the hotel and be responsible to the owner. The hotel operator's approval shall be obtained on all matters required by the management agreement. Often, the question of who, owner or architect, owns the design and the drawings becomes an issue during the negotiation of the contract. Generally, all documents should be the property of the owner.

The architect's fees for the scope of services described below are normally a lump sum amount ranging from 4 to 6 percent of the agreed estimate of the construction cost of the work designed by the architect and related consultants. The exact fee depends on the size and complexity of the hotel. If full technical services are not provided by the hotel company, the architect's fees may be increased by up to 1 percent. Fees may vary from the above averages due to unique conditions. But more than any other factor, information, decisions, and approvals provided rapidly by the client save time and expense for the consultants, enabling them to reduce their fees accordingly.

Basic Services

Basic services shall consist of the following six phases including normal structural, mechanical, electrical, fire protection, elevators, civil engineering, landscaping, sitework, parking, acoustical, audiovisual, standard lighting, security, estimating, and coordination of all required consultants as approved by the owner. The architect shall provide value design and value-engineering services consisting of evaluation of all reasonable design components, systems, and methods for efficiency, economy, life safety, and adaptability to the site. The architect warrants that documents shall be in full compliance with all applicable codes and regulations. All construction estimates shall be prepared by a qualified estimator in adequate detail to evaluate the work at each phase, according to the following schedule, not to be exceeded, except for reasonable cause, by either the architect or owner. [Insert here agreed completion dates for each phase.] The owner shall have the right to require modifications to achieve its desired goals with respect to overall design and operation of the hotel.

- *Schematic design*: based on the hotel facilities list and design program, technical guides, construction budget, and other data furnished by the owner, the architect shall prepare single-line plans and variations of buildable schemes, indicating the relationships of all hotel components. The architect shall further refine the concept selected by the owner, presenting all floor plans, exterior elevations, building sections, exterior color perspectives, and cost estimates.
- *Design development*: based on the approved schematic design documents, the architect shall prepare further detailed drawings and outline specifications describing all aspects of the hotel's size and character, including architectural, structural, mechanical, electrical, and fire protection systems, materials, and an updated cost estimate. In compliance with energy conservation codes and standards, the architect shall prepare a comparative analysis of capital costs and operating expenses of alternate mechanical, electrical, and energy-saving systems so that the owner can select between them.
- *Construction documents phase I (50 percent complete documents)*: based on approved design development documents, the architect shall prepare final detailed drawings and specifications of all construction requirements for the hotel, coordinating in the documents all data provided by the owner and consultants on guestroom layouts, kitchen, bars, and laundry equipment layouts, exterior signs, and other standard details. The architect shall provide the interior designer with drawings of fixed interior elements of the hotel, but not including movable furnishings or other work directly provided by the owner's consultants. The architect shall refine engineering subsystems and advise the owner of any adjustments to the cost estimate.
- *Construction documents phase II (90 percent complete documents)*: the owners and their consultants shall give the architect material and color selections and data on any additional systems or equipment to be incorporated in final documents including front desk, communications and computer equipment. The architect shall submit updated drawings and specifications, advise of any adjustments to the cost estimate, and assist the owner in preparing necessary bidding documents.
- *Construction documents phase III (100 percent complete documents and bidding)*: the architect shall finalize drawings and specifications and file them on behalf of the owner with appropriate regulatory agencies for issuance of the building permit, with the owner paying all associated fees. The architect will submit an updated cost estimate and assist the owner in clarifying documents during bidding. Where mutually considered necessary to ensure that the budget is met, the architect will organize specified portions of the design as bid alternates.
- *Construction phase*: the architect shall promptly review and take appropriate action on the contractor's submittals to make sure they conform with the design concept and construction documents and forward them to the owner. The architect shall visit the site as appropriate, but not less than once each month, to make recommendations to the owner about progress of the work, evaluate the contractor's applications for payment, endeavor to guard against defects in the work, but not to guarantee performance by the contractor or supervise construction means, methods, or safety precautions. The architect shall interpret all documents and provide certificates of substantial and final completion of the work.

Construction Budget

The architect agrees that the construction budget is a maximum of [insert amount here] and its best efforts shall be made to delineate the design biddable within this sum, but if exceeded by lowest *bona fide* bids, the owner shall: (1) approve increase;

(2) authorize re-bidding; or (3) cooperate in revising the scope, materials, or details to reduce the cost. In such case, the architect, without additional charge, shall modify final documents to bring the cost within the construction budget.

Compensation to Architect

The owner's payments shall be made on approved invoices at the completion of each of the following phases:

■ Schematic design	10%
■ Design development	35%
■ Construction documents phase I	55%
■ Construction documents phase II	70%
■ Construction documents phase III	80%
■ Construction (payable monthly in accordance with construction progress)	100%

If the scope of the hotel is changed substantially after approval of the schematic design phase or the architect's services, through no fault of the architect, have not been completed within six months after the originally scheduled completion date, the architect's compensation for the then uncompleted portion shall be subject to renegotiation.

Insurance

The architect shall maintain during service, and for a minimum of five years after their completion, professional liability insurance specifically covering errors and omissions, as well as during service, worker's compensation, employer's liability, and comprehensive general liability insurance. The architect shall submit certificates of insurance naming the owner and operator as additional insureds to the extent permitted by the carrier. Such insurance shall not limit the architect's liability. The architect shall hold the owner and operator harmless from the liability, loss, or property damage resulting from the architect's acts or omissions.

Interior Designer's Agreement

In hotel work the interior designer generally is hired directly by the owner, rather than the architect as is done for some other buildings. The interior designer works collaboratively with the architect and other design consultants to prepare a cohesive concept for the hotel or resort. The agreement should include phrasing that the operator's approval shall be obtained on all matters required by the management agreement between the owner and operator. Also, it should define clearly the complete scope of work, that is, a detailed listing of the spaces to be designed. Besides all guestroom areas and the hotel public spaces, the interior designer's scope usually includes the elevator cab interiors, public restrooms, administration offices, and occasional outdoor areas such as dining and pool terraces. In addition, the designer may be called on to design interior signage, uniforms, the restaurant 'table top,' and other special items.

Basic Services

Basic interior design services shall consist of the following six phases including normal interior design services for furniture, fixtures, and equipment (FF&E), accessories, special finishes, graphics, uniforms, and table top items and coordination of consultants approved by the owner. The designer shall coordinate with the architect and other consultants. The designer warrants that documents shall be in full compliance with all applicable codes and regulations. All interior design estimates shall be prepared by a qualified estimator in adequate detail to evaluate the work at each phase, according to the following schedule, not to be exceeded, except for reasonable cause, by either the designer or the owner. [Insert agreed completion dates for each phase.] The owner shall have the right to require modifications to achieve the desired goals with respect to overall design and operation of the hotel.

- *Concept phase*: based on the hotel facilities list and design program, technical guides, room mix, suggested operating and design themes for food and beverage areas, budget for FF&E and special finishes, available architectural plans, and other data furnished by owner, the designer shall prepare preliminary floor plans and variations indicating proposed furniture layouts for public areas and guestrooms; sketch perspectives of overall design concepts; colors and samples of proposed materials, photos of furnishings, and alternate selections; and cost estimates.
- *Design development*: based on approved concept documents, the designer shall prepare preliminary room layouts for all public areas, guestrooms and suites including furniture, ceiling and lighting designs, electrical outlet locations, with color perspective renderings and presentation boards containing color, fabric, and material samples of floor, wall, and ceiling finishes, window treatments, furniture and furnishing fabrics and materials including drawings and photos of standard and custom-fabricated furniture, fixtures, and accessories for presentation to the owner. The designer shall present a preliminary design direction for graphics, uniforms, and artwork to the

owner and submit a preliminary line-item estimate of interior FF&E and special finishes.

- *Documentation phase I (working drawings of furniture and special finishes and mock-up room specifications and review)*: the designer shall prepare complete working drawings including floor plans showing all furnishings identified by type, size, and total number of each item, coded on the drawings and cross-referenced to all other specification data. Drawings shall include elevations, sections, and ceiling plans identifying all wall and window treatments, location of special finishes and materials, variations in ceiling heights and floor levels, location of lighting and outlets for electricity, communications, and TV. The designer shall prepare specifications for a mock-up of a typical guestroom and assist in installation and adjustments to meet the owner's approval.
- *Documentation phase II (millwork and special finishes drawings, complete specifications, and confirmation of budget)*: the designer shall prepare final working drawings and bid specifications for all millwork and special finishes including floor and ceiling plans, sections, elevations, and details of all fixed furniture, furnishings, fixtures, and finishes including floor, wall, and ceiling decorative elements and level changes, and coordination of all engineering outlets. Each decorative item shall be detailed and identified by manufacturer. The designer shall provide a finish schedule and specification books of swatches illustrating all materials, fabrics, colors, details, or catalog cuts of interior FF&E, cross-referenced to drawings and specifications; carpet and fabric designs including color tufts or samples; itemized schedules and bid specification sheets including alternate sources of supply; design and procurement coordination for artwork and special accessories; and a final estimate breakdown conforming with the budget for FF&E and special finishes for approval of the owner, operator, and their designated purchasing agent.
- *Documentation phase III (graphics, uniforms and table tops)*: the designer shall provide a graphics program throughout the hotel including specialty signage for each food and beverage area and required drawings, specifications and color samples for all interior signs for the owner's approval. Estimates shall be included in the budget for FF&E. The designer shall assist the owner in reviewing uniform design and selections of table-top items including glassware, china, linen, and related service pieces, menus, and accessories designed by others.
- *Construction and installation phase*: the designer shall verify that construction and installation of interior spaces conform to documents; review and approve color and material samples, shop drawings, and manufacturers' detail submittals of furniture, fixtures, and millwork; provide onsite coordination with the installation contractor to approve furniture arrangements; locate decorative materials, artwork, and accessories; and prepare a final punch-list of defective items.

Cost of FF&E and Special Finishes

The designer agrees that the budget for FF&E and special finishes is a maximum of [insert amount here] and best efforts shall be made to delineate a design biddable within this sum, but if exceeded by lowest *bona fide* bids, the owner shall: (1) approve increase; (2) authorize rebidding; or (3) cooperate in revising scope, materials, or details to reduce cost. In such case, the designer, without additional charge, shall modify final documents to bring costs within the FF&E and special finishes budget.

Compensation to Designer

The owner's payments shall be made on approved invoices at completion of each of following phases:

■ Concept design	25%
■ Preliminary design	40%
■ Documentation phase I	50%
■ Documentation phase II	70%
■ Documentation phase III	80%
■ Construction and installation (payable monthly in accordance with progress of services)	100%

Provisions for renegotiation of compensation, ownership of documents, and insurance should be similar to those discussed under the architect's agreement above. The interior designer's fees for the scope of services defined in the agreement are normally a lump sum amount ranging from 6 to 10 percent of the agreed cost estimate of the work designed and specified by the interior designer and their consultants. The exact fee depends on the size and complexity of the hotel (for example, the number of restaurants or special suites). But, for extensive renovation services, fees may range to 12 percent.

Food-service Consultant's Agreement

Given the importance of the food and beverage outlets and the banquet and social functions in a hotel, the food-service consultant takes on an increasingly important role. The consulting agreement may be either with the owner or the architect. It should require that the operator's approval be obtained on all matters required by the management agreement. The scope of work includes all food preparation and service areas including restaurant exhibition and display areas, bars, F&B storage areas, receiving, employee cafeteria, and related areas.

Basic Services

The usual food-service design consists of the following four phases including normal design services for all food-service equipment (FSE) layouts, and coordination with the architect, interior designer, and other consultants. The consultant warrants that documents shall be in full compliance with all applicable codes and regulations. All equipment estimates shall be in adequate detail to evaluate the work at each phase according to the following schedule not to be exceeded, except for reasonable cause. [Insert agreed completion dates for each phase.]

- *Preliminary design phase*: based on hotel facilities list and design program, hotel design guide, suggested operating and design themes for food and beverage areas, budget for FSE, available architectural plans and other data furnished by the owner, the consultant shall prepare preliminary plans indicating all equipment, counters, shelving and hoods; a schedule describing types and quantities of equipment; and a cost estimate with equipment set in place ready for final utilities connections.

- *Documentation phase*: based on approved preliminary designs, the consultant shall prepare final plans with dimensions and locations of all equipment, shelving, counters, and hoods; dimensions, sizes, and capacities of all required plumbing, electrical, gas, and steam services and exhaust hoods; schedule and specifications of all equipment by their manufacturers, models, and utilities requirements as well as specially fabricated items by their sizes, shapes, materials, and finishes. Documents shall be in adequate detail for bidding and contracting supply and setting in place of all required FSE. The consultant shall submit an updated cost estimate for approval.

- *Bidding phase*: the consultant shall recommend at least three qualified bidders; review any clarifications or proposed alternatives to documents with bidders; assist the owner in analyzing bids and making acceptable revisions, if required, to negotiate a contract within the approved estimate.

- *Construction phase*: the consultant shall review and approve shop drawings, manufacturers' equipment cuts, and samples; coordinate with the architect and other consultants as required; inspect installation, prepare a corrective punch list, verify compliance, and recommend final acceptance of all equipment.

Cost of Food-service Equipment

The consultant agrees that the budget for the FSE is a maximum of [insert amount here], and best efforts shall be made to delineate designs biddable within the sum, but if exceeded by lowest *bona fide* bids, the owner shall: (1) approve increase; (2) authorize rebidding; or (3) cooperate in revising scope, materials, or details to reduce cost. In such case, the consultant, without additional charge, shall modify the final documents to bring costs within the FSE budget.

Compensation to Consultant

The owner's payments shall be made on approved invoices at completion of each of the following phases:

■ Preliminary design	35%
■ Documentation	80%
■ Bidding	90%
■ Construction	100%

Provisions for renegotiation of compensation, ownership of documents, and insurance should be similar to those described under the architect's agreement. The food-service consultant's fees for the scope of services defined in the above agreement are a lump sum amount ranging from 4 to 5 percent of the agreed estimate of the FSE designed or specified.

Purchasing Agent's Agreement

The purchasing agent's (PA) agreement should define their role to coordinate, schedule, estimate, order, expedite, and supervise installation of the FF&E, accessories, operating supplies, and inventories for the hotel. They are involved throughout the design phase during which they coordinate with the hotel operator, architect, interior designer, and other consultants to monitor design, recommend different materials, vendors, and possible alternates. Once the design is set, the PA provides itemized price take-offs comparing actual vendor quotes to the line-item budget, and supervises the bidding, negotiating, and awarding of purchase orders. As the project moves ahead, the PA issues schedules and reports on procurement and regularly updates shipping status including highlighting any item that might affect on-time completion. Finally, the PA supervises the installation of interior FF&E and delivery of operating supplies and equipment. The purchasing agent's fees usually range from 4 to 5 percent of the cost of work procured.

Construction Management Agreement

Construction management (CM) often is provided directly by the owner, developer, or management company through its construction staff or by a professional CM firm (see Chapter 21). Agreements with construction managers should be on a fixed fee basis of about 3 percent of construction costs, depending on the project's size. Their responsibilities and reimbursable expenses should be clearly defined and the fees and reimbursable expenses divided into separate guaranteed maximum amounts for the pre-construction and construction phases. It should require that the CM prepare itemized cost estimates at each phase of the architect's and interior designer's services. Where these exceed the construction budget, the construction manager must advise the owner on possible cost reductions to meet the budget.

Budgeting, Estimating, and Cost Control

The foremost goal of budgeting and estimating systems is to establish a reliable capital budget that works throughout the entire development and construction program, beginning with appropriate allowances and adding detail as the design takes shape. A fully detailed facilities outline and area program based on the market demand study (see Chapter 22) enables the developer to set initial project budgets and prepare a 10-year business proforma and financial forecast for the project.

The complexity of hotel development demands that the developer estimate and monitor a budget with hundreds of individual line items. The earliest budgets, based on preliminary plans and sketches, and before undergoing value design, value-engineering, or substantial interior detail, are too preliminary to use for sound budgetary purposes.

However, the developer should make certain that the budget estimates are (1) complete and do not omit any category or item and (2) properly indexed to the local area—not based on broad regional or national indexes averaging all types of hotel construction. In addition, it is important, where the hotel structure or concept might be unusually costly, that the CM offers value design and ensures that the market concept is strong enough to carry the extra initial cost as well as debt service.

Budget Control Steps

Maintaining the budget control requires careful monitoring of the project during both the design and construction phases. Throughout the design period, the owner needs to rely on the accuracy of estimates for all categories, updated monthly or at the end of each documentation phase. In addition to the budget estimates for architecture and engineering, for site development and interior design, for kitchen equipment and operating supplies—those submitted by the architect and other consultants—the project manager or, where applicable, an outside quantity estimating firm should prepare a second estimate, with any differences in the budget estimates resolved by mutually agreed revisions to the drawings and specifications. Design consultants must be held responsible for redesigning, revising, and re-specifying to meet the initial agreed upon budget without an additional fee.

Due to the clear link between project cost and floor area, maintaining control of the budget, to a large extent, is a matter of space control. The owner, through its project manager or CM, during schematic design and design development, must ensure that the architect's plans don't contain areas beyond those required in the facilities program. As the project proceeds into contract documents, the team needs to watch for the introduction of special equipment or costly finishes unless they can be justified based on their additional revenue-producing potential.

Budget control is no less important during the construction phase. All bidding must be competitive and, where bids exceed the budget, the architect and design consultants must redesign or respecify or the owner needs to consider whether to reduce the project scope or increase the budget. Construction commitments should not be made until virtually all major items are under guaranteed maximum contract or reasonably firm allowances have been established, and required design reductions already implemented to meet the budget.

Among the most important tools for controlling costs is 'value design,' as required under many agreements. It eliminates waste space that does not contribute to the market concept or hotel revenue and carefully evaluates the building plan for configurations that are most appropriate to a site and to the internal layout of the particular type of hotel. For example, through careful value design the Embassy Suites prototype became more cost efficient than that of other suite hotels (see Chapter 8). Its 'shotgun' style suite requires less corridor area and exterior wall, thereby reducing overall construction costs, and incorporates an atrium, enhancing the public experience and increasing both the average rate and occupancy percent. In addition, value design enabled such high-performing hotels as the Crowne Plaza in New Orleans, the Hyatt Regency in Maui, and The Buttes near Phoenix to be developed for lower comparable costs than their competitors. Each of these hotels included certain costly features essential to their market concept but which generated additional revenue or increased market share, enhancing their financial performance and real estate value.

While the more attractive finish on a door knob costs pennies, a more efficient building configuration easily can save $1–2 million or more. During the early phases value design focuses on those basic planning issues which result in excessive costs, including:

- *Expensive construction*: suburban hotels often spread their public and support functions over one floor; instead, a main public level and lower back-of-house level greatly reduces construction cost and simplifies circulation.
- *Inefficient circulation*: double-loaded corridor configurations save 50 percent in corridor area compared with single-loaded schemes and may provide a 15–20 percent space savings overall (see Chapter 15).
- *Inefficient building systems*: one elevator core for both public and service functions is more efficient than separate elevator banks in different locations; back-to-back guestrooms greatly reduce plumbing cost.
- *High net to gross area factor*: study alternative layouts to reduce the amount of nonusable and nonrevenue producing space. For example, increasing the number of rooms per floor and reducing the building height requires a lower gross factor and generally is more economical.

Improvements such as these, often referred to as 'tightening up the design,' normally make the building more serviceable to guests, reducing distances between functions, and easier for management to operate.

Early cost estimates for hotels that are based on average cost per unit of floor area or cost per guestroom are only preliminary, at best, because of the range of planning and design variables. The project manager must prepare increasingly accurate estimates during the design development and construction document phases, reducing the contingency from 15 percent at the earliest point to no more than 5 percent when the construction contract is awarded:

	Contingency
■ Program and conceptual design:	15%
■ Schematic design	10%
■ Design development	7%
■ Construction documents	5%
■ Bid or award contract	5%

Value Design, Value-engineering, and Life-cycle Analysis

The goal of achieving value design, or value-*added* design, extends from the initial space program to the construction award. It generally includes both profound and minor economies which, in total, can easily make a difference in a project's viability. For example, the boutique hotel concept, in addition to its many marketing advantages, generally has smaller rooms and narrower corridors (because of the number of older buildings converted to boutique hotels) with more efficient space adjacencies and circulation. The smaller boutique hotel room reduces total area by about 15 percent compared to a mid-rate hotel of the same size. This results in a saving of an average of 75 ft^2 (7 m^2) per room or over $1 million on a 150-room hotel.

But value design extends to most minute detail. In *The Art of the Deal* developer Donald Trump cites using three hinges on each ballroom door, instead of four smaller ones, thereby saving 25 percent of the installation cost with no change to the material cost. The process is pure 'cost common sense' and every project can benefit from it. In the same manner, each and every net area of the hotel should answer positively to the question: 'Is this space essential to the market concept?'

In 'value-engineering' the architect, engineers, manufacturers' representatives, and hotel technical staff develop cost-benefit analyses of the maintenance, reliability, and durability of major materials, systems, and equipment being considered for the hotel. For example, they request and evaluate alternate proposals from at least two different elevator companies or air conditioning manufacturers. In addition, the developer should have the engineering consultants undertake a 'life-cycle cost' analysis including estimated energy, maintenance, and replacement costs before selecting the final system. Value engineering extends well beyond the building systems. For example, several contractors have adopted re-usable steel tunnel form systems to create poured-in-place concrete guestroom walls and floors, saving time and labor in erecting the guestroom tower.

Successful cost management also requires both an effective control system to monitor the progress of the work in relation to its completion schedule and a measurement system to compare actual expenditures against the budget. These systems closely track the rate and amount of resource consumption in terms of schedule, cost, material, and labor, alerting the development team sufficiently in advance of any potential variances in the work plan, budget, technical performance, quality-standard, or schedule. This permits early corrective action to head-off problems before they create a major delay, cost overrun, or affect the project's investment return. The same systems are used to identify potential cost savings opportunities. However, the greatest opportunities for reducing project costs occur at the early stages and decrease sharply with the contract bid and award.

Technical Guides

The major management companies provide technical design and engineering guides to hotel developers and their consultants. These manuals assist the team in developing imaginative, efficient, and marketable design solutions as well as ensure a safe and environmentally sound structure. Developed over many years and through the experience of scores of projects worldwide, the comprehensiveness of the guides is evident in their typical outline. A typical corporate standard may have a first volume containing proprietary planning and technical standards and a second volume covering the recommended systems and procedures (checklists, reference documents and coordination methods) used during the development and construction period. The guides also may include a third volume covering 'prototype' plans and typical details customized for internal use (see Table 19.3).

Architectural and Engineering Systems

Whether the hotel is a high-rise 'ultratel' or luxury resort with the guestrooms arranged in spread out villas, its market type and program help to determine appropriate solutions to the myriad architectural and engineering alternatives. These involve a number of structural issues, many based on differing require-

Table 19.3 Technical guides

Volume 1 Design, Planning and Development Standards
Introduction, purpose and intent
General requirements, reviews, and approvals
Site planning, zoning, massing, and exterior design considerations
Building codes including structural, life-safety, and handicap requirements
Facilities and space programming standards
Site and environmental planning requirements including parking and roadways, recreation, and landscape
Guestroom, suite, and villa standards
Public space standards including restaurants and lounges, function and conference areas, indoor recreational amenities, themed shopping, and entertainment features
Back-of-house service requirements
Furniture, fixtures, and equipment (FF&E) standards
Special systems requirements including fire protection, security, communications, television and in-room entertainment, audiovisual, and property management systems
Keying and guest security standards
Building systems including electrical, mechanical (heating, ventilation, and air-conditioning; energy conservation), plumbing, vertical transportation (elevators and escalators), and fire-protection systems
Volume 2 Technical Services
General description: scope of technical services, types of agreements, list of consultants, and development sequence
Market surveys and feasibility studies: scope of surveys and analysis, types of agreements, and proforma development software
Facilities programming systems: area matrix and programming software, and facilities checklists
Budgeting and estimating systems: budget estimating software, progress confirmation cost reviews, and value-engineering by CM, A&E firm, or cost consultant; definitive estimate format; and operations pre-opening expense budget format
Progress scheduling and reporting systems: CPM system for scheduling, reporting and approvals; design and construction phase scheduling formats; checklist of early areas for FF&E installation and training; and project manager's coordination checklists
Design requirements: selection process format and agreements for architect, interior designer, food service, site survey, geotechnical report and other required consultants; environmental, location, and parking checklists including circulation diagrams, parking analysis, and basic building configuration alternatives; checklists for life safety, security, audiovisual, and special hotel systems; checklists for guestroom types, food and beverage, recreation and health spa amenities, conference, lobby, front office, administration and back-of-house services; checklists for renovations and additions
Construction contracting, bidding and negotiation process: selection format for alternate construction contracting systems
Construction contracts and field supervision requirements
Construction contracts and general conditions including provisions for inspection, testing, reporting and insurance guarantees; construction management agreements as required
FF&E procurement and installation requirements: purchasing agent's agreement, checklists of required FF&E items, and format for preliminary FF&E information and estimate
Required inspections, permits and approvals: format for local checklist of permits and licenses
Confirmation of staff training and early occupancy requirements
Soft opening and building acceptance procedures: checklist for construction closeout
Opening
Volume 3 Prototype Plans and Typical Details
New prototype hotel plans
Recommended protopart plans: guestroom layouts, health club plans, back-of-house layouts
Typical details: brand logos, standard and selected details for special applications

ments of the guestroom areas versus the public and support facilities. For example, by their nature the guestrooms utilize a short-span structure while the public areas, especially the ballroom, require medium to long spans. These areas also have different needs for mechanical systems, ceiling heights, and fall under different sections of the building code.

The number of general planning and design issues continues from these larger conceptual aspects to the smallest detail. Where the hotel is based on a prototype, it needs to adapt to the site and the surrounding environs. In addition, the architect should consider how many areas in the hotel will need to adapt to future changes—certainly the restaurants and lounges will undergo frequent retheming to keep them current—and all areas will be regularly updated and refreshed. Meeting room technology will change, fitness center equipment must follow health trends, and guestrooms may need to adapt elements of an office or spa. Therefore, the building infrastructure needs to be highly adaptable to future innovation and change.

While the architect and engineers may evaluate different structural and mechanical systems, the nuances of hotel design tend to limit available choices. Table 19.4 identifies many of the more common building system alternatives, which have different but direct application to guestroom and public/support areas. For example, depending on the location and type of hotel, it may be appropriate to use a frame structure, bearing wall system, or even pre-fabricated guestroom modules. The decision is based on available technology and skills of the building trades, but more on issues related to bay-spacing and the need to integrate mechanical and other systems into the structure.

Table 19.4 Alternative building system configurations

Massing
Ultra-high-rise: over 70 stories
High-rise: 20–70 stories
Mid-rise: 6–19 stories
Low-rise: 3–5 stories
Disbursed: 1–2 stories
Guestroom configuration
Slab: guestrooms on double- or single-loaded corridors
Tower: guestrooms clustered around a central core
Atrium: rooms around or overlooking multistory interior space
Hybrid: combination of configurations
Villa: individual units or low-rise clusters of rooms
Type structure
Reinforced concrete frame: flat plate, poured-in-place, prefabricated, pre-stressed, post-tensioned, reusable tunnel forms, etc.
Combination poured-in-place concrete with precast floors and walls
Steel frame: heavy or light steel frame
Masonry bearing wall
Panel: factory or onsite precast floor and wall units
Modular: prefabricated guestroom modules
Wood frame (villas)
Indigenous methods and materials
Column spacing
Single-bay: columns at each guestroom partition
Double-bay: columns at every other partition
At thirds: usually four columns across the width of a guestroom wing, the two interior ones being approximately at the one-third and two-third positions
No interior columns: staggered truss
Building materials
Exterior: consider glass to wall ratio; performance criteria of all materials
Interior architectural finishes
Interior decorative finishes
Mechanical, electrical, and environmental
Central vs. individual package units
Relative first cost vs. life-cycle cost
Heat recovery alternatives
Submetering of individual areas
Cogeneration and other systems
Environmental technology

Frame Structures

The principal structural system for all mid- and high-rise buildings is the steel or reinforced concrete frame structure. Office buildings, which require an open plan and suspended ceilings, generally utilize the steel frame. However, the guestroom portions of a hotel are more easily built with a flat-plate concrete or precast concrete floor slabs. With no need for HVAC ducts or extensive recessed lighting, the underside of the slab can easily be given an appropriate ceiling finish. While the typical steel frame is less appropriate for guestroom structures, it has been used for ultra-high-rise megatels and in locations where it is cost competitive with concrete structures. All high-rise buildings must be designed to resist wind and seismic conditions which often require diagonal bracing or other accommodation within the structural system.

Steel is much more suitable for long-span spaces and, therefore, commonly is used for the public and service areas of a hotel. The column spacing and frame system should be designed so that it can flexibly accommodate a variety of hotel functions in case the market changes and the property needs to renovate in the future.

Bearing-wall Structures

A second approach is to eliminate the structural frame entirely and, since the guestrooms contain parallel walls roughly 13 ft (4 m) apart, to use these as load-bearing partitions. While the early skyscrapers used masonry bearing walls several feet thick at their base, 8 in (20 cm) thick concrete block partitions support up to 24 floors at the Clarion and Rosen Centre convention hotels in Orlando, Florida. A bearing-wall system is low cost and can be constructed relatively quickly and, in addition, offers acoustical and fireproofing benefits. While logical for the guestroom structure, the bearing walls limit the flexibility of the public and service areas on the lower floors. Therefore, the bearing walls must be combined with another system; at the Rosen Centre they are built on top of a two-story concrete frame structure.

Pre-fabricated Modular Construction

A third structural approach that has found support uses factory-manufactured modular room units (each unit may contain one or two rooms), precast structural members, and panelized systems. The main advantages of these systems are in the speed and quality control of their assembly-line production. The modular guestroom system has the advantage of providing full room units, bathrooms fully plumbed and complete with all finishes and furniture. On the site they are lifted from a truck and stacked by crane needing only final plumbing and electrical connections. Generally the public areas are built by conventional means or with a pre-fabricated panel system. The concrete modules date from the late 1960s when they were developed for the World's Fair in Montreal and have been used for hotels from the 1970s to the present in the US, Middle East, and Pacific area including the 515-room high-rise Hilton Palacio del Rio in San Antonio, Texas, and the 326-room Hyatt Regency in Macau.

The differences between the architectural, structural, and mechanical requirements of the guestrooms and those of the public/service areas suggests that they be separated so that the most appropriate engineering systems can be used for each. For example, architects may select flat plate slabs on masonry bearing walls for the guestroom structure and lightweight steel for the larger span public and service areas. The separation allows more flexibility in the building orientation, massing, and location of HVAC equipment closer to the public and service areas; shorter distribution lines to the guestrooms; and related savings in energy costs. The initial construction costs are somewhat higher per unit of area for the public spaces, because of the additional structural requirements and mechanical systems. Table 19.5 identifies the cost breakdown of the basic building shell and the principal engineering systems. The public areas have more complex HVAC requirements while the guestrooms have denser electrical and plumbing needs.

Atrium Engineering

Since the open atrium concept returned to hotels in the late-1960s, it has been considered an energy saver and source of natural light as well as providing the visually dramatic central public space. Especially in office/hotel mixed-use developments, where the office lighting normally consumes nearly half the energy, the atrium skylight provides substantial light to the work spaces, thereby reducing their demand for electricity.

In the event of a fire in the atrium, smoke evacuation is accomplished by introducing a jet column of air at the center of the atrium floor and exhausting it through the operable skylight. Building codes require sprinklers throughout the building, including the guestrooms, and pressurized smoke-proof fire stairs, similar to nonatrium hotels of a similar height. Because the guestroom corridors overlook the major atrium space, engineers have developed an approach to isolate the fire and control the spread of smoke, which includes these characteristics:

- Fire zone kept at negative pressure (air supply ducts are closed).
- Nonfire floors kept at positive pressure (fresh air is supplied at corridor ends remote from atrium; return air fans shut off; dampers closed).
- Atrium kept at negative pressure (induction jet directing smoke in atrium upward; exhaust doors in skylight open to emit smoke through roof).
- Stairwells kept at positive pressure (fresh air is supplied, often by dedicated HVAC systems; all doors well sealed against smoke infiltration)
- Computer-controlled smoke dampers in supply and return ducts; all air-handling units not part of smoke control system shut down; manual back-up system at the fire control room.

Table 19.5 Construction cost percentages

Cost category	*Guestrooms*	*Public/service*
Architecture and structure	60–65%	60–65%
Heating, ventilation, and air-conditioning	10–12%	16–18%
Electrical	11–13%	8–10%
Plumbing	8–9%	4–5%
Sprinklers	3–4%	3–4%
General conditions (site overhead)	4–5%	4–5%

Cogeneration Systems

Hotel operators increasingly are aware of the cost of energy and seek new approaches for controlling and reducing the expense. One solution is cogeneration, which offers a combination of onsite electrical generation with the reuse of waste heat for heating, air-conditioning, and domestic hot water. It is most appropriate in areas with high electric rates (such as New York City and the Caribbean) and with demand charges and for those hotels with emergency generators.

The typical system includes a reciprocating motor/generator set, fueled with either natural gas or diesel fuel, sized to meet the required electrical base load (public area lighting, guestroom corridor lighting; pumps and fans; and refrigerator compressors) and whatever additional load might be economically feasible. Where utilities add extra charges for 'peak demand' or 'time of day' billing, it might be cost effective to generate all of a hotel's electrical power. Equally important is harnessing the waste heat from the cooling exhaust and other systems and using it to meet the thermal requirements for the hotel. These typical sources of waste heat may be cost effective where compatible with local codes and where energy costs are high: domestic hot water, steam for kitchen and laundry, space heating, air conditioning (with an absorption chiller), and swimming pool heating.

Acoustical Considerations

Guest surveys are a consistent reminder of the importance of a noise-free guestroom and soundproof partitions between meeting rooms. But almost every part of the hotel including the public areas (lobbies, meeting room foyers, entertainment lounges, bars), recreation facilities, service areas (kitchens, laundries, mechanical, receiving and trash areas), and the audio-entertainment and hospitality functions of the guest suites are subject to unwanted noise. In addition, proximity to highways and airports, while important in attracting guests, creates additional noise problems.

Noise level standards have been established to identify the required acoustic separation needed between areas to reduce noise levels. For example, meeting room dividing partitions are rated at 44–48 STC (sound transmission class), which reflects the average reduction in decibels achieved by a particular construction. Guestroom partitions should be rated at 50 or higher, while others may vary between 35 and 50. The more severe acoustic separation problems that must be addressed by the architect and consultants occur between:

- adjoining guestrooms (including guest bathrooms)
- adjoining meeting rooms
- exterior areas and meeting rooms or guestrooms
- elevators/elevator lobby and guestrooms
- entertainment rooms and guestrooms
- kitchen and restaurants
- service pantries and banquet rooms
- mechanical areas and public rooms or guestrooms
- rooftop cooling towers and penthouse suites
- laundries and adjoining public and guest areas.

Lighting

The electrical systems are a major part of any building project and no less important in a hotel. However, the designer should consider hotel lighting more a design element than a building science. Lobbies, atriums, restaurants, entertainment areas, meeting and banquet rooms, and guestrooms owe their success to comfortable and creative lighting as much as to any other single design element. As in other disciplines, the requirements are often based on common sense. For example, guestroom lighting needs to be adequate for reading in bed, working at the desk or table, and shaving or applying makeup. If any of these is poor, the guest registers at least subconscious irritation. Meeting room lighting also must be highly adaptable. It should combine incandescent lighting for ambiance with fluorescent fixtures for meeting use and track lighting for displays or accents. Special decorative restaurant lighting is essential in creating the desired mood in food outlets.

The responsibility for such lighting design normally is assigned to the interior designer and its lighting consultant, while architects and engineers provide the lighting design for the offices and back-of-house areas. However, many locations have special restrictions for overall energy. For example, Massachusetts requires that hotels not have over 1 watt per square foot of lighting.

Exterior areas also require proper illumination effects. The architect must consider exterior lighting of the building, parking, grounds, and exterior recreational areas for identification and security. The night illumination of a hotel helps create a memorable image and must be considered a part of the lighting program.

Building and Life-safety Codes

All structures, particularly hotels, are subject to thorough regulation ranging from fire-protection and health and satety codes to sign ordinances. Once the proposed hotel meets the applicable planning and zoning codes regulating use, height, site coverage, density and additional environmental requirements, the detailed design must comply with the local building codes. Their intent is to protect the public against faulty design or construction; therefore, they principally address structure (including materials and live and dead loads) and emergency conditions. The goal is a structure that will resist fire or other emergencies and protect the occupants until they can exit from the building. Electrical, mechanical, elevators, plumbing, and sprinkler systems as well as interior furnishings are also carefully regulated by codes. Other important codes which must be followed in the US include the Americans with Disabilities Act (ADA) Accessibility Guidelines and Environmental Protection Agency (EPA) Rules and Regulations.

While codes are continually updated based on new experience, they do vary internationally as well as nationally within specific countries, including the US. For example, in some locations, updating the entire building in a renovation is not always required. Hotel technical guides often require that higher standards be met beyond local codes. This policy recognizes the principle of consistency in maintaining a higher quality at all properties, regardless of the extra expense or lower standards allowed by local codes. Typical fire and life-safety standards addressed by codes include (see pp. 345–347):

- *Fire resistance*: codes define for different construction elements the number of hours they should withstand fire, ranging from 45 minutes to four hours.
- *Compartmentalization*: codes outline the required fire separation between different uses (for example, assembly and parking).
- *Flame spread*: codes rate interior finishes according to their ability to limit fire growth as measured by 'flame spread rating,' ranging from 0 (nonflammable) to 100 (red oak) to over 500.
- *Fire resistance of furnishings*: codes describe furnishings in terms of both fire and smoke propagation, especially to reduce toxicity.
- *Fire detection alarm and fire suppression systems*: codes require fire detection and alarm systems and, for multistory hotels, full sprinkler protection.
- *Limited building height and single floor area*: in special cases, codes may limit the height and maximum area per floor.
- *Occupant load*: codes establish maximum room occupancies based on floor area and define the number and size of the exits for a particular type and size of space.
- *Exit requirements*: codes require at least two independent routes of egress and establish requirements for their width and protection from flame and smoke.

Table 19.6 Fire resistance and compartmentalization

Fire resistance of construction elements	*Separation of hotel uses*
3-Hour rating	**3-Hour separation**
Structural frame	Ballroom, meeting and banquet rooms, exhibit halls
Load-bearing and fire walls	Enclosed restaurants and lounges
Doors in 3-hour walls	Offices and computer rooms
2-Hour rating	Laundries and dry-cleaning areas
Floor construction	Projection booths
Roofs	Maintenance shops (carpentry, painting, furniture refinishing)
Walls enclosing vertical shafts (stairs, elevators, chutes)	Boiler, transformer, switchgear and emergency generator rooms
Most nonbearing exterior walls	Parking garage
	Storage area
1.5-Hour rating	**1-Hour separation**
Doors in 2-hour walls	Guestrooms
Windows in 2-hour walls	Mechanical areas
1-Hour rating	Kitchen
Interior partitions	
0.75-Hour rating	
Doors in 1-hour partitions	
Openings in most exterior walls	

However, even the most advanced codes sometimes differ, or are subject to various local interpretations. For example, the number of sprinklers required in a typical guestroom ranges from two to five, depending on the local code and whether it faces into an atrium. Also, different codes establish alternate methods for maintaining smoke-free exit stairs, either through positive pressure in the stair or by means of a smoke evacuation system in the stair vestibule. Amid these differences the international hotel industry maintains what it believes are the highest standards, but any situation where a government insists on its own local code must be decided on an individual basis.

The basic fire protection considerations for a new or renovated hotel begin by rating the construction materials and assemblies and defining the different use categories (e.g. public assembly or storage) with their needed separation and hours of resistance to the spread of fire. For example, from the accompanying tables, ratings are established for the structural frame based on its component elements, as well as separations required between different hotel uses. Where mixed uses occur, such as in storage areas adjacent to a hotel ballroom or restaurants next to a kitchen, the more stringent requirement prevails. Similarly, in calculating the occupancy of an area, the higher occupancy is assumed, such as assembly type seating in a ballroom, rather than table seating.

The furniture, fixtures, and interior finishes are, as a rule, a hotel's single largest fire hazard, with its furnishings, primarily bedding, the source of a majority of hotel fires. Fire- and flame-resistant materials are rated according to their ability to limit the spread of fire and minimize the danger from smoke (see Table 19.7). Even though mathematical models can predict how different furnishings will behave during fire and various laboratories have tested actual samples, many materials act differently in a unique application or situation. For example, flame spread ratings vary depending on fabric dyes, cleaning solvents, wear, and varying installation techniques. Custom-built products, common in guestrooms as well as public areas, usually are not tested or the results are averaged. To counteract these problems, architects and interior designers need to fully document the selection and specification of furniture and finishes, assigning responsibilities at each stage to the manufacturer, fabricator, installer, or owner as appropriate. It is essential that the specifier record any substitutions, retain product and material samples, and verify that the product guarantees cover the type of installation envisioned.

Table 19.7 Flame-spread ratings

Hotel area	
Guestrooms and suites	200
Ballrooms, meeting, and banquet rooms	200
Restaurants and lounges	200
Ballroom foyer and hotel lobby	75
Stairs and exit corridors	75
Interior finishes	
Carpet	75
Furniture and upholstery	75
Curtains, drapes, and wall-coverings	25

Because of the highly decorative nature of many hotels, the interior designer assumes major responsibility for the selection of the materials, and the relationship between the designer and architect is more important than for other building types. There are numerous areas in which they must share in the decision making, resulting in unclear responsibility for specification, purchasing and budgeting. As a result, hotel companies have developed checklists that define the responsibilities among the design professionals and assign the items to an appropriate category (see the Coordination Matrix in Appendix B).

The one component that leads to the most difficult coordination problems is the 'fixed décor,' the decorative finishes applied to walls and ceilings in restaurants, lounges, meeting and boardrooms; as well as such millwork as the front desk, bar, built-in planters, and level changes.

Flame-spread Rating

Building finish materials and furnishings are rated according to their relative ability to resist combustion or cause toxic smoke. For example, the assigned flame-spread rating is 0 for nonflammable materials, 100 for red oak, and may be as high as 500 for highly flammable fabrics. Hotel companies do not permit the use of any interior finishing materials, fabrics or other furnishings that have a tested smoke development rating of over 300. The standards in the cruise ship industry are much more restrictive. Decorative finish fabrics must be selected carefully to assure compliance and highly flammable materials such as polyurethane foam must be avoided.

Flame-resistant Guestroom

A project by Owens Corning Fiberglas Corporation's Life Safety Laboratory developed six prototype flame-resistant guestrooms for economy, business,

Table 19.8 Fire-resistant guestroom characteristics

Materials
Glass fiber wall coverings
Fire-resistive drapes, sheers, and blackout liners
Fire-resistive bedspread, fabrics, mattress ticking, and pillow covers
Fire-retardant foam cushions, fire-resistant liners, and upholstery fabrics
Flame-resistant nylon carpeting
Wood furniture in place of plastic laminates
Nonflammable materials (mirror, glass, tile, metal furnishings)

Equipment
Built-in cabinets with fire blankets and fire extinguishers
Television used as annunciator
Smoke detectors that activate exhaust fans to create negative pressure
Halon gas extinguishers in rehabilitation projects where permitted

Space design
Hard floor entry foyer as fire break
Fire-rated door with drop seal as smoke barrier
Second door between room foyer and guestroom to isolate room from corridor
Furniture with a minimum of folds, buttons, or pillows to limit the opportunity for cigarettes to ignite upholstery

Table 19.9 Occupant load and exit requirements

Floor area per person		
Guestrooms	200 ft^2	(18.6 m^2)
Offices	100 ft^2	(9.3 m^2)
Retail at grade	30 ft^2	(2.8 m^2)
Retail on upper floors	60 ft^2	(5.6 m^2)
Assembly spaces	7 ft^2	(0.7 m^2)
Theaters (fixed seating)	Actual number of seats	
Parking garage	Number parking spaces	
Number of exits *(based on the room capacity)*	*Exits*	
1000 people or more	4	
601–999	3	
50–600	2	
Capacity of exits *(based on number of people per 22 in [0.55 m] exit unit)*		
Guestroom and assembly area stairs	113	
Guestroom and retail doors	150	
Office and retail stairs	90	
Office and retail doors	150	
Maximum travel distance to protected exit *(for sprinklered hotels)*		
Guestroom areas	150 ft	(46 m)
Assembly areas	200 ft	(60 m)
Through atrium space	100 ft	(30 m)
Dead-end corridor	20 ft	(6 m)
Sample calculation *(based on 10,000 ft^2 [929 m^2] ballroom)*		
Capacity	1,428	(10,000/7)
Number of exits	4	(capacity > 1000 people)
Total width of exit doors	220 in	(1428/150 = 10 × 22)
Total width of exit stairs	286 in	(1428/113 = 13 × 22)

and luxury resort hotels. The room layouts, designed by GKR, Inc., The Walker Group, and Hirsch Bedner and Associates, focused on the use of fire-resistant materials, especially glass fiber fabrics and fire-resistant liners for foam cushions, protective equipment, and space design concepts. Table 19.8 identifies many of the principles developed in these designs.

Occupant Load and Exit Requirements

Exit requirements including the number and size of doors, width of corridors and stairs, and travel distance are based on the assumed maximum capacity of a space, usually determined by dividing the floor area by an appropriate amount of area per person. Code officials generally calculate a conservative occupant load. They may require that any assembly space be rated at 7 ft^2 (0.7 m^2) per person, even if, for example, the restaurant is furnished to accommodate one-half to one-third that number. The necessary exit calculations can be extremely involved. Consider the simplified analysis for a hotel ballroom of 10,000 ft^2 (929 m^2), as shown in Table 19.9. In addition, each meeting room, foyer space, and so on must be added and exit routes from the building specifically identified.

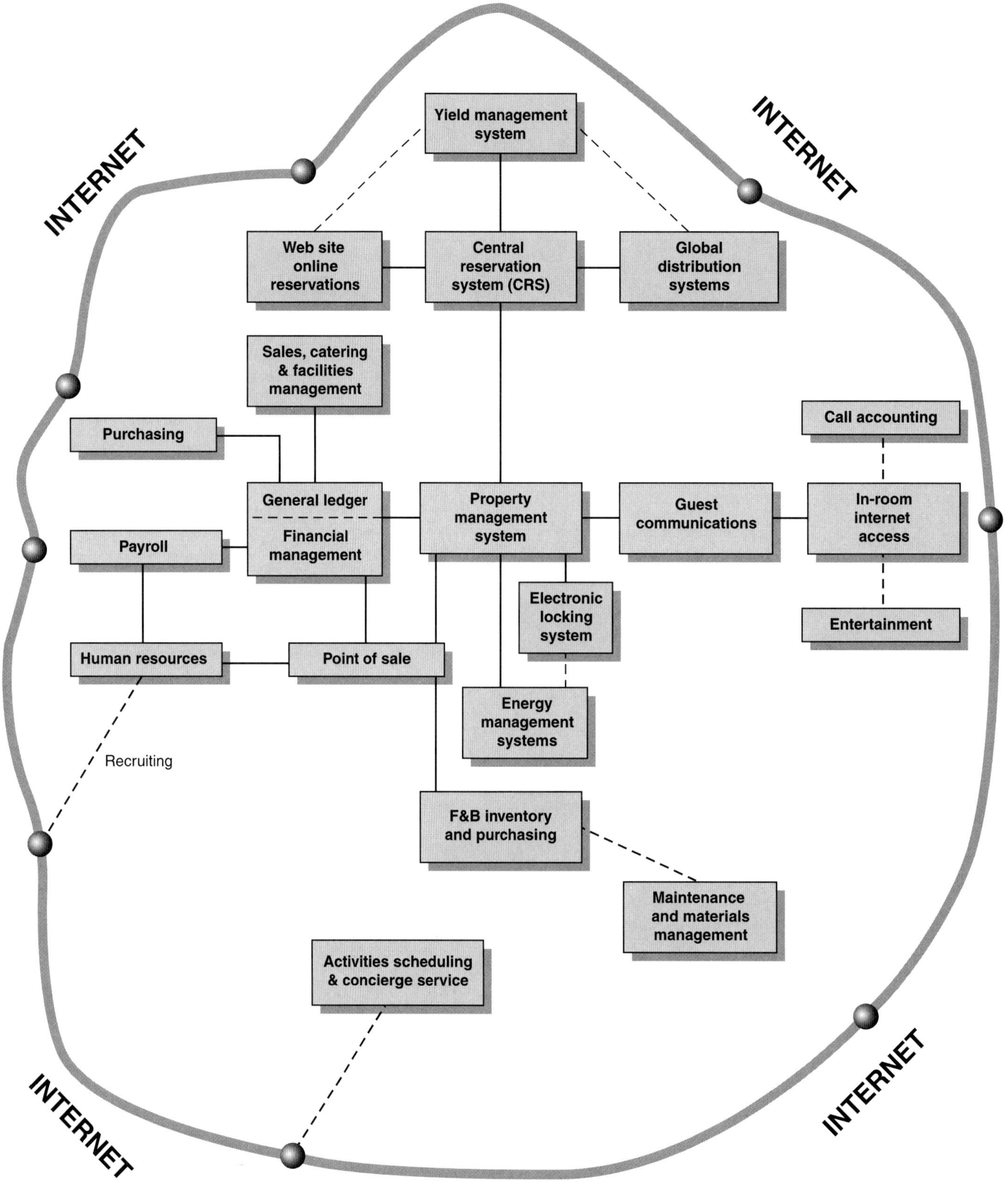

The automated services **Hotel systems diagram.** The property management system sits at the center of an integrated technology infrastructure that links front office, back office, marketing, and decision support systems with increasing reliance on the Internet for outside communication (courtesy of HVS International).

Special Systems 20

Technology is evolving at such a fast pace that within the past decade advances in the various systems have dramatically changed both hotel operations and the services that guests expect. The end of the twentieth century saw the almost universal adoption of computerized check-in and automatic wake-up calls, electronic guestroom locks, satellite television, sophisticated security protection systems, and teleconferencing. Few buildings have a greater variety of computerized or other specialized systems than do today's lodging properties. These fall into six broad categories:

- information processing
- telecommunications
- energy control
- life safety systems
- security systems
- audio and video systems.

The rapid advances and changes are not limited to one or two categories; they cross all lines, reflecting the pervasive influence of computers and related electronic controls. While some of these technologies were available in the 1980s, albeit in a very different form, the ensuing period has made them much more sophisticated as well as cost effective.

The technology is readily available, for instance, to create an automated front desk pod, much like a bank-teller machine, which would handle guest registration—although many operators are unsure how the public would respond to such an impersonal transaction. Yet the system could easily accept the input of a name, check this against a reservation, record credit card information or accept cash, assign a room, and issue a magnetic card-key that would be good only until a designated check-out day and time. Not only would the card-key provide access to the room, it would activate the telephone, turn on the heating and air-conditioning, and permit use of in-room electronic services (computer, fax, movies, and entertainment) and the refreshment center. Guests would approve their bill and check-out through the television, making it possible not to have contact with any staff during the entire stay. These automated operations are routine at many hotels around the world.

Information Processing

Computerized reservations systems were first centrally organized by Sheraton in 1956 and further developed by Holiday Inns in the early 1960s. Now every major hotel chain has its own computerized international reservation system, integrating Internet-based inquiries with the more typical telephone contracts.

Central to computerized hotel operations today is the property management system (PMS). These integrated systems link the several operational areas of the hotel and feature components to access the hotel reservations network and accept credit card authorization. The PMS integrates a wide range of potential guest charges such as restaurant charges, guestroom movie purchases, and long-distance phone calls with in-house recording tasks and general office systems. Among the most important features involve front office requirements that clearly identify room inventory and can track guest history information including room preferences and membership in airline frequent flyer programs.

The last decade has seen the number of proprietary systems that perform a host of management tasks at the property level grow exponentially, each one offering a new twist or gimmick. The future should see more innovation such as wider use of touch-screens and wireless terminals. Central to every system is the ability to interface with the most critical applications such as telephone call-accounting and point-of-sale systems. The most common functions of today's PMSs include:

- guest reservations
- guest registration and folio accounting (the record of guest charges for room, food and beverage, and telephone)
- accounting, including night audit, city ledger, accounts payable, and general ledger
- travel agency accounting (record of commissions to be paid)
- guest history and other marketing reports
- daily and monthly operating reports
- payroll and related reports
- inventory.

Following the lead of airlines, larger hotels and resorts have adopted yield management techniques. Sometimes called 'revenue management,' these systems, which must be integrated with the PMS, match past history with existing reservations to forecast demand for future dates. The goal is to adjust the room rate in order to maximize total room revenue. Too often in the past management would begin to discount room rates in order to increase bookings. But the yield management program looks at historical patterns and, for example, projects that full-rate guests will book rooms only days out; it thereby eliminates certain discount rates for likely higher revenues. Or the system may not accept a one-night reservation even at a high rate when it anticipates that later longer-stay guests will materialize.

Among the most visible systems may be the point-of-sale units that have become ubiquitous in most retail operations including hotel restaurants and lounges. The system allows the server to place an order at a terminal located in the dining room; the system then prints out the order in the kitchen where the production staff begins to prepare the food. In addition to saving steps and time, the restaurant systems reduce errors in calculating and totaling the final check, immediately post the charge to the guest's room account, and provide a variety of analyses including daily accounting and food inventory reports.

The many vendors now competing to satisfy the individual requirements of a particular hotel or resort can be expected not only to supply the computer equipment and the software but to modify them to accommodate the specific needs of the property. The typical systems, whether Windows-based or other older but highly reliable platforms, run on conventional PCs networked together. A few larger hotels, such as each of the four Mirage properties in Las Vegas, including the 3,025-room Belagio (see Chapter 13) work off one large central processor connected to scores of less-costly workstations. Sheraton, where it has hotels very close together in New York City, connects all of the properties to a single main server with dedicated lines between the hotels. They cite the advantage of sharing rooms inventory, a single night-audit, and a central systems support group among the several hotels.

The final choice on a PMS vendor depends on the type of hotel and what functions are most important. Part 1 of this book describes the incredible variety of lodging properties; consider how these place very different demands on the choice of technology:

- Smaller hotels such as roadside and suburban properties need straightforward reservations and accounting systems.
- Convention hotels need a flexible system to handle special functions and such features as group billing.
- Resorts need to track a variety of guest-related activities such as golf club or spa use.
- Boutique and super-luxury hotels need to maintain detailed guest history files.

Telecommunications

The second technological area that has had a major influence in the hotel industry recently is telecommunications. Among the most important systems as far as guest satisfaction is the phone system, based on the PBX or 'private branch exchange.' Today's electronic systems offer hotels the same advantages that guests are used to at home or work: quicker dialing, data transmission (increasingly important as more guests carry laptop computers on business), and such expanded features as voice mail and caller ID. A number of companies already have developed sophisticated telephone systems that:

- include dual line phones to accommodate call-waiting and computers
- include message systems with the ability for guests to record their own personal messages
- control room amenities including television remote control features, room temperature, and open or close drapes
- provide fire safety information by serving as a loudspeaker for emergency messages
- notify the hotel automatically when guests place an emergency call from a guestroom
- transmit alarms to front desk from smoke or motion detector or from other security sensors

- function as a room status system to track cleaning of occupied rooms and preparation of unoccupied rooms.

Telephone call-accounting systems are profitable because they permit the hotel to automatically identify long-distance calls, charging the guest with an accurate and specific record of all calls placed. Among other savings, the newer systems automatically route the calls through private interconnect companies to obtain the least expensive rate. Telecommunications requirements will continue to grow steadily in the future and the hotel operator must consider how to best expand the communications infrastructure. For example, the steady increase in the use of laptop computers by guests will require the installation of additional trunk lines to accommodate more and longer connection times.

Some hotels are specifying full-featured cordless phones in the guestrooms. Many of these units, depending on the manufacturer, provide two lines (for voice and computer), a speaker-phone base instrument, illuminated dials, message waiting indicator, and the usual guest-service keys (housekeeping, room service, etc.). The cordless phone allows the guest to comfortably roam the room while talking, and even can eliminate the need for a second or third phone in the room.

Energy Control

Energy management features have become increasingly important since the first drastic rise in energy prices created by the Middle East oil embargo in 1973. Technological advances that formerly were cost prohibitive have become common as a result of rising energy prices, increased efficiencies of the systems, and reductions in capital equipment costs. The greatest savings are in the design and operation of the heating, ventilation, and air-conditioning (HVAC) systems, lighting, and water heating and in their controls. Of course, the relative benefit depends on the type and size of hotel and its climate, orientation, and construction materials.

A survey by the American Hotel & Motel Association (AH&MA) identified the most common energy control technologies, many of which have become standard in nearly every hotel or resort. These include:

- *Water flow restrictors*: limit water flow in guestroom showers reducing the use of hot water.
- *Automatic lighting controls*: provide programmed control of lights by cycling or dimming particular areas and time clocks to turn lighting on and off according to a pre-established schedule.
- *Load cyclers/programmable controllers*: provide programmed control of motors and other equipment according to schedule.
- *Peak demand controllers*: limit the total energy consumed at any one time by turning off equipment.
- Heat recovery systems: reuse waste heat from the kitchen, laundry, and mechanical areas.
- *Occupancy sensors*: automatically turn off lights in meeting rooms, offices, and other areas when unoccupied.
- *Guestroom occupancy sensors*: infrared occupancy sensor, in addition to controlling lights, automatically turns down guestroom heat and air-conditioning and provides real-time information on occupied rooms.

Other energy-related technologies such as total building automation, co-generation, or solar or wind-based systems may become more practical and cost efficient in the future. Overall, energy control technologies vary from the extremely simple to the complex. Plastic or metal disc water flow restrictors, which reduce the diameter of the opening in a faucet, cost only pennies and can be installed in minutes. At the other end of the scale are central building systems that combine the sophisticated controllers from the above list and that include the ability to integrate security, fire alarm, telephone, and data processing components. They include computers that continuously monitor building functions, turning on equipment only when it is needed.

Energy management technology is rapidly increasing to meet the rising expectations of the industry. Unfortunately, hotel operators often do not comprehend the value of energy conservation techniques as easily as they see the virtues of new accounting or security systems. One general manager expressed this disconcerting opinion: 'My engineer and I have never heard of some of the types of energy control technology [you describe]. I'm busy greeting guests and paying the electric company. My engineer can't keep up with the light bulb changes and clogged sinks. How the hell can we tell what technology we should have?'

Life-safety Systems

Fire protection systems in hotels were greatly enhanced in the 1980s and 1990s because of a number of devastating hotel fires that raised public awareness to life-safety issues. Among those with the most fatalities were fires at the MGM Grand Hotel in Las Vegas, Nevada, the DuPont Plaza in San Juan, Puerto Rico, and the Stouffer's Hotel in Westchester, New York. Testing and research on the causes of these and other hotel fires have improved design methods and standards and new technology has advanced the quality of detection, alarm, and fire extinguishing systems. As a result, most hotels in western countries incorporate state-of-the-art fire protection systems; those without these systems should not be considered safe.

One issue that affects the provision of life-safety systems is the mandate of building codes. For example, an electrical fire at a Boston hotel caused the city to modify its standards for the protection of emergency generators. Other hotels under construction at that time upgraded their plans even though they had complied with previous codes. A serious fire at a Fort Worth, Texas, hotel was the impetus for requiring sprinklers even in low-rise guestroom wings. Concern after a fire in an atrium hotel near Chicago resulted in code changes that required increased exhaust systems to draw smoke away from atrium guestroom corridors.

As a result of these and several other fires, the National Fire Protection Association (NFPA) and the AH&MA have urged developers to incorporate new technology even where codes do not require it. The ultimate goal, of course, is to install fail-safe protection in all hotels worldwide. Life safety technology includes the following:

- automatic fire detection and alarm systems
- fully sprinklered building
- central annunciator panels
- guest evacuation sound systems
- firefighters' voice communication system
- smoke-proof and pressurized exit stairs
- emergency generator (alarm systems, lighting, smoke exhaust).

Also, building codes specify numerous construction details to further protect the building occupants as well as the property. The US has several building codes in addition to the NFPA life safety code on which most individual city or state codes are based. The UK, France, Germany, and many other nations also have precise building regulations. Although similar, the detailed requirements vary somewhat from code to code—the number of sprinklers required in a hotel guestroom, for example, varies from two to five depending on the code in force, even more in such special situations as rooms looking into an atrium—so that hotel standards must be designed to meet the most stringent requirements of all codes. (Building codes are discussed in more detail in Chapter 19.)

Because of the high priority given to fire safety by the hotel industry, large national and international hotel companies have established their own fire safety standards that exceed most local codes, thereby reducing the problem of satisfying varying regulations in different localities. Up-to-date, consistent company standards that go beyond codes also are becoming the key to 'legal safety' as well. Today, owners who fail to apply the latest safety or security measures throughout a hotel or chain may risk liability. For example, after a hotel in Washington, DC, installed electronic locks in its new addition, it was held liable for a theft in the older building because those locks were less secure. Attempts have been made to apply this legal principle also to life safety issues; therefore, operators and designers must carefully consider safety standards and consistently implement them in all hotels under the same ownership or management.

Smoke or heat detectors are now required by most codes in all hotel guestrooms as well as public areas. These usually are placed above the bed and at regular intervals along the guest corridors. Additional heat detectors in such service areas as kitchens, laundries, and mechanical areas are set to recognize the usual high temperatures in these spaces. Critical is how any alarm is recorded: In addition to sounding a local alarm, an integrated system automatically notifies the local fire department; sends a signal to a fire control panel near the hotel entrance—which is easily accessible to firefighters; and alerts hotel staff in the telephone PBX room—the main point from which directions can be quickly communicated to hotel guests.

A major issue in hotel fires is the approach taken to notify guests of the emergency. Some hotels have attempted to put out a local fire without evacuating the building. Often, in emergencies, guests have been uninformed about whether they should try to leave their room or remain there until the emergency is over. Various approaches to establishing sound systems connected to hotel guestrooms have been implemented, including speakers in the corridors loud enough to be heard in the guestrooms. Some regulations insist that a guest evacuation sound system be carried over the telephone system, master television antenna (MTV), or independent low-voltage systems.

The Sensible Application of High Technology to Hotel Design

Valentine A. Lehr,
Lehr Associates,
Consulting Engineers

High technology continues its invasion of all aspects of our lives, including the lodging industry. That technology can be a great boon, or the source of endless frustration, cost, and guest dissatisfaction. Understanding and controlling technology is ever more important and the key to successful applications in hotels.

For example, the wireless telephone has immense benefit in allowing unrestrained communication throughout the guestroom, indeed throughout a hotel property. At the same time, unlimited access to phone service, especially in restaurants, ballrooms, and other areas can be a major annoyance to guests. A balance is needed to restrain available technology. In a similar manner, emerging voice control offers immense possibilities in hotel properties, but the question of privacy (if it can hear my commands and route them to a computer, it can hear everything I say) may limit or negate this technology in hotels.

Certainly, technology will greatly expand guest control in rooms, both through occupancy sensors, and wireless multi-function control devices. High speed data links will allow the guestroom to be a true remote workspace, and the expanded entertainment technology will redefine guestroom use. The bathroom fixtures will all be automated. Technology will also permit significantly higher guest comfort, visually, thermally, and acoustically.

Applying high technology to hotels requires strict adherence to some fundamentals:

- The technology must be intuitively apparent to users. Too many applications confuse and frustrate rather than assist.
- High technology must be easily maintainable.
- The technology must not threaten users, as with voice control systems.
- The technology must be relatively enduring. There is little sense in investing in early obsolescence.

High technology is everywhere and there is much more to come. We can't avoid it, so sensible application is our only logical choice.

Recognition that much of the danger from fires comes from smoke rather than the fire itself has created an increased awareness of the importance of controlling the spread of smoke. This goal is accomplished horizontally by closers on guestroom and other doors and by the installation of fire doors at elevator lobbies that are held open magnetically but which close automatically when detectors sense a fire. The problem is more severe vertically because of elevators, stairs, mechanical ducts and shafts, and numerous small penetrations through the floor slabs. Any vertical openings must be protected with fire-rated automatic dampers to isolate smoke and fire between floors. These dampers, adding substantially to the capital costs of a project, can be designed to also help control energy use.

Vertical stair towers present a similar smoke problem. Two common solutions are to pressurize the stairs so that when any door is opened the higher air pressure keeps the stair clear of toxic smoke or to provide for smoke evacuation in stair vestibules. Elevator shafts require similar specialized systems. In Germany codes require pressurization of elevator shafts, while in France all elevator openings are further protected by automatic fire shutters. In the US many jurisdictions require automatic smoke doors between the elevator lobby and the guestroom corridor.

Security Systems

While improved life safety systems protect the public against fire or such other emergencies as earthquakes, new security systems protect guests, employees, and the physical property from crime. The systems and the procedures set up by management may be developed, at least in part, to meet the requirements established by the hotel's legal and insurance advisors and to help ward off lawsuits. To protect people and property against theft, physical assault, vandalism, arson, and terrorism, the hotel security system has three principal components: locking systems, television surveillance cameras, and various types of alarms.

The keying system is the largest element in hotel security and has undergone the most change over the past few years. Mechanical locks have practically disappeared from guest areas where electronic card-key systems now are standard. Before the card-keys became common hotels were under intense pressure to physically change each lock after a key had been lost or stolen. However, due to the time involved and expense this was not done sufficiently often. The same card-key systems are becoming more common in back-of-house areas because of the ability to generate a record of what cards, that is which employees, attempt entry.

A second major part of the hotel's security systems is closed circuit television (CCTV). The television surveillance system is controlled and monitored in larger hotels at a security office and in smaller properties at the receiving office or telephone PBX. Cameras can be used to scan outdoor areas and specific indoor locations where theft or unauthorized access is a problem. They may be programmed to run only when an alarm is sounded or when a particular door is opened. In other cases, especially in casinos, the CCTV systems monitor areas continuously. The hotel areas most often protected by closed circuit television include the several hotel entrances, storage rooms, and areas where large amounts of cash are handled.

The third element in a security plan is the installation of intrusion alarms at critical points. These incorporate various types of electrical circuits, light beams, and motion detectors. Obviously, these depend on standby or emergency power systems to protect the hotel completely. Intrusion detectors can be used for all areas of the hotel: grounds, doors and windows, unoccupied rooms including guestrooms and storage areas, and selected locations such as the safe and safety deposit boxes. Connecting these alarms to a security console permits the operator to notify authorities of the exact location of the alarm, before taking action.

All these security systems, in addition to effective staff training, increase the safety of the guests and employees and help reduce the hotel operator's insurance premiums. As with other specialized systems, the security components generally are available as part of an overall, integrated package including life safety and energy management.

Audio and Video Systems

With the increased emphasis on group business hotels are investigating new audio and video technologies that can give them a competitive advantage. But operators also are finding that some systems offer a variety of guestroom entertainment and general business options that offer additional benefits beyond those common to the meeting areas. As with most technologies, each year the systems offer new features, added reliability and, sometimes, even lower cost. Typical systems include:

- hand-held technologies
- employee paging
- meeting room sound reinforcement
- closed circuit television
- video conferencing
- large screen television entertainment
- guestroom information/entertainment systems
- master antenna systems including entertainment information, and integrated fire safety, security, and energy management.

For the most part, these systems have been available in some form for many years but, as with other technology, they are quickly becoming more sophisticated with the addition of new innovations and features. The hand-held technologies should continue to explode as computer and communications systems become increasingly integrated. Engineering or housekeeping staff, for example, will be able to stay in close contact with their supervisors and make notations at remote locations directly into the hotel maintenance database. Another area—the use of guestroom computer terminals for entertainment, business, and information purposes—is seeing exploding growth. Videotel, a supplier of in-room electronic services, recently surveyed hotel guests in Boston and found that more than 20 percent were willing to pay additional charges for special services. These included cable TV, video games, online airline schedules, local information (about restaurants, films, shopping, and so on), wire service news, and daily stock prices and other financial news.

Both frequent industry surveys, which indicate increased investment in systems, and new product introductions at annual technology conferences give evidence of exciting innovations that should begin to appear in upscale hotels and resorts. Some experts anticipate, for example, that large screen flat wall units that can project multiple screen images will replace the standard television. As more components are added to the basic low-voltage network the cost of each system will be reduced significantly to the point where it becomes both cost effective and competitively essential.

The 2-day cycle **Four Seasons Hotel, New York.** Fast-track construction schedules are called for in many urban locations where the high cost of land accelerates the need for return on investment. On high-rise buildings with poured-in-place concrete super-structures, the construction sequencing may employ a 2-day cycle where forms are stripped and set up on day one and concrete is poured on day two—then repeated on the following two days, yielding two-and-a-half or three floors a week (see pp. C-2 and 171).

Construction 21

Managing the construction of a hotel or resort requires a well-organized system. The owner's project manager and other financial and operational members of the project team now take on major leadership roles, closely follow the progress of construction, and, especially, pay particular attention to any modifications of the project scope, budget, schedule, or quality. They must establish a methodical control system that tracks each change, measures expenditures against a variety of construction and line budgets, and updates the project schedule. Once the building is largely completed, the owner needs to purchase and install literally thousands of furniture, fixtures, and equipment (FF&E) items, then train staff and test special systems, all well before the anticipated opening date.

The first step in establishing an effective control system is to fully plan the construction project well in advance. Each aspect of the work must be reduced to a group of tasks and subtasks that will allow adequate monitoring and timely reporting of any sign of schedule delays or potential cost overruns. The owner/developer's project manager must carefully identify and diagram the scope and priority of all tasks. Just as marketing and design are crucial to the project's image, so, too, are the construction methods critical to its schedule and budget, and eventual success.

Construction completion dates generally are more critical for hotels than for most other types of buildings. Hotels under construction—even those late in the design phase—sell large blocks of guestrooms and meeting space to convention groups often years before the hotel opens. Any delay entails not only lost revenue but can negatively affect the hotel's reputation among travel agents, corporate groups, and disaffected guests. In addition, staff payroll, training, and other fixed pre-opening expenses are further extended. To help ensure that opening dates are met, the construction contract may include liquidated damage and bonus clauses to penalize or provide incentives for the contractor.

An essential step is to define clearly the roles of the project construction team to avoid potential overlapping—or gaps—in key areas of responsibility. While the 'general conditions' of the construction contract establishes a legal relationship between the contractor or construction manager and the owner, additional roles and detailed work scope descriptions should be prepared to better tie them to the various subcontractors and suppliers.

Project Delivery

The complexity of the mixed-use aspects of hotels—lodging, assembly, commercial, and other uses combined in one facility—presents significant challenges in construction as well as operation. Therefore, the choice of the construction contract form can greatly influence the quality, timeliness, and cost of the final product. While there are various ways to combine the typical contract types, the most common arrangements are (1) the traditional 'design/bid/award' contract, (2) 'construction management,' often including 'fast track' elements, and (3) 'design/build.' Generally, the owner or developer designates a staff executive or consultant to act as the overall project manager, with clear authority and appropriate staff for the size and complexity of the project. Table 21.1 illustrates the key advantages and disadvantages of each type of project delivery method.

Among the three most prevalent variations, the design/bid/award contract separates each of the roles: the architect completes the design and construction documents, contractors review these and submit a lump sum bid, and the owner, with the advice of the architect, selects a contractor, who then completes the building expressly as designed and specified. Construction management integrates these elements more fully by offering construction and budgeting advice throughout the design process. Also, the process may provide the option to fast track the schedule and deliver the project earlier by overlapping the design and construction phases. In the design/build variant, the owner preselects a contractor who directs the design effort, seeking techniques that offer greater potential for cost savings and design improvements during construction. The final selection will depend on the unique special conditions of the project but, generally, design/bid/award best establishes a firm price, construction management offers greater flexibility and the potential to shorten the schedule, and design/build offers a 'turnkey' solution appropriate for less complex lodging types. The availability and productivity of skilled labor also may affect the choice of contract and delivery options.

Owners without in-house project management experience may hire a for-fee developer to represent them throughout the process. Or the developer may initiate the project, investing some funds but seeking joint-venture partners for the majority share, while managing the entire process. Whichever, the project manager performs the following tasks:

- represent the owner at project meetings
- apply for required approvals from city agencies
- review applications for payment
- prepare minutes of meetings
- organize planning information for the owner
- guide and organize the project team.

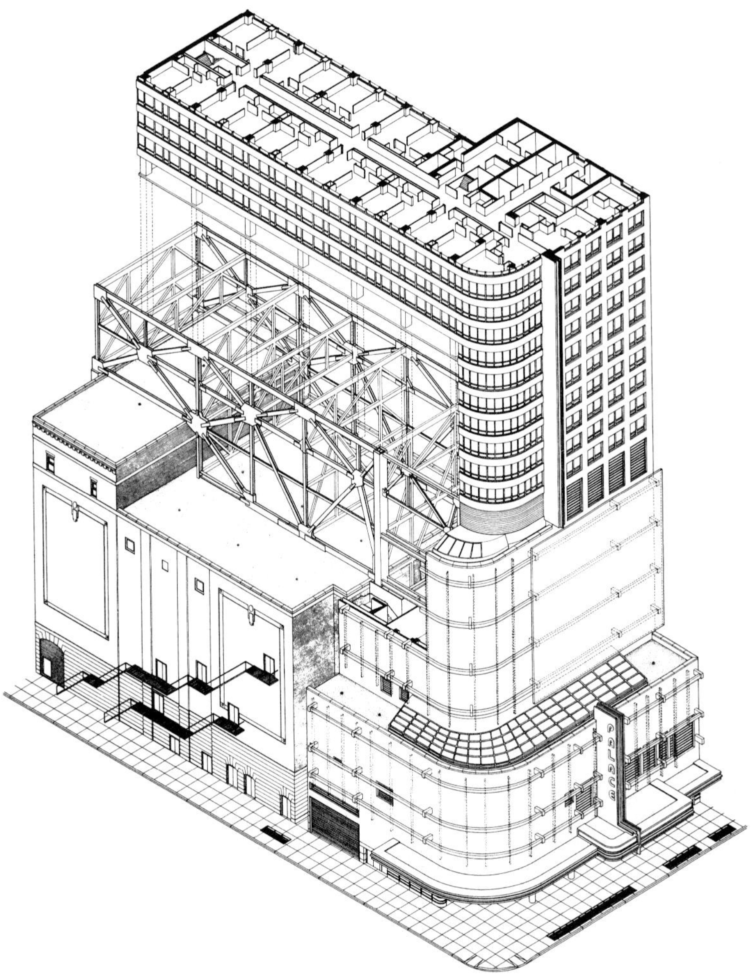

A hotel tower above a theater **Embassy Suites Times Square Hotel, New York.** Structural gymnastics are often called for in tight urban sites where cramped conditions and existing structures pose obstacles to construction. In this 460-suite Times Square hotel a massive steel truss system was employed to allow the 43-story tower to be built above an existing landmark theater.

Design/Bid/Award Contract

The traditional design/bid/award contract is widely used by the hotel industry. It may require the most time, several months (see p. 398) for the architect and design team to prepare full drawings and specifications, then time to allow several general contractors (GC) to calculate their bids and the owner to analyze these before awarding the contract. In this contract form the emphasis is on tight construction documents from the architect and independent management by the general contractor, who takes full responsibility for managing and scheduling the construction. Allowing the architect sufficient time to produce clear, complete, and concise documents provides the owner with the best opportunity to purchase the entire project at a competitive cost and reduces the risk of price overruns. While some people feel that the GC and, in turn, the many subcontractors, may submit a low bid expecting to recoup money later through change orders, to minimize that potential the owner/developer and project manager should accept bids only from qualified and reputable contracting firms.

In the design/bid/award form the GC takes more risk in that its bid must anticipate future material and labor costs and depends on the timely work of countless subcontractors and suppliers. This contract form makes it more difficult for the owner or architect to modify the scope or design—which requires negotiating price and schedule changes—but helps to keep the project on budget and schedule.

Construction Management

The construction management method, developed over the last half of the twentieth century, draws together and integrates the construction, cost estimating, architecture, and engineering disciplines. The construction manager (CM), in effect, acts as both the owner's agent and project manager, providing a continuous involvement from early conceptual design to hotel opening, during which he or she is responsible for the overall budget and schedule, creating value in the design, and value-engineering. The main advantage is that the owner, early in the project, has access to advice on construction methods and costs. Also, the owner has greater flexibility to make modifications in scope or design during the project and can easily work with subcontractors and suppliers to seek out equivalent but more competitive systems and products.

Construction management often assumes some degree of fast tracking, in which construction may begin before the full drawings and specifications are complete. Consider that the contractor can begin the excavation, even the foundations and lower floors, before the architects, engineers, and designers specify every detail of the interior systems and finishes. While reducing the overall construction schedule is a great boon, and may allow the hotel to open and generate revenues earlier, the owner must recognize the risk in beginning a project before the design is complete and final costs are known.

Generally, the architect completes schematic design and, with the construction manager, agrees on the major design elements including structure, principal materials, mechanical systems, and vertical circulation. For example, they may establish the column spacing based on the garage bay or the guestroom module and choose between, say, steel and reinforced concrete structural systems. This sets a number of key elements that should not be changed and allows the contractor to order long-lead-time items in advance of the completion of the design. While early construction proceeds, the architect and design consultants complete the documentation of the remaining details. The owner must carefully analyze the benefits of an accelerated construction timetable and earlier opening versus the potential increases in project cost due to deferring important design and construction decisions.

Without complete drawings it is impossible to agree on a lump sum. The CM process, instead, often utilizes a 'guaranteed maximum price' (GMP) based on a clear definition of the scope of the work and outline specifications detailing the quality levels. The contract usually is structured so that owner and contractor share any savings below the GMP, giving the contractor an incentive to lower construction costs.

The construction manager may select a general contractor but usually manages separate contracts with individual subcontractors. Therefore, the CM plays a strong onsite role coordinating many diverse trades, but has the flexibility to go back to the owner or architect as opportunities arise to add a feature or modify a design, within reasonable constraints. Sometimes, where subcontractors are rushed to complete a task, the quality of workmanship may become an issue. Thus, the CM needs to balance the owner's objectives for quality against the real needs to keep on schedule and budget. The major difficulty with fast track projects is that there is the potential for costs to rise when the design is not fully documented until the middle of the construction process. An experienced CM should be able to shorten the construction period, particularly if using familiar subcontractors and building components, without jeopardizing the quality of the finished hotel.

Design/Build

The design/build format was developed to reduce the delivery time of a project and centralize the design and construction responsibility in a single entity. This approach is best used where the project has fairly simple design requirements and all parties recognize a range of appropriate solutions. Full responsibility is placed in the design/build team, generally headed by the construction side. In this variation, the design aspects usually are secondary to simplifying construction and reducing costs, which, while not unattractive to hotel owners, may not fully meet the needs and expectations of the hotel guest.

The design/build method also has a useful application where the project can be defined very narrowly and the owner benefits from the guaranteed price and schedule. For example, a 'turnkey' approach may be suitable to a guestroom renovation where the owner approves a particular design direction and leaves it to the contractor to complete the renovation, replacing bathroom fixtures and finishes, adding new electronic locks, upgrading electrical and data lines, and purchasing and installing the guestroom FF&E, all for an established price.

Construction Schedule

Most contractors and construction management firms use the 'critical path method' (CPM) to schedule a construction project. These, now, are computer programs such as by Primavera or Microsoft Project that identify each separate task and its relationship to others in the project. The CPM requires that the contractor carefully organize the project ahead of time, making these precise decisions:

- identify each discrete task or subtask
- determine its duration in days or weeks
- identify the task's dependence on other, earlier, steps.

The program calculates the relationship among all the tasks and prepares a graphical representation, highlighting milestones or major events, such as topping out of the structural frame or completion of the enclosure. The diagram clearly shows each step of the process, the amount of time each one requires,

Table 21.1 Construction contract options

	Design/bid/award	*Construction management/ fast track*	*Design/build*
Client/owner			
Advantages	Professional advice on contract and construction quality issues Good industry understanding of how method operates Budgets most accurately resemble actual costs Easier guaranteed maximum price negotiations Clear penalties for cost overruns Unambiguous chain of responsibility	Shorter project delivery time Lower project costs Builder is agent to the owner Professional advice on contract and construction quality issues Clearly defined sharing of cost overruns and savings	Shorter project delivery time Lower project costs Single responsible party Inventive design/construction solutions Reduced project management workload Reduced number of claims Single fee to pay
Disadvantages	Longer start-to-finish time Inability to negotiate subcontractor costs Multiple fees to pay	Project management increases workload Decision-making responsibilities unclear	No independent professional design advice
Contractor/construction manager			
Advantages	Definitive plans and specifications on which to base bids Role clearly understood by all parties	Reduced financial risk Early completion bonuses Easier to recommend substitutions	More control over project Minimum risk and uncertainty Improved design Direct communication with design professionals Opportunity to increase profits
Disadvantages	Less flexibility for substitutions of materials, equipment and systems Adversarial relationships with design professionals	Difficulty in establishing guaranteed maximum price Coordination failures result in delays Penalties Gaps in insurance coverage	Responsible for design errors and omissions
Architect/designer			
Advantages	Greatest control over design and construction quality Role clearly understood by all parties	More involvement in the field Quick decisions by all parties Input from builder during design process	More control over project quality Opportunity to increase profits Field experience Greater credibility with clients Reduced number of claims from contractor
Disadvantages	Adversarial relationships with contractors	Decision-making responsibilities unclear Priorities blurred Timeliness more important than quality Coordination workload increased	Responsibility for errors and omissions of the contractor

Adapted from *Hotel Development*, PKF Consulting, © 1996 by the Urban Land Institute, p. 102. Used with permission.

Precast systems in hotels **Hyatt Regency Greenwich, Old Greenwich, Connecticut.** Advancements in precast concrete systems, a technique that dates back to early Roman architecture, has provided architects with an excellent and economical substitute for carved stone. Lightweight systems such as GFRC (glass-fiber reinforced concrete) are used in ornamental restorations where a rubber mold is made of a complex shape and reproduced in exacting precision.

and the task's dependency on other activities. The graphical organization of the staging and sequencing of tasks helps to identify the importance of long-lead items to the entire schedule. Integrated programs add other features. For example, if each task includes an estimate of the required labor, the program will generate work schedules. Or another module ties the owner's cash flow to the schedule.

As the project moves forward, the program monitors the real-time performance against the schedule and helps to organize and track the work flow. Its overriding advantage is to alert project managers to a potential problem or delay so that they can solve it before one becomes critical.

A key skill the right general contractor or construction manager brings to the project is an ability to organize the site so that the work proceeds in an orderly manner. For example, work can be completed more efficiently when the several trades work separately from each other, rather than share space. Materials need to be delivered in sufficient quantities and stored, sometimes under cover, convenient to their final placement. Similarly, equipment needs to be available when it is needed and the site kept clean and free of debris and potential hazards. In the US, the Occupational Safety and Health Act (OSHA) places very specific rules on the construction site, such as temporary railings on above-ground areas, which must be fully obeyed and enforced. Where the supervisors manage the project in all its details, work flow, efficiency and, ultimately, the quality of the project all are enhanced.

Furniture, Fixtures, and Equipment

At the completion of the design phases of a hotel project, the architect and interior designer have detailed designs and specifications describing the fixed décor and the furniture, fixtures, and equipment (FF&E) for the hotel. Other FF&E items include carpets and rugs, artwork and accessories, window treatments, decorative lighting, decorative hardware, bathroom accessories, and planters. The hotel operator also specifies and purchases additional FF&E items such as linens, china, glassware, uniforms, banquet equipment, and other operating items. The specifications include information required to buy and coordinate FF&E items. For each project these come from hundreds of sources and, frequently, one vendor is dependent on another's product to complete their work. For example, before a lobby sofa can be delivered to a site, the purchasing agent orders fabric from one source, has it sent to another vendor for flame- and soil-treatment, if applicable, and shipped to the sofa manufacturer to be upholstered. Each step must be completed on schedule for the manufacturer to meet the timetable for the project. The architect, interior designer, purchasing agent, or in-house staff may send the specifications to various manufacturers for competitive pricing or, alternatively, may send the packages directly to vendors with whom they have a good relationship.

The construction manager or FF&E installer must develop a systematic approach to ensure the developer and operator that the property will be complete and ready for occupancy before the scheduled soft opening. Once vendors have been selected, the management team uses purchase orders, tracking forms, delivery schedules, and punch-lists to expedite and document the process. The number of FF&E purchase orders can be in the thousands for a large-scale hotel project. For example, one style of sofa might be ordered in several sizes and with a variety of fabrics and trims, each one intended for a difference location. Properly documenting all of these details, if coordinated at the specification and purchase order stage, not only sets up a smooth installation but also helps protect the owner and consultants from manufacturing and delivery mistakes. Table 21.2 identifies the type of detail required to adequately purchase and track FF&E items.

The purchasing agent typically develops a tracking system to catalogue and chart all items that have

Table 21.2 Purchase order information

Project name and location
Purchase order number, coded for easy reference such as 'f' for fabric, 's' for sofa, etc. and number for each different item
Order date
Delivery date required
Product manufacturer's name, address, telephone, and contact person
Item number, description, and quantity
Unit price, extended price, and total price (including applicable taxes and shipping)
Deposit required and balance due after receipt and/or installation
Special requirements (e.g. finish sample, dye lot cutting, shop drawings, or mock-up required for approval; field measurements required prior to manufacturing)
Ship to address (vendor to vendor, vendor to storage warehouse, vendor to hotel site)
Side-mark (indicate on the outside of the shipping package the final destination of the item, such as lobby, guestroom type, etc.)
Specification (attach full spec, often with catalog photo or physical sample of fabric or wood finish)

been purchased and create a simple form for follow-up. The architect, interior designer, or in-house personnel make frequent calls to check whether a particular product is on schedule. The tracking forms help ensure that all items are delivered on schedule—or identify potential shipment problems in a time frame that allows the team to react. New computerized systems make this information readily available on the Internet to members of the team, allowing them to find almost instantly the status on any particular item.

The FF&E installation is part of the overall project schedule, and included in the CPM matrix. Typically, the FF&E is phased to follow construction completion but, as the opening date approaches, contractors, delivery people, and installation crews often are working in the same areas—and vying for use of the loading dock, delivery entrance, and freight elevators—making schedule coordination critical. Architects and interior designers prepare FF&E plans and elevations, coded to the specifications and purchase orders, indicating the precise location for each specific item.

Depending on the schedule, furniture and other items may be delivered directly at the site or arrive, first, at an intermediate warehouse facility where they are received, inspected, and stored until needed. When the FF&E arrives directly at the site, it is important for the designer or another person to inspect the delivery for damage and to match the items to the tracking forms. Often, the hotel ballroom is the last space to be completed, so that it can be used as a staging area for temporary storage of other items during the FF&E installation phase. As the construction project nears completion, contractors, furniture installers, pre-opening staff, inspectors, and others all need access to the same spaces. Therefore, it is important that the delivery and installation proceed in an orderly way (see Table 21.3).

After the FF&E is installed, the team prepares a punch-list, identifying missing or damaged items that need to be replaced or repaired. Often, there has not been time to complete a separate punch-list of deficiencies in each room before the furniture is placed, so the same list identifies paint and electrical items, for instance, which need correcting. Only after all items have been properly installed and operate as designed, should the construction manager or designer authorize final payment.

Table 21.3 Order for FF&E installation

Contractor-installed Items
Back-of-house equipment
Decorative light fixtures (chandeliers and wall sconces)
Special hardware
Bathroom accessories
Floor coverings
Window treatments
Guestroom items
Wall-mounted items (headboards, framed mirrors)
Large furnishings
Small furnishings
Art and accessories
Public space Items
Large furnishings
Small furnishings
Art and accessories (rugs, throw pillows, interior planting)

Part 3

Entertainment atrium

Development Guide

The successful hotel development requires a familiarity with more than the distinct variety of hotel types and the design criteria outlined in Parts 1 and 2. Equally essential is an understanding of the development process itself and how the many financial, operational, marketing and organizational objectives of an owner and developer influence the project and its eventual ability to be successful. Only if these objectives are in balance with the demand for hotel facilities, with the site's capacity to support a hotel or resort, and with the programmatic and design decisions, can the project prosper.

The chapters in this third section trace the hotel development process beginning with the initial concept—the idea to develop a lodging property. The process includes a number of key steps: analyzing the feasibility, assembling the development and design team, establishing the building program, and managing the budget, schedule, and the hotel opening. In addition, the team should understand the issues of hotel operation and how the planning and design decisions influence many of the practical and technical aspects of running a hotel. This allows the team to consider solutions that effectively reduce staff numbers or accommodate important life safety or mechanical requirements.

Finally, the book considers the future, whether it is increasing numbers of focused niche lodging types, broad socioeconomic trends, or creative proposals for new resorts under the sea or in outer space. The future is wide open, the industry is dynamic, and a truly collaborative partnership among developer, design team, and operator should see a continuing explosion of creative hotels and resorts in the twenty-first century.

The boutique hotel lobby prototype **Mondrian, Hollywood, California.** This smashing urban resort incorporates many Ian Schrager and Philippe Starck trademarks and features a collection of 200 pieces of furniture and other *objets d'dart* which are regularly repositioned throughout the public spaces.

Development Planning

22

On the surface, the idea of developing a lodging property seems fairly simple: the developer conceives a new project, buys the land, hires the architect, acquires financing, builds the structure, and opens the hotel or resort—to great success. But, in reality, it is more complex and fraught with risk. Part 1 of this book describes the tremendous variety of competitive hotel types—which one is best for a particular site and market? How are the market needs assessed? Who is the customer and what facilities does he or she really need and expect? What skills are needed in the design team and what specialized consultants should be hired? And so forth.

Therefore, developing the successful hotel requires bringing together the experience of scores of professionals from real estate, finance, design, construction, hotel operations, and many other disciplines, whose work then must be coordinated and channeled to complete the project—defined by the market requirements and the architect's design—both on time and on budget. The bubble diagram on the next page suggests one simple way to conceive a project: programming, design, cost estimating, construction, and operations. It is easiest to describe the development process as a linear one, complete the first step, then proceed to the next, and so forth. But it seldom happens that way. Development is messy, with lots of false starts and circling back to reassess a decision. The diagram implies just that. At each step you may need to consider altering some of the previous decisions, to change the market orientation, for example, or to reduce the project scope in order to save money. This chapter will discuss some of the key aspects of development—project sequence, feasibility, and facilities programming—and will introduce the concept of prototype development.

Project Sequence

Hotel projects follow the same general sequence as other development projects but with some important nuances. The future operator, for instance, usually is involved from nearly the first step, influencing the site selection, program, choice of consultants, and so forth. Therefore, it is best to consider how the principal management companies, the organizations with the development and operating experience, think about a new project, and incorporate their methods.

Most of these companies have real estate professionals and architects on staff, who field perhaps dozens of inquiries a day, from developers with an idea for a new hotel or desire to reposition one. The prospective operator needs to carefully assess the developer's experience and financial wherewithal and balance this against the company's own strategic goals. Do they have an appropriate lodging product to meet the developer's goals? Do they want to expand in that region? At that type of site (airport, downtown)? At that quality level? And so forth. If some of these can be answered in the affirmative, the technical staff from the management company may help coordinate and provide guidance and feedback during some of these basic steps:

- evaluate the prospective site
- complete a feasibility study
- select the architect and design consultants
- prepare a facilities program (concept statement, area program, operational description, project budget)
- obtain financing
- review the project design (schematic, design development, construction documents)
- monitor construction and the hotel opening

One of the first steps, of course, is to confirm the location and particular site and assess its suitability for a hotel. This is partly carried out in the feasibility study from a market standpoint but, equally importantly, the site needs to be evaluated from a design and construction perspective.

Feasibility Analysis

Among the first steps that the developer of a new hotel must take is to prepare a market study and financial projections. The study, usually assembled by a consulting firm and further refined by the management company's senior operations staff (if it is to be chain operated), has two key aspects. First, it assesses present and future demand for lodging and such other hotel services as meeting areas, restaurants and bars, and recreational facilities. Second, it estimates operating income and expenses for 10 years after the hotel opens.

There is no single formula for success. Projects with optimistic feasibility studies may do poorly while, occasionally, those built despite a negative report do surprisingly well. However, the more successful projects combine several ingredients: good location, continuing strong demand, the proper mix of facilities, and professional management. To some extent, the prototypical feasibility study common to the hotel industry critically assesses all these factors. What these studies don't consider is the impact that outstanding design—whether architectural, interior, or landscape—can make on a future property's success.

Feasibility studies have differing objectives. Most are used to increase the confidence of others in a project's success and to obtain permanent financing. Thus, often, it is a basic component of the developer's package to prospective lenders. Other feasibility studies may be used to obtain an operating franchise or management contract or to attract equity participation. Similar reports but with different emphases may be used in negotiations with city officials to support a developer's request for a zoning variance or to reinforce his or her contention that the project will increase local sales and real estate taxes and add new jobs. Occasionally, in recent years, feasibility studies have been commissioned by a municipality or public agency or—in developing countries—by the national government, in an attempt to attract new private development.

Only infrequently do these studies actually assess the feasibility of a project. This is because any calculation of relative success depends on much more than the objective analysis of the lodging market. Not only does it depend on accurate projections of future conditions, but it also must take into account such confidential factors as the developer's investment strategies and tax status.

Assuming the study does not go beyond projecting cash flow available after fixed charges (real estate taxes, property insurance, and management fee), the typical outline includes:

- *Local area evaluation*: analyze the economic vitality of the city or region; describe the suitability of the project site for a hotel.
- *Lodging market analysis*: assess the present demand for lodging (and other revenue generators) and future growth rates for each of several market segments; identify the existing supply of competitive properties and anticipate additions to the supply; assess the competitive position of the subject property.
- *Proposed facilities*: propose a balance of guestroom and public facilities including restaurants, bars, meeting and banquet rooms, retail shops, recreation facilities, and parking.
- *Financial analysis*: estimate income and expenses for the hotel over a 10-year period to show its potential cash flow.

However, these sections are not treated in equal detail in the typical study. The parts that have the most direct relationship to the architectural solution—the site analysis and the facilities program—are the least highly refined. The supply and demand analyses and the financial projections, on the other hand, are the most specific, understandably, since the study is prepared by market and economic consultants. Unfortunately, too often the study does not give full enough consideration to trends beginning to influence the market and their possible impact on the project design. The following discussion and the accompanying tables adapted from an actual report highlight the principal aspects of a typical hotel feasibility analysis.

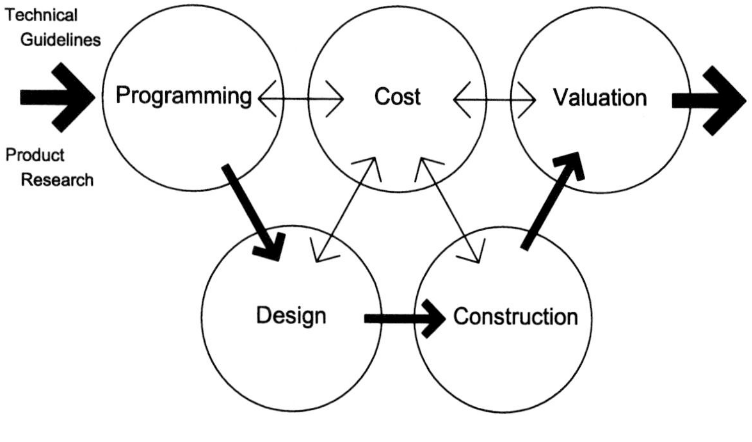

The process **Development flow chart.** Based on market data and other research, the design team continually refines program, budget, and design, utilizing development software to perfect new projects and prototypes.

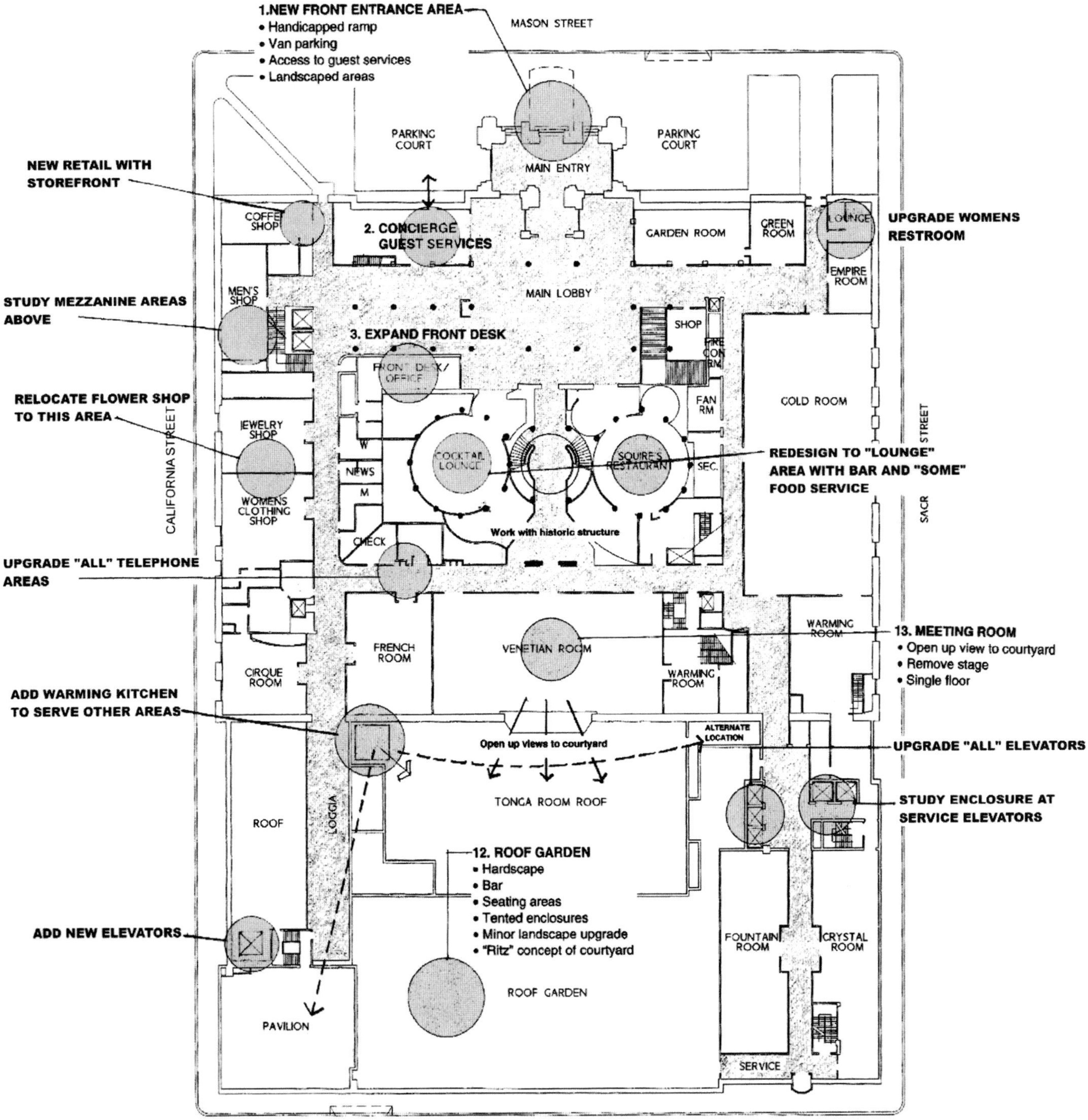

Diagramming the renovation opportunities **Fairmont Hotel, San Francisco, California.** Hotel renovations require balancing changing functional requirements and building system upgrades with the need to accommodate increasingly complex code requirements and building constraints within budgetary limits. Here, the architects, Gensler, prepared simple yet clear diagrams of the proposed scope of work as a first step in gaining the owner's approval and estimating project cost.

Analyzing the Local Area

As a prelude to the market analysis, most feasibility studies present data illustrating the economic climate in the area—from the entire city or region to the particulars of the specific project site. Many critics consider them no more than 'boiler plate,' yet they are helpful in providing necessary background to lenders from outside the local community and in establishing a relative sense of the lodging markets. In broad terms the local analysis includes:

- Growth trends in population, employment, income, tax receipts, new construction, airport data, etc.
- Major public and private facilities including those for education, health, government, transportation, religion, tourism, etc.
- Travel and visitor analysis, including volume and percentage of traffic by car, air, train, bus, and ship, as appropriate.

The emphases of the study should reflect the probable type of hotel project. For example, a resort hotel would be only marginally concerned with industrial and commercial influences, perhaps only as secondary markets for off-season periods. Instead, it should focus on natural attractions and recreational opportunities in the area and on airline and highway networks from the principal market areas. For the same reason, area analyses for hotels sited near a university, a major medical complex, or a 'Silicon Valley' development should deal with trends influencing these specialized demand generators—perhaps high-level training sessions—rather than with those of the larger industrial and commercial sector.

The area evaluation also should include a detailed site analysis. In addition to the obvious site description—size, boundaries, topography, and so forth—the analysis should emphasize visibility, accessibility, and suitability to hotel use. The first two are most critical for motel and other roadside properties that attract predominantly highway business, much of it from travelers without reservations. The suitability discussion may emphasize such site advantages or potential constraints as views, natural features, proximity to local attractions or businesses, adjacent uses, room for expansion, zoning, or utility availability.

Analyzing the Lodging Market

The largest part of the feasibility study is the analysis of the demand for guestrooms and other hotel services and the enumeration of existing competitive hotel rooms. The study must acknowledge future shifts in demand, as individual market segments expand or contract and as neighborhoods undergo change. Making assumptions about these future changes, as well as about growth rates, improves the sophistication of the analysis but adds considerably to the risk. Therefore, the developer must be prepared to analyze and review the consultant's assumptions.

The demand for lodging can be calculated in two complementary ways. In one approach, estimates of the need for guestrooms are assembled from interviews and meetings with local business people representing the various generators of lodging demand: industries, government and commercial offices, universities, medical centers, amusement parks, and so forth. For the most part, the demand is separated into three major market segments: convention and other group business, commercial business, and tourists. Occasionally, the report may identify airline crews or tour groups, for example, where these or other specific markets are a key component of the business. It analyzes each segment thoroughly in terms of its weekday/weekend characteristics, seasonality, price sensitivity, amount of double occupancy, and, most important, its anticipated growth over the succeeding several years. At the same time, the report should assess the potential for group meeting business, restaurant demand, and requirements for other hotel services and amenities.

Table 22.1 Existing lodging demand by hotel and market segment

Property	*Rooms*	*Occupancy*	*Commercial*	*Group*	*Leisure*	*Local*	*Total*
Hotel A	200	85%	34,500	9,500	12,000	6,050	62,050
Hotel B	200	82%	29,300	8,200	14,160	8,200	59,860
Hotel C	165	74%	22,000	4,500	13,500	4,560	44,561
Hotel D	135	80%	6,200	12,800	19,340	1,190	39,530
Total	700	80.6%	92,000	35,000	59,000	20,000	206,000

Table 22.2 Future areawide lodging demand by market segment

Market demand segment	*Growth factor*	*Current demand*	*Year 1*	*Year 2*	*Year 3*	*Year 4*	*Year 5*
Commercial	3%	92,000	94,750	97,600	100,500	103,500	106,400
Group	5%	35,000	36,750	38,500	40,500	42,500	44,600
Leisure	3%	59,000	60,700	62,600	64,500	66,400	68,400
Local	3%	20,000	20,600	21,200	21,800	22,500	23,200
Total demand		206,000	212,800	219,900	227,300	234,900	242,600
Competitive supply		255,500	255,500	365,000*	365,000	365,000	365,000
Estimated area-wide occupancy		80.6%	83.3%	60.2%	62.3%	64.4%	66.5%

*Note, the competitive supply increases in Year 2 with the opening of the proposed 300-room hotel. The growth factors represent an annual increase; current demand is the number of rooms sold by market segment.

The second and quicker way to estimate total demand—although with important limitations—is to know the current year's occupancy rates at the competitive hotels. A simple calculation for each hotel (number of rooms × average occupancy percentage × 365 days) results in a figure that represents the total area-wide annual demand for guestrooms. Unfortunately, the use of the average occupancy rates fails to take into account daily or seasonal fluctuations in demand and, importantly, does not identify the 'fill days' when the local hotels are at 100 percent occupancy and must turn away potential guests.

The consultant estimates future demand for each segment by extending the current demand figures using various growth rates. These inflation factors—critical to the conclusions of the market study—are based on identifiable trends, economic projections, and the consultant's judgment and experience. A simplified market segment analysis, including the application of the growth factors, is shown in Tables 22.1 and 22.2.

Similarly, the consultant prepares a table which sets out the competitive hotels or 'supply' showing their physical characteristics (number of guestrooms, size of restaurants, bars, meeting and banquet areas, recreation facilities, and parking) and fundamental operating statistics (occupancy percentage, 'rack' or listed rates, average rate—the result of group discounts or promotional rates—and double occupancy). In smaller communities, where there are few or no competitors in the subject property's class, less competitive properties may be added to the analysis. The supply analysis includes adjustments for future years to reflect the construction of new hotels, the expansion of existing properties, the renovation and repositioning of lower quality hotels, as well as any anticipated deletions from the market.

Next, the consultant establishes the competitive standing of the proposed hotel by assessing its location, size, facilities, rate, and level of quality versus the existing properties. This part of the analysis focuses on guestroom occupancy percentage and average room rate. The 'fair share' concept, which assumes that a new hotel will attract at least its proportionate share of the aggregate market demand, is at the center of the competitive evaluation. On occasion, the consultants may propose that a par-

Table 22.3 Future lodging demand by hotel and market segment (Year 2)

Property	*Rooms*	*Occupancy*	*Commercial*	*Group*	*Leisure*	*Local*	*Total*
Existing total demand			97,600	38,500	62,600	21,200	219,900
Proposed hotel fair share (30%)			29,280	11,550	18,780	6,360	65,970
Proposed hotel penetration			90%	120%	100%	80%	97.1%
Proposed hotel	300	58.5%	26,352	13,860	18,780	5,088	64,080
Hotel A	200	64.7%	26,718	6,675	8,940	4,865	47,198
Hotel B	200	62.4%	22,655	5,765	10,515	6,605	45,540
Hotel C	165	56.2%	17,030	3,180	9,990	3,675	33,875
Hotel D	135	59.3%	4,845	9,020	14,375	967	29,207

The existing total demand comes from Year 2 in the previous table. The proposed hotel's fair share of each market segment is 30% (300 of 1,000 total rooms); its penetration of the total market depends on relative location, facilities, chain affiliation, etc.

ticular hotel will capture more than its fair share of a specific market segment because of its location, facilities, chain affiliation or, perhaps, nothing more than its newness.

This refinement of the aggregate demand figures allows the consultant to begin to assign occupied guestrooms to area hotels in proportion to their current standing as modified by the introduction of the new property in the marketplace. Commonly, occupancy during the first two or three years is several percentage points below a stabilized or target operating year because the hotel needs this time to develop its full sales potential. The third year is frequently used as the standard to represent the probable operating results in a stable year. Table 22.3, carrying forward the earlier example, illustrates how all hotel occupancies suffer when additional rooms are added to the market.

In addition to guestroom occupancy, the feasibility report projects estimated average room rates for the new hotel based on existing rates at similar quality hotels inflated to 'future dollars.' The average rate is expanded to represent room sales for each year, and this figure, based on numerous assumptions and estimates, provides the basis for many of the financial projections, briefly discussed later in this chapter.

Defining the Proposed Facilities

Feasibility consultants include in the body of the report a general description of the proposed facilities. As illustrated here, this description includes the following elements, outlined in only the broadest terms:

- number and mix of guestrooms and suites
- number of restaurants and lounges with their capacities
- amount of meeting and banquet facilities with their capacities or floor area
- health club and other recreational facilities
- parking
- additional amenities, such as retail shops, entertainment, and any special services.

The facilities description, substantially based on the supply and demand analysis, is the one section of the report that most directly influences the pre-design and planning phases of the hotel development project. It establishes the number of guestrooms and outlines the major public facilities that provide the order-of-magnitude framework for the preliminary space program (Table 22.4). Although the report describes the public areas briefly, it neglects entirely the back-of-house service areas and administrative offices.

Some developers feel that the typical definition of the public areas isn't detailed enough. They request that the consultants identify specific operational and design features that will help assure the hotel's success and discuss how these influence the positioning of the hotel. Many studies, though, do little more than suggest that the property 'will be developed as a first class hotel and be expertly managed and promoted.'

It is common for the hotel management company, the future operator, to review the feasibility recommendations critically and to modify them to reflect their own operating strategies as well as perceptions about the local market. Though depending on the feasibility report for background material and for the objective judgment of experienced hospitality consultants, experienced and sophisticated developers

Table 22.4 Proposed facilities list

Guestrooms	*Keys*	*Bays*
Double-double	180	180
King	100	100
Sico room (wall bed/meeting room)	6	6
Suite (one-bay, connects to two guestrooms)	8	8
Suite (two-bays; connects to two guestrooms)	6	12
Club floor executive lounge	0	4
Manager's apartment	0	0
Total	300	310
Food and beverage outlets		*Seats*
Three-meal restaurant		120
Specialty restaurant		80
Cocktail lounge		70
Lobby bar		30
Total		300
Function rooms		*Seats*
Ballroom		700
Meeting rooms, total		400
Boardroom (included above)		0
Total		1,100
Other public facilities		
Indoor swimming pool		
Health club, sauna, exercise room		
Retail shops		2,000 ft^2 (185 m^2)
Parking		350 spaces

may alter significant portions of the facilities outline or the occupancy and rate assumptions to better support their own image of the project.

Preparing the Financial Analysis

In addition to the main body of the feasibility study, which analyzes the local area, identifies supply and demand characteristics, and proposes a project of a specific size, the full report includes a second part, the financial projections. This section contains 15–30 pages of financial tables projecting income and expenses for the subject property for 10 years following its opening (see Appendix D). A snapshot of such financial projections is shown in the example of a cash flow statement, Table 22.5.

The financial analysis is based on averages of hotel operations established by several major financial services and consulting firms, including PricewaterhouseCoopers, PKF Consulting, and Hospitality Valuation Services. These and other international consulting firms, as well as Smith Travel Research, regularly publish annual statistics comparing hotels by size, region, type, age, and, for smaller properties, those with and without restaurants. The developer of a new property should be familiar with the basic organization of and approximate values reflected in these industry statistics.

In selecting the feasibility consultant, the developer should seek a firm with experience and high industry credibility. The consultant must be neutral and objective if he or she is to prepare an independent report that will be accepted by lenders. In addition, the developer must insist on complete documentation of sources and explanations of assumptions. The developer may provide data that are biased in favor of the project and other people and companies interviewed for the study may purposely exaggerate or simply be too optimistic. Similarly, such assumptions as growth rates, inflation, and market penetration, if even slightly in error, can substantially alter the reliability of the study.

A well-prepared feasibility study can establish the basis, in terms of both financial and facilities goals, for a profitable and clearly defined hotel. The developer who begins the project with a relatively narrow focus, whose instinct defines the approximate size, facilities, quality level, services and amenities, etc., can better target the market analysis, select truly competitive hotels, define rate and occupancy, identify important trends, and outline the needed facilities. The developer, then, must critique the drafts of the study and insist on a clear and logical presentation of the competitive environment.

Table 22.5 Cash flow statement

Revenue	
Rooms	$6,000,000
Food	2,500,000
Beverage	700,000
Telephone	300,000
Minor operated departments	400,000
Rents and other income	100,000
Total	**$10,000,000**
Departmental expenses	
Rooms	$1,500,000
Food and beverage	2,500,000
Telephone	150,000
Minor operated departments	250,000
Total	**$4,400,000**
Departmental income	**$5,600,000**
Operating expenses	
Administrative and general	$850,000
Management fee	300,000
Marketing	600,000
Property operation and maintenance	350,000
Energy	300,000
Total	**$2,400,000**
Gross operating profit	**$3,200,000**
Fixed expenses	
Property taxes	$250,000
Insurance	50,000
Reserve for replacement	300,000
Total	**$600,000**
Net operating income	**$2,600,000**

Facilities Programming

While the general concept of the hotel may be known early in the project and tested during the feasibility phase, establishing the hotel program is especially important because of the highly competitive nature of the hotel business. The pre-design documentation for a new project or for a major expansion or repositioning of a hotel must fully describe and define both the space needs and the operational requirements. Without such information, the architect and design consultants are not able to fine tune standard rule-of-thumb numbers or create a unique hotel for a precise market. Much of this documentation is required to obtain a lender's package to finance hotel.

Table 22.6 Conceptual area requirements

	Roadside inn mid-scale		*Downtown hotel first-class*		*Resort hotel luxury*		*Convention hotel first-class*	
Number of guestroom keys	150		300		300		600	
Number of guestroom bays	150		315		360		650	
Net guestroom area	310	(29)	350	(32)	420	(39)	350	(32)
Gross guestroom area	430	(40)	500	(46)	610	(57)	510	(47)
Total guestroom area	64,500	(5,985)	157,500	(14,615)	219,600	(20,380)	331,500	(30,765)
Guestroom percentage	80%		75%		70%		65%	
Total hotel area*	80,625	(7,480)	210,000	(19,490)	313,700	(29,110)	510,000	(47,330)
Total area/key	537	(50)	700	(65)	1,045	(97)	850	(79)

*Total area figures in ft^2 (m^2) exclude parking.

Complete facilities programming is much more than a list of the space requirements; it also must address a variety of needs: location, market demand, competition, quality level, operational features, restaurant concepts, staffing, budget, and market trends (see Appendix E). Feasibility consultants generally recommend a mix of certain facilities, but the hotel management company, working with the owner and architect, develop the final program. Table 22.6, illustrating different types of hotels, shows how widely the program for a hotel can vary depending on its purpose, market orientation, and other issues. Note that hotels of different types can vary from about 550 ft^2 (51 m^2) per room to over 1,000 ft^2 (93 m^2) because of the substantially different mix of facilities.

The facilities program includes not only the area requirements but also a narrative discussion which defines the project in qualitative terms and outlines many of the operational requirements and constraints.

Defining the Project

With so many designers and consultants at work on a major hotel project, a consensus on the goals and objectives of the development is essential: What market is it supposed to attract? What class and what type of hotel might it be? What services and amenities should it provide? Which public functions should be emphasized? Therefore, it is helpful to prepare a concise definition of the project to identify these issues, to outline the primary public facilities, and to provide a gross estimate of the size of the project. The extract below illustrates the type of statement that clearly defines the project's intent.

The hotel will be a first-class, full-service, high-rise, convention hotel with 800 rooms and 50,000 ft^2 (4,640 m^2) of meeting space. Located in a growing retail and entertainment district near the proposed new convention center, the project should accommodate, besides convention attendees, both the individual business traveler and weekend 'vacationer.' Facilities should include two restaurants, two lounges, a health club/spa, a business center, ground level retail, and parking for 600 cars.

The second part of the preliminary definition of a new or expanded hotel project is a summary of the principal public facilities. Before the developer and his team can move on to the program and later design phases, they need a precise list of the revenue-producing areas, those on which the support and service areas are based. This list forms the core of the expanded space program. For example, even a cursory listing of the restaurant and banquet requirements influences the size and design requirements of the kitchen, food storage, and employee locker areas. As the developer focuses on the projections for operating income and expenses, the designers refine their summary list of major facilities to better meet the project objectives, which include:

- *guestrooms*: number of room 'keys' (separate rental units); number of room 'bays' (total equivalent room modules); number and description of suites; typical room and suite dimensions
- *lobby and public areas*: architectural image and ambiance; amount of retail space
- *food and beverage*: capacity of each restaurant; capacity of each lounge; quality level and theme for each
- *function space*: dimensions of the ballroom (including ceiling height); amount of other meeting and banquet space; need for exhibition space

- *recreation facilities*: quality level of health club/spa; outline of any additional facilities
- *parking requirements*
- *technical requirements*: special building systems and guest amenities.

The early estimates of project size generally are little more than the application of basic rules-of-thumb. The experienced hotel developer and architect calculate gross project floor area from an understanding of the typical guestroom dimensions—to which they apply factors to increase the area to allow for circulation (corridors, elevators, stairs), walls, and other unusable space—and the relative amount of public and support space required for a particular type of hotel. Until a more detailed program is established, this gross approximation of project size is the critical basis for all cost estimates. In the detailed program examples later in this chapter, the area requirements vary tremendously depending on the type, quality level, and architectural configuration.

Allocating Program Areas

The development of the architectural space program does not occur at one time nor does it result in a static document. The early definition establishes an approximate total area for the project; later, the architect develops a space list at the beginning of the conceptual design and refines a more detailed program during the schematic and design development phases. Because the technical-services staffs of the major hotel-operating companies have the experience to react quickly and accurately to requests for programmatic information, many developers never prepare comprehensive space programs. Instead, the detailed planning and space-use information is transmitted through a comprehensive management company Design Guide or bit-by-bit during the ensuing design phases, as the architect requires more specific technical information. But, with computer programs such as Strategic Hotel Area Program Estimate and Evaluation (SHAPEE) now available, detailed area information can be issued early and can be updated easily during the design phases.

The preliminary program permits the architect to begin the schematic studies for the project. Usually, the management company staff prepare the list based on their own standards as well as on their experience with similar projects and on the market information provided in the feasibility report. They analyze the broad guidelines established in the earlier estimates to see whether the estimates still accurately reflect the size, class, and hotel type of the project. The staff then expands these guidelines to include a list of the principal guestrooms and suites as well as public, administration, and service areas.

Development Software

Robert E. Kastner, MBA, 9 Tek Ltd.

Sophisticated software programs are essential in the development and construction process. Particularly useful are those systems that integrate multiple steps in hotel development and build upon each other, such as software that combines the building program, construction budgeting, and proforma financial analyses.

One example of such a program which has been continually refined over more than 15 years is the SHAPE Software System, a series of Excel templates that allows developers and consultants to generate detailed planning and analysis information for a proposed hotel or resort project anywhere in the world.

The first module, Strategic Hotel Area Program Estimate and Evaluation (SHAPEE) provides a programming template which allows the user to input such basic assumptions as typical guestroom area, number of restaurants and their capacities, and amount of function space. From this foundation the program generates a detailed area program (square feet or meters), expanding these public areas and adding all the back-of-house support functions, which can be modified further as members of the design team develop a fuller sense of the hotel and its market.

The second module, Strategic Hotel Area and Project Estimate (SHAPEST) links SHAPEE to cost data which calculates total project cost and other budget data on a per key or per bay basis. The cost estimates are dependent on such hotel attributes as quality level and location.

The last module, Strategic Hotel Analysis Program Evaluation and Proforma (SHAPEPRO) further builds on the previous modules and, by adding its own set of capital and operating assumptions, generates a ten-year cash flow projection. The developer may find most useful the integrated internal rate of return (IRR) and present value calculations, as well as a value-added (V-A) analysis which allows the user to run through any number of 'what-if' scenarios: changing the program; modifying construction, FF&E, or technical costs; or adjusting operating assumptions. Together, these programs, and others that may accomplish similar objectives, provide an essential tool to the developer and other members of the team.

Table 22.7 Hotel area program

	Size of hotel (number of rooms):					
	200	*500*	*1,000*	*200*	*500*	*1,000*
Guestroom mix (number of rooms)						
King (50%)	100	250	500	100	250	500
Double-double (42%)	84	210	430	84	210	430
Handicapped (2–3%)	6	15	20	6	15	20
Suite (5%)	10	25	50	10	25	50
Hotel area program	*Area in square feet*			*Area in square meters*		
Guestrooms						
Guestrooms, at 350 ft^2 (32.5 m^2)	66,500	166,250	332,500	6,175	15,450	30,875
Suites, at 700 ft^2 (65 m^2)	7,000	8,750	17,500	325	815	1,625
Support (linen storage, vending, ice)	2,000	4,000	8,000	186	371	742
Lobby						
Flow area	2,000	4,000	8,000	186	371	742
Seating	200	500	1,000	19	46	93
Retail	300	800	2,000	28	74	186
Assistant manager	0	100	100	0	9	9
Support (bellman, luggage, toilets, phones)	400	600	1,000	37	56	93
Food and beverage outlets						
Coffee shop	2,700	3,200	3,600	251	297	334
Specialty restaurant	0	2,000	2,400	0	186	223
Theme restaurant	0	0	2,000	0	0	186
Quick service/coffee retail	0	600	800	0	56	74
Lobby lounge	600	1,200	2,000	56	111	186
Cocktail lounge	1,500	0	2,000	139	0	186
Entertainment lounge/sports bar	0	3,000	4,000	0	278	371
Pool bar	0	0	400	0	0	37
Support (bar storage, toilets, coats, phones)	400	800	1,500	37	74	139
Function areas						
Ballroom	4,000	10,000	25,000	371	928	2,320
Ballroom foyer	1,000	2,500	6,000	93	232	557
Junior ballroom	0	4,000	12,000	0	371	1,114
Junior ballroom foyer	0	1,000	3,000	0	93	278
Banquet rooms	0	3,000	6,000	0	278	557
Meeting rooms	1,200	2,400	6,000	111	223	557
Boardroom	0	400	1,000	0	37	93
Amphitheater	0	1,200	1,500	0	111	139
Exhibit hall	0	0	20,000	0	0	1856
Support (function and AV storage, projection booth, toilets, coats, phones)	1,000	4,000	10,000	93	371	928
Recreation						
Swimming pool	0	1,000	1,500	0	93	139
Pool including deck, whirlpool	0	2,400	4,000	0	223	371
Lockers, toilets, sauna	300	600	1,000	28	56	93
Exercise room	500	800	1,000	46	74	93
Spa facilities	0	1,000	3,000	0	93	278
Children's playroom	0	0	600	0	0	56
Reception/manager	0	200	400	0	19	37
Support (pool equipment and storage)	100	400	800	9	37	74

	Size of hotel (number of rooms):					
	200	500	1,000	200	500	1,000
Administration						
Front office						
Front desk	160	250	420	15	23	39
Front office manager	120	120	120	11	11	11
Assistant manager	0	120	120	0	11	11
Credit manager	100	100	100	9	9	9
Director of rooms	0	150	150	0	14	14
Reception/secretary	100	100	100	9	9	9
Reservations area	80	200	250	7	19	23
Reservations manager	0	120	120	0	11	11
Telephone operators	80	150	200	7	14	19
Safe deposit boxes	30	60	60	3	6	6
General cashier	0	120	120	0	11	11
Count room	125	150	200	12	14	19
Work area/mail	40	100	150	4	9	14
Storage	40	80	120	4	7	11
Executive office						
Reception/waiting	200	250	300	19	23	28
General manager	150	200	250	14	19	23
Executive assistant manager	0	180	180	0	17	17
Resident manager	0	0	180	0	0	17
Food and beverage manager	120	150	175	11	14	16
Secretary	100	150	200	9	14	19
Conference room	0	200	250	0	19	23
Copying and storage	60	120	200	6	11	19
Sales and catering						
Reception/waiting	150	200	300	14	19	28
Director of sales	150	150	200	14	14	19
Sales representatives	0	300	600	0	28	56
Director of public relations	0	150	150	0	14	14
Secretary	0	225	375	0	21	35
Catering manager	0	150	200	0	14	19
Banquet managers	0	200	400	0	19	37
Beverage manager	0	120	120	0	11	11
Convention services	0	120	240	0	11	22
Secretary	0	150	225	0	14	21
Copying and storage	60	150	300	6	14	28
Accounting						
Reception/waiting	0	100	100	0	9	9
Controller	120	150	180	11	14	17
Assistant controller/auditor	0	100	100	0	9	9
Accounting work area	150	600	800	14	56	74
Payroll manager	120	120	150	11	11	14
Secretary	0	100	100	0	9	9
Copying and storage	100	200	300	9	19	28
Computer room	0	100	150	0	9	14
Accounting record archive	100	200	400	9	19	37
Food preparation						
Main kitchen	2,000	9,000	13,000	186	835	1,206
Banquet pantry	0	1,200	2,000	0	111	186
Specialty restaurant pantry	0	1,000	1,200	0	93	111
Bake shop	0	850	1,000	0	79	93
Room service area	100	300	500	9	28	46

Table 22.7 Hotel area program—*continued*

	Size of hotel (number of rooms):					
	200	*500*	*1,000*	*200*	*500*	*1,000*
Chef's office	100	120	120	9	11	11
Dry food storage	300	1,000	1,800	28	93	167
Refrigerated food storage	200	800	1,200	19	74	111
Beverage storage	150	500	1,000	14	46	93
Refrigerated beverage storage	100	250	400	9	23	37
China, silver, glass storage	200	500	1,000	19	46	93
Food controller office	100	120	120	9	11	11
Toilets	100	150	150	9	14	14
Receiving and storage						
Loading dock	200	400	800	19	37	74
Receiving area	250	500	1,200	23	46	111
Receiving office	120	150	150	11	14	14
Purchasing office	120	175	200	11	16	19
Locked storage	100	150	250	9	14	23
Trash/recycling area	200	400	800	19	37	74
Grounds equipment storage	200	400	600	19	37	56
General storage	1,000	2,000	4,000	93	186	371
Employee areas						
Personnel						
Personnel/reception	120	150	200	11	14	19
Personnel manager	120	140	160	11	13	15
Assistant personnel manager	0	120	120	0	11	11
Interview rooms	100	100	200	9	9	19
Training room	0	250	400	0	23	37
Files and storage	100	150	200	9	14	19
First aid	80	100	150	7	9	14
Timekeeper	100	120	120	9	11	11
Security	0	120	120	0	11	11
Employee facilities						
Men's lockers/toilets	400	900	1,800	37	84	167
Women's lockers/toilets	500	1,200	2,400	46	111	223
Banquet staff lockers	0	400	600	0	37	56
Employee cafeteria	600	1,000	1,800	56	93	167
Laundry and housekeeping						
Laundry						
Soiled linen room	100	150	250	9	14	23
Laundry	1,000	2,500	4,000	93	232	371
Laundry supervisor	0	100	120	0	9	11
Valet laundry	0	250	400	0	23	37
Supplies storage	50	125	200	5	12	19
Housekeeping						
Housekeeper	100	125	150	9	12	14
Assistant housekeeper	0	100	120	0	9	11
Secretary	0	100	100	0	9	9
Linen storage	500	1,500	3,000	46	139	278
Uniform issue/storage	250	500	800	23	46	74
Supplies storage	0	100	200	0	9	19
Lost and found	100	150	200	9	14	19
Sewing room	0	100	200	0	9	19

	Size of hotel (number of rooms):					
	200	*500*	*1,000*	*200*	*500*	*1,000*
Engineering						
Engineer	100	125	150	9	12	14
Assistant engineer	0	100	100	0	9	9
Secretary	100	100	100	9	9	9
Carpentry shop	300	400	600	28	37	56
Plumbing shop	0	200	300	0	19	28
Electrical shop	0	200	300	0	19	28
Paint shop	0	200	300	0	19	28
Energy management computer	0	120	120	0	11	11
Engineering storeroom	300	600	1,000	28	56	93
Mechanical areas (estimated)						
Mechanical plant	1,200	3,000	6,000	111	278	557
Transformer room	400	1,000	1,500	37	93	139
Emergency generator	300	500	800	28	46	74
Meter room	50	100	150	5	9	14
Fire pumps	0	100	200	0	9	19
Electrical switchboard	200	600	1,000	19	56	93
Elevator machine room	100	400	800	9	37	74
Telephone equipment room	100	400	800	9	37	74

Additional factor required to increase program net areas to total gross area. Recommend using +45% in guestroom areas, +25% in public areas, and +20% in back-of-house areas.

Often, the mix of food and beverage outlets or the balance between a large ballroom and the smaller meeting and banquet rooms will be modified to reflect the operator's knowledge of a local market or to exploit the management company's development strategies. Thus, the operator's programming and planning expertise should influence the project at the earliest date.

The space list prepared by the operating company begins to set the framework for a clear understanding of the facilities and of the image that the hotel wants to project to the public. The operating company identifies the mix of guestrooms and suites; defines the specific dining rooms, lounges, and function areas; details the amount of administrative office space; and allocates area to service functions—kitchens, receiving, storage, employee areas, laundry, housekeeping, engineering, and maintenance spaces. Table 22.7 proposes a space program checklist for hotels of three very different scales.

Operating companies issue their programming material in a variety of forms. Many hotel companies have developed extremely detailed space programs for different size hotels and for different locations or markets. These programs specify precise area requirements. For example, the lobby program may list public seating, bell stand, luggage storage, sundries shop, house and public phones, and so forth. Hyatt Hotels, on the other hand, although it provides a moderately detailed list of most functional areas and their space requirements, simply states that the lobby should be a 'function of the architectural design, of ample space and character appropriate to its function of welcoming guests and serving as a popular meeting place.' These two approaches illustrate the different development strategies of today's management companies. Still, all these firms regularly modify and update their standards to introduce new ideas and accommodate growing market trends.

Therefore, a precise program depends on understanding the interconnection between a variety of planning and design aspects of hotels. It is clear that the relative size of the guestroom is a major determinant of total project area; it is less obvious that the eventual choice of a particular configuration for the guestroom structure (see Chapter 15) can influence the project's total size and budget by 15–20 percent.

Developing a clear project statement may help to define some of the quality, facilities, and architectural alternatives that are basic to establishing an accurate program. The following factors, many of which are undetermined until the schematic design phase is complete, greatly influence the space requirements for hotels and resorts:

- architectural configuration
- number of floors (added floors greatly increase amount of vertical circulation)
- location of food and beverage outlets (may require various satellite kitchens)
- location of the ballroom (may require pantry; also establishes column-free zone that affects guestroom tower placement)
- availability of basement space
- ratio of land to gross building area (affects stacking of public areas, duplication of circulation and lobbies, and need for parking structure).

Table 22.8 Operational program decisions

Guest services	
Parking	Valet or self-park? Garage or on-grade?
Luggage handling	By guest or bellman? Use public or service elevator?
Front desk procedures	Safe deposit?
Guestroom food service	Hours, menu, cart or tray service?
Restaurant service	Hours, types of service, theme dining, retail operations, outdoor, etc.?
Recreation	Hours, open to public, children, lockers nearby, food-service?
Guestroom communications	Telephone(s), TV cable/movies, Internet, etc.?
Guestroom amenities	Coffee maker, iron/ironing board?
Guestroom services	Evening turndown, concierge floor or butler?
Guest security	Card-key system, fire alarm, and evacuation procedures?
Staff operations	
Employee entrance	Timekeeper, security?
Employee uniforms	Issuing, laundering, storage?
Employee facilities	Cafeteria, lounge, recreation, housing?
Staff communications	Cell phone, pager?
Information technology	Property management system, revenue management, point of sale, etc.
Accounting/controls	F&B control, purchasing/receiving, drop safe, closed circuit television?
Food preparation	Central or decentralized?
Material handling	
Receiving area	Weather protection, separate from trash, security?
Trash and garbage	Holding, compactor, recycling?
Laundry	In-house, guest valet, hours/shifts?
Vertical circulation	Stocking of linen rooms, rooftop restaurant, linen/trash chutes?

Describing the Operations

The facilities program is incomplete until the future hotel operations, as well as the basic space requirements, are fully defined and described. Usually developed by the hotel operator, the description of the operations includes various checklists of guest services, staffing numbers, and back-of-house activities in addition to schematic diagrams that show the designer which spaces must be adjacent to each other. Because services vary greatly from property to property, the complexity and the importance of their description also differs.

Among the most challenging aspects of hotel design is the necessity to develop a plan that accommodates both the great variety of guest markets and the operational requirements of the hotel. These often are in conflict, and the cost of providing for every need is likely to be prohibitive. Architects and operators have to make countless value judgments, for example, about whether the hotel will cater primarily to individuals or to groups, the relative prominence of the several restaurants and lounges, or the need for direct food service to the secondary meeting rooms.

For the most part, the key planning objective is to group public functions around the lobby, to position service functions convenient to the receiving area, and to cluster food outlets and function rooms around the kitchen. These functional planning principals are fully described in the several chapters in Part 2, Design Guide.

Many operating decisions are changing because of the increased automation and computerization of the hotel industry. Its labor-intensive character forces hotel management to create innovative procedures and systems to reduce the necessity for repetitive staff work while they maintain a quality level of service. Table 22.8 identifies the range of the necessary operational program decisions that management must make which influence planning and design decisions.

One area that directly affects the guests' perception of the entire hotel is the food and beverage operation. The operator or a qualified restaurant consultant must provide highly detailed descriptions for each individual restaurant and lounge so that the architect, interior designer, and kitchen planner can develop a unified design and operation. The description of the food and beverage concept should detail every aspect of the operation, including capacity, floor area, name and graphics, menu, theme, hours, staffing, special equipment, uniforms, and table service requirements. Chapter 17 includes basic outlines for food and beverage concept checklists.

The description of the hotel operations also should include a complete staffing program. The number of employees and their assignments affect the space requirements in three primary areas: administrative offices, employee lockers and toilets, and employee cafeteria. In resorts and some international hotels, staff housing may even be required. In addition, the staffing program dictates the need or desirability for different systems and equipment in the numerous office and back-of-house areas.

Preparing the Project Budget

A final part of the facilities program is the preparation of an outline budget summary (see Appendix B). Because the total project cost varies 10-fold or more—from less than $40,000 for small inns to over $400,000 per guestroom for the top luxury hotels—strict budget control throughout the entire design and construction process is critical. Budgeting is made more difficult by the common practice in hotel work of using separate architectural and interior design firms. Therefore, the developer must define precisely the design and budget responsibilities of the architect, interior designer, and other consultants, for example differentiating between the general construction budget and the furniture, fixtures, and equipment (FF&E) budget. This is further defined in the Coordination Matrix in Appendix B.

In addition, the entire FF&E category, with which the architect and many developers often are unfamiliar, frequently approaches 20 percent of the total project budget. It is important that the FF&E and pre-opening budgets are developed collaboratively by the consultants and hotel operator to assure that sufficient amounts are allocated to these key lines. The extraordinary amounts of nonconstruction dollars required to equip and open a hotel emphasizes the need to establish sound budgetary controls at the outset (see Chapter 19).

Prototype Development

The growth in hotel prototypes became most prevalent in the mid-1980s as a development system for launching new hotel brands. Many of the major management companies, such as Marriott and Holiday Inn, realized that they were saturating their traditional downtown or roadside locations, and needed new products in order to continue to grow. Marriott launched its Courtyard brand, to compete with mid-price roadside properties; Holiday Inn countered with Embassy Suites and Crowne Plaza, although very different in physical characteristics, to appeal to the business market. In each case, the new products were based on imaginative and well-studied designs and market concepts. The range of significant prototypes that have become virtual 'household names' includes:

- Embassy Suites, the largest of the early all-suite prototypes (see Chapter 8).
- Residence Inn, the leading prototype not originated but acquired by a major chain.
- Courtyard by Marriott, initially developed as a roadside inn and organized around a central landscaped courtyard, but so successful that Marriott now builds many urban high-rise 'courtyard' projects.

The modern atrium prototype **Marina Center Mandarin, Singapore.** The hotel, part of a huge shopping and entertainment complex near Singapore's waterfront, successfully blends Asian service with dramatic international design. The 21-story light-filled atrium features a 120 ft (36 m) hanging sculpture.

Table 22.9 Influential hotel prototypes of the past century and into the future

Design concept	*Major originator*	*Hotel design*
Modern multistory hotel	Ellsworth M. Statler	Statler Hotel, Buffalo, New York
Mixed-use hotel-office building	Ellsworth M. Statler	Park Plaza Hotel and Statler Office Building, Boston
Family roadside hotel	Kemmons Wilson	Holiday Inn, Memphis, Tennessee
Super-budget motel	Jean Marc Epalioux	Formule 1 prototype, France
Airport terminal hotel	Conrad Hilton	Hilton Chicago O'Hare Airport, Chicago
Medical hotel	Kahler Corp.	Kahler Hotels, Rochester, Minnesota
Convention headquarters hotel	Tisch Brothers and architect Morris Lapidus	Americana Hotel, New York City
	Uris Brothers and architect William B. Tabler	New York Hilton, New York City
Modern atrium hotel	John C. Portman, Jr.	Hyatt Regency Hotel, Atlanta
Conference center	Walter Green	Harrison Conference Center, Glen Cove, New York
Extended-stay hotel	Jack DeBoer	Residence Inn, Wichita, Kansas
All-suite hotel	Robert Wooley	Granada Royal, San Antonio, Texas
	Walter A. Rutes	Embassy Suites prototype
Modern beach resort	Morris Lapidus	Fontainebleau, Miami Beach
	Carl Fisher	Development of Miami Beach
Fantasy resort	Chris Hemmeter	Hyatt Regency Hotels, Hawaii
Modern spa resort	Allard Roen and Ward Hutton	La Costa, Carlsbad, California
Ecoresort	Stanley Selengut	Harmony Bay Camps, St. John, US Virgin Islands
Environmental resort	Laurence Rockefeller and architects Nathaniel Owings and Charles Bassett	Mauna Kea Beach Resort (Rockresorts), The Big Island, Hawaii
	George (Pete) Wimberly	Inter-Continental Hotel, Tahara, Tahiti
Vacation village	Serge Trigano	Club Med, France
Resort theme park	Walt Disney	Polynesian Resort, Walt Disney World, Orlando
Boutique hotel	Steven Rubell, Ian Schrager, and designers Andrée Putman and Philippe Starck	Morgans and The Royalton, New York City
	William Kimpton	Vintage Court, San Francisco
The Entertainment Hotel	John C. Tishman and architects	Westin New York at Times Square, New York City
Show business themes	Arquitectonica and D'agostino Izzo Quirk	
	Forest City Ratner and architect Beyer Blinder Belle	Hilton Times Square, New York City
	Madison Equities and architect Frank Williams	W Times Square, New York City
Educational themes	The Moody Foundation and Morris Architects	Moody Gardens, Galveston, Texas
Multi-themes	Bayindir Holding and architect Oktay Nayman with HHCP Intl.	Bati Tourism Center and Tatilya Theme Park, West Istanbul, Turkey
Sports themes	Tankanaka Corp. and architect Cesar Pelli	Sea Hawk, Fukuoka, Japan
	Robbie/Young + Wright; Adjeleian Allen Rubeli; and NORR Partnership	Renaissance Hotel at Toronto SkyDome, Toronto
Super-luxury chain hotel	Four Seasons Hotels and architects Pei Cobb Freed and Frank Williams	Four Seasons Hotel, New York
Mega-hotel	William J. Marriott	Orlando World Center Marriott Resort, Orlando
Ultratel	John C. Portman, Jr.	The Westin Peachtree Plaza, Atlanta
	I.M. Pei	Westin Stamford Hotel, Raffles City, Singapore
Spacetel	International consortia	NASA, Houston
	Design Studies	WAT&G, Honolulu
	Design Studies	Space Island Group, Los Angeles

- Crowne Plaza, Holiday Inn's successful response to the franchisee's requests for an upscale prototype for a downtown or suburban business hotel.
- Hampton Inn, Holiday Inn's most successful mid-market product since the original Holiday Inn.
- Ian Schrager Hotels and Kimpton/Palomar Hotels, the earliest boutique hotel chains (see Chapter 2).
- W hotels by Starwood, the first boutique prototype by a major chain (see Chapter 2).
- Formule 1, the economically innovative product from the French company Accor, not launched in regions where it is considered too Spartan (see Chapter 3).
- Studio 6, created by Motel 6 as a super-budget extended-stay prototype (see Chapter 8).

Creating a new lodging prototype has several obvious advantages. One, the company can focus greater research and design resources on developing one superior concept adaptable to a wide variety of conditions and sites. Many prototypes feature low- and mid-rise options, sometimes with both indoor and outdoor corridor-schemes or with an atrium alternative. Also, they may include different public area options: one version may have no F&B areas, another a small breakfast lounge, while others feature a full-service restaurant, the decision depending on the size of the hotel and its immediate surroundings. Two, the product, through repeated analysis, should be able to better meet the customers' expectations. The physical asset is the largest single investment over the life of a hotel or inn and it is imperative that it be 'right' from the start. Three, prototype development saves reinventing the wheel on each new project. The company should be able to test market its new concepts and closely monitor the customers' reactions, fine-tuning the project in its successive versions.

Companies developing different prototype lodging products may proceed along either of two separate paths. One is to develop a standard property design, and to expand it in a 'cookie-cutter' approach across a region or the country. Often, the prototype includes a series of design options to overcome excessive standardization, but the basic goal must be justified by substantial savings in project cost or design and construction time that otherwise could not be achieved. One example is La Quinta inn's early prefabrication system. Very different but equally viable is the 'protopart' or 'kit-of-parts' approach as illustrated by Embassy Suites' partial plans of buildings, from typical guestrooms and suites to health spa, kitchen, and laundry layouts—as well as scores of standardized details.

In the first case, the prototype system should not dictate a standardized appearance to the extent where its usefulness is diminished. Therefore it must provide flexibility for site differences and alternate designs appropriate to different regions. The second example, the 'protopart' system, encourages greater flexibility for adapting the program and design to meet the requirements set out by local authorities that, to their credit, may require the design to blend in with its surrounding environment. Some of the original cookie-cutter products completely reversed their initial strategy to one of encouraging flexibility in their exterior designs. Table 22.9 lists significant examples of major prototypical developments since 1900, many of which are illustrated throughout the book.

Hotel Management 23

Hotel design affects two major groups: the guests and the employees. The best designs not only anticipate the guests' needs and expectations, but also consider the functional requirements of the management and staff. For example, hotel management companies are exploring different locations for and ways to staff the business center: some choose to locate it adjacent to the meeting space, others place it near the front desk, or decide to outsource the business center and treat it as a retail function. As the more creative operators explore new ways to deliver guest services cost-effectively, it is important that those involved in developing and designing hotels take an increasing interest in hotel operations and management.

A standard hotel organization plan does not exist. The size of the staff and their specific duties are determined by such factors as the type, size, and location of the hotel, its chain affiliation, the abilities of the management team, and the type of ownership. In small hotels, many functions may be combined and performed by one person. In larger hotels, the staff will be larger and more specialized in order to service the guests properly. The basic divisions, however, are straightforward:

- administration and general (general manager, marketing and sales, accounting, human resources, conference services)
- rooms (front office, concierge, housekeeping, security)
- food and beverage (restaurants and lounges, banquets, room service)
- property operations (engineering and maintenance).

Because hotels vary not only in size but also in the type of clientele and in the activities offered, priorities differ from one hotel to the next. Security, for example, may be a separate department in a 1,000-room downtown property, but under the control of the rooms executive in a suburban hotel. Similarly, in a convention hotel where the meeting and banquet facilities produce a substantial share of the total income, the banquet manager may be moved from the food and beverage department and elevated to a department-head position.

Table 23.1 lists the major departments for a medium-size hotel and identifies the department heads who report directly to the general manager (or, in larger hotels, to a resident manager). The list, an expansion of the four divisions above, may be altered even further to suit a particular hotel's operating policies. One of the key pre-opening tasks for the general manager is to develop a staffing program for the hotel, determining the departmental structure and projecting different numbers of staff at, say, 55, 70, and 85 percent occupancy. This staffing schedule, then, is used to refine the space program for administration offices and for staff areas (lockers, employee dining, etc.) as well as to project payroll and related expenses at different levels of business.

Rooms Department

A hotel can be defined most simply by the number and quality of its guestrooms and suites; simply stating that a property has, for example, 100 rooms or 500 rooms immediately provides the key descriptor. Therefore, the rooms department, which is responsible for managing the basic elements of the overnight stay, is the key department at nearly every hotel or resort. It performs the following functions:

- front office (registration, checkout, reservations, and telephone)
- guest services (doormen, bellmen, concierge, and club floor)
- security.

Clearly, a critical policy decision within the rooms department is establishing the room rate structure and guidelines for discounting to the corporate, convention, and tour group markets during weekends and off-season periods. The full-price overnight charge, or 'rack rate,' initially positions the hotel among a group of competitive properties. Setting the rate too high may discourage business and even permit rival hotels to inch their rates up profitably without losing occupancy. Setting it too low, on the other hand, may contribute to increasing occupancy percentages but make it difficult to meet fixed costs.

Like that of the airlines, the hotel's product is highly perishable. The lost revenue from an unoccupied guestroom never can be recovered. Therefore, the rooms department attempts to accurately forecast demand for each night many months in advance, fine tuning the room rate for short periods and even overbooking when they project a sufficient number of 'no-shows.' New yield management software increasingly is being used to help senior management find that balance between rate and occupancy which results in the greatest profit. Thus, while reservations, guest registration and checkout, and other visible functions are routine, behind the scenes management is continually adjusting the price and availability of guestrooms in a highly competitive market.

To serve guests better and to assure their return business, operator regularly implements new procedures and services. These include express check-in and check-out (the guest indicates he or she is leaving by using the guestroom television remote control or by depositing a card at the front desk), club floor services (registration and check-out at an upper floor concierge desk), and electronic systems that handle wake-up and messages. Such services usually are established as corporate operating policies and utilize systems selected through competitive bidding; occasionally they may be proposed by the front office or rooms department manager and adopted by the hotel's senior management. Of course, another objective of such innovations is to reduce payroll and other operating costs.

Many commercial and convention properties have added club or 'executive' floors that combine guest check-in, concierge services, and an open lounge where continental breakfast, coffee, tea, cocktails, and snacks are available throughout the day. In a few super-luxury hotels, the operator requires a pantry on each guestroom floor where staff can assemble made-to-order breakfasts and a range of special food and beverage amenities. Though the pantry system is extremely labor intensive, it permits the hotel to provide more consistent and personalized service to the guest.

A recent organizational trend has been to create a 'guest services' department that is responsible to handle any guest need. Therefore, guests no longer call room service for a meal, housekeeping to make-up the room, engineering to adjust the heat, the front desk for help with luggage, or whatever. Instead, a single call to the guest service number is facilitated by a single person, who logs the request into the computer and electronically forwards it to the proper department. This greatly simplifies the guest's interface with the hotel, but requires better organization and follow-through from the staff.

Security is an increasingly important consideration of guests when selecting a hotel. To better coordinate anti-crime and life-safety measures, large downtown and convention hotels create a separate security department. In step with the advances in technology, today most hotels uniformly install sophisticated electronic devices such as keyless locks, closed circuit television, and intrusion detectors, no longer

Table 23.1 Staffing program

General manager rooms (executive assistant manager—rooms)	
Front office manager	Front desk, reservations, telephone
Guest services manager	Doormen, bellmen, concierge, club floor
Executive housekeeper	Housekeeping and laundry
Recreation manager	Health club and spa
Security director	
Food and beverage (executive assistant manager—F&B)	
Executive chef	
Restaurant manager(s)	
Beverage manager	
Room service manager	
Banquet manager(s)	
F&B controller	F&B storage, inventory
Human resources (human resources director)	
Assistant HR director	Recruitment, training, benefits, staff scheduling
Accounting (controller)	
Assistant controller	Payroll, accounts receivable, accounts payable, financial reporting
Purchasing director	
Marketing and sales (marketing director)	
Sales manager(s)	
Conference services manager	
Director of public relations	
Property operations (chief engineer)	
Assistant chief engineer	Energy, repairs and maintenance, building systems, grounds
Projects manager	Renovations

prohibitively expensive, even for smaller properties. It is important to note, however, that simple installation of state-of-the-art security systems does not ensure the safety of guests and property. The hotel must include training programs to equip staff to deal fully with security and safety issues.

Housekeeping Department

The hotel housekeeping function, while important to the guest's perception of quality and service, tends to be fairly routine. The department includes an executive housekeeper, assistant housekeepers ('inspectors'), and a cadre of maids ('room attendants') and housemen, responsible for cleaning all areas in the hotel. The laundry operations may be under the executive housekeeper or directly supervised by the rooms executive. The principal housekeeping activities include:

- cleaning (guestrooms, public areas, and back-of-house areas)
- linen supply (linen storeroom and uniform issue)
- laundry (hotel linens and terry, guest laundry, and dry cleaning)
- minor refurbishing.

Well into the late twentieth century some operating companies still recommended planning guestroom floors in multiples of 14 rooms (that is, 14 or 28 or 42 rooms per floor), the standard day's work for one maid. On the surface, this policy may have been beneficial to scheduling the housekeeping staff and assigning rooms; however, in general, the many other architectural and functional considerations do not permit such strict planning. In reality, the maid's room assignments differ based on the hotel's daily occupancy.

There is some flexibility in the operating details of guestroom housekeeping. For example, there are alternative procedures for stocking linen carts or the guestroom floor storerooms depending on such planning aspects as number of service elevators, size of guest floor linen rooms, and use of linen and trash chutes: if the hotel has an insufficient number of service elevators, management may decide to stock the linen rooms on the guestroom floors in the mid-afternoon in preparation for the next day, to avoid putting extra demand on the elevators during the heavy morning room service period.

The executive housekeeper often directs the management and coordination of small-scale repair and refurbishing projects. Larger renovation and major redecoration projects more often are directed by the engineer, an assistant manager, or a projects manager (a newer staff position in larger hotels). Nevertheless, the housekeeper should maintain a database of the furnishings for each room and record both regular maintenance and any unusual repairs or replacement of furnishings.

Food and Beverage Department

Despite the fact that rooms usually provide the largest source of income for a hotel, a quality food and beverage operation can be a hotel's best advertisement. While hotel rooms at some quality levels have become a generic commodity, the restaurants, lounges, and catering functions represent one area that differs greatly from hotel to hotel. For an otherwise fairly typical downtown or suburban property, the restaurant may be the single most identifiable feature and be used as a marketing tool to measure demand for other facilities. Even the smaller property may benefit from a restaurant operation: industry statistics show that motels with restaurants operate at a higher average occupancy than those without.

While about half of the total revenue in the industry comes from food and beverage sales, little more than 15 percent of the overall operating profit comes from F&B due to the complexity of departmental operations. The limited food and beverage profitability is the result of such factors as high staffing levels, inadequate control of inventory, fluctuating food costs, and highly variable customer demand. The food and beverage department is responsible for the following functions:

- F&B storage (food storage, beverage storage, and issuing)
- food preparation (cooking, baking, restaurant prep, and banquet prep)
- stewarding (dishwashing and potwashing)
- restaurant service
- beverage service
- room service
- banquet service.

In addition to the food and beverage service to restaurants and lounges, banquet service is an important function at many hotels—generally the largest profit maker in the food and beverage area. After the sales staff books a banquet, reception, or other event in one of the hotel function rooms, a banquet manager works with the customer to coordinate the meal and the room setup and with the food and beverage department to plan food preparation and service. Because of their importance to a smoothly efficient and profitable operation, catering managers are among the highest paid mid-level hotel staff.

Human Resources Department

The human resources department in a hotel is a relatively modem phenomenon. Well into the 1950s and 1960s, the owner or general manager personally selected department heads who, in turn, hired their own staffs. Each manager ran their own fiefdom. There were few written procedures and little attention to employment law. But today, with international management agreements, complex labor laws and regulations, comprehensive benefits packages, and increasing pressure to reduce staff turnover—with the resulting need to rehire and retrain, the human resources department has become a key management area. The following primary activities occur in the human resources department:

- recruitment
- training
- administration (staff planning, benefits administration, scheduling, and safety).

More than ever before, the hotel industry is making a real effort to train employees systematically. Larger hotels establish training departments to structure and control this process better, not only for lower-level employees but for managers as well. Nearly every hotel company requires that people entering managerial positions first participate in a corporate training program. A few companies, such as Hilton International, have developed a centralized management development program to help retain the most effective managers and provide them with opportunities for advancement within the company.

While the human resources department has growing authority, many personnel decisions are made at the corporate level. These include the initial staffing of a hotel, uniform wage and salary guidelines, benefits packages, and guidelines for changing staffing levels due to increases or decreases in business volume.

Accounting Department

The accounting department continues to provide support for operations and financial information to management and ownership. With increasing competition, changing corporate structures, and industry-wide consolidation there now is more pressure on the department to forecast revenues and expenses accurately. General managers are held to performance standards based on meeting rate, occupancy, revenue, and other financial targets.

Generally, the controller joins the pre-opening team 6–12 months before the hotel opens to prepare the final pre-opening budget. While a tentative budget has been prepared as part of the development process, the controller adds new precision with input from the general manager and department heads, including sales data on tentative and guaranteed bookings, more accurate occupancy projections, food and beverage forecasts, FF&E (furniture, fixtures, and equipment) figures from purchasing, and detailed staffing requirements for the each department.

In most cases the purchasing function is organized within the accounting department, although from a physical location, near the loading dock, it may seem to be more food and beverage related. Hotel organizations seek to establish clear sets of controls and checks and balances, for example by separating the purchasing and receiving functions.

Marketing and Sales Department

For much of the late twentieth century the individual hotel's focus was on 'sales,' on selling guestrooms and function space. However, increasing competition has changed the orientation so that now most management companies and individual hotels develop a marketing strategy based on the consumer rather than on the product to be sold. By identifying potential customers and understanding their needs and wants, the sales personnel in the field can be more effective. This realization that hotels are offering a service, not a product, encourages the marketing department to better understand the competitive nature of the myriad market segments that it might attract to purchase lodging, meals, or meeting functions. The following activities occur in the marketing department:

- sales
- conference services
- public relations.

A major function of the marketing department is to attract group business, which results in large blocks of rooms, meeting space, and F&B functions. Industry sources project that by 2005 there will be over 35,000 conventions annually in the USA with a total attendance in excess of 20 million people. Not only convention hotels but smaller properties—downtown, suburban, and airport hotels, conference centers, and others lodging types—are rushing to accommodate some part of this huge segment. Convention business also has proven beneficial to resort hotels, which have added function space to attract groups during the shoulder and off-season periods to boost occupancy and revenues.

But many groups are not convention or conference-oriented and hotels should seek out opportunities from such potential business groups as performing arts organizations, sports teams, airlines, or the government, that need to reserve blocks of rooms on a regular basis but may not need large amounts of function space. Many hotels attract leisure groups as well—bus tours, for example—or sell blocks of rooms to tour consolidators. Group bookings usually are made at discounts from the normal rack rate. Discounting is also a strategy to attract individual guests. The emergence of weekend packages and Internet specials are marketing efforts to bring in new guests during seasonal or weekend occupancy lulls.

Just as catering staff coordinate the individual banquet or reception, the convention and conference services staff play a critical role in assuring that larger multiday functions proceed successfully. They work with the meeting planner to schedule each individual session, plan function room set-ups, confirm audiovisual and other technical requirements, and provide support throughout a meeting or other event.

Property Operations Department

The engineering and maintenance function may be taken for granted by hotel guests but provides one final key component of the successful hotel operation. Consider that a 200-room hotel may represent something over a $30 million physical asset, and large urban hotels or destination resorts more than $100 million. The daily operation of the rooms, restaurants, and meeting activities pales in comparison with the importance of operating and protecting such an investment.

The property operations function supports this need. And it is not insubstantial: the property operations budget typically runs about 5-6 percent of gross revenues and energy expense another 3–4 percent. Keeping these unallocated expenses in check is the responsibility of the chief engineer and staff, who perform the following tasks:

- repairs and maintenance
- energy management
- building systems
- grounds care
- renovation management.

In the early years in the life of a hotel property, engineering work consists of establishing a preventive maintenance program and making minor repairs. Much of the routine work is completed by the hotel staff but, increasingly, hotels outsource major maintenance contracts, especially where technical expertise or special equipment is required, such as for elevators or escalators, or window washing. As the hotel ages, scheduling of major renovation and refurbishing projects becomes important in order to minimize the downtime of a guestroom, guestroom floor, restaurant, or other public area. Consequently, the work often is done during slow periods or the off-season.

Over the last decade, hoteliers have recognized the need to continually update public and guestroom areas. Large properties hire a projects manager who reports to the chief engineer and who is responsible for coordinating all capital projects. These projects can become highly complicated, with their own group of specialized contracts, budgets, and schedules. The hotel must supervise major capital projects in order to assure that they do not extend beyond a reasonable completion date, and to participate in the 'punch list' to identify incomplete or unsatisfactory work.

Concern for managing the utility expense often varies depending, in part, on media attention placed on energy prices worldwide. However, because of the not insubstantial magnitude of this expense, energy conservation strategies are vital, demanding staff training as well as systems decisions. Even the choice of light fixtures in public spaces, though seemingly a minor concern, can have a real impact on a hotel's annual utility bill. New property management software offers great flexibility in scheduling the operation of major equipment to reduce energy costs. But management may search for other means as well: one of the largest Toronto hotels schedules its laundry operations on the night shift, despite having to pay staff overtime, in order to move the substantial energy use to a lower off-peak rate. This is the essence of energy management.

Multiunit Operations

The previous discussion centered on typical management structures and responsibilities common to most lodging properties. But with increasing numbers of consolidations and mergers, the larger hotel companies are seeing a growing supply of rooms within one region or city and are exploring ways to combine staff or operate several properties under the control of a single management team. Marriott pioneered this clustering with its Courtyard chain in the mid-1980s, where a group of several inns shared a single general manager, human resources director, executive housekeeper, chief engineer, and so forth. Each property had a front office manager and a head housekeeper, but little other management staff—the centralized department heads might be 30–60 minutes away, but could respond fairly quickly in case of an emergency.

The several new resort projects being developed by Universal Studios and Loews Hotels (see Chapter 4) are being managed in a similar way. Table 23.2 outlines their organization, where a regional vice president leads a central group that includes human resources, finance, information systems, engineering, laundry, and marketing. The individual hotels include managers-on-duty and department heads for the individual departments providing guest services, food and beverage operations, housekeeping, and conference services. As companies reinvent themselves, we are likely to see ever increasing changes to traditional hotel organizations and methods of management.

Table 23.2 Multiunit organization

Regional vice president and managing director	*Centralized management for a cluster of hotel or resort properties*
Human resources (regional) Recruitment Training Benefits Hotel HR managers	All recruitment, training, and employment administration is done centrally. The individual hotel human resources managers report to the regional director of HR rather than to the hotel GM
Operations (regional) Retail operations Telecommunications Security Laundry Engineering	Many of the traditional technical and back-of-house functions are managed centrally. For example, the company operates one central laundry rather than several satellite operations; the individual hotel engineers report to the regional director of operations instead of the hotel general manager
Administration (regional) Controller Insurance/risk management Information systems Purchasing Operations analysis	
Resort marketing (regional) Marketing planning Reservations Public relations and advertising Sales	Marketing and sales is controlled centrally by the regional staff in collaboration with the destination theme park rather than at each hotel
Hotel general managers (unit) Guest services Food and beverage Housekeeping Conference management and catering	Guest services consolidates all guest requests for all service departments including room service, valet laundry, parking, housekeeping, etc.

The oasis ultratel **Al Faisaliah Center and Rosewood Hotel, Riyadh, Saudi Arabia.** This design represents the latest variation of the ultratel concept by the hand of architect Sir Norman Foster. The 873 ft (267 m) office tower is topped by a communications spire and a dramatic three-level restaurant within a glass dome, just below its apex. The 224-room luxury Rosewood Hotel is located at the base of the tower, along with an upscale retail mall, 100 apartment units, and parking. In addition, the project includes a vast banquet hall below the plaza, providing a column-free space of 49,730 ft^2 (4,620 m^2) for international conferences and banquets/weddings. The hotel and apartments feature indigenous materials in a multilayered façade of concrete, limestone, and wood.

Future Development 24

The coming age should witness the continuing worldwide expansion of lodging systems serving residential, leisure, and business markets. As described in Part 1, the new mix will range from vertically tiered ultratel towers and serviced condominiums to low-density residential communities with resort-like amenities and concepts as different as flexible office suites in downtown and suburban locations, entertainment hotels, and destinations in futuristic undersea habitats and outer space. New ecotourist areas will attract adventure seekers to the peaks of Belize, the edges of the Patagonian rainforest, and to places as unique as the scenic wonders of Siberia's Lake Baikal. Both independent development groups and hotel management companies will be prime catalysts for new concepts incorporating a variety of strategies, including healthtels, spa-tels, floatels, and marinetels and eventually, spacetels.

Innovative Trends

The earlier sections detail the constant innovation taking place throughout the hotel and resort industries. Developers and operators market to increasingly targeted segments, finding success in fine-tuning their design and services to the needs of particular guests. Owners identify new sites, long overlooked by traditional developers and designers imagine incredible themed resorts based on fantasy storylines and distant landmarks and civilizations. For instance, airport hotels once were little more than conventional business hotels located close to a major terminal. But in the 1990s a number of high-profile hotels were built close to the largest international airports, with soaring atrium lobbies not unlike nearby hangars, or constructed immediately above the main public concourse, a new mixed-use type.

The program mix at many new hotels is substantially changed as well. While most hotels focus on lodging, many place an increasing emphasis on outside business by providing a dedicated conference facility, high-visibility food and beverage outlets, and a sports or fitness-orientated recreational complex. The most successful are sensitively matched to local business and lifestyle trends.

Hotels in different segments adopt and embrace techniques and operational features of the others. The incredible growth in the economy segment proves that the industry's cost-effectiveness in serving price-conscious consumers is here to stay. Note that just as luxurious attributes trickle down to improve mid-rate and budget hotels, economical applications filter up to make luxury hotels more viable. This is illustrated by the latest innovative resort design in northern California, where developers may adapt spacious movie-star-quality trailers to provide themed luxury guestroom villas.

Theming

Stunning themed resorts such as The Palace of the Lost City, Atlantis, and the Portofino Bay Hotel greatly expand the role of theme design—an influence on hotels as far back as the 1870s (see Chapter 4). By providing market data to theme design consultants, owners can raise the project's bottom line. And with more visitors heading to Las Vegas and Orlando resorts than to any of the individual venues they portray, the effectiveness of theming, even planned for the inner walls of spacetels, is unquestioned.

Customization

Hotel companies are perfecting more sophisticated methods of market specialization including in-hotel segmentation and mass customization that creates popular prototypes and imaginative protoparts. Among the latest examples is the entertainment hotel, the most spontaneous and diverse pre-segmented prototype to date, offering different guest markets different experiences. At another scale is the robotic kiosk, a protopart element that provides flexible food and beverage service in the assembly areas of conference-oriented properties. With new and innovative applications, hotels will become even more specialized in responding to the needs of each guest segment.

Other important advances include hotel companies taking the lead in innovating flexibility for the residential inventory with all-suite and extended-stay products and serviced condominiums. These satisfy the growing demand for housing serving career relocation and long-term training programs. Other companies specialize in virtual home officing, business and educational conferencing, and senior residential and assisted-living centers, all with advanced amenities and leisure activities (see Chapters 6, 8, 12 and 22).

Entrepreneurship

While the industry is dominated by the big chains, many of which have a number of individual brands to target particular segments and price categories, there remain many development opportunities for the entrepreneur who can respond quickly with a unique property, whether in a primary or secondary market. The first is more competitive, often going head-to-head with the major brands. But an owner-operated hotel may thrive on a special theme, such as art or music or local history, which gives the property a special cache and ambiance. In secondary markets, for example, the small downtown hotel or suburban country inn, the property may thrive in part because the multibrand chains ignore these locations (see Chapter 3). The booming boutique hotel market has succeeded due to the creativity of its entrepreneurial originators—many of whom now have formed new national and international chains (see Chapter 2).

Technology

The larger chains and construction management firms specializing in the hospitality industry are adapting new techniques and materials to reduce costs and cut construction schedules, helping to bring more competitive hotels to market. Most of the engineering systems in hotels, and especially their controls, have undergone radical redesign and now substantially out-perform systems only 10 years old. Some of these innovations are available to the guest: luxury hotels now typically provide cordless phones in the rooms, an advance that allows the guest one of the simple niceties of home. New advanced entertainment systems will remain TV-based but will be liberated by more economical high quality super-thin video units which provide greater convenience and space in the guestroom. Hotels will benefit from occupancy sensors, automatically conserving resources, turning off lights, and cycling the HVAC systems without inconveniencing the guest.

The imaginative high-rise hotel tower **RIHGA Royal, New York.** With its contextual architecture and innovative interior suite design, the luxury suite hotel provides a modern example of the future advances promised by this genre.

Automated Services

The past decade has seen unprecedented expansion of the economy segment, operating efficiently due to increased automation and productivity. Price-sensitive guests willingly accept limited levels of service but the industry has found, not surprisingly, that more affluent travelers also appreciate self-service systems that deliver speed and efficiency. Increased computerization and the adoption of new systems in practically all types of hotels, in both guest and operational areas, will continue to evolve. All hotels, from economy to super-luxury, are pursuing sensible forms of automation.

Research

Many companies increasingly use trend and mega-trend research to evaluate alternative strategies for growth, new market segments, or potential reengineering of operations. These include changing attitudes towards site selection criteria for the increasing variety of new hotels. Interestingly, many traditional development 'rules' are now considered no more than myths (see Appendix E, Market Trend Checklist).

- *Never locate two major hotel chains in the same tower*: in Las Vegas, the Four Seasons and Mandalay Bay hotels are imaginatively and functionally combined into a single high-rise tower with each hotel maintaining its individuality, yet enhanced by its proximity to the features of the other (see Chapter 13).
- *The three most important factors in development are location, location, and location*: in today's super-sophisticated market, where quality quite

Spacetels and Marinetels

Howard J. Wolff, Senior Vice President, Wimberly Allison Tong & Goo

Our firm, Wimberly Allison Tong & Goo (WAT&G), has designed a concept for a space resort utilizing recycled external fuel tanks salvaged from future space shuttle launches. The hotel is expected to be operating by 2017 and will accommodate 100 guests as it orbits 200 miles above Earth. A cross between a theme park and a cruise ship, the resort takes into account the needs of paying guests rather than well-trained astronauts.

Our designers conceive the hotel being divided between areas of zero gravity in the hub and artificial gravity in the perimeter ring, which would rotate. This will allow guests to experience weightlessness, but also provide refuge for those guests expected to suffer from space sickness. An area with partial-Earth gravity will give guests an opportunity to take a shower or sit down for a meal. Zero gravity, on the other hand, will provide them the chance to dance on the ceiling, observe the Earth, and play sports in three dimensions.

The project presented the design team with a new twist on the challenges inherent in the normal work of creating hotels and resorts on Earth. The number one issue, of course, is safety. But, in addition, we are trying to strike a balance between creating an out-of-this-world experience and providing creature comforts and amenities that travelers have come to expect in destination resorts.

A 'room with a view' will take on a whole new meaning for guests in an undersea hotel. Underwater tourism has the potential to be the travel industry's fastest-growing sector. Currently, the only existing underwater hotel, Jules' Undersea Lodge in Key Largo, Florida, accommodates just those who can dive 21 ft (6.4 m) to its two guestrooms. Its creator, Ian Koblick, describes it as 'the first and last underwater hotel that you will have to get wet to enter.'

Our firm is designing an 80-room underwater hotel and observatory that could be located in Maui or Belize. Multi-level suites will have sub-surface chambers and curved glass windows for watching sea life. The resort, attached to shore by a long boardwalk, will have two stories of underwater guestrooms plus above-sea-level recreational areas, including upper dry decks for sunbathing, and docks to accommodate pleasure boats.

Ian Koblick is involved in the design and engineering of a 4,000-acre (1,620 ha) underwater theme park and 300-room hotel (with sub-surface disco and casino) that a Panamanian developer hopes to build at the Pacific end of the Panama Canal. According to Koblick: 'It will be kind of a Disney of the deep. You would drive across a big causeway, then take little bridges to bases with elevators for descending to different parts of the resort, all connected by acrylic tunnels.'

Travelers are getting increasingly sophisticated. They've been to Europe, to Asia, maybe even to Costa Rica. What could be more interesting and novel than experiencing an undersea vacation and interacting with the creatures that inhabit 70% of our earth's surface?

often is more important than location, applying trend analysis and spending savings in land cost on a superior design concept can greatly improve the viability of the property. For example, conventional wisdom may dictate not to locate a major luxury resort on the X side of a city. The Buttes-A Wyndham Resort, in the Phoenix, Arizona, regional market proved that investing the savings from lower land costs in better design could create strong demand in a breakout location well removed from the long-established luxury resorts.

- *Do not locate a resort more than 1 hour from a major airport*: while the feasibility analysis for a destination resort must assess transportation systems and feeder markets, resorts with advanced design features in more remote locations often have been more successful with their character enhanced by their remoteness.

- *Do not locate a major New York City hotel outside the mid-town area (not in the financial district, or on the waterfront, or in the surrounding boroughs)*: traditionally, successful hotels in New York were all in the mid-town area, close to business, luxury shopping, museums and theaters. Far-sighted developers who dared to challenge this assumption, supported by leading consultants, were amply rewarded with such successful and much needed properties as: (1) the luxury UN Plaza Hotel on Manhattan's East Side; (2) the upscale Vista Hotel at the World Trade Center; (3) Embassy Suites' largest hotel at Battery Park City in Lower Manhattan; and (4) the Brooklyn Marriott Hotel, outside Manhattan. More hotel sites are under review, in the Wall Street area and riverfront locations proposed by developers and community groups.

Preservation

Many major hotels and resorts built in the nineteenth century are still operating, as well as a small number more than 200 years old (see Chapter 10). These

The innovative future designs of the urban entertainment resort **Hard Rock Hotel, Orlando, Florida.** Reminiscent of popular southern California hotels, the exterior of the Mission style resort features traditional clay tile roofs, textured stucco surfaces, and Spanish detailing, with the main courtyard a stage set of a southern California beach. The interior spaces of this new type of entertainment hotel showcase the culture's most celebrated and legendary rock stars.

historic properties have a quality and ambiance that can not readily be copied and, as a result, dedicated owners continue to restore and preserve the older hotels. That restoration and adaptive reuse are more prevalent in hotels than in any other building type demonstrates the industry's ability to convert its long-standing renovation experience into leadership in urban preservation.

Environment

Given the large amount of construction taking place worldwide, it is commendable that all major developers respect environmental stewardship and promote and encourage environmental practices in new hotels, resorts, and leisure-time projects (with only scant exceptions, noted in Chapter 4). Also, 'green hotels' espouse an environmentally responsive sustainable design, both in their systems, which have a lower environmental impact, and in their furnishings that may use, for example, only renewable woods and nontoxic coatings. These concepts are popular with guests and can be achieved at relatively slight cost.

Economics

The continuing advances in the hotel field as demonstrated by many exciting, efficient, and highly successful new products will greatly improve the industry's occupancy and lower its breakeven point, as described in Bjorn Hanson's Foreword. In addition, the next decades should see vastly increasing public investment in hotels through the capital markets, forcing developers to target new segments with even better concepts.

Memorable Spaces

The major influences and highest design quality of the era are expressed in its greatest, most successful spaces. For example, in the US, the most significant hotel spaces include the original atrium lobby in Denver's Brown Palace (1892), the ballroom of New York's world-famous Waldorf=Astoria (1931), and John Portman's seminal modern atrium design for the Hyatt Regency Atlanta (1967). Equally important are the splendidly landscaped outdoor spaces at the Mauna Kea Beach Hotel in Hawaii (1965), technological marvels such as the former Imperial Hotel in Tokyo (1915), or the smashing avant-garde interiors in today's boutique hotels. With this in mind, we recall some favorites from among the outstanding examples of this extraordinarily fertile era, pictured on these pages:

- Singapore's restored Raffles Hotel expresses the utmost in hospitality (p. C-1).

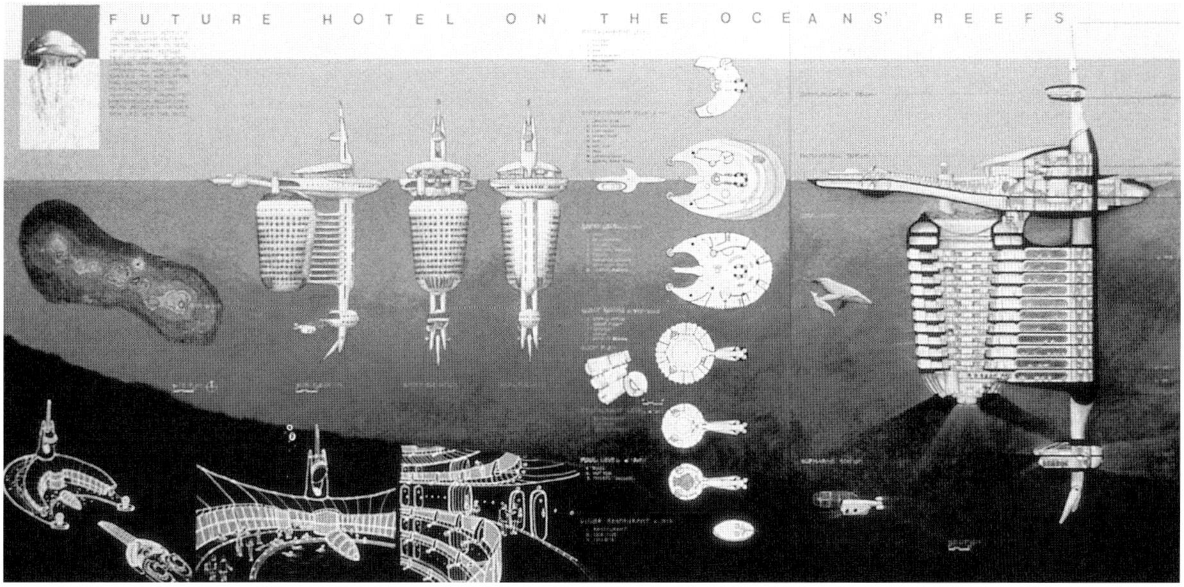

The widest choice of sites **Floatel/Marinetel.** Dubbed The Jellyfish, the winning concept of the Hotels of the Future design competition is an imaginative ocean-based resort, designed by Oklahoma State University architectural students. Its intriguing concept derives from the jellyfish, an organism whose upper portion propels its buoyant, mainly underwater, volume. It combines advantages of 'floatels' (see Chapter 14) and 'marinetels'.

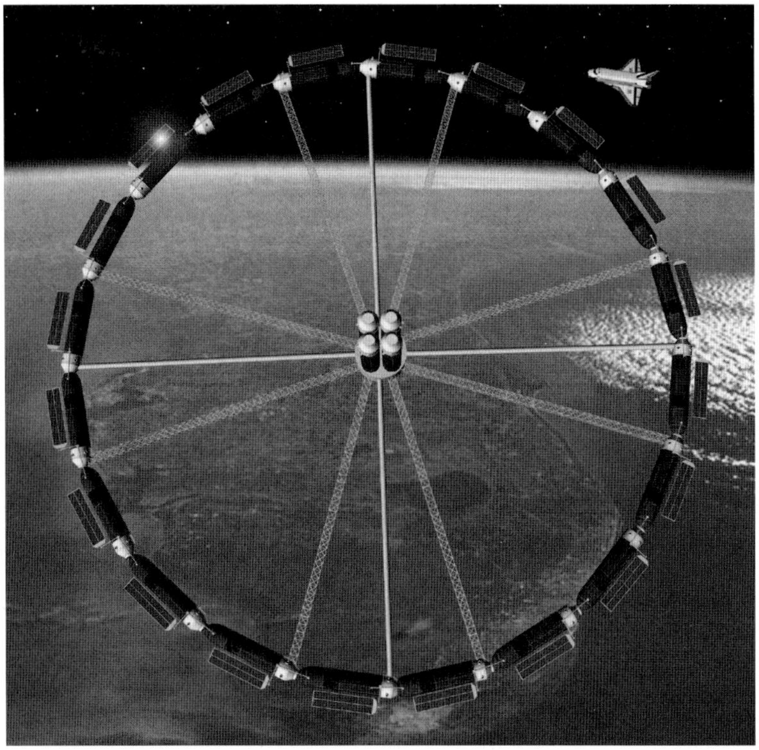

The configuration **Spacetel.** Developers describe a 12-module circular guestroom configuration, assembled in space, as the most efficient prototype, with its midsection used as a zero gravity guest recreation center.

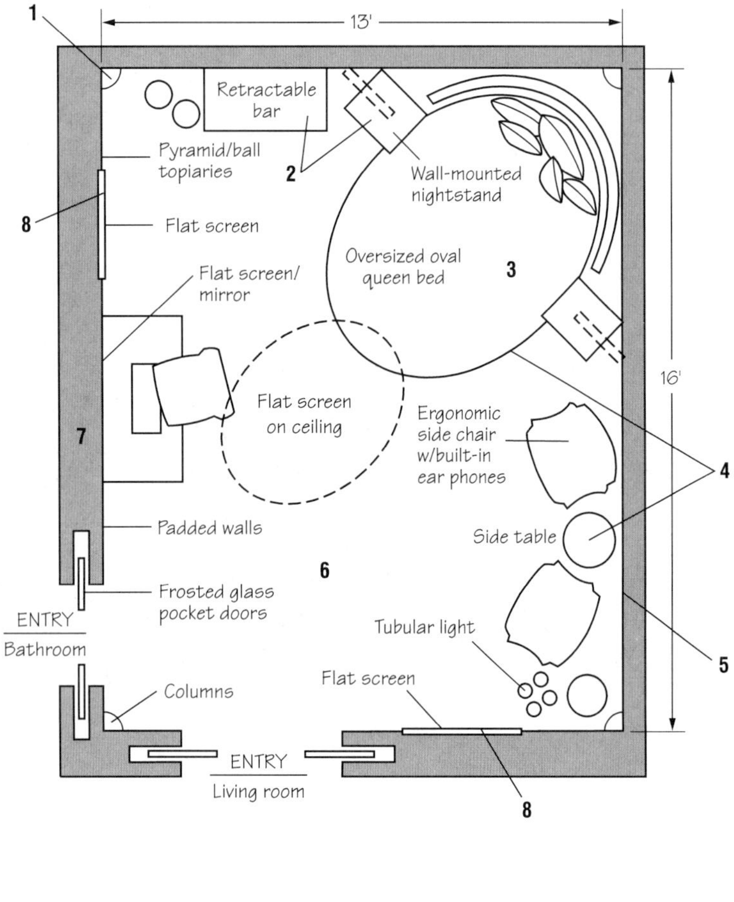

- The modern lobby of the Four Seasons Hotel New York exudes the greatest grandeur (p. C-2).
- The Palace of the Lost City in Sun City, South Africa, is conceived with the greatest imagination (pp. C-31, 229, 249, 280, and 293).
- Ultratels are the most impressive and inspiring mixed-use structures. Examples include Baiyoke Sky Hotel, Bangkok (p. 20), Shanghai World Financial Center (p. x), Kowloon MTR Tower, Hong Kong (p. C-3), Daewoo Marina City, Pusan (p. 211), and Jin Mao Tower, Shanghai (p. 210).
- The Sheraton Miramar Resort, el Gouna, Egypt, by architect Michael Graves, presents the most original architectural vocabulary, completely at home with Pharaonic traditions (pp. C-24 and 76).
- The Westin Regina Golf and Beach Resort at Los Cabos, Mexico, symbolizes the region's newly found natural modernism (pp. C-20 and 64).
- At Atlantis on Paradise Island in the Bahamas, the underwater walkway through a shark habitat provides a thrill to remember (pp. C-29, 97, and 194).
- The boat harbor at the Portofino Bay Hotel at Universal Orlando, a Loews Hotel, authentically recreates the most endearing themed resort setting of the era (pp. C-28 and 196).
- The Hotel Cheyenne, at Disneyland Paris Resort, authentically preserves the history of the Western

The checklist **Spacetel Guestroom**. Designers conceive innovative layouts and new systems for space resorts, incorporating high-tech lighting and audiovisual components to assure guest safety in a weightless environment.

Legend

1 Tube lights in the corners of the room provide additional light and create a softer feel.
2 Orbital shifts and reduced gravity are acknowledged by attaching items, such as nightstands and a retractable bar, to the wall or floor.
3 Lightweight materials, including a temper-pedic mattress developed by NASA, are used to reduce transporting costs.
4 Rounded items, such as beds and tables, increase guests' safety during orbital shifts.
5 Lighting equipment installed behind the crown molding floods the walls with colorful light selected by the guest.
6 The use of cork as flooring addresses the need for lightweight and low-fume building materials.
7 Padded walls assist in sound absorption and provide additional safety during orbital shifts.
8 Flat screens, which are substituted for windows, show live video from space. Windowpanes, which disappear for regular viewing, complete the effect.

hotel exactly as it was created by Hollywood (p. 121).

- With the area's authentic adobe style, the Hyatt Regency Tamaya in New Mexico blends a Native American casino with a 400-year-old Spanish Pueblo (p. 236).
- At the Four Seasons Resort, Sharm el Sheikh, Egypt, the luxurious domed guest villas cascading down a hillside provide Red Sea views to remember (pp. 77 and 248).
- The tall windowed lounge of the Amangani ski resort in Jackson Hole, Wyoming, indelibly etches the region's peaks and valleys as far as the eye can see (pp. C-23 and 100).
- The porch of the Lodge at Koele in the Central Highlands of Lana'i, Hawaii, re-creates the relaxing mood of a Hawaiian plantation estate (p. 72).
- The all-villa Four Seasons Resort Hualalai, Kona, on The Big Island of Hawaii, fashions the natural relaxing design of the future (pp. 71 and 279).
- The residential setting of The Westin Kierland Resort of Phoenix/Scottsdale, Arizona, the centerpiece of the planned community, offers a comfortable and relaxing environment for the mega-resort of the future (see pp. 199, 216, and 392).
- The interior elegance of the Four Seasons Hotel in Las Vegas, contrasting with its gaudy surroundings, strangely, makes both more delightful (p. 233).
- Entertainment hotels provide exciting spaces in the urban landscape ranging from Broadway extravaganzas and major league sports events to museum-quality exhibits with outstanding seminars. On the rise in major worldwide cities, top hotel executives, developers, architects, and designers continue creating novel prototypes including the 'E Walk' Westin New York at Times Square (pp. C-32 and 34), Moody Gardens, Galveston, Texas (p. 37), Bati Tourism Center and Tatilya Theme Park, West Istanbul, Turkey (p. 206), Sea Hawk Hotel & Resort, Fukuoka, Japan (pp. C-30 and 41), SkyDome Renaissance Hotel, Toronto (p. 37), and Hard Rock Hotel at Universal Orlando (p. 388).

These outstanding future-oriented successes clearly chart the course of an unbridled industry so free that it advances in a multitude of dynamic directions at once.

The 'reverse' aquarium concept **Marinetel Guestroom.** Designers envision this typical underwater guestroom in a marine habitat.

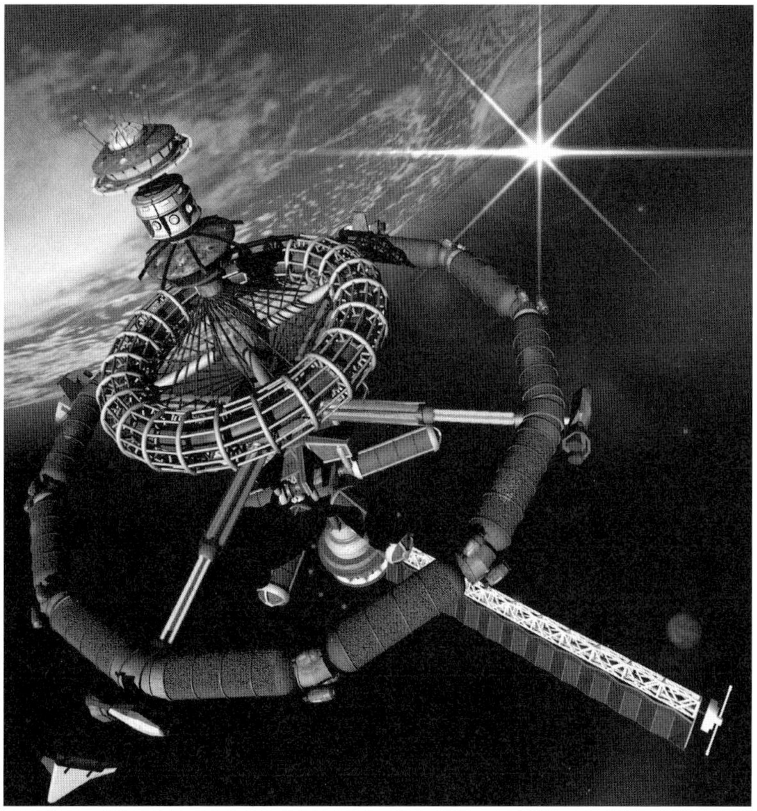

The planned schedule **Spacetel.** Sized for approximately 100 guests, lodging structures hurtling through space are on the drawing boards, scheduled to be operating by 2017.

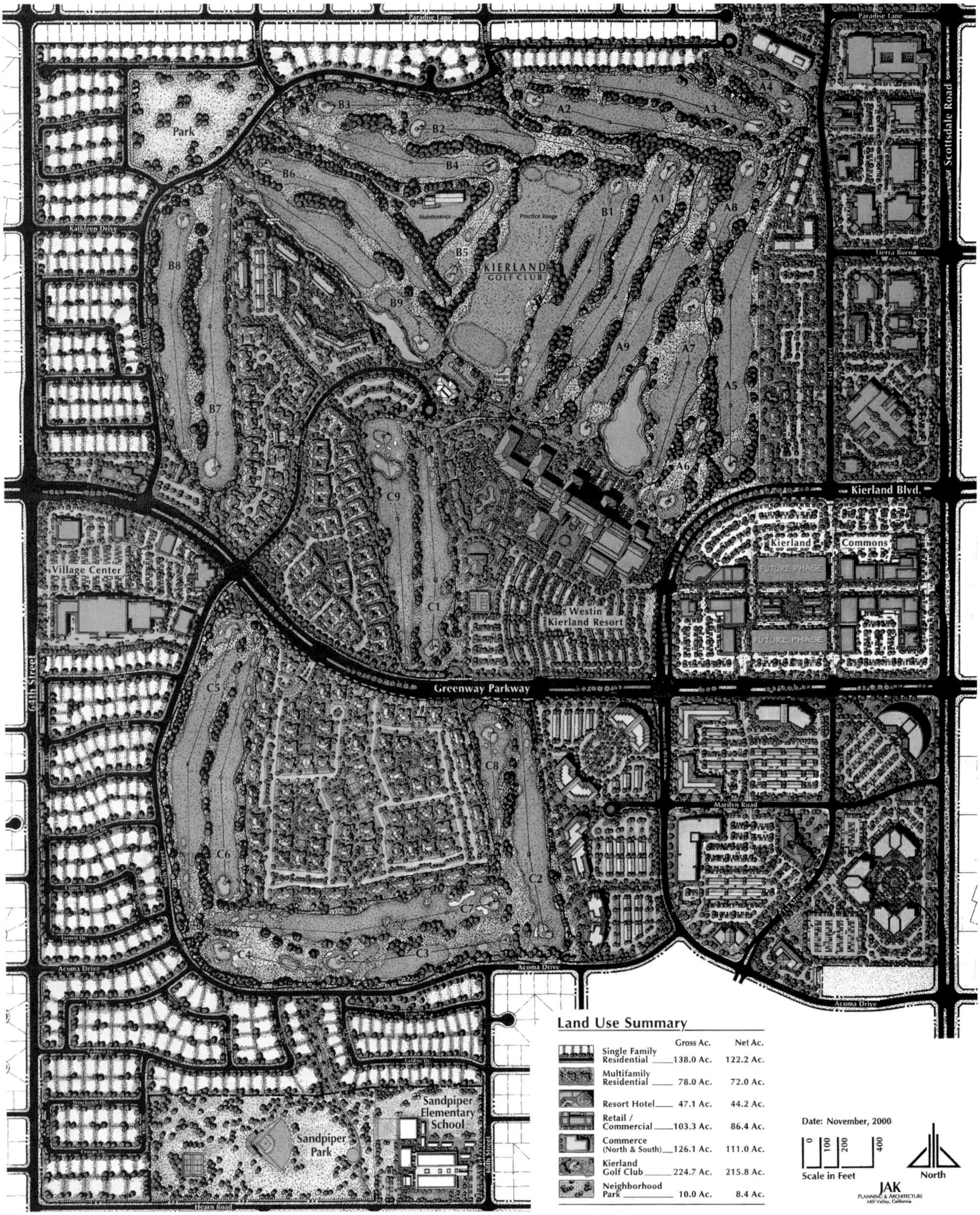

The community mega-hotel **The Westin Kierland Resort of Phoenix/Scottsdale, Arizona.** Centered on an idyllic 750-room megaresort, this vibrant community of neighborhoods for 1,738 residences with extensive public and recreation amenities and lively retail and office features expresses the true meaning of community. Launched by highly respected developers Woodbine Southwest Corp. and the Herberger Interests, the project is the work of leading multidisciplinary consultants: urban planners Sasaki Associates; land planners Larsen, Voss Associates; commerce planner John A. Kricensky; hardscape architect Studio API; golf course architect Scott Miller Design; traffic engineers Kirkham, Michael & Associates and Boldue & Smiley; civil engineers Coe & Van Loo Consultants and Primas & Associates; and hotel architect Hill Glazier (see hotel views on pp. 199 and 216). By combining historic concepts and new dynamic megatrends, such as the grand hotel with the planned community, broad environmental teams are creating better prototypes for the future (see Appendices A and E, pp. 393 and 402).

A Environmental Planning Checklist

Data	*Description*	*Source*
Location map	Indicate limits of project site in relation to the surrounding area	Planner
Topographic map	Provide contour map at 1 in = 100 ft (1:1000), or scale as appropriate depending on the site.	Surveyor
Land use analysis	Study compatibility with surrounding uses, plans, and policies; approximate mix of uses and phases in which market would absorb them.	Planner
Traffic analysis	Calculate average number of daily trips generated, distributed to road systems; identify roadway capacity problems; evaluate traffic count data; analyze intersection capacities; provide data for air quality and noise analysis; consider use of mass transit, monorails; pedestrian walks, and bridges.	Traffic consultant
Air quality and noise analysis	Confirm that project and traffic-generated impacts meet local standards.	Environmental engineer
Urban design analysis	Preserve scenic qualities of the site; study effect on views; consider shadows cast by buildings; confirm compatibility with adjacent land uses and existing built environment; analyze building orientation to save energy; locate parking to minimize impact; study character of landscape.	Planner
Growth inducement	Consider use and popularity of project to local population.	Planner
Employment opportunities	Confirm availability of labor supply and distance of travel.	Economist
Public services	Identify critical police, fire, and emergency medical services; confirm location of health facilities; locate public recreational facilities including parks, waterfront activities, marinas, jogging trails, bicycle paths, nature walks, etc.	Planner
Archaeological resources	Undertake test excavation near known sites or wherever artifacts are found.	Archaeologist
Grading plan	Provide detailed plan with grade elevations and show existing contours; specify area to be graded (acres or hectares), volume of cut and fill and its disposition or source; describe any proposed retaining walls (location, height, length, material).	Civil engineer
Site utilities design	Show location and configuration of water and sewer mains; design storm drainage system including quantity, direction, and velocity of projected surface run-off; locate retention ponds; confirm electric, telephone, and natural gas supply; identify required off-site improvements.	Civil and mechanical engineers
Site plan and building elevations	On plan show building(s) location; describe principal uses and area in ft^2 (m^2); locate site access, roads and walkways, parking and service areas. On elevations indicate principal building materials and colors.	Architect
Landscape concept	Provide general description of types of landscaping proposed including plant species list; preserve existing vegetation as appropriate; show lakes, lagoons, fountains, and other water features; identify terraces and outdoor recreation.	Landscape architect
Geotechnical report	Describe existing geologic conditions including stratigraphy of bedrock and soils; identify any geologic hazards or constraints (faults, landslides, adverse soil conditions, significant mineral resources); provide engineering recommendations to reduce adverse impacts on the project from grading, slope stability, or seismic potential; assess surface water, drainage, water table, fresh water or salt tidal ponds; consider potential for flooding or hurricane damage and identify mitigating measures.	Soils engineer
Sustainable design measures	Consider potential applications for solar energy, wind power, thermal storage, gray water, waste treatment, etc.	Specialty engineers

B Budget Coordination Checklist

Typical Budget Summary for 500-room Mid-rate Hotel*

	Ten-line summary budget	*Amount $*	*Percent*
1.	**Land**†	**3,250,000**	**6.02**
2.	**General construction**	**31,996,242**	**59.26**
	Basic building	28,615,242	53.00
	Interior special finishes for above	1,200,000	2.22
	Sitework, pools, utilities, landscaping†	1,541,000	2.85
	Surface parking, roads	640,000	1.19
3.	**Furniture, fixtures & equipment**	**10,047,149**	**18.61**
	Furniture and fixtures	5,068,478	9.39
	Kitchen, laundry, and back-of-house equipment	2,303,853	4.27
	Inventories (linen, china, glassware, supplies)	1,382,312	2.56
	Purchasing agent's fee	460,771	0.85
	Special systems (communications, computer, audiovisual equipment)	831,735	1.54
4.	**Technical expenses** (Consultant fees, site survey, soils testing, field administration, typical guestroom mock-ups, construction testing, building permit, feasibility study, reimbursables, and miscellaneous)	**2,537,670**	**4.70**
5.	**Legal, financial & administration** (Loan commitment, brokerage or syndication fees, owner's and lender's legal fees, developer's fee, appraisal, impact fees, real estate taxes, title, builder's risk, liability insurance, permits, licenses, relocation fees, and miscellaneous)	**678,812**	**1.26**
6.	**Marketing & preopening expenses** (Advertising, staff recruiting, training and pre-opening activities)	**1,272,492**	**2.36**
7.	**Working capital**	**250,000**	**0.46**
8.	**Employee housing**	**None**	**0**
9.	**Interest during construction**	**2,607,728**	**4.83**
10.	**Contingency**†	**1,349,746**	**2.50**
	Operating deficit reserve	**None**	**0**
	Total cost	**53,989,839**	**100.00**
	Total cost/room	**107,980**	

*See table below for luxury, upscale, and economy hotels.

†Allowances vary.

Courtesy of Frank F. Homiah, Cost Consultant.

Hotel Cost Indices

Classifications	*Cost index*	*Cost/room ($)*	*Total cost (500 rooms)*
Luxury	1.33	143,613	71,806,500 +
Upscale	1.20	129,576	64,767,800
Mid-rate	1.00	107,980	53,990,000
Economy	0.80	86,384	43,191,900 –

Dollar estimates are approximate and subject to revised location cost indexes. Courtesy of Frank F. Homiah, Cost Consultant.

Coordination Matrix

To avoid duplications or omissions in the budget, responsibility should be assigned on the 'design, construction, purchasing and installation costs of all structures, equipment and furnishings,' as in the following or an equivalent system (see Chapters 19–21) often referred to as the 'differentiation document.'

Basic budget categories

C Building construction and sitework
FD Fixed décor, millwork, and special finishes
FFE Furniture, fixtures, and equipment
OP Operating supplies, inventories, and consumables
SS Special hotel systems

Design team members and consultants

A Architect
AC Acoustical consultant
AV Audiovisual consultant
CE Construction estimator or consultant
CIV Civil engineer
EV Elevator consultant
EE Electrical engineer
F Fire protection consultant
G Graphics designer
GC General contractor
I Interior designer
IN Installation contractor for FF&E items
K Kitchen, bar, and food-service consultant
L Laundry consultant
LS Landscape architect
LT Lighting consultant
MC Millwork contractor
ME Mechanical engineer
O Operator's purchasing department
O* Subject leasing option
PA Purchasing agent for FF&E items
S Systems consultant
ST Structural engineer
V Vendor

Areas of responsibility	*Budget category*	*Estimated by*	*Designed by*	*Contract doc's by*	*Purchased by*	*Installed by*
1. **General construction**	**C**	**CE**	**A/ST/AC/F**	**A/ST**	**GC**	**GC**
2. **Furniture** (seating, casepieces, etc.)						
a. Movable	**FFE**	**I**	**I**	**I**	**PA**	**PA/IN**
b. Fixed/millwork	**FD**	**I**	**I**	**I**	**GC/MC**	**GC/MC**
3. **Artwork and artifacts**	**FFE**	**I**	**I**	**I**	**PA**	**PA/IN**
4. **Flooring**						
a. Carpeting and pad	**FFE**	**I**	**I**	**I**	**PA**	**PA/IN**
b. Marble, decorative tile, and wood	**FD**	**I**	**I**	**I**	**GC**	**GC**
c. Concrete, resilient tile, ceramic tile bathrooms, quarry tile kitchens and pantries, etc.	**C**	**CE**	**I/A**	**A**	**GC**	**GC**
5. **Wall covering**						
a. Vinyl in guestrooms	**C**	**CE**	**I**	**A**	**GC**	**GC**
b. Vinyl in public areas	**FD**	**I**	**I**	**I**	**PA**	**GC**
c. Paneling/marble/other decorative finish	**FD**	**I**	**I**	**I**	**GC/MC**	**GC/MC**
d. Masonry and plaster, drywall, and paint or ceramic tile in bathrooms, kitchens, and pantries	**C**	**CE**	**I**	**A/I**	**GC**	**GC**
6. **Ceiling finish**						
a. Paint or acoustic tile	**C**	**CE**	**I/A**	**A**	**GC**	**GC**
b. Coffered or other decorative treatments	**FD**	**I**	**I/A**	**I/A**	**GC/MC**	**GC/MC**
7. **Doors** (finishes, hardware, door frames, etc.)	**C**	**CE**	**I/A**	**A**	**GC**	**GC**
8. **Moveable partitions** (ballrooms and meeting rooms)	**C**	**CE**	**I/A**	**A**	**GC**	**GC**
9. **Lighting**						
a. Plug-in decorative fixtures	**FFE**	**I**	**I**	**I**	**PA**	**PA/IN**
b. Fixed decorative fixtures	**FFE**	**I**	**I/LT**	**I/A/EE**	**PA**	**PA/IN**
c. General lighting	**C**	**CE**	**I/A/EE**	**A/EE**	**GC**	**GC**
d. Conduit, wiring and dimming systems	**C**	**CE**	**A/EE**	**A/EE**	**GC**	**GC**
10. **Mechanical, electrical, life-safety, and security systems** (sprinklers, standpipes, fire hoses, smoke detectors, alarms, fire extinguishers, etc.)	**C**	**CE**	**A/ME/EE/F**	**A/ME/EE**	**GC**	**GC**

Areas of responsibility	*Budget category*	*Estimated by*	*Designed by*	*Contract doc's by*	*Purchased by*	*Installed by*
11. Elevators and escalators						
a. Equipment	**C**	**CE**	**A/EV**	**A/EV/EE**	**GC**	**GC**
b. Cab interiors, doors and frames	**C**	**CE**	**I/A**	**A**	**GC**	**GC**
12. TV system						
a. Conduit	**C**	**CE**	**A/EE/S**	**A/EE**	**GC**	**GC**
b. Equipment and wiring	**SS**	**S**	**S/V**	**S/V**	**O***	**V**
13. TV surveillance systems						
a. Conduit	**C**	**CE**	**A/EE/S**	**A/EE**	**GC**	**GC**
b. Equipment and wiring	**SS**	**S**	**S/V**	**S/V**	**O***	**V**
14. Telephones						
a. Conduit	**C**	**CE**	**A/EE**	**A/EE**	**GC**	**GC**
b. Equipment and wiring	**SS**	**S**	**S**	**S**	**O***	**V**
c. Public phones	**SS**	**O**	**O/V/I**	**V/I/A**	**O***	**V**
15. Computer, Internet, and reservations systems						
a. Uninterrupted power supply (UPS) and conduit for computer systems	**C**	**CE**	**A/EE/S**	**A/EE**	**GC**	**GC**
b. Equipment and wiring	**SS**	**S**	**S/V**	**S/V**	**O***	**V**
16. Audiovisual systems						
a. Fixed equipment and wiring	**SS**	**S**	**A/S/AV**	**A/AV**	**GC**	**V**
b. Movable equipment	**SS**	**S**	**S/AV**	**S**	**O***	**V**
c. Conduit	**C**	**CE**	**A/S/EE**	**A/E**	**GC**	**GC**
d. Built-in projection screens	**C**	**CE**	**A/AV**	**A**	**GC**	**GC**
17. Food-service equipment						
a. Kitchen, bar, and pantry equipment set in place	**FFE**	**K**	**K**	**K**	**PA**	**GC**
b. Ice and vending machines	**FFE**	**K**	**K**	**K**	**O***	**GC**
c. Mechanical and electrical rough-in, final connections, and ventilation	**C**	**CE**	**K/A/ME/EE**	**K/A/ME/EE**	**GC**	**GC**
d. Food-service carts	**FFE**	**K**	**K**	**K**	**O**	**O**
18. Laundry and dry-cleaning						
a. Equipment (set in place)	**FFE**	**L**	**L/A/ME/EE**	**L/A/ME/EE**	**PA**	**GC**
b. Mechanical and electrical rough-in, final connections, and ventilation	**C**	**C**	**L/A/ME/EE**	**L/A/ME/EE**	**GC**	**GC**
c. Linen chute	**C**	**CE**	**A**	**A**	**GC**	**GC**
19. Housekeeping and maintenance equipment (vacuum cleaners, maid's carts, floor polishers, tools, maintenance shop equipment, etc.)	**FFE**	**O**	**O**	**O**	**O**	**O/V**
20. Storage shelving						
a. Fixed wood	**C**	**CE**	**A**	**A**	**GC/MC**	**GC/MC**
b. Metal movable	**FFE**	**O**	**A/O**	**A/O**	**O**	**IN**
21. Office and front desk equipment						
a. Office furniture, files, vaults, business machines, copiers, etc.	**FFE**	**O**	**O**	**O**	**O**	**O**
b. Safe deposit boxes	**FFE**	**O**	**O**	**O**	**O**	**GC**
c. Baggage carts	**OP**	**O**	**O**	**O**	**PA**	**PA/IN**
22. Meeting room equipment (movable stages, dance floors, lecterns, easels, etc.)	**FFE**	**O**	**I/O**	**I/O**	**PA**	**PA/IN**
23. Recreation facilities						
a. Pools, tennis courts, etc.	**C**	**CE**	**A**	**A**	**GC**	**GC**
b. Equipment	**FFE**	**O**	**O/A**	**O/A**	**O**	**O**

Areas of responsibility	Budget category	Estimated by	Designed by	Contract doc's by	Purchased by	Installed by
24. Window coverings						
a. Draperies, tracks, and blinds	FFE	I	I	I	PA	PA/IN
b. Valances	FD	I	I	I	GC/MC	GC/MC
25. Shower curtains	FFE	I	I	I	O	IN
26. Shower rods/door assemblies	C	CE	I/A	A	GC	GC
27. Vanities	C	CE	I/A	A	GC	GC
28. Mirrors						
a. Public areas and guestrooms	FD	I	I	I	GC/MC	GC/MC
b. Bathrooms	C	CE	I	A/I	GC	GC
29. Accessories						
a. Towel bars and shelves, tissue dispensers, paper holders, robe hooks, etc.	C	CE	I/A	A	GC	GC
b. Closet shelving and clothes rods	C	CE	I/A	A	GC	GC
c. Luggage racks	FFE	I	I/O	I	PA	PA/IN
30. Bedspreads	FFE	I	I	I	PA	PA/IN
31. Mattresses and boxsprings	FFE	O	O	O	O	IN
32. Linens, bedding and terry	OP	O	I/O	I	O	O
33. Uniforms	OP	O	I/O/V	O	O	O
34. Tableware (china, glassware, flatware, holloware, table linen, etc.)	OP	O	I/O	I	O	O
35. Kitchen and bar utensils and smallwares	OP	O	O	O	O	O
36. Food and beverage consumables	OP	O	O	O	O	O
37. Working inventories						
a. Office supplies; cleaning, laundry and maintenance supplies; guestroom and bathroom supplies (wastebaskets, soaps, tissues, etc.)	OP	O	O	O	O	O
b. Menus and printed forms	OP	O	O	O/G	O	O
38. Interior signage	FFE	I	I/G	I	GC	GC
39. Exterior signage						
a. Building identification signs	SS	O	O/A	O/A/V	O	V
b. Directional, traffic, and parking signs	C	CE	A/G	A	GC	GC
40. Interior landscaping						
a. Fixed planters	C	CE	I/A/LS	A	GC	GC
b. Movable planters	FFE	I	I/LS	I	PA	PA/IN
c. Plants	FD	I	I	I	O*	V
d. Water features	FD	I	I/A/ME	I/A/ME	GC	GC
41. Exterior landscaping						
a. Planters	C	CE	A/LS	A	GC	GC
b. Irrigation and drainage	C	CE	A/CIV/LS	A/CIV	GC	GC
c. Planting, water-features and hardscape	C	CE	A/LS	ALS	GC	GC
42. Roadways, parking, and walks	C	CE	A/CIV/LS/SS	A/CIV	GC	GC
43. Vehicles (vans, golf carts, grounds care trucks, etc.)	OP	O	O	O	O*	O

Typical project schedule and global development cost index map*

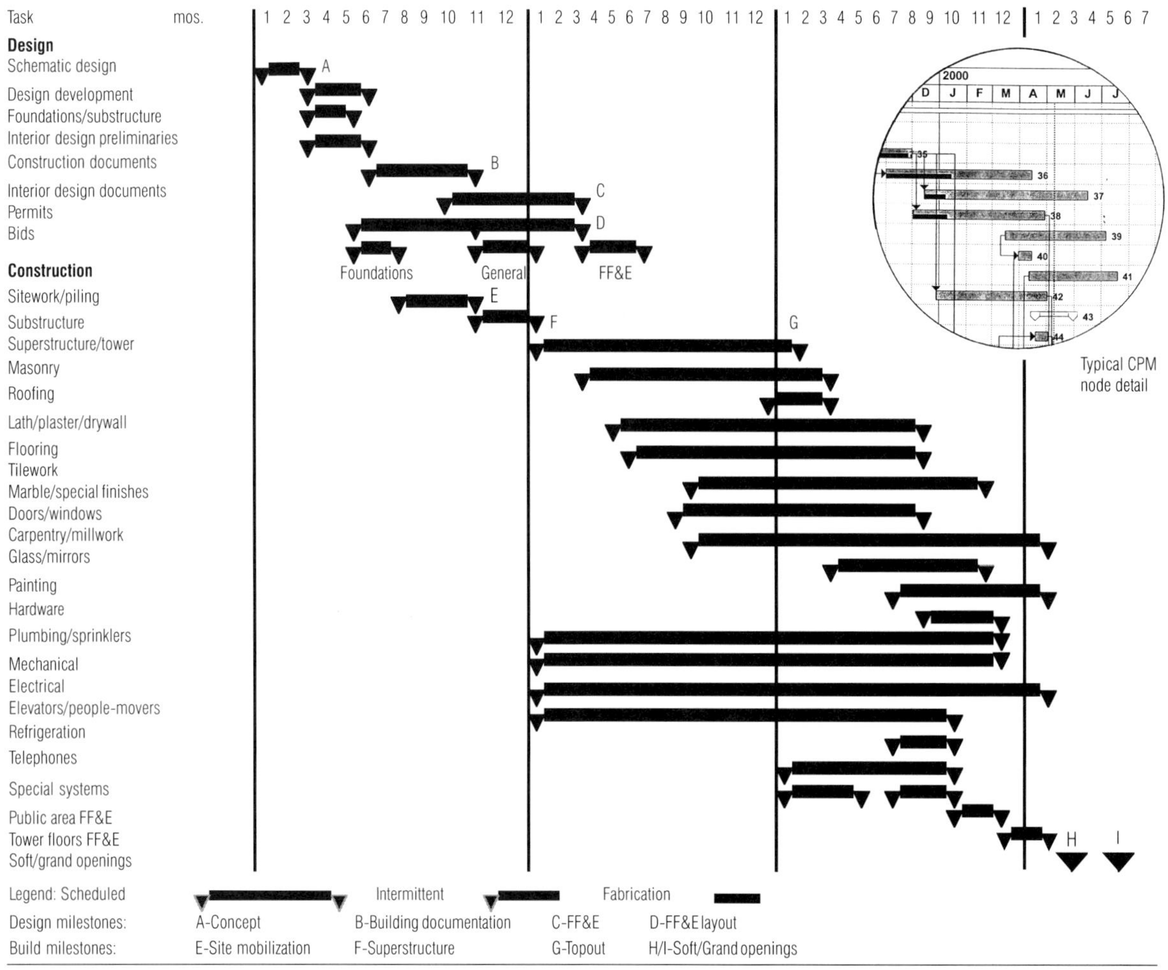

*Schedule is based on Design/Bid/Award Construction System with early foundation build option. Indexes are approximate and subject to change.

C Hotel Classifications

1 Super-luxury (selected examples)
[$400 and higher]
Four Seasons Hotel, New York
Hotel de Crillon, Paris
The Lanesborough, London

2 Luxury-deluxe
[$300 and higher]
Aman Resorts
Four Seasons
Mandarin
Peninsula
Regent
Ritz-Carlton
Rosewood
St. Regis Collection

3 Luxury
[$160–300]
Club Med
Concorde
Conrad International
Doral
Fairmont
Gran Melia
Hilton
Hilton International
Hyatt
Inter-Continental
Kempinski
Marriott
Melia
Meridien
Nikko
Oberoi
Omni
Park Hyatt
Sandals
Shangri-La
Sheraton
Sofitel
Swissotel
Taj Group
Vista
W Hotels
Westin
Wyndham

4 Upscale
[$100–160]
Adam's Mark
Bilderberg
Clarion
Courtyard by Marriott
Crowne Plaza
Dorint
Doubletree
Golden Tulip
Hilton Inn
Holiday Inn Select
Novotel
Provobis
Radisson
Red Lion
Riu
Thistle
Wyndham Garden

5 All-suite
[$120–180 and higher]
Doubletree Suites
Embassy Suites
Marriott Suites
RIHGA Royal

6 Extended-stay
[$70–180 or $200–700 weekly]
Candlewood Suites
Extended StayAmerica
Hawthorn Suites
Homewood Suites by Hilton
MainStay Suites
Residence Inn by Marriott
Staybridge Suites
Studio 6
Studio Plus
Summerfield Suites
TownPlace Suites
Woodfin Suites

7 Mid-rate
[$70–110]
Best Western
Blue Marine
Country Inn by Carlson
Four Points Sheraton
Holiday Inn
Holiday Inn Sunspree
Howard Johnson
Little America
Melia Comfort
Mercure
Moat House
Musa
Outrigger
Posthouse
Quality Inns
Ramada Inns
Scandic
Sol Elite

8 Mid-rate Limited-service
[$70–110]
Amerhost Inn
Amersuites
Comfort Inn
Drury Inn
Hampton Inns
Hilton Garden Inn
Holiday Inn Express
La Quinta
Wingate Inn

9 Economy
[$60–70]
Baymont Inns
Best Inns
Days Inn
Etap
Fairfield Inns
Ibis
Ramada Limited
Red Roof Inns
Rodeway Inn
Travel Inn
Travelodge

10 Budget
[to $60]
Budget Host
Budget Inn
Cross Country Inns
EconoLodge
Formule 1
Knight Inn
Microtel
Motel 6
Sleep Inns
Super 8

See Chapter 1 for discussion of classifications. Average rate of standard unit [approximate US$] subject to change. Full listings are not included.

D Ten-year Forecast of Net Operating Income

Calendar year	*Year 1*		*Year 2*		*Year 3*		*Year 4*		*Year 5*	
No. of rooms	275		275		275		275		275	
No. of occupied rooms	65,244		70,263		73,274		74,278		74,278	
Occupancy	65.0%		70.0%		73.0%		74.0%		74.0%	
Average rate	$127.32		$131.14		$135.07		$139.12		$143.30	
	$000	*% of gross*	*$000*	*% of gross*	*$000*	*% of gross*	*$000*	*% of gross*	*$000*	*% of gross*
Revenue										
Rooms	$8,307	62.1	$9,214	62.7	$9,897	62.9	$10,334	63.2	$10,644	63.2
Food	3,438	25.7	3,738	25.4	3,972	25.3	4,134	25.2	4,258	25.2
Beverage	619	4.6	673	4.6	715	4.6	744	4.5	766	4.5
Telephone	316	2.4	348	2.4	372	2.4	388	2.4	399	2.4
Minor operated depts.	569	4.3	599	4.1	625	4.0	646	3.9	665	3.9
Rents and other income	114	0.9	120	0.8	125	0.8	129	0.8	133	0.8
Total	13,363	100.0	14,692	100.0	15,706	100.0	16,375	100.0	16,865	100.0
Departmental expenses*										
Rooms	2,051	24.7	2,173	23.6	2,275	23.0	2,356	22.8	2,427	22.8
Food & beverage	3,168	78.1	3,340	75.7	3,488	74.4	3,610	74.0	3,718	74.0
Telephone	170	53.8	179	51.4	187	50.3	194	50.0	200	50.1
Minor operated depts.	377	66.3	393	65.6	407	65.1	420	65.0	432	65.0
Total	5,766	43.1	6,085	41.4	6,357	40.5	6,580	40.2	6,777	40.2
Departmental income	7,597	56.9	8,607	58.6	9,349	59.5	9,795	59.8	10,088	59.8
Operating expenses										
Administrative & general	1,129	8.4	1,185	8.1	1,234	7.9	1,275	7.8	1,314	7.8
Management fee	401	3.0	441	3.0	471	3.0	491	3.0	506	3.0
Marketing	748	5.6	785	5.3	817	5.2	845	5.2	870	5.2
Franchise fees	415	3.1	461	3.1	495	3.2	517	3.2	532	3.2
Property oper. & maint.	489	3.7	582	4.0	677	4.3	737	4.5	759	4.5
Energy	462	3.5	479	3.3	495	3.2	510	3.1	525	3.1
Total	3,644	27.3	3,933	26.8	4,189	26.8	4,375	26.8	4,506	26.8
Gross operating profit	3,953	29.6	4,674	31.8	5,160	32.7	5,420	33.0	5,582	33.0
Fixed expenses										
Property taxes	300	2.2	309	2.1	318	2.0	327	2.0	337	2.0
Insurance	58	0.4	60	0.4	62	0.4	64	0.4	66	0.4
Reserve for replacement	134	2.0	471	3.0	655	4.0	675	4.0	695	4.0
Total	492	3.7	663	4.5	851	5.4	1,046	6.4	1,078	6.4
Net operating income	$3,461	25.9	$4,011	27.3	$4,309	27.4	$4,374	26.7	$4,504	26.7

Revenue and expense amounts are expressed in thousands of dollars.
*Departmental expense ratios are expressed as a percentage of departmental revenues. Forecast courtesy of HVS International, New York.

Year 6		Year 7		Year 8		Year 9		Year 10	
275		275		275		275		275	
74,278		74,278		74,278		74,278		74,278	
74.0%		74.0%		74.0%		74.0%		74.0%	
$147.60		$152.02		$156.59		$161.28		$166.12	
$000	*% of gross*	*$000*	*% of gross*	*$000*	*% of gross*	*$000*	*% of gross*	*$000*	*% of gross*
$10,963	63.2	$11,292	63.2	$11,631	63.2	$11,980	63.2	$12,339	63.2
4,385	25.2	4,517	25.2	4,652	25.2	4,792	25.2	4,936	25.2
789	4.5	813	4.5	837	4.5	863	4.5	888	4.5
411	2.4	423	2.4	436	2.4	449	2.4	463	2.4
685	3.9	706	3.9	727	3.9	749	3.9	771	3.9
137	0.8	141	0.8	145	0.8	150	0.8	154	0.8
17,370	100.0	17,892	100.0	18,428	100.0	18,983	100.0	19,551	100.0
2,500	22.8	2,575	22.8	2,652	22.8	2,731	22.8	2,813	22.8
3,829	74.0	3,944	74.0	4,062	74.0	4,184	74.0	4,310	74.0
206	50.1	212	50.1	218	50.0	225	50.1	231	49.9
445	65.0	459	65.0	473	65.1	487	65.0	501	65.0
6,980	40.2	7,190	40.2	7,405	40.2	7,627	40.2	7,855	40.2
10,390	59.8	10,702	59.8	11,023	59.8	11,356	59.8	11,696	59.8
1,353	7.8	1,394	7.8	1,435	7.8	1,478	7.8	1,523	7.8
521	3.0	537	3.0	553	3.0	569	3.0	587	3.0
896	5.2	923	5.2	951	5.2	979	5.2	1,009	5.2
548	3.2	565	3.2	582	3.2	599	3.2	617	3.2
782	4.5	805	4.5	829	4.5	854	4.5	880	4.5
541	3.1	557	3.1	574	3.1	591	3.1	609	3.1
4,641	26.8	4,781	26.8	4,924	26.8	5,070	26.8	5,225	26.8
5,749	33.0	5,921	33.0	6,099	33.0	6,286	33.0	6,471	33.0
347	2.0	358	2.0	369	2.0	380	2.0	391	2.0
68	0.4	70	0.4	72	0.4	74	0.4	76	0.4
716	4.0	737	4.0	759	4.0	782	4.0		
1,110	6.4	1,144	6.4	1,178	6.4	1,213	6.4	1,249	6.4
$4,639	26.7	$4,777	26.7	$4,921	26.7	$5,073	26.7	$5,222	26.7

E Market Trend Checklist

Trends, particularly long-range megatrends, are increasingly useful in creating successful market prototypes. The successful development of worldwide hotels, resorts, and related amenities will depend, to a large extent, on more effective market research and trend analysis, in which consumer feedback is key, typically obtained through highly motivated researchers trained in the latest techniques for probing preferences of consumers from 'Generation X' in markets from Shanghai to Detroit. For example, 'fitness and health consciousness': the megatrend chosen by President Kennedy as a mantra for his administration, benefited consumers as well as health foods, sports fashions, and spa resorts. Its effect was equaled by only one other megatrend—the aging population. Using Aristotle's principle of generative systems, the skill of the market design team in incorporating the maximum megatrends in the facilities program greatly affects the hotel's success.

Years of case studies on outstanding projects, ranging from the 1960s era's most successful Hyatt Regency Atlanta atrium hotel, to its later fantasy resort counterpart, the Hyatt Regency Kaanapali in Maui, Hawaii, The Boulders and The Buttes resorts in Arizona, such prototypes as Residence Inn, Embassy Suites, and Courtyard-by-Marriott, plus the wave of extended-stay, vacation ownership, spa, boutique, mixed-use 'ultratel,' and entertainment hotels, demonstrate that hotel values grow far greater when based on advanced trends. Therefore this approach forms a valuable fundamental tool for future development. Popular megatrends effecting hotels and their potential product types are listed below and discussed in the trend sections of the related chapters:

- *Emerging free-market economies*: growing international trade requiring more effective business hotel infrastructure, product exhibition, and world trade centers.
- *Peaceful conditions*: easing travel to formerly unstable areas now permitting world-class tourist resorts and hotel infrastructure from luxury hotels to budget inns.
- *Multinational business communities*: requiring international conference, training and trade centers, suburban office park hotels, and hotel business centers.
- *Special conference and convention markets*: including dedicated growing university centers and affordable convention hotels for not-for-profit organizations.
- *Sophisticated independent travelers*: combining various types of fantasy resorts, island getaways, vacation villages, spa, ecotourist, and boutique hotels.
- *Perception of value*: focusing on efficient all-suite and extended-stay hotels as well as the latest limited-service, economy, and super-budget prototype models.
- *Perception of choice*: growing variety of new segments ranging from boutique hotels to urban resort waterfront, entertainment, sports stadium, and spatel types.
- *Environmental conservation*: pioneering ecotourist hotels and resorts with exotic wildlife preserves, aviary sanctuaries, and animal and marine habitats.
- *Sense of place, tradition, and historic preservation*: ensuring contextual relationship of hotel to location, with appropriate restoration and design sensitivity.
- *Fitness and health consciousness*: including exercise and stress relief from high-tech living through relaxing health and spa resort techniques.
- *Aging population*: requiring senior residences and communities with pre-care wellness centers, specialty clinics, and outpatient healthtels at medical campuses.
- *Increased opportunities for self-development*: including professional interest group and seminar retreats with specialty libraries and research facilities.
- *Increased family vacations*: including trend toward greater family vacation opportunities enhanced by further advances in vacation ownership.
- *Greater opportunities and business travel for women*: requiring privacy, comfort, and security, including outdoor areas, and suites for business meetings.
- *Informality and functionality*: including clear preferences for informal but highly styled residential decor as well as functional furnishing layouts.
- *Sense of style and theater*: including high quality of art, architecture, and interior design as well as performing arts and entertainment at hotels and resorts.
- *Exciting cuisine*: offering gourmet buffet food fair, multithemed hybrid cuisines, health/juice sandwich bar, and bistro/coffee/tea lounges often tied to shopping.
- *Entertainment activities*: including mini-theme parks, festival atrium plazas, sports events, teen centers, themed shopping, retail villages, and airline-style lounges.
- *Gaming*: Chapter 13, casino hotels.
- *Scenic golf*: Chapter 4, the golf resort.
- *Island getaways*: Chapter 4, the island resort.
- *Unique natural site contexts*: Chapter 4, the site context resort.
- *Vacation ownership and shared yachting*: Chapter 4, vacation ownership and condominium resorts, the marina hotel, and the ski lodge.
- *Multiuse communities*: including master planned developments in Chapter 4, the multiresort destination complex and Chapter 12, planned community developments.
- *Varied mixed-use complexes*: including teamwork between public and private sectors in developing major mixed-use urban sites and senior residence, assisted-living, and medical outpatient hotels (see Chapter 12).
- *Vertically-tiered ultratel towers*: featuring guestrooms in varied locations of shared towers depending on local market factors (see Chapter 12).
- *New technology and futurist concepts*: introducing spacetels, marinetels and floatels (see Chapters 14 and 24).
- *Convenient automated travel info/reservation systems*: creating an Internet buyers' virtual electronic bazaar and dynamic hotel classifications.
- *Wholesome curiosity*: ensuring the development of ever more popular concepts.

F International Hotel and Travel Organizations

Acronym	*Organization name and address*
AIT	*Alliance Internationale du Tourisme* International Touring Alliance Geneva, Switzerland www.aitgva.ch
AH&MA	American Hotel & Motel Association Washington, DC, USA www.ahma.com
ASTA	American Society of Travel Agents Alexandria, VA, USA www.astanet.com
ATME	Association of Travel Marketing Executives Washington, DC, USA www.atme.org
CTO	Caribbean Tourist Organisation Barbados, British West Indies www.caribtourism.com
EHMA	European Hotel Managers Association Rome, Italy www.ehma.com
ETC	European Travel Commission *Commission Européenne du Tourisme (CET)* Brussels, Belgium www.etc-europe-travel.org
HCIMA	Hotel & Catering International Management Association London, UK www.hcima.org.uk
HOTREC	Confederation of National Associations of Hotels, Restaurants, and Cafés in the EU Brussels, Belgium www.hotrec.org
HSMAI	Hospitality Sales and Marketing Association International Washington, DC, USA www.hsmai.org
IATA	International Air Transport Association Geneva, Switzerland www.iata.org
IACC	International Association of Conference Centers St. Louis, MO, USA www.iacconline.org
ICCA	International Congress & Conventions Association Amsterdam, The Netherlands www.congresscity.com/icca
IFTO	International Federation of Tour Operators East Sussex, UK www.world-tourism.org/omt/affiliate/ifto.htm
HEI	International Hotels Environment Initiative London, UK www.ihei.org/main.htm
IHRA	Internatiional Hotel & Restaurant Association Paris, France www.ih-ra.com
IOTO	Indian Ocean Tourism Organisation Perth, Australia www.ioto.org
OTEM	*Organisation du Tourisme Euro-Méditerranéen* Euro-Mediterranean Tourism Organisation (EMTO) Nice, France www.otem.org/anglais
PATA	Pacific Area Travel Association Bangkok, Thailand www.pata.org
SITE	Society of Incentive & Travel Executives New York, USA www.site-intl.org
UFTAA	Universal Federation of Travel Agents' Associations Monaco www.uftaa.com
UIC	*Union Internationale des Chemins de Fer* International Union of Railways Paris, France www.uic.asso.fr
WATA	*World Association of Travel Agencies* *Organisation Mondiale des Agents de Voyage* Geneva, Switzerland www.wata.net
WTO	World Tourism Organisation *Organisation Mondiale du Tourisme (OMT)* Madrid, Spain www.world-tourism.org
WTTC	World Travel and Tourism Council London, UK www.wttc.org/

G Bibliography

Hotel and resort development and planning guidelines

Baucom, Alfred H. *Hospitality Design for the Graying Generation*. New York: Wiley, 1996.

Baud-Bovy, Manuel and Fred Lawson. *Tourism and Recreation: Handbook of Planning and Design*. Oxford: Architectural Press, 1998.

Berens, Carol. *Hotel Bars and Lobbies*. New York: McGraw-Hill, 1997.

Davies, Thomas D. and Kim A. Beasley. *Design for Hospitality: Planning for Accessible Hotels & Motels*. New York: Nichols, 1993.

Gee, Chuck Y. *Resort Development and Management*. East Lansing, MI: Educational Institute of AH&MA, 1988.

Henderson, Justin. *Casino Design: Resorts, Hotels, and Themed Entertainment Spaces*. Gloucester, MA: Rockport, 1999.

Huffadine, Margaret. *Project Management in Hotel and Resort Development*. New York: McGraw-Hill, 1993.

——. *Resort Design: Planning Architecture, and Interiors*. New York, McGraw-Hill, 2000.

Kaplan, Michael. *The New Hotel: International Hotel and Resort Design 3*. Glen Cove, NY: PBC International, 1998.

Lawson, Fred. *Hotels and Resorts: Planning, Design and Refurbishment*. Oxford: Butterworth Architecture, 1995.

Mill, Robert Christie. *Resorts, Management and Operation*. New York: Wiley, 2001.

Penner, Richard H. *Conference Center Planning and Design*. New York: Whitney Library of Design, 1991.

PKF Consulting. *Hotel Development*. Washington, DC: ULI—the Urban Land Institute, 1996.

Portman, John and Jonathan Barnett. *The Architect as Developer*. New York: McGraw-Hill, 1976.

Raleigh, Lori E. and Rachel J. Roginsky (ed). *Hotel Investments: Issues & Perspectives*. East Lansing, MI: Educational Institute of the AH&MA, 1999.

Ransley, Josef and Hadyn Ingram, eds. *Developing Hospitality Properties and Facilities*. Oxford: Butterworth-Heinemann, 2000.

Rushmore, Stephen, Dana Michael Ciraldo and John M. Tarras. *Hotel Investments Handbook*. New York: West Group, 1999.

Rutes, Walter A. and Richard H. Penner. *Hotel Planning and Design*. New York: Whitney Library of Design, 1985.

Schwanke, Dean, et al. *Resort Development Handbook*. Washington, DC: ULI—the Urban Land Institute, 1997.

Stipanuk, David M. and Harold Roffman. *Hospitality Facilities Management and Design*. East Lansing, MI: Educational Institute of the AH&MA, 1992.

Suchman, Diane R., et al. *Developing Timeshare and Vacation-Ownership Properties*. Washington, DC: ULI—the Urban Land Institute, 1999.

Hotel and resort projects (illustrated)

Banger, Albrecht and Otto Riewoldt. *Designer Hotels*. New York: Vendome Press, 1993.

Beng, Tan Hock. *Tropical Retreats: The Poetics of Place*. Singapore: Page One Publishing, 1996.

Black, Wendy. *International Hotel and Resort Design 2*. Glen Cove, NY: PBC International, 1991.

Clubs and Resorts: Designing for Recreation and Leisure. Glen Cove, NY: PBC International, 1993.

de Vleeschouwer, Olivier. *New Hotel Designs*. Paris: Telleri, 1998.

The Hospitality and Leisure Architecture of Wimberly Allison Tong & Goo. Gloucester, MA: Rockport, 1997.

Hotel Facilities: New Concepts in Architecture and Design. Tokyo, Meisei, 1997.

Knapp, Frederick. *Hotel Renovation Planning and Design*. New York: McGraw-Hill, 1995.

Moreno, Elena Marcheso. *Hotels: International Design Portfolios*. Gloucester, MA: Rockport, 1998.

Mostaedi, Arian. *Design Hotels*. Barcelona: LINKS, 1998.

New Hotel Architecture: Modern Hotel Design, a Pictorial Survey. Tokyo: Meisei, 1993.

Radulski, John P. and William Weathersby, Jr. *Pleasure Paradises: International Clubs and Resorts*. Glen Cove, NY: PBC International, 1997.

Riewoldt, Otto. *Hotel Design*. Corte Madera, CA: Gingko Press, 1998.

Schmid, Anne M. *International Hotel Redesign*. New York: PBC International, 1990.

Schmid, Anne M. and Mary Scoviak-Lerner. *International Hotel and Resort Design*. New York: PBC International, 1988.

Tackach, James. *Great American Hotels, Luxury Palaces and Elegant Resorts*. New York: Smithmark, 1991.

Ypma, Herbert. *Hip Hotels: City*. London: Thames & Hudson, 1999.

——. *Hip Hotels: Escape*. London, Thames & Hudson, 2000.

Hotel, motel, and resort history

Belasco, Warren James. *Americans on the Road, From Autocamp to Motel, 1910–1945*. Cambridge, MA: The MIT Press, 1979.

Curl, Donald Walter. *Mizner's Florida: American Resort Architecture*. Cambridge, MA: MIT Press, 1996.

Donzel, Catherine, Alexis Gregory and Marc Walter. *Grand American Hotels*. New York: Vendome Press, 1989.

Jakle, John A., Keith A. Sculle and Jefferson S. Rogers. *The Motel in America*. Baltimore: Johns Hopkins, 1996.

Kramer, J. J. *The Last of the Grand Hotels*. New York: Van Nostrand Reinhold, 1978.

Lapidus, Morris. *An Architecture of Joy*. Miami: Seemann, 1979.

Liebs, Chester H. *Main Street to Miracle Mile*. New York: Graphic Society, 1985.

Limerick, Jeffrey, Nancy Ferguson and Richard Oliver. *America's Grand Resort Hotels*. New York: Pantheon, 1979.

McGinty, Brian. *The Palace Inns*. Harrisburg, PA: Stackpole, 1978.

Meade, Martin and Jean Larteguy. *Grand Oriental Hotels*. New York: Vendome Press, 1987.

Pevsner, Nikolaus. *A History of Building Types*. Princeton, NJ: Princeton University Press, 1976 (chapter 11, pp. 169–192).

Watkin, David. *Grand Hotel*. New York: Vendome Press, 1984.

Williamson, Jefferson. *The American Hotel: an Anecdotal History*. New York: Alfred A. Knopf, 1930.

H Illustration List and Idea Finder

The island environmental resort **Four Seasons Resort Hualalai, Kona, The Big Island, Hawaii**
The island ocean-view resort **The Orchid at Mauna Lani, The Big Island, Hawaii**
The island inland-view resort **The Lodge at Koele, Lana'i, Hawaii**
The island coastal-view resort **Manele Bay Hotel, Lana'i, Hawaii**
The island plantation resort **The Ritz-Carlton Kapalua, Maui, Hawaii**
Europe's island convention resort **Gran Hotel Costa Meloneras, Canary Islands, Spain**
China's island gaming resort **West Island Golf and Casino Hotel, Hainan Island, China**
Egypt's well conceived resort expansion program, more ambitious than the Pyramids **Red Sea rim resort map**
An original resort design vocabulary **Sheraton Miramar Resort el Gouna, Egypt**
A multicourt resort design **Inter-Continental Taba Heights Resort, Sinai Coast, Egypt**
The resort with the spectacular Red Sea views **Four Seasons Resort, Sharm el Sheikh, Egypt,**
A Cracker-style resort design **Hyatt Regency Coconut Point Resort, Naples, Florida**
An ideal site-blended resort design **Long Point Resort Hotel, Palos Verdes, California**
A nineteenth-century themed resort design **The Ritz-Carlton Half Moon Bay, California**
The growing US golf resort experience **Doral Golf Resort and Spa, Miami, Florida**
The growing global golf resort experience **The Greenbrier at West Village Golf Resort, Fukushima, Japan**

Spa resorts

A pristine waterfront spa design **The St. David's Hotel & Spa, Cardiff, Wales**
The market 'value' of the spa experience **Canyon Ranch SpaClub, Las Vegas, Nevada**
Varied spa venues **Canyon Ranch in the Berkshires, Lenox, Massachusetts**
Effective spa planning/standards **The spa circulation flow diagram**
The guestroom spa **The In-Room Spa-tel concept plan**
Spa enhancement through design **Sandals Royal Bahamian Resort & Spa, Nassau, Bahamas**

Vacation villages

Cancun's popular prototypical vacation village **Club Méd Cancun, Mexico**
Vacation village theming **Sandals St. Lucia Golf Resort & Spa, West Indies**
Entertainment at vacation villages **Sandals Antigua Resort & Spa**
The botanical/hydroponic resort **CuisinArt Resort & Spa, Rendezvous Bay, Anguilla, BWI**

Vacation ownership and condominium resorts

The themed vacation ownership resort **Hilton Grand Vacations Club at Hilton Seaworld International Center, Orlando, Florida**
The vacation ownership golf resort **Marriott Vacation Club International at Marriott's Grand Vista Resort, Orlando, Florida**
The vacation ownership oasis resort **Hyatt Regency Lake Las Vegas Resort, Nevada**
The vacation ownership ski lodge resort **Hyatt High Sierra Lodge, North Lake Tahoe, California**
The vacation ownership desert mountain resort **Four Seasons Resort Club, Scottsdale at Troon North, Arizona**
Vacation ownership unit design **Vacation ownership unit plans**
The island multiresort condominium **Cayman Grand Harbour, Grand Cayman, BWI**

Marina hotels

The Caribbean marina resort **The Marina at Atlantis, Paradise Island, Bahamas**
The Mediterranean marina resort **The Porto Cervo Marina at Costa Smeralda, Sardinia, Italy**
Florida's island marina resort **Fisher Island Marina, Miami Beach, Florida**

Ski resorts

The modern ski lodge with dramatic views **Amangani, Jackson Hole, Wyoming**
The ski lodge renovation and addition **Sun Mountain Lodge, Winthrop, Washington**
The Alpine ski lodge **The Ritz-Carlton Bachelor Gulch, Vail, Colorado**
The mega-ski village second home resort community **WestRock Resort, Lake Cascade, Idaho**

Ecotourist resorts

The ecotourist resort perched on water **Pangkor Laut Resort, Lumut, Malaysia**
The ecotourist resort of solar, wind, and rainwater **Harmony Maho Bay Camps, US Virgin Islands**
The eco-ethno-tourist resort **Amandari, Kedewatan, Bali, Indonesia**
The ecotourist resort at the rainforest's edge **Sheraton Timika Hotel, Irian Jaya, Indonesia**
The ecotourist wilderness resort **Hotel Explora en Patagonia, Lake Pehoe, Chile**
The ecotourist desert resort **Hotel Explora en Atacama, San Pedro de Atacama, Chile**

Multiresort destination complexes

The island contextual multiresort **Costa Smeralda, Sardinia, Italy, The Luxury Collection, Starwood Hotels and Resorts**
The multiresort 'nautical' conference center **Jumeirah Beach Resort Conference Center, Dubai, UAE**
The multiresort booming gaming community **Laughlin, Nevada**
The multiresort booming entertainment community **Branson, Missouri**

Resort theme parks

A fantasy waterpark-based theme park **Caribbean Bay Waterpark, Seoul, South Korea**
The focused entertainment and activity-based theme park **Tatilya Park, West Istanbul, Turkey**
The cultural/historic-based theme park **Taiwan Folk Village, Chang Hua, Taiwan**
The movie and islands themed resort **Universal Orlando, Florida**
The Rosetta Stone of theme park design **Park attraction matrix**
The hub-and-spoke plan theme park **Magic Kingdom, Walt Disney World Resort, Orlando, Florida**
The random plan theme park **Fantasy Island Waterpark, Sentosa Island, Singapore**
A nostalgic resort theme **Disney's BoardWalk at Walt Disney World Resort, Orlando, Florida**
An integrated waterpark resort theme park **Caribbean Bay Hotel, Seoul, South Korea**
A wild-west themed resort **Hotel Cheyenne at Disneyland Paris Resort, France**
An integrated nautical/historic resort theme park **Ship of Dreams, Orlando, Florida**

Cruise ships

The cruise ship resort **Royal Caribbean, Voyager of the Seas**

5 Convention Hotels

Chicago's convention center/hotel complex **Hyatt Regency McCormick Place, Chicago, Illinois**
The urban destination convention hotel **San Antonio Marriott Rivercenter, Texas**

The convention center headquarters hotel **Sheraton Atlantic City Convention Center Hotel, New Jersey**

The convention center hotel **Hyatt Regency McCormick Place, Chicago, Illinois**

The convention resort mega-hotel **Orlando World Center Marriott, Florida**

The compact urban convention hotel **Grand Hyatt, Washington, DC**

The casino hotel convention center addition **MGM Grand Conference Center, Las Vegas, Nevada**

A versatile convention resort with a daylight ballroom **Loews Miami Beach Hotel, Florida**

The efficient convention-resort hotel **Hyatt Regency Coconut Point Resort & Spa, Naples, Florida**

6 Conference Centers

The medical research conference center **Howard Hughes Medical Institute, Chevy Chase, Maryland**

The convention hotel executive conference center **Sheraton New York Executive Conference Center**

The environmentally-focused not-for-profit conference center **Lied Conference Center, Arbor Day Farm, Nebraska City, Nebraska**

Accommodating the needs of the small meeting **Conference Center Prototype**

The suburban executive conference center **Palisades Executive Conference Center, Palisades, New Jersey**

The ski resort conference center **Resort at Squaw Creek, Olympic Valley, California**

The resort retreat conference center **Brasstown Valley Resort, Young Harris, Georgia**

The luxury nature-retreat conference center **Rough Creek Lodge, Glen Rose, Texas**

The corporate training center **AT&T Learning Center, Basking Ridge, New Jersey**

The university conference center **Emory Conference Center Hotel, Atlanta, Georgia**

The blended campus conference center **Kingsgate Conference Center, University of Cincinnati, Ohio**

The medical research conference center **Howard Hughes Medical Institute, Chevy Chase, Maryland**

7 Residential and Condominium Hotels

The serviced condominium and hotel tower overlooking New York Harbor **The Ritz-Carlton Battery Park, New York**

The integrated condominium and hotel tower **The Ritz-Carlton Battery Park, New York**

The mixed-use condominium and hotel tower **Four Seasons Hotel and Tower, San Francisco, California**

Florida's towering mixed-use condominium, vacation ownership, and hotel tower **Four Seasons Hotel and Tower, Miami, Florida.**

8 All-suite and Extended-stay Hotels

The luxury all-suite hotel unit **RIHGA Royal, New York**

A boutique lobby for the luxury all-suite hotel **RIHGA Royal, New York**

The community all-suite hotel **Embassy Suites Hotel, Battery Park City, New York**

The all-suite hotel unit **All-suite prototype plans**

The extended-stay hotel unit **Extended-stay prototype plans**

The flexible luxury extended-stay hotel unit **Trump International Hotel & Tower, New York**

The all-suite high-rise hotel central core floor plan **Al Ain Center, Abu Dhabi, UAE**

9 Super-luxury Hotels

The royal suite at the super-luxury hotel **The Lanesborough, London, England**

The exemplary London super-luxury hotel **The Lanesborough, London, England**

The exemplary Paris super-luxury hotel **Hotel de Crillon, Paris, France**

The exemplary New York super-luxury hotel **Four Seasons Hotel, New York**

The super-luxury resort **Ocean Club, Paradise Island, Bahamas**

The exotic super-luxury lodge **Zimbali Lodge, KwaZulu-Natal, Africa**

10 Updating Existing Hotels

The elegant addition to a Grand Dame **The Peninsula, Hong Kong, China**

Renovations

The adaptive modern high-rise office landmark hotel **Loews Philadelphia Hotel, Pennsylvania**

The golf inn renovation **Old Course Hotel, St. Andrews, Scotland**

The 'hotel of the stars' renovation **The Beverly Hills Hotel, California**

Restorations

The convention hotel restoration **Hilton Chicago & Towers, Illinois**

The atrium hotel restoration **Brown Palace Hotel, Denver, Colorado**

The high-rise landmark hotel restoration **The St. Regis, New York**

Hotel restoration in a seismic zone **Mission Inn, Riverside, California**

Additions

The hotel tower addition **Le Meridien Cairo, Egypt**

Adaptive re-use

The landmark adaptive reuse **The Ritz-Carlton San Francisco, California**

The urban infill adaptive reuse hotel **Courtyard by Marriott at Scott Circle, Washington, DC**

The innovative adaptive reuse hotel **Hotel im Wasserturm, Cologne, Germany**

The adaptive 'mixed-use-reuse' hotel **Le Meridien Lingotto, Turin, Italy**

The 'unadaptive' reuse hotel **The Crowne Plaza Hotel, Washington, DC**

11 Mega-hotels

The multifaceted mega-hotel **Atlantis, Paradise Island, Bahamas**

The culturally-themed lobby **Mohegan Sun Casino Resort, Uncasville, Connecticut**

The themed site contextual resort **Portofino Bay Hotel at Universal Orlando, a Loews Hotel, Florida**

The community mega-hotel **The Westin Kierland Resort of Phoenix/Scottsdale, Arizona**

12 Mixed-use Developments

A democratically planned complex **AOL Time Warner Center and Mandarin Hotel, New York**

18 Administration and Back-of-house Design

19 Technical Coordination

20 Special Systems

21 Construction

22 Development Planning

23 Hotel Management

24 Future Development

List of Properties and Credits

Key

A, Architect; DC, Development Consultant; ID, Interior Designer; LA, Landscape Architect; LP, Land Planner; P, Photographer; R, Renderer

Adelphi Hotel, Melbourne, Australia; A/ID: Denton Corker Marshall Group; P: John Gollings

Al Ain Center, Abu Dhabi, UAE; A: Ahuja Priya Architects; DC: 9 Tek Ltd.; R: Louis Blanc

Al Faisaliah Center and Rosewood Hotel, Riyadh, Saudi Arabia; A: Sir Norman Foster & Partners; ID: DiLeonardo International; P: Courtesy of Al Khozama Management Co. Ltd.

Amandari, Bali, Indonesia; A: Peter Muller; ID: Neville Marsh: P: Courtesy of Amanresorts

Amangani Jackson Hole, Wyoming; A/ID Ed Tuttle; P: Courtesy of Amanresorts

AOL Time Warner Center and Mandarin Hotel, New York; A: Skidmore, Owings & Merrill and Brennan Beer Gorman, Architects (hotel); R: Thomas W. Schaller

AT&T Learning Center, Basking Ridge, New Jersey; A: AT&T Resource Management Corp.; ID: Smallwood, Reynolds, Stewart, Stewart & Associates; P: Courtesy of Benchmark Hospitality

Atlantis, Paradise Island, The Bahamas; A: Wimberly Allison Tong & Goo (WAT&G), HKS, and Jackson Burnside; ID: Wilson & Associates; LA: EDSA; P: Courtesy of Sun International

Baiyoke Sky Hotel, Bangkok, Thailand; A: Plan Architects; P: Courtesy of Baiyoke Sky Hotel

Bati Tourism Center and Tatilya Park, West Istanbul, Turkey; A: Oktay Nayman Architect; Consultant: HHCP International; P: Courtesy of HHCP Design International

Bellagio, Las Vegas, Nevada; A: The Jerde Partnership International, Atlandia Design; ID: Thomas Design Group; P: Dennis Keeley

Bentley Village, A Classic Residence by Hyatt, Naples, Florida; A: HHCP Design International; ID: Stanzione & Associates; P: Courtesy of Classic Residence

The Beverly Hills Hotel, California; A: Gensler; ID: Hirsch Bedner Associates; P: Robert Miller, Fred Licht

Blakes London, England; A/ID: Anouska Hempel; P: Courtesy of Anouska Hempel

Boeing Leadership Center, Florissant, Missouri; A/ID: HOK; P: Steve Hall

Boston Harbor Hotel, Boston, Massachusetts; A: Skidmore, Owings & Merrill; ID: Wilson & Associates; P: Courtesy of SOM

The Boulders, Carefree, Arizona; A: Robert Bacon; ID: Warner Interiors; P: Courtesy of The Boulders

Branson, Missouri; P: Courtesy of Branson/Lakes Area Chamber of Commerce & CVB

Brasstown Valley Resort, Young Harris, Georgia; A: Cooper Carey; ID: Marcia Davis & Associates; P: Gabriel Benzur

Brown Palace Hotel, Denver, Colorado; (renovation) ID: Forrest Perkins Tuttle; P: Robert Reck

Burj Al Arab Hotel, Dubai, UAE; A: W.S. Atkins and Partners; ID: KCA International Designers; P: Courtesy of Burj Al Arab Hotel

Canyon Ranch in the Berkshires, Lenox, Massachusetts; A: Jung/Brannen Associates; ID: Lenox Design Resources; P: Courtesy of Canyon Ranch

Canyon Ranch SpaClub, Las Vegas, Nevada; A: The Stubbins Group; ID: Interior Design Network International; P: Courtesy of Canyon Ranch

Caribbean Bay Hotel and Carribean Bay Waterpark, Seoul, South Korea; A: HHCP Design International; P: Courtesy of HHCP Design International

Cayman Grand Harbour, Grand Cayman, BWI; A: HHCP Design International; R: Courtesy of HHCP Design International

Celebration Hotel, Celebration, Florida; A: Graham Gund Architects and Lindsay, Pope, Brayfield & Associates; ID: Lew Oliver, Julie Wilde, Lori Amis; P: Raymond Martinot

Chambers, New York; A/ID: Rockwell Group, Adams Soffes Wood; R: Louis Blanc

Club Méd Cancun, Mexico; A/ID: Daniel Paterne; P: Courtesy of Club Med

Costa Smeralda Resort Complex, Sardinia; LP: Sasaki Associates; A: Luigi Vietti, Michele Busiri-Vici, Jacques Couelle; P: Courtesy of Starwood Hotels & Resorts Worldwide

Courtyard by Marriott at Scott Circle, Washington, DC; A/ID: Brennan Beer Gorman Monk/Architects & Interiors; P: Dan Cunningham

Courtyard by Marriott, prototype; Plans courtesy of Marriott Hotels and Resorts

The Crowne Plaza Hotel, Washington, DC; A: Brennan Beer Gorman/Architects; ID: Brennan Beer Gorman Monk/Interiors; P: Dan Cunningham

CusinArt Resort and Spa, Anguilla; A: Culpen & Woods Architects; P: Courtesy of CuisinArt Resort and Spa

Daewoo Marina City 21, Pusan, South Korea; A: Kohn Pederson Fox; R: Courtesy of KPF

Delano, Miami Beach, Florida; ID: Philippe Starck; P: Todd Eberle

Desert Kingdom Resort Theme Park, Aqaba/Eilat, Jordan/Israel; A: CYP International, Battaglia Associates; ID: Hirsch Bedner Associates; P: Bott Aeb Basbo

Disney's BoardWalk at Walt Disney World Resort, Orlando, Florida; A: Robert A.M. Stern Architects; ID: Design One; Drawing courtesy of Robert A.M. Stern Architects

Doral Golf Resort and Spa, Miami, Florida; P: Doral Golf Resort & Spa

Embassy Suites Hotel, New York; A: Perkins Eastman Architects; Drawing courtesy of Perkins Eastman Architects

Embassy Suites Hotel, Times Square, New York; A: Fox & Fowle Architects; Drawing courtesy of Fox & Fowle

Emirates Towers Hotel, Dubai, UAE; A: Hazel Wong, NORR Group Consultants International; ID: Design Division; P: Courtesy of Jumeirah Beach International

Emory University Conference Center, Atlanta, Georgia; A: Rabun Hogan Ota Rasche Architects; ID: Ai Group; P: Gary Knight

Eola Hotel, Natchez, Mississippi; A: Charles Moore, Perez Associates; ID: Deborah Forrest; P: Mark Coffee

Fairmont San Francisco, California; (renovation) A: Gensler; Plan courtesy of Gensler

Fairmont San Jose, California; A: HOK; ID: Intradesign; P: George Cott

Fantasy Island Waterpark, Singapore; P: Courtesy of HHCP Design International

Far Eastern Plaza Hotel, Taipei, Taiwan; A: P&T, C. Y. Lee; ID: Chhada Siembieda & Associates; P: Courtesy of Shangi-La Hotels

Fisher Island Marina, Miami Beach, Florida; A: Sandy & Babcock; P: Courtesy of Fisher Island Holdings

Floatel/Marinetel ("Jellyfish Hotel"); A: Oklahoma State University School of Architecture: students Brian Fitzsimmons, John Campbell, Chad Schmidt, Peng Hun Tan

Formule 1; P: Courtesy of Accor

Four Seasons Hotel and Tower, Miami, Florida; A: Gary Edward Handel + Associates; ID: Frank Nicholson; LA: Dan Kiley; P: IO Media

Four Seasons Hotel and Tower, San Francisco, California; A: Gary Edward Handel + Associates; ID: Frank Nicholson; R: Vladislav Yeliseyev

Four Seasons Hotel, Budapest; Kitchen plan courtesy of Cini-Little International

Four Seasons Hotel, Las Vegas, Nevada; A: Klai-Juba Architects; ID: Anita Brooks; LA: Mackenzie & Partners P: Courtesy of Four Seasons Architects

Four Seasons Hotel, Mexico D.F., Mexico; A: Wimberly Allison Tong & Goo (WAT&G) and Sergio Alvarez Aleman/GTM International; ID: Inter Art; P: Robert Miller

Four Seasons Hotel, New York; A: Pei Cobb Freed & Partners, Frank Williams & Associates; ID: Chhada Siembieda & Associates; P: Jeff Goldberg/Esto, Peter Vitale

Four Seasons Hotel, Tokyo at Chinzan-so, Japan; A: Wimberly Allison Tong & Goo (WAT&G) and Kanko Kikaku Sekkeisha; ID: Frank Nicholson; P: Robert Miller

Four Seasons Resort, Hualalai, Kona, The Big Island, Hawaii; A: Hill Glazier Architects; ID: James Northcutt & Associates; P: Peter French, Courtesy of Four Seasons Hotels and Resorts (aerial)

Four Seasons Resort, Scottsdale at Troon North, Arizona; A: Hill Glazier Architects; ID: Wilson & Associates; P: Courtesy of Four Seasons Hotels and Resorts

Four Seasons Resort, Sharm el Sheikh, Egypt; A: Hill Glazier Architects; ID: Brayton & Hughes Design Studio; R: Clay Perry

Gran Hotel Costa Meloneras, Canary Islands, Spain; A: Hill Glazier Architects; R: Clay Perry

Grand Hyatt Bali, Nusa Dua, Indonesia; A: Wimberly Allison Tong & Goo (WAT&G) and Shimizu Corporation; ID: Hirsch Bedner Associates; LA: Tongg Clarke & Mechler; P: Jaime Ardiles-Arce

Grand Hyatt Fukuoka, Canal City Hakata, Japan; A: The Jerde Partnership International; ID: Bilkey Llinas Design; P: FJUD

Grand Hyatt Shanghai, Jin Mao Tower, China; A: Skidmore, Owings & Merrill; ID: Bilkey Llinas Design; R: Courtesy of SOM

Grand Hyatt Washington, DC; A: RTKL; ID: Hirsch Bedner Associates; P: Courtesy of Grand Hyatt Washington

Great Wall Sheraton Hotel, Beijing, China; A: Welton Becket; ID: Hirsch Bedner Associates; P: Courtesy of Hirsch Bedner Associates

Greenbrier at West Village Golf Resort, Fukushima, Japan; A/ID: Robert A. M. Stern; P: Kawasumi Architectural Photograph Office

Hard Rock Hotel at Universal Orlando, Florida; A: Hill Glazier Architects and Milton Pate Associates; ID: Henriksen Design Associates (guestrooms), Mazie Wiepper & Associates (public areas); LA: Burton & Associates, Meyer Bongirno & Craig; P: Courtesy of Hill Glazier Architects

Harmony Maho Bay Camps, US Virgin Islands; A: Real Goods Trading Corporation; P: Maho Bay Camps

Healthtel prototype; A: 9 Tek Ltd; Plans courtesy of 9 Tek Ltd

The Hempel, London, England; A/ID: Anouska Hempel; P: Kim Zwarts

Hilton Boston Logan Airport, Massachusetts; A: Cambridge Seven Associates; ID: Ahern Schopfer Interior Design; P: Steve Rosenthal and Peter Vanderwarker

Hilton Chicago & Towers, Illinois; ID: Hirsch Bedner Associates; P: Jaime Ardiles-Arce

Hilton Grand Vacations Club, Orlando, Florida; A: HHCP Design International; LA: EDSA; P: Courtesy of HHCP Design International

Hilton Short Hills, New Jersey (spa); A: Brennan Beer Gorman; ID: Brennan Beer Gorman Monk; P: Paul Warchol

Hilton Times Square, New York; A: Beyer Blinder Belle Architects; ID: Alexandra Champalimaud & Associates; R: AMD Rendering

Hotel Cala di Volpe, Costa Smeralda, Sardinia; A: Jacques Couelle; P: Courtesy of Starwood Hotels & Resorts Worldwide

Hotel Cheyenne at Disneyland Paris Resort, France; A/ID: Robert A.M. Stern Architects; Drawing courtesy of Robert A.M. Stern Architects

Hotel de Crillon, Paris, France; (renovation) A: Jean Lou Roubert; ID: Sonia Rykiel; P: Courtesy of Hotel de Crillon

Hotel Explora en Atacama, San Pedro de Atacama, Chile; A: German del Sol; P: Guy Wemborne

Hotel Explora en Patagonia, Lake Pehoe, Chile; A: José Cruz; P: Guy Wemborne

Hotel im Wasserturm, Cologne, Germany; ID: Andrée Putman; P: Courtesy of Hotel im Wasserturm

Hotel Kyocera, Kagoshima, Japan; A/ID: Kisho Kurokawa; P: Tomio Ohashi

Hotel Martinspark, Dornbirn, Austria; A/ID: Baumschlager & Eberle; P: Eduard Hueber

Hotel Rey Juan Carlos I, Barcelona, Spain; A/ID: Joseph Cartana, Carlos Ferrater; P: Louis Casals

Hotel Seiyo Ginza, Tokyo, Japan; A: Seirun Kikutake; ID: Noel Lee; P: Courtesy of Rosewood Hotels and Resorts

Hotel Sofitel, New York; A: Brennan Beer Gorman/Architects; R: Yann LeRoy

Howard Hughes Medical Institute, Chevy Chase, Maryland; A/ID: The Hillier Group; P: Jeff Goldberg/Esto, William F. Geiger (exterior) and Mark Ross (interior)

Hyatt High Sierra Lodge, North Lake Tahoe, California; A: Hill Glazier Architects; ID: Brayton & Hughes Design Studio; P: John Sutton

Hyatt Regency Aruba Resort & Casino; A: Thompson, Ventulett, Satinback & Associates (TVS); ID: Hirsch Bedner Associates; LA: EDSA; P: Courtesy of Hyatt Hotels

Hyatt Regency Atlanta, Georgia; A: John Portman Associates; TVS/Thompson, Ventulett, Stainback Associates (ballroom); ID: Culpepper, McAuliffe and Meaders; P: Brian Gassel/TVS

Hyatt Regency Coconut Point, Naples, Florida; A: Hill Glazier Architects; ID: Culpepper, McAuliffe & Meaders; R: Clay Perry

Hyatt Regency Fukuoka, Japan; A/ID: Michael Graves & Associates and Maeda Corporation; P: Toyota Photo Studio, Courtesy of Maeda Corporation

Hyatt Regency Greenwich, Connecticut; A: Kohn Pederson Fox; ID: Graham-Solano; P: Courtesy of KPF

Hyatt Regency La Jolla at Aventine, San Diego, California; A: Michael Graves & Associates and Langdon Wilson Architect; ID: Michael Graves with Wilson & Associates; P: David Hewitt/Anne Garrison

Hyatt Regency Lake Las Vegas Resort, Nevada; A: Hill Glazier Architects; ID: Wilson & Associates; P: Courtesy of Hill Glazier Architects

Hyatt Regency Mainz, Germany; A: JSK Architects; ID: Hirsch Bedner Associates; P: Ken Kirkwood

Hyatt Regency McCormick Place, Chicago, Illinois; A: TVS/Thompson Ventulett, Stainback & Associates; ID: Wilson & Associates; P: Brian Gassel/TVS

Hyatt Regency Orlando International Airport, Florida; A: KBJ Architects; ID: Lynn Wilson & Associates; Plan courtesy of KBJ Architects

Hyatt Regency Paris–Charles de Gaulle, Roissy, France; A: Murphy/Jahn Architects; ID: Hirsch Bedner Associates; P: Courtesy of Hyatt International

Hyatt Regency Tamaya Resort & Spa, New Mexico; A: Hill Glazier Architects; ID: Wilson & Associates; R Clay Perry

Hyatt Regency Thessaloniki, Greece; A: Wimberly Allison Tong & Goo (WAT&G); ID: Hirsch Bedner Associates; P: Jaime Ardiles-Arce

Inn on Biltmore Estate, Asheville, North Carolina; A: TVS/Thompson, Ventulett, Stainback & Associates; ID: Hughes Design Associates; P: Brian Gassel/TVS

Inter-Continental Taba Heights Resort, Sinai Coast, Egypt; A/ID: Michael Graves & Associates and Rami El Dahan & Soheir Farid; ID: Ibrahim Nagy; P: Courtesy of MGA

Inverness Hotel & Golf Club, Denver, Colorado; A: Friis Moltke Larson and RNL; Plans courtesy of Friis Moltke Larson

JR Central Towers and Station, Nagoya, Japan; A: Kohn Pederson Fox; P: Courtesy of KPF

Jumeirah Beach Resort Conference Center, Dubai, UAE; A: W.S. Atkins & Partners; ID: Leo A. Daly; P: Courtesy of Jumeirah Beach Resort; Plan courtesy of Leo A. Daly

Kempinski Hotel Airport Munich, Germany; A: Murphy/Jahn Architects; ID: Jan Wichers; P: Engelhardt Sellin

Kingsgate Conference Center, University of Cincinnati, Ohio; A/ID: VOA Associates; P: Hedrich Blessing and Stewkamp/Ballogg

Kowloon MTR Tower, Hong Kong, China; A: Skidmore, Owings & Merrill; R: Courtesy of SOM

Lakeside Village, A Classic Residence by Hyatt, Lantana, Florida; A: Mauriz, Salazar & Associates; ID: Interior Design Associates; P: Courtesy of Classic Residence

The Lanesborough, London, United Kingdom; (renovation) ID: Ezra Attila; P: Courtesy of Rosewood Hotels and Resorts

Las Ventanas al Paraiso, Los Cabos, Mexico; A: HKS Architects; ID: Wilson and Associates; LA: SWA Group; P: Tom Fox

Laughlin, Nevada; P: Courtesy of Riverside Resort Hotel and Casino

Le Meridien Cairo, Egypt; A: William B. Tabler Architects and RBSD Associates; ID: Bilkey Llinas Design; P: Jock Pottle/Esto

Le Meridien Lingotto, Turin, Italy; A: Renzo Piano; ID: Franco Mirenzi; P: Mollica

Lied Conference Center, Arbor Day Farm, Nebraska City, Nebraska; A: Alley Poyner Architecture; P: Assassi Productions

The Lodge at Koele, Lana'I, Hawaii; A: Arnold C. Savrann; P: Photo courtesy of Lana'i Company

Loews Miami Beach Hotel, Florida; A: Nichols Brosch Sandoval; ID: Hirsch Bedner Associates; P: Erhard Pfeiffer

Loews Philadelphia Hotel, Pennsylvania; A: Bower Lewis Thrower Architects; ID: Daroff Design; P: Michael Kleinberg

Long Point Resort Hotel, Palos Verdes, California; A: Hill Glazier Architects; R: Clay Perry

Magic Kingdom, Walt Disney World Resort, Orlando, Florida; P: Courtesy of HHCP Design International

The Mandalay Bay Resort & Casino, Las Vegas, Nevada; A: Klai-Juba Architects; ID: Anita Brooks (guestrooms), Dougall Design (public areas); LA: Mackenzie & Partners; P: Courtesy of Mandalay Resort Group

Manele Bay Hotel, Lana'i, Hawaii; A: Arnold C. Savrann; P: Photo courtesy of Lana'i Company

Manhattan Hotel, Makuhari, Japan; A: RTKL Associates and Kajima Corporation; P: Satashi Asakawa

Manila Diamond, Philippines; A: K. Hara Associates, GW Architects & Engineers; ID: Hirsch Bedner Associates; P: Robert Miller

Marina Center Mandarin, Singapore; A: John Portman Associates; P: Courtesy of John Portman Associates

Marriott Desert Springs Villas II, Palm Desert, California; P: Courtesy of Marriott Vacation Club International

Marriott's Grande Vista Resort, Orlando, Florida; A: HHCP Design International; P: Courtesy of HHCP Design International

The Mercer, New York; A: Tsao McKown and Mark Markowitz; ID: Christian Liaigre; P: Dana Gallagher, William Waldron

MGM Grand Conference Center, Las Vegas, Nevada; A: HOK; ID: Hirsch Bedner Associates; P: Erhard Pfeiffer

Mission Inn, Riverside, California; A: ELS Architecture and Urban Design; P: Timothy Hursley (aerial)

Mohegan Sun Casino Resort, Uncasville, Connecticut; A/ID: Kohn Pederson Fox and Rockwell Group; R: Courtesy of Rockwell Group

Mojiko Hotel, Kitakyushu, Japan; A: Aldo Rossi, Shigeru Uchida; P: Courtesy of Mojiko Hotel

Mologne Guest House at Walter Reed Army Hospital, Washington, DC; A/ID: Brennan Beer Gorman Monk/Architects & Interiors; P: Dan Cunningham

Mondrian, West Hollywood, California; ID: Philippe Starck; P: Todd Eberle

Moody Gardens Hotel, Galveston, Texas; A: Morris Architects; P: Childs/Muniz Photography

Motel 6 prototype; P: Courtesy of Motel 6

Naoshima Contemporary Art Museum and Annex, Japan; A: Tadao Ando Architect; P: Mitsuo Matsuoka

Noto Monzen Family Inn, Ishikawa, Japan; A/ID: Mozuna Kikoo Architects; P: Fujitsuka Mitsumasa, Taisuke Ogawa

Ocean Club, Paradise Island, Bahamas; A: Hill Glazier Architects; ID: Barry Design Associates; R: Van Strauhal

Old Course Hotel, St. Andrews, Scotland; A: RTKL Associates and Hurd Roland Partnership; ID: Wilson & Associates; P: Hedrich Blessing

The Orchid at Mauna Lani, The Big Island, Hawaii; A: Wimberly Allison Tong & Goo (WAT&G); ID: Philpotts & Associates; P: Douglas Peebles

Orlando World Center Marriott, Florida; A: RTKL Associates; ID: Jutras + Nobili; P: Courtesy of Orlando World Center Marriott

The Palace of the Lost City, Sun City, South Africa; A: Wimberly Allison Tong & Goo (WAT&G) and Burg Doherty Bryant & Partners; ID: Wilson & Associates; LA: Top Turf & Associates; P: Courtesy of Sun International

Palisades Executive Conference Center, Palisades, New Jersey; A/ID: Mitchell/Giurgola Architects; P: Mick Hales

Pan Pacific Hotel Vancouver, Canada; P: Courtesy of Pan Pacific

Pan Pacific Hotel Yokohama, Japan; A: Nikken Sekkei Co.; ID: Hirsch Bedner Associates; P: Jaime Ardiles-Arce

Pangkor Laut Resort, Lumut, Malaysia; A: Lek Bunnang; LA: Bill Bensley; P: Courtesy of Fox Global Communications

Paramount, New York; ID: Philippe Starck; P: Todd Eberle

Park Hyatt Hamburg, Germany; A: SGS and Partners; ID: Hirsch Bedner Associates; P: Ken Kirkwood

Park Hyatt Johannesburg, South Africa; A: GAPP; ID: Hirsch Bedner Associates; P: Ivan Muller

Park Hyatt Tokyo, Japan; A: Kenzo Tange & Associates; ID: John Morford; P: Courtesy of Hyatt International Corp.

The Peninsula, Hong Kong, China; (addition) A: Rocco Design Partners; ID: Philippe Starck (restaurant); P: Courtesy of The Peninsula Group

Porto Cervo Marina at Costa Smeralda, Sardinia, Italy; LP: Sasaki Associates; A: Luigi Vietti; P: Courtesy of Sasaki Associates

Portofino Bay Hotel at Universal Orlando, a Loews Hotel, Florida; A: WAT&G and Morris Architects; ID: Wilson & Associates; P: Courtesy of Universal Studios

Raffles Hotel, Singapore; A: Callison Partnership; ID: Bent Severin; P: Courtesy of Raffles Hotel

Resort at Squaw Creek, Olympic Valley, California; A: Ward Young; ID: Simon, Martin-Vegue, Winkelstein, Moris; P: Courtesy of Benchmark Hospitality

RIHGA Royal, New York; A: Frank Williams & Associates; ID: Birch Coffee Design Associates; P: Jeff Goldberg/Esto; Peter Paige

The Ritz-Carlton, Aspen Highlands, Aspen, Colorado; A: Robert A.M. Stern; R: Michael McCann

The Ritz-Carlton, Bachelor Gulch, Vail, Colorado; A: Hill Glazier Architects; ID: Wilson & Associates; R: Clay Perry

The Ritz-Carlton, Battery Park, New York; A: Polshek & Partners and Gary Edward Handel + Associates; ID: Frank Nicholson; P: Robert Frank

The Ritz-Carlton, Half Moon Bay, California; A: Hill Glazier Architects; ID: Brayton & Hughes Design Studio; P: Model photo courtesy of Hill Glazier Architects

The Ritz-Carlton, Kapalua, Hawaii; A: Wimberly Allison Tong & Goo (WAT&G); ID: Frank Nicholson; LA: Peridian Group; P: Howard J. Wolff

The Ritz-Carlton, Millenia, Singapore; A: Kevin Roche John Dinkeloo and Associates; ID: Hirsch Bedner Associates; P: Peter Mealin

The Ritz-Carlton, San Antonio, Texas; A: Hill Glazier Architects; Plan courtesy of Hill Glazier Architects

The Ritz-Carlton, San Francisco, California; A: Kajima Associates, Whistler-Patri; ID: Frank Nicholson; P: Courtesy of Ritz-Carton

The Ritz-Carlton, San Juan Hotel, Spa & Casino, Isla Verde, Puerto Rico; A: Nichols Brosch Sandoval; ID: Hirsch Bedner Associates; P: Robert Miller

Rotary House International, Anderson Cancer Center, Houston, Texas; A: Morris Architects; P: Aker/Zvonkovic Photography

Rough Creek Lodge, Glen Rose, Texas; A: Larry Speck; ID: Vivian/Nichols Associates; P: Michael French

Royalton, New York; ID: Philippe Starck; P: Tom Vack and Andrew Garn

Sackett Lake Resort, Monticello, New York; A: Adams Soffes Wood; LA: SWA Group

San Antonio Marriott Rivercenter, Texas; A: RTKL Associates; ID: Marriott Corporation; P: Hedrich Blessing

Sandals Antigua Resort & Spa; P: Courtesy of Sandals Resorts

Sandals Royal Bahamian Resort & Spa, Nassau, Bahamas; P: Courtesy of Sandals Resorts

Sandals St. Lucia Golf Resort & Spa; P: Courtesy of Sandals Resorts

Sea Hawk Hotel & Resort, Hakata, Japan; A/ID: Cesar Pelli & Associates; P: B. Davis, T. Sato/Courtesy of Cesar Pelli & Associates

Seaport Hotel, Boston, Massachusetts; A: Stubbins Associates; ID: Kenneth Hurd; P: Peter Vanderwalker

Seaside, Florida; A: Andres Duany and Elizabeth Plater-Zyberk; P: Steven Brooke; Alex MacLean (aerial)

Seven Seas Resort, Side, Turkey; A: Mustafa Tatlici, Ali Kolsal; ID: Graham Design Ltd.; LA: SWA Group; P: Tom Fox

Sheraton Atlantic City Convention Center Hotel, New Jersey; A: David Habib & Associates and Cope Linder Associates; ID: Vivian/Nichols Associates; P: Michael French

Sheraton Miramar Resort el Gouna, Egypt; A/ID: Michael Graves & Associates and Rami El Dahan & Soheir Farid; ID: Ibrahim Nagy; P: Courtesy of MGA

Sheraton New York Hotel & Towers, Executive Conference Center, New York; A/ID: Brennan Beer Gorman Monk/Interiors; P: Peter Paige

Sheraton Paris Airport Hotel Charles de Gaulle, Roissy, France; A: Martinet Architecture; ID: Group Ecart; P: Deidi von Schaewen

Sheraton Timika Hotel, Irian Jaya, Indonesia; A/ID: HOK; P: Nick Merrick

Ship of Dreams, Orlando, Florida; A: HHCP Design International; ID: Hirsch Bedner Associates; R: Courtesy of HHCP Design International

Shoreham Hotel II, New York; A/ID: Pasanella + Klein Stolzman + Berg; P: Paul Warchol

Silver Legacy Resort Casino, Reno, Nevada; A: Mitchell Cohen; ID: Yates-Silverman; P: Courtesy of Silver Legacy Resort Casino

SkyDome Renaissance, Toronto, Canada; A: Robbie/Young and Wright Adjeleian Allen Rubeli and NORR Partnership; P: Courtesy of SkyDome Renaissance Hotel

SoHo Grand Hotel, New York; A: Helpern Architects; ID: William Scofield; P: Peter Mauss/Esto

Spacetel guestroom; ID: Interlsland Group and Myhome.com; P: Courtesy of Myhome.com

Spacetel; A: WAT&G; P: Courtesy of WAT&G

St. David's Hotel & Spa, Cardiff, Wales; A: Richard Davies; ID: Olga Polizzi; P: Fritz vor der Schulenburg

St. Martins Lane, London, United Kingdom; ID: Philippe Starck; P: James Mortimer

The St. Regis, New York; (renovation) ID: Brennan Beer Gorman/Architects; P: Anthony Albarello

The Standard, Los Angeles, California; A: Arquitectonica; ID: Shawn Hausman and The Standard Design Team; P: Tim Street-Porter, Todd Eberle

Star City, Sydney Harbour Casino Hotel, Australia; A: The Hillier Group and Cox Richardson Architects & Planners; P: Patrick Bingham-Hall

Statler Hotel, Cornell University, Ithaca, New York; A: The Architects Collaborative; ID: Kenneth Hurd; P: Sam Sweezy

Steigenberger Resort el Fanadir, Hurghada, Egypt; A: William B. Tabler Architects; LA: Belt Collins Hong Kong

Studio 6 room prototype; Courtesy of Studio 6:

Summerfield Suites room prototype; Plan courtesy of Summerfield Suites

Sun Mountain Lodge, Winthrop, Washington; A/ID: NBBJ; P: Paul Warchol

Taiwan Folk Village, Chang Hua, Taiwan; P: Courtesy of Taiwan Folk Village

Tanjong Jara Beach Resort Hotel, Kuala Trengganu, Malaysia; A: Wimberly Allison Tong & Goo (WAT&G) and Arkitek Berskutu; ID: Juru liasan Consultant; LA: Belt Collins Hawaii; P: Courtesy of Tanjong Jara Resort

TidePointe, A Classic Residence by Hyatt, Hilton Head, South Carolina; A: The Martin Group; P: Courtesy of Classic Residence

Toyoko Inn Capsule Omori, Tokyo, Japan; P: Courtesy of Hiroshi Hamada and PC International, Tokyo

Trump International Hotel & Tower, New York; A: Philip Johnson and Costas Kondylis & Associates; ID: Hirsch Bedner Associates; P: Courtesy of Trump International Hotel & Tower

Twin Farms, Barnard, Vermont; A/ID: JWA; P: John M. Hall

Undersea Hotel; A: Wimberly Allison Tong & Goo (WAT&G); P: Courtesy of WAT&G

Universal Orlando, Florida; P: Courtesy of Universal Studios

Venetian Resort-Hotel-Casino, Las Vegas, Nevada; A: Wimberly Allison Tong & Goo (WAT&G) and TSA of Nevada; ID: Wilson & Associates (hotel) and Dougall Design (casino): LA: Lifescapes International; P: Cormier/Malinowski InSite Architectural Photography

Voyager of the Seas, Royal Caribbean International; P: Courtesy of Royal Caribbean International

W New York; A: Rockwell Group and Helpern Architects; ID: Rockwell Group; P: Paul Warchol, Todd Eberle

W San Francisco, California; A: Hornberger + Worstell; ID: W Design Group; P: Whittaker Photography

W Times Square Hotel, New York; A: Frank Williams & Associates; ID: W Design Group; R: David Williams

Walt Disney World Swan & Dolphin, Orlando, Florida; A: Michael Graves, Alan Lapidus; ID: Michael Graves

WAT&G Space Resort; A: Wimberly Allison Tong & Goo (WAT&G); P: Courtesy of WAT&G

West Island Golf and Casino Hotel, Hainan, China; A: Kohn Pederson Fox; P: Courtesy of KPF

The Westin Kierland Resort at Phoenix/Scottsdale, Arizona; LP: Sasaki Associates; A: Hill Glazier Architects; R: Clay Perry; Plan courtesy of Herberger Interests

The Westin New York and E Walk; A: Arquitectonica and D'Agostino Izzo Quirk; ID: Arquitectonica; R: Courtesy of Tishman Realty

The Westin Park Towers, San Diego, California; A: Hornberger + Worstell; ID: Chhada Siembieda Remedios; R: Michael Reardon

The Westin Regina Golf and Beach Resort Los Cabos, Mexico; A: Javier Sordo Madaleno; ID: Architecture and Design International; P: Fernando Cerdero, courtesy of Westin Regina Resort

The Westin Stamford and Westin Plaza towers, Singapore; A: I.M. Pei & Partners; ID: Forma; Plan by Adams Soffes Wood

WestRock Resort, Lake Cascade,Idaho; A: Dennis Taggart Architect; R: Courtesy of Dennis Taggart Architect

World Financial Center, Shanghai, China; A: Kohn Pederson Fox; P: Courtesy of KPF

Wyndahm El Conquistador Resort & Country Club, Fajardo, Puerto Rico; A: Edward Durrell Stone Associates, Ray Melendez & Associates; LP/LA: EDSA; ID: Jorge Rossello & Associates; P: Courtesy of EDSA

Wyndham Buttes Resort, Tempe, Arizona; A: Corneyer Hedrich; P: Courtesy of Wyndham Buttes Resort

Yokohama Grand Inter-Continental Hotel, Japan; A: Nikken Sekkei Ltd.; ID: Media Five, Cheryl Rowley, Lee Interior Design, Pierre Yves Rochon; P: Kouji Horiuchi, Courtesy of Nikken Sekkei Ltd.

Yusuhara Visitors Center, Japan; A: Kengo Kuma; P: Mitsumasa Fujitsuka

Zimbali Lodge, KwaZulu-Natal, Africa; A: Theunissen Jankowitz; ID: Wilson & Associates; P: Francki Burger

Drawings: Back-of-house schematic diagrams, Stephani Robson; **Ballroom schematic diagram,** Stephani Robson; **Development team flow chart,** Roque Rey; **Development sequence diagram,** Daniel Rutes; **Evolutionary tree diagram,** Carlos Fernandez and Roque Rey; **Guestroom floors and unit plans,** Carla di Silva, Eduardo Quintero, Stephani Robson; **Spa-tel plan,** Stephani Robson; **Ultratel profiles,** Carlos Fernandez

Index

Page numbers in *italics* refer to illustrations.